Lecture Notes in Computer Science 15993

Founding Editors

Gerhard Goos
Juris Hartmanis

The series Lecture Notes in Computer Science (LNCS), including its subseries Lecture Notes in Artificial Intelligence (LNAI) and Lecture Notes in Bioinformatics (LNBI), has established itself as a medium for the publication of new developments in computer science and information technology research, teaching, and education.

LNCS enjoys close cooperation with the computer science R & D community, the series counts many renowned academics among its volume editors and paper authors, and collaborates with prestigious societies. Its mission is to serve this international community by providing an invaluable service, mainly focused on the publication of conference and workshop proceedings and postproceedings. LNCS commenced publication in 1973.

Mila Dalla Preda · Sebastian Schrittwieser ·
Vincent Naessens · Bjorn De Sutter
Editors

Availability, Reliability and Security

20th International Conference, ARES 2025
Ghent, Belgium, August 11–14, 2025
Proceedings, Part II

 Springer

Editors
Mila Dalla Preda ⓘ
University of Verona
Verona, Italy

Sebastian Schrittwieser ⓘ
University of Vienna
Vienna, Austria

Vincent Naessens ⓘ
KU Leuven
Ghent, Belgium

Bjorn De Sutter ⓘ
Ghent University
Ghent, Belgium

ISSN 0302-9743 ISSN 1611-3349 (electronic)
Lecture Notes in Computer Science
ISBN 978-3-032-00626-4 ISBN 978-3-032-00627-1 (eBook)
https://doi.org/10.1007/978-3-032-00627-1

This Springer imprint is published by the registered company Springer Nature Switzerland AG
The registered company address is: Gewerbestrasse 11, 6330 Cham, Switzerland

If disposing of this product, please recycle the paper.

Preface

The Twentieth International Conference on Availability, Reliability, and Security (ARES 2025) brings together researchers and practitioners to advance the fields of availability, reliability, and computer security. Following the tradition of previous editions, the conference fosters collaboration and the exchange of ideas across these critical areas of research.

This year, the conference was hosted in Ghent, a vibrant and historic city whose rich cultural heritage, distinguished academic tradition, and welcoming atmosphere offer an ideal setting for scholarly exchange and research collaboration.

This year, the main conference was organized in eleven technical sessions, including a session dedicated to the candidates for the Best Paper Award. We were also honored to host two brilliant keynote speakers: Christian Collberg, Professor at the University of Arizona, renowned for his work in the fields of software protection, intellectual property protection, and reverse engineering resistance, and Bart Preneel, Professor at the Katholieke Universiteit Leuven in Belgium, renowned for his work in the fields of cryptography, information security, and privacy.

ARES 2025 received 162 full papers, 11 SoK papers, and 20 short papers. After desk rejecting 12 papers, we accepted 33 full papers, 1 SoK paper, and 8 short papers that were originally submitted as full papers. For full and SoK papers, this yields an acceptance rate of 19.7%. Each paper, including those submitted by Program Committee members, received a minimum of three reviews. The three best papers were selected by the PC chairs and organizing team for inclusion in the Best Paper Sessions, based on the highest review scores. The Best Paper award was then chosen by the PC chairs and organizing team during the conference, following the Best Paper Sessions, in order to also consider the quality of the presentations.

We thank all the authors for submitting a high volume of quality papers to ARES this year. We are also particularly grateful for the hard work, insights, and support displayed by each of the Program Committee members. Thanks to them, we were able to offer a technically solid program to the attendees. We further thank all workshop chairs for their efforts in organizing engaging workshop sessions.

After years of being organized by a dedicated team from SBA Research, the ARES conference was now for the first time organized by a team from the local host. We specifically want to thank Bettina Jaber from SBA research for the manner in which she prepared the handover, providing tons of documentation and guidance. From the local team, we deeply thank Vicky Wandels, Inge Lason, and Eneko Illarramendi for successfully managing the registrations, the finances, the website, the conference rooms, the social events, the catering, etc.

The General Chair and the Proceedings Chair are included as editors of this volume to reflect their contributions in the preparation of the proceedings.

August 2025

Bjorn De Sutter
Mila Dalla Preda
Vincent Naessens
Sebastian Schrittwieser

Organization

General Chair

Bjorn De Sutter   Ghent University, Belgium

Program Committee Chairs

Mila Dalla Preda   University of Verona, Italy
Sebastian Schrittwieser   SBA Research and University of Vienna, Austria

Steering Committee

Abdelmalek Benzekri   University of Toulouse, France
Francesco Buccafurri   University of Reggio Calabria, Italy
Dominik Engel   Salzburg University of Applied Sciences, Austria
Mathias Fischer   University of Hamburg, Germany
Steven Furnell   University of Nottingham, UK
Stefanie Rinderle-Ma   University of Vienna, Austria
Shujun Li   University of Kent, UK
Christian Doerr   Delft University of Technology, Germany
Pierangela Samarati   Università degli Studi di Milano, Italy
Melanie Volkamer   Karlsruher Institute for Technology (KIT),
      Germany

Steering Committee Chairs

Edgar Weippl   SBA Research, Austria
A Min Tjoa   TU Vienna, Austria

Workshop Chairs

Bart Coppens   Ghent University, Belgium
Bruno Volckaert   Ghent University, Belgium

Workshop Chair EU Projects Symposium

Florian Skopik   AIT Austrian Institute of Technology, Austria

Proceedings Chairs

Vincent Naessens   KU Leuven, Belgium
Michiel Willocx   KU Leuven, Belgium

Organization Chairs

Vicky Wandels   Ghent University, Belgium
Inge Lason   Ghent University, Belgium

Conference Management

Vicky Wandels   Ghent University, Belgium
Eneko Illarramendi   Ghent University, Belgium

Program Committee

Bert Abrath   Ghent University, Belgium
Isaac Agudo   University of Malaga, Spain
Esma Aïmeur   University of Montreal, Canada
Magnus Almgren   Chalmers University of Technology, Sweden
Saed Alrabaee   United Arab Emirates University, UAE
Todd Andel   University of South Alabama, USA
Mikael Asplund   Linköping University, Sweden
Ali Ismail Awad   United Arab Emirates University, UAE
Sebastien Bardin   CEA LIST, France
Cataldo Basile   Politecnico di Torino, Italy
Ingmar Baumgart   Karlsruhe Institute of Technology, Germany
Bernhard J. Berger   University of Rostock, Germany
Monowar Bhuyan   Umeå University, Sweden
Pascal Birnstill   Fraunhofer, Germany
Gregory Blanc   Institut Mines-Télécom, Télécom SudParis,
                                 Institut Polytechnique de Paris, France
Olivier Blazy   Ecole Polytechnique, France

Aymen Boudguiga	IRT SystemX, France
Nora Boulahia-Cuppens	Polytechnique Montréal, Canada
Alessandro Brighente	University of Padova, Italy
Francesco Buccafurri	Università Mediterranea di Reggio Calabria, Italy
Krzysztof Cabaj	Warsaw University of Technology, Poland
Jordi Castellà-Roca	Universitat Rovira i Virgili, Spain
Marta Catillo	Università del Sannio, Italy
Luca Caviglione	CNR - IMATI, Italy
Mariano Ceccato	University of Verona, Italy
Bo Chen	Michigan Technological University, USA
Sherman S. M. Chow	The Chinese University of Hong Kong, China
Nathan Clarke	University of Plymouth, UK
Marijke Coetzee	North-West University, South Africa
Emilio Coppa	LUISS University, Italy
Tiago Cruz	University of Coimbra, Portugal
Michel Cukier	University of Maryland, USA
Frederic Cuppens	Polytechnique Montreal, Canada
José Maria de Fuentes	Universidad Carlos III de Madrid, Spain
Laurens D'Hooge	Ghent University, Belgium
Nicolás E. Díaz Ferreyra	Hamburg University of Technology, Germany
Tassos Dimitriou	Computer Technology Institute, Greece and Kuwait University, Kuwait
Niels Dossche	Ghent University, Belgium
Pavlos Efraimidis	Democritus University of Thrace, Greece
Günther Eibl	Salzburg University of Applied Sciences, Josef Ressel Center for User-Centric Smart Grid Privacy, Security and Control, Austria
Andreas Ekelhart	SBA Research, Austria
Christian Engelmann	ORNL (Oak Ridge National Laboratory), USA
Santiago Escobar	Universitat Politècnica de València, Spain
Hannes Federrath	University of Hamburg, Germany
Anna Lisa Ferrara	Università degli Studi del Molise, Italy
Umberto Ferraro	Università di Roma, La Sapienza, Italy
Mathias Fischer	University of Hamburg, Germany
Panagiotis Fouliras	University of Macedonia, Greece
Virginia Franqueira	University of Kent, UK
Steven Furnell	University of Nottingham, UK
Sarah Gaballah	Ruhr-Universität Bochum, Germany
Dimitrios Georgoulias	Aalborg University, Denmark
Giorgio Giacinto	Università degli Studi di Cagliari, Italy
Karl M. Goeschka	Vienna University of Technology, Austria
Lorena González Manzano	Universidad Carlos III de Madrid, Spain

Rudolf Mayer	Vienna University of Technology, Austria
Wojciech Mazurczyk	Warsaw University of Technology, Poland
Michael Meier	University of Bonn, Germany
Per Håkon Meland	SINTEF Digital, Norway
Weizhi Meng	Lancaster University, UK
Francesco Mercaldo	University of Molise, Italy
Massimo Merro	University of Verona, Italy
Joachim Meyer	Tel Aviv University, Israel
Rodrigo Miani	Federal University of Uberlândia (UFU), Brazil
Aleksandra Mileva	Goce Delcev University, North Macedonia
Lorenzo Musarella	Università Mediterranea di Reggio Calabria, Italy
Stephan Neumann	SaarLB, Germany
Zhenyu Ning	Hunan University, China
Maximilian Noppel	Karlsruhe Institute of Technology, Germany
Christoforos Ntantogian	Ionian University, Greece
Marc Ohm	University of Bonn & Fraunhofer FKIE, Germany
Rolf Oppliger	eSECURITY Technologies, Switzerland
Vinod P.	Cochin University of Science and Technology, Kochi, Kerala, India
Federica Paci	University of Verona, Italy
Miguel Pardal	Universidade de Lisboa, Portugal
Sergio Pastrana	Universidad Carlos III de Madrid, Spain
Sikhar Patranabis	IBM Research India
Sven Peldszus	Ruhr University Bochum, Germany
Günther Pernul	Universität Regensburg, Germany
Pablo Picazo-Sanchez	Halmstad University, Sweden
Alexander Ponticello	CISPA Helmholtz Center for Information Security, Germany
Marie-Laure Potet	University Grenoble Alps, France
Masoom Rabbani	Chalmers University of Technology, Sweden
Pawel Rajba	University of Wroclaw, Poland
Silvio Ranise	University of Trento and FBK, Italy
Pascal Reisert	University of Stuttgart, Germany
Karen Renaud	University of Strathclyde, UK
Christian Reuter	Technical University of Darmstadt, PEASEC, Germany
Junghwan Rhee	University of Central Oklahoma, USA
Golden G. Richard III	Louisiana State University, USA
Giulio Rigoni	Sapienza, University of Rome, Italy
Thomas Rosenstatter	Salzburg University of Applied Sciences, Austria
Michael Rossberg	Technische Universitaet Ilmenau, Germany
Christoph Saatjohann	FH Muenster, Germany

Morteza Safaei Pour	San Diego State University, USA
Pierangela Samarati	Università degli Studi di Milano, Italy
Luis Enrique Sanchez Crespo	University of Castilla-la Mancha, Spain
Riccardo Scandariato	Hamburg University of Technology, Germany
Joern-Marc Schmidt	IU International Hochschule GmbH, Germany
Guido Schmitz	Lancaster University Leipzig, Germany
Jan Seedorf	HFT Stuttgart, Germany
Arnaldo Sgueglia	University of Sannio, Italy
Siamak Shahandashti	University of York, UK
Hervais Simo	Fraunhofer SIT, Germany
Paulo Simões	University of Coimbra, Portugal
Dario Stabili	University of Bologna, Italy
Nazatul Haque Sultan	University of Newcastle, UK
Shamik Sural	Indian Institute of Technology Kharagpur, India
Anum Talpur	University of Hamburg, Germany
Oliver Theel	Carl von Ossietzky University of Oldenburg, Germany
Simon Tjoa	St. Pölten UAS, Austria
Jacob Torrey	Thinkst Applied Research, USA
Katja Tuma	Eindhoven University of Technology, Netherlands
Johanna Ullrich	SBA Research, Austria
Andreas Unterweger	Salzburg University of Applied Sciences, Austria
Emmanouil Vasilomanolakis	Technical University of Denmark, Denmark
Umberto Villano	University of Sannio, Italy
Corrado Aaron Visaggio	University of Sannio, Italy
Stijn Volckaert	KU Leuven, Belgium
Ahmad Samer Wazan	Zayed University, United Arab Emirates
Christos Xenakis	University of Piraeus, Greece
Koen Yskout	KU Leuven, Belgium
Nicola Zannone	Eindhoven University of Technology, Netherlands
Ephraim Zimmer	Technical University of Darmstadt, Germany

Additional Reviewers

Diego Soi	Franziska Schneider
Nikolaos Tsinganos	Dejan Radovanovic
Andreas Menegatos	Tiago Roxo
Soumyadyuti Ghosh	Riccardo Ceccaroni
Reeshav Chowdhury	Daniele Canavese
Jack P. K. Ma	Laurent Mounier
Yagmur Yigit	Pierangelo Loi

Philipp Kühn

Ijeoma Faustina Ekeh

James Ghawaly

Silvia Lucia Sanna

Thrasyvoulos Giannakopoulos

Clemente Galdi

Timo Pohl

Riccardo Ziglio

Anindya Sundar Das

Jef Jacobs

Harry W. H. Wong

August See

Giulia Grani

Georgios Gkoktsis

Konstantinos Giapantzis

Marvin Banse

Riccardo Longo

Aristeidis Farao

Andes Y. L. Kei

Bernardo Sequeiros

Caroline König

Jeetesh Gupta

Ricardo Yaben

Joana C. Costa

Karina Elzer

Max Schirl

Martin Dukek

Chiara Spadafora

Alexander Wallis

Eleni Briola

Nikolaos Pavlidis

Stelvio Cimato

Matthias Börsig

Frank Nelles

Obaidullah Zaland

Josh Dafoe

Simon Althaus

Kilian Demuth

Contents – Part II

Supply Chain Security, Malware and Forensics

Machine Learning and Security

Contents – Part I

IoT ànd Embedded Systems Security

Machine Learning and Privacy

Usable Security and Awareness

QRisk: Think Before You Scan QR Codes

Abhishek Kumar Mishra[1]([✉]) [iD], Guillaume Gagnon[2] [iD], Mathieu Cunche[1] [iD], and Sebastien Gambs[2] [iD]

[1] INSA-Lyon, Inria, University of Lyon, CITI Lab., Lyon, France
{abhishek.mishra,mathieu.cunche}@insa-lyon.fr
[2] Université du Québec à Montréal, Montréal, Canada
gagnon.guillaume.5@courrier.uqam.ca, gambs.sebastien@uqam.ca

Abstract. QR codes are pervasive in modern digital interactions, but despite their convenience, they pose significant privacy risks that are often underestimated. For instance, privacy issues escalate when scanned URLs trigger HTTP redirections involving QR URL shorteners and third-party domains, exposing user data to external entities. However, a comprehensive study of the privacy implications of QR code interactions concerning cookie exploitation and query strings remains lacking in the literature. To address this, we collected a dataset of 860 QR codes over a two-year period from France, China, Austria, India, and Canada to analyze the privacy risks associated with QR code usage. We find in this paper titled QRisk, that 39.2% of redirected URLs set cookies, including tracking, analytics, and advertising cookies, enabling potential cross-session behavioral profiling. Additionally, over 25% of QR URLs embed query strings that not only contain sensitive user identifiers but also carry information such as location data in them, leading to user profiling and social link inference.

Keywords: QR codes · URL shorteners · Privacy · Cookies · URL strings

1 Introduction

Quick-Response (QR) codes have become an integral part of modern digital communication, allowing seamless access to digital information in the physical world [9]. For instance, they are commonly used in various domains, from marketing campaigns to payment systems, and play a pivotal role in bridging physical and digital spaces. In addition, QR codes are closely associated with user smartphones, as they are primarily accessed through mobile devices via the camera app's built-in reader or a dedicated scanning application. This association makes users potentially vulnerable to various privacy breaches.

Indeed, QR codes transform analog interactions, such as ordering at a restaurant, into digital ones, enabling data collection like order histories and contact information [5, 21]. More broadly, interacting with QR codes creates *a digital trail* from everyday movements [1], activities and consumption habits [13]. This can

M. Dalla Preda et al. (Eds.): ARES 2025, LNCS 15993, pp. 3–24, 2025.
https://doi.org/10.1007/978-3-032-00627-1_1

lead to the vast collection of data on previously untracked aspects of our lives, often without explicit consent [14], thereby posing significant privacy threats.

From a technical point of view, QR codes often contain Uniform Resource Locators (URLs) with query strings (key-value pairs) that enable server-side functionalities like referral tracking and analytics. Potentially, these query strings can carry sensitive information, such as user identifiers, location data and other contextual information. Additionally, although a standalone QR code URL may appear harmless, its risks are magnified when scanned and subjected to a series of HTTP redirections. These chains frequently involve URL shorteners and potential third-party tracking domains, exposing user data to entities beyond their control. This ecosystem can be a fertile ground for tracking cookies and analytics scripts for gathering detailed user behavior profiles.

The security of QR codes has been studied previously, and various attack strategies have been demonstrated [6]. In contrast, the privacy risks associated with specific URL access encoded in QR codes remain largely unexplored in the literature. Indeed, while some studies have explored the risks associated with URL query strings [20] or shorteners [9,11,12] separately, they have not comprehensively examined vulnerabilities specific to QR code interactions from a user-centric perspective. Moreover, they lack privacy threat investigation across diverse geographical locations with various internet regulations.

Our work, titled QRisk, aims at addressing this gap by analyzing the privacy implications of query strings, cookies and redirection chains in QR-scanned URLs across three continents, including heavily censored countries [19] such as China. Our findings highlight significant risks, ranging from invasive tracking to the inadvertent exposure of personal information. In addition to unveiling these privacy risks, one of our objectives is to raise the awareness of stakeholders about the vulnerabilities inherent in QR code practices as well as to encourage users to adopt more secure practices.

In summary, the main contributions of our paper are:

- We investigate the use of URL shortening services (USS) in QR code workflows, demonstrating their role in obfuscating URLs, potentially enabling user profiling and tracking.
- We perform an in-depth examination of cookies set by third parties (USS) during URL redirection chains, categorizing them and identifying highly intrusive ones.
- We investigate query strings in QR-scanned URLs, revealing their widespread use for tracking metrics and location.
- We release a diverse and public dataset[1] of QR codes, providing a valuable resource for further research into their privacy and security challenges.

The outline of the paper is as follows. First, we introduce the related works in Sect. 2 and formulate our research questions. Next, we present the required

---

[1] Available at https://www.dev-null.ca/~gg/ARES25/ARES25-QR_Codes.zip.

background on QR codes in Sect. 3 before detailing the QR code dataset that we have collected in Sect. 4. Then, we investigate the redirections and USS in Sect. 5 and demonstrate that QR USS does deploy privacy intrusive cookies in Sect. 6. We then review the privacy implications of URL paths and query strings in Sect. 7. Finally, we conclude by discussing how the revealed privacy risks could be mitigated and regulated in Sect. 8.

2   Related Work and Research Questions

2.1   Related Work

The existing literature on the privacy and security challenges of QR codes and their associated workflows can be categorized into three types of studies.

QR Code Usage and Ecosystem Analysis. To understand the ecosystem of QR code usage, Lerner and collaborators have conducted a large-scale analysis of QR and barcode scans [8,9], uncovering general usage patterns from conventional Web links to emerging applications like Bitcoin wallets. While these studies show the growing ubiquity of QR codes, they have not analyzed the privacy threats posed by URLs and associated metadata.

Security Mechanisms in QR Code Scanners. Securing QR code scanning applications is emphasized by Krombholz and co-authors [7], who propose design recommendations to mitigate phishing attacks. SafeQR [22] leverages APIs like Google Safe Browsing and Phishtank for enhanced detection of malicious URLs. Similarly, Wahsbeh and Luccio [18] offer recommendations for creating applications that are secure, privacy-conscious and user-friendly, demonstrating their approach with BarSec Droid, a prototype Android application adhering to these guidelines. While these works focus on malicious QR codes and scanner vulnerabilities, they do not address privacy risks related to sources like query strings, cookies or redirection behaviors.

URL Query Strings and Shortening Services. Generic privacy risks of URL query strings and shortening services have been explored by [11,12,20]. Encoding of sensitive data, such as usernames and passwords, within query strings across user-submitted URLs, is highlighted by West [20], who ultimately propose a prototype framework called CleanURL to sanitize URLs. Another work focuses on ad-based URL shortening services, and concludes that the greater risks posed by it to users compared to traditional shortening services are due to the involvement of third-party advertising networks [12]. Finally, Neumann, Barnickel and Meyer [11] have investigated the vulnerabilities of URL shortening services (USS), claiming the leakage of URLs to search engines and also hinting at USS setting long-term cookies, without digging deeper into the nature of these cookies.

All of these studies focus on generic URLs and do not delve into the specific in-depth privacy challenges (*i.e.*, intrusive cookies, URL strings exploited in QR

URLs, issues with redirections) associated with QR codes and the services that provide shortened URLs for them. Thus, to the best of our knowledge, `QRisk` is the first work to investigate such critical aspects of QR code scanning.

2.2 Research Questions

Based on the results of the literature review, in this work we aim to explore and address critical questions regarding the privacy implications of QR code usage, which we detail hereafter.

Q_1 - *Information collected by QR URL shorteners without user consent.* URL shorteners play a central role in QR code workflows by deferring the final destination URL. This layer of re-direction raises significant privacy concerns:

- $Q_{1.1}$ - **Are QR URL shorteners setting cookies?** We investigate if URL shorteners set cookies during the redirection process without consent to gain insights into their role in tracking and profiling users (*cf.* Sect. 6.1).
- $Q_{1.2}$ - **What types of cookies are being set?** Cookies vary in purpose, from functional and session-based to tracking and advertising. We identify and classify the types of cookies set by QR URL shorteners to reveal the extent to which they contribute to privacy risks (*cf.* Sect. 6.2).

Q_2 - *Information collected by the target party:* The end destination of a QR code scan–the landing page (server)–has multiple opportunities to collect user data. This aspect of the workflow leads to the following questions:

- $Q_{2.1}$ - **What mechanisms are employed to transfer information?** Information can be transferred through cookies, URL paths, query strings as well as other techniques during the redirection chain. We investigate these possible mechanisms for assessing the scale of sensitive data inference (*cf.* Sect. 5).
- $Q_{2.2}$ - **How prevalent are these mechanisms?** We quantify the frequency of these mechanisms to evaluate how common privacy-intrusive practices are in QR code workflows (*cf.* Sect. 6 and 7).
- $Q_{2.3}$ - **What types of data are being transferred?** Data such as user location, session identifiers or demographic information can be encoded in query strings. We analyze the nature of this data and identify scenarios in which it can be exploited to compromise user privacy (*cf.* Sect. 7).

3   Background on QR Codes

Quick-Response (QR) codes are 2-dimensional codes that can be read via the camera, typically from a smartphone. A QR code can encode various types of data, such as digital identifiers, emails, phone numbers or URLs. There exist multiple *versions* of QR codes, corresponding to capacity ranging from 25 up to 4296 characters in version 40 [15].

URL Shortening. QR codes have a limited capacity that cannot always accommodate the needs of the application. Hence, URL Shortening Services (USS) are regularly used to convert a long URL into a short one that can easily fit in a QR code. For instance, the service QR-Code-Generator[2] (affiliated to `bit.ly`) uses the domain `qrco.de` for URL shortening purposes. Other USS, not related to QR code services, may also be used. QR code services are offered by a number of companies through both free and paid plans. In addition to the generation and customization, they usually offer additional services, including dedicated URL shortening, analytics and reporting, as well as dynamic link management.

In the situation in which a URL is encoded, QR codes are used according to the following model described in Fig. 1. First, a QR code is scanned by the smartphone of a user and the browser on the smartphone then opens the URL and retrieves the landing page. A URL shortening may be involved, in which case the browser will first contact the USS, which will redirect the browser to the landing page. In practice, additional redirection may occur on the website as well as on the USS.

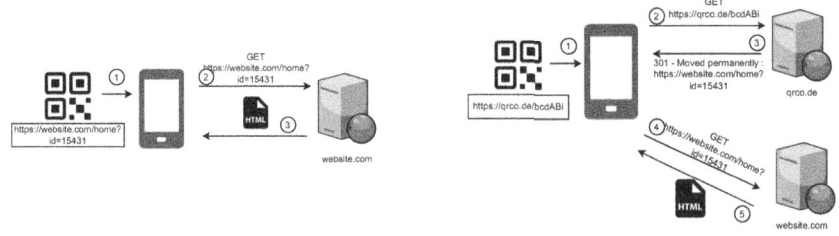

(a) Without URL shortener.   (b) With URL shortener.

Fig. 1. Process of scanning a QR code to access a URL, with and without a URL shortener.

4   QR Code Dataset

Collection. We have collected the dataset from QR codes displayed in the wild in public places across France, China, Austria, India and Canada over a two-year period (January 2023 – December 2024). It encompasses diverse real-world settings such as restaurants, bus stops, malls, public transport hubs, academic complexes and supermarkets as shown in Fig. 2.

After de-duplication and filtering out invalid entries, non-functional URLs, and corrupted codes, the curated resulting dataset contains 860 unique QR codes. Due to the diversity of locations used for the collection, we believe that this dataset captures diverse user experiences and privacy implications.

---

[2] https://www.qr-code-generator.com/.

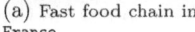

(a) Fast food chain in France.   (b) University campus in India.   (c) Hotel premise in China.   (d) Restaurant in Canada.

Fig. 2. Illustration of collected QR codes in various contextual scenarios across diverse geographic locations.

Characteristics. Table 1 outlines the key features of our dataset, highlighting how QR codes predominantly contain URLs (>93%). First, we can also observe a strong adoption of secure protocols, with 81% of URLs using `https`, and a wide range of URL lengths, ranging from a minimum of 12 characters to a maximum of 203, with an average length of 45 characters. To analyze the diversity of remote content types when accessing a URL, we extract the `Content-Type` header from HTTP responses. Most URLs point to web content, while static files like PDFs are also present, reflecting a broad mix of applications. The dataset further showcases diverse top-level domains (TLDs), with `.com`, `.fr`, `.de` and `.cn` being the most common among the top 10, underscoring the breadth of QR code use cases across various contexts.

Table 1. Characteristics of the QR Dataset

Feature	Description/Statistics
Number of QRs	860
Countries	France (721), China (60), Austria (58), India (15), and, Canada (6)
Collection Period	Jan. 2023 – Dec. 2024
HTTPS Usage	81%
Average URL Length	45 characters
Shortest URL Length	12 characters
Longest URL Length	203 characters
Content Types	web, plain-text, PDFs
Top 10 TLDs	`.com`, `.fr`, `.de`, `.cn`, `.co`, `.link`, `.org`, `.to`, `.me`, `.gouv.fr`, `.eu`

QR Code Capacity Utilization. Figure 3 presents the distribution of URL lengths, with the objective of illustrating the fraction of each QR code's total capacity that is used, along with the necessity of using USS. Vertical lines denote the capacity of various QR code versions. The plot reveals that version V4 or lower suffices for 85% of the QR codes. This suggests that QR codes are often not optimized for storage efficiency, as even higher-capacity versions such as V29 and above are either completely unused or significantly underutilized. This observation contradicts the assumption that USS is required due to URL length constraints. While the use of USS may be motivated by other reasons (analytics, dynamic link, etc.), due to the privacy and security risks associated with USS [12], URL shortening only for capacity reasons should be avoided.

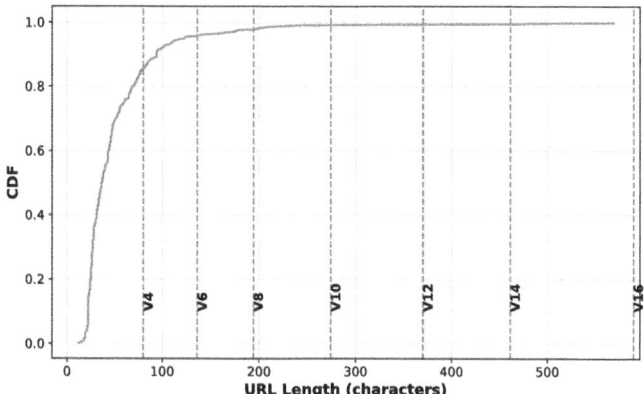

Fig. 3. Cumulative distribution function (CDF) of URL lengths in the analyzed QR codes, overlaid with capacity limits of selected QR code versions (byte mode, level L error correction, UTF-8 encoding).

Unresolvable QR Codes. Figure 4 presents an analysis of various failure modes encountered when attempting to resolve URLs encoded within QR codes. These categories include *Connection Timeout, Failed to Establish Connection, SSL Certificate Failure,* and *Redirection Issues.* Among these, connection failures and timeouts are observed to be the most frequent errors, suggesting that a notable fraction of QR codes point to unavailable or misconfigured web resources at the time of our access. SSL certificate failures indicate the presence of expired or untrusted certificates, which may compromise the security of interactions initiated through QR scans. The occurrence of redirection issues highlights cases in which excessive or broken redirections hinder access to the intended content. These results underscore potential usability and security concerns associated with QR code scanning, reinforcing the need for caution when interacting with encoded URLs.

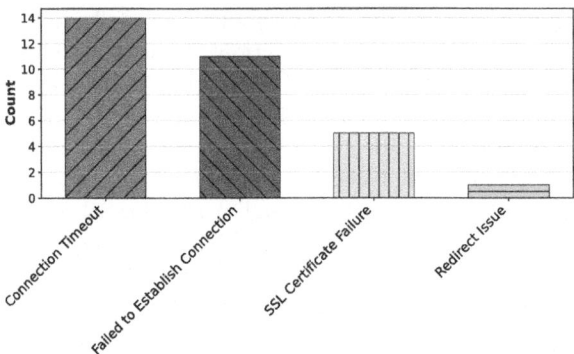

Fig. 4. Error in fetching encoded URLs

5 Redirections and USS

Redirection is a common mechanism in USS, in which a user is directed from a shortened URL to its destination URL. Analyzing redirections provides insights into user navigation patterns and potential privacy concerns.

5.1 Redirection

We explore three key metrics related to redirection: the proportion of URLs that involve redirection, the distribution of redirection type and the cumulative distribution function (CDF) of redirection chain lengths.

First, approximately 55% of the URLs exhibit at least one redirection, indicating that a majority of the shortened URLs require additional hops to reach their final destinations. Second, we have analyzed the distribution of redirection types, as shown in Fig. 5a. The majority of redirections are HTTP 301 (*i.e.*, Moved Permanently) responses, accounting for close to 60% of the total redirections while HTTP 302 (Found) responses follow at around 40%. This distribution suggests that most redirections (301) are designed to be persistent.

Finally, the CDF of redirection chain lengths, depicted in Fig. 5b, provides insight into the depth of redirection paths. The result shows that 60% of URLs involve only one redirection, while 40% require two or more redirections. Notably, 10% of URLs undergo three or more redirections, which may heighten privacy risks due to users' navigation paths passing through multiple intermediate domains, particularly when managed by distinct entities. This is particularly concerning as it can lead to increased exposure of user data to multiple parties, potentially without the user's knowledge or consent.

5.2 Top Providers

Identifying popular QR code generators and providers is crucial to understanding the USS ecosystem within QR codes. In particular, we examine the reuse of domain names across different QR codes, as illustrated in Fig. 6.

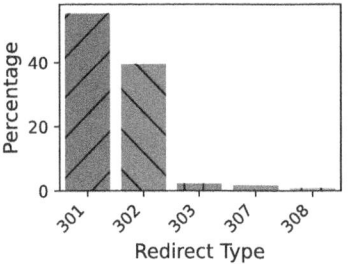

(a) Redirection types.

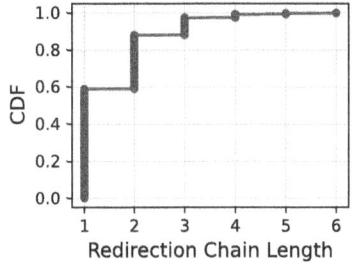

(b) Lengths of redirection chains.

Fig. 5. HTTP redirections in QR URLs.

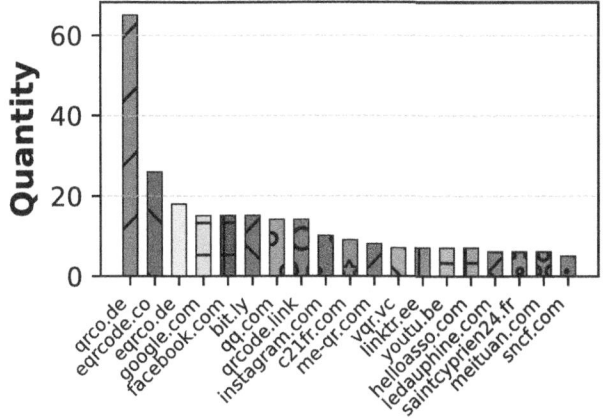

Fig. 6. Reuse of domain names across different QR codes.

Our findings highlight a diverse set of top domains frequently associated with QR codes, indicating their widespread adoption and reuse. These include dedicated QR code providers like qrco.de, eqrcode.co, qrcode.link, me-qr.com and vqr.vc, as well as general-purpose URL shorteners such as bit.ly. These domains dominate the QR USS landscape, with significant reuse across different QR code deployments.

In addition to dedicated providers, search engines and social networks also play a role in this space. For instance, we also notice in our dataset that google.com is occasionally used for URL shortening. Social network platforms like facebook.com, youtu.be and instagram.com sometimes provide short URLs and QR codes to facilitate content sharing. These cases complement the activities of specialized QR code generators and emphasize the multi-faceted nature of URL shortening in the QR code ecosystems. In the next section, we will be specifically focusing on dedicated QR USS.

6   Cookie Exploitation by QR USS

The use of cookies in USS linked to QR codes poses significant privacy risks, particularly due to their involvement as a third party. These services can set cookies during redirection, often collecting user data without explicit consent. Domains frequently involved in redirections could use tracking and analytics cookies to monitor user behavior, including link clicks, browsing patterns and locations.

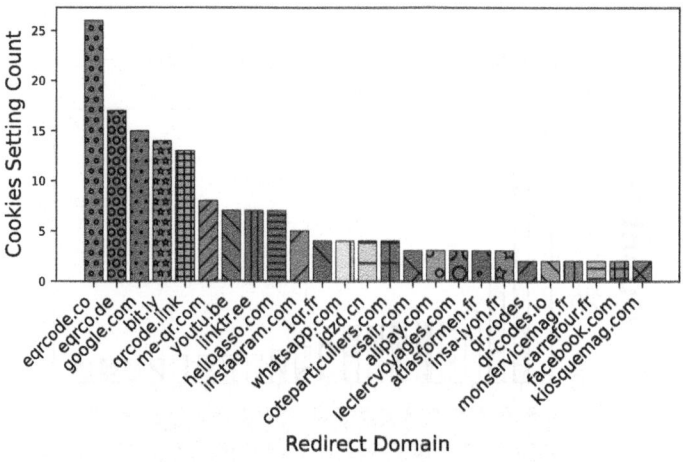

Fig. 7. Number of instances that top redirectors set cookies.

6.1   Cookies in Redirections

Cookies' potential for misuse raises significant privacy concerns, especially when they collect data without users' explicit consent. Our analysis reveals that 39.2% of URLs with external redirections set cookies, potentially involving third-party domains that engage in tracking and analytics. Top redirectors using cookies (see Fig. 7) include prominent domains like `qrcode.co`, `eqrco.de`, `google.com`, `bit.ly` and `qrcode .link`, which leverage cookies for a variety of purposes, which we investigate in Sect. 6.2. Social networks and content-sharing platforms such as `instagram.com`, `whatsapp.com`, and `linktr.ee` also integrate cookies into redirection chains.

An analysis of individual cookie usage by top redirectors (Fig. 8) reveals that certain redirection domains consistently set cookies in 100% of their QR services. Domains such as `qrcode.link`, `eqrco.de`, `eqrcode.co`, `linktr.ee`, `bit.ly`, `helloasso.com`, `youtu.be` and `google.com` exemplify this trend. This uniform behavior underscores their reliance on cookies as a mechanism for enabling functionalities like session tracking, personalization and data collection.

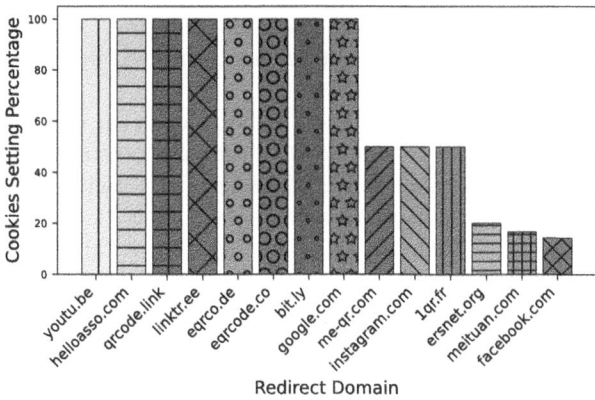

Fig. 8. Individual cookie usage by top redirectors.

6.2 Classifying Cookies Set by QR USS

Inspired by prior work [2,10], we have used `Cookiepedia` [16] as a key resource for classifying cookies. `Cookiepedia` is a comprehensive database of cookies maintained by the Consent Management Platform (CMP) OneTrust [2,4]. Table 2 lists potentially intrusive cookies (analytics/advertising/tracking) classified by `Cookiepedia`.

Table 2. Intrusive (tracking/advertising/analytics) Cookies collected by QR USS [16].

Cookie Names
NID, dwanonymous_7ad186a87c92467d3c0495460d6555fc, _fbp, mgrefby, cquid, SS, AS, SP, dwac_10e76b50b2189fd2b0a7ed1e4f, VISITOR_INFO1_LIVE, mgref, __wpdm_client, G

Targeting/Advertising/Analytics Cookies. We found 13 targeting/advertising cookies set by QR USS. By tracking activities across multiple QR scans, these cookies may enable advertising networks to understand shopping habits, interests and preferences. In the following, we highlight some of the notable cookies and their purposes mentioned in `Cookiepedia`:

- `VISITOR_INFO1_LIVE`, monitors YouTube video interactions on external sites, influencing video recommendations and optimizing ad placements tailored to user engagement.
- `SP`, associated with event-booking, collects click data to enhance advertising campaigns across multiple platforms, ensuring the effectiveness of ad delivery strategies.

- `dwanonymous_7ad186a87c92467d3c0495460d6555fc`, tracks anonymous interactions for dynamic ad targeting, analyzing patterns without directly identifying users.
- `dwac_10e76b50b2189fd2b0a7ed1e4f`, collects data on user navigation and interaction to fine-tune real-time ad targeting and personalization.
- `cquid`, supports advanced ad delivery by identifying user sessions and linking them to ad content most likely to drive engagement.
- `__wpdm_client`, facilitates tailored advertising by tracking interactions with dynamic web content.
- `mgref`, tracks referrer information to analyze the origin of user traffic, such as from websites, ads or social media campaigns, enabling precise attribution of ad performance.
- `mgrefby`, captures intermediate interactions to provide a detailed view of multi-step browsing paths, enhancing the granularity of campaign evaluations.
- `SS` (Session Source), gathers session data in real-time, including clicks and page visits, allowing advertisers to dynamically adjust campaigns to reflect user behavior.

The integration of these cookies within QR USS poses serious privacy challenges, as they can aggregate data across platforms to build detailed user profiles. Furthermore, there is no consent collection nor information of the user, which prevents the exercise of user rights with respect to privacy, in contrast to other online situations.

Extended Cookie Analysis. We identify 22 out of 89 cookies that are not included in the `Cookiepedia` classification in Table 2 and are labeled as *unclassified.* We start by still using `Cookiepedia` insights to dive into four key aspects of such cookies to know their prevalence: i) the host domains setting such cookies, ii) the websites reporting them as third-party cookies, iii) the websites reporting them as persistent cookies and iv) the websites reporting them as session cookies.

Figure 9 provides a distribution of the above four key attributes. The figure reveals that these unclassified cookies exhibit diverse behaviors in terms of their presence across different domains and classifications. The first plot illustrates that while most cookies are confined to a small number of host domains, a few are widely distributed, spanning nearly 300 domains. The second and third plots highlight that these unclassified cookies are frequently observed as third-party and persistent cookies, with some instances exceeding 1000 occurrences. The final plot shows that session cookies, which typically exist only for a single browsing session, have a significantly higher number of occurrences, with some appearing in over 6000 instances. This suggests that these unclassified cookies may be extensively used for tracking purposes, particularly through session-based mechanisms, reinforcing the need for further investigation into their role and privacy implications.

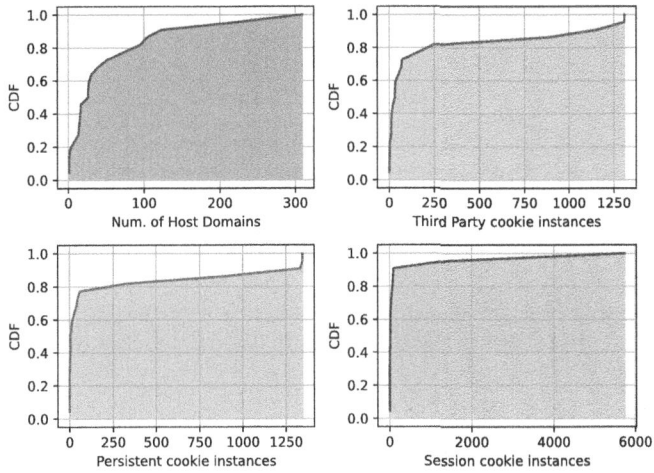

Fig. 9. Characteristics of unclassified cookies.

Moreover, an extended investigation revealed that among these *unclassi-fied* cookies are the tracking cookies _bit[3] from Bitly, which stands out for monitoring interactions with shortened URLs, such as clicks and timestamps, potentially uncovering behavioral patterns. On the advertising front, cookies like adsStatData[4] and trackingId[5] enable targeted advertising by assigning unique user identifiers and tracking ad performance. Given the large lifetimes of several other cookies (see next section) like qB, msv4_idCookieUser, qrm and QoSID, their classification as an intrusive cookie looms large.

6.3   Cookie Lifetimes

We analyze the lifetimes of all the above-identified potentially intrusive cookies to understand the duration of data collection. Figure 10 illustrates the distribution of privacy-intrusive cookies' lifetimes in days. Results show that intrusive cookies persist way beyond a single browsing session, with more than 95% of cookies lasting between 30 and 7300 days. This indicates QR USS sets cookies potentially enabling the construction of detailed user profiles over extended periods. Among all cookies, COMPASS stands out with a lifetime of less than a day, suggesting that it is primarily used for session-based tracking. In contrast, QoSID cookies persist for 2315 days, while qrm, msv4_idCookieUser and qB last respectively for 3650, 4166 and 7300 days, indicating long-term tracking capabilities. In comparison, we observed that more than 27% of cookies that are not classified as privacy-intrusive by Cookiepedia expire when the browser is closed or have a lifetime of less than a day.

---

[3] https://bitly.com/pages/privacy.
[4] https://me-qr.com/privacy-policy.
[5] https://www.facebook.com/privacy/policy.

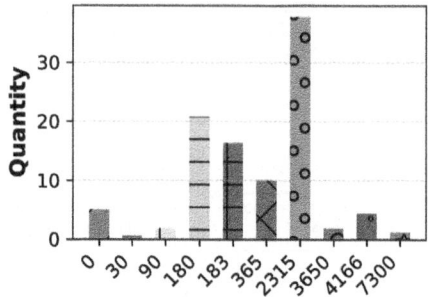

Fig. 10. Lifetimes of intrusive cookies (in days).

6.4   Set-Cookie Prevalence Across Geographic Locations

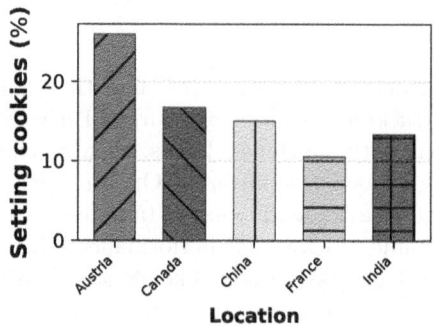

Fig. 11. Variance of set-cookies across geographic locations.

Figure 11 illustrates the distribution of websites that actively set cookies across different geographic locations from which the QR codes were collected. The results reveal notable differences in cookie-setting behaviors among countries. Austria and Canada exhibit a relatively higher prevalence of websites that set cookies, whereas Canada, China and India also show higher percentages. These variations can be attributed to differences in privacy regulations, enforcement levels and common industry practices. The elevated presence of set cookies may be influenced by factors such as the widespread use of analytics and tracking services. The results indicate that user privacy experiences may vary substantially depending on geographic location, reinforcing the need for a global perspective on cookie regulation and enforcement.

7 Privacy Implications of URL Path and Query Strings

Independent of the resource they point to, QR codes are often associated with a specific context. Information related to this context can be transmitted to web servers through the URL associated with the QR code. The USS may also have access to this information, though it is unclear whether they process it. Such contextual information is typically encoded via the Query String part of the URL (*e.g.*, the URL path can also be used for this purpose). In our analysis, we found that 25.7% of the URLs contained query parameters, increasing even more when also taking into account those hidden behind URL shorteners and redirections, indicating their significant presence in QR code usage.

Table 3 provides an overview of the most frequent query parameters extracted from URLs embedded in QR codes. These query strings often encode metadata related to marketing campaigns (`utm_source`, `utm_campaign`, `utm_medium`), user identifiers (`id`, `token`, `cid`), payment information (`pa`, `pn`, `mc`) and other contextual data such as session details, venue and timestamps. The presence of structured tracking parameters suggests a significant potential for user profiling and behavioral tracking across multiple web domains. Notably, the high occurrence of payment-related identifiers indicates that QR codes are increasingly used in financial transactions, raising concerns regarding potential data exposure and security risks. In the following, we perform a detailed analysis of the privacy threats posed by these query strings, investigating their implications for user tracking, data retention and third-party sharing mechanisms.

7.1 Privacy Implications

A manual analysis of the dataset uncovered a number of data items transferred via query string parameters. Representative examples are presented in Tables 4, 5 and 6. In the following, we review those items as well as some personal information that can be inferred from them.

Generic User Profiling. Query parameters embedded in QR codes can reveal various types of personal information that could be exploited for user profiling. Beyond consumption habits, QR codes can also be linked to medical contexts. For instance, QR codes associated with clinical trials may contain parameters disclosing the *medical center* conducting the research and the *trial date* (see Table 4). Additionally, event-related QR codes often include details about *time, venue, and session types*, allowing organizations to track attendance patterns and user interests in specific topics. Even seemingly minor details, such as a *flyer ID*, can be leveraged to infer which promotional materials a user has interacted with, along with the location.

Table 3. Most frequent query strings

Query	Count	Examples of values
utm_source	35	seatbackad, AfficheVitrine, INSA, akilux, QR code, QR-code, qr, VersionFemina, affichage, lbpcatcadeau, QR_Code, qr_code, affiche, tag2d, maline, print, Print
utm_campaign	25	Bien, fermeture-covid, op12-aout-2023, jeu-rugby, carrefour, 2023_03_01_Aidants_VersionFemina, work_info, b.nouveau_programme_de_fidelite.2024-01-31 Epigenetic, ZT, QR-code-revetsens, akilux-21-22, vuelingsyteng, store4574, INSA_Partnership_FRA_TutRecruit, francais-parlent-anglais
utm_medium	25	ooh, qrcode, akilux, QR code, qr, Vitrophanie, Display_Branding, informative_sign, affichage, Print, metro, QRcode, stopper, Partnership
id	14	com.freetnessenergy, 100057276736505, CNU85387, 5d985bd8-1a52-49c4-b177-a3186016aa0a, 1394140769041321986, CNU66119, 100087057884876, 192189, com.keolis.ruban, 61153, prod.maasify.evian, 61553441277844
r	10	qr
pa	9	Q751854265@ybl, gpay-11240877578@okbizaxis, paytmqr1w14125ijv@paytm
pn	9	PhonePeMerchant, Paytm, Google Pay Merchant
mc	5	5399, 0000
utm_content	5	Presse, iledefrance, 2557, NW_zt, revetsens
purpose	4	00
token	4	q1ZKLUvNK4nPTFGy...
cid	4	B2010120080300323, B64105231128C2999, B72106230517A0809
table	4	438, B02, 506, T5
COUNTRY	4	1
questlist	4	COUNTRY;CDPF;SOURCE
CDPF	4	31122, 32048, 17501
mode	4	02
starts_at_from	3	2024-09-08 08:00:00, 2024-09-10 08:00:00, 2024-09-10 12:30:00
day	3	2024-09-07
days	3	2024-09-10, 2024-09-08
cu	3	INR
contentsessiontype_ids	3	7585
order	3	room_title
filterbox	3	true
ends_at_to	3	2024-09-10 09:30:00, 2024-09-08 09:30:00, 2024-09-10 14:00:00
timezone	3	false
room_ids	3	8374,8373

QR codes found on product packaging frequently contain *product identifiers* or *descriptive details*, revealing specific consumption behaviors (see toothpaste and liquor entries in Table 4). Similarly, QR codes in print advertisements may include query parameters identifying *the publication source and issue number*, thereby exposing *reading habits and preferences* (see magazine entries in Table 4). These findings highlight how query parameters in QR codes serve as *silent carriers of personal information*, emphasizing the need for stricter privacy considerations when embedding tracking elements in consumer-facing QR campaigns.

Location Data. Query string parameters embedded in QR codes often contain location-related information, allowing third parties to infer a user's whereabouts. In some cases, these parameters provide *coarse-grained geographical details*, such as a *region* or a *postal code*, revealing the general area in which the QR code was

Table 4. Generic profiling through query string parameters from QR codes.

Information	Query String	Notes
Medical information	cid=qr%3ANucleus_Global%3Arespiratory%2Fongoing-clinical-trials%3A29_07_2024%3ALanding_Page	*Center* and *date* of the clinical trials
Event tracking	'contentsessiontype_ids': ['7585'], **'starts_at_from':** **['2024-09-10 08:00:00'], 'ends_at_to':** **['2024-09-10 09:30:00'], 'room_ids': ['8374,8373'],** 'grade': ['1'], 'filterbox': ['true'], 'legendbox': ['false'], 'timezone': ['false'], **'days': ['2024-09-10'], 'day':** **['2024-09-07'],** 'viewType': ['list'], 'segment': ['poster'], 'segmentname': ['Abstract Sessions'], 'order': ['room_title']	*Time* and *venue* of the event
Flyer ID	**'flyerCode': ['bonapp106ja983'],** 'redirectURL': ['https://bit.ly/3A3SIG6']	*ID* of the information flyers
Toothpaste	qrcode=onpack&utm_source=PackSecondary&utm_medium=QR&utm_campaign=Alma-BH0437-BE-FR&utm_content=Sustainability&Purpose-BOP&utm_term=**I8_White**&evt_**product_id=** **VyeH9t7wKCVgaUxT dnYAwbab**&evt_implicit_scan_id=VET5myhUd9CPr2e2GBYAUkhr	Name (*Signal Integral 8 white*) and identifier of the toothpaste
Liquor	utm_source=onpack&utm_medium=qr&utm_campaign=**get-27**&utm_content=**70cl-SEU**	Name of the liquor and size of the bottle
Cheese	utm_source=pack&utm_campaign=**camembert**&utm-source=QR_CODE	Type of cheese
Name of the magazine and issue	utm_source=Presse&utm_medium=QRCODE&utm_campaign=LEGS24&utm_content=**Diverto1+S2+24**	Name of the magazine and issue (2nd semester 2024)
Name of the magazine and issue	utm_source=**FEMINA-OCT**&utm_medium=QRCODE&utm_campaign=24LEGS&utm_content=PRESSE	Name of the magazine (*Femina*) and issue (*October*)

Table 5. Location inference through query string parameters from QR codes.

Information	Query String	Notes
Region	v=iledefrance-affichage&utm_source=affichage&utm_medium=metro&utm_campaign=francais-parlent-anglais&utm_content=**iledefrance**	Region *Ile de France*
City	CD_ACCESS=NF8E4X&**CP=35300**&QR=1&utm_source=lbpcatcadeau&utm_medium=qrcode	Postal code
Train station	**uicDeparture=8738249**	Train station identifier
Store	**store=store4574**&utm_campaign=store4574	Store identifier
Restaurant venue and table	**restaurant=K0076**&**table=T5**&terrace=false&token=6A5D2166CB73A75F34141DC991350B2C	Restaurant identifier and table identifier
Points of interest	'continue': [**placeid=ChIJo82WsnB9EcRj og** **UKxUEHhg**&source=g.page.m.rc._&laa=merchant-web-dashboard-card]	Unique location ID
GPS coordinates	country=FR&articleId=IN7017&**lat=48.73085021972656**&**lon=2.174370050430298**	Latitude and longitude

scanned (see Table 5). Additionally, store identifiers and train station references can be leveraged to infer visits to specific commercial venues or transportation hubs. These identifiers serve as digital breadcrumbs that, when combined with other contextual data, can contribute to behavioral profiling.

Beyond regional and commercial location data, query parameters may also expose *precise location details*. This includes parameters containing *GPS coordinates*, allowing the tracking of exact user movements or *unique place identifiers* associated with points of interest (*e.g.*, restaurants and review pages). The presence of restaurant-specific table numbers further suggests the capability to monitor *in-store seating preferences*. Consequently, if users open these QR codes on-site (as is typically the case), external parties can correlate location data with *timestamps* to reconstruct detailed visit timelines, raising significant privacy concerns. Hereafter, we discuss in detail the extended version of this threat.

Social Link Inference. Location-specific QR codes could potentially be leveraged to infer social links between users, as spatio-temporal coincidence [3] (being in the same place at the same time) is a strong indicator of social ties. For instance, in some restaurants, QR codes provided to access the menu and place orders are specific to the venue and the table: https://restaurant.com/restaurants/564/commander/eat_in?table=506.

A group of people dining together would access this QR code at approximately the same time, revealing that they are all seated at the same table and, therefore, part of the same social group (see Fig. 12). Although we found no indication that such an inference is currently being performed, we observed that the underlying information is readily available in many cases, as these table-specific QR codes are commonly used by major fast-food restaurant chains.

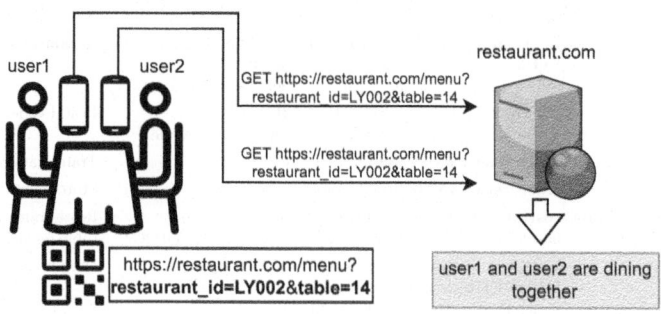

Fig. 12. Scanning a QR code to access the menu at a restaurant can reveal that two persons are dining together.

Other Privacy Leaks. Beyond user profiling and location inference, QR code query strings may also expose *sensitive security-related information*. Notably, some URLs contain *API keys* or *authentication tokens* embedded directly within the request parameters (see Table 6). These keys, if leaked or intercepted, could allow unauthorized access to protected resources, potentially leading to data breaches or system compromises. The presence of authentication keys further exacerbates security risks, as malicious actors could exploit them to impersonate legitimate users or access restricted services. Additionally, query strings reveal *application identifiers* used for tracking and analytics. These identifiers allow third parties to monitor user interactions across different digital platforms, facilitating targeted marketing and behavioral profiling.

Table 6. Other leaks.

Information	Query String	Notes
API key	**'apiKey':** **['gQpFZIioRDSOCYMoeFLY5Kbo3Dl19Quz']**	Security threat
Auth key	'fiche_type': ['publique'], 'lang': ['fr'], 'idann': ['26472'], 'internal': ['1'], 'idag': ['1'], **'authKey':** **['ab7127222e4ac2f3d0fdc7a8e8486f4f']**	Security threat
Application ID	**'appId': ['3']**, 'campaignId': ['1699281368256960'], 'utm_source': ['cobranding'], 'utm_campaign': ['vpfr-migration-1223'], 'utm_medium': ['cobrandingnoel']	User-analytics

7.2 Encoded and Non-Human-Readable Parameters

The previous cases were identified because the data was in plaintext and understandable. However, other parameters may carry similar information in an encoded or non-human-readable format, which can be associated with contextual information by the website owner. Our dataset includes 38 QR codes in which the URL contains an alphanumerical identifier of at least 6 characters[6]. However, we were unable to determine whether these were used to convey context information. Thus, the cases identified in Sect. 7.1 should be considered as the visible part of the iceberg.

7.3 Query Strings Across Countries

Figure 13 presents the distribution of query strings embedded in QR code URLs across different geographic locations. The variation in the presence of query strings suggests differences in how QR codes are generated and utilized globally. Notably, India exhibits the highest proportion of URLs containing query strings, surpassing 60%, highlighting a high potential for embedding tracking or identification parameters. China also shows high levels, with approximately 40% of QR codes embedding such parameters. In contrast, France, Canada, and Austria have significantly lower occurrences, suggesting a lesser reliance on query-based tracking in QR-linked services.

---

[6] Examples of identifiers: `utm_campaign=042022_media_mdlz_ritz`, `token=cd0d80288 ae42eef94b4132d982064e9d7f37834`, `products_id=51658860`, `id=1730457376655- ddaf88af-1fe6-4f5b-b657-6426c82d4ce3`, `scenario_uid=11f23a77f5a8a186f444`.

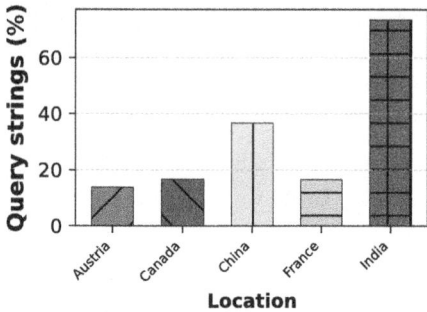

Fig. 13. Variance of present query strings across geographic locations.

However, these discrepancies must be interpreted with caution, as the dataset exhibits sampling biases, particularly the over-representation of French QR codes and the limited number of samples from certain countries such as India (only 15 codes). Addressing this imbalance will require a more representative and geographically diverse dataset, which we leave as future work. The presence of query strings in QR codes has already raised privacy concerns, underscoring the necessity for location-specific privacy considerations when assessing QR code-related risks.

8   Discussion and Conclusion

Discussion. Tech-savvy users might attempt to assess potential privacy risks by inspecting the URL embedded in a QR code before scanning it. However, problematic parameters may be concealed through obfuscation or only become visible further in the redirection chain (*e.g.*, after passing through a USS). Thus, users are often unaware of the usage of information. Addressing this issue requires better disclosures and mechanisms for informed user consent.

Another challenge is due to the role of USS providers as third parties in the data collection process. These intermediaries are often not explicitly mentioned in privacy policies, leaving users unaware of their involvement. This omission complicates accountability, and it has already been shown that many privacy policies fail to account for such third-party roles [17]. Regulations need to ensure that USS providers are clearly identified in policies. While laws like the General Data Protection Regulation (GDPR) emphasize transparency and consent, they do not specifically address the unique privacy risks associated with QR codes and USS. To mitigate the risks of unauthorized data collection and profiling, policymakers should consider updating existing frameworks to encompass emerging technologies, and service providers must proactively inform and protect users.

Conclusion. This paper provides a comprehensive analysis of the privacy risks associated with QR code usage and URL shortening services (USS). Our study leverages a unique and diverse dataset of 860 QR codes collected over two years, highlighting real-world practices across multiple domains, regions, and internet regulations. Unlike prior work, we examine the interplay between QR codes, USS and tracking mechanisms, uncovering significant risks such as invasive behavioral profiling and geolocation tracking. Our findings reveal the significant presence of tracking/advertising/analytics cookies set in redirected URLs. Moreover, we find that URLs embed sensitive data like user identifiers and location data in the query strings, enabling user profiling and social link inference.

Acknowledgements. Sébastien Gambs is supported by the Canada Research Chair program and a Discovery Grant from NSERC. The authors also acknowledge support from Inria, PEPR IPOP, and ANR GTTP projects.

References

1. Bernholz, L.: Philanthropy and Digital Civil Society: Blueprint 2022 (2021). https://pacscenter.stanford.edu/publication/philanthropy-and-digital-civil-society-blueprint-2022/
2. Bollinger, D., Kubicek, K., Cotrini, C., Basin, D.: Automating cookie consent and {GDPR} violation detection. In: 31st USENIX Security Symposium (USENIX Security 2022), pp. 2893–2910 (2022)
3. Crandall, D.J., Backstrom, L., Cosley, D., Suri, S., Huttenlocher, D., Kleinberg, J.: Inferring social ties from geographic coincidences. Proc. Natl. Acad. Sci. **107**(52), 22436–22441 (2010)
4. Hils, M., Woods, D.W., Böhme, R.: Measuring the emergence of consent management on the web. In: Proceedings of the ACM Internet Measurement Conference, pp. 317–332 (2020)
5. Hunter, T.: QR codes are a privacy problem but not for the reasons you-ve heard. Washington Post (2021). https://www.washingtonpost.com/technology/2021/10/07/are-qr-codes-safe/
6. Kieseberg, P., et al.: QR code security. In: Proceedings of the 8th International Conference on Advances in Mobile Computing and Multimedia, pp. 430–435 (2010)
7. Krombholz, K., Frühwirt, P., Rieder, T., Kapsalis, I., Ullrich, J., Weippl, E.: QR code security – how secure and usable apps can protect users against malicious QR codes. In: 2015 10th International Conference on Availability, Reliability and Security, pp. 230–237 (2015). https://doi.org/10.1109/ARES.2015.84
8. Lerner, A.: Measuring and Improving Security and Privacy on the Web: Case Studies with QR Codes, Third-Party Tracking, and Archives. Ph.D. thesis, University of Washington (2017)
9. Lerner, A., et al.: Analyzing the use of quick response codes in the wild. In: Proceedings of the 13th Annual International Conference on Mobile Systems, Applications, and Services, pp. 359–374 (2015)
10. Munir, S., Siby, S., Iqbal, U., Englehardt, S., Shafiq, Z., Troncoso, C.: Cookiegraph: understanding and detecting first-party tracking cookies. In: Proceedings of the 2023 ACM SIGSAC Conference on Computer and Communications Security, pp. 3490–3504 (2023)
11. Neumann, A., Barnickel, J., Meyer, U.: Security and privacy implications of URL shortening services. In: Proceedings of the Workshop on Web 2.0 Security and Privacy (2010)

12. Nikiforakis, N., et al.: Stranger danger: exploring the ecosystem of ad-based URL shortening services. In: Proceedings of the 23rd International Conference on World Wide Web, pp. 51–62 (2014)
13. Rotsios, K., Konstantoglou, A., Folinas, D., Fotiadis, T., Hatzithomas, L., Boutsouki, C.: Evaluating the use of QR codes on food products. Sustainability **14**(8), 4437 (2022)
14. Smith, J.J.: Corporate tips: Are QR codes problematic from a Privacy Law standpoint? (2021). https://www.lexology.com/library/detail.aspx?g=fe9e7b45-fbbf-4906-972f-9d541f5516d1
15. Tiwari, S.: An introduction to QR code technology. In: 2016 International Conference on Information Technology (ICIT), pp. 39–44 (2016). https://doi.org/10.1109/ICIT.2016.021
16. Trust, O.: Cookiepedia (2024). https://cookiepedia.co.uk. Accessed 13 Nov 2024
17. Utz, C., Amft, S., Degeling, M., Holz, T., Fahl, S., Schaub, F.: Privacy rarely considered: exploring considerations in the adoption of third-party services by websites. arXiv preprint arXiv:2203.11387 (2022)
18. Wahsheh, H., Luccio, F.L.: Security and privacy of QR code applications: a comprehensive study, general guidelines and solutions. Information **11**(4), 217 (2020). https://doi.org/10.3390/info11040217
19. Warf, B.: Geographies of global internet censorship. GeoJournal **76**, 1–23 (2011)
20. West, A.G., Aviv, A.J.: On the privacy concerns of URL query strings (2014)
21. Woo, E.: QR Codes Are Here to Stay. So Is the Tracking They Allow. The New York Times (2021). https://www.nytimes.com/2021/07/26/technology/qr-codes-tracking.html
22. Yao, H., Shin, D.: Towards preventing QR code based attacks on android phone using security warnings. In: Proceedings of the 8th ACM SIGSAC Symposium on Information, Computer and Communications Security, ASIA CCS 2013, pp. 341–346. Association for Computing Machinery, New York (2013). https://doi.org/10.1145/2484313.2484357

Evaluating Argon2 Adoption
and Effectiveness in Real-World Software

Pascal Tippe$^{(\boxtimes)}$ and Michael P. Berner

FernUniversität in Hagen, Hagen, Germany
`pascal.tippe@fernuni-hagen.de`

Abstract. Modern password hashing remains a critical defense against credential cracking, yet the transition from theoretically secure algorithms to robust real-world implementations remains fraught with challenges. This paper presents a dual analysis of Argon2, the Password Hashing Competition winner, combining attack simulations quantifying how parameter configurations impact guessing costs under realistic budgets, with the first large-scale empirical study of Argon2 adoption across public GitHub software repositories. Our economic model, validated against cryptocurrency mining benchmarks, demonstrates that OWASP's recommended 46 MiB configuration reduces compromise rates by 42.5% compared to SHA-256 at \$1/account attack budgets for strong user passwords. However, this protection offers a linear trade-off: increasing memory 44.5-fold to the stronger 2048 MiB RFC 9106 setting further reduces compromise rates by a valuable, but costly, 11.8% points. Crucially, both configurations fail to mitigate risks from weak passwords, with 96.9–99.8% compromise rates for RockYou-like credentials regardless of algorithm choice. Our repository analysis shows accelerating Argon2 adoption, yet weak configuration practices: 46.6% of deployments use weaker-than-OWASP parameters. Surprisingly, sensitive applications (password managers, encryption tools) show no stronger configurations than general software. Our findings highlight that a secure algorithm alone cannot ensure security, effective parameter guidance and developer education remain essential for realizing Argon2's theoretical advantages.

Keywords: password hashing · Argon2 · cryptographic adoption

1 Introduction

As reliance on digital systems grows, ensuring secure user authentication has become a critical challenge. Password hashing functions are pivotal in protecting credentials, yet legacy algorithms like SHA-256 exhibit vulnerabilities when deployed in authentication systems. While theoretically secure, these fast algorithms are ineffective against modern attacks that leverage specialized hardware (GPUs/ASICs) to test billions of passwords per second. This mismatch between the intended use of fast hashing functions and the capabilities of modern attackers highlights the need for algorithms specifically designed to resist acceleration

© The Author(s), under exclusive license to Springer Nature Switzerland AG 2025
M. Dalla Preda et al. (Eds.): ARES 2025, LNCS 15993, pp. 25–46, 2025.
https://doi.org/10.1007/978-3-032-00627-1_2

from specialized parallel hardware. Argon2, the winner of the 2015 Password Hashing Competition, represents a significant advancement by building on the principle of memory-hardness, first popularized by scrypt, to increase costs for attackers [2]. By requiring substantial RAM allocation, Argon2 leverages the fact that memory is more expensive for attackers to scale in parallel than raw computation, thereby disadvantaging adversaries who use specialized cracking hardware. However, its effectiveness depends heavily on parameter selection, with configurations like the OWASP-recommended 46 MiB of memory differing significantly from the RFC 9106 proposal of 2 GiB. This disparity underscores the importance of standardized, context-aware parameterization.

While Argon2's advantages are documented, its real-world adoption remains inconsistent. Our preliminary scans suggest a reliance on older algorithms, including fast hashing functions like SHA-256 and iterative functions like PBKDF2. Even when Argon2 is implemented, suboptimal parameter configurations are common, reflecting systemic barriers to cryptographic modernization. This study addresses four key questions: (1) How does Argon2, as the modern standard, compare to a legacy fast hash like SHA-256 in resisting modern attacks, and what is the impact of its parameter choices? (2) What is the current state of Argon2 adoption among software projects? (3) How have Argon2 parameters in new projects evolved over time? (4) Do applications with heightened security requirements implement stronger parameter configurations? While other memory-hard functions are surveyed in our real-world analysis, our initial security comparison focuses on the stark contrast between the legacy (SHA-256) and modern (Argon2) approaches to provide a clear baseline.

The remainder of this paper is organized as follows: Sect. 2 reviews related work. Section 3 describes our methodology, while Sect. 4 details our attack simulations. Section 5 presents our cracking results, Sect. 6 explores data from software repositories, and Sect. 7 analyzes this data. Section 8 discusses our findings before we conclude in Sect. 9.

2   Background and Related Work

Online platforms continuously suffer from breaches that expose user passwords en masse. To mitigate this risk, traditional password storage relies on cryptographic hashing to prevent credential exposure. Unlike encryption, deterministic hash functions like SHA-256 produce fixed-length digests that cannot be feasibly reversed. However, attackers can enumerate password candidates until they find a matching hash value. This attack vector fundamentally depends on two factors: the computational efficiency of the hash function and the statistical distribution of password *guessability* across user populations. To prevent attackers from using precomputed rainbow tables and attacking multiple breached credentials simultaneously [14], defenders add a randomly generated string (called a salt) to passwords, forcing attackers to target each individual salted password hash. While salting prevents batch attacks, it does not address the fundamental vulnerability of fast hash algorithms to brute-force and dictionary attacks. Instead of exhaustively iterating over all possible character combinations, attackers exploit users' tendency to follow predictable patterns during password creation: combining words, replacing characters with numbers, or appending special symbols. Deprecated password metrics like Shannon entropy fail to capture these human-chosen password patterns, leading researchers to develop more accurate estimation techniques. The zxcvbn algorithm's [19] pattern-aware entropy and models like Markov chains [18] or context-free grammars [18] better reflect real-world password weaknesses by analyzing dictionary matches, spatial keyboard patterns, and breach recurrence patterns. Bonneau [6] formalized the concept of guessability, establishing a direct connection to practical password strength measurement by quantifying the average number of guesses required to breach a target percentage of user accounts. This approach better captures systematic risks. For example, Dell'Amico et al. [8] determined an attacker would require 149,053,078 attempts on average to crack over half the passwords in three real-world datasets (approximately $2^{27.14}$). Bonneau [6] calculated median attack costs ranging between $2^{19.8}$ and $2^{21.6}$ attempts across multiple leaked datasets, including RockYou, to crack 50% of the passwords. Florencio and Herley [9] found an average bit-strength of approximately 40.54 bits using naive calculations across half a million users over three months.

Memory-hard functions represent a paradigm shift in password hashing by imposing substantial RAM requirements. The interplay between memory-hardness and guessability becomes apparent in Blocki et al.'s framework [5], where attackers maximize compromised accounts within fixed budgets. The objective is not to linearly increase costs for both defenders and attackers by iterating hash functions but to create asymmetric costs that disproportionately disadvantage attackers using specialized hardware such as ASICs. Argon2, the winner of the 2015 Password Hashing Competition, implements this approach through three tunable parameters: memory cost (m), iterations (t), and parallelism (p). Argon2 comes in three variants: Argon2d (fast but vulnerable to side-channels), Argon2i (side-channel resistant but slower), and Argon2id (a hybrid approach). This study focuses exclusively on Argon2id, which RFC 9106 recommends as the default for password hashing. Its design prioritizes time-memory tradeoff resistance, forcing attackers to spend either prohibitive time or memory resources, directly impacting guessability economics. Blocki et al. [5] modeled this increased strength against guessing attacks as an optimization problem, using Bitcoin mining hardware and blockchain hashrate as proxies for determining attacker strength, finding that memory-hard hash functions substantially increase guessing costs. Argon2's security relies on selecting appropriate values for its parameters, yet many developers in user studies struggle to implement even basic password hashing correctly [13]. Furthermore, while OWASP recommends 46 MiB of memory for general use cases [15], the RFC 9106 standard [2] advocates for significantly higher values (2048 MiB). This 44.5 × difference reflects a tension between practical deployment constraints and theoretical security requirements, potentially leaving developers uncertain about which configuration is suitable for their specific applications. Our work bridges this gap by analyzing real-world Argon2 implementation patterns across GitHub repositories, quantifying the security impact of different parameter configurations through attack simulations, and identifying systemic mismatches between academic parameter recommendations and developer implementation practices. This research extends prior work by providing concrete evidence of how theoretical security advantages translate, or fail to translate, into practical security improvements in deployed software.

3   Methodology

This study employs a comprehensive methodology to evaluate the technical performance and real-world adoption of Argon2 as a password hashing algorithm. The analysis is divided into two interconnected components: a security analysis of Argon2 configurations compared to SHA-256 and an empirical investigation into the adoption trends of Argon2 across software repositories on GitHub. By combining cryptographic modeling, password strength estimation, attack simulation, and repository analysis, this methodology provides a holistic view of both theoretical efficacy and practical implementation.

3.1   Security Analysis Framework

The security analysis focuses on Argon2's resistance to offline password cracking under realistic attacker constraints. The threat model assumes an attacker with offline access to hashed credentials and computational resources comparable to large-scale cryptocurrency mining operations. Attackers are assumed to prioritize cost-efficiency, spending a fixed budget for cracking passwords. We leverage public password datasets for strength estimation. To model cryptographic costs, we analyze the economics of cryptocurrency mining as a proxy for attacker resources. Bitcoin's SHA-256 implementation serves as the baseline for traditional fast, non-memory-hard hashing costs, while Monero's RandomX, a memory-hard proof-of-work algorithm based on Argon2d, provides insights into memory-dependent computation costs. These models are validated using energy consumption benchmarks from consumer-grade CPUs, ensuring real-world applicability. Password strength estimation is conducted using zxcvbn's pattern-aware entropy metric. The RockYou 2009 dataset, containing leaked cleartext passwords from an online platform, is used as the baseline for password distributions, filtered to include only passwords meeting modern length requirements (≥ 8 characters). For modeling enhanced password policies, we generated a synthetic dataset by doubling the zxcvbn bit-strength values from the filtered RockYou data. This transformation simulates passwords with significantly higher guessing resistance (e.g., a 20-bit password becomes a 40-bit password) while preserving the overall distribution characteristics. Attack simulations evaluate the effectiveness of different hashing configurations under three budget scenarios for attackers: $0.1, $1, and $20 per targeted account. Analyzed configurations include SHA-256 as a baseline and

Argon2 implementations with both RFC 9106 recommended parameters (2048 MiB memory) and OWASP-suggested hardened parameters (46 MiB memory).

3.2 Data Collection and Repository Analysis

To assess Argon2's adoption in real-world software projects, we systematically collect data from public repositories on GitHub using its REST API. GitHub was chosen due to its prominence in open-source development and its extensive repository metadata, which includes indicators such as stars that we use as a proxy for repository quality. While acknowledging that user motivations for starring repositories vary, prior research suggests that stars are more reliable indicators of relevance than other metrics like the number of forks [7]. The analysis employs two complementary search methods: repository metadata search and code search. Repository searches query titles, descriptions, and topics for keywords related to password hashing algorithms (*Argon2, bcrypt, scrypt, yescrypt* and *PBKDF2*). The selection was driven by their prominence as widely recognized password hashing algorithms, providing a comparative baseline to evaluate Argon2's adoption and security properties against established standards with distinct characteristics in memory-hardness and performance. Since GitHub limits search results to 1,000 entries per query, searches are segmented by repository creation date to capture a comprehensive dataset. Code searches identify instances of password hashing algorithm implementations within source code files. To address GitHub's indexing limitations for code searches, results are segmented by programming language. Languages were selected based on their support for symbol extraction on GitHub and manual reviews of preliminary data[1]. To ensure accuracy in both search methods, filtering mechanisms are applied to exclude false positives (e.g., repositories unrelated to password hashing or those associated with cryptocurrencies). Automated exclusion based on keywords is supplemented by manual refinement to further reduce noise in the dataset.

3.3 Manual Review and Parameter Analysis

Repositories identified through searches undergo manual review to extract Argon2 parameter configurations and classify software types. This step ensures accuracy by accounting for variations in parameter naming conventions and library usage that automated tools might miss or misclassify. Additionally, this process verifies that Argon2id is used appropriately within repositories and not in contexts such as cryptocurrency mining. Repositories where parameter configurations cannot be assessed or that serve non-productive purposes (e.g., specifications or benchmarking tools) are excluded from further analysis. To focus

---

[1] Selected languages: Bash, C, C#, C++, CodeQL, Dart, Elixir, Erlang, Go, Haskell, Java, JavaScript, Kotlin, Lua, PHP, Python, R, Ruby, Rust, Scala, Starlark, Swift, TypeScript.

on high-quality implementations, only repositories with a significant number of stars are included in the final dataset. The extracted parameter configurations are analyzed to evaluate their alignment with recommended security practices. Repositories are categorized by software type (e.g., web applications, password managers), allowing comparisons between parameter strengths across different application domains. To analyze trends in Argon2 adoption over time and across software categories, statistical hypothesis testing is employed. Non-parametric tests such as chi-square goodness-of-fit and independence tests examine whether observed distributions deviate significantly from uniformity or exhibit associations between variables (e.g., repository type and parameter strength). A significance level of $p = 0.05$ is used throughout the analysis.

4   Attack Simulation Framework

The attack simulation framework evaluates Argon2's economic resistance to offline password guessing by modeling adversarial cost structures under realistic resource constraints. Our analysis compares two recommended parameter configurations representing different security philosophies: the RFC 9106 recommendation (2048 MiB memory), which prioritizes ASIC resistance through substantial memory demands, and OWASP's pragmatic guidelines (46 MiB memory), which balance security with server resource limitations. These configurations create a $44.5\times$ difference in memory allocation, enabling a direct comparison of their effectiveness in thwarting large-scale attacks.

4.1   Parameter Configurations

To explore the trade-offs between security and resource efficiency, we analyze two widely referenced Argon2 parameter configurations: the RFC 9106 recommendation and OWASP's pragmatic guidelines. The RFC 9106 configuration prioritizes resistance to attacks by allocating 2048 MiB of memory per hash computation, thereby imposing significant memory demands on attackers and defenders. In contrast, OWASP's configuration uses a reduced memory allocation of 46 MiB, reflecting a balance between security and server-side performance constraints. These configurations represent distinct security philosophies, with the former emphasizing robustness against specialized hardware and the latter accommodating practical deployment scenarios. Both are the first recommended configuration and use parameters $t = 1$ and $p = 1$, allowing a direct comparison. The $44.5\times$ difference in memory allocation between these configurations provides a valuable basis for evaluating their relative effectiveness in thwarting large-scale attacks. In our simulations, attackers are modeled as having fixed budgets of \$0.10, \$1.00, and \$20.00 per targeted account. These budgets reflect varying levels of attacker investment, from low-cost opportunistic attacks to more resource-intensive campaigns targeting higher-value accounts. The budgetary constraints are used to calculate the number of hash computations an attacker can afford under each parameter configuration, enabling direct comparisons of their economic resistance.

4.2   Cost per Hash Evaluation

The computational cost of Argon2 is central to its ability to resist offline attacks. To estimate this cost, we use cryptocurrency mining as a proxy for adversarial resource expenditures due to its well-documented economic metrics and operational similarities to password cracking. Specifically, we derive baseline costs for SHA-256 from Bitcoin mining data and extrapolate Argon2 costs using Monero's RandomX algorithm, which incorporates Argon2d to create an initial cache and extends it with additional computations inside a virtual machine. For SHA-256, Bitcoin's network hashrate (701.72 EH/s) and block rewards as of February 20, 2025 [3] provide a per-hash cost estimate of approximately 7.079×10^{-19}. Argon2's memory-hardness complicates direct benchmarking. However, RandomX [16] serves as a functional analog due to its use of approximately 2 GiB memory allocations and its use of Argon2d as a base element. Adjusting for RandomX's additional computational overhead (conservatively estimated at $100\times$), we estimate Argon2's base cost at 2.729×10^{-12} per hash for 2 GiB configurations with the network statistics on February 20, 2025 (4.54 GH/s, 32 blocks per hour, and $232.31 per unit) [4]. This cost scales linearly with reduced memory allocations, allowing us to model the economic impact of different parameter settings.

To validate these estimates, we conducted energy consumption calculations using processor thermal design power (TDP) values and measured hashes per second on consumer-grade CPUs[2]. For example, using an energy price of $0.05/kWh and considering only CPU power consumption, the cost per hash was calculated as 4.17×10^{-7}, which exceeds our baseline estimate derived from RandomX mining data. This discrepancy highlights that our cryptocurrency-based estimate represents a highly-optimized, lower-bound cost achievable by a resourceful attacker. It thus confirms our baseline is a pessimistic (i.e., worst-case) estimate from a defender's perspective, strengthening the validity of our attack simulations.

4.3   Dataset Preparation

The datasets used in this study are critical for simulating realistic attack scenarios and evaluating password strength distributions under different hashing configurations. We employ two datasets: the RockYou dataset and a synthetic dataset, D_{syn}, derived from it. The RockYou dataset, leaked in 2009, contains over 32.6 million user passwords and is an important resource in password security research due to its size and real-world origins [5,6]. To ensure consistency and relevance to contemporary minimal security standards, we preprocessed this dataset. First, all passwords were normalized to UTF-8 encoding using Python scripts equipped with the `chardet` library to resolve character encoding inconsistencies; entries with unresolvable issues were removed (affecting 242 passwords). Next, passwords shorter than eight characters were excluded to align with modern minimum policy requirements, reducing the dataset by approximately 16.18

---

[2] Intel Core i3-7130U, AMD FX-6300, Intel Core i5-10300H, Intel Core i5-9400F, AMD Ryzen 5 2600X.

million entries and yielding a curated subset of 16.42 million passwords. The filtered RockYou dataset exhibits a median password length of nine characters ($M = 9.46, \sigma = 2.43$). Notable outliers include lengthy HTML fragments or URLs used as passwords that likely reflect user behavior anomalies rather than deliberate choices. These entries were retained to preserve the dataset's authenticity despite their slight skewing effect on bit-strength calculations. Password entropy was estimated using zxcvbn's pattern-aware algorithm and showed a mean (median) entropy of 21.9 (21.7) bits with a standard deviation of 9.6 bits, a third quartile of 26.8, and a first quartile of 15.6. Recognizing that RockYou reflects pre-2010 user behavior patterns, we constructed D_{syn} by systematically doubling the bit-strength values of each password in our filtered set accounting for improved password policies and heightened user awareness. This process preserves the original distribution's shape while creating an updated benchmark in higher-security contexts with a median strength of 43.4 bits, reflecting password strengths observed in systems with robust security requirements [12].

5   Attack Simulation Results

Our attack simulations reveal fundamental security trade-offs between hashing algorithms, parameter configurations, and password strength. In Figs. 1 and 2, we illustrate these dynamics. Each plot shows the underlying password strength as a cumulative distribution (the blue curve), where the y-axis represents the percentage of passwords and the x-axis represents the password bit strength. The vertical lines indicate the percentage of accounts compromised by an attacker with a specific budget for SHA-256 and two Argon2 configurations.

RockYou Dataset: As depicted in Fig. 1, SHA-256's susceptibility to low-cost attacks is pronounced, with near-total compromises (99.77%) at just $0.10 per account, increasing to 99.83% at a $1.00 budget. Conversely, Argon2 introduces modest resistance. The 46 MiB parameters reduce compromise rates to 98.81% at $1 budgets, while the 2048 MiB configuration cuts down success to 96.89% under identical conditions which is a notable 2.94% improvement compared to SHA-256, protecting more than 475,000 accounts. While Argon2 impacts the attackers success to a limited extent, the weak passwords are the decisive factor.

Synthetic Dataset (D_{syn}): Figure 2 shows a shift when modeling stronger user passwords and policies. Here, SHA-256 exhibits higher resistance due to improved password bit-strength. Due to the exponential effects of password bit-strength, the gap between hashing algorithms widens. At $1.00 budgets, 88.31%, 50.74%, and 38.92% of all passwords are compromised for SHA-256, Argon2 with 46 MiB, and Argon2 with 2048 MiB, respectively. For the $20 budget, this rate increases to 91.85%, 59.16%, and 48.69%. This demonstrates that the stronger 2048 MiB configuration provides stronger protection compared to 46 MiB, with an 11.82 (10.48) percentage point lower compromise rate under the $1 ($20) budget. However, the largest difference is the change from SHA-256 to the lower Argon2 configuration, indicating that it provides significantly more protection.

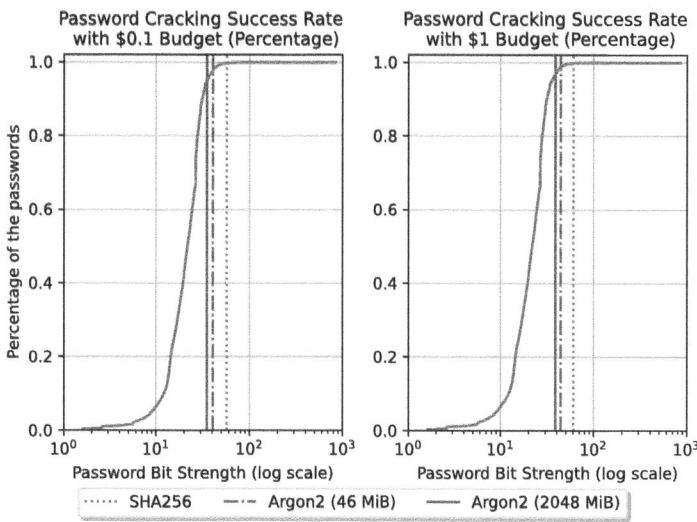

Fig. 1. Password cracking success rates for the RockYou dataset under $0.1 and $1 budgets for SHA-256 and Argon2 configurations (46 MiB and 2048 MiB).

These results highlight the reliance on the strength of user passwords: for RockYou's median 21.7-bit passwords, even the strongest Argon2 configuration could not prevent an attacker from cracking almost all passwords on small budgets. However, simulations using D_{syn}'s median 43.4-bit passwords show that Argon2 additionally protects 43.16% of all accounts compared to SHA-256 with a $20 budget. For defenders, increasing Argon2's memory parameter provides a linear increase in cracking costs for an attacker, a valuable gain especially when protecting strong passwords. The most significant leap in security comes from adopting Argon2 over SHA-256. Subsequent increases to memory parameters offer incremental, yet important, improvements at a higher operational cost.

6   Real-World Data Collection

Following our analysis of Argon2's theoretical security properties and its resilience under simulated attacks, we shift our focus to research questions 2–4 by analyzing Argon2's adoption trends through a systematic examination of GitHub repositories.

6.1   Repository Search

The dataset was constructed through systematic GitHub [10] repository searches for five password hashing algorithms (Argon2, bcrypt, scrypt, yescrypt, and PBKDF2) across GitHub's entire availability period (2008–2024). Table 1 shows the number of repositories through the filtering steps. For each algorithm, we

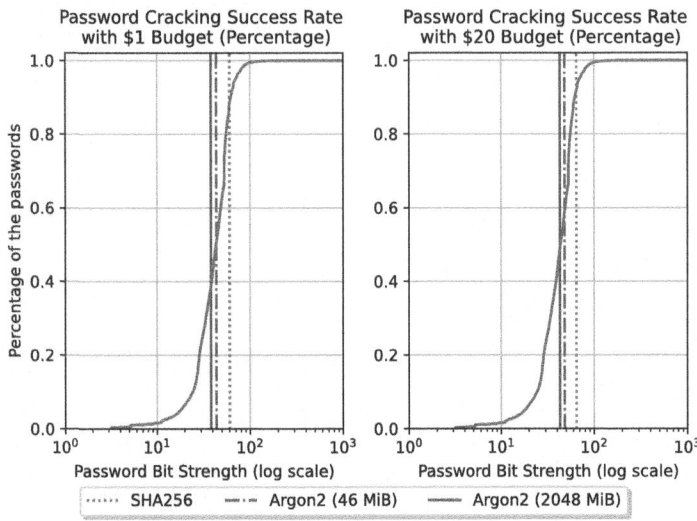

Fig. 2. Password cracking success rates for the synthetic dataset (D_{syn}) under \$1 and \$20 budgets for SHA-256 and Argon2 configurations (46 MiB and 2048 MiB).

executed temporal searches segmented by repository creation time, followed by a filtering phase. Effectively, we decided to include 31 repositories from one user for PBKDF2 and set the cutoff at 66 or more repositories per user. After manual review, we created a keyword list[3] related to common cryptocurrency themes to exclude irrelevant projects. After the filtering, we checked random samples from the results for each hashing algorithm and noticed that the 1,520 scrypt repositories still contained many repositories unrelated to password hashing but included similar terms (e.g., scrypto, bash scrypt, python scrypt), some of which we attribute to (intentional) misspellings. Therefore, we continued to filter the results and created an additional keyword list to ensure relevancy with words commonly used with hashing and key derivation functions: *password, hash, auth, kdf, key derivation, percival* (the author of scrypt). Of these 1,520 repositories, 1,279 contained none of these additional keywords, a number we judged to be too high. Therefore, we used an additional list containing similar names[4] that only excluded 439 repositories. Among these 439 repositories, all but three contained none of the relevancy words and were subsequently excluded. The three outliers were manually reviewed, and one was marked as relevant, resulting in 1,081 remaining hits (1,520-439). Out of these, only 238 contained at least one relevancy word, which led us to manually review the other results by analyzing the URL name and project description. We excluded projects if they were clearly not

---

[3] *miner, mining, proof-of-work, proof of work, currency, coin, wallet, bitzeny, doge, mint, blockchain, contract.*

[4] *scrypta, scrypto, scrypts, scrypted, scrypting, inscription, scryptic, scrypture, ipsa-scrypt.*

related to password hashing, marked them as *yes* if we clearly connected them, and coded them as *possible* if we could not conclude with high certainty. The latter was the case for 326 repositories that did not contain any description. This resulted in 595 repositories, including the 219 possible hits, identified as scrypt password hashing repositories. Including the possible hits overestimates rather than underestimates the prevalence of scrypt password hashing. Since Argon2 was included in five repositories with a creation date before 2015 (the year it won the Password Hashing Competition), we reviewed them manually. Two of them included Argon2 later, while the others are abandoned or just include Argon2 references in non-productive parts.

Table 1. Repository collection and filtering statistics per algorithm

Algorithm	Initial Repos	Spam Removed (%)	Mining Filtered (%)	Final Count
Argon2	1,602	534 (33.33%)	36 (2.25%)	1,032
bcrypt	12,727	604 (4.75%)	58 (0.46%)	12,065
scrypt	2,396	528 (22.04%)	1,273 (51.13%)*	595
yescrypt	76	0 (0%)	36 (47.37%)	40
PBKDF2	1,006	0 (0%)	12 (1.19%)	994

* Includes extended relevance checks for scrypt repositories (see Subsect. 6.1).

6.2   Code Search

The code search was performed using the GitHub Search API for programming languages supporting symbol extraction and additional programming languages that we assessed as relevant after our manual review of repositories, as listed in Subsect. 3.3. The primary search term for each query was the name of the password-hashing algorithm itself, refined with negative keywords to exclude cryptocurrency-related projects, which are outside the scope of this research. These negative keywords were the same as used in the repository search (see Subsect. 6.1). Furthermore, we excluded files with the *.md* extension (to avoid *README* files and other documentation) and files located within directories containing *test* in their name to minimize irrelevant results. Due to the potential for a single repository to contain multiple instances of a given hashing function across different files, our search results often included duplicate entries for the same repository. To address this redundancy and estimate the number of unique repositories, we calculated a duplication quota based on the ratio of distinct repository IDs within the first 1,000 search results. This quota was then applied to the total number of search results to approximate the underlying number of unique repositories implementing each hashing algorithm.

Table 2 shows the code search results. Initial searches without programming language differentiation yielded total code hits of 48,768 for Argon2, 519,168 for bcrypt, 36,592 for PBKDF2, 131,328 for scrypt, and 3,232 for yescrypt. Calculating repository redundancy required estimating a repository duplication quota based on unique repositories within the first 1,000 results (5.9% for Argon2, 1.2% for bcrypt, 13.6% for PBKDF2, 26.2% for scrypt, and 67.3% for yescrypt). This resulted in estimated total repositories of 45,891, 512,938, 31,615, 96,920, and 1,057, respectively. The search separated by programming languages and hash function has 115 combinations. For 52 combinations, the query results were below 1,000, and the repository number could be counted directly without using the duplication quota. The overall results are shown in Table 2. Since we could not conduct the additional filtering steps for scrypt that we did for the repository search, we used the filtering ratio from the repository search to estimate the filtered number of scrypt results. Table 3 shows the quotas for different result sizes and hashing functions.

Table 2. Total hits and estimated number of repos, separately for the different password hashing methods and searches.

	Argon2	bcrypt	PBKDF2	scrypt	yescrypt
Code Search with Programming Language Differentiation:					
Total Code Hits	41,464	226,768	75,521	88,211	905
Estimated Total Repos	33,170	213,012	64,645	64,416	531
				(29,116*)	
Simple Code Search:					
Total Code Hits	48,768	519,168	36,592	131,328	3,232
Estimated Total Repos	45,891	512,938	31,615	96,920	1,057
				(43,808*)	
Repository Search Results:					
Results from Repo Search	1,032	12,065	994	595	40

* After applying the scrypt false positive removal rate of 54.8% as determined in Subsect. 6.1 after only applying the initial cryptocurrency filter.

6.3 Parameterization

For manual identification of Argon2 configurations, we decided to focus only on high-quality repositories. To focus on high-quality repositories from the 1,068 found in our search, we selected those with at least three stars, resulting in a set of 253. We further excluded repositories that were archived or not productive (e.g., described as homework assignments, demos, or trials). We then divided the remaining 206 repositories into four equal sets based on their star count (3–4, 5–10, 11–30, and more than 30). We further excluded 21 repositories tied to cryptocurrency applications or password cracking. Afterward, we classified each

Table 3. Repository redundancy quotas for password hashing methods from code search analysis with programming language differentiation. For large result sets (>3,500 hits, n = 30) and medium-sized sets (1,000-3,500 hits, n = 26), quotas were estimated from the first 1,000 results. For small result sets (<1,000 hits, n = 52), exact quotas were determined. Analysis covers 108 of 115 programming language and hash function combinations.

Repo Redundancy	Argon2	bcrypt	PBKDF2	scrypt	yescrypt	Total
Estimated	5.50%	9.89%	11.83%	24.03%	—	13.67%
(>3500, n = 30)	n = 3	n = 12	n = 7	n = 8		n = 30
Estimated	32.59%	23.60%	26.97%	44.15%	—	32.36%
(≤ 3500, n = 26)	n = 9	n = 4	n = 7	n = 6		n = 26
Exactly	59.73%	51.17%	50.83%	64.11%	37.24%	50.87%
determined (n = 52)	n = 11	n = 7	n = 9	n = 9	n = 16	n = 52
Total	42.03%	24.84%	31.70%	44.96%	25.90%	33.89%
(n = 108*)	n = 23	n = 23	n = 23	n = 23	n = 16*	n = 108*

* In 7 of the total 115 cases, there were no matches for yescrypt and therefore not considered here.

project into the following categories: components (libraries, wrappers, bindings), applications, and sensitive applications (password managers and file encryption). Then we proceeded to manually extract the Argon2id configuration with a focus on iterations (t) and memory (m). In 24 repositories, we were unable to determine the parameters because they did not offer a (complete) default parameterization, were specifications, or were benchmarking tools. If the software code used a library and did not modify the parameter settings, we extracted the library's default settings as parameters. In sum, parameterization data was collected for 161 repositories.

7 Real-World Implementations Analysis

7.1 Adoption

Figure 3 shows the number of repositories for the hash functions per creation year. To put this into the context of general repository developments, we decided to introduce two more search terms, with *VPN* being related to computer security and *video editing*, which is unrelated to the field. The development of bcrypt aligns with that of these additional search terms. Argon2 shows continuous growth in newly created projects since its inception in 2015. scrypt and PBKDF2 show notably less development, which we assume is due to the introduction of Argon2. Argon2 also managed to overtake the number of new repositories for scrypt, PBKDF2, and yescrypt from 2018 onwards. yescrypt, a competitor of

Argon2 in the Password Hashing Competition, did not succeed in keeping up with Argon2's adoption and shows stagnating, low creation numbers. Focusing on the time between 2015 and 2024, the average number of repositories with a creation date in the respective years has a mean value of 102.7 for Argon2 ($\sigma = 59.95$), 85.3 for PBKDF2 ($\sigma = 25.47$), and 51 for scrypt ($\sigma = 27.52$). We used the Kruskal-Wallis test to determine a statistically significant difference between the three groups ($H(2) = 6.07, p = .048$) and then conducted Dunn tests to compare the hashing functions with each other. Argon2 and scrypt differ significantly ($z = 2.13, p = .033$), and PBKDF2 and scrypt differ significantly ($z = 2.13, p = .033$), while there is no statistically significant difference between Argon2 and PBKDF2 ($z = 0, p = 1.0$). This indicates that Argon2 clearly overtook scrypt, but due to the larger variance in the number of Argon2 repositories created over the years, no statistically significant overall difference is evident between Argon2 and PBKDF2.

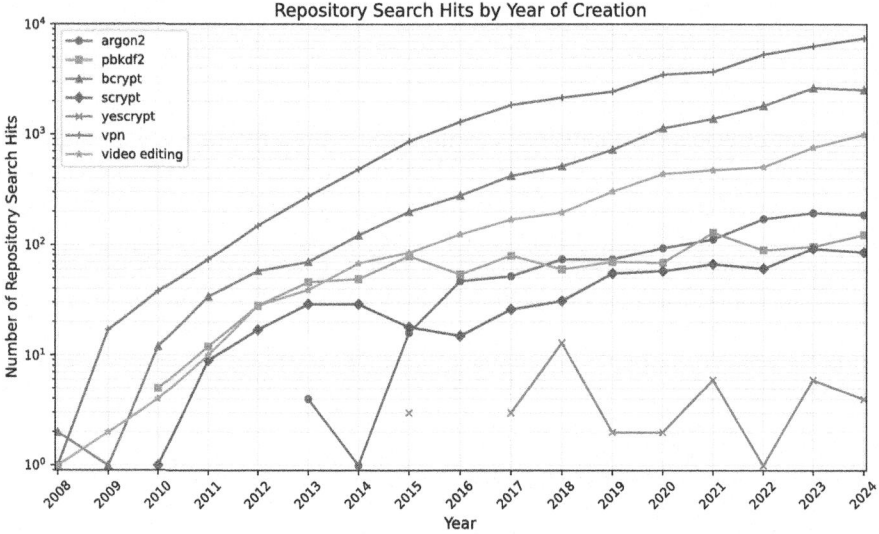

Fig. 3. Repository search hits for various password hashing algorithms (2008–2024).

During the repository analysis, we found that 141 repositories offered multiple hashing algorithms. The majority (93) implements exactly two functions (of the five in the scope of this analysis), 33 offer three functions, and 15 offer four functions. Of the possible 26 combinations, only 13 appear in our dataset. yescrypt appears in only two of these 13 combination repositories and is therefore excluded from the following significance test. A chi-square goodness-of-fit test shows that there is no clear evidence that the distribution differs from a uniform distribution ($\chi^2(3) = 0.25, p = .969$). Therefore, we did not find evidence that some of the analyzed hashing functions are overrepresented in combination repositories.

The code search had more uncertainties since the number of repositories was estimated for search queries with more than 1,000 results based on the repository redundancy quota in the accessible results. Table 3 shows that the determined quotas clearly differ. Evidently, the estimated repository duplication quotas are closer to the precisely calculated ones when the number of code search results is smaller (below 3,500). This is plausible since the subset of 1,000 accessible code search results will be more representative if the selection pool is smaller. To ensure that the observed differences in repository duplication quotas are not systematically influenced by the interplay between hashing method and the size of the result set, we performed a chi-square test of independence, excluding yescrypt to avoid potential bias. The non-significant result $(\chi^2(6) = 8.36, p = .213)$ supports the validity of comparing methods, indicating that the identified trends likely reflect genuine differences rather than sampling artifacts. Overall, the results from the general code search and the one segmented by programming languages support the results from the repository search, as shown in Table 2. The repository search and simple code search results generally followed a consistent pattern. However, PBKDF2 was an exception, as the programming-segmented code search yielded more PBKDF2 results than the simple code search. We could not identify a plausible explanation for this anomaly. The other hash functions led to a smaller number of estimated repositories in the segmented code search since the redundancy quota was more accurately calculated. The code search results support the repository search results for the adoption of Argon2, confirming its growing prominence among password hashing algorithms.

7.2 Parameterization over Time

During the data collection phase, we used the star count as a quality proxy to focus on high-quality repositories. We set the minimum star count to three to conduct the initial filtering. To test our assumption, we divided this initial set of 253 repositories into four equal-sized classes: 3–4 stars, 5–10 stars, 11–30 stars, and more than 30 stars. We created a contingency table with the star sets and the number of productive and non-productive repositories that we filtered in the following step. A chi-square independence test shows the distribution is not independent $(\chi^2(6) = 12.53, p = .006)$ and that higher star counts are associated with fewer non-productive repositories. This supports our assumption of the star count as a quality proxy. After successfully extracting the parameter configurations from the selected 161 repositories (as described in Subsect. 6.3), we noticed that the configurations were clustered around the following most popular configurations:

- $t = 3, m = 4096$ KiB (33 times)
- $t = 3, m = 65536$ KiB (28 times),
- $t = 2, m = 19456$ KiB (11 times),
- $t = 1, m = 65536$ KiB (10 times),

– $t = 2, m = 65536$ KiB (9 times)

We attribute this clustering especially to the default values of used libraries. We compared the parameter strength by linearly extrapolating the OWASP Argon2 recommendations and classifying the extracted configurations as weaker or stronger. Figure 4 shows the OWASP extrapolation and the observed repository configurations. 75 repositories were weaker and 86 were stronger than the OWASP recommendations. To see the development over the years, we created a contingency table shown in Table 4 and grouped the repository creation years 2013–2024 into three groups: before 2018, 2019–2021, and 2022-2024. The grouping helped to reach the minimum number of entries for the chi-square test and takes the publication dates of RFC 9106 and OWASP recommendations into account. A chi-square independence test confirms that these factors are not independent $(\chi^2(2) = 8.42, p = .015)$. This shows an increase in parameterization strength over time.

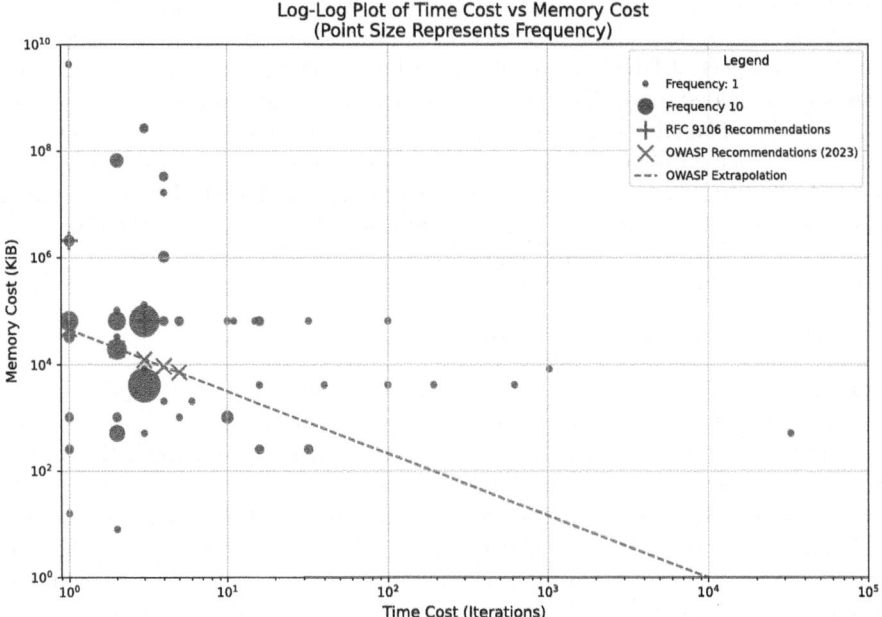

Fig. 4. Log-log plot of time cost (t) versus memory cost (m). The size of each blue dot represents the frequency of data points with a specific combination of t and m. The red crosses represent OWASP recommendations, while the purple crosses represent RFC 9106 recommendations. The dashed red line extrapolates OWASP recommendations using a linear regression in log-log space.

Table 4. Repository age and categorical strength of parameterization.

Parameterization Strength	Repository Age			Total
	≤2018	2019–2021	2022–2024	
Weaker	38 (60.3%)	23 (41.1%)	14 (33.3%)	75 (46.6%)
Stronger	25 (39.7%)	33 (58.9%)	28 (66.7%)	86 (53.4%)
Total	63 (100.0%)	56 (100.0%)	42 (100.0%)	161 (100.0%)

7.3 Parameterization by Program Type

Table 5 shows the parameterization strength for the different software types. Weaker configurations are more prevalent in components, while the configurations are stronger for applications. A chi-square test confirms this hypothesis by showing a statistically significant effect of the software type variable $(\chi^2(2) = 7.38, p = .007)$. When the applications are separated into sensitive (file encryption, password managers) and general-purpose password hashing applications, there is no statistically significant difference $(\chi^2(1) = 0.002, p = .967)$ between them. So, the hypothesis that sensitive software programs use stronger parameterizations could not be confirmed. To exclude effects from the star count on the software type, we tested with a contingency table if there is a statistically significant effect of the repository star count (divided in four equal-sized groups) on the software type (application vs. component) and determined no significant effect $(\chi^2(3) = 3.41, p = .332)$.

Table 5. Cross table: Software type x categorical strength of parameterization.

Parameterizations	Sensitive Application	Application	Component	Total
Weaker	4 (26.7%)	6 (27.3%)	65 (52.4%)	75 (46.6%)
Stronger	11 (73.3%)	16 (72.7%)	59 (47.6%)	86 (53.4%)
Total	15 (100.0%)	22 (100.0%)	124 (100.0%)	161 (100.0%)

Additionally, we analyzed how parameterization is affected by the star count. Surprisingly, stronger configurations dominate the repositories with lower star counts (3–10), while repositories with more stars (more popular repositories) exhibit weaker configurations (see Table 6). A chi-square test confirmed this effect as statistically significant $(\chi^2(3) = 8.71, p = .033)$. While this seems counterintuitive, we noticed that the star count (popularity) is also tied to age. This hypothesis would fit with the finding from Subsect. 7.2 that older repositories exhibit weaker configurations than newer ones. Therefore, we tested the influence of repository age on star count and confirmed with the chi-square independence test that older repositories have a higher star count ($\chi^2(6) = 32.53, p < .001$). This is also intuitive since older projects have more time to gain popularity and accrue stars. Finally, we tested the influence of repository age on software type and found that there is a statistically significant effect such that the number of components is higher for older repositories while the younger repositories include more applications ($\chi^2(2) = 20.25, p < .001$). This weakens the finding that components exhibit weaker configurations, since repository age is a confounding factor here as well, suggesting that the observed difference may be more strongly associated with when repositories were created rather than their functional purpose as components versus applications.

Table 6. Star categories and categorical strength of parameterization.

Parameterization Strength	Repository Star Count				Total
	3–4 Stars	5–10 Stars	11–30 Stars	>30 Stars	
Weaker	13 (34.2%)	12 (35.3%)	28 (62.2%)	22 (50.0%)	75 (46.6%)
Stronger	25 (65.8%)	22 (64.7%)	17 (37.8%)	22 (50.0%)	86 (53.4%)
Total	38 (100.0%)	34 (100.0%)	45 (100.0%)	44 (100.0%)	161 (100.0%)

8 Discussion

Our analysis reveals a key tension: while Argon2 is technically superior to legacy functions, its real-world impact is moderated by practical adoption challenges and parameterization trade-offs. Unlike cryptography that requires strict interoperability, password hashing is an internal control where established, *good enough* solutions might persist due to legacy constraints and risk perception. This context is crucial for understanding our findings.

8.1 Main Findings

Argon2's Security Advantages over SHA-256: Our simulations confirm Argon2's clear security advantage. On a synthetic dataset (D_{syn}) modeling modern passwords, even a modest Argon2 configuration (46 MiB) cuts compromise rates by 37.57% over SHA-256 (at a $1 budget). Increasing memory provides a valuable but linear defensive gain: the 2048 MiB configuration further reduces compromises by 11.82% points, but at a 44.5x higher memory cost, highlighting a key operational trade-off for defenders. Ultimately, our results underscore that strong algorithms cannot compensate for weak passwords, which remain vulnerable regardless of the hashing configuration.

Growing Adoption Trend: Argon2 adoption has steadily increased since its introduction in 2015, surpassing competing algorithms like scrypt and PBKDF2 in the number of new GitHub repositories created annually starting in 2018.

However, its adoption lags behind bcrypt, which remains the most widely implemented password hashing algorithm, likely due to its age and familiarity among developers. Our analysis of over 161 manually reviewed repositories revealed that Argon2 is present in a diverse range of software projects, with both applications (38 repositories) and components (124 repositories) incorporating it into their cryptographic workflows. Interestingly, the frequency of Argon2's coexistence with other algorithms (e.g., bcrypt, PBKDF2, scrypt) in multi-algorithm implementations underscores its growing acceptance as part of a broader cryptographic toolbox. However, the absence of statistically significant overrepresentation of any specific combinations suggests that Argon2 adoption is not yet widespread enough to dominate as a preferred choice.

Parameter Evolution: Our analysis of Argon2 parameter configurations in real-world implementations reveals a shift towards stronger configurations over time. Before 2018, 60.3% of repositories adopted weaker-than-OWASP-recommended settings, but this proportion decreased to 33.3% in repositories created after 2022. This trend aligns with the publication of the RFC 9106 standard in 2021 and evolving OWASP guidelines, which have likely increased awareness of the importance of using secure configurations. The observed clustering of common configurations suggests a heavy reliance on default library settings rather than deliberate customization by developers.

Context-Dependent Configuration: Contrary to our expectations, sensitive applications such as password managers and file encryption software did not consistently implement stronger Argon2 parameter configurations compared to general-purpose applications. While 73.3% of sensitive applications used stronger settings than OWASP recommendations, this proportion was similar to general application repositories (72.7%). This finding highlights unclear practices for parameter selection, even among software with higher security stakes. Interestingly, components (e.g., libraries and cryptographic bindings) exhibited weaker parameterization (52.4% below OWASP standards), possibly due to the need to balance performance and usability across diverse deployments. This correlation is likely influenced by confounding factors: older repositories, which are more likely to be components, also tend to have weaker configurations, while repositories with higher star counts also tend to be older and thus have weaker parameters.

8.2   Practical Recommendations

Our comprehensive analysis reveals that while Argon2 offers theoretical security advantages, these are not fully realized in practice. To bridge this gap, we offer actionable recommendations. Argon2's benefits are amplified when combined with robust user passwords. Studies indicate that password meters and password policies significantly increase password strength, aiding users in creating more secure credentials [12,17]. Developers should implement strength estimation tools, enforce password policies, and integrate techniques like password blacklisting to ensure users generate stronger passwords. Facilitating secure implementation requires simplifying the developer experience. Integrating comprehensive documentation and automated parameter selection tools into cryptographic libraries can increase adoption [1]. Providing sane default configurations (OWASP and RFC 9106 recommendations) directly within libraries streamlines the process, reducing configuration errors. Additionally, automated checks in vulnerability scanners or compilers could flag weak settings, ensuring password-hash hardening remains a priority. Argon2 parameters may create a configuration challenge for some developers. Implementing adaptive benchmarking tools, as noted in some repositories, automates parameter selection tailored to local environments. To protect servers from potential denial-of-service attacks resulting from intensive hash computation, partial client-side hashing can be considered. Clients precompute their passwords with Argon2 before transmitting the resulting hash to the server, which then performs fast hashing functions [11]. While OWASP suggests a conservative 46 MiB of memory on the client side, current devices often possess capabilities to accommodate higher allocations, allowing for more robust defense multipliers without compromising usability.

8.3   Limitations and Future Work

The economic models for hash computation costs use cryptocurrency mining practices as a proxy for large-scale computational attacks. While this provides a validated cost structure, it does not fully capture the nuances of different attackers who can hardly compete with large, centralized mining pools. Using cryptocurrency mining as a proxy for attacker costs introduces uncertainty into our budget-scenario analyses, which could systematically underestimate the true protection levels afforded by Argon2 in production environments. Also, the used budget may vary significantly: while $1 might be appropriate for low-relevance credentials, accounts with cryptocurrency assets carry significantly more wealth that in turn justifies substantially increased attack budgets. The password datasets we employed (RockYou and D_{syn}) serve as benchmarks for password strength but carry inherent limitations. RockYou is over a decade old, and its password distribution might not accurately reflect current practices. While our synthetic dataset addresses this by doubling bit-strength values, it remains an approximation. Real-world password behavior, influenced by contemporary policies, user awareness, and cultural factors, might deviate significantly from our modeled datasets.

Our real-world study focuses on open-source projects hosted on GitHub. This selection bias may skew our results towards projects developed in a particular community culture, potentially missing trends in proprietary software or repositories on alternative platforms. Similarly, our adoption analysis is based on project creation dates, capturing trends in new software but not the migration of existing projects, which would require a complex longitudinal analysis of commit histories. The reliance on GitHub's prominence means that our findings might underestimate the adoption and implementation trends of Argon2 in closed-source or enterprise environments, where different regulations and development practices could influence cryptographic choices. Moreover, developer motivations for starring repositories are heterogeneous (e.g., bookmarking, acknowledgment of quality, personal interest), adding variability to our quality proxy metric. Additionally, the manual extraction process restricted our parameter analysis to 161 high-star repositories, potentially missing patterns present in a broader sample. While we believe this selection provides a representative set of quality implementations, broader sampling might reveal different distributions in parameter configurations. Addressing these limitations requires further research, potentially incorporating a broader range of software implementations, cost models derived from real-world attackers, and conducting user studies with programmers to explore barriers to Argon2 adoption.

9   Conclusion

This research evaluated Argon2, revealing a significant gap between its cryptographic potential and its real-world implementation. Our attack simulations confirm that Argon2 provides substantial security advantages over legacy algorithms like SHA-256, but its effectiveness is highly dependent on parameter choice and, most critically, cannot compensate for weak user passwords, reinforcing the critical need for strong password policies. Beyond technical performance, the analysis of GitHub repositories revealed that real-world adoption of Argon2 has grown steadily, surpassing other modern algorithms like scrypt and PBKDF2 in new implementations since 2018. Despite this, bcrypt remains the dominant choice, and parameter configurations in many repositories still fall short of OWASP and RFC 9106 recommendations. This trend may reflect a perception that password hashing is less critical than other cryptographic functions. Moreover, parameter strength has improved over time, aligning with updated standards and adoption, but a significant number of implementations have weaker-than-recommended configurations. Sensitive applications do not consistently implement stronger Argon2 configurations compared to other applications, challenging assumptions about the correlation between software security demands and cryptographic diligence. These results suggest that while Argon2 holds significant cryptographic advantages for password hashing, its real-world security effectiveness depends on proper parameterization and user practices.

Disclosure of Interests. The authors have no competing interests to declare that are relevant to the content of this article.

References

1. Acar, Y., et al.: Comparing the usability of cryptographic APIs. In: 2017 IEEE Symposium on Security and Privacy, SP 2017, San Jose, CA, USA, 22–26 May 2017, pp. 154–171. IEEE Computer Society (2017)
2. Biryukov, A., Dinu, D., Khovratovich, D., Josefsson, S.: Argon2 Memory-Hard Function for Password Hashing and Proof-of-Work Applications. RFC 9106, IRTF (2021). https://www.rfc-editor.org/info/rfc9106

3. Bitbo: Bitcoin Market and Mining Statistics (2025). https://bitbo.io. Accessed 20 Feb 2025

4. BitInfoCharts: Monero (XMR) statistics (2025). https://www.bitinfocharts.com/monero/. Accessed 20 Feb 2025

5. Blocki, J., Harsha, B., Zhou, S.: On the economics of offline password cracking. In: 2018 IEEE Symposium on Security and Privacy (SP), pp. 853–871 (2018)

6. Bonneau, J.: The science of guessing: analyzing an anonymized corpus of 70 million passwords. In: 2012 IEEE Symposium on Security and Privacy, pp. 538–552 (2012)

7. Borges, H., Tulio Valente, M.: What's in a GitHub star? Understanding repository starring practices in a social coding platform. J. Syst. Softw. **146**, 112–129 (2018)

8. Dell'Amico, M., Michiardi, P., Roudier, Y.: Password strength: an empirical analysis. In: Proceedings of the 29th Conference on Information Communications, INFOCOM 2010, pp. 983–991. IEEE Press (2010)

9. Florencio, D., Herley, C.: A large-scale study of web password habits. In: Proceedings of the 16th International Conference on World Wide Web, WWW 2007, pp. 657–666. Association for Computing Machinery, New York (2007)

10. GitHub, Inc.: Github (2025). https://github.com. Accessed 28 Jan 2025

11. Harsha, B., Blocki, J.: Just in time hashing. In: 2018 IEEE European Symposium on Security and Privacy (EuroS&P), pp. 368–383 (2018)

12. Komanduri, S., et al.: Of passwords and people: measuring the effect of password-composition policies. In: Proceedings of the SIGCHI Conference on Human Factors in Computing Systems, CHI 2011, pp. 2595–2604. Association for Computing Machinery, New York (2011)

13. Naiakshina, A., Danilova, A., Gerlitz, E., von Zezschwitz, E., Smith, M.: "If you want, I can store the encrypted password": a password-storage field study with freelance developers. In: Proceedings of the 2019 CHI Conference on Human Factors in Computing Systems, CHI 2019, pp. 1–12. Association for Computing Machinery, New York (2019)

14. Oechslin, P.: Making a faster cryptanalytic time-memory trade-off. In: Boneh, D. (ed.) CRYPTO 2003. LNCS, vol. 2729, pp. 617–630. Springer, Heidelberg (2003). https://doi.org/10.1007/978-3-540-45146-4_36

15. OWASP: Password Storage Cheat Sheet (2023). https://github.com/OWASP/CheatSheetSeries/blob/master/cheatsheets/Password_Storage_Cheat_Sheet.md. Accessed 02 Feb 2025

16. tevador: RandomX: Proof of work algorithm based on random code execution (2023). https://github.com/tevador/RandomX. Accessed 10 Jan 2025

17. Ur, B., et al.: How does your password measure up? The effect of strength meters on password creation. In: Proceedings of the 21st USENIX Conference on Security Symposium, Security 2012, p. 5. USENIX Association, USA (2012)

18. Weir, M., Aggarwal, S., Medeiros, B.d., Glodek, B.: Password cracking using probabilistic context-free grammars. In: Proceedings of the 2009 30th IEEE Symposium on Security and Privacy, SP 2009, pp. 391–405. IEEE Computer Society, USA (2009)

19. Wheeler, D.L.: Zxcvbn: low-budget password strength estimation. In: Proceedings of the 25th USENIX Conference on Security Symposium, SEC 2016, pp. 157–173. USENIX Association, USA (2016)

AdvisoryHub: Design and Evaluation of a Cross-Platform Security Advisory System for Cyber Situational Awareness

Marc-André Kaufhold$^{(\boxtimes)}$ (iD), Julian Bäumler(iD), Nicolai Koukal,
and Christian Reuter$^{(\boxtimes)}$ (iD)

Science and Technology for Peace and Security (PEASEC), Technical University of
Darmstadt, Pankratiusstraße 2, 64289 Darmstadt, Germany
`{kaufhold,baeumler,koukal,reuter}@peasec.tu-darmstadt.de`

Abstract. Computer Emergency Response Teams (CERTs) provide advisory, preventive, and reactive cybersecurity services for authorities, citizens, and businesses. However, their responsibility of establishing cyber situational awareness by monitoring and analyzing security advisories and vulnerabilities has become challenging due to the growing volume of information disseminated through public channels. Thus, this paper analyzes semi-structured interviews (N = 17) with CERT employees to identify user requirements, which are translated into the design of a system for automatically retrieving and extracting security advisory documents from Common Security Advisory Framework (CSAF), HTML, and RSS sources. The evaluation using a CERT-based list of trusted security advisory sources (N = 53) shows that the developed system can retrieve 90% of the published advisory documents, which is a significant improvement over systems only relying on the retrieval from RSS feeds (30%).

Keywords: Cyber Situational Awareness · Security Advisories · Computer Emergency Response Teams

1 Introduction

The importance of cybersecurity is not only motivated by the advancing digitization and networking of society but also by the increasing frequency and sophistication of cyberattacks [8]. Recognizing the need for incident management, Computer Emergency Response Teams (CERTs) have been established in public and private sectors [20] to provide reactive, proactive, and security quality services internally or externally for authorities, citizens, and enterprises [10]. To provide these services, CERTs must first establish Cyber Situational Awareness (CSA) by monitoring, analyzing, and communicating cyber threats and security vulnerabilities [6]. CSA describes a level of understanding possessed by individuals that allows them to perceive pertinent elements in the cyber environment within a defined timeframe and spatial context, interpret their significance, and anticipate their future status [7].

© The Author(s), under exclusive license to Springer Nature Switzerland AG 2025
M. Dalla Preda et al. (Eds.): ARES 2025, LNCS 15993, pp. 47–68, 2025.
https://doi.org/10.1007/978-3-032-00627-1_3

Yet, the establishment of CSA is becoming more difficult due to the increasing volume of information accessible through public channels, including feeds, social media, vulnerability databases, third-party services, and websites [8]. To enhance CSA, security advisories provide vulnerability information, enabling users to identify vulnerable products and services and take action to remediate the vulnerabilities [13]. Empirical studies with German state CERTs indicate a lack of efficient mechanisms for extracting and seamlessly incorporating real-time threat intelligence [20]. Moreover, CERTs often encounter irrelevant, duplicated, and occasionally implausible information, whose curation for stakeholder reports can consume multiple hours per day [9].

However, we identified a lack of design studies focusing on tools for the cross-platform collection and analysis of security advisories [8]. Thus, this paper examines the following research question: **What are user requirements and design implications for a cross-platform security advisory content retrieval and extraction system to facilitate the cyber situational awareness of CERTs?** Based on a literature review (Sect. 2) and semi-structured interviews (N = 17) with CERT employees (Sect. 3), this paper analyses the context of use and specifies user requirements (Sect. 4) to describe the design of a cross-platform security advisory system (Sect. 5). Thereafter, it presents the evaluation with security advisory sources (N = 53), highlighting the successful retrieval of 90% of the published advisory documents (Sect. 6), and discusses the findings of our first design iteration (Sect. 7).

2 Related Work

CERTs need to overview the general threat landscape to align organizational security measures and provide services to external clients, requiring the identification of suspicious behaviours, current information on external threats, and participation in security communities to stay updated on emerging threats [14].

2.1 Distribution and Standardization of Security Advisories

Thus, numerous manufacturers, public sector CERTs and other private sector organizations release information regarding vulnerabilities and solutions, i.e. security advisories, through their own communication channels [13]. These platforms can be divided into sources, aggregators, and hybrid sources/aggregators of information [16]. Product CERTs primarily publish advisories which are focused on concrete vulnerabilities related to their products and are thus classified as sources of advisories. In contrast, publications from public sector CERTs typically reference advisories first published by the product CERTs. Acting as advisory aggregators, they often group related vulnerabilities into one report, e.g., when the same type of vulnerability was found in multiple products within a narrow time frame. However, existing studies outline the lack of standardization regarding the representation and provision of security advisories, forcing German public CERTs to gather security advisories from diverse manufacturer websites manually on a daily basis [20], as obstacles for deploying security-relevant updates in a timely manner. Although some vendors have been providing security advisories via email subscriptions or RSS feeds, a considerable amount of daily manual checking for new security advisories is still needed in order to prepare stakeholder reports or warnings. Thus, the Common Security Advisory Framework (CSAF) was developed recently and is supported by other well-known organizations such as Redhat, Cisco, and the German Federal Office for Information Security (BSI) [23]. It is based on JSON and supports the use of CPE, CVSS, and CWE. Vulnerabilities may be referenced using the CVE system, or other forms of vulnerability IDs, such as vendor-specific systems, may be used. Additionally, the Traffic Light Protocol (TLP) can be used to label advisory information regarding their sensitivity to sharing.

2.2   Crawling and Processing of Security Advisories

Due to the relative novelty and thus lacking distribution of the CSAF standard, multiple approaches have been designed to gather security advisories differently. [5] proposed a system that collects security advisories, converts them into a standardized and machine-readable format, and distributes them to its subscribers. Compared to text-based security advisory systems, the system offers precise automated filtering and enables the user to map the advisories to the existing infrastructure. The authors stated that the message transformation module should contain conversion rules that convert the unstructured web data into structured vulnerability data for each data source. The system, however, does not automatically create these extraction rules, which hinders the scalability of advisory sources and only supports the retrieval of advisories via RSS. [9] have developed an automatic real-time cybersecurity dashboard that ingests, processes, and displays not only security advisory data, but also indicators of compromise, social media data, and data from vulnerability databases. Furthermore, Taranis3 was developed to assist in retrieving, structuring, and analyzing vulnerability information from various sources as well as writing and publishing advisories [19]. It supports the retrieval of web, email, and social media-based sources. While the retrieved documents can be automatically clustered, the content of security advisory documents is not parsed. As a consequence, the analysis of security advisories is only semi-automated, as the analysis process still requires significant manual effort. While SK-CERT created the Python-based tool Taranis NG, the latest iteration of the tool is Taranis AI, which aims to integrate modern natural language processing (NLP) methods into the analysis process, allowing the efficient identification and extraction of relevant entities [21].

3   Problem Identification: Empirical Pre-Study

To better understand how CERTs use security advisory documents and how this process could be enhanced by technology, transcripts of semi-structured interviews ($N = 17$) were analyzed. These were conducted prior to this work and focused not only on security advisory documents but, more broadly, on the technology use and processes in CERT operations. While this prior work [20] outlines collaborative, organizational and technological challenges and implications concerning German CERTs, it does not derive user requirements for and the actual design of a security advisory system. The interview guidelines encompassed (1) the roles and affiliations of the interviewees, (2) their procedures for reporting cyber incidents, (3) methods for monitoring cyber incident data, such as indicators of compromise, (4) processes for analyzing, prioritizing, and validating collected evidence, (5) collaborations among CERTs, and (6) how recommendations and warnings are communicated. We used a purposive sampling strategy in order to primarily involve personnel on operational (e.g., incident managers as technology operators), but also tactical level (e.g., internal team leaders) among German state CERTs. In summary, our interviews comprised eight internal incident managers (I01, I04-I07, I14, I17), six internal team leaders (I02, I08-I10, I12, I16), three external information security officers (I11, I12, I15), and one external public safety answering point (I13). Overall, participants (15 male and two female) from eleven organizations, including eight CERTs and three other organizations, were included in our pre-study interviews. Each interview session, conducted with the acceptance and informed consent of the participants, lasted approximately 60 min.

3.1   Data Analysis

The analysis was conducted by three researchers (two white males and one white female) from the domains of HCI, CSCW, and information security. Given its flexibility, *thematic analysis* appeared to be a well-suited approach for understanding how CERT staff work with security advisory documents [2]. The themes that form the core of thematic analysis can be identified either inductively or deductively. Given that there is a theoretical framework for establishing situational awareness but no framework for processing advisory documents, the use of inductive theme discovery seemed more appropriate. We followed the step model of inductive category development by [15], which comprises the determination of category definition, formulation of inductive categories, revision of categories, and a final working through the texts before interpreting and presenting the results. We clustered the themes into meta themes to present the themes more clearly and to show content-related references between the identified themes that were lost during the categorization process (Table 1). Although the original thematic analysis by [2] does not include such a procedure, [15] allows the use of main categories, which reflects our idea of meta themes. During biweekly team meetings, we discussed and revised these codes until we reached consensus.

3.2   Results

Both the **selection of relevant information sources and the retrieval of the vulnerability information** are challenging for CERT staff. For example,

Table 1. Identified themes, meta themes, and prevalences

Themes	Meta Themes	n
Sources, Social Media, Privacy	Sources Selection & Advisory Retrieval	57
Dissemination	Reporting & Spread of Information	40
Classification, Cognitive Aspects	Vulnerability Scoring & Classification	41
Time, Interfaces, Tools	(Lack of) Automation	44
Assets	IT Asset Management (ITAM)	20
Timeliness, Quality, Deduplication	Information Quality	27
Context, Summarization, Trends	Manual Vulnerability Analysis	15

one CERT employee stated that the lack of a catalogue of relevant sources is perceived as a problem: "[...] you would simply have to put together a catalogue of sites that you want to monitor. This certainly also happens in a different context, when in the business sector you want to be aware of certain things that someone publishes and that is difficult" (I10). According to six participants, their CERTs mostly rely on self-curated lists of sources and use information provided by the German national CERT (CERT-Bund) or other upstream CERTs. Some CERTs also use information provided by other CERTs, such as by the US-CERT, to close potential blind spots in the data. In addition to information provided by other CERTs, five employees report the use of information provided by hard- and software vendors. This information is usually retrieved manually from the vendor's websites. One respondent stated that they rely solely on vendors actively alerting them of new vulnerabilities according to contractual obligations. Other sources of information include RSS feeds, mailing lists, online IT news, and social media. Three interviewees specifically stated that they try to use as much information as possible to maximize their situational awareness.

According to seven participants, nearly all CERTs **disseminate situational reports** to their stakeholders. Most commonly, a daily report is generated. Reports of lower frequency are sometimes created additionally or alternatively to daily reports: "Yes, we have a wide range of recommendations that we send out, so we create various products for our customers. These are, on the one hand, a situational report - that is a vulnerability report - and, more recently, a cyber situational report where we try [...] to provide information that is tailored to the target group and clientele at various levels" (I01). The reports contain vulnerability details, information about incidents that affected the network, and information about threats that are not directly related to vulnerabilities, e.g., in the case of recent phishing waves. The reports often contain a high-level threat indicator, such as a traffic light: "Yes, [the situation report includes] the incident reports, vulnerabilities, and exploits. General information from the internet, e.g., what is being discussed in the press, what security topics can be found in the news, and of course, the general topic of IT security, what is a current topic in the press that is being discussed, should be included there" (I05). Three participants stressed that important elements of the reports are the CERT's recommendations or instructions on what steps should be taken in response to the vulnerability, which help to achieve the overall goal of remediating the vulnerabilities as soon as possible. Some CERTs contact the operational teams directly in cases of severe vulnerabilities, e.g., via email or phone, so that the vulnerabilities can be mitigated before the next situational report is sent.

CERTs **score, categorize, and classify vulnerabilities** in terms of their severity, relevance, and potential impact on handling cognitive challenges of CSA, such as information overload and alert fatigue. One example of such a score is the CVSS. According to five participants, the initial score provided by the vendors or the upstream CERT is an important input for the scoring process conducted by the CERT. However, due to differences in infrastructure in different organizations, there is a subjective component in scoring systems. For that reason, some CERTs incorporate their own logic and weights into the scoring process, such as disregarding vulnerabilities for products which are not used by their constituents: "[...] so of course, we only try to subscribe to information that is relevant to us or to our target groups, as we usually call them. So we have a very good overview of the software that is used in the state, of course not in detail" (I10). Some CERTs use information on how often a product is used in the organization or information on the patch level of the infrastructure. Sometimes, it is also considered whether a vulnerability is actively being exploited in the wild. Four respondents reported that the calculated scores and classifications are used to sort, filter, and prioritize vulnerabilities.

CERTs are interested in a **higher degree of automation** in vulnerability information retrieval and processing, which is discussed by six interviewees. The first reason is that manual labour can be saved to improve in-depth analyses of selected vulnerabilities and achieve a better overall analysis result. If vulnerability information retrieval processes are not automated, they may take between 0.5h and 1.5h per day. Smaller organizations, in particular, cannot devote that many resources to retrieving vulnerability information. The second reason is that CERTs could shorten query intervals. With manual retrieval, sources are typically queried and inspected once a day. In addition to retrieval, six participants would like to use automation to merge information from different sources, determine the reliability of sources, simplify report creation, fill in missing information in vulnerability descriptions, or remove redundant information: "It would be a huge relief if the information from different sources were brought together [automatically] in one place and an evaluation could somehow be created from this" (I15). There have been some concerns about information accuracy, particularly in cases where machine learning technologies are used for the prioritization of vulnerabilities. Two respondents thus suggested displaying percentage-based confidence levels and data sources of the algorithm alongside the information generated. According to four interviewees, the most difficult challenge for automation is that security advisories are not offered in a standardized format. Furthermore, due to a lack of standardization, the data format in which a vendor publishes their advisories in may change at any time. This would then break possible automation solutions.

Furthermore, it is essential for CERTs to **know whether a particular product (both software and hardware) is being used** by the constituents to reliably predict the risk of new vulnerabilities. As mentioned by five participants, CERTs often do not have a complete picture of the products their constituents use: "So it's just way too much that I really know what software is used here. I'm aware of maybe 80 per cent, maybe 90, but I can't reach 100" (I11). Some CERTs warn not only about vulnerabilities affecting software that runs on organization-managed devices but also software that is likely to run on the employees' personal devices. IT asset management is important for both knowing whether a certain product is used within an organization, and also for identifying the responsible technical contact that is necessary for mitigating vulnerabilities and other incidents. This information can be used to send vulnerability information only to those who are affected by them and thereby ensure that the report is actionable for the receiver: "So if we were, for example, informed of a critical SAP error, then we would only send it to [department name] because the [department name] has an SAP [instance] running and we know that no one else uses it" (I11). Some CERTs stated that they have minimal information about what software is used by their constituents, and they thus forward all vulnerabilities without changing the scores provided by the vendors or upstream CERTs.

Various aspects of **information quality** were mentioned during the interviews, especially timeliness. For example, three CERT employees specifically mentioned that in addition to the information provided by the national CERT, vendor websites are monitored to avoid the national CERT's reporting delay: "Usually, we set the criticality higher and next we check around a hundred websites for security advisories so that we can simply publish security warnings before the BSI [publishes the vulnerabilities]" (I02). The timeliness of the information enables CERTs to remediate the vulnerabilities as quickly as possible. Besides timeliness, it is also important that the processed information is dated properly. This allows for displaying the course of events chronologically and helps in the selection process when there are two conflicting pieces of information. Another important quality metric is the correctness of information. Since the accuracy often cannot easily be verified by the CERTs, they deploy different strategies to determine the factuality of information. One CERT relies primarily on vendor advisories as an authoritative source of information: "Of course, we also look through the normal standard sources that every other user uses. Sometimes something is discovered that isn't yet published on the vendor's website or additional information. Those are the things [we additionally use], but they are all things that we then confirm through the vendors" (I13). More generally, five participants discussed the importance of determining the primary source in order to gain insight into the reliability of information. Using and cross-checking multiple sources can help with improving the reliability of information. In cases where automation is used, it is not only important to know where the underlying information came from, but also how a system derived a result from that data. Some CERTs also use social media as an indicator that some information may be more reliable than others. One concern raised regarding the use of machine learning for automation was the risk of biases. As stressed by five participants, redundant and duplicated data is a common issue related to data quality in CERT processes. The interviewees suggested different solutions to this problem, such as more standardization or the use of artificial intelligence.

There are various steps which CERTs take to gain CSA, including the often **manual vulnerability analysis** and the preparation of the information for dissemination. According to three participants, CERTs add recommendations to security advisories to ensure that their constituents, the receivers of the disseminated reports, can work with actionable information. In cases where CERTs use information from their upstream CERTs, they supplement and enrich the information to better match the needs of their constituents. Similarly, sometimes the information is summarized and unnecessary information is removed. They also may merge information from different sources and reference the respective original publications in their report: "The vulnerabilities of vendors are copied, briefly summarized and tagged with a link so that further information can be looked up again by the interested party who receives it" (I14).

4   Defining the Objectives of Solution: Conceptualization

Based on the literature review and interview data, we envisioned a potential pipeline for the technical processing of security advisories (Fig. 1) that is based on functional requirements (R1-10), which can also be mapped to non-functional requirements (U1-11). To identify both functional and non-functional requirements, we first analyzed the empirical material alongside the identified themes and then correlated it with selected related work, which is detailed in our GitHub appendix [12]. The reason for this approach was that the literature mainly dealt with threat-focused but not vulnerability-focused CSA and could, therefore, only be supplementary because many literature findings did not apply to the topic of investigation.

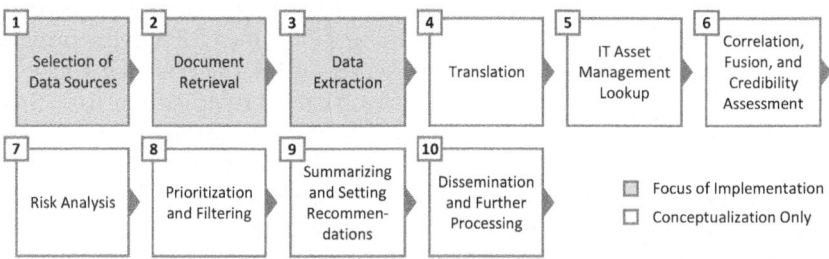

Fig. 1. Steps for handling security advisory documents.

4.1   Functional Requirements

First, there should be a comprehensive prefilled catalogue of relevant sources (R1, Facilitate the Selection of Security Advisory Sources), which should be monitored for automated advisory retrieval (R2, Continuously Monitor Security Advisory Sources for Document Retrieval) and then transformed into a standardized format (R3, Extract and Convert Data into a Standardized Format). Considering that advisories can originate from different national CERTs, language translation steps using specific APIs or code libraries (R4, Translate Foreign Language Content for the System Operator) might be required before automatically determining whether a vulnerability is relevant for the respective stakeholder group (R5, Integrate an IT Asset Management to Check Stakeholder Affectedness), or even merging complementary data from different advisory sources might be advisable (R6, Enable the Fusion of Data from Multiple Sources). In case of a relevant security vulnerability, there is a need to assess the criticality, timeliness, and risk of compromise (R7, Support the Risk Analysis of Vulnerability Exploitation) before prioritizing the urgency of concurrent threats (R8, Provide Functionality for Sorting, Prioritizing and Filtering Security Advisories). Given the potentially large amount of security advisories, a functionality for recommendations and summarization (R9, Summarize Security Advisory Content and Provide Recommendations for Action) and support for creating and disseminating reports (R10, Facilitate the Creation and Dissemination of Stakeholder Reports) was requested. In Sect. 5, we present the first design iteration of a system supporting the envisioned pipeline's first three steps.

4.2   Non-functional Requirements

Besides the functional requirements that describe *which* steps need to be performed by the system, there are non-functional requirements that describe *how* the steps must be carried out. The non-functional requirements include ensuring data quality (U1) and maintaining data origin (U2), which involves the trustworthiness, completeness, and freshness of data. Trustworthiness can be enhanced by correlating data from multiple sources and maintaining data origin information. Automation (U3) and resilience (U4) are essential for efficient data collection. The system must handle incomplete or contradictory data by calculating missing data or making predictions. Timeliness (U5) and timestampedness (U6) are critical, as faster retrieval and interpretation of vulnerability information enable more frequent querying. Precise timestamps are necessary for creating accurate event timelines. Standardization (U7) and configurability (U8) are required for consistent communication between pipeline steps, with the core data format aligning with CSAF to ensure all information is conveyed effectively. Scalability (U9) is important as the architecture must support a high data volume from diverse sources. Finally, the system should be adaptable to the cognitive needs of users (U10), presenting only necessary information to avoid overload.

4.3   Mapping of Pipeline Steps to Non-functional Requirements

The identified non-functional requirements have an impact on the functional requirements and, therefore, also on the pipeline steps. However, not all non-functional requirements are applicable to every step. To visualize dependencies between non-functional requirements and pipeline steps, an approach similar to Quality Function Deployment (QFD) is chosen, which is a method for mapping customer requirements to engineering requirements [17]. We opted for this approach because it helps to clearly separate functional and non-functional requirements (which were mentioned intermixed, especially in the interviews) along the two axes of the matrix (Table 2). It shows which non-functional requirements are related to which functional requirements (e.g., that the non-functional requirement of adaptability to the user's cognitive needs is not related to the front steps of the pipeline), which should help in the later implementation. It is also helpful to show relationships between the individual functional requirements and thus define a sequence of pipeline steps (e.g., the risk calculation step requires standardized data, so the earlier step of data extraction must establish standardization). The mapping of pipeline steps to non-functional requirements in Table 2 visualized dependencies and technical implications, showing how different steps enable (e), require (r), or are challenged (c) by these requirements.

Table 2. Mapping pipeline steps to non-functional requirements, showing how different steps enable (e), require (r), or are challenged (c) by these requirements.

$\longrightarrow$	Source Selection	Document Retrieval	Data Extraction	Translation	Asset Management	Correlation Fusion	Risk Calculation	Prioritization	Summarizing	Dissemination
Data Quality			e			e	r		c	r
Data Origin Principle		e	e	e		e				
Automation	e	e	e	e	e	e	e	e	c	e
Resilience			c		c	e				
Timeliness			e							
Timestampedness		e	e				r			
Standardization			e		r	r	r			r
Configurability	e	e	e	e	e	e	e	e	e	e
Scaleability	e	e					r			
Cognitive Adaptability									e	e

5   Design: Cross-Platform Security Advisory System

Overall, we designed a Python application whose code and implementation details are published at GitHub [12]. The frontend web interface for configuring monitoring and retrieval of the advisory sources was implemented using the Bootstrap framework in combination with the JavaScript library D3.js, which was utilized to render charts. The backend is divided into four layers. The app layer forms the counterpart to the frontend by receiving the HTTP requests and responding to them accordingly. The batch layer is responsible for continuously running processes in the background to monitor **overview pages** (e.g., lists or tables) that contain references to advisory document detail pages, as well as monitoring these **detail pages** (including detailed attributes) and analyzing the retrieved content. To retrieve overview pages and process the content on the detail pages, the monitoring functions of the batch layer spawn retriever, extractor, and constructor function in the parallel layer. The data layer is responsible for persisting both the configuration data and the retrieved security advisory documents. While the configuration data and selected metadata are stored in an SQLite database, the retrieved security advisory documents are stored as files on disk. While the overall system is designed to address the functional requirements of data source selection (R1), document retrieval (R2) and data extraction (R3), we will discuss the consideration of non-functional requirements within the following subsections.

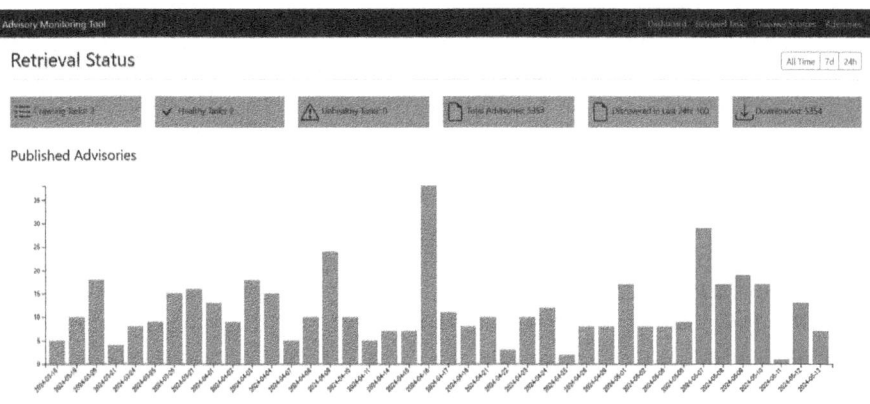

Fig. 2. Screenshot of the dashboard view.

5.1   Backend: Monitoring of Overview Pages

The system is able to monitor a variety of different data sources such as CSAF, HTML, and RSS content. To account for the differences between the data source categories, different retriever classes were developed. Each of these retriever classes ultimately inherits from the Python class *threading.thread* to enable asynchronous and parallel retrieval. First, the **HTML Table Retriever** allows the system to extract data from static websites containing the desired data within HTML table tags. The rows of these tables represent the advisory detail pages and their columns represent advisory metadata, including a link to the respective detail page for the advisory document. Second, the **HTML XPATH Retriever** allows the system to create detail tasks not only from table tags but arbitrary HTML elements that are part of the Document Object Model (DOM) of the monitored site. A representative application for this retriever are sites that contain multiple div elements that represent the advisories and their respective metadata attributes. The elements of interest are selected via the XPATH expression language. For example, the XPATH string *//div[contains(@class, 'advisory')]* can be used to select all div elements in the page DOM that have the string advisory in their class name and subsequently extract relevant values. Third, the **HTML URL Retriever** acts similarly to the XPATH retriever but only extracts a-tags from the DOM. To filter out references to pages that are not detail pages, the results are filtered with a prefix provided by the user. This prefix must be common to all the detail pages; however, it must be specific enough to distinguish detail pages from not detail pages. An example could be a string such as *http://www.example.com/advisories/*. The URL retriever is more robust than the Table retriever, but it is not able to extract the same amount of metadata provided by the detail page, such as the publishing data or the affected products.

Fourth, the **HTML Ajax Retriever** allows the system to extract the advisory information directly from JSON APIs that are called by the JavaScript code to populate the overview pages. For setting up the retriever, the user must manually inspect the overview site and determine the URL and the request parameters of the called API. This information is provided to the retriever to request the JSON data containing the desired information. The retriever is able to automatically find the required data within the JSON response and transform it into a table. After transforming relative URLs into absolute URLs, the selected table can be processed in the same way the other HTML retriever classes process the constructed table. Fifth, the **RSS Retriever** transforms an XML-based RSS feed into a list of elements representing the different advisories. The list is then transformed into a table and used to construct detail tasks, as in the other tables. The advisory content, which is often already part of the RSS feed, is stored in the detail task content field. Finally, the **CSAF Retriever** transforms the JSON-based CSAF feed into a table, which is used to construct detail tasks. Overall, the designed backend seeks to ensure data quality (U1) by trying the best possible retrievers for the construction of as complete as possible, standardized (U7) CSAF files, while maintaining the data origin principle (U2) by referencing the URL from which it was retrieved. Furthermore, it lays the foundation for automatic (U3) cross-platform retrieval of security advisories and also provides resilience (U4) against changes because the system can at least fall back to less optimal retrievers.

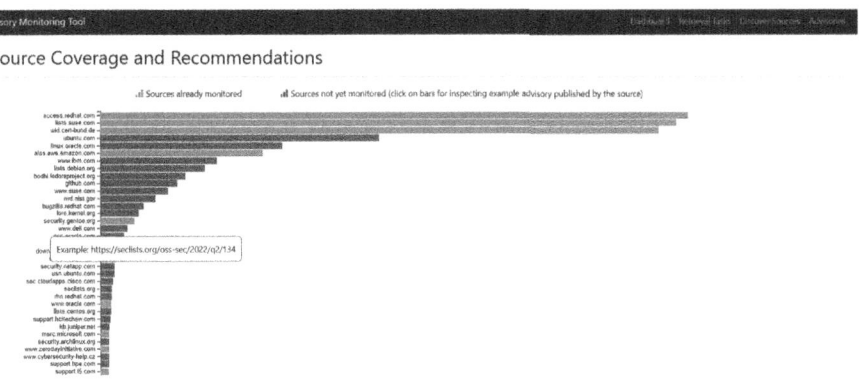

Fig. 3. Suggestions for additional sources to monitor.

5.2   Frontend: Cross-Platform Management of Security Advisories

The interface starts with a **dashboard page**, which consists of status elements indicating whether the retriever works properly and metrics, such as the number of new advisory documents discovered in the last 24 h (Fig. 2). Additionally, there is a time-series column chart showing how many advisory documents were published on a given date. This allows the user to quickly identify abnormalities, such as a higher-than-usual number of new vulnerabilities. By clicking on the date in question, the user can investigate the advisories published on that date in the preview menu.

On the **overview task page**, the user can inspect the running tasks. By clicking on the individual tasks, the user can inspect the task properties, such as the configured request body and header or error messages in case the retriever failed to poll a data source. New sources can be either added individually via a web form or in bulk via a CSV import function. When adding new sources via the web form, the user must first select the retriever type the system should use and then set the other task properties. After submitting the task, a test request is conducted to verify that the task was configured properly. If the task was configured incorrectly, or the polled server returned for other reasons, the user is displayed an error message. In case the request worked, the user needs to set column types in the tabularized form of the response. The system automatically suggests column types based on the column names coming from the server. After the column types, e.g., *URL*, *title*, or *identifier* were set, the user can add the task to the database. The system then automatically executes the retrieval in the background and creates detailed tasks if new advisory documents are detected.

The system automatically suggests new data sources based on the references of the documents already ingested and analyzed. In the **recommendation view**, which can be seen in Fig. 3, the user sees how often a particular provider was referenced by the ingested advisories. If there is already a monitoring task for that vendor, the respective bar is marked as green; otherwise it is marked red. The user can, therefore, screen the suggested sources by clicking on the red bars. This forwards the user to one example referenced detail page. After deciding whether the advisory source may be of interest, the user needs to navigate to the overview site of the provider and add it as a new task.

The implementation also includes a **preview page** that displays the retrieved and extracted advisory documents. The user can access the original resource by clicking on the link symbol left of the title. By clicking on the provider of an advisory document, the user can filter for documents that were published by that particular provider. This functionality is also offered for the name of the affected vendor and CVE numbers. The preview does not contain all advisory attributes, but they are stored in the CSAF files that were saved to disk. Overall, the designed frontend enhances the automation (U3) of security advisory gathering and ensures timeliness (U4) since new security advisories are constantly added to the dashboard. Furthermore, it facilitates the configuration (U7) of plenty of data sources, which is supplemented by the recommendations view, and thus constitutes a scalable (U9) cross-platform system for security advisory retrieval.

6   Demonstration: Formative Lab Evaluation

The evaluation aims to prove the utility and efficacy of the designed and implemented artefact. For choosing an appropriate evaluation methodology, [22] distinguish between naturalistic and artificial contexts, such as with real users of the artefact or in a simulated environment, as well as whether an evaluation is conducted ex-ante or ex-post, i.e. before or after the artefact is created. While an artificial evaluation comes with a lower cost compared to a naturalistic evaluation, it is not as well-suited to evaluate sociotechnical artefacts. Since the development of the system is in its first of multiple design iterations, the selected evaluation methodology should also result in knowledge that can be used formatively to improve future iterations of the artifact. To ensure the technical functionality of the system, an artificial evaluation seems more appropriate for the first round of evaluation. Given that the evaluation is based on the developed artefact, an ex-post evaluation can be conducted. First, the ability of the system to monitor sources and, second, the ability of the system to extract information from retrieved documents is evaluated by the third author.

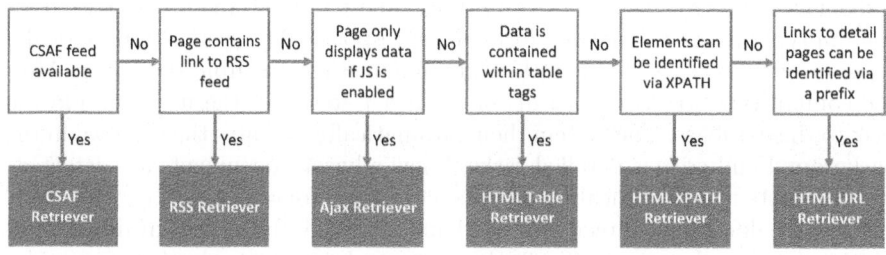

Fig. 4. Application of the retriever classes during the evaluation.

6.1   Retrieval Functionality Evaluation

The retrieval functionality is evaluated in a lab setting modelled after real challenges a CERT may face when working with advisory documents. The lab experiment builds upon a list of links to advisory providers that was made available by one of the CERTs involved in the interviews. For the evaluation, every advisory provider on the list is checked for retrievability and whether it can be monitored by the developed system. A provider is considered to be retrieved successfully if at least one of the retrievers can successfully be configured to generate detail tasks based on the page content. For selecting the appropriate retrievers, the decision scheme depicted in Fig. 4 was developed. The order of the decision scheme is based on the individual advantages and disadvantages of the retrievers, which are illustrated in Table 5. For example, as the CSAF retriever provides the most comprehensive data and the greatest stability over time against changes in templates, the user should first check if a CSAF feed is offered by the provider.

Table 3. Ability of retrievers to monitor overview pages

n = 53	CSAF	RSS	AJAX	TABLE	XPATH	URL	FAIL
Fetched	4	16	9	10	19	26	-
Best	4	13	6	8	9	8	5

The list provided by the CERT contained 53 links pointing primarily to pages on which security advisory information is published, but also pages on which new software releases are announced. The results documented in Table 3 show that the CSAF feeds are still not a common way of publishing security advisory information, as only 4 of the 53 surveyed sources offered advisories in the CSAF format. Of those sources, two were services provided by national CERTs and the other two were product CERTs publishing advisories. The results also indicate that approximately 30% of the surveyed data sources offer the option to subscribe to an RSS feed, which in consequence also means that cyber situational awareness systems only ingesting RSS data can merely retrieve 30% of the published vulnerabilities. The developed system, on the other hand, was able to monitor 90% of the advisory sources, which is a significant improvement. The 10% that could not be monitored consisted of sites that did not follow the overview-page-detail-page structure but instead contained all vulnerability data within a single page. Also, there were some JavaScript-dependent websites, where the API data could not be accessed. For example, one site executed JavaScript code to generate a token that was required for the API request.

6.2   Extraction and Standardization Evaluation

The evaluation of the extraction and standardization functionality was conducted similarly to the evaluation of the retrieval function. For each of the 48 sites that were successfully monitored by the retrieval modules, one random extracted document was manually inspected and rated regarding the quality of the extraction of its most important attributes. The attributes selected were title, vendor, product, text content, a timeline consisting of publication and update dates, a severity string, a CVSS score, and references. The extraction quality was rated on a scale from 0 to 3, with 0 meaning an attribute was not extracted or a wrong value was extracted that would be detrimental to the situational awareness of the operator. The used coding is detailed in our GitHub appendix [12]. One example of such a case would be the extraction of a CVSS score of 2.1 when the real score was 9.3 since that could lead to the advisory document being omitted by an automatic filtering system or being disregarded by a human operator. While value 1 was used for extractions that contained some correct pieces of information but were mainly incorrect, value 2 was used for extracted attributes that were inaccurate but were not detrimental to establishing situational awareness. An example of this would be the extraction of an unrelated link as a reference. The value 3 was used for cases where the extracted value was identical to the value a human would extract.

Table 4. Extraction Performance for Advisory Attributes

n = 48	NA	#0	#1	#2	#3	AVG
Vendor	1	8	0	10	29	2,28
Product	1	23	0	5	19	1,43
Vulnerability	8	9	0	1	30	2,30
Timeline	0	16	3	6	23	1,75
Title	0	4	1	2	41	2,67
Content	3	7	5	8	25	2,13
Severity	14	10	2	4	18	1,88
Score	25	9	0	1	13	1,78
References	3	12	5	9	19	1,78

Table 4 shows that the extraction worked well for some arguments, such as title, vulnerability, and vendor, but did not perform well for other attributes, such as the product names. The low score for the product name extraction is caused by a high false positive rate, as many product names were not recognized. Besides the extraction quality, the evaluation also shows that not all advisories contained all attributes to begin with. Especially, the attributes of vulnerability, severity, and score were not provided for several advisory documents. Some of the missing attributes can be ascribed to the advisories being focused on the release of a patch, rather than the publication of vulnerabilities. While the recognition worked well in general due to the prevalence of the CVE numbers, some vulnerabilities without CVE numbers were not extracted.

7 Discussion and Conclusion

Based on requirements from literature and interviews with security profession-als, we proposed a system that automatically retrieves new security advisory documents and transforms them into a machine-readable format. In addition to standardizing advisories by transforming them into the CSAF file format, the system offers improvements regarding the different types of advisory sources that can be polled for new documents. These improvements result in an overall retrieval rate of over 90%. Furthermore, we found that the retriever classes have different characteristics regarding their configuration, the amount of advisory metadata they extract from the overview page, such as the publishing date, and their stability against changes in the structure of the retrieved overview page.

Table 5. Characteristics of the Retriever Classes

Retriever	Config	Metadata	Flexibility	Robustness
Table	Easy	Good	Average	Average
XPATH	Hard	Average	High	Low
URL	Easy	Low	High	Good
Ajax	Hard	Good	High	Low
RSS	Easy	Good	Low	Good
CSAF	Easy	Good	Low	Good

These insights are summarized in Table 5. Compared to the work of [9] and [5], vulnerabilities are processed from a wider variety of sources, includ-ing websites. This makes the system more robust compared to other systems that depend on individual aggregated sources, such as the NVD. The system offers an improvement compared to the work of [5], as the addition of new data sources was simplified. The extraction of metadata from overview pages, in addi-tion to the extraction of data from the detail page content, is an improvement over Taranis NG, which only extracts data from monitored detail pages.

7.1 Implications for Design

By reflecting on the findings and identified user requirements of our study, we want to discuss the following five implications for designing systems for the retrieval and extraction of security advisory documents (RQ1).

Requirement Satisfaction for the Selection, Retrieval, and Extraction of Security Advisories (D1). For the processes of source selection, document retrieval, and data extraction, the non-functional requirements of data quality, data origin, automation, resilience, timeliness, timestampedness, standardiza-tion, configurability, and scalability were identified. The requirements of config-urability and scalability were satisfied by the ability of the system to monitor hundreds of sites, that can either be added manually or imported via a CSV file. The system is more scalable than comparable systems since it avoids using headless browsers but instead directly retrieves data from the back-end APIs of the providers, thus saving both bandwidth and processing time. The requirement for automation is only partially met by the source selection process since the recommendation of new advisory sources is only semi-automatic and still needs manual work. The user needs to manually evaluate whether the recommended site is suitable for ingestion, find the corresponding overview site, and configure the correct retriever for the recommended provider. The overview and detail page monitoring fulfilled the requirements of configurability, automation, and timeliness since the user can configure arbitrary sites to be monitored, and new advisories are automatically detected shortly after they have been published. Resilience against changes and data quality was challenging for the data extraction step since the extractor did not perform well for some attributes, such as product names. While the data origin principle was maintained on a document level, since each created CSAF contains a reference to the URL from which it was retrieved, maintaining data origin on an attribute level was not possible. The CSAF format, which was used as a central data structure for security advisory documents, does not allow storing metadata on how exactly attributes were extracted from a document.

Lack of Support for Automatic Retrieval (D2). While the advisory providers did not take any measures to hinder non-human access to their published documents, they also did not take any significant measures to support automatic retrieval. Many of the overview pages were JavaScript-dependent, effectively locking out non-human parties such as search machine indexing agents. The effect of that was somewhat mitigated by the providers offering RSS feeds, but the majority (70%) of sites still did not offer such a service. Since the system of [9] solely depends on RSS for retrieval of security advisory documents, the developed system can retrieve a significantly larger share of advisory documents. To compensate for the missing advisory documents, [9] also ingested data from the NIST National Vulnerability Database (NVD). However, this approach is considered risky due to the NVD being a single point of failure, compared to the decentralized nature of different individual vendors. That the risk associated with centralization is not unfounded is demonstrated by the fact that there is a significant backlog of unenriched vulnerabilities in the NVD as of April 2024 [18]. While 30% of the surveyed sites offered security advisory information as an RSS feed, only 8% of the sites offered a feed in the CSAF format, once again showing the difficulties of the standard being adopted and thus justifying the importance of this research.

Issues with Data Origin and Uncertainty (D3). The CSAF format cannot preserve data origins on an attribute level, since no information can be stored on how a particular value was extracted from a document. For instance, in the implementation, multiple approaches were taken for the extraction of CVSS scores: They were either taken from the metadata displayed on the overview page, extracted directly from the text content of the detail page, or calculated from extracted CVSS vectors. In the interviews, it was mentioned that the data can only be trusted if the system is transparent about how the presented information was obtained. This is especially true once conventional extraction methods are mixed with machine learning-based extraction methods. Similarly, the CSAF format was designed to represent absolute and not probabilistic information. For example, one may want to use multiple extraction techniques and then store their results together with a probability that the extracted information is correct. The current architecture only supports this up to the point where a CSAF file is created, and the system needs to decide on which results to accept or discard. However, if the probabilities and alternative values were kept, they could later be used during the correlation step to cross-check them with data from other providers and resolve conflicting information better. The concept of probability extraction and attribute-level data origin could be implemented by changing the data structure so that instead of atomic values, a 3-tuple is inserted into the CSAF scaffold. This 3-tuple would contain the attribute's value, the probability of it being correct, and the information on how it was derived from the source document. Alternatively, the whole CSAF could be wrapped in a dictionary and metadata could be stored alongside the CSAF document in a subdictionary.

Advisory Documents as CSA Objects (D4). While existing approaches have been applying the CSA concept to cyber defence [1], not much work has been done on how security advisory documents fit into the picture. This work presents a model where security advisory documents and the referenced vulnerabilities correspond to the elements of [3]. While the notion of "time" can be interpreted as the timestamps at which an advisory document was published or changed, the notion of "space" can be interpreted as the site on which the information was published, as well the location of the document within a network of documents interlinked by references. By combining the timeline of the published documents and the extracted references to other documents, one can model the flow of information between the retrieved sources. While this has already been done in academic settings for a limited number of sites, as in the work of [16], there exist no systems that present users with this information, allowing them to make projections. For example, if multiple independent advisory providers reference the same advisory in quick succession, this may be interpreted as a signal for a high-severity vulnerability. Thus, to make temporal and spatial aspects of security advisories understandable to humans, vulnerability-centered CSA systems should make use of timeline graphs and network graphs. For example, the visualization of timelines could help the user to make projections on how the risk of exploitation will evolve over time [8].

Vulnerability Front-Running and Ethical Concerns (D5). According to our interviewees, quicker access to information is the main reason why they invest a significant amount of time in directly retrieving advisory documents from vendors instead of solely relying on the feed of the upstream CERT. This raises the question of whether adversaries could use the developed system too, as a form of *vulnerability front-running*, to gain an advantage over CERTs not using such a system but instead relying on an aggregated feed. The concept of front-running is taken from the field of finance, where dishonest participants use non-public information on an impending market-changing transaction to their own advantage. The problem of vulnerability front-running is not only exacerbated by the delay between initial publication and publication in aggregated feeds, which can be observed in the case of the NVD but also in the decreasing time between the publication of vulnerabilities and their exploitation [18]. The work of [4], which uses Large Language Models (LLMs) to generate exploits for new vulnerabilities automatically, shows that we can soon expect publication-to-exploitation timeframes of a few seconds. This development shows that a CSA system should help humans make better and quicker decisions. These developments may lead to a technological arms race between CERTs and adversaries to retrieve and interpret advisory documents as quickly as possible, ultimately questioning the role of the human *in* the advisory processing loop, or in advisory providers taking steps against the automatic retrieval of advisory documents, such as CAPTCHAs.

7.2   Limitations and Future Work

Overall, since the interviews touched upon multiple topics, it cannot be guaranteed that the process model covers all vulnerability-handling activities and more empirical research, such as cognitive walkthroughs of the vulnerability management processes, should be conducted on how CERTs gain CSA from security advisories. Furthermore, limited resources were spent on the development of the preliminary system, especially the extraction component. Due to the high variability of content on detail pages, more effort is needed to develop a robust extraction solution that can gracefully handle the many potential edge cases. In particular, the extraction and standardization of vendor and product names should receive more attention, since having a high level of accuracy in extracting these arguments is essential for later processing steps such as correlation and filtering. Lastly, only the first three steps of the processing pipeline were implemented. Thus, cognitive aspects, which play an essential role in CSA, were not yet examined. This work focused on the base processes required for establishing vulnerability-centred CSA but did not answer the question of how the retrieved and extracted data should be best presented to enhance CSA. For this reason, the subsequent steps of the processing pipeline should also be implemented, ideally informed by a user-centred design process which iteratively incorporates user evaluations to assess the acceptance, functionality, and usability of the system.

Acknowledgments. This research work has been co-funded by the German Federal Ministry of Education and Research (BMBF) and the Hessian Ministry of Higher Education, Research, Science and the Arts (HMWK) within their joint support of the National Research Center for Applied Cybersecurity ATHENE, as well as by the BMBF in the project CYLENCE (13N16636). A preliminary version of this study was presented at a workshop [11], which did not comprise the (I) results of our empirical pre-study, (II) discussion of non-functional requirements, (III) extraction and standardization evaluation, nor a (IV) thorough discussion of design implications.

References

1. Albanese, M., et al.: Computer-aided human centric cyber situation awareness. In: Theory and Models for Cyber Situation Awareness, pp. 3–25 (2017). https://doi.org/10.1007/978-3-319-61152-5_1

2. Braun, V., Clarke, V.: Using thematic analysis in psychology. Qual. Res. Psychol. 3(2), 77–101 (2006). https://doi.org/10.1191/1478088706qp063oa

3. Endsley, M.R.: Situation awareness global assessment technique (SAGAT). In: Proceedings of the IEEE 1988 National Aerospace and Electronics Conference, pp. 789–795. IEEE (1988). https://ieeexplore.ieee.org/abstract/document/195097/

4. Fang, R., Bindu, R., Gupta, A., Kang, D.: LLM Agents can Autonomously Exploit One-day Vulnerabilities (2024). http://arxiv.org/abs/2404.08144. arXiv:2404.08144

5. Fenz, S., Ekelhart, A., Weippl, E.: Fortification of IT security by automatic security advisory processing. In: 22nd International Conference on Advanced Information Networking and Applications (AINA 2008), pp. 575–582. IEEE (2008). https://ieeexplore.ieee.org/abstract/document/4482758/

6. Franke, U., Brynielsson, J.: Cyber situational awareness - a systematic review of the literature. Comput. Secur. 46, 18–31 (2014). https://doi.org/10.1016/j.cose.2014.06.008

7. Husák, M., Jirsík, T., Yang, S.J.: SoK: contemporary issues and challenges to enable cyber situational awareness for network security. In: Proceedings of the 15th International Conference on Availability, Reliability and Security, pp. 1–10 (2020). https://doi.org/10.1145/3407023.3407062

8. Jiang, L., Jayatilaka, A., Nasim, M., Grobler, M., Zahedi, M., Babar, M.A.: Systematic literature review on cyber situational awareness visualizations. IEEE Access 10, 57525–57554 (2022). https://doi.org/10.1109/ACCESS.2022.3178195

9. Kaufhold, M.A., Riebe, T., Bayer, M., Reuter, C.: We do not have the capacity to monitor all media': a design case study on cyber situational awareness in computer emergency response teams. In: Proceedings of the Conference on Human Factors in Computing Systems (CHI), Honolulu, HI, USA (2024). https://doi.org/10.1145/3613904.3642368

10. Kaufhold, M.A., Bäumler, J., Bajorski, M., Reuter, C.: Cyber threat awareness, protective measures and communication preferences in Germany: implications from three representative surveys (2021–2024). In: Proceedings of the Conference on Human Factors in Computing Systems (CHI), CHI 2025, Yokohama, Japan. Association for Computing Machinery (2025). https://doi.org/10.1145/3706598.3713795

11. Kaufhold, M.A., Bäumler, J., Koukal, N., Reuter, C.: Towards a security advisory content retrieval and extraction system for computer emergency response teams. In: Mensch und Computer 2024 - Workshopband. Gesellschaft für Informatik e.V., Karlsruhe, Germany (2024). https://doi.org/10.18420/muc2024-mci-ws13-133

12. Kaufhold, M.A., Bäumler, J., Koukal, N., Reuter, C.: GitHub: Appendix and Source Code of the AdvisoryHub Application (2025). https://github.com/PEASEC/advisory-hub

13. Lekkas, D., Spinellis, D.: Handling and reporting security advisories: a scorecard approach. IEEE Secur. Priv. 3(4), 32–41 (2005). https://doi.org/10.1109/MSP.2005.98

14. Mancuso, V., McGuire, S., Staheli, D.: Human centered cyber situation awareness. In: Ahram, T., Karwowski, W. (eds.) AHFE 2019. AISC, vol. 960, pp. 69–78. Springer, Cham (2020). https://doi.org/10.1007/978-3-030-20488-4_7

15. Mayring, P.: Qualitative content analysis. Forum Qual. Soc. Res. **1**(2) (2000). https://doi.org/10.17169/fqs-1.2.1089
16. Miranda, L., et al.: On the flow of software security advisories. IEEE Trans. Netw. Serv. Manag. **18**(2), 1305–1320 (2021). https://ieeexplore.ieee.org/abstract/document/9427134/
17. Morrell, N.E.: Quality function deployment. SAE Trans. 1090–1097 (1987). https://www.jstor.org/stable/44470091
18. Munshaw, J.: What's the deal with the massive backlog of vulnerabilities at the NVD? (2024). https://blog.talosintelligence.com/nvd-vulnerability-backlog-the-need-to-know/
19. Overmeer, M.: Taranis3 Documentation (2018). https://github.com/markov2/taranis3
20. Riebe, T., Kaufhold, M.A., Reuter, C.: The impact of organizational structure and technology use on collaborative practices in computer emergency response teams: an empirical study. Proc. ACM Hum. Comput. Interact. (PACM) Comput.-Supported Coop. Work Soc. Comput. **5** (2021). https://doi.org/10.1145/3479865
21. Skopik, F., Akhras, B.: Taranis AI: applying natural language processing for advanced open-source intelligence analysis. ERCIM News **2024**(136), 50–51 (2024). https://ercim-news.ercim.eu/en136/r-i/taranis-ai-applying-natural-language-processing-for-advanced-open-source-intelligence-analysis
22. Venable, J., Pries-Heje, J., Baskerville, R.: A comprehensive framework for evaluation in design science research. In: Peffers, K., Rothenberger, M., Kuechler, B. (eds.) DESRIST 2012. LNCS, vol. 7286, pp. 423–438. Springer, Heidelberg (2012). https://doi.org/10.1007/978-3-642-29863-9_31
23. Wunder, J., Aurich, J., Benenson, Z.: From chaos to consistency: the role of CSAF in streamlining security advisories. In: Proceedings of the 2024 European Symposium on Usable Security, pp. 187–199 (2024). https://doi.org/10.1145/3688459.3688463

Service-Aware Password Risk Meter – Helping Users to Choose Suitable Passwords in Services

Roi S. Serna⬤, Ana I. González-Tablas⁽⊠⁾⬤, Lorena González-Manzano⬤,
and Jose María de Fuentes⬤

Computer Science and Engineering Department, Universidad Carlos III de Madrid,
Av. de la Universidad, 30, 28911 Leganés, Madrid, Spain
roisanch@pa.uc3m.es, {aigonzal,lgmanzan,jfuentes}@inf.uc3m.es

Abstract. Passwords remain as a widespread authentication mechanism for online services. Users are required to adopt complex and unique passwords. Since human memory is limited, it is important to adapt the password complexity to the severity of an eventual account compromise. To the best of authors' knowledge, this has not been addressed yet. Indeed, our analysis of 352M passwords from 25 online services reveals that users do not consider the service at stake. This paper proposes a service-aware password risk model and a meter that consider user-, password- and service-related features. It aims to (1) make users aware of the risk associated with their account compromise depending on the service features and (2) encourage them to choose passwords with appropriate robustness. Our approach is assessed by 31 cybersecurity experts and 284 regular users, confirming the effectiveness of the metric and its usefulness for the users.

Keywords: Passwords · Authentication · Risk-meter · Risk-model

1 Introduction

The use of passwords is a common practice, specially in web services [2]. Each user manages 168 passwords for personal uses and 87 for business-related issues on average[1]. Single sign-on, on the other hand, is not seen as a perfect solution [18] and alternatives such as passwordless authentication, while being a promising solution, face obstacles to rapid adoption [14].

User (mis)practices. According to BitWarden, 85% of users reuse passwords across services[2], and over half rely on memory—often using personal data or lyrics. These habits increase attack success, especially with widespread data

---

[1] https://nordpass.com/blog/how-many-passwords-does-average-person-have/, last access Feb. 2025.

[2] https://bitwarden.com/blog/a-closer-look-at-password-statistics/, last access Feb. 2025.

The extended version of this article is available at https://hdl.handle.net/10016/47287.

M. Dalla Preda et al. (Eds.): ARES 2025, LNCS 15993, pp. 69–79, 2025.
https://doi.org/10.1007/978-3-032-00627-1_4

breaches: 49% involve passwords[3]. Thus, improving password selection has been emphasized [1]. Password managers could help, but adoption remains low (only 30% use them[4]).

Password Risk and Metering. A first step to handle this threat is to measure the security level of passwords, e.g., with password meters.

At first, [4] introduced the use of probability and the Monte Carlo method. Later, [25] employed probabilistic context-free grammars, and [27] proposed heuristic-based approaches. Recently artificial intelligence has facilitated studies such as [16] using RNNs and [12] using deep learning. Nevertheless, classical approaches, like [3], using rank estimation, have continued to evolve.

Motivation. Human memory limitations make it unrealistic to expect users to create long, complex, and unique passwords for every service. Instead, password complexity should be adapted to the risk level of each service. For example, using simple passwords is particularly dangerous on platforms without two-factor authentication (2FA), contrasting with approaches that assess passwords without considering their context of use.

Contribution. This paper proposes a password risk meter that considers the service in which it is used. Given the type of service as well as the sensitivity of the data it manages, it is possible to help users make informed decisions on the required security level for each password. Specific contributions are listed next, while additional data, all experimental materials and the developed prototype are publicly released in a GitHub repository[5]:

C1 **Characterize user awareness on service-related factors when picking passwords**: More than 352M passwords from 25 services are analysed to study if their strength is related to any service-related feature. Our findings show that users do not consider this aspect when picking their passwords.
C2 **A risk metric supported by a model based on services' features**: Features of services are analysed to develop a risk model and metric against threats to password-based authentication (e.g., leaked, revealed or guessed passwords and leaked hashed passwords). Security experts have contributed to adjust the model's risk parameters (40) and validate the risk metric (31).
C3 **Development of service-aware password risk meter**: To enhance users' security awareness, the risk meter is materialized as a user assistance tool. It is tested with 284 real users of different profiles, showing its suitability.

2   Related Work

Prior research on password security has largely focused on understanding user habits through leaked password datasets and on developing metrics and tools to

---

[3] https://www.smbguide.com/password-statistics/, last access Feb. 2025.
[4] https://explodingtopics.com/blog/password-stats, last access Feb. 2025.
[5] https://github.com/serna-r/Service-aware-password-risk-meter-Helping-users-to-choose-suitable-passwords-in-services.

Table 1. Related work

Ref.	Year	Description	Password related techniques	Service aware	Users validation
[4]	2015	Use probabilistic methods to approximate password strength	Guesses estimation	×	×
[16]	2016	Apply neural networks to estimate password strength	Strength meter	×	×
[25]	2016	Decide password strength based on PCFGs	Strength meter	×	×
[27]	2016	Create a lightweight password strength estimator	Strength meter	×	×
[24]	2017	Combine neural networks with heuristics to create a password meter	Strength meter	×	×
[23]	2018	Design an educational tool to show password creation strategies to users	Creation tool	×	30
[6]	2019	Create an algorithm to create strong passwords from users' information	Generation algorithm	×	×
[10]	2020	Design a game to train users to choose better passwords	User awareness	×	4,906
[9]	2022	Development of a password policy based on analyzed user leaked passwords	Policy	×	×
[19]	2022	Improve have I been PWNED including the risk of credential stuffing	Reuse evaluation	×	×
[12]	2023	Improve password strength meters using deep learning	Strength meter	×	×
[20]	2023	Combine neural networks with user auxiliary information to improve password strength approximations	Strength meter	×	×
[28]	2023	Test bi-directional transformers for password guessing and propose a password strength meter	Strength meter	×	×
[13]	2023	Create a password meter using the LLM ChatGPT	Password evaluation	×	×
[17]	2024	Create a system to recommend better passwords for users	Recommender system	×	758
Ours	2025	Service-aware password risk meter	Risk meter	✓	284

evaluate password strength. Although effective at guessing or scoring passwords, most of these systems ignore the context in which the password is used. A complementary line of work addresses user behavior and awareness, However, existing proposals tend to treat password creation independently from the specific risks associated with the services being accessed. Our work introduces a novel perspective by integrating empirical analysis, service-specific risk modeling, and user interaction. It is the first to explicitly incorporate potential data exposure into password evaluation and to validate this approach with a functioning prototype tested by users. Table 1 summarizes the contributions of previous proposals and our work comparing the following aspects: (a) development of techniques to enhance or help creating better passwords, (b) involvement of services where passwords are used for login purposes; and (c) evaluation of the techniques by real users.

3   Characterizing Password Selection

This section analyses the relationship, from different perspectives, between passwords' strength and services in which they are used.

Experimental Data: Passwords and Services. This study analyzes password leaks from 25 online services, sourced from Leakbase[6] and [5]. Only breaches preserving real password prevalence and containing at least 50,000 passwords were selected. In total, over 353 million passwords are considered, from leaks spanning from 2008 to 2019. Services are grouped into 11 categories: social, adult, game, entertainment, network operations, email, shopping, finance, business, digital tools, and news. This classification is based on the leaked datasets

---

[6] https://leakbase.io/, last access February 2025.

and the most visited website categories according to Similarweb[7]. Mean password lengths of each leak range from 7 to 10 characters, with an overall average of 8.48 and low standard deviation, consistent with NIST's minimum recommendation of 8 characters [7]. Additional details on the characteristics of each leak can be found in the GitHub repository[8].

Password Strength vs. Service. Password strength is evaluated across services using the zxcvbn score [27], which estimates password strength based on attacker-relevant heuristics, it scores each password from 0 to 4. For each service, the score distribution is represented by the tuple $S = (p_0, p_1, p_2, p_3, p_4)$, where p_i denotes the normalized frequency of score i. All services exhibit similar distributions: low frequencies for scores 0 and 4, and a dominant frequency for score 1 ($p(\text{score} = 1) \approx 0.43$ on average). Some outliers include dubsmash (score 0), myheritage (score 1), and clearvoicesurveys (score 3). Temporal analysis shows no significant variation in score distributions over time. A Kruskal-Wallis test confirms this, yielding a p-value close to 1, indicating that the distributions are statistically indistinguishable across years.

Password Strength vs. Composition Requirements. This section explores if stricter password requirements yield stronger passwords. Based on LUDS classification [12], most services require 6 or 8 characters (each in 28%), and only two demand more than 8. A linear regression using minimum length as predictor yielded low explanatory power ($R^2 = 0.10$). Kruskal–Wallis tests comparing password strength by length ($p = 0.18$) and mask ($p = 0.21$) found no significant differences. Thus, stricter rules do not necessarily result in stronger passwords.

Password Strength vs. Service Category. Based on the service classification, we analyze the relationship between password strength distributions—represented by the zxcvbn score tuple S—across services within the same category (cohesion) and between different categories (separation).

We evaluate whether service category impacts password strength by comparing clustering metrics using two strategies: (i) predefined service categories and (ii) unsupervised clustering via K-means ($k = 6$, selected empirically). Results indicate no strong alignment between password strength and service category. Specifically, the silhouette index (SI) improves from -0.24 (category-based) to 0.42 (K-means). Cohesion, measured by the Sum of Squared Within-cluster distances (SSW), improves from 0.86 to 0.15, and separation, measured by the Sum of Squared Between-cluster distances (SSB), increases from 0.10 to 0.81 under K-means. These changes suggest that real password strength distributions cluster more coherently than predefined categories allow.

To further examine intra-category cohesion, we compute the Kullback-Leibler (KL) divergence between password score distributions for all service pairs within each category. Most categories exhibit high internal variability, suggesting heterogeneous user behaviors. However, the games category shows consistently low

---

[7] https://www.similarweb.com/es/top-websites, last access February 2025.

[8] https://github.com/serna-r/Service-aware-password-risk-meter-Helping-users-to-choose-suitable-passwords-in-services.

KL divergence, indicating high cohesion. A similar but weaker pattern is observed in the shopping category, possibly due to its limited number of datasets.

Password Strength vs. Services Features. This section explores whether specific service features influence the strength of user-chosen passwords. Features were identified through manual analysis of the 50 most visited websites (Similarweb, February 2025) and services from the leak datasets. Two categories were considered: (i) authentication practices (e.g., 2FA, password policies, blacklist usage) and (ii) types of user data managed (17 types, including location, email, birthdate, photos, etc.).

To evaluate impact, a Mann–Whitney U test compared password strength distributions between services with and without each feature. No statistically significant associations were found ($p > 0.05$) except for "location" data, with a marginal p-value of 0.04. This suggests weak evidence of an effect. Overall, service features do not strongly influence password strength.

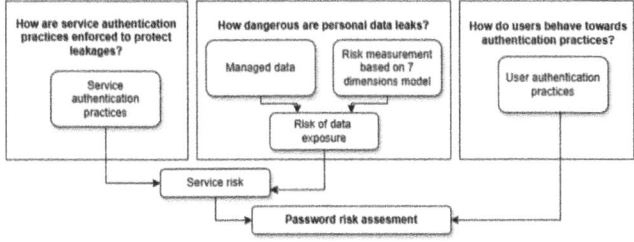

Fig. 1. Password risk assessment model

4 Service-Aware Password Risk Model and Metric

Results in the previous section confirm that users do not adapt their passwords to the service, to its category or any service-related feature. Thus, this section develops a risk model (Sect. 4.1) and a metric (Sect. 4.2) to improve security awareness. Experts finally validate the proposal (Sect. 4.3).

4.1 Risk Model

This section presents a model to guide users in choosing stronger passwords based on service context. It combines three aspects: u the privacy risk of the user's data exposure, and the authentication practices of the service and the user (see Fig. 1). While this paper proposes a specific instantiation, the model is flexible and can be extended with additional elements.

Risk of Data Exposure. The privacy risk of data exposure arising from threats to password-based authentication is evaluated using the multidimensional measurement scales proposed in [11]. This framework conceptualizes seven distinct privacy risk dimensions ($nd = 7$): physical, social, resource-related, psychological, prosecution-related, career-related, and freedom-related. Each dimension reflects a specific adverse effect users may perceive from disclosing personal information digitally.

In this work, user data corresponds to the $k = 17$ items dat_j mentioned in Sect. 3, which can be accessed upon successful login. For each pair of dimension d_i and data item dat_j, a privacy risk score r_{d_i, dat_j} is assigned using a 7-point Likert scale based on expert evaluations. These scores form a risk matrix R_d with dimensions $nd \times k$.

To ensure reliability, 40 subject-matter experts (mainly from Spain, with some from France and Iran) provided 80 total responses, rating the perceived impact of exposing each dat_j across pairs of dimensions d_i. The distribution of responses per dimension was: $d_1 \sim 14$, $d_2 \sim 8$, $d_3 \sim 7$, $d_4 \sim 10$, $d_5 \sim 12$, $d_6 \sim 13$, and $d_7 \sim 16$. The final score r_{d_i, dat_j} for each entry is computed as the median of expert responses to account for non-normal sample distributions.

Each service s_i is then characterized by a binary vector $D_{s_i} \in \{0, 1\}^k$, indicating which user data items dat_j the service manages. The overall estimated privacy risk of data exposure for a service is calculated by the matrix-vector product $R_d \times D_{s_i}$.

Service Authentication Practices. This work examines two authentication practices in services: the implementation of password policies aligned with NIST guidelines [7], focusing on password length and composition to balance security and usability; and the use of two-factor authentication (2FA). Services with 2FA—using time-based one-time passwords, SMS codes, or hardware tokens—offer stronger protection against attacks like credential stuffing and better prevent unauthorized access.

User Authentication Practices. The behavior of users towards security may affect the overall risk, thus reaching a more tailored value. In this work we have included the strength of the user chosen password and the user indication of reuse of that password.

4.2   Risk Metric

Based on the previous model, a metric is proposed by combining the three aforementioned factors. Specific details on the computation of each factor are presented next, showing their combination at the end. For simplicity, $\mathcal{N}_{[a;\, b]}^{[c;\, d]}(x)$ represents the normalization of x from range $[a;\, b]$ to $[c;\, d]$ as shown in Eq. 1. On the other hand, $||\cdot||_F$ represents the Frobenius norm [15] and $\times$ is the matrix multiplication.

$$\mathcal{N}_{[a;\, b]}^{[c;\, d]}(x) = c + \frac{(x - a) \cdot (d - c)}{b - a} \tag{1}$$

Risk of Data Exposure $(D_{EXP}(s_i))$. This service-related factor measures the severity of the user's data exposure if the password gets compromised. As previously explained, the privacy risk attributed to all data items d_j handled by a service s_i can be computed by multiplying the privacy_dimensions–data_items risk score matrix R_d by the vector D_{s_i}. The normalized risk value $D_{EXP}(s_i)$ is computed as shown in Eq. 2. Note that the normalizations are applied to keep the relative weight of this factor in the global risk value.

$$D_{EXP}(s_i) = \mathcal{N}_{[1;\,\|R_d\|_F]}^{[1;\,20]}(\|R_d \times D_{s_i}\|_F) \tag{2}$$

Service Authentication Practices $(S_{AUTH}(s_i))$. This factor assesses the compliance of service s_i with NIST policies [7], password guidelines, and the use of 2FA. Compliance with NIST recommendations is quantified as $P = c_p + b_p + m_p$, where c_p, b_p, and m_p represent the composition, blacklist, and minimum length requirements, respectively. Each is assigned a value of 0 if the requirement is met and 1 otherwise. Additionally, the password length recommendation is included as m_r, valued at 0 if passwords longer than 8 characters are advised, and 1 otherwise. The use of 2FA is modeled by the variable fa, set to 0.99 when 2FA is implemented and 0 when not. This choice follows CISA's statement that 2FA can reduce compromise likelihood by up to 99%[9]. The overall authentication score for service s_i, denoted $S_{AUTH}(s_i)$, is computed as a normalized combination of these components, as shown in Eq. 3.

$$S_{AUTH}(s_i) = \mathcal{N}_{[0;4]}^{[0;2]}((P + m_r) \cdot (1 - fa)) \tag{3}$$

User Authentication Practices $U_{AUTH}(pwd_j)$. This work considers two user decisions when signing into a service: password strength and reuse. Password strength is measured by the zxcvbn score, $P_{STR}(pwd_j)$. Password reuse, $P_{USE}(pwd_j)$, adjusts risk based on how many times a password is unique to the user—whether it is used only in service s_i or reused elsewhere. To balance security and usability, reuse impact is modulated by user trends. Studies [21,22,26] find passwords are typically reused about 3–4 times. Thus, reuse up to this threshold is tolerated, while exceeding it is penalized. If n is the reuse count, a penalty of 0.5 is applied as follows:

$$P_{USE}(pwd_j) = \begin{cases} 0.1 \cdot (n-1), & \text{if } pwd_j \text{ is used } 1 \leq n \leq 3 \text{ times} \\ 0.5, & \text{if } n \geq 4. \end{cases}$$

Globally, the normalized user authentication practices factor $U_{AUTH}(pwd_j)$ is computed according to Eq. 4. Note that the value 4 is set because it is the maximum zxcvbn score.

$$U_{AUTH}(pwd_j) = \mathcal{N}_{[0;\,4.5]}^{[0;\,2]}(4 - P_{STR}(pwd_j) + P_{USE}(pwd_j)) \tag{4}$$

---

[9] https://www.cisa.gov/topics/cybersecurity-best-practices/multifactor-authentication, accessed February 2025.

Global Metric $R(s_i, pwd_j)$ and Usage. The proposed risk metric $R(s_i, pwd_j)$ for a password pwd_j in service s_i combines three factors: data exposure $D_{EXP}(s_i)$, service authentication $S_{AUTH}(s_i)$, and user authentication $U_{AUTH}(pwd_j)$. It is computed as shown in Eq. 5. Each service has an inherent risk from the data it manages, which is adjusted based on the security measures of the service and the user. The normalization of each factor ensures the final risk score lies within the $[0, 100]$ range, facilitating communication to average users.

$$R(s_i, pwd_j) = D_{EXP}(s_i) \cdot (1 + S_{AUTH}(s_i) + U_{AUTH}(pwd_j)) \tag{5}$$

4.3 Expert Validation

The metric validation was performed via an expert survey. Experts reviewed case studies and rated their agreement with $R(s_i, pwd_j)$. A total of 31 experts—participants from the R_d elicitation in Sect. 4.1—completed the survey, using a 5-point Likert scale to express their level of agreement with the metric values for each case study. Results in Fig. 2a show experts largely agree with the proposed metric, with most responses at 4 (agree) on the Likert scale. While consensus is clear, total agreement is lower (19%, 32%, and 19% for case studies 1, 2, and 3, respectively). Agreement rates are 51% for case study 1 and 45% for cases 2 and 3. Total disagreement is minimal, with only 1 expert in case 2 and 2 in case 3.

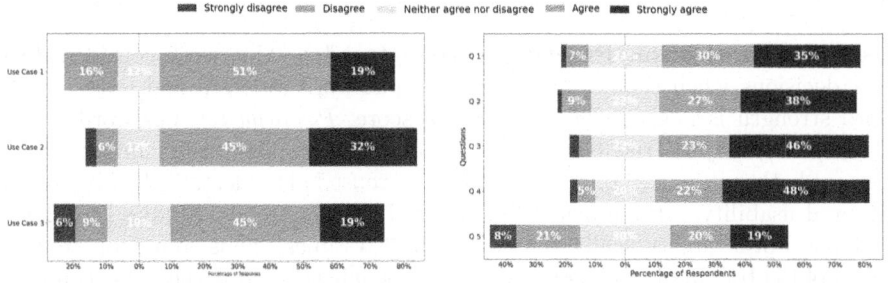

(a) Metric validation: Expert answers   (b) Meter validation: User answers

Fig. 2. Validation results

5 Service-Aware Password Risk Meter

Once the risk metric has been presented and validated by experts, it is necessary to assess its usefulness to real-world users. This section presents the implemented prototype (Sect. 5.1) and the results of the user validation (Sect. 5.2).

5.1   Prototype Description

A prototype was developed to test if a risk meter improves users' password choices. The interface lets users select a service, review collected data and authentication, and input a password with its reuse count. It then dynamically shows risk indicators—data exposure, service authentication strength, password strength, and overall risk—using a color scale based on a geometric progression. The prototype is publicly available online[10].

5.2   User-Based Validation

Design of the Study. To evaluate the password risk meter, participants used the prototype and completed a survey assessing their understanding, usability, and willingness to adopt the tool. Demographic data—age, nationality, gender, and education level—were also collected.

Survey Results. A total of 284 users participated, mostly aged 25–54 (87%), with 37% aged 25–34. Gender distribution was 62% female and 38% male. Most (92%) were from Spain; others from Colombia, Argentina, the US, and Europe. Regarding education, 84% had a University degree, 7% vocational training, and 9% high school or less. Figure 2b shows users generally agreed or strongly agreed that the tool helps understand password risk and are willing to adopt it. However, responses to Q5 showed less agreement, indicating reluctance to switch services despite high risks. Kruskal-Wallis tests [8] found no significant response differences across demographics ($p > 0.1$), e.g., $p = 0.87$ for Q1 by age and $p = 0.48$ by education, suggesting consistent perceptions regardless of profile.

6   Conclusion

This work examines whether users adapt password strength according to service sensitivity. A risk model and metric were introduced, showing that users generally ignore contextual risk when selecting passwords. A validated prototype risk meter demonstrated potential to improve user awareness and behavior, despite certain limitations. Future research will explore its applicability in workplace environments and assess the service-awareness of AI-generated password suggestions.

Acknowledgments. This work was supported by the Spanish National Cybersecurity Institute (INCIBE) grant APAMciber within the framework of the Recovery, Transformation and Resilience Plan funds, financed by the European Union (Next Generation).

Ethical Issues. This research was supervised by UC3M's data protection officer. Usernames were never stored or processed. Expert and user contact data were handled in compliance with the GDPR, with informed consent obtained and rights communicated. Notably, the prototype did not collect any personal data or passwords.

---

[10] https://serna-r.github.io/risk-meter---V2/.

References

1. Amador, J., Ma, Y., Hasama, S., Lumba, E., Lee, G., Birrell, E.: Prospects for improving password selection. In: Nineteenth Symposium on Usable Privacy and Security (SOUPS 2023), Anaheim, CA, pp. 263–282. USENIX (2023)
2. Barkadehi, M.H., Nilashi, M., Ibrahim, O., Zakeri Fardi, A., Samad, S.: Authentication systems: a literature review and classification. Telematics Inform. **35**(5), 1491–1511 (2018)
3. David, L., Wool, A.: PESrank: an explainable online password strength estimator1. J. Comput. Secur. **30**(6), 877–901 (2022)
4. Dell'Amico, M., Filippone, M.: Monte Carlo strength evaluation: fast and reliable password checking. In: Proceedings of the 22nd ACM SIGSAC Conference on Computer and Communications Security, CCS 2015, pp. 158–169. ACM, New York (2015)
5. Dionysiou, A., Vassiliades, V., Athanasopoulos, E.: HoneyGen: generating honeywords using representation learning. In: Proceedings of the 2021 ACM Asia Conference on Computer and Communications Security, Virtual Event Hong Kong, pp. 265–279. ACM (2021)
6. Glory, F.Z., Ul Aftab, A., Tremblay-Savard, O., Mohammed, N.: Strong password generation based on user inputs. In: 2019 IEEE 10th Annual Information Technology, Electronics and Mobile Communication Conference (IEMCON), pp. 0416–0423 (2019). ISSN: 2644-3163
7. Grassi, P.A., et al.: NIST Special Publication 800-63B: Digital Identity Guidelines – Authentication and Lifecycle Management. Special Publication 800-63B, National Institute of Standards and Technology (2017)
8. Guo, S., Zhong, S., Zhang, A.: Privacy-preserving Kruskal-Wallis test. Comput. Methods Programs Biomed. **112**(1), 135–145 (2013)
9. Güven, E.Y., Boyaci, A., Aydin, M.A.: A novel password policy focusing on altering user password selection habits: a statistical analysis on breached data. Comput. Secur. **113** (2022)
10. Jayakrishnan, G.C., Sirigireddy, G.R., Vaddepalli, S., Banahatti, V., Lodha, S.P., Pandit, S.S.: Passworld: a serious game to promote password awareness and diversity in an enterprise. In: Sixteenth Symposium on Usable Privacy and Security (SOUPS 2020), pp. 1–18. USENIX (2020)
11. Karwatzki, S., Trenz, M., Veit, D.: The multidimensional nature of privacy risks: conceptualisation, measurement and implications for digital services. Inf. Syst. J. **32**(6), 1126–1157 (2022)
12. Kim, S.J., Lee, B.M.: Multi-class classification prediction model for password strength based on deep learning. J. Multimedia Inf. Syst. **10**(1), 45–52 (2023)
13. Kim, S.J., Lee, B.M.: A novel approach to password strength evaluation using ChatGPT-based prompt metrics. IEEE Access **12**, 175071–175080 (2024)
14. Lassak, L., Pan, E., Ur, B., Golla, M.: Why aren't we using passkeys? Obstacles companies face deploying fido2 passwordless authentication. In: Proceedings of the 33rd USENIX Conference on Security Symposium, SEC 2024. USENIX (2024)
15. Ma, C., Kamp, Y., Willems, L.: A Frobenius norm approach to glottal closure detection from the speech signal. IEEE Trans. Speech Audio Process. **2**, 258–265 (1994)
16. Melicher, W., et al.: Fast, lean, and accurate: modeling password guessability using neural networks. In: 25th USENIX Security Symposium (USENIX Security 2016), pp. 175–191. USENIX (2016)

17. Morag, A., David, L., Toch, E., Wool, A.: Improving users' passwords with DPAR: a data-driven password recommendation system (2024)
18. Morkonda, S.G., Chiasson, S., van Oorschot, P.C.: Influences of displaying permission-related information on web single sign-on login decisions. Comput. Secur. **139**, 103666 (2024)
19. Pal, B., et al.: Might I get pwned: a second generation compromised credential checking service. In: Proceedings of the 31st USENIX Security Symposium, Security 2022. USENIX (2022)
20. Pasquini, D., Ateniese, G., Troncoso, C.: Universal neural-cracking-machines: self-configurable password models from auxiliary data. In: 2024 IEEE Symposium on Security and Privacy (SP), pp. 1365–1384. IEEE (2024)
21. Stobert, E., Biddle, R.: Expert password management. In: Stajano, F., Mjølsnes, S.F., Jenkinson, G., Thorsheim, P. (eds.) PASSWORDS 2015. LNCS, vol. 9551, pp. 3–20. Springer, Cham (2016). https://doi.org/10.1007/978-3-319-29938-9_1
22. Taneski, V., Heričko, M., Brumen, B.: Systematic overview of password security problems. Acta Polytechnica Hungarica **16**(3), 143–165 (2019)
23. Tsokkis, P., Stavrou, E.: A password generator tool to increase users' awareness on bad password construction strategies. In: 2018 International Symposium on Networks, Computers and Communications (ISNCC), pp. 1–5 (2018)
24. Ur, B., et al.: Design and evaluation of a data-driven password meter. In: Conference on Human Factors in Computing Systems - Proceedings, vol. 2017-May (2017)
25. Wang, D., He, D., Cheng, H., Wang, P.: fuzzyPSM: a new password strength meter using fuzzy probabilistic context-free grammars. In: 2016 46th Annual IEEE/IFIP International Conference on Dependable Systems and Networks (DSN), pp. 595–606 (2016)
26. Wash, R., Rader, E., Berman, R., Wellmer, Z.: Understanding password choices: how frequently entered passwords are re-used across websites. In: Twelfth Symposium on Usable Privacy and Security (SOUPS 2016), pp. 175–188 (2016)
27. Wheeler, D.L.: zxcvbn: low-budget password strength estimation. In: 25th USENIX Security Symposium (USENIX Security 2016), Austin, TX, pp. 157–173 (2016)
28. Xu, M., et al.: Improving real-world password guessing attacks via bi-directional transformers. In: 32nd USENIX Security Symposium (USENIX Security 2023), Anaheim, CA, pp. 1001–1018. USENIX (2023)

System Security

TEE-Assisted Recovery and Upgrades for Long-Running BFT Services

Ines Messadi$^{(\boxtimes)}$ ⓘ, Markus Elias Gerber,
Tobias Distler ⓘ, and Rüdiger Kapitza ⓘ

Friedrich-Alexander-Universität Erlangen-Nürnberg, Erlangen, Germany
{ines.messadi,tobias.distler,ruediger.kapitza}@fau.de

Abstract. Integrating Byzantine fault-tolerant (BFT) replication with trusted execution environments (TEEs) offers an unprecedented degree of resilience and confidentiality. Nevertheless, vulnerabilities in both the underlying infrastructure and the application software still exist, which means that for long-running services there typically is a substantial risk that eventually the number of faulty or compromised replicas exceeds a system's fault-tolerance threshold. We address this issue with NABORIS, the first approach in the area of confidential computing to provide long-term resilience for critical BFT services. To achieve this, NABORIS combines (1) proactive recovery of replicas to remove faults with (2) support for software upgrades to patch newly discovered vulnerabilities at run-time. For both of these procedures, NABORIS afterwards provides remote entities with verifiable evidence that they actually took place. We implement NABORIS using AMD SEV-SNP and show that its performance overhead is low compared to the state of the art in recovery procedures.

Keywords: Byzantine Fault Tolerance · Trusted Execution Environments · Long-Term Resilience · Recovery · Replica Evolution

1 Introduction

Byzantine fault-tolerant (BFT) replication [29,40] is an effective technique to build systems that provide their service even if a subset of its replicas (usually up to f out of $3f+1$ [15]) are subjected to arbitrary faults caused by hardware errors, software bugs, or intrusions. However, by itself Byzantine fault tolerance is not able to address additional aspects that are vital for practical deployments such as privacy or defense measures to reduce the probability of successful attacks.

In an effort to mitigate these issues, organizations are increasingly turning to hardware-based trusted execution environments (TEEs) to shield sensitive code and data, for example in the form of confidential virtual machines (CVMs). As a reaction to the growing demand, CVMs based on technologies such as AMD SEV-SNP and Intel TDX have already been integrated into major public-cloud platforms [3,8], allowing customers to rent virtual machines while the provider cannot access their private data. Following this emergence of hardware-based protection, several BFT systems have adopted TEEs [10,11,14,31,39].

M. Dalla Preda et al. (Eds.): ARES 2025, LNCS 15993, pp. 83–105, 2025.
https://doi.org/10.1007/978-3-032-00627-1_5

Sadly, TEEs are not a panacea but themselves susceptible to vulnerabilities [16,37,41,48], including software-based attacks that exploit application-level bugs (e.g., synchronization bugs [48]) and can cause the bypassing of the CVM protection [49]. Even worse, attacks are getting stealthier and detection techniques are limited, giving adversaries more time to gather information and learn from previous attacks on already compromised replicas. In such a stealthy attack on the Ronin Blockchain Network, for example, attackers recently gained undetected access for over a week, resulting in a loss of $615 million [47].

Taking these circumstances into account, for long-running services it is likely that more than f replicas become faulty or compromised during a system's lifetime. Thus, it is essential to enable such BFT systems to self-heal by automatically recovering replicas from faults [15,38,42]. In addition, they should offer mechanisms that allow replicas to evolve [32], meaning to dynamically modify the replica code during recovery in order to eliminate (known) vulnerabilities [26,36,43]. Unfortunately, despite some approaches specifically targeting virtualized environments [21,22,38,46], to our knowledge there are currently no solutions supporting both the recovery and the evolution of CVM-based replicas.

In this paper we address this problem with NABORIS, an approach that offers resilience for long-running CVM-based services by proactively recovering replicas and enabling upgrades during execution. Since many faults and attacks are inherently difficult to identify, NABORIS recovers replicas *proactively* [15] in configurable intervals. As part of the recovery process, NABORIS creates an entirely new CVM instance for the affected replica containing the latest security patches, safely transfers the current agreement-protocol and application state into this instance, and refreshes the replica's cryptographic keys. This way, attackers have a reduced window of vulnerability and face a constantly changing attack surface.

To achieve flexibility with regard to deployment options, we designed NABORIS to be as independent from the underlying infrastructure as possible. Ruling out the use of special-purpose hardware components [15,42], this goal required us to develop a new methodology for ensuring that recoveries actually took place. More precisely, while traditional approaches rely on trusted subsystems to always execute recovery procedures in a reliable and timely manner [15,21,22,38,42], NABORIS enables its replicas to present a *proof of recovery and upgrade* that is verifiable by both its peers as well as external parties (e.g., service customers). Only after a recovering replica provides such a proof, the other replicas in the system allow the replica to rejoin their group.

In summary, this work makes the following contributions: (1) It presents NABORIS, the first confidential-computing-aware approach to offer both replica recovery and evolution. (2) It describes NABORIS's multi-phase recovery protocol that performs replica rejuvenation with only negligible impact on overall system performance due to replacing the old CVM instance of a replica with a new CVM instance hosted on the same machine. (3) It offers details on the NABORIS prototype implementation based on AMD SEV-SNP. (4) It outlines our vision of how to provide "NABORIS as a service" in public-cloud environments. (5) It evaluates NABORIS for multiple applications and in the presence of recovery procedures.

2   Background

In this section, we provide background on BFT state-machine replication and give an overview of how trusted execution environments are able to offer verifiable proofs of integrity in the context of confidential computing.

2.1   BFT State-Machine Replication

Our target systems achieve resilience against arbitrary faults by replicating the user application across multiple servers and executing a BFT agreement protocol (e.g., PBFT [15]) to keep the application state consistent (see Fig. 1). To tolerate up to f faulty replicas, these systems require a total of $3f+1$ replicas. In the use-case scenarios we address, the fault threshold f is typically small (e.g., $f = 1$) which is why support for recovering replicas from faults is crucial.

In a nutshell, BFT state-machine replication works as follows. To invoke operations at the replicated service, clients submit requests to one of the replicas, the leader, which then initiates a multi-phase consensus protocol that enables all correct replicas in the system to agree on a common order in which to execute the requests in the application. With the application designed as a deterministic state machine [40], this approach ensures that all correct replicas produce the same replies to requests and also end up with the same application states. To garbage-collect information belonging to completed consensus-protocol runs, replicas periodically create checkpoints of the application state in predefined intervals [24]. If necessary, such checkpoints can later be used by trailing replicas to catch up with the rest of the group by performing a state transfer between replicas. In case the leader is suspected or confirmed to be faulty, the other replicas initiate a view-change mechanism that reassigns the leader role to a different replica and consequently allows the overall system to make progress again.

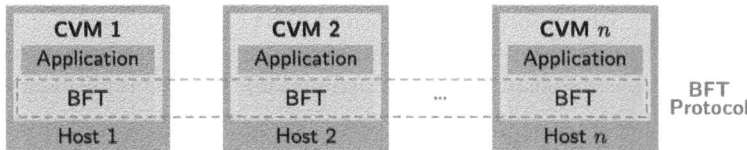

Fig. 1. BFT state-machine replication architecture for CVM-based replicas.

2.2   Trusted Execution Environments

Trusted execution environments (TEEs) promise a hardware-encrypted environment for computations beyond the observation and control of hosting entities, thereby laying the foundation for confidential computing. Depending on the technology, the CPU has the ability to protect the integrity and encrypt either specific application components [17] or entire virtual machines, which are then referred to as confidential virtual machines (CVMs) [3].

In this paper, we focus on AMD SEV [2] as technology for CVMs because it has a lower adoption barrier than more fine-grained approaches. For the recent release of Secure Nested Paging (SNP), a CVM mitigates attacks of a malicious hypervisor. In the SEV-SNP architecture, the memory controller encrypts the initial set of VM pages using a key unique to the VM. This is monitored by a secure processor to provide essential security services for SEV-SNP. In addition, when a CVM is executed, its memory pages are decrypted by the memory controller and reencrypted when the data leaves the CPU. Any communication between the CVMs and the hypervisor occurs through shared memory pages.

SEV-SNP incorporates an attestation mechanism that allows communicating parties to prove the TEE's genuineness. Attestation starts with the CVM requesting an *attestation report* (including the initial measured pages) from the secure processor. The report is signed with the versioned chip endorsement key (VCEK) that is unique to the secure processor firmware and a unique chip ID to ensure that the report originated from a specific machine and that the system is properly patched. In addition, the verification process also involves a remote key distribution service (KDS) that supplies certificates to authenticate the VCEK's validity. Existing works have proposed a variety of options when it comes to leveraging TEEs for enhancing resilience and confidentiality in BFT systems. Some approaches like Engraft [46] and CCF [39] encapsulate consensus and transaction handling while maintaining untrusted storage and network layers. Others aim to strengthen resilience by reducing the trusted computing base, protecting only safety-critical components (e.g., message signing [11,31]).

2.3   System and Threat Model

As illustrated in Fig. 1, with this work we target systems in which there is a clear separation between, on the one hand, the customer application running inside CVMs and, on the other hand, the underlying host infrastructure, which is typically provided by a different entity. For fault tolerance, the application is replicated using a BFT protocol that ensures safety in the presence of at most f concurrent Byzantine replica faults, and liveness under partial synchrony [15]. We assume that by exploiting an existing vulnerability in the implementation of an application replica, an adversary may cause the replica to behave in an arbitrary way. For this reason, despite running replicas inside TEEs, our target systems cannot employ TEE-based BFT protocols such as Hybster [11] or DAMYSUS [18], as those protocols require their TEE-based components to be fully trusted. Hence, we rely on full-fledged BFT agreement provided by approaches like PBFT [15] to ensure consistency among $n = 3f + 1$ replicas.

Besides direct attacks on the application, another potential strategy of an adversary involves gaining access to the host infrastructure. If the adversary takes control over a server, we assume the TEE to ensure the confidentiality of the local replica (i.e., our approach does not offer improvements regarding (rollback or side-channel) attacks against the TEE itself [33,44,45]). However, during these kinds of attacks the replica is no longer guaranteed to make progress; as discussed in Sect. 7, such scenarios commonly do not pose a major problem in practice.

3   Challenges

Next, we identify the main challenges associated with ensuring resilience for long-running CVM-based BFT services and highlight how NABORIS addresses them.

3.1   Long-Term Resilience for CVM-Based Services

As discussed in Sect. 2.1, the replicated BFT systems we target in our work typically consist of a small number of replicas, therefore making it necessary to provide some form of automated recovery to support long-running applications [20]. Specifically, the recovery of replicas ensures that faults do not accumulate over time, and hence allows a system to tolerate more than f faulty replicas over the course of its lifetime.

In the past, several strategies have been proposed to address this issue, including reactive-recovery procedures that are initiated once a fault was either detected or at least suspected [27], proactive-recovery mechanisms that are time-triggered [15,21,22,38], as well as combinations of both [42]. To further increase the effectiveness of such measures, the recovery should be combined with the concept of replica evolution [32] which entails modifications to the replica code to remove existing vulnerabilities. Among other things, this may involve the use of randomization techniques [13], recompiling replica executables to enhance the diversity of implementations [36], and substitutions of port numbers and passwords [43]. Unfortunately, despite the large body of previous works on these topics, it is still an open question how to perform replica recovery and evolution in BFT systems consisting of a group of CVM-based replicas.

➤ *Our Approach in a Nutshell.* NABORIS offers long-term resilience for replicated BFT services by supporting proactive recovery of CVM-based replicas, including the opportunity to dynamically eliminate vulnerabilities at runtime by installing upgrades as part of the recovery process.

3.2   Proof of Recovery

In a nutshell, recovery procedures remove faults by replacing an existing (potentially faulty) replica instance with a new instance that is created from a verified state [20]. For this approach to be effective it is essential that an adversary must not be able to prevent the initiation, execution, and completion of the recovery process. Traditionally, this problem is addressed by introducing a trusted component that cannot be compromised through attacks and takes care of handling critical recovery steps. Examples for such components include a hardware-based watchdog timer [15], a dedicated replica-local synchronous subsystem [42], or an entire virtualization layer that is considered to be trustworthy [22,38].

For our target use cases, and especially potential future scenarios in which NABORIS is deployed as a service in a cloud environment (see Sect. 7), none of these options represents a practical solution due to conflicting with our goal of minimizing infrastructure dependence. Specifically, relying on any type of low-level component to control the recovery process would mean to shift additional responsibilities to the underlying infrastructure, and hence makes it more difficult to develop a generic design. Furthermore, to our knowledge no cloud provider currently offers this kind of reliable-recovery functionality to upper layers. Thus, there is no possibility to directly force faulty replicas to perform a timely recovery under all circumstances and to the same extent as traditional approaches do.

➢ *Our Approach in a Nutshell.* To circumvent the lack of recovery support from the underlying infrastructure, NABORIS pursues a novel strategy that focuses on reliably detecting scenarios in which faulty replicas try to avoid recovery. More precisely, once a recovery is due, the other replicas temporarily exclude the affected replica from participating in the BFT protocol and only allow the replica to rejoin after presenting a proof that it actually has recovered. To create such a *proof of recovery*, we extend a CVM's attestation report with a recovery counter whose value is dictated by the other replicas and changes on each recovery.

3.3   Proof of Upgrade

Besides trying to hinder the execution of recovery procedures, an adversary may also aim at preventing upgrades in an effort to keep the replica vulnerable, and consequently make it easier to compromise a replica even after a recovery. To solve this problem, replicas should not only prove that a recovery indeed took place, but also that they are currently running the latest firmware and software versions. For systems that do not support upgrades at runtime, the latter can be achieved by assuming that the replica code is obtained from a non-modifiable medium [15]. Otherwise, existing approaches typically resort to a trusted component to perform upgrades in a reliable and timely manner [36, 43], which is why their designs do not incorporate mechanisms to dynamically validate the replica code during execution.

➢ *Our Approach in a Nutshell.* As it is the case for recovery, NABORIS does not simply rely on the assumption that a replica upgrade has actually been performed, but instead offers the other replicas in the system to verify such a scenario based on a *proof of upgrade*. In general, NABORIS replicas validate the integrity of their peers by comparing the attestation measurements of other replicas to their own, thereby ensuring that all participating replicas execute the identical (unaltered) code; if a replica on such occasion presents a diverging measurement, it is not allowed to (re)join the system. To support verifiable upgrades (which change the code of the affected replica and hence its measurement), NABORIS utilizes a special command that is sent through the agreement protocol to inform all replicas about the new measurement in a consistent manner.

4   NABORIS

NABORIS is a TEE-based framework that offers long-term resilience for critical BFT services by supporting both replica recovery as well as replica evolution. In this section, we first present an overview of our approach and then discuss the most important techniques and components in more detail.

4.1 Overview

NABORIS provides Byzantine fault tolerance by running multiple replicas of the
same application on different servers and connecting them through a BFT agreement protocol (PBFT [15] in our prototype). To protect the integrity of the replicated service, each replica is located inside its own CVM. As illustrated in Fig. 2,
in addition to the replica CVM every participating server also accommodates an
auxiliary NABORIS system component, the *recovery agent*, which is responsible for
assisting in proactive-recovery procedures for its local replica. Specifically, whenever the NABORIS protocol (which itself is running inside the replica CVM) decides
that the recovery of a replica is due, the recovery agent starts a second CVM on
the same host which at the end of the recovery process becomes the new replica
and fully replaces the old CVM. Among other things, this approach has three main
advantages: (1) By creating a new replica instance in a separate CVM, from the
overall replica's perspective the NABORIS recovery process is able to remove any
effects that a (potential) intrusion might have had on the old CVM. (2) The use
of a second CVM enables NABORIS to not only eliminate existing faults, but also
close vulnerabilities by installing security patches in the new CVM. (3) Hosting
both the old and the new CVM on the same server allows NABORIS to bring the
application state of the new replica instance up to date via a state transfer that primarily relies on local operations [21,22], and therefore has only negligible impact
on system availability and performance.

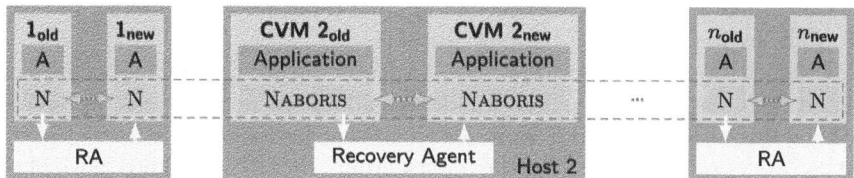

Fig. 2. NABORIS replication infrastructure.

4.2 Proof of Recovery

Since Byzantine faults and successful attacks do not necessarily result in detectable
faulty behavior, NABORIS recovers replicas in a periodic and proactive manner,
thereby ensuring that faults are removed after a configurable window of time.
Specifically, replicas are recovered individually using a round-robin strategy to
minimize the impact of recovery on overall system performance. To be compatible with different underlying infrastructures, in contrast to other approaches (see
Sect. 3.2) NABORIS does not rely on special-purpose hardware to trigger recovery
procedures but instead applies a *coordinated timer* to decide when the next recovery is due. In a nutshell, NABORIS's coordinated timer works as follows.

To participate in the timer subprotocol, replicas maintain a *recovery counter* as part of the state that is replicated using NABORIS's BFT agreement protocol. Using a deterministic mapping to replica ids, the current value *recno* of this counter indicates which replica i to recover next (e.g., $recno \% n = i$, with n denoting the total number of replicas). At the beginning of every recovery period, each replica starts a local timer that is set to the end of the period (i.e., when the next recovery should take place). Once its local timer expires, a replica signals this event by distributing a message demanding the recovery counter to be incremented. Combining such notifications from $f+1$ different replicas (i.e., at least one correct replica), the current leader creates a special request and passes it through the agreement protocol. When this request is committed, the execution of the request causes the recovery counter to be updated, thereby informing all replicas (including the one to be recovered) about the fact that the recovery is due. At this point, the other replicas exclude the recovering replica from their group and only allow the replica (more precisely: its new CVM instance running on the same machine) to rejoin after supplying them with a proof of recovery.

To produce such a proof of recovery for NABORIS, we extend a CVM's attestation report by adding the corresponding recovery-counter value. Specifically, we instruct the hypervisor to add the recovery-counter value as *host data* during the startup of the new CVM. Once such host data is set for a CVM, it is included in all of its attestation reports and cannot be changed by either the host or the CVM. Correct replicas only accept an attestation report if it contains the expected recovery-counter value. This way, and as a consequence of the report of a CVM being immutable at runtime, the old replica CVM is unable to rejoin the group by impersonating the new instance.

A replica's recovery agent (i.e., the NABORIS infrastructure component running on each host server, see Sect. 4.1) learns about the need to perform a recovery by acting as a special BFT-protocol client that periodically retrieves the current recovery-counter value from the replica group. Based on the knowledge of the deterministic mapping of counter values to replica ids, a recovery agent is able to determine when the time has come to recover its local replica. In particular, this approach offers two key benefits: (1) Triggering a recovery by evaluating the recovery counter allows the recovery agent to directly obtain the counter value to use for the configuration of the new CVM instance. (2) Having the recovery agent fetch the recovery-counter value by sending a read request to the replica group ensures that faulty replicas are unable to prevent recovery procedures.

4.3   Proof of Upgrade

To enable NABORIS replicas to evolve by applying upgrades at runtime, we first put each replica in the position to verify the integrity of other replicas, and then further extend this mechanism to support dynamic changes.

Verifiable Integrity. Overall, system integrity in NABORIS builds on three principles: (1) a verifiable boot chain ensures the integrity of each replica CVM right from the beginning, (2) a running code-hash validation enables each replica to verify the integrity of the code that is currently executed by another replica, and (3) a read-only filesystem prevents adversaries from retroactively modifying system files even in case of successful intrusions.

The SEV-SNP attestation process is limited to measuring the initial VM context before the VM begins execution. The context is typically used only to place and measure the initial firmware (Open Virtual Machine Firmware, OVMF), which is sufficient to continue booting a VM. This is a significant weakness because it allows adversaries, for example, to load a malicious kernel undetected because only the firmware is reflected in the attestation report. To mitigate this risk, the initialization and boot process was updated to include the kernel, initrd, and command-line hashes as part of the OVMF, referred to as Direct-Measured Boot. However, this still leaves the system vulnerable to runtime attacks (e.g., privilege escalation) where a privileged attacker could replace critical system binaries or files, persisting across reboots. For this reason, for NABORIS we extend the verified boot process to protect the entire CVM state against tampering [25]. Apart from the hashes incorporated during the directly measured boot, the root hash of a Merkle tree created from the root file system is also added. Upon the start of the CVM, the OVMF validates the hashes while loading the kernel and initrd. Furthermore, the initrd mounts the root file system and verifies its integrity using dm-verity. To secure and persist CVM runtime data across reboots, we provide support for encrypted file systems using dm-crypt. The required disk encryption key is wrapped and unwrapped using the sealing key provided by the AMD secure processor. The wrapped key is stored on the disk in an unencrypted partition and is therefore persisted and accessible across reboots. The sealing key is unique to the CVM measurement and machine identification and can only be retrieved by a running CVM with that particular measurement. Therefore only the CVM can access the encrypted file systems.

Supporting Upgrades. During periods without upgrades, a NABORIS replica is able to validate the integrity of other (recovering) replicas by comparing their attestation measurements to its own. However, with NABORIS recovering replicas using a round-robin strategy, this is no longer possible once an administrator applies a patch to fix a discovered vulnerability, because changes to the code result in diverging attestation reports. To address this issue, when performing upgrades NABORIS administrators not only update the replica code but also submit a corresponding command to the replica group (via the BFT replication protocol) that informs replicas of the new attestation value to use for the measurement comparison. This way, NABORIS enables upgrades while at the same time allowing continuous integrity verification.

4.4 Recovery Protocol

We use the established PBFT-PR [15] protocol as basis for the NABORIS recovery mechanism and adapt it to fit our needs. In the following, we highlight the differences to PBFT-PR and describe the NABORIS recovery phases in detail.

Properties. In order to be applicable to our target use cases, the NABORIS recovery protocol offers improvements over PBFT-PR with regard to several properties that are summarized in Table 1 and further discussed next.

Table 1. Comparison between PBFT-PR and NABORIS

Aspect	Property	PBFT-PR [15]	NABORIS
Recovery strategy		Proactive	Proactive
Code protection	Ⓤ	ROM	Read-only rootfs
Rejuvenation	Ⓐ	Same server	New CVM
Trusted component	Ⓒ	Secure co-processor	CVM protection
Recovery trigger	Ⓒ	HW watchdog	Coordinated timer

Ⓤ Upgrade Support As part of the recovery process, PBFT-PR ensures the integrity of the operating-system and application code by verifying the code based on a digest that was stored in read-only memory prior to the system start. Since this digest cannot be modified, PBFT-PR does not support dynamic code changes and hence makes it impossible to fix newly discovered vulnerabilities. In contrast, NABORIS replicas validate the integrity of their peers by comparing attestation measurements and allow an administrator to consistently update the expected measurement, thereby enabling upgrades while the system is running.

Ⓐ Availability In PBFT-PR, a replica spans a whole server and is recovered by rebooting the physical machine. As a consequence, the recovery of a PBFT-PR replica is typically associated with a significant period of time during which the replica is not able to regularly participate in the system. For services requiring high availability, this only leaves two options: counting the recovering replica as a temporary fault with regard to the fault-tolerance threshold f (and hence being able to tolerate fewer actual faults during this period), or extending the system with additional replicas at the cost of an increased resource footprint [42]. In NABORIS, we circumvent this problem by implementing the recovery as a switch from the old replica CVM to a new replica CVM hosted on the same physical machine. As a key benefit, this allows NABORIS to keep the old replica CVM running while the new replica CVM is started, initialized, and brought up to date, thereby minimizing unavailability to a negligibly short period during the local switch.

Ⓒ Cloud Readiness Involving the reboot of an entire physical machine, the recovery process in PBFT-PR is triggered by a trusted hardware-based watchdog timer. For potential cloud-based use-case scenarios (see Sect. 7), neither the reboot of an entire physical machine nor the reliance on a special-purpose hardware component is feasible, especially for approaches that seek to offer provider independence. To enable the use of NABORIS in these kinds of environments, we designed the NABORIS recovery protocol in such a way that it can be operated within CVMs using standard cloud infrastructure services (e.g., starting and terminating CVMs) and without requiring additional specialized hardware.

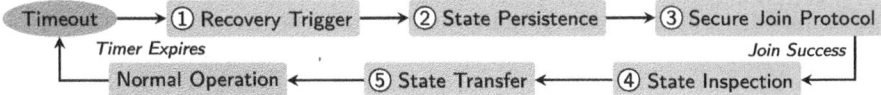

Fig. 3. NABORIS recovery protocol phases.

Recovery Phases. As illustrated in Fig. 3, NABORIS's protocol for recovering replicas consists of several phases. Once the replicas' local timers signal that the next recovery is due, the replicas ① execute the coordinated-timer subprotocol to trigger the recovery in a consistent manner (see Sect. 4.2). In response to this, ② the old replica CVM instance saves its volatile application state to disk; this data serves as basis for the new replica CVM instance, which is subsequently started by the recovery. If the old replica instance is faulty and fails to comply in this phase, the recovery agent fetches the necessary data from another replica. Once the new replica instance is running, ③ it provides the other replicas with its proof of recovery (and upgrade) in order to rejoin the group. After that, with assistance from the group, ④ the new replica instance executes a subprotocol that allows the replica to clear faulty residue that the old replica instance potentially left on disk. Finally, in a last step ⑤ the new instance fetches recently updated application-state parts from other replicas to compensate for the state changes that occurred while the replica was recovering, before eventually returning to normal operation. In the following, we discuss each of these phases in detail.

Recovery Trigger. The expiration of the timer in each replica marks the recovery start. At this point, NABORIS replicas execute a consensus round to establish the new recovery-counter value for the recovering replica (see Sect. 4.2). For this purpose, each replica sends an $\langle$INIT-REC, $recno_i + 1\rangle$ message to propose a value to the leader. The leader waits for matching INIT-REC messages from $f + 1$ different replicas (possibly including its own) to start the agreement. This prevents both accidental and malicious recovery triggers from individual replicas. Upon reaching an agreement, replicas notify clients to reject messages from the recovering replica, and then set up a timeout to wait for the rejuvenated replica to reconnect. If the replica fails to return within this interval, the protocol triggers failure handling (e.g., sending a blame signal to the administrator), as this situation implies a problem with the underlying infrastructure that is beyond NABORIS's control. Finally, the retreating replica instance sends a $\langle$SIGNAL, $recno\rangle$ message with the newly agreed counter value to the recovery agent to inform the agent about the value to use in the attestation report of the new replica instance.

State Persistence. After the recovery is triggered, the old replica instance writes its state (including consensus and application data) to an encrypted disk. This step occurs for two reasons that are explained in the following.

Firstly, in order to ensure protocol safety, it is essential that the recovery process does not cause correct replicas to become faulty by losing their states [15]. More precisely, due to the correctness of BFT agreement protocols depending on the decisions made by a quorum of correct replicas, after recovery a correct replica must remember all statements it made to other replicas before the recovery took place. In NABORIS, we fulfill this condition by having the old replica instance flush all necessary state to disk and afterwards attaching this disk to the new replica instance. Notice that the aforementioned requirement does not apply to faulty replicas. Specifically, if the state of a faulty replica is lost, or a malicious replica refuses to persist its current state, the new replica instance may be initialized with an older checkpoint (e.g., provided by another replica in the system).

Secondly, this approach allows to leverage the fact that in many use-case scenarios the replicated application already maintains large parts of its state on disk. As a consequence, forwarding the state via the same medium represents an efficient method to load the data into the new replica instance.

Secure Join Protocol. Upon initialization by the recovery agent, the newly started replica instance generates a fresh pair of keys and broadcasts a JOIN-REQUEST message (Algorithm 1, Line 6). The other replicas validate the joining replica by comparing its measurement against their attestation values (Lines 21–27). As part of the process, this verification requires reproducible CVM builds to ensure consistent measurements across all replicas, as discussed in Sect. 4.3. Since the join request contains the versioned chip endorsement key, there is no need for the other replicas to perform a query to the key distribution service (see Sect. 2.2). A replica accepts a join request provided that: (1) the key digest in the join request report matches the computed digest of the public key pk_{irej}; (2) the recovery number $recno_i$ matches the agreed-upon number in the current view; (3) the report data in $attReport_{irej}$ matches the report data from at least $2f+1$ replicas in the current view; (4) the SNP certificate chain verifies correctly using the $vcek_{irej}$ included in the join-request message.

State Inspection. Once accepted back into the group, the new replica instance examines the state that the old replica instance supplied via encrypted disk as part of the state-persistence phase. For this purpose, the new instance requests the corresponding disk encryption key (`dm-crypt` key) from the old instance, which, upon successful attestation verification, transmits this key and afterwards instructs the recovery agent to shut it down. Similar to the scenarios discussed above, if the old instance is faulty and does not cooperate, NABORIS resorts to a stable checkpoint provided by another replica to initialize the new instance.

Apart from being non-cooperative, a faulty old instance may also try to trick the new instance into using a corrupted state. To handle such cases, NABORIS executes a mechanism that closely resembles PBFT-PR's estimation subprotocol [15], which is why we omit specifics. In a nutshell, this subprotocol enables the new instance to determine an upper bound (in the form of a high water mark hm, see Algorithm 1, Line 10) up to which the old instance at most may have contributed to the consensus progress. Consequently, if the provided state contains information beyond this point, the old instance must have deliberately planted it there, meaning that the new instance can safely ignore it.

Algorithm 1. Secure Join Protocol

```
 1: as a rejuvenated replica
 2:     upon connection to all do
 3:         pk_i ← generatePublicKey()
 4:         attReport_i ← requestReport(Hash(pk_i))
 5:         vcek_i ← requestVcek(attReport_i)
 6:         send ⟨JOIN-REQUEST, attReport_i, pk_i, vcek_i⟩ to all
 7:         verify remote replicas' report
 8:     upon receiving ⟨JOIN-RESPONSE, status, recno, c, p, v⟩ do
 9:         if status = accept then
10:             (hm, view_i) ← estimateHm(c, p, v)          ▷ Get high water mark and view estimate
11:             joinProcessingRequests()
12:         else                                                          ▷ status = reject
13:             send ⟨SIGNAL, recno⟩ to agent                  ▷ Use correct recno
14:         end if
15: as a remote replica
16:     upon receiving ⟨JOIN-REQUEST, attReport_{irej}, pk_{irej}, vcek_{irej}⟩ do
17:         keyHash ← getHash(attReport_{irej})
18:         recno ← getRecCounter(attReport_{irej})
19:         c ← ∅
20:         p ← ∅
21:         if keyHash = Hash(pk_i) ∧ verifyCertifChain(vcek) ∧ recno = agreedRecno then
22:             c ← lastCheckpointSeqNum()
23:             p ← lastPreparedReq()
24:             status ← accept
25:         else
26:             status ← reject
27:         end if
28:         send⟨JOIN-RESPONSE, status, recno, c, p, view_i⟩ to rejuvenated replica
```

State Transfer. If during the state-inspection phase the new instance determines that parts of its state are corrupted or missing, the new instance in a final step initiates a secure state transfer to repair/obtain the affected partitions. As part of this procedure, other replicas not only provide the requested state parts but also verifiable proof (in the form of quorum certificates that are backed up by $2f+1$ replicas [15]) of the transmitted data's correctness. Once the state transfer finishes, the recovery process of the replica is complete.

4.5   Discussion

As discussed in Sect. 3.2, our decision to forgo trusted recovery support from the underlying infrastructure in order to achieve a more flexible design may result in scenarios in which a timely recovery cannot always be guaranteed if an adversary managed to launch a successful intrusion of the host machine. Specifically, there may be situations where the recovery of a replica does not proceed as expected or is delayed due to a malicious actor at the host level, causing the recovering replica to become unavailable. If this happens to more than f hosts at the same time, the service is no longer live, however its safety is still ensured even under such circumstances. We argue that such cases of delayed recovery can be detected early by monitoring the NABORIS protocol's control messages using a special monitoring client. If a replica fails to recover within a specified time, this is detected by the monitoring client and the administrator is contacted to resolve the problem at the host-system level.

Having compromised a host, an adversary may try to exploit CVM reboots to launch forking attacks that violate state continuity, which can create divergent replica groups serving inconsistent responses to clients. To prevent such attacks, we can adopt Narrator's blockchain-based approach [35], where each CVM registers its unique identifier (provided by the AMD secure processor) with a trusted tamper-proof blockchain during initialization, or let the leader dictate the CVM instance the group should communicate with. In AMD CVMs, each fork is a new instance for which the platform security processor generates a unique `REPORT_ID`. By registering this identifier, other replicas can detect forked identities.

5   Implementation

Our implementation builds on the PBFT components of the Themis codebase [5], reusing its core consensus functionality and extending it with our proactive recovery implementation. We realized the NABORIS prototype in 2,802 lines of code (LOC), the PBFT-PR [15] protocol (which serves as baseline in our evaluation, see Sect. 6) in 2,297 LOC, and the agent logic using the Rust nightly 2023-04-01. To digitally sign protocol messages, we rely on the 256-bit ED25519 from the ring library (v0.16.20). The attestation functionality in our prototype is embedded as a Rust module (304 LOC) using the VirTEE API [6].

NABORIS and PBFT-PR handle replica recoveries through different mechanisms. NABORIS involves the recovery agent and starts new replica instances with the recovery-counter value determined by the replica group. Besides, SEV-SNP CVMs are architecturally restricted from performing internal reboots. In contrast, PBFT-PR replicas autonomously shut down and restart using `systemd` services on the host to maintain CPU pinning configurations across reboots.

Providing CVMs via AMD SEV-SNP. NABORIS's prototype runs inside a CVM built using a modified Revelio assembling scripts as a base [25]. The root filesystem is constructed through a Docker-based build process that incorporates an SEV-SNP-capable kernel and other essential packages. The build process eliminates nondeterministic elements to guarantee reproducible measurements across different instances. The resulting CVM integrates additional mechanisms: `dm-verity` for root filesystem integrity verification in the initramfs and `dm-crypt` for disk encryption. Furthermore, we added a service started at boot time to request the necessary VCEK from the KDS keyserver in order to enable the validation of attestation reports. Some configuration information (e.g., basic network settings) that is not critical to the integrity of the CVM but needed for a proper integration into the system is injected via a separate partition that is not part of the measurement of the CVM. During transition to the rejuvenated CVM, the retreating CVM's disk is mounted as removable storage, enabling state recovery by the rejuvenated CVM.

Can NABORIS be Implemented Based on Other CVM Technologies Such as Intel TDX? The NABORIS protocol is CVM-agnostic and can be realized using other TEE architectures that provide similar confidentiality and integrity properties, host-provided data (i.e., for the recovery counter), and trusted timers using accurate instruction timing (i.e., recovery triggers). In our case, the AMD trusted-timer feature [2] queries timestamps from the AMD secure processor using encrypted communication, preventing time manipulation attacks. Furthermore, using a distributed consensus between CVMs, our design strengthens the timing guarantees. To enable verifiable recovery counters in attestation reports, we leverage `host_data` in AMD SEV-SNP. Intel TDX provides equivalent functionality via its measurement registers (`mrconfigid`, `mrowner`, and `mrownerconfig`) [30]. For cloud-based deployments (see Sect. 7), some features in Azure such as the configuration of `host_data` in the interface for creating SEV-SNP CVMs may be restricted, however this is not a fundamental problem as the `host_data` setting could be made available to customers.

6   Evaluation

In this section, we evaluate NABORIS using PBFT-PR (see Sect. 4.4) as baseline. For this purpose, we conduct experiments with two different applications: (1) A counter (incremented on each client request) to measure the overhead of the recovery protocol in isolation. (2) An in-memory key-value store (KVS) that operates at a workload of 50%/50% read/write operations using 10,000 keys.

In our evaluation, we primarily focus on examining how NABORIS performs compared to a system (PBFT-PR) which also supports proactive recovery, but offers lower security guarantees than NABORIS. In this context, it is important to note that we do not claim NABORIS to be a means for improving throughput or latency in TEE-based replicated systems, which is why our experiments neither include protocols that exploit TEEs for enhancing the performance of Byzantine agreement [11,18], nor approaches that speed up the recovery process by optimizing the state transfer between old and new replica instance [21,22]. As discussed in Sect. 3, our goal in this paper is to provide proofs of recovery and upgrade for CVM-based replicas, hence in the evaluation we are interested in studying whether NABORIS is able to achieve this without notable performance overhead.

6.1   Experimental Setup

We evaluate NABORIS using virtual machines with SEV-SNP-enabled kernels, comparing it against PBFT-PR running on virtual machines without SEV-SNP. Each virtual machine is configured with 4 vCPUs and 8 GiB memory, running Ubuntu 20.04. To optimize performance, each virtual machine is pinned to cores sharing the same physical CPU to prevent context switching. Both prototypes comprise 4 replicas and utilize a thread pool of 4 workers implementing the work stealing algorithm from the Tokio library, where networking and message authentication are parallelized while maintaining sequential protocol execution.

Client requests carry 100-byte payloads and the agreement on them is performed in batches of 50 requests. In all experiments, the checkpointing interval is set to 1,000 requests and the workload is produced by 100 client threads. Each client continuously issues synchronous requests and measures the time it takes after the submission of a request to obtain a stable result. During the experiments, a new recovery procedure is triggered 40 s after the completion of the previous recovery procedure. Before a leader replica is recovered, the replica group initiates a view change to reassign the leader role to another replica.

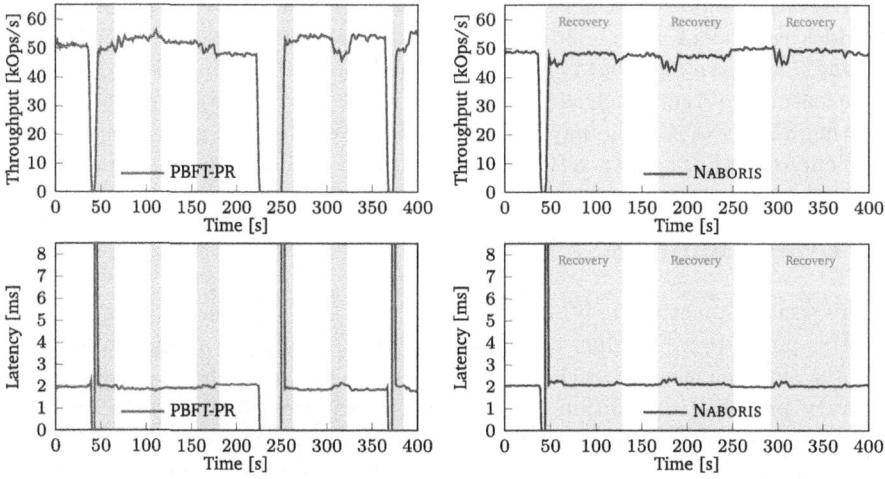

Fig. 4. Comparison of throughput and latency results for PBFT-PR (left) and NABORIS (right) during and outside of recovery procedures for the counter application.

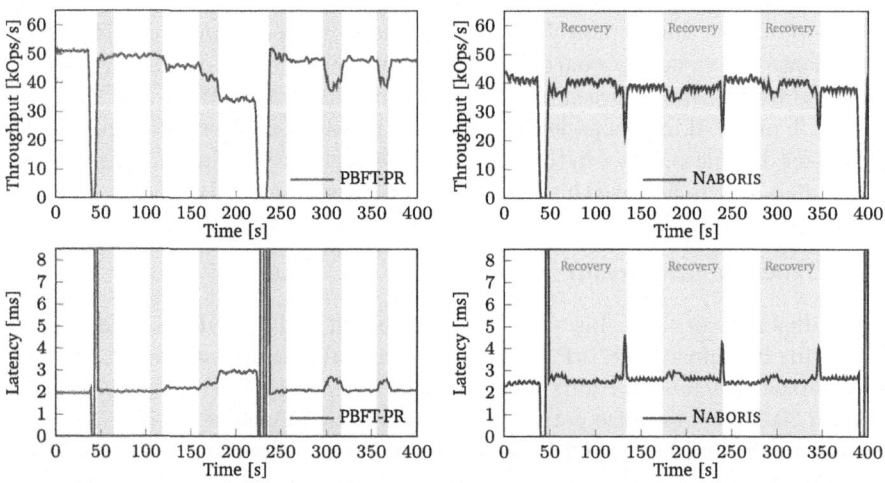

Fig. 5. Comparison of throughput and latency results for PBFT-PR (left) and NABORIS (right) during and outside of recovery procedures for the key-value store.

6.2   Impact of Recoveries on Performance

The results of our experiments in Figs. 4 and 5 show that the recovery process in NABORIS requires approximately 64 s on average from start to finish, while PBFT-PR completes recovery in 19 s. This difference is due to several factors: Firstly, CVM boot times are 220% higher compared to VM boot times in non-SEV environments due to the additional memory pre-allocation and initialization required for SEV-SNP CVMs. Secondly, the NABORIS recovery protocol (see Sect. 4.4) involves additional steps compared to PBFT-PR, including VM disk mounting and secure exchange of disk encryption keys. However, despite the longer recovery period NABORIS maintains stable throughput outside of view changes even during recoveries. For both NABORIS and PBFT-PR, the temporary drops in throughput (and the associated spikes in latency) that are observable in the graphs (e.g., at $t = 45$ s in Fig. 4) are a result of the systems performing a view change prior to recovering the active leader replica. In a production setting, the windows between two recoveries are typically significantly longer than in our experiments (e.g., up to several hours), which is why the higher duration of NABORIS's recovery procedure does not pose a problem, especially due to the fact that over the course of this process NABORIS is able to provide normal-case performance.

6.3   The Cost of SEV-SNP CVM Mechanisms

To better understand the difference between NABORIS and PBFT-PR, we measure the average latency of the protocols' main phases. Table 2 presents a detailed comparison. The total boot time shows that SEV-SNP CVMs have approximately $3.2\times$ higher latency than non-SEV VMs, primarily due to the additional memory initialization and pre-allocation. The most significant performance difference appears in the key-exchange mechanism. NABORIS's attestation exchange requires 8 ms, compared to PBFT-PR's new-key message which takes about 53 μs (99% faster). The attestation message also carries a larger payload (876 bytes total: 748-byte report, 32-byte key, 96-byte VCEK) compared to PBFT-PR's simple 32-byte public-key message.

At boot time, a NABORIS replica must request a report from the AMD secure processor and in principle a VCEK from the key distribution service. The key distribution service introduces rate limiting when multiple similar CVMs request VCEKs running on the same host and it could be unavailable. However, the VCEK of a machine does not change unless the firmware of the SVE-SNP is upgraded, so the VCEK can be prefetched, cached and included in attestation messages. The duration of the estimation protocol varies based on replica load and message processing queues, particularly after performing a view change.

Updating the entire CVM requires about 5 min in which the VM is reassembled from scratch including rebuilding the base Docker image. However, this occurs outside the critical path by pre-preparing assembled VMs. Similarly, the one-time partition decryption and mounting cost of 1,217 ms (including a 1 s sleep to wait for decryption) is only necessary because NABORIS, in contrast to PBFT-PR, is designed for use in confidential-computing environments.

Table 2. Comparison of system functions

Primitive	NABORIS	PBFT-PR
Booting Time	32 s	10 s
Pre-kernel	7 s	4 s
Integrity protection (dm-verity)	4 ms	-
Disk encryption (dm-crypt)	33 ms	33 ms
Attestation vs. new-key message	8 ms	53 µs
Verifying report	4 ms	-
Requesting report from AMD-SP	833 ms	-
Requesting VCEK from KDS	794 ms	-
Decryption and mount partition	1,217 ms	-
Saving state in files (KVS)	464 ms	123 ms
Estimation protocol	20 ms	10 ms
Re-assembling the VM (Upgrades)	5 m	-

7 NABORIS as a Service

With more and more critical applications being moved to the cloud, we envision that it can be beneficial to provide the NABORIS functionality as a cloud service to customers who need long-term resilience for their applications. For this purpose, it is important to avoid vendor lock-in by not relying on a specific provider so that the NABORIS service is able to run on different clouds. Fortunately, by designing NABORIS in such a way that it requires the underlying infrastructure to only offer basic operations like starting and terminating CVMs, from a technical perspective there are no additional barriers in this regard. Hence, in the following we focus our discussion on the question how provider independence can be achieved. The key to solve this is to take the special characteristics of cloud environments and its stakeholders into account, which we do by distinguishing between different roles that each are associated with a distinct set of privileges and responsibilities. Specifically, we separate the tasks that are related to the cloud infrastructure (→ cloud provider) from the tasks necessary to perform replica recovery and evolution (→ NABORIS operator).

Cloud Provider. The cloud provider's central task is to maintain and operate the underlying infrastructure, offering the trusted execution environment that NABORIS relies on for confidentiality and integrity. For this purpose, the cloud provider does not require any knowledge about NABORIS in general, or of the recovery procedures and the replicated application in particular. In fact, as a result of the trusted execution environment ensuring confidentiality, the application state is completely hidden from the cloud provider.

   If the cloud provider fails to preserve the availability of its infrastructure (e.g., by unilaterally shutting down CVMs), the liveness of the replicated service can no longer be guaranteed, however even in this case NABORIS's BFT agreement protocol ensures that safety is not at stake. Overall, we do not expect provider-induced liveness issues to become a major problem in practice for two reasons. On the one hand, cloud providers typically do not have an incentive to violate service level agreements, because doing so hurts their reputation and consequently their business. On the other hand, if the dependability of an individual cloud provider is of concern, NABORIS's provider-independent design makes it possible to distribute a NABORIS deployment across different clouds in order to reduce the reliance on a specific provider [12].

NABORIS **Operator** The NABORIS operator leverages the cloud infrastructure to offer NABORIS as a service to its customers. In this context, the operator is primarily responsible for running the NABORIS recovery agent associated with each replica and for performing timely upgrades to the replica CVMs to fix critical bugs. To ensure that a newly started CVM is co-located with the old CVM of the same replica, the operator may either rent a bare-metal instance [7] or rely on a dedicated host service [1,4]. As with the cloud provider, the trusted execution environment prevents the NABORIS operator from learning application secrets.

Using a CVM's attestation report measurement, customers (and other external entities) are able to validate the code by accessing a public repository that features a deterministic build process, and hence allows them to recompute the measurement offline. This way, they can verify whether upgrades were actually performed, and if necessary (i.e., when the replica code does not match the expected version) blame the NABORIS operator for not meeting its responsibilities.

8 Related Work

We consider works on recovery and rejuvenation of Byzantine fault-tolerant systems and approaches that build on TEEs to implement a hybrid fault model and support recovery as most relevant to NABORIS.

BFT Fault Recovery and Rejuvenation. The problem of replica recovery with the goal of evicting adversaries has been studied in previous works [15, 22,38,42]. Castro and Liskov's work [15], PBFT-PR, inspired the development of several approaches in this area. PBFT-PR relies on trusted subsystems and watchdogs to proactively rejuvenate replicas one by one after a predefined time. As discussed in Sect. 4.4, the NABORIS approach shares similarities with the protocol when triggering a stateful recovery, but offers advantages with regard to properties such as upgrade support, availability, and cloud readiness.

VM-FIT [38] proposes a virtualization-based recovery initializing a new virtual machine replica in parallel to the normal execution to minimize the recovery overhead. SPARE [22] represents a design with $f + 1$ active replicas handling request processing and voting, while f passive replicas in a paused state receive periodic state updates; during proactive-recovery procedures, the passive replicas serve as foundation for the new replica instances. Sousa et al. [42] explored a reactive-recovery scheme introducing wormholes as trusted subsystems that coordinate rejuvenation, an approach that demands additional resources. Other systems, like Dynamic BFT [23], treat recovery as a reconfiguration problem, replacing faulty replicas rather than simply restarting them.

Various evolution techniques modify replica configurations across recoveries to prevent attackers from repeatedly compromising recovered replicas. These include code obfuscation [34] and parameter updates [43]. Building on this concept of evolution, our system generates a new CVM instance with distinct configurations after each recovery. The Eternal system [32] enables live software upgrades, where one replica can be upgraded while others maintain service availability. Compared to these works, NABORIS is the first to propose proactive recovery and upgrade support using commodity hardware support for TEEs such as CVMs.

Recovering TEE-Based Replication Systems. Several works have explored protecting consensus protocols using TEEs [10, 28, 46]. However, they commonly assume that code running inside a TEE cannot be exploited and focus on handling crash failures and their consequences, particularly state recovery and rollback attack prevention. Dinis et al. [19] propose a restart-rollback model for state replication during TEE restarts, with replicas verifying state freshness through digest comparisons. Engraft [46] encapsulates Raft consensus in TEEs and uses a two-phase protocol for state recovery after restarts. Nimble [9] prevents rollback attacks using trusted TEE endorsers that maintain signed ledger states and require majority consensus. While CCF [28] provides disaster recovery through ledger recovery and node restart protocols, its recovery model is purely reactive, initiating only after failures occur. NABORIS assumes that the hardware and firmware support implementing the TEE mechanisms can only fail by crashing, but imposes no further restrictions regarding Byzantine failures. Hence, it has a smaller trusted computing base than previous TEE-based replication systems.

9   Conclusion

NABORIS provides long-term resilience for CVM-based BFT services by supporting both proactive recovery and dynamic software upgrades. In contrast to existing recovery approaches, NABORIS does not rely on trusted special-purpose (hardware) components, but instead applies a novel concept that builds on the idea of only allowing recovering replicas to rejoin the system after having presented verifiable proof (in the form of CVM attestation reports) confirming that recoveries and upgrades indeed took place.

Acknowledgements. This work was funded by the Deutsche Forschungsgemeinschaft (DFG, German Research Foundation) – 446811880, 541017677.

References

1. Amazon EC2 dedicated hosts. https://aws.amazon.com/ec2/dedicated-hosts/
2. AMD secure encrypted virtualization (SEV). https://developer.amd.com/sev/
3. AMD SEV-SNP on Amazon EC2 instances. https://docs.aws.amazon.com/AWSEC2/latest/UserGuide/sev-snp.html
4. Azure dedicated host. https://azure.microsoft.com/en-us/products/virtual-machines/dedicated-host
5. Themis: BFT framework in Rust. https://github.com/ibr-ds/themis
6. VirTEE: Virtualized Trusted Execution Environments. https://github.com/virtee
7. What is BareMetal infrastructure on Azure? https://learn.microsoft.com/en-us/azure/baremetal-infrastructure/concepts-baremetal-infrastructure-overview
8. Announcing the public preview of Azure confidential VMs with Intel TDX (2023). https://azure.microsoft.com/en-us/updates/confidential-vms-with-intel-tdx-dcesv5-ecesv5-public-preview/
9. Angel, S., et al.: Nimble: Rollback protection for confidential cloud services. In: OSDI 2023 (2023)
10. Bailleu, M., Giantsidi, D., Gavrielatos, V., Quoc, D.L., Nagarajan, V., Bhatotia, P.: Avocado: A secure in-memory distributed storage system. In: ATC 2021 (2021)
11. Behl, J., Distler, T., Kapitza, R.: Hybrids on steroids: SGX-based high performance BFT. In: EuroSys 2017 (2017)
12. Bessani, A., Correia, M., Quaresma, B., André, F., Sousa, P.: DepSky: Dependable and secure storage in a cloud-of-clouds. ACM Trans. Storage **9**(4) (2013)
13. Bhatkar, S., DuVarney, D.C., Sekar, R.: Address obfuscation: An efficient approach to combat a board range of memory error exploits. In: USENIX Security 2003 (2003)
14. Brandenburger, M., Cachin, C., Kapitza, R., Sorniotti, A.: Trusted computing meets blockchain: Rollback attacks and a solution for Hyperledger Fabric. In: SRDS 2019 (2019)
15. Castro, M., Liskov, B.: Practical byzantine fault tolerance and proactive recovery. ACM Trans. Comput. Syst. **20**(4) (2002)
16. Chen, Z., Vasilakis, G., Murdock, K., Dean, E., Oswald, D., Garcia, F.D.: VoltPillager: Hardware-based fault injection attacks against Intel SGX enclaves using the SVID voltage scaling interface. In: USENIX Security 2021 (2021)
17. Costan, V., Devadas, S.: Intel SGX explained. IACR Cryptology ePrint Archive **2016**(86) (2016)
18. Decouchant, J., Kozhaya, D., Rahli, V., Yu, J.: DAMYSUS: Streamlined BFT consensus leveraging trusted components. In: EuroSys 2022 (2022)
19. Dinis, B., Druschel, P., Rodrigues, R.: RR: A fault model for efficient TEE replication. In: NDSS 2023 (2023)
20. Distler, T.: Byzantine fault-tolerant state-machine replication from a systems perspective. ACM Comput. Surv. **54**(1) (2021)
21. Distler, T., Kapitza, R., Reiser, H.P.: State transfer for hypervisor-based proactive recovery of heterogeneous replicated services. In: SICHERHEIT 2010 (2010)
22. Distler, T., Popov, I., Schröder-Preikschat, W., Reiser, H.P., Kapitza, R.: SPARE: Replicas on hold. In: NDSS 2011 (2011)
23. Duan, S., Zhang, H.: Foundations of dynamic BFT. In: SP 2022 (2022)
24. Eischer, M., Büttner, M., Distler, T.: Deterministic fuzzy checkpoints. In: SRDS 2019 (2019)

25. Galanou, A., Bindlish, K., Preibsch, L., Pignolet, Y.A., Fetzer, C., Kapitza, R.: Trustworthy confidential virtual machines for the masses. In: Middleware 2023 (2023)
26. Garcia, M., Bessani, A., Neves, N.: Lazarus: Automatic management of diversity in BFT systems. In: Middleware 2019 (2019)
27. Haeberlen, A., Kouznetsov, P., Druschel, P.: PeerReview: Practical accountability for distributed systems. In: SOSP 2007 (2007)
28. Howard, H., et al.: Confidential consortium framework: Secure multiparty applications with confidentiality, integrity, and high availability. arXiv preprint arXiv:2310.11559 (2023)
29. Lamport, L., Shostak, R., Pease, M.: The Byzantine generals problem. In: Concurrency: The Works of Leslie Lamport (2019)
30. Li, X.: QEMU patch submission (2024). https://patchew.org/QEMU/20241105062408.3533704-1-xiaoyao.li@intel.com/20241105062408.3533704-15-xiaoyao.li@intel.com/
31. Messadi, I., Becker, M.H., Bleeke, K., Jehl, L., Mokhtar, S.B., Kapitza, R.: SplitBFT: Improving Byzantine fault tolerance safety using trusted compartments. In: Middleware 2022 (2022)
32. Moser, L.E., Melliar-Smith, P.M., Narasimhan, P., Tewksbury, L.A., Kalogeraki, V.: Eternal: Fault tolerance and live upgrades for distributed object systems. In: DISCEX 2000 (2000)
33. Murdock, K., Oswald, D., Garcia, F.D., Van Bulck, J., Gruss, D., Piessens, F.: Plundervolt: Software-based fault injection attacks against Intel SGX. In: IEEE S&P 2020 (2020)
34. Padilha, R., Pedone, F.: Belisarius: BFT storage with confidentiality. In: NCA 2011 (2011)
35. Peng, W., Li, X., Niu, J., Zhang, X., Zhang, Y.: Ensuring state continuity for confidential computing: A blockchain-based approach. IEEE Trans. Dependable Secure Comput. (2024)
36. Platania, M., Obenshain, D., Tantillo, T., Sharma, R., Amir, Y.: Towards a practical survivable intrusion tolerant replication system. In: SRDS 2014 (2014)
37. Puddu, I., Schneider, M., Haller, M., Capkun, S.: Frontal attack: Leaking control-flow in SGX via the CPU frontend. In: USENIX Security 2021 (2021)
38. Reiser, H.P., Kapitza, R.: Hypervisor-based efficient proactive recovery. In: SRDS 2007 (2007)
39. Russinovich, M., et al.: CCF: A framework for building confidential verifiable replicated services. Technical Report MSR-TR-2019-16 (2019)
40. Schneider, F.B.: Implementing fault-tolerant services using the state machine approach: A tutorial. ACM Comput. Surv. **22**(4) (1990)
41. Shih, M.W., Lee, S., Kim, T., Peinado, M.: T-SGX: Eradicating controlled-channel attacks against enclave programs. In: NDSS 2017 (2017)
42. Sousa, P., Bessani, A.N., Correia, M., Neves, N.F., Verissimo, P.: Highly available intrusion-tolerant services with proactive-reactive recovery. IEEE Trans. Parallel Distrib. Syst. **21**(4) (2010)
43. Sousa, P., Bessani, A.N., Obelheiro, R.R.: The FOREVER service for fault/intrusion removal. In: WRAITS 2008 (2008)
44. Van Bulck, J., et al.: Foreshadow: Extracting the keys to the Intel SGX kingdom with transient out-of-order execution. In: USENIX Security 2018 (2018)
45. Van Bulck, J., Piessens, F., Strackx, R.: SGX-Step: A practical attack framework for precise enclave execution control. In: SysTEX 2017 (2017)

46. Wang, W., Deng, S., Niu, J., Reiter, M.K., Zhang, Y.: Engraft: Enclave-guarded Raft on Byzantine faulty nodes. In: CCS 2022 (2022)
47. Warren-Kachelein, D.: Crypto hackers exploit Ronin network for $615 million (2022). https://www.bankinfosecurity.com/crypto-hackers-exploit-ronin-network-for-615-million-a-18810
48. Weichbrodt, N., Kurmus, A., Pietzuch, P., Kapitza, R.: AsyncShock: Exploiting synchronisation bugs in Intel SGX enclaves. In: ESORICS 2016 (2016)
49. Zhang, R., et al.: CacheWarp: Software-based fault injection using selective state reset. In: USENIX Security 2024 (2024)

Fast and Efficient Secure L1 Caches for SMT

Lukas Giner[(✉)] , Roland Czerny , Simon Lammer , Aaron Giner ,
Paul Gollob , Jonas Juffinger , and Daniel Gruss

Graz University of Technology, Graz, Austria
{lukas.giner,roland.czerny,simon.lammer,aaron.giner,
paul.gollob,jonas.juffinger,daniel.gruss}@tugraz.at

Abstract. Secure randomized caches use the latency budgets of last-level caches to isolate data by security domain. In contrast, L1 caches are very latency- and size-constrained (by cache ways and page size), hindering both the adoption of secure randomized designs and increases in size without losing backward compatibility due to page size changes.

We propose a new secure and larger L1 cache design for SMT cores: SMTCache. SMTCache uses separate, identical L1 caches (slices) to isolate security domains. The overall cache size scales with the number of SMT threads, with individual slices mirroring current designs without changing the page size. SMTCache consumes less power than larger sets and does not increase hit latency. We show that SMTCache is a principled mitigation against L1 cache attacks and fundamentally precludes vulnerabilities like L1TF. Further, we measure that SMTCache improves L1 cache performance compared to current designs and even remains competitive with larger caches. For instance, on a system with SMT-2, SMTCache provides equivalent hit ratios across the SPEC CPU2017 suite to a state-of-the-art L1 cache of comparable size while improving system security and significantly reducing energy costs.

1 Introduction

Caches hide the high access times of main memory by storing recently used data within the CPU. With low latency, limited space, and sharing across security contexts, they are an attractive target for attacks. Attacks range from side channels [7,16,22,35,46] to severe vulnerabilities like Meltdown [29] and its variants [8,45,47,49,54,56]. All of these attacks rely on the cache being a shared resource without security domain isolation.

While recent secure cache proposals address this problem for the large last-level caches [10,14,41,43,51,57], low latency is crucial for L1 caches. Hence, we cannot simply apply last-level secure cache designs to the L1 cache. Furthermore, partitioning the L1 cache is costly as it is already very size-constrained. Due to the virtual indexing, the L1 size is determined by the number of ways times the page size, which for commodity laptop, desktop, and server CPUs has been 4 KiB for over a decade. This limits an 8-way L1 cache to a maximum size of $4\,\text{KiB} \cdot 8 = 32\,\text{KiB}$. Thus, there are currently only two options to increase the L1 cache size, without even taking security considerations into account: First, like some recent

M. Dalla Preda et al. (Eds.): ARES 2025, LNCS 15993, pp. 106–126, 2025.
https://doi.org/10.1007/978-3-032-00627-1_6

Intel server CPUs, the number of ways per set is increased (e.g., from 8 to 12), at the cost of a super-linear increase in energy consumption [1, 37]. Second, like recent Apple CPUs, the page size could be increased (e.g., to 16 KiB [12]). However, this is only possible given Apple's firm control of both hardware and software on their machines, reducing the need for backward compatibility. Still, with this change, Apple increased the L1 cache size to 128 KiB. While this shows that *die area near the execution core is available*, it further emphasizes the page size as a limiting factor to efficiently scale the L1 and its lack of security that becomes increasingly interesting for attacks.

This leads us to investigate the following research questions:
How can we prevent L1 cache attacks in a principled way? Is it possible to increase L1 cache size and security without substantial efficiency loss or software-breaking changes? What is the energy cost of scaling the L1 cache?

In this paper, we propose SMTCache, a secure L1 data cache (L1D) design that offers advantages in L1 cache size, security, and energy efficiency on CPUs with simultaneous multithreading (SMT). SMTCache stays within the existing ISA specifications as well as power and latency budgets of commodity off-the-shelf CPUs. We achieve this by creating independent L1D *slices* (like L3 slices) accessed by a memory address and a security domain. Every domain has its own L1 slice, ensuring principled data separation.

In our default configuration, SMTCache does not require operating system support and switches domains based on existing mechanisms, *i.e.*, user mode and kernel mode. This provides out-of-the-box data separation between processes and the operating system. From the point of view of processes, they have their own private L1D cache without interference or data leakage from one SMT thread or process to another. Often, the number of processes active on a core is higher than the number of L1D slices (we evaluate up to 9 slices per core). If a process is scheduled to run on a core where it does not have a slice assigned, the least recently used (LRU) slice is flushed to higher cache levels, and the new process gets this slice exclusively until it is eventually flushed for a different process.

Each slice can be the same size as current L1D caches, as sets are addressed by their domain in addition to the virtual address, thereby sidestepping the page-size limitation while scaling the cache. The maximum active number of slices is limited to the number of SMT threads. For SMT-2, this doubles the effective available L1D cache space for simultaneously running processes. When the operating system schedules only a small number of processes on a core, this markedly increases performance as processes are not competing over cache space. With more slices than SMT threads, inactive slices store currently unused data for different processes that are not running while only drawing static power.

We evaluate the performance of SMTCache in CacheSim [15] and on traces recorded on a native Linux server running different workloads, as well as the functionality via micro-benchmarks with Linux on gem5 [5, 33]. Our evaluation shows that performance scales very well with SMT and often exceeds the performance of an equivalently large standard cache due to the inherent thrashing protection. For SMT-2, and especially SMT-4 (Sect. 6.1), SMTCache increases the available L1 cache per thread while guaranteeing fairness and security. We find that a number of slices higher than SMT ways + 1 only minimally improves performance, as processes rarely return to an empty L1D cache at that point.

Contributions. In summary, our main contributions are:

- We propose a novel secure L1 cache design, SMTCache, providing strict isolation between security domains on the hardware level.
- SMTCache builds on the synergetic introduction of security and performance enhancements to expand cache sizes without breaking backward compatibility.
- We provide a security argument for SMTCache, showing that it mitigates a range of state-of-the-art attacks in a principled way.
- We evaluate the performance of SMTCache in many different configurations and demonstrate that it offers competitive hit ratios even when compared to larger monolithic L1 caches like Apple's M1.

Outline. Sect. 2 presents background and Sect. 3 the design. Section 4 discusses energy and area costs and Sect. 5 security. Section 6 evaluates the performance. Section 7 presents related and future work. Section 8 concludes.

2   Background

In this section, we discuss caches, limiting factors for their size, traditional and secure L1 designs as well as their attack surfaces.

Caches. CPU caches are buffers close to the CPU, orders of magnitude smaller than main memory. They hide high memory access latencies for recently used data. In modern set-associative caches, addresses are statically mapped to one of many sets of cache lines and occupy any of the ways within that set.

Traditional caches are organized in a 3-level hierarchy, with the cache closest to the CPU (L1) being the smallest and fastest, with a critical impact on CPU performance. Unlike higher-level caches, most L1 caches use the virtual address to index the cache set to reduce latency by already looking for a cache line while translating the address. To not map a physical address to multiple sets, the index is taken only from bits shared with the virtual address, *i.e.*, the page offset, typically 12 bit. This limits the L1 cache size by the page size and number of ways, e.g., $4\,\text{KiB} \cdot 8\,\text{ways} = 32\,\text{KiB}$. Hence, traditional L1 cache size can only be increased with the page size, the number of ways, or by dropping the virtually indexed design. Intel increased the L1D cache size of the "Core" CPUs from 16 KiB to 32 KiB and 48 KiB with the number of ways, from 4 to 8 and 12. In the Apple M1, the 16 KiB page size allows for a 128 KiB L1D cache and a 192 KiB L1 instruction cache (L1I).

The drawback of increasing the associativity is a rising energy cost per access due to two factors: Firstly, the number of tags that need to be searched to determine a cache hit increases proportionally to the number of ways. Implementations may also load the data of all lines in a set at the time of the tag comparison [36], further adding to the increased energy demand. Secondly, super-linear components to the power draw grow with the size of a cache set [1,37].

Cache Coherence. When multiple cores access the same memory location on a CPU with private, per-core caches, writes on one core need to become visible to other cores as soon as possible. There are various coherence protocols that ensure this memory consistency. In the simplest case, caches need to know if a local copy of a cache line is modified, shared, or invalid (MSI). There are two common methods to implement coherence protocols, *snooping* and *cache directories* [38]. Snooping protocols work by broadcasting each memory request to all caches but are only viable for a low number of caches. Directories can solve this problem by centralizing the protocol's state information at a point of coherence. In inclusive cache hierarchies, the last-level cache (LLC) stores all cache lines found in lower levels and can, therefore, also act as the directory.

Cache Attacks. As caches are shared and introduce timing differences, they have been a popular target for side-channel research. In a cache attack, an attacker observes different access times to their data to infer a victim's behavior. With knowledge about cache architecture, refined cache attacks are possible.

Attacks on Cache Metadata. The simplest form of these attacks are time-driven attacks, such as Bernstein's attack [4] or **Evict+Time** [39]. The latter, for example, evicts an AES T-Table entry by filling the cache set with attacker memory. By timing the victim's execution the attacker can infer if this entry was used. A more noise-resilient evolution is **Prime+Probe**, where the attacker first *primes* a set by filling it, and then *probes* it by timing accesses. If the victim used a line in this set in between, the attacker measures a longer access and can observe the victim's accesses at the granularity of cache sets. Prime+Probe requires a set of addresses that map to the same cache set, called an *eviction set*. The **Flush+Reload** [60] attack enables cache line accuracy if attacker and victim share memory, by not relying on set conflicts but measuring the target line directly. The attacker uses the `clflush` instruction to evict the targeted address precisely, and later measures it again to see if the victim has brought it into the cache. Achieving shared memory with a victim is more challenging than co-location, and `clflush` might be unavailable. **Evict+Reload** [17,27] removes the need for `clflush` by replacing it with set eviction like Prime+Probe.

Attacks with Caches. Meltdown, Spectre, etc. [28,49,54] use caches for their covert-channel to recover data encoded during speculative execution. This is possible because the state of the caches is not reversed when a speculatively execution is aborted. Meltdown variants leaking from the L1 Cache (or the Line Fill Buffer) exploit caches that does not check permissions when data is served.

Secure Cache Designs and Related Work. With some of the attacks known for decades, many secure cache designs have been proposed, generally based on two methods: randomization or partitioning. The former tries to obscure access patterns by making them seemingly random, while the later tries to make accesses unobservable. Many designs require complex functions whose latency is too large for the L1 and only target the LLC [10,14,30,40–43,51–53,57] assuming the other caches are secure. In Sect. 7 we detail these secure caches and highlight

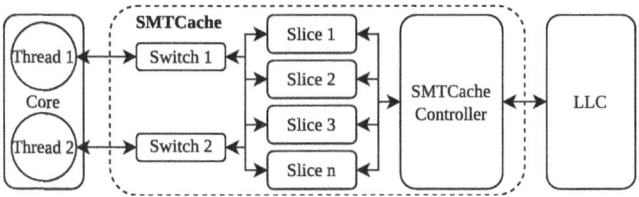

Fig. 1. SMTCache abstract design for n slices. At most 2 slices are active at the same time, one per SMT thread. The SMTCache controller ensures coherence between slices and that SMTCache appears like a normal cache to higher cache levels.

how SMTCache is orthogonal to many of them and discuss how SMTCache can complement them for improved security and performance.

3   The SMTCache Architecture

At the heart of SMTCache are a number of n identical *slices*; complete L1 data caches with standard parameters, e.g., 8 ways, 32 KiB size as shown in Fig. 1. At each context switch (security domain switch), one slice is assigned to the process. Until the next context switch, requests from the SMT thread are statically routed to this slice by a switch. From the perspective of the core, cache hits on this slice behave identical to a standard L1 design cache hit. The communication with the higher-level caches, however, runs through the SMTCache controller (Sect. 3.3), presenting SMTCache as a standard L1 cache. This, of course, adds extra latency. While our design could also be used for instruction caches, we focus on L1 data caches to limit the scope.

3.1   Domains

An important aspect of isolation-based designs is how security domains are derived. We propose a basic in-hardware implementation augmented with optional software control. The default configuration changes the slice assignment when the process (PCID/CR3) or the protection ring change. When the protection ring is 3, the CR3 register represents the domain ID, when it is less than 3, it is considered the kernel domain, regardless of the CR3 value. All kernel threads therefore share one slice, while userspace processes are isolated. This ensures security boundaries in line with standard OS process isolation. This is the backward-compatible mode of the design that works regardless of OS version.

With OS support, this could be enhanced to be more or less precise via MSRs. A process might, e.g., want to isolate its threads to maximize its L1D cache size, while another might want to share one slice among an entire process group. As this is highly workload dependent, we do not evaluate OS support in this work.

Hypervisors and SGX. With a hypervisor, we can simply consider ring -1 the only mandatory domain in the default configuration. Thus, the hypervisor and

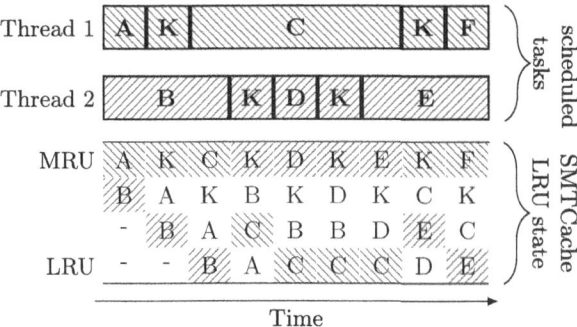

Fig. 2. Domain swapping with modified LRU for SMTCache with 4 slices. Context switches cannot replace active caches and bring the last active slice to the second-most recently used position. As the context switches are performed by the kernel (**K**) its slice is always most or second-most recently used automatically and can never be evicted.

guest can never share an L1. Intel SGX [21] has the unique situation that the hardware is generally under the control of the untrusted OS, yet SGX must be secure. We can accommodate this by always treating each enclave as a unique domain, irrespective of any configuration the OS might have chosen.

3.2 Slice Swapping

When a new domain not currently associated with a slice is assigned to a core, one of the slices is chosen to be evicted. On eviction, the hardware flushes all modified (dirty) cache lines to the higher cache levels, unmodifed (clean) cache lines can simply be dropped. When the number of slices equals the number of SMT ways $n = n_{SMT}$, the slices can be statically assigned to logical cores, and the current slice will be reused. For $n = n_{SMT} + 1$, the additional slice is always used for the kernel.

When $n > (n_{SMT} + 1)$, SMTCache chooses the slice to be evicted with a modified LRU algorithm. Domains scheduled often are therefore likely to keep their data in an inactive slice while they are descheduled, ready to resume work when they are scheduled again (see Sect. 6.2).

Figure 2 shows an example of our modified LRU for 4 slices and SMT-2. A thread is moved to the MRU position the moment it is newly scheduled on the core. Because the process scheduling is always performed by the kernel (**K**) it can always only be at the most or second-most recently used position. This ensure that the slice of the kernel is "reserved" and never evicted, guaranteeing fast kernel entries when there are more slices than SMT ways. We modify standard LRU such that active threads can never have their slice taken from them, regardless of their LRU position. Additionally, swapped-out threads are placed in the second-most recent position. This prevents long-running threads from immediately being the new eviction candidate (see switch from B to D or C to F in Fig. 2). For a configuration of 5 slices, this means that 4 slices will be

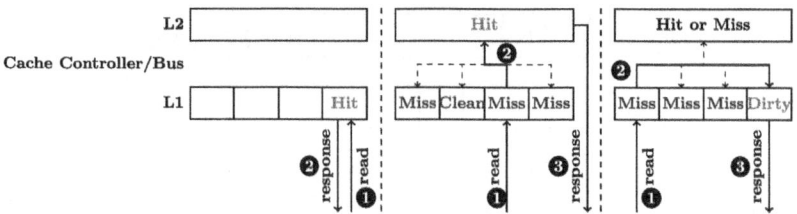

Fig. 3. A read request can be satisfied by the same slice (left), by the L2 (middle), and by a sibling slice (right). Hits on clean lines in sibling core are served from upper levels to prevent side-channel leakage.

available for user space domains. If the kernel is scheduled on both SMT threads at the same time, they share one cache slice similar to normal CPUs where both SMT threads share the L1 cache.

3.3   SMTCache Controller and Coherence

Multi-core processing with several simultaneously executing threads and shared, writeable memory requires caches to implement a coherence protocol that ensures all threads work with consistent copies of modified data. Information about changes to a location in one cache is propagated to other caches as soon as possible. SMTCache includes an extra coherency controller that facilitates security-aware snooping for the L1 slices (see Fig. 1) to support shared memory, stay coherent between threads and processes, and curb high lookup latency for writeable shared memory. It handles misses from currently active L1 caches and requests from higher cache levels.

The snooping protocol works like the standard coherence between L1I and L1D caches. It avoids moving the attack surface from the L1 cache slice one layer higher to a directory [59], as there are no evictions from underprovisioning. Contrary to caches on different cores, the slices are also in much closer physical proximity, which reduces the cost of snooping. To reduce the energy costs of querying all slices for data, we propose a dual-mode line lookup for each cache line's tag and state data. When answering a request from the local core, only the currently active slice's set is searched, and tag, state, and data can be loaded in parallel. In response to a sibling-slice or remote miss, tag and state information from all slices is requested in parallel, without loading cache line data simultaneously.

Requests from the core first go to the assigned slice, then, for a miss, are forwarded to other slices and L2 cache at the same time (Fig. 3). The cache controller can also aggregate cache line states w.r.t. upper levels, it can distinguish between a total miss in SMTCache and a hit on a clean or dirty line in a sibling slice. When a miss occurs in the controller, the request is served from the L2 cache. Likewise, when the data is found but is clean, the request is still served from the L2 cache to prevent Flush+Reload (see Sect. 5). When a sibling slice contains the requested data and it is dirty, it can be served directly from there

Table 1. Area and power overheads estimated with McPAT [26] and CACTI [37].

Number of Ways	8-way	12-way	16-way	2 slices (8-way)	24-way	3 slices (8-way)	32-way	4 slices (8-way)	40-way	5 slices (8-way)
Total L1 Cache Size	32 KiB	48 KiB	64 KiB	64 KiB	96 KiB	96 KiB	128 KiB	128 KiB	160 KiB	160 KiB
Number of SMT Cores†	1	1	2	2	2	2	4	4	4	4
Bus Area [mm²]	0.37	0.37	0.38	0.38	0.39	0.40	0.41	0.42	0.53	0.54
Bus Peak Dynamic [W]	2.04	2.08	2.11	2.13	2.15	2.13	2.27	2.14	2.41	2.45
Bus Subthreshold Leakage [W]	0.05	0.05	0.06	0.06	0.06	0.06	0.06	0.06	0.06	0.06
Bus Runtime Dynamic [W]	2.04	2.08	2.11	2.13	2.15	2.13	2.27	2.14	2.41	2.45
L1 Dynamic read energy [nJ]	2.53	6.87	11.22	2.53	29.16	2.53	47.09	2.53	81.55	2.53
L1 Dynamic write energy [nJ]	2.58	7.01	11.45	2.58	29.73	2.58	48.01	2.58	82.72	2.58
L1 Standby Leakage [mW]	42.50	64.41	86.33	85.83	132.47	127.49	178.61	169.98	276.95	212.48
L1 Area [mm²]	3.77	9.26	14.75	7.63	36.52	11.32	58.30	15.10	100.54	18.87
L1 Max. Total Leak. (2 loads+stores/cycle) [W]	10.26	27.84	45.42	10.30	117.90	10.34	190.38	10.38	328.83	10.43
L1 Max. Total Leak. (4 loads+stores/cycle) [W]	-	-	90.77	20.52	235.70	20.56	380.63	20.60	657.47	20.64
L1 Max. Total Leak. (8 loads+stores/cycle) [W]	-	-	-	-	-	-	761.04	41.02	1314.59	41.07

† For a fair comparison, we adjusted the number of SMT cores to reflect the L1 cache sizes: 1 SMT core below 64 KiB, 2 SMT cores for the 64 KiB to 96 KiB range, and 4 SMT cores above. We simulate the results for 3 different configurations for the load and store ports from 2 to 8 loads and stores per cycle. The maximum total leakage significantly changes with the number of SMT cores and the number of loads and stores per cycle. As the slices of SMTCache act as independent caches, they scale almost linearly in the maximum total leakage.

with limited security concerns. Since the position of the line is already known from the lookup request, the corresponding set does not need to be searched again, saving time and energy.

The slices together with the controller also keep track of copies and only forward modified data when the last copy is evicted or a coherence message from the upper level requires it. This avoids generating unnecessary traffic up the hierarchy when a line is evicted from one slice but still present in others. From a top-down view, SMTCache presents as a standard cache controller within the larger coherency protocol while maintaining its own internal state. Upon a request from a remote core, the controller can locate the address in the slices and adjust the cache lines accordingly, *i.e.*, changing ownership, responding with data, or flushing lines. Again, finding an address via the first broadcast already includes the location in the slice's set, so an extra lookup is unnecessary.

4   Energy and Area Estimation

Estimating energy and area overheads for commercial large-scale CPUs is difficult as CPU vendors do not open-source competitive state-of-the-art designs. Therefore, we follow the methodology of prior work [43,52] and use McPAT [26] with CACTI [37] to estimate energy and area overheads, close to the actual hardware costs for commercial large-scale CPUs [26]. Like Townley et al. [52], we use the most recent Intel Xeon that McPAT supports. For the cache, we configure CACTI [37] directly, providing more fine-grained configuration and detailed information. The slices of SMTCache behave like separate caches that each contribute to the static power consumption of the CPU. We interpolate unsupported non-power-of-two values.

Area. The main area overhead of SMTCache is storage area, closely resembling that of L1 caches in recent Apple CPUs. An increase from 32 KiB to a 128 KiB cache (like Apple's) comes with a proportional area growth of factor 4. The bus area increase is entirely negligible compared to the storage. SMTCache has a about 1% area overhead from a basic 8-way cache due to additional complexity and tag bits added. However, SMTCache scales much better than a naive extension of current cache designs with a higher number of ways.

Energy. The dynamic read and write energy for a single operation (2.53 nJ and 2.58 nJ respectively) stays at the level of the initial cache design (see Table 1). While standby leakage increases significantly it is negligible compared to overall power consumption. For the maximum total leakage, we use the metrics of a current CPU, *i.e.*, a throughput of 0.5 cache reads and writes per cycle. On a CPU with a 4 cycle cache latency, two load and two store ports, and 4 GHz clock, the upper bound for the throughput is 2 billion cache reads and cache writes each per second, which we also empirically tested on an Intel i7-8565U CPU.

For a fair comparison across all designs, we compute the maximum total leakage for 1 SMT core for all caches with less than 64 KiB, 2 SMT cores for all caches from 64 KiB to 96 KiB, and 4 SMT cores for 128 KiB or more. As SMT Cache slices act as entirely separate L1 caches, their energy consumption only increases linearly with the number of slices. The two slice variant of SMTCache has twice as much maximum total leakage, as both caches can be fully utilized by the two SMT threads. However, even at this point the maximum total leakage is lower than the 12-way L1 cache without SMT and significantly lower than the 16-way L1 cache with two SMT threads. This trend continues for the 96 KiB to 160 KiB caches. The energy costs for the 40-way L1 cache are particularly prohibitive, whereas SMTCache with SMT-4 support stays below the maximum total leakage of the 16-way L1 cache.

5   Security

SMTCache provides strong isolation guarantees for the L1 cache. Therefore, we discuss how different cache contention and cache utilization channels are mitigated by our design. However, equally importantly, we show how SMTCache is a defense-in-depth against data leakage attacks.

Data Leakage (Defense in Depth). The strict separation of L1 slices ensures that the L1 cache can no longer be a source for leakage of data at rest, such as Meltdown [29,49] and L1TF [49,54,56]. As requests from one domain are never directly routed to the slice of a different domain, the active L1 slice can never respond with data outside its domain. The request to other domains is only issued with the request to the L2, which happens after the permission check on Meltdown-affected hardware. Though orthogonal to SMTCache, a similar separation (or static partitioning) of the line fill buffer (LFB) could be implemented to additionally prevent leaking data in use, as seen in several microarchitectural data sampling (MDS) attacks [8,45,47]. Though these vulnerabilities have been mitigated in current CPU generations, designs with clear isolation boundaries provide defense in depth against possible future leakage from similar sources. We conclude that had these processors already followed a design like

SMTCache, Meltdown [29,49] and L1TF [49,54,56] would have had very little security impact.

Kernel Domain. As mentioned in Sect. 3.1, the kernel shares a single domain. This is in line with standard process isolation but leaves open the possibility of (transient) confused deputy attacks. We weigh this against the significant overhead of providing each process with a separate kernel slice. We consider this an acceptable tradeoff, primarily because confused deputy attacks in the case of SMTCache require both a disclosure gadget in the victim's kernel code and a leakage gadget in the attacker's. Additionally, this attack surface is known, and gadgets have been systematically reduced in recent years.

OpenSSL AES. The AES T-Table implementation in OpenSSL is often considered as a benchmark for side channels. The typically page-aligned block of T-Tables (`Te` and `Td`) is accessed during the encryption, e.g., in the first round with a byte-wise xor of plaintext and key. With SMTCache, the initial `prefetch256` call loads the tables into the L1 cache, *i.e.*, they are placed in separate slices of SMTCache. Consequently, we cannot observe any contention.

mbedTLS RSA. Another side-channel attack commonly used as a benchmark is the mbedTLS RSA implementation. mbedTLS uses a windowed square-and-multiply implementation. However, prior attacks [32,48] exploited that a window size of 1 results in a simple square-and-multiply where the buffer containing the exponent is used in different ways, allowing to observe different contention patterns With SMTCache, the buffer is first loaded into the L1 cache, *i.e.*, again in separate slices of SMTCache where we cannot observe any contention.

Generic Side Channels. In general, Prime+Probe builds on the foundational assumption that an attacker can find the set that the victim process' targeted address is cached in and interact with it. Specifically, the *Prime* step fills the entire set, thereby evicting the victim cache line. The *Probe* step then measures how many of the attacker's own addresses are still cached after the victim has executed some code. If an address has been replaced, the attacker infers that, with some likelihood, an address from the victim was loaded. SMTCache cuts this primitive off at the root, as two different security domains cannot interact with each other's cache line allocation anymore. As the sets are separated in both the slice and the L1 directory, the victim's set contents are unaffected by Prime+Probe or other attacks that manipulate the replacement algorithm.

Flush+Reload and Flush+Flush rely on shared memory between victim and attacker. However, with SMTCache, sibling slices do not respond to requests for unmodified data (see Fig. 3 middle). Thus, neither Flush+Reload nor Flush+Flush on unmodified data are possible on SMTCache.

Cache side channels on writeable shared memory are still possible. However, this is a special case that was not handled by prior work on secure last-level caches either, as writeable shared memory already requires trust between victim and attacker for these shared memory regions. Hence, we also conclude that given the lack of a plausible threat model it is no case that SMTCache should cover.

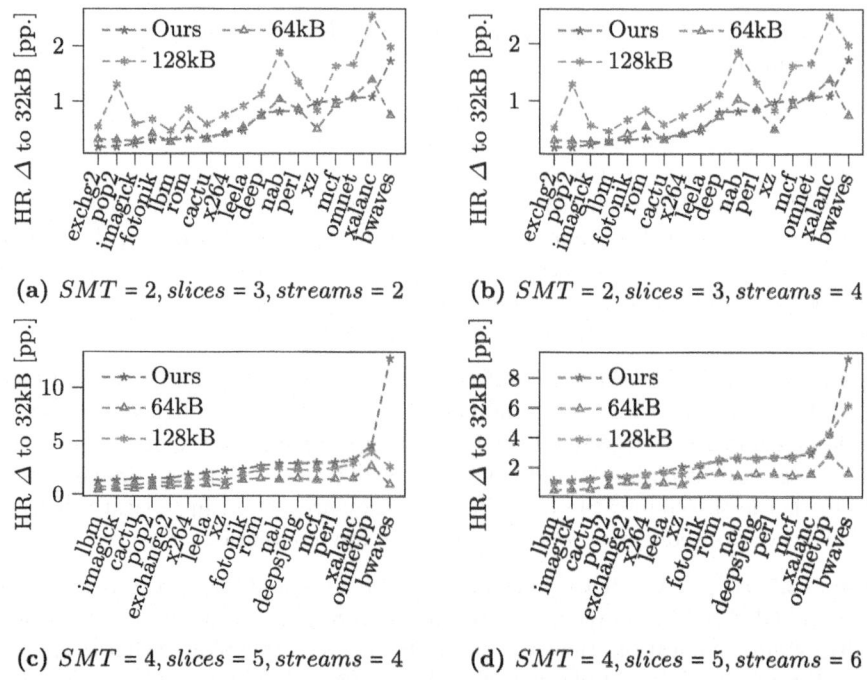

(a) $SMT = 2, slices = 3, streams = 2$ **(b)** $SMT = 2, slices = 3, streams = 4$

(c) $SMT = 4, slices = 5, streams = 4$ **(d)** $SMT = 4, slices = 5, streams = 6$

Fig. 4. Average simulator hit ratios over SPEC-speed 2017 benchmark combinations of different L1D cache configurations compared to a standard 32 KiB cache. Each datapoint represents the average hitrate of that benchmark measured in all combinations with other benchmarks. Base hit ratios are around 90–99%. Benchmarks sorted by ascending SMTCache hit ratio.

6   Performance Evaluation

As gem5 lacks SMT support, we cannot use it to test SMTCache performance, as its benefits only materialize with SMT. Instead, we evaluate performance in CacheSim [15] and on an Intel CPU, both with SMT, using the SPEC benchmark. We evaluate real-world single-threaded and SMT switching behaviour on Linux server workloads over several hours, resulting in data for SMTCache performance estimates for different numbers of slices.

6.1   CacheSim Hit Ratio Simulation

We use CacheSim [15] to evaluate hit ratios in SMTCache in different SMT configurations and two levels of cache. Like prior work [11,14,57], we use a representative sample of 250 million instructions from SPECspeed CPU 2017 benchmarks. We use a standard 8 way, 32 KiB L1 instruction cache, combined with the different L1 data caches we evaluate.

SMT workloads are simulated by interleaving memory accesses of the currently active workloads. We test all 153 pairwise combinations (with repetition) of 17 SPEC workloads. To fill up to 8 SMT threads, we use multiples of the pairs to create up to 8 workload streams and avoid an explosion of simulation time. We shift the recorded addresses of streams such that no two workloads share memory addresses. To simulate context switches by the operating system, threads change their workload in regular intervals of 3 000 000 accesses, which roughly equals 500 Hz on a 3 GHz machine, assuming 2 memory accesses per cycle. Between each switch, the implementation of SMTCache briefly loads a fictitious kernel domain. In addition to context switches, we also add the option to simulate a number of syscalls in every context switch interval, e.g., 5 syscalls for every context switch. A syscall here is simulated simply by loading the kernel domain and switching back to the last workload.

We examine the hit ratio of these combinations in Figs. 4 and 5. In Fig. 4, we plot the averages for each benchmark combination. We simulate configurations where the number of workloads is equal or higher than the number of slices. This shows an ideal and non-ideal case for SMTCache. SMTCache performs about on par with a standard cache of equivalent size to the maximum active number of slices, *i.e.*, the number of SMT ways. We only see a significant deviation for the benchmark combinations that include *bwaves* (and, to a minor extent, *xz*), as this workload seems to use a particularly large working set. The example of *bwaves* also demonstrates the thrashing resistance of SMTCache, as thrashing can only spill over to the second thread via evictions caused by inclusivity in higher caches. The combination of 2 *bwaves* workloads (Fig. 4a) produces a 1.73 pp. higher hit ratio on SMTCache than a standard cache on SMT-2 with 3 slices, compared to 1.98 pp. for the 128 KiB standard cache with twice the concurrently available cache memory. This becomes even more pronounced for SMT-4 (Fig. 4c) with hit ratio increases of 12.78 pp. vs 2.64 pp. for SMTCache (5 slices) vs. a 128 KiB cache.

Figure 5 reinforces the result that thrashing resistance becomes increasingly more pronounced with more logical cores. In this graph, the size of SMTCache increases with the number of SMT ways. While SMTCache starts with hit ratios very similar to the standard cache with the corresponding size, we can see that the hit ratio of standard caches quickly drop as the 8 workloads start to interfere more and more, while SMTCache remains somewhat static.

As Fig. 6 shows, the increase in hit ratio for each extra slice beyond $SMT + 1$ is fairly small, compared to the benefit from increasing the effective cache size. This coincides with our observations in other benchmarks (cf. Sect. 6.2) that returning to an empty cache is not a significant cost when the uninterrupted runtime is significantly larger than the time it takes to refill the cache. The overhead of the full-flush mitigation is mostly small, but some applications see a significant loss in performance [25]. In our tests, when we add a number of simulated syscalls per context switch similar to what we find in Sect. 6.2, we see that the gap from 2 to 3 slices grows slightly. Specifically, this occurs when the number of slices is not higher than the number of SMT ways, as then each syscall results in a full cache eviction. For example, in the depicted configuration with 2 slices, 6 workloads and SMT-2, we see the average hit ratio drop from 94.16 pp.

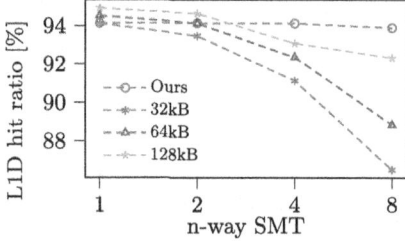 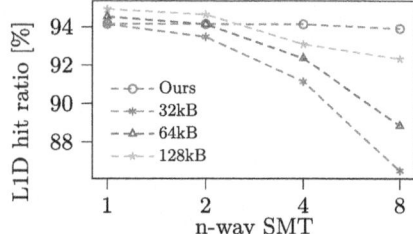

Fig. 5. Mean simulator hit ratio over SPEC combinations for different number of slices with standard designs for reference. 1,2,4,8-way SMT. 8 workloads. $n = n_{SMT} + 1$ for SMTCache.

Fig. 6. Mean simulator hit ratio over SPEC combinations for different number of slices with different numbers of syscalls per context switch. Standard designs for reference. SMT-2, 6 workloads.

to 93.50 pp. when we increase number of syscalls per context switch from 0 to 10. Therefore, the number of slices in our proposed default configuration of SMT Cache is the number of SMT ways + 1. This ensures that applications always return to a full cache from a syscall.

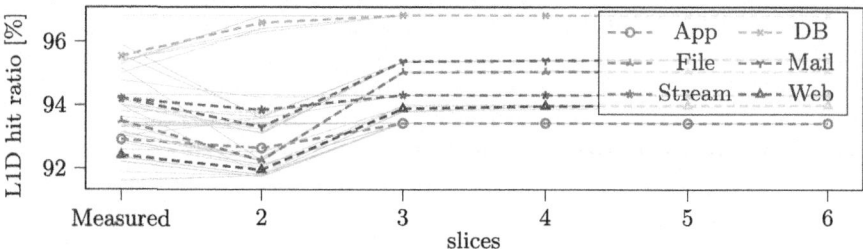

Fig. 7. Measured hit ratios from conventional cache architecture compared to expected hit ratios for different numbers of slices in SMTCache. SMT-2.

6.2   Server Context-Switch Evaluation

We analyze real-world switching behavior with SMT-2 by running several server workloads in different configurations on a native Linux system and simulate the impact of our design. We use the applications proposed by prior work [19,58] to evaluate the performance of SMTCache in a realistic cloud scenario. These benchmarks include the following server applications combined in pairs of two to form our server workloads: Apache Tomcat (application server), MySQL (DB server), Postfix (mail server), Samba (file server), FFserver (streaming), and Apache (http server). We run all experiments on an Intel i7-6700K CPU with 4 cores and SMT. We isolate one physical core to eliminate interference from unrelated tasks and execute the workloads on the two SMT cores.

We modify a Linux v5.13 Kernel to record all context switches and syscalls with tracepoints in the `context_switch` and `do_syscall_64` functions. In addition to information about the current and next process, we also record L1D performance counters of hit ratios for all applications. The context switching and syscall information now lets us simulate LRU replacement for varying numbers of slices for each application in different workload combinations. The EER indicates how often a process receives a cleared cache upon being scheduled. A higher number of slices results in a lower EER. With the performance counters, we create two L1 cache hit ratio baselines for each server application on an isolated core. The first baseline is standard switching without flushing, yielding the highest possible hit ratio for each application (HR_{high}). For the second baseline, we evict the cache in every context switch and syscall, producing each application's lowest possible hit ratio (HR_{low}). We assume that the hit ratio decreases linearly from an EER of 0% (HR_{high}) to an EER of 100% (HR_{low}), that a process with a dedicated cache performs roughly the same as a process running on an isolated core, and that kernel threads only interfere minimally on isolated cores. Based on these assumptions, a process receiving a cleared cache each time it is scheduled (EER 100%) has the hit ratio of the process operating on a dedicated core, where the cache is flushed at every context switch and syscall (HR_{low}) and vice versa (EER 0%, HR_{high}).

For the evaluation, we record the application's L1 hit ratios, context switches, and syscalls in all workload combinations. We use the information about context switches and syscalls to compute the EER for each application and varying numbers of slices. We then use the EER values to interpolate between the hit ratio baselines. This yields the expected hit ratios of each application in a SMT Cache architecture with different numbers of slices.

Figure 7 shows the expected hit ratios for all workload combinations with different numbers of slices. The leftmost values represent the measured hit ratios for each application in all workload combinations in a conventional cache architecture. The other values are the expected hit ratios for the respective number of slices in a SMTCache architecture. The grey lines represent specific workload combinations. The colored lines show the average hit ratio for each application. Our evaluation shows an expected performance improvement for SMT workloads when there are *SMT ways + 1* slices compared to the measured value in a conventional cache architecture. We observe a decrease in performance when using as many slices as *SMT ways* in most workload combinations. The cause for this expected performance decrease roots in syscalls. Since syscalls constantly refresh the kernel to be the most recently used cache domain, only one slice is left for parallel tasks. Table 2 shows that, on average, between 4 and 46 syscalls occur during a scheduled period, depending on the application.

Figure 8 depicts each server application's average expected eviction ratios in a SMTCache architecture for different numbers of slices. We see a high eviction ratio when using as many slices as *SMT ways*. For some workloads, the computed eviction ratio is almost 100% when using 2 slices on our machine with 2 *SMT ways*. Moreover, we see that using more than *SMT ways + 1* slices brings almost

Table 2. Comparison of measured syscall and scheduling metrics.

	App	DB	File	Mail	Stream	Web
Syscalls per scheduled period	6.86	4.84	10.56	10.98	46.34	4.12
Avg. scheduled period (ms)	0.033	0.088	0.066	0.298	9.843	0.028
Avg. time to context switch or syscall (ms)	0.004	0.015	0.006	0.025	0.208	0.005

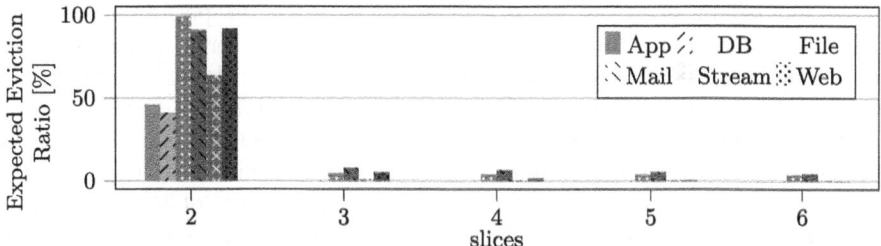

Fig. 8. Expected eviction ratios computed from context switch and syscall information for different numbers of slices. SMT-2.

no performance improvement, given that the eviction ratio is already almost as low as 0% for 3 slices for all applications.

The average time for a full L1D cache flush in our applications is 3836 cycles (2332 cycles to 10272 cycles, median 2401 cycles). We flush the L1D cache upon every syscall and context switch to record this value. We observe a higher duration of 10 272 cycles for the stream testcase compared to the other server applications. The average L1D flush duration correlates with the average time between syscalls and context switches for each application. The stream testcase runs uninterrupted for 0.208 ms between syscalls and context switches on average (Table 2), allowing a longer time for data to be written to the L1D cache. As all dirty cache lines are flushed to higher cache levels, the L1D cache flush duration increases with the number of writes.

To confirm these L1 flush delays, we also micro-benchmark the full-cache-flush duration in gem5. The results show 350 writebacks on average taking an average of 1700 cycles, comparable to our real-world results.

7   Related and Future Work

Many secure cache designs have been proposed to curb these attacks. We can divide these designs into two groups: designs based on randomization and on partitioning. The former tries to obscure access patterns by making them seemingly random to an attacker, while the latter tries to make accesses unobservable. Many designs require complex functions whose latency is too large for implementation in an L1 cache or simply target the LLC because they assume the underlying caches are secured in a different way. These designs therefore only target the LLC [10, 14, 30, 40–43, 51–53, 57].

While prior partition-based designs may be applicable to the L1, they have so far come at a reduced cache utilization or available cache size. Only way-based partitioning even has the option to increase cache size, though as examined in Sect. 4, may come with increased energy needs. In this sense, SMTCache achieves an orthogonal goal of offering security and an increase in the overall L1 size, which is complementary to the partition-based designs. We anticipate that for a fully secure system memory subsystem, SMTCache will be combined with one or more of the secure cache approaches for L2 and L3 caches.

Wang et al. [55] presented *PLCache* and *RPCache*. *PLCache* has the ability to lock critical cache lines dynamically in the cache. While less wasteful than static partitioning, the programmer has to mark secrets. Instead, *Random Permutation Cache* tries to prevent observable interference between cache lines of different processes by randomizing their locations with a permutation table. Both *PLCache* and *RPCache* have low-overhead implementations, though Kong et al. [24] point out security-related shortcomings of both. Further approaches have been proposed that offer fine-grained specification of cache partitions, on a cache-line and cache bank granularity respectively [3,44]. Still, all these designs are size-limited, where SMTCache offers an orthogonal approach to increase the overall L1 size.

Some works explored way-based partitioning [11,23] similar to Intel CAT [18, 20] with additional security by disabling cross-domain cache hits and moderate performance costs. We believe that compared to our work, these way-split designs could not benefit from power savings in the way SMTCache does because of the dynamic nature of the designs. *Hybcache* [9] proposes selective cache partitioning that incurs only a low overhead and only for protected code. It does so by combining random replacement with a small but fully-associative sub-set of the cache for a trusted execution environment. *Jumanji* [50] partitions the L3 cache dynamically by splitting it into software-defined shares. Still, partitioning reduces the effective cache size, which is unsuitable for the size-limited L1 cache. *Newcache* [31] is a pseudo-fully-associative cache with random replacement, that maps address and domain ID of a load to a possible random location in the cache, at moderate performance, area, and energy costs.

TEE-SHirT [2] is a design with partitioned L3 caches and private L2 caches, and non-partitioned private L1 caches. To secure the L1 cache, they simply flush the cache on context switches, which is not overly expensive, given that refills from L2 and L3 are possible. Ge et al. [13] estimated the overhead for L1 flushing to be as low as 1 cycles on the L4 kernel. However, benchmarks on the Linux kernel showed a significantly higher cost of 10 cycles [25] on commodity CPUs. SMTCache complements *TEE-SHirT* from a security perspective while offering better performance than L1 flushing. Similarly, for *MI6* [6], SMTCache offers a better alternative to simple L1 flushing.

Future Work. Our experiments have shown that while scaling the number of slices with the number of SMT threads provides a performance boost very similar to an equivalent increase in cache size, going beyond has quickly diminishing returns. The impact of context switches and syscalls, however, shows that an extra domain for the kernel is useful. An open question for future work is, therefore, if a separate but smaller slice dedicated to the operating system would be a good tradeoff between performance and chip area.

To maintain energy consumption on par with current designs, we assumed the same bandwidth between the core and SMTCache as in standard caches. SMT Cache supports twice that bandwidth for SMT-2. Future work could investigate dynamic scaling of the amount of issued loads and stores by the core to optimally fit power budgets and provide increased performance.

8   Conclusion

We proposed SMTCache, a secure L1D cache increasing cache size and thrashing resistance while being energy efficient. SMTCache achieves strong domain isolation, as security critical memory accesses from one domain are never served from another. With CacheSim and a simulation based on traces from native Linux benchmarks, we also showed that increasing the cache size with multiple slices provides not only the performance boost from simply increasing the cache size, but also from preventing interference between workloads. Lastly, our CACTI power simulation revealed that SMTCache design is significantly more energy-efficient than a traditional design of comparable size. We conclude that the SMTCache design shows promising results in terms of security, performance, and energy efficiency.

Acknowledgments. This research is supported in part by the European Research Council (ERC project FSSec 101076409), and the Austrian Science Fund (FWF SFB project SPyCoDe 10.55776/F85 and FWF project NeRAM 10.55776/I6054). Additional funding was provided by generous gifts from Intel, Red Hat and Google. Any opinions, findings, and conclusions or recommendations expressed in this paper are those of the authors and do not necessarily reflect the views of the funding parties.

A   Implementation of SMTCache in gem5

To demonstrate the functionality of SMTCache we implemented it in gem5. At the moment, the gem5 simulator does not support simultaneous multithreading in full system mode. Therefore, we cannot use it to estimate full system-level performance overheads for SMTCache, as it scales with simultaneous multithreading. We still modelled the additional latencies caused by our design realistically, allowing for micro-benchmarks of specific operations. Our implementation aims to functionally represent the features of the design described in Sect. 3, while working within the limitations of the gem5 codebase.

A.1   Implementation Overview

The gem5 framework simulates a freely configurable set of CPU cores, caches, crossbars (XBar), peripheral devices, etc. connected through ports on with each other. To avoid a complete overhaul of the memory subsystem, our implementation works within the system as much as possible, only swapping the default cache configuration with our SMTCache implementation.

Because all the SMTCache L1 slices behave like independent caches, we can build SMTCache on top of the existing L1 cache implementation. More specifically, we add functionality to perform a full cache flush (Appendix A.3). In a typical CPU, the gem5 CPU core is directly connected to a L1 data cache. For SMTCache, we instead add multiple L1 caches and connect all of them to the CPU core through a custom SMTCache-XBar that implements the switch, as shown in Fig. 1. Additionally, this XBar also simulates the SMTCache coherence behavior. The design of the XBar is described in detail in Appendix A.2. The L2 cache in our system is shared between cores and the point of coherence. Usually gem5 connects all L1 caches of all cores to the shared L2 cache through the L2XBar. For SMTCache we do exactly the same, with all L1 data slices of all cores connected to the L2XBar. Finally, we customize the move-into-control-register instruction implementation (MOV_C_R) to inform our custom SMTCache-XBar about a CR3 change.

A.2   SMTCache-XBar Coherence Controller

The CPU core communicates with its SMTCache-XBar by writing to a special address, whenever the CR3 register is written. This communication is necessary to allow the SMTCache-XBar to respond to a switch in the active domain. The SMTCache-XBar implements the LRU slice eviction and causes a full flush of all lines in the slice about to be assigned to a new domain.

Finally, the SMTCache-XBar also simulates the snooping coherence behavior. In a real implementation, every memory access would go to the active L1 slice, which may then forward the request to the controller if it is a miss. The controller then forwards the request to a slice that contains the cache line if there is one, or the L2 cache. In our gem5 implementation, the SMTCache-XBar directly checks all connected L1 slices and forwards the request to the correct one, if appropriate (*i.e.*, the line is found in the current slice or is modified in a different slice). By adding the correct latencies differentiating a cache hit vs a miss in the active L1 slice, our implementation can simulate the correct overhead. For the tag-matching in the slices, we budget one extra cycle. With this, we implement the behavior of the SMTCache coherence controller without requiring a separate component.

A.3   Flushing

Whenever a process without an associated slice is scheduled, the least recently used cache slice must be flushed and write back dirty data into higher cache levels or the main memory. Because we only have to write back dirty data, the flush latency is dependent on the number of dirty cache lines. Intel Skylake and later CPUs have a bandwidth of 1 cache line per cycle between the L1 and L2 [34]. This gives a lower bound of 512 cycles for a full flush if every single line is dirty.

The flushing can take longer if, e.g., the L2 has to write data into the main memory to make space for the flushed data from the L1 slice. We implement our cache flushing to simulate this behavior and latency.

In gem5, caches can tell the CPU that they are blocked for various reasons. We use this mechanism to block the cache while flushing, as this can take many clock cycles. The CPU waits for the flushing to be finished, treating it as a fully serializing operation. This is important to avoid speculative loads or stores to the wrong slice during this step.

References

1. Al-Tarawneh, M.: An investigation of the impact of instruction cache (i-cache) organization on power-performance trade-offs in the design of scalar processors. Eur. J. Sci. Res. **115**, 7–26 (2013)
2. Arıkan, K., et al.: TEE-SHirT: scalable leakage-free cache hierarchies for TEEs. In: NDSS (2024)
3. Beckmann, N., Sanchez, D.: Jigsaw: scalable software-defined caches. In: PACT (2013)
4. Bernstein, D.J.: Cache-Timing Attacks on AES (2005). http://cr.yp.to/antiforgery/cachetiming-20050414.pdf
5. Binkert, N., et al.: The gem5 simulator. ACM SIGARCH Comput. Archit. News (2011)
6. Bourgeat, T., Lebedev, I., Wright, A., Zhang, S., Devadas, S.: MI6: secure enclaves in a speculative out-of-order processor. In: MICRO (2019)
7. Brasser, F., Müller, U., Dmitrienko, A., Kostiainen, K., Capkun, S., Sadeghi, A.R.: Software grand exposure: SGX cache attacks are practical. In: WOOT (2017)
8. Canella, C., et al.: Fallout: leaking data on meltdown-resistant CPUs. In: CCS (2019)
9. Dessouky, G., Frassetto, T., Sadeghi, A.R.: HybCache: hybrid side-channel-resilient caches for trusted execution environments. In: USENIX Security (2019)
10. Dessouky, G., Gruler, A., Mahmoody, P., Sadeghi, A.R., Stapf, E.: Chunked-cache: on-demand and scalable cache isolation for security architectures. In: NDSS (2022)
11. Domnitser, L., Jaleel, A., Loew, J., Abu-Ghazaleh, N., Ponomarev, D.: Non-monopolizable caches: low-complexity mitigation of cache side channel attacks. ACM TACO **8**(4) (2011)
12. Frumusanu, A.: Apple Announces The Apple Silicon M1: Ditching x86 - What to Expect, Based on A14 (2020). https://www.anandtech.com/show/16226/apple-silicon-m1-a14-deep-dive
13. Ge, Q., Yarom, Y., Chothia, T., Heiser, G.: Time protection: the missing OS abstraction. In: EuroSys (2019)
14. Giner, L., et al.: Scatter and split securely: defeating cache contention and occupancy attacks. In: USENIX Security (2023)
15. Giner, L.: CacheSim Cache Simulator (2023). https://github.com/isec-tugraz/CacheSim
16. Götzfried, J., Eckert, M., Schinzel, S., Müller, T.: Cache attacks on intel SGX. In: EuroSec (2017)
17. Gruss, D., Spreitzer, R., Mangard, S.: Cache template attacks: automating attacks on inclusive last-level caches. In: USENIX Security (2015)

18. Herdrich, A., et al.: Cache QoS: from concept to reality in the Intel Xeon processor E5-2600 v3 product family. In: HPCA (2016)
19. Huang, D., Ye, D., He, Q., Chen, J., Ye, K.: Virt-LM: a benchmark for live migration of virtual machine. In: ACM/SPEC ICPE (2011)
20. Intel: Improving Real-Time Performance by Utilizing Cache Allocation Technology: Enhancing Performance via Allocation of the Processor's Cache (2015). https://www.intel.com/content/dam/www/public/us/en/documents/white-papers/cache-allocation-technology-white-paper.pdf
21. Intel: Intel Software Guard Extensions (Intel SGX) (2024). https://www.intel.com/content/www/us/en/products/docs/accelerator-engines/software-guard-extensions.html
22. Jiang, Z.H., Fei, Y.: A novel cache bank timing attack. In: ICCAD (2017)
23. Kiriansky, V., Lebedev, I., Amarasinghe, S., Devadas, S., Emer, J.: DAWG: a defense against cache timing attacks in speculative execution processors. In: MICRO (2018)
24. Kong, J., Acıiçmez, O., Seifert, J.P., Zhou, H.: Deconstructing new cache designs for thwarting software cache-based side channel attacks. In: CSAW, p. 25 (2008)
25. Larabel, M.: An Early Look At The L1 Terminal Fault "L1TF" Performance Impact on Virtual Machines (2018). https://www.phoronix.com/review/l1tf-early-look
26. Li, S., Chen, K., Ahn, J.H., Brockman, J.B., Jouppi, N.P.: CACTI-P: architecture-level modeling for SRAM-based structures with advanced leakage reduction techniques. In: ICCAD (2011)
27. Lipp, M., Gruss, D., Spreitzer, R., Maurice, C., Mangard, S.: ARMageddon: cache attacks on mobile devices. In: USENIX Security (2016)
28. Lipp, M., et al.: Meltdown: reading kernel memory from user space. In: USENIX Security (2018)
29. Lipp, M., et al.: Meltdown: reading kernel memory from user space. Commun. ACM **63**(6) (2020)
30. Liu, F., et al.: Catalyst: defeating last-level cache side channel attacks in cloud computing. In: HPCA (2016)
31. Liu, F., Wu, H., Mai, K., Lee, R.B.: Newcache: secure cache architecture thwarting cache side-channel attacks. IEEE Micro **36**(5), 8–16 (2016)
32. Liu, F., Yarom, Y., Ge, Q., Heiser, G., Lee, R.B.: Last-level cache side-channel attacks are practical. In: S&P (2015)
33. Lowe-Power, J., et al.: The gem5 simulator: version 20.0+ (2020)
34. Mandelblat, J.: Technology Insight: Intel's Next Generation Microarchitecture Code Name Skylake (2015). https://en.wikichip.org/w/images/8/8f/Technology_Insight_Intel%E2%80%99s_Next_Generation_Microarchitecture_Code_Name_Skylake.pdf
35. Moghimi, A., Irazoqui, G., Eisenbarth, T.: CacheZoom: how SGX amplifies the power of cache attacks. In: CHES (2017)
36. Mohammad, B.: Embedded Memory Design for Multi-Core and Systems on Chip, Analog Circuits and Signal Processing, vol. 116. Springer (2014)
37. Muralimanohar, N., Balasubramonian, R., Jouppi, N.P.: CACTI 6.0: a tool to model large caches. HP Lab. **27**, 28 (2009)
38. Nagarajan, V., Sorin, D.J., Hill, M.D., Wood, D.A.: A primer on memory consistency and cache coherence. Springer Nature (2020)
39. Osvik, D.A., Shamir, A., Tromer, E.: Cache attacks and countermeasures: the case of AES. In: CT-RSA (2006)

40. Qureshi, M.K.: CEASER: mitigating conflict-based cache attacks via encrypted-address and remapping. In: MICRO (2018)
41. Qureshi, M.K.: New attacks and defense for encrypted-address cache. In: ISCA (2019)
42. Saileshwar, G., Kariyappa, S., Qureshi, M.: Bespoke cache enclaves: fine-grained and scalable isolation from cache side-channels via flexible set-partitioning. In: SEED (2021)
43. Saileshwar, G., Qureshi, M.K.: MIRAGE: mitigating conflict-based cache attacks with a practical fully-associative design. In: USENIX Security (2021)
44. Sanchez, D., Kozyrakis, C.: Vantage: scalable and efficient fine-grain cache partitioning. In: ISCA (2011)
45. van Schaik, S., et al.: RIDL: rogue in-flight data load. In: S&P (2019)
46. van Schaik, S., Minkin, M., Kwong, A., Genkin, D., Yarom, Y.: CacheOut: leaking data on intel CPUs via cache evictions. In: S&P (2021)
47. Schwarz, M., et al.: ZombieLoad: cross-privilege-boundary data sampling. In: CCS (2019)
48. Schwarz, M., Weiser, S., Gruss, D., Maurice, C., Mangard, S.: Malware guard extension: using SGX to conceal cache attacks. In: DIMVA (2017)
49. Schwarzl, M., Schuster, T., Schwarz, M., Gruss, D.: Speculative dereferencing of registers: reviving foreshadow. In: FC (2021)
50. Schwedock, B.C., Beckmann, N.: Jumanji: the case for dynamic NUCA in the datacenter. In: MICRO (2020)
51. Tan, Q., Zeng, Z., Bu, K., Ren, K.: PhantomCache: obfuscating cache conflicts with localized randomization. In: NDSS (2020)
52. Townley, D., Arıkan, K., Liu, Y.D., Ponomarev, D., Ergin, O.: Composable cachelets: protecting enclaves from cache {side-channel} attacks. In: USENIX Security, pp. 2839–2856 (2022)
53. Unterluggauer, T., Harris, A., Constable, S., Liu, F., Rozas, C.: Chameleon cache: approximating fully associative caches with random replacement to prevent contention-based cache attacks. In: SEED (2022)
54. Van Bulck, J., et al.: Foreshadow: extracting the keys to the intel SGX kingdom with transient out-of-order execution. In: USENIX Security (2018)
55. Wang, Z., Lee, R.B.: New cache designs for thwarting software cache-based side channel attacks. ACM SIGARCH Comput. Archit. News **35**(2), 494 (2007)
56. Weisse, O., et al.: Foreshadow-NG: Breaking the Virtual Memory Abstraction with Transient Out-of-Order Execution (2018). https://foreshadowattack.eu/
57. Werner, M., Unterluggauer, T., Giner, L., Schwarz, M., Gruss, D., Mangard, S.: ScatterCache: thwarting cache attacks via cache set randomization. In: USENIX Security (2019)
58. Wu, H., Liu, F., Lee, R.B.: Cloud server benchmark suite for evaluating new hardware architectures. IEEE CAL **16**(1), 14–17 (2017)
59. Yan, M., Sprabery, R., Gopireddy, B., Fletcher, C., Campbell, R., Torrellas, J.: Attack directories, not caches: side channel attacks in a non-inclusive world. In: S&P (2019)
60. Yarom, Y., Falkner, K.: Flush+reload: a high resolution, low noise, L3 cache side-channel attack. In: USENIX Security (2014)

FatPTE - Expanding Page Table Entries for Security

Lukas Lamster[1]([✉]) [iD], Martin Unterguggenberger[1] [iD], Moritz Waser[1] [iD], David Schrammel[2] [iD], and Stefan Mangard[1] [iD]

[1] Graz University of Technology, Graz, Austria
{lukas.lamster,martin.unterguggenberger,moritz.waser,
stefan.mangard}@tugraz.at
[2] Rivos Inc., Santa Clara, USA
davidschrammel@rivosinc.com

Abstract. Modern computing systems have a strong need for security and require protection against attacks such as control-flow hijacking, information leakage, or data manipulation. As a solution, academia and industry propose essential security technologies operating on page granularity. Through metadata bits located in page table entries (PTEs), these technologies provide security with high efficiency. While PTE bits allow for highly efficient implementations, the reliance on spare bits is not future-proof. Due to the steady increase in memory capacity and the introduction of new security features, the spare bits are exhausted. Thus, the implementation of new features is impossible while the security of existing features is severely limited.

In this work we introduce FatPTE, a novel approach that enhances page table entries with dedicated metadata regions for security features. Our design provides up to 192 metadata bits, thus far exceeding the 7 reserved bits of x86-64 and RISC-V. We perform a case study on academic and commercial PTE-based control-flow integrity, memory protection, and confidential computing features. Our findings show that FatPTE easily accommodates all bits needed by the considered features, thus highlighting the practical relevance of our design. We implement an x86-64 prototype using the gem5 system simulator as well as a RISC-V FPGA prototype using the CORE-V CVA6 processor. We evaluate FatPTE in four configurations derived from the requirements identified in our case study. Our evaluation using SPEC CPU 2017 workloads yields a geomean performance overhead of 0.21% to 1.34% for the gem5 simulator and 0.51% to 1.99% for the FPGA prototype.

1 Introduction

Software vulnerabilities allow attackers to hijack a program's control flow, disclose secret information, corrupt victim data, or even take over the complete system. Thus, strong security measures protecting against a range of attack vectors

---

D. Schrammel—The work was done while the author was at Graz University of Technology.

M. Dalla Preda et al. (Eds.): ARES 2025, LNCS 15993, pp. 127–148, 2025.
https://doi.org/10.1007/978-3-032-00627-1_7

are necessary. CPU vendors and academic researchers proposed a variety of security features mitigating the increasing number of vulnerabilities [11,17,19,21,33].

A core principle of such security features is memory protection. Memory Protection Keys (MPK) efficiently isolate in-process memory through page-granular access restriction [2,15,21]. Confidential computing technologies protect memory through cryptographic isolation and facilitate secure virtual machines, page-granular encryption, and the secure execution of mutually untrusted software [2,13,14]. Shadow stacks provide control-flow integrity by confining return addresses to access-protected memory regions [15,37]. Due to the strong need for *efficient page-granular protection*, most security features implemented in commercial processors store metadata in spare bits of the system's page table entries (PTEs) [11,17,19,21,33]. With the constant increase in system memory capacity the number of spare bits is steadily decreasing. While repurposing PTE bits has worked in the past, this approach has ultimately reached its limits in current CPU generations. Not only does the scarcity of PTE bits prevent the implementation of additional PTE-based security features, *it also severely limits the security of existing features.* The memory protection keys of AMD and Intel, for example, are constrained to four bits per page, thus only allowing for 16 protection domains per page. Memory encryption schemes require up to 15 key identifier bits, yet only 7 bits are available in x86-64 and RISC-V systems. Thus, they repurpose physical address bits in the PTE and reduce the amount of addressable system memory to a degree that is unsustainable for current-generation server systems. Upcoming academic and commercial security features are unable to use PTE bits and must rely on more inefficient methods of storing the required metadata. Hence, *the adaptation of novel security features using PTE bits is hindered and existing features are strongly limited.*

In this work, we present FatPTE, a design that extends page table entries such that all required security-critical metadata is co-located with the paging information *without repurposing any PTE bits.* By increasing the size of PTEs to *explicitly account for security-critical metadata*, we eliminate the limitations imposed by the increase of system memory capacity and the growing number of competing schemes. We propose two variants of FatPTE allowing for 64 or 192 metadata bits, which is a vast improvement over the 7 remaining bits in existing x86-64 and RISC-V processors. We conduct a case study on commercial and academic memory protection and confidential computing security features [11,17,19,21,33]. Not only does FatPTE allow the implementation of all considered page-granular security schemes *without repurposing PTE bits*, it also increases the security of certain schemes, e.g., by increasing the number of available protection domains or the amount of encryption keys. Based on the case study, we identify parameterizations that allow the efficient implementation of existing security features using FatPTE. We use the gem5 computer architecture simulator system [4] to implement an out-of-order prototype of FatPTE for x86-64. Moreover, we implement an in-order FPGA prototype by integrating FatPTE into the CORE-V CVA6 application-class RISC-V processor. Our prototypes allows us to perform a performance evaluation for the previously identified configurations using SPEC CPU 2017.

Our evaluation yields a maximum geomean performance overhead of 1.34% for x86-64 and 1.99% for RISC-V, showcasing the feasibility of our approach. We find that FatPTE allows to *implement all the security schemes discussed in our case study with minimal performance and memory overhead.*

Contributions. We make the following key contributions:

- We present FatPTE, a lightweight hardware extension that enhances PTEs with metadata regions, providing up to 192 bits for security features.
- We perform an extensive case study demonstrating that FatPTE enables the integration of all discussed countermeasures while increasing the security of most of them.
- We provide an x86-64 prototype based on the gem5 simulator and a RISC-V FPGA implementation of FatPTE using the CORE-V CVA6 processor.
- We evaluate FatPTE, showcasing a maximum geomean overhead of 1.34% and 1.99% for x86-64 and RISC-V, respectively.

Outline. The paper is structured as follows. Section 2 provides the background on virtual memory in modern operating systems and hardware support for paging. Section 3 discusses the current issues faced when implementing schemes that rely on spare PTE bits and motivates our approach. Section 4 presents the design space and possible configurations of FatPTE. Section 5 conducts a case study showing the wide applicability and feasible parameterizations of FatPTE. Section 6 discusses the prototype implementations of FatPTE and provides the respective evaluation. Section 7 compares FatPTE to related work, while Sect. 8 concludes this work.

2   Background

In this section, we discuss virtual memory and paging in modern operating systems. Furthermore, we elaborate on hardware support for paging in modern CPUs.

2.1   Virtual Memory and Paging

Virtual memory is a fundamental feature of modern computing systems. With virtual memory, processes do not directly access to physical memory. Instead, the OS provisions virtual addresses, which are translated to physical addresses upon use. From an application's perspective, virtual memory is a continuous range, while the OS can allocate and map physical memory on demand in a fragmented fashion. This provides an elegant solution to several problems that arise in modern multithreaded and multiprocessed environments. It enables efficient management of memory, allows for access permission control, and provides strong isolation between processes that operate in disjunct virtual memory spaces.

Pages and Page Sizes. Modern virtual memory systems divide their physical memory into *pages*, which serve as memory granules that are distributed to processes by the operating system. This smallest provisioned memory granule is sometimes called the *translation granule* [3]. The actual granule and the number of available page sizes depend on the instruction set architecture (ISA). In x86-64 and RISC-V systems, the translation granule is 4 KiB and regular pages hold 4 KiB of data. On AArch64, the translation granule can be 4 KiB, 16 KiB, or 64 KiB. Each virtual memory page has a virtual page number and maps to one physical page in memory. While each virtual page points to *exactly one* physical page, the opposite is not necessarily true. Through *alias mappings*, multiple virtual addresses can refer to the same physical page, which enables features such as shared memory or shared libraries.

Page Tables and Translation Tables. The mappings from virtual to physical pages are stored in hierarchical data structures called *page tables* (PTs) or *translation tables*. A PT holds *page table entries* (PTEs), which contain a *physical page number* (PPN) and its associated access permissions. Typically, one bit of a PTE determines if the referred physical page is a leaf node, *i.e.*, it holds data, or if it contains another level of the paging hierarchy. The translation consists of a multi-stage table lookup where parts of the virtual address are used as indices for PTs. Depending on the number of layers n in the hierarchy, we talk about *n-level paging*. In current x86-64 systems, a page table may consist of up to five layers, allowing the operating system to provision virtual addresses with at most 57 address bits. Since the translation requires a starting point, every process is assigned a root page table as the base of virtual address translation. Providing each process with a separate paging hierarchy isolates their views of virtual memory against each other. Through these disjoint views, each process can use the full virtual address space without interfering with other processes.

In modern systems, the PTEs in each layer are 64 bits wide. However, the physical address indexing the underlying memory does not use the full number of available bits. Current x86-64 CPUs allow up to 52-bit physical addresses, thus theoretically supporting petabytes of main memory. However, in practice the amount of supported DRAM is often limited to a few terabytes. The lowermost 12 bits of the physical address in a leaf PTE are not explicitly stored as they determine the offset within the page and are instead taken from the virtual address during memory accesses. The remaining PTE bits are typically used to encode status and permission bits, while some bits remain unused.

Figure 1 illustrates 5-level paging with a 4 KiB page size, as used by x86-64 or RISC-V processors. Each level in the paging hierarchy except for the last layer (*i.e.*, PTL4 to PTL0) represents a page table indexed by 9 bits of the virtual address. With 9 index bits for each of the five layers and a 12-bit index for the leaf page, the 7 topmost bits of each 64-bit virtual address remain unused. Thus, current paging implementations of the Linux kernel for these ISAs support up to 57-bit virtual addresses. Translating a virtual to a physical address requires a sequential table lookup called *page table walk*. The paging structure's root is formed by the physical page number (PPN) of the root page table. This PPN is stored in a control register (CR3 on x86-64, SATP on RISC-V, TTBR0_ELx on ARM). The root page table holds the topmost entries of the paging hierarchy. The least significant bits of the virtual address act as a byte-granular offset for

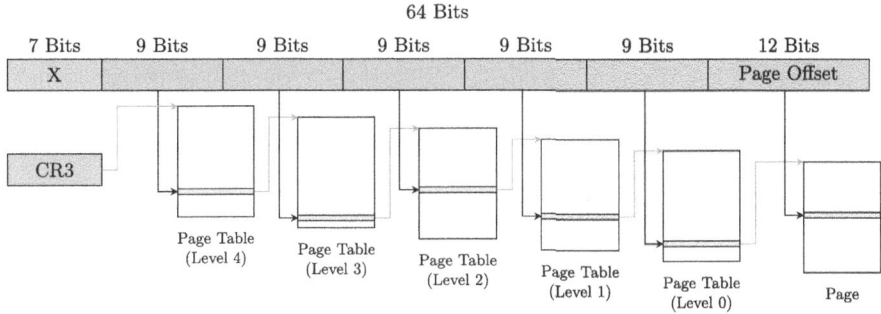

Fig. 1. 5-level paging in x86-64. On the lowermost level, 12 bits are used to address individual bytes within a page while the 9-bit values in the upper levels act as indices that select 64-bit entries within page tables.

the leaf page. Note that the number of offset bits equals the base-2 logarithm of the number of bytes per leaf page.

Huge Pages. Virtual memory systems often support *huge pages*, which cover a larger continuous memory region than the basic translation granule [34]. A huge page can be mapped by removing a translation layer and extending the offset bits with the former page table index bits. For instance, in a 4 KiB virtual memory system, a 2 MiB page can be mapped by removing the final translation layer and extending the 12-bit offset to a 21-bit offset using the 9 bits that were used as an index for the final page table. Depending on the translation granule and the presence of hardware support, varying sizes of huge pages can be mapped. Mapping huge pages reduces the metadata required for continuous memory regions and can improve performance for large allocations.

2.2   Hardware Support for Paging

In the case of 5-level paging, a single memory access may entail six loads from memory as each layer must be fetched sequentially. The first five loads fetch the PTEs, while the sixth memory load fetches the accessed memory location. Loading data from main memory frequently has a detrimental performance impact as DRAM is significantly slower than the on-chip caches. Memory-related operations such as loading data, checking access permissions, and performing address translations are handled by the *memory management unit* (MMU). Due to the high frequency of memory operations and their performance-critical nature, this component is deeply integrated into the CPU. When performing an address translation, the *page table walker* (PTW), which is a part of the MMU, iteratively fetches the PTEs according to the page tables of the current process. To further reduce the performance impact of address translations, recently used mappings are cached in the *translation lookaside buffer* (TLB). Modern CPUs use multiple TLBs in different layers of the caching hierarchy. A TLB entry maps a combination of an address space identifier (ASID), which is required to distinguish processes, and a virtual page number, to a physical page and its associated permissions. When accessing a virtual address the CPU checks if the required translation can be directly served from the TLB. If a valid entry is present, a *TLB hit* occurs and the costly page table traversal is completely avoided.

3   The Need for Larger PTEs

Historically, PTEs consisted of a physical page number, permission bits, and a set of software-defined bits. This only left a small number of bits available for future use. 64-bit systems increase the PTE size from 32 bits to 64 bits, increase the size of the PPN field, and add more page attributes and permission bits such as the no-execute bit. Modern Intel x86-64 CPUs with 5-level paging allow for up to 53 physical address bits [15]. Combined with the other PTE bits in use, PTEs that map 4 KiB pages only provide seven bits for future use. Similarly, RISC-V's Sv57 format provides seven reserved bits for future use [23].

The introduction of security features like control-flow integrity, memory protection keys, and confidential computing [15, 17, 19] has decreased the number of available PTE bits drastically. Memory Protection Keys (MPK) use four bits to tag a page with a protection key and allow quick page permission modifications from userspace without a context switch [2, 15]. Intel's Total Memory Encryption requires up to 15 bits to be stored in the PTE and currently repurposes physical address bits to store their key identifiers [15]. Intel Control-Flow Enforcement Technologies (CET) [33] introduces a *shadow stack* whose pages are identified by an unused combination of permission bits in the PTEs. Confidential computing architectures like Intel TDX [12, 14] and AMD SEV [1] both require one PTE bit to indicate whether a memory page is encrypted or not [17]. This bit is also taken from the physical address, thus further reducing the physical address space.

Besides commercially available security features, a range of academic designs proposes repurposing the available PTE bits for added security. For example, PT-Guard [24] co-locates a MAC to detect Rowhammer attacks, and Multi-Tag stores a memory tag for memory safety [36].

All features requiring PTE bits compete for the few available spare bits. This hinders the adoption of new features, limits the achievable security, and ultimately slows the progress of innovation. Intel's shadow stack already resorts to using a special encoding of the regular permission bits to avoid using an additional PTE bit [15]. Features like TME-MK must repurpose physical address bits, thus limiting the amount of usable DRAM [11]. Finally, Intel's Sub-Page Write-Permission (SPP) feature requires 64 bits to be stored per page [15]. This per-page metadata must be fetched on-demand and accessed through a number of indirections, similar to existing page tables.

Clearly, per-page metadata is essential for many security features. The existing PTE structure is the ideal location for metadata, as it contains all other paging information. Furthermore, for most security features the metadata must be fetched and checked synchronous to the associated PTEs. Hence, there is a clear need for larger PTEs that can co-locate security-critical metadata.

4   Design

In this section, we discuss the design principles of FatPTE. When discussing page tables and their modifications, we must distinguish between the different levels in the paging hierarchy. We refer to the lowest hierarchy level as the *last* layer and to the highest level as the *first* layer, according to the order in which they are fetched during a page table walk. A layer is considered *above* another layer if it is fetched first when traversing the hierarchy. We use *PTE* to refer to all entries of the paging structure, regardless of the layer. For clarity, we refer to the PTEs modified by our approach as fat page table entries (FPTEs). An FPTE consists of a legacy PTE and the associated metadata. A *leaf PTE* or *leaf node* refers to an entry that does not point to another translation layer but to a page containing arbitrary data. Upon reaching a leaf node, the translation is finished. In our design exploration, we identify four key parameters $\mathcal{P}_1$ to $\mathcal{P}_4$.

4.1   Metadata Region Size $\mathcal{P}_1$

The main goal of FatPTE is to extend the available number of bits for security features. Our approach enhances PTEs with a dedicated *page table entry metadata region* (PTE-MR), thus transforming them to FPTEs. Assuming a constant page size, using FPTEs instead of legacy PTEs reduces the overall number of entries that fit on a single page. Thus, the amount of mappable memory covered by the same number of hierarchy levels is also reduced. As each PTE points to a single page, using FPTEs which are twice as large halves the size of the memory region that can be mapped by an entry in the layer directly above (cf. Fig. 2). Note that the overall amount by which the mappable memory decreases is *independent of the layer* at which FPTEs are used. It only depends on the *number* of layers with FPTEs and the size difference between FPTEs and PTEs. Increasing the size of FPTEs too much increases memory overheads as more entries are required to map the same amount of memory.

Each doubling in FPTE size halves the number of mappable memory and decreases the number of available virtual address bits by one. Thus, we are bound to power-of-two sizes. Using any other factor results in a mapping scheme requiring complex encodings of virtual addresses. Ultimately, this would lead to issues in pointer arithmetic and greatly increase the complexity of the PTW.

Given the constraints of a power-of-two size increase and the implications on the amount of mappable memory, we propose two parameterizations.

64-bit PTE-MR. First, we consider the case in which the additional metadata region holds 64 bits. With this configuration, the overall size of each FPTE equals 128 bits. We can illustrate the consequences of this size increase through a concrete example. Consider replacing the last-layer PTEs of a system with 4 KiB pages by FPTEs. The page containing the last-layer PTEs originally holds 512 64-bit entries. This number decreases to 256 FPTEs as the page size stays constant. A single 4 KiB page of PTEs originally maps a memory range of 2 MiB. When using FPTEs, the mappable memory decreases to 1 MiB (cf. Fig. 2).

In commodity CPUs, the memory system operates on a 512-bit (cache line) granularity. Thus, a single 4 KiB page encompasses 64 cache lines. With the above configuration, we provide one metadata bit per cache line of the page, which can already be suitable for simple schemes at cache line granularity.

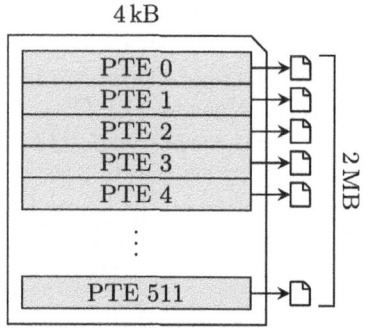
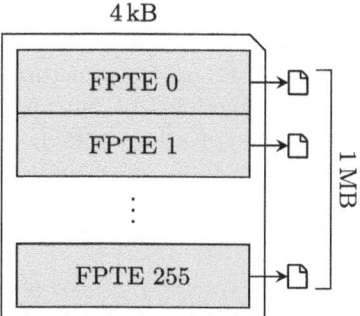

(a) A 4 KiB page contains 512 64-bit PTEs and can map 2 MiB.

(b) Only half as many FPTEs fit on the same page which can map 1 MiB.

Fig. 2. Using FPTEs reduces the amount of mappable memory. For an x86-64 system with 4 KiB pages, a single page of last-level PTEs can map 2 MiB. Doubling the size of each entry decreases this amount to 1 MiB.

192-bit PTE-MR. In this configuration, we further increase the size of the metadata region to hold up to 192 bits. This results in 256-bit FPTEs. As we further increase the size of the FPTEs, the number of FPTEs per page continues to decrease. Thus, with this configuration, a single page of FPTEs can only map a quarter of the memory that was originally mappable by the same number of entries. While this parameterization reduces the amount of mappable memory more significantly than the 64-bit variant, it simultaneously allows for the implementation of more complex schemes. The 192-bit variant provides three bits per cache line on 4 KiB pages, thus allowing for more complex schemes.

4.2   Metadata Region Layout $\mathcal{P}_2$

When enhancing PTEs with additional metadata, we cannot use a dedicated metadata storage region akin to tagged memory architectures. As we associate metadata with PTEs, the required metadata memory changes during runtime.

Hence, we cannot statically reserve a memory region for metadata during system initialization. Storing the metadata in a disjunct location causes further issues, as the PTW must fetch the metadata during page table walks. This can only be achieved using a lookup table or a shadowed paging structure dedicated to locating the associated metadata. Both cases require additional memory transactions with potentially poor spatial locality. To avoid such issues, *FatPTE always co-locates PTEs and metadata within the same memory page.*

When co-locating mapping information with metadata, the layout of the PTEs and the associated metadata regions within a page can be chosen arbitrarily. However, a complex mapping function for the metadata region may have a detrimental impact on the system performance and would require additional logic in the PTW. It is, thus, favorable to keep the layout as simple as possible. When discussing the layout of PTEs and metadata regions within the same page, we use the term *index* to refer to their 64-bit aligned locations in the page. Thus, index 0 denotes the first byte on the page, index 1 the 8th byte, and so on. We consider two variants of how the FPTEs are stored within a page.

Split-Page Layout. In the first variant the upper part of the page exclusively accommodates legacy PTEs. Thus, this portion of the page is equivalent to the case of using unmodified PTEs. The metadata for each entry is located on the remaining portion of the page. We denote this type of layout as the *split-page layout* due to the content of the page being clearly divided. When accessing a FPTE, the PTE and the corresponding metadata are fetched from their respective parts of the page. While this layout has the advantage that the PTW can directly use the index extracted from the virtual address to access the FPTE, it also entails disadvantages. As the index of the metadata region is determined by the formula given above, the PTW must implement additional logic to determine the location from which the metadata must be fetched. Furthermore, separating the PTE and the metadata may cause additional latency due to low spatial locality as the metadata may reside in a different cache line.

Cache-Line Localized Layout. In modern systems, the memory subsystem operates on cache line granularity, which spans 512 bits. Thus, a single cache line can hold eight 64-bit legacy PTEs. For 64-bit metadata regions, a cache line can accommodate four FPTEs. For the 192-bit metadata regions, the number of FPTEs per cache line decreases to two. Organizing the PTEs and their associated metadata such that they are co-located in the same cache line has the advantage that all data can be *fetched in one single memory transaction.* Furthermore, the fact that the metadata is directly co-located to the PTE simplifies the function computing the indices in the PTW. By co-locating the PTE and the metadata in the same cache line, the additional pressure imposed on the memory subsystem is kept to a minimum, as no additional memory requests are required.

4.3   Affected Levels $\mathcal{P}_3$

Only using FPTEs on the last paging level limits the usage of security-relevant metadata to the case where default-sized pages are used. As modern systems allow to directly map a leaf page instead of the next-lower table (*i.e.*, huge pages), one must decide on the layer up to which FPTEs are supported. We denote a configuration in which only the last-level page table supports FPTEs as a *PTL0* configuration. Consequently, a configuration supporting FPTEs in the last level and the level directly above is called a *PTL1* configuration (cf. Fig. 1). This naming scheme continues for all layers of the hierarchy and we assume the configurations includes all lower levels.

PTL0 Configuration. The PTL0 configuration is the most straightforward configuration, as only one layer in the paging hierarchy is modified. As only the last-level PTEs are replaced by FPTEs, the PTW only requires additional fetches in the last translation stage in the case of the split-page layout. Also, the virtual address bit decrease is minimized as even a 192-bit PTE-MR only causes an overall decrease of two bits. However, a PTL0 configuration limits security schemes to requiring metadata on the smallest paging granule. Larger mappings consequently cannot utilize any of the additional bits, which may be a limiting factor for certain features.

PTL1 Configuration. With a PTL1 configuration, FPTEs are available on the second-to-last layer and on the last layer of the paging hierarchy. Thus, this configuration allows for the implementation of security schemes even in the case of huge pages. A single entry in the second-to-last layer maps a larger continuous virtual memory range than an entry in the last layer. Hence, the granularity on which this metadata is assigned is coarser than for PTL0 configurations. Security schemes that require fine-grained metadata may consequently not profit from PTL1 configurations. Furthermore, the memory overhead of such a configuration is also increased compared to PTL0 as the number of FPTEs increases. As the PTEs of the last two layers are modified in a PTL1 configuration, the amount of available virtual address bits decreases by at least two bits. In the case of 192-bit PTE-MR, the overall decrease sums up to four bits.

Depending on the implemented scheme, it may be possible that even more levels of the paging hierarchy use FPTEs. In such cases, the memory overhead increases with each additional level and the number of available virtual address bits decreases further. We do not consider implementing FPTEs on a higher level without including all levels below as this would introduce the same address space reductions while yielding a coarser granularity of metadata bits.

4.4   TLB Entry Size $\mathcal{P}_4$

As each FPTE consists of a legacy PTE and associated metadata, we must consider whether to increase the size of the TLB entries as well. Each TLB entry holds a mapping from a virtual page to the associated physical page and the accompanying permission bits. Furthermore, each entry holds a tag and potentially additional data.

The exact number of required additional metadata bits in each TLB entry is dictated by the implemented security scheme. If the metadata is only relevant during the initial translation process, *i.e.*, when performing a page table walk, no additional TLB bits are required. If, however, the additional bits are checked on every access, the relevant bits must be stored in the TLB entries, thus increasing their size. This size increase necessitates a tradeoff between the overall TLB area and the number of TLB entries. As the TLB is implemented in hardware, its size is static and the TLB entry size cannot be configured during runtime. Consider the case in which the size of each TLB entry is doubled and assume that each entry only consists of storage and no additional logic. Keeping the number of TLB entries constant roughly doubles the overall storage space requirements of the TLB. Contrarily, doubling the entry size while halving the number of entries keeps the overall TLB size constant. However, reducing the number of TLB entries has a detrimental impact on the system performance as the number of page table walks due to TLB misses increases. At the same time, increasing the TLB size is increasingly costly due to its close proximity to the core and L1 caches. In our design, we consider both options to underline the tradeoff between performance and area overhead resulting from modifying the TLB.

5   Case Study

The main objective of FatPTE is to support as many security schemes depending on additional metadata located in the page table entries as possible. We perform a case study to showcase the applicability of FatPTE for commodity and academic security features. In our case study, we provide a detailed comparison of security features and demonstrate that their required metadata can be effectively stored using FPTEs. Furthermore, we analyze whether each scheme would benefit from an even larger number of metadata bits. For each security scheme, we investigate whether additional TLB bits are required and, if necessary, the number of additional bits. Additionally, we explore how the findings influence our choice of the design parameters $\mathcal{P}_1$ to $\mathcal{P}_4$.

Considered Applications. Various academic designs and commercial security features rely on metadata located in page table entries. These designs utilize PTE bits to associate metadata for *essential security technologies*, such as control-flow integrity (CFI), memory protection, and confidential computing. Table 1 provides a concise overview of the analyzed security technologies, which are discussed below. In our study, we discuss commercial security features and academic designs separately. A scheme is designated as a commercial product if it is present in commodity off-the-shelf CPUs or will be available in upcoming CPU generations. We do not consider schemes using tagged memory architectures [16], *i.e.*, store metadata in a dedicated tag storage, such as ARM MTE [31] as physical memory tagging is an orthogonal technology to implement security features.

Table 1. A comparison of commercial and academic designs that use PTE metadata to enable key security technologies.

Mechanism	Application	ISA	# PTE bits
Intel CET SHSTK [33]	Access Permission	x86-64	1-bit[†]
ARM BTI	Legacy Compatibility	ARMv8.5	1-bit
Intel MPK [21]	Protection Key	x86-64 ✪	4-bit
ARM Domains [39]	Protection Key	ARMv7 ✪	4-bit
Intel TME-MK [13]	Key Identifier (KeyID)	x86-64 ✪	15-bit[‡]
IMIX [9]	Access Permission	x86-64	1-bit
Donky [29]	Protection Key	RISC-V ✪	10-bit
Multi-Tag [36]	Page-granular Tag	x86-64 ✪	16-bit
PT-Guard [24]	Cryptographic MAC	x86-64 ✪	12-bit
SecWalk [25]	Redundancy Code	RISC-V ✪	25-bit

✪ Profits from additional bits   † Implicitly encoded   ‡ Up to 15-bit

5.1 Commercial Security Features

Intel Control-Flow Enforcement Technologies (CET) [33] introduce the indirect branch tracking (IBT) and shadow stack (SHSTK) features to protect forward-edge and backward-edge control-flow transfers. The shadow stack protects return addresses and, thus, mitigates attacks like return-oriented programming [6,32]. As the shadow stack holds security-critical data, it must be protected from unauthorized access. This is achieved by uniquely marking shadow stack pages using a previously unused combination of the read/write bit and the dirty bit in the PTE. Shadow stack pages can only be accessed using dedicated instructions, such as the wrss instruction. Other architectures, such as ARM and RISC-V, provide comparable features to enforce control-flow integrity. The RISC-V SHSTK also relies on memory protection using a new, previously unused, page type. This type is encoded by setting the page permissions in the PTE to write-only. The ARM guarded control stack (GCS) implements a shadow stack feature for the ARM architecture by leveraging a memory attribute for page protection. ARM branch target instructions (BTI) also provide landing pads for forward-edge CFI. However, ARM BTI leverages the GP-bit in the translation table to enable compatibility with legacy binaries. For all of the above schemes, it is essential to include the access permissions for the page in the TLB entry.

Apart from control-flow integrity, fine-grained and efficient control over page-granular access permissions can protect against memory safety issues. Intel memory protection keys (MPK) [21] leverage a 4-bit protection key encoded in the PTE to enforce read and write access policies during runtime. Memory protection is achieved by comparing the protection key with the user space protection keys register (PKRU), reflecting the currently active access permissions. PKRU implements read and write permission bits for each distinct protection key and is software-controlled from user space. MPK reduces performance overheads when partitioning the virtual address space through logical integrity checks, as no context switch is required to change permissions. ARM memory domains [39] introduce a 4-bit domain identifier for page-granular memory protection. As the memory protection keys and the domain identifiers are checked on every access, they both must be included in the corresponding TLB entries.

Transparent memory encryption technologies like Intel Total Memory Encryption (TME) [11] and AMD Secure Memory Encryption (SME) [17] have been available in commodity CPUs for several generations. However, TME and SME only allow for one encryption key when encrypting DRAM data. Recent CPUs introduce new features, allowing for multiple encryption keys, thus paving the way for cryptographically isolated domains. Intel total memory encryption multi-key (TME-MK) [13] provides up to 15 key identifiers (keyID) bits located in the PTE for DRAM encryption. Intel TME-MK is used to encrypt guest memory for Intel's confidential computing technology [7]. To encode the keyIDs, TME-MK changes the specification of the physical address, *i.e.*, physical address bits are repurposed to encode the keyID into the PTE, thus reducing the overall addressable physical memory. The secure memory encryption (SME) feature of AMD uses a single bit in the physical address to indicate whether a page is encrypted or not. This *C-bit* thus reduces the available physical address size by one bit. Building on SME, AMD secure encrypted virtualization (SEV) [1] leverages the same C-bit to identify encrypted pages but provides per-VM encryption keys to cryptographically isolate virtual machines against each other and the host. As the keyID and the C-bit are part of the physical address, they are implicitly stored in the TLB entries.

We find that FatPTE increases the achievable security of certain commercial security features. Intel MPK is often criticized for allowing only 16 unique keys [29,30]. Schemes that use MPK for in-process isolation are thus constrained to 16 domains, which can be a limiting factor for their applicability. FatPTE facilitates the usage of more PTE bits for security and, thus, allows for an increased number of protection domains. This enables a more fine-grained compartmentalization of the application, resulting in increased security properties. Similarly, the security of ARM memory domains would improve by offering more domain identifiers. Consider, for example, a configuration with 64-bit PTE-MR. By providing 64-bit identifiers, we support a number of isolation domains that far exceeds the currently possible maximum of 16. In its current form, Intel TME-MK, which is essential for the cryptographic isolation of VMs, introduces a trade-off between the number keyIDs and addressable physical memory. While this approach works in current generations, future CPUs may require a larger number of keyIDs. As each additional keyID bit comes at the cost of halving the available physical address space, the maximum number of keyIDs is inherently limited. Through FatPTE, it is possible to increase the number of key bits without forfeiting any of the physical address bits.

5.2   Academic Designs

Security researchers proposed various security features that repurpose PTE bits [5,9,24,25,29,36]. Like the commercial features discussed above, academic schemes suffer from the same limitations due to the scarcity of spare PTE bits.

Donky [29] proposes the extension of MPK to use 10-bit protection keys on the RISC-V platform. Here, MPK greatly benefits from an increased number of protection keys, e.g., 10-bit protection keys enable the use of more than 1000 memory domains. Additionally, multiple designs leverage Intel TME-MK memory encryption for security beyond VM memory encryption [20,26,27,35]. However, the number of available keys is platform-specific. Schemes based on Intel TME-MK significantly benefit from an increased number of available keyIDs. Due to the steady increase in physical memory capacity, it is vital to allow for a large number of keyIDs without reducing the addressable physical memory.

Multi-Tag [36] proposes a multi-granular tagging strategy combining tagged memory with PTE-based tags to perform logical integrity checks for memory safety. As the integrity checks are performed at every access, Multi-Tag must use TLB entries for the page-granular tag bits. PT-Guard [24] repurposes 12 PTE bits for a cryptographic MAC that protects the integrity of the PTE itself. In the case of PT-Guard, the MAC is only required when performing the page table walk to detect tampering of the paging structures. Once the PTE is stored in the TLB, it is considered valid and does not require additional authentication. SecWalk [25] requires 25 bits in the PTE (thus significantly reducing the addressable physical memory) to provide fault protection with redundancy codes. Furthermore, SassCache [10] explores the use of available PTE bits for their secure randomized cache architecture.

Other academic designs rely on a single-bit in the PTE to enforce dedicated security policies and protect memory resources. IMIX [9] leverages one bit in the PTE for in-process isolation to mark security-critical memory. Similarly, CETIS [37] repurposes Intel CET SHSTK protection for in-process isolation. Cornucopia Reloaded [8] proposes the extension of one PTE bit to block capability loads, which is beneficial for implementing a fast memory sweep.

These academic designs highlight the strong need for more feature-specific PTE bits. Similar to commercial security features, FatPTE improves the security for several of the presented designs. While Donky proposed extending the protection key size from 4 to 10 bits, FatPTE allows for an even larger amount of protection domains. FatPTE also allows Multi-Tag to increase the number of tag bits beyond 16 bits without reducing the addressable physical memory. PT-Guard greatly benefits from FatPTE in terms of security and performance as it can compute a single MAC for each PTE, thus eliminating the need for additional fetches. When using 192-bit PTE-MR, the probability of a MAC collision becomes vanishingly small, thus providing exceedingly strong security against attacks. Similarly, SecWalk's security is significantly increased by allowing larger redundancy codes, resulting in stronger fault detection capabilities.

5.3   Insights

Our case study underlines the need for dedicated PTE bits for essential security features. In current CPU generations the spare PTE bits of major CPU manufacturers, such as Intel, are exhausted. Due to PTE size constraints, promising academic designs requiring additional PTE bits are hard to adopt for industry use. Not only can FatPTE provide enough bits for all of the considered security features, *it even allows the implementing multiple features without compromising on their security.* Thus, FatPTE is an effective approach that facilitates easy adaptation and combination of commercial and academic security technologies. Furthermore, we find that 7 out of the 10 investigated security features benefit from additional PTE bits, thus underlining the relevance of adding security-specific bits to page table entries.

While the parameterization of FatPTE depends on the implemented security feature, we find that many of these features share common characteristics and requirements. We find that most schemes profit strongly from a 64-bit PTE-MR. The schemes with further security gains from using 192-bit PTE-MR are PT-Guard and SecWalk. Thus, we conclude that a 64-bit metadata region is feasible for all of the analyzed security features. All of the investigated security schemes can, in theory, operate on the granularity of huge pages. However, the effectiveness of schemes like Multi-Tag suffers when using larger mappings due to the coarser granularity of the metadata. We thus consider both a PTL0 configuration and a PTL4 configuration as feasible. However, note that none of the schemes requires the metadata to be present in all layers *at the same time.* The metadata is only required if a FPTE is a leaf entry, *i.e.*, if it points to a page and not another level in the hierarchy. Thus, even in the case of a PTL4 configuration, only one additional memory transaction for the metadata is necessary.

6   Implementation and Evaluation

To evaluate the performance impact of FatPTE, we create exemplary prototype implementations for x86-64 and RISC-V. Both variants implement 4 KiB pages and a 64-bit PTE-MR. It is not possible to include FatPTE's hardware changes on commodity x86-64 hardware. Thus, we use the gem5 system simulator [4] to implement FatPTE for the x86-64 ISA. We modify the PTW so that the number of index bits fits the number of entries in each level. In the case of the PTL0 configuration we change the indexing used for last-level pages such that the lowest level uses 8 instead of 9 index bits. We implement both the split-page and the cache-line localized layout. When using the split-page layout, our modified PTW fetches the metadata associated with a PTE by accessing the 64 bits located 256 indices lower on the same page. For the cache-line localized layout, the fetches are cache-line aligned and the fetch width increases to 512 bits. We implement the PTL4 configuration by modifying the PTW such that the index modification applies to all levels of the hierarchy.

Besides the gem5 prototype we also implement FatPTE for RISC-V using the CVA6 core [38], which uses 39-bit virtual addresses. We extend the core's PTW to support the additional fetches required by FatPTE and synthesize it for a Digilent Genesys 2 FPGA board. Here, we assume the cache-line localized layout with 64 bits of metadata, analogous to the x86-64 prototype. Our implementation supports configurable metadata fetching at all layers which we can control using a dedicated control and status register (CSR). The metadata of intermediate layers can be checked directly after it was fetched and we store the metadata of the last translation layer in the TLB. We synthesize our prototype using a Digilent Genesys 2 FPGA board.

Depending on the feature implemented with FatPTE, it is necessary to extend the TLB entries by a certain number of bits. Thus, TLB entries increase in size as the amount of metadata bits increases. We implement two TLB configurations for the simulator prototype and the hardware prototype. The first configuration extends the size of each TLB entry by 64 bits while keeping the number of TLB entries constant, thus increasing the overall TLB area. The second configuration increases the TLB entry size while reducing the number of TLB entries to model the case in which the TLB area is limited.

6.1   Performance Evaluation

We evaluate the performance of FatPTE using the SPEC CPU 2017 benchmark suite. Our evaluation consist of multiple configurations to exemplify the design choices discussed above.

Simulation Setup. For our simulation, we model an x86-64 system with 4 KiB pages. We implement FPTEs on the lowest level of the hierarchy (PTL0) and on all levels (PTL4). Each FPTE holds 64 bits of metadata. We implement the cache-line localized and the split-page layout and investigate two TLB configurations. In the full-TLB configuration (TLB-F), the amount of TLB entries stays constant, which represents the case in which the TLB area increases. For the half-TLB configuration (TLB-H), we reduce the number of TLB entries by halving it, thus representing the case in which the area is limited. We base our gem5 configuration on the CPU model used by LeMay et al. [18] which represents current Intel Ice Lake CPUs. We use the out-of-order (O3) CPU model as this is the most accurate gem5 CPU model. We evaluate four variants of FatPTE (PTL0 TLB-F, PTL0 TLB-H, PTL4 TLB-F, PTL4 TLB-H). Our baseline system uses legacy PTEs, 128 iTLB entries, and 64 dTLB entries.

As the simulation duration using the O3 CPU can become infeasibly high for complex workloads, we use simpoints [22]. The simpoints tool identifies representative regions within the workload for its different execution phases. Simulating these regions and computing a weighted sum of the partial results provides a performance estimation for the complete workload. We use *cycles per instruction* (CPI) as the performance metric. Each simulation interval consists of a constant number of instructions. Thus, CPI values of different runs are normalized to the same instruction count.

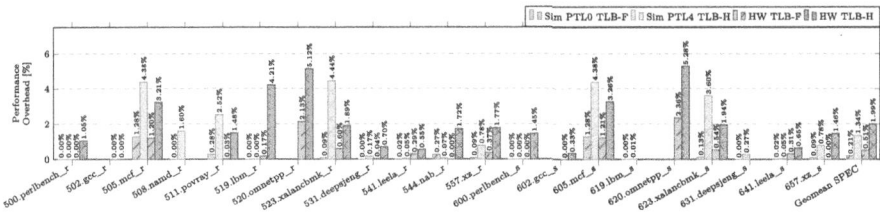

Fig. 3. The simulated and measured overheads using the SPEC CPU 2017 benchmark suite. The geomean overheads range from 0.21% to 1.99%.

Hardware Evaluation. We use our hardware prototype in two different configurations to evaluate the performance implications of FatPTE. Both models implement a PTL0 configuration and differ in the number of TLB entries. Our baseline features 64 iTLB and 32 dTLB entries and does not fetch metadata. While the TLB-F configuration leaves the TLB size unchanged, TLB-H reduces the number of iTLB entries to 32 and the number of dTLB entries to 16.

For both evaluation platforms, we exclude SPEC CPU 2017 benchmarks that fail to compile, crash due to runtime issues, or do not finish within a reasonable amount of time (e.g., less than 100 h).

6.2   Performance Evaluation Results

Figure 3 illustrates the relative performance overheads for our simulation and our FPGA prototype. For the simulation, we consider PTL0 TLB-F and PTL4 TLB-H using a cache-line localized layout. For our hardware prototype, we use a PTL-0 configuration with TLB-F and TLB-H. We select these configurations as they are the lowest and highest overheads, respectively.

We find that using FPTEs has an overall low impact on the system performance with geomean overheads ranging from 0.21% to 1.34% and most benchmarks experience overheads below one percent. For the benchmarks that show larger overheads, the performance impact is still within a reasonable range. We find that the number of TLB entries ($\mathcal{P}_4$) has a far stronger impact on the measured performance overhead than the paging levels on which the PTEs are extended ($\mathcal{P}_3$). This is mainly due to the fact that performing cache-line aligned requests synergizes with the granularity of the memory subsystem and the caching layers. Furthermore, reducing the number of TLB entries increases the amount of TLB misses and, thus, the need for costly page table walks. For the split-page layout, we observe larger overheads ranging from 1.04% for the (PTL0, TLB-F) configuration to 2.66% when using a (PTL4, TLB-H) configuration.

Similar to the simulation, the performance impact on the FPGA is low, with a geomean of 0.51% for TLB-F and 1.99% for TLB-H. Note that our hardware implementation requires an additional fetch during the page table walk to fetch the required metadata. While we use a cache-line localized layout, the hardware

Table 2. FPGA Utilization of our modified CVA6 core. The TLB-Full configuration increases the number of lookup tables (LUTs) and flipflops (FFs). For TLB-Half, the total area decreases slightly compared to an unmodified system.

	iTLB	dTLB		LUTs	FFs
Base	64	32	Total	45626	29843
			TLB	7072	8990
TLB-F	64	32	Total	51700 (+13.3%)	36152 (+21.1%)
			TLB	11040 (+56.1%)	15134 (+68.3%)
TLB-H	32	16	Total	45544 (−0.2%)	28519 (−4.4%)
			TLB	3801 (−46.3%)	7566 (−15.8%)

operates on word-sized granularity. As we run our benchmarks using a PTL0 configuration, the additional fetch is performed at the end of the walk. The given results suggest that FatPTE imposes feasible overheads, even in the case of resource-constrained systems with lower TLB capacity and smaller caches.

6.3   Memory and Area Overhead

Increasing the size of PTEs also increases the memory footprint of the paging structures which scale with the amount of mapped virtual memory. We compute the relative overhead introduced by the different parameterizations assuming 64-bit PTE-MR metadata, 5-level paging, 4 KiB pages and that memory pages are mapped in virtually contiguous regions. Mapping a single page requires a PTE in each of the five layers and causes an overhead of 0.98%. As the amount of mapped memory increases, the overhead converges to a lower bound of 0.196%. When using FPTEs on the last layer (PTL0 configuration), the overhead converges to 0.391%. In a PTL4 configuration, this limit further increases to 0.392%. When using 192-bit PTE-MR, the overheads increase to 0.783% and 0.787% for PTL0 and PTL4, respectively.

For most of the security features analyzed in Sect. 5, the metadata bits are checked on every access and, thus, cached in the TLB. A TLB entry typically consists of the PTE bits and additional information for TLB lookups and security checks. Keeping the number of entries constant while increasing the entry size increases the total area of the TLB. Alternatively, an area-constrained TLB can provide larger entries at the cost of a reduced overall number of entries. The CVA6 CPU uses 135-bit TLB entries. Adding a 64-bit PTE-MR increases the required bits by 47% but does not necessarily translate to an area increase of that same amount.

Table 2 shows synthesis results with different numbers of TLB entries. The values are relative to the unmodified CVA6 (*Base*). Most of the area overheads stem from caching the extra metadata in the TLB. The TLB itself grows by 56% and 68% in lookup tables (LUTs) and FlipFlops (FFs), respectively. When halving the TLB (TLB-H), the area stays roughly the same compared to the baseline. Hence, when the TLB is constrained by area, the number of entries would have to be halved to cache the full 64-bit PTE-MR.

7   Related Work

SPEAR-V [28] implements enclaves for RISC-V using a page-granular tagged memory architecture. In contrast to FatPTE, SPEAR-V associates metadata with physical memory pages by reserving an access-restricted fixed memory region. FatPTE associates metadata with virtual memory, thus scaling better in terms of memory overhead. Furthermore, FatPTE profits from increased spatial locality as metadata is co-located with the paging information.

Intel Sub-Page Write-Permission (SPP) allows granting write-access for 128-byte memory regions within a read-only page [15]. The used metadata is fetched on-demand since current PTEs cannot accomodate it. SPP metadata is accessed through a number of indirection layers which are traversed on every write access. Thus, SPP may cause non-negligible overheads in the case of frequent write accesses to protected pages. Note that FatPTE can directly encode such permission bits in the PTE metadata, thus eliminating the need for additional lookups.

ARMv9 introduced a new translation table format that increases each descriptor's size to 128 bits. Similarly to FatPTE, this allows for a larger addressable physical memory size and new attribute fields. However, the translation descriptors of ARM can only provide a subset of the available bits for security-critical features. In its current form, it is not possible provide one metadata bit for each cache line of a 4 KiB page. Thus, schemes that scale with the number of bits (e.g., PTGuard) may not be usable due to a loss of security. In contrast, FatPTE provides at least 64 metadata bits per PTE, thus allowing for at least cache-line granular metadata and the efficient implementation of schemes requiring a certain lower bound of bits for them to be effective. Furthermore, the PTE layout of FatPTE does not depend on the layer at which the entry resides.

8   Conclusion

In this work we introduced FatPTE, a design that facilitates the implementation of security features relying on metadata bits in page table entries.

As the number of spare PTE bits is exhausted the adoption of new features is hindered and the security of existing features is limited. FatPTE transforms PTEs to FPTEs by enhancing them with dedicated metadata for security-critical bits (PTE-MR). We identify the metadata region size, the metadata layout, the number of affected levels, and the modification of TLB entries as possible parameters for our design. By performing a case study on commercial and academic security features we uncover suitable parameterizations of FatPTE.

We implement an x86-64 software prototype using gem5 and a RISC-V hardware prototype to evaluate our design. Using the insights gained in our case study, we configure and benchmark multiple parameterizations of FatPTE using workloads of the SPEC CPU 2017 benchmark suite.

We find that the imposed performance overheads are low, ranging from 0.21% to 1.34% for our simulated prototype and from 0.51% to 1.99% on our hardware implementation. Furthermore, we show that our design imposes negligible page table storage overheads.

Acknowledgements. We thank the anonymous reviewers for their valuable feedback. This project has received funding from the Austrian Research Promotion Agency (FFG) via the SEIZE project (FFG grant number 888087) and the AWARE project (FFG grant number 891092).

References

1. Advanced Micro Devices: Strengthening VM isolation with integrity protection and more. White Paper (2020)
2. Advanced Micro Devices: AMD64 Architecture Programmer's Manual Volume 2: System Programming (2024). https://www.amd.com/content/dam/amd/en/documents/processor-tech-docs/programmer-references/24593.pdf. Revision 3.42. Accessed 01 Aug 2024
3. ARM: Translation granule. https://developer.arm.com/documentation/101811/0103/Translation-granule. Version 1.3. Accessed 01 Aug 2024
4. Binkert, N.L., et al.: The gem5 simulator. SIGARCH Comput. Archit. News **39**, 1–7 (2011)
5. Bratus, S., Locasto, M.E., Ramaswamy, A., Smith, S.W.: Traps, events, emulation, and enforcement: managing the yin and yang of virtualization-based security. In: Proceedings of the 1st ACM Workshop on Virtual Machine Security, VMSec 2008, Alexandria, VA, USA, 27 October 2008, pp. 49–58 (2008)
6. Buchanan, E., Roemer, R., Shacham, H., Savage, S.: When good instructions go bad: generalizing return-oriented programming to RISC. In: Proceedings of the 2008 ACM Conference on Computer and Communications Security, CCS 2008, Alexandria, Virginia, USA, 27–31 October 2008, pp. 27–38 (2008)
7. Cheng, P., et al.: Intel TDX demystified: a top-down approach. ACM Comput. Surv. **56**, 238:1–238:33 (2024)
8. Filardo, N.W., et al.: Cornucopia reloaded: load barriers for CHERI heap temporal safety. In: Proceedings of the 29th ACM International Conference on Architectural Support for Programming Languages and Operating Systems, Volume 2, ASPLOS 2024, La Jolla, CA, USA, 27 April 2024–1 May 2024, pp. 251–268 (2024)
9. Frassetto, T., Jauernig, P., Liebchen, C., Sadeghi, A.: IMIX: in-process memory isolation extension. In: 27th USENIX Security Symposium, USENIX Security 2018, Baltimore, MD, USA, 15–17 August 2018, pp. 83–97 (2018)
10. Giner, L., et al.: Scatter and split securely: defeating cache contention and occupancy attacks. In: 44th IEEE Symposium on Security and Privacy, SP 2023, San Francisco, CA, USA, 21–25 May 2023, pp. 2273–2287 (2023)
11. Intel: Intel Architecture Memory Encryption Technologies (2022), revision 1.4. https://www.intel.com/content/www/us/en/content-details/679154/intel-architecture-memory-encryption-technologies-specification.html. Accessed 31 Jan 2023
12. Intel: Intel Trust Domain Extensions (2022). https://cdrdv2-public.intel.com/690419/TDX-Whitepaper-February2022.pdf. Accessed 27 May 2024

13. Intel: Runtime Encryption of Memory with Intel Total Memory Encryption-Multi-Key (Intel TME-MK) (2022). https://www.intel.com/content/www/us/en/developer/articles/news/runtime-encryption-of-memory-with-intel-tme-mk.html. Accessed 27 May 2024
14. Intel: Architecture Specification: Intel Trust Domain Extensions (Intel TDX) Module (2023). https://cdrdv2-public.intel.com/733568/tdx-module-1.0-public-spec-344425005.pdf. Accessed 27 May 2024
15. Intel: Intel® 64 and IA-32 architectures software developer manual (2024). https://www.intel.com/content/www/us/en/developer/articles/technical/intel-sdm.html
16. Jero, S., et al.: TAG: tagged architecture guide. ACM Comput. Surv. **55**, 124:1–124:34 (2023)
17. Kaplan, D., Powell, J., Woller, T.: AMD memory encryption. White paper **13** (2016)
18. LeMay, M., et al.: Cryptographic capability computing. In: MICRO 2021: 54th Annual IEEE/ACM International Symposium on Microarchitecture, Virtual Event, Greece, 18–22 October 2021, pp. 253–267 (2021)
19. Li, X., et al.: Design and verification of the arm confidential compute architecture. In: 16th USENIX Symposium on Operating Systems Design and Implementation, OSDI 2022, Carlsbad, CA, USA, 11–13 July 2022, pp. 465–484 (2022)
20. Nasahl, P., et al.: EC-CFI: control-flow integrity via code encryption counteracting fault attacks. In: IEEE International Symposium on Hardware Oriented Security and Trust, HOST 2023, San Jose, CA, USA, 1–4 May 2023, pp. 24–35 (2023)
21. Park, S., Lee, S., Kim, T.: Memory protection keys: facts, key extension perspectives, and discussions. IEEE Secur. Priv. **21**, 8–15 (2023)
22. Perelman, E., Hamerly, G., Van Biesbrouck, M., Sherwood, T., Calder, B.: Using simpoint for accurate and efficient simulation. ACM SIGMETRICS Perform. Eval. Rev. **31**(1), 318–319 (2003)
23. RISC-V Foundation: The RISC-V Instruction Set Manual, Volume II: Privileged Architecture (2024). https://github.com/riscv/riscv-isa-manual
24. Saxena, A., Saileshwar, G., Juffinger, J., Kogler, A., Gruss, D., Qureshi, M.K.: PT-guard: integrity-protected page tables to defend against breakthrough rowhammer attacks. In: 53rd Annual IEEE/IFIP International Conference on Dependable Systems and Network, DSN 2023, Porto, Portugal, 27–30 June 2023, pp. 95–108 (2023)
25. Schilling, R., Nasahl, P., Weiglhofer, S., Mangard, S.: SecWalk: protecting page table walks against fault attacks. In: IEEE International Symposium on Hardware Oriented Security and Trust, HOST 2021, Tysons Corner, VA, USA, 12–15 December 2021, pp. 56–67 (2021)
26. Schrammel, D., et al.: MEMES: memory encryption-based memory safety on commodity hardware. In: Proceedings of the 20th International Conference on Security and Cryptography, SECRYPT 2023, Rome, Italy, 10–12 July 2023, pp. 25–36 (2023)
27. Schrammel, D., et al.: Memory tagging using cryptographic memory integrity on commodity X86 CPUs. In: 9th IEEE European Symposium on Security and Privacy, EuroS&P 2024, Vienna, Austria, 8–12 July 2024. IEEE (2024)
28. Schrammel, D., Waser, M., Lamster, L., Unterguggenberger, M., Mangard, S.: SPEAR-V: secure and practical enclave architecture for RISC-V. In: Proceedings of the 2023 ACM Asia Conference on Computer and Communications Security, ASIA CCS 2023, Melbourne, VIC, Australia, 10–14 July 2023, pp. 457–468 (2023)
29. Schrammel, D., et al.: Donky: domain keys - efficient in-process isolation for RISC-V and x86. In: 29th USENIX Security Symposium, USENIX Security 2020, 12–14 August 2020, pp. 1677–1694 (2020)

30. Schwarzl, M., et al.: Robust and scalable process isolation against spectre in the cloud. In: Computer Security - ESORICS 2022 - 27th European Symposium on Research in Computer Security, Copenhagen, Denmark, 26–30 September 2022, Proceedings, Part II, pp. 167–186 (2022)
31. Serebryany, K.: ARM memory tagging extension and how it improves C/C++ memory safety. Login Usenix Mag. **44** (2019)
32. Shacham, H.: The geometry of innocent flesh on the bone: return-into-LIBC without function calls (on the x86). In: Proceedings of the 2007 ACM Conference on Computer and Communications Security, CCS 2007, Alexandria, Virginia, USA, 28–31 October 2007, pp. 552–561 (2007)
33. Shanbhogue, V., Gupta, D., Sahita, R.: Security analysis of processor instruction set architecture for enforcing control-flow integrity. In: Proceedings of the 8th International Workshop on Hardware and Architectural Support for Security and Privacy, HASP@ISCA 2019, 23 June 2019, pp. 8:1–8:11 (2019)
34. The kernel development community: HugeTLB Pages (2024). https://docs.kernel.org/admin-guide/mm/hugetlbpage.html
35. Unterguggenberger, M., Lamster, L., Schrammel, D., Schwarzl, M., Mangard, S.: TME-box: scalable in-process isolation through intel TME-MK memory encryption. In: 32nd Annual Network and Distributed System Security Symposium, NDSS 2025, San Diego, California, USA, 24–28 February 2025 (2025)
36. Unterguggenberger, M., Schrammel, D., Nasahl, P., Schilling, R., Lamster, L., Mangard, S.: Multi-tag: a hardware-software co-design for memory safety based on multi-granular memory tagging. In: Proceedings of the 2023 ACM Asia Conference on Computer and Communications Security, ASIA CCS 2023, Melbourne, VIC, Australia, 10–14 July 2023, pp. 177–189 (2023)
37. Xie, M., et al.: CETIS: retrofitting intel CET for generic and efficient intra-process memory isolation. In: Proceedings of the 2022 ACM SIGSAC Conference on Computer and Communications Security, CCS 2022, Los Angeles, CA, USA, 7–11 November 2022, pp. 2989–3002 (2022)
38. Zaruba, F., Benini, L.: The cost of application-class processing: energy and performance analysis of a linux-ready 1.7-GHz 64-bit RISC-V core in 22-nm FDSOI technology. IEEE Trans. Very Large Scale Integr. Syst. **27**, 2629–2640 (2019)
39. Zhou, Y., Wang, X., Chen, Y., Wang, Z.: ARMlock: hardware-based fault isolation for ARM. In: Proceedings of the 2014 ACM SIGSAC Conference on Computer and Communications Security, Scottsdale, AZ, USA, 3–7 November 2014, pp. 558–569 (2014)

CHERI UNCHAINED: Generic Instruction and Register Control for CHERI Capabilities

Moritz Waser[1]([✉]) [ID], Lukas Lamster[1] [ID], David Schrammel[2] [ID],
Martin Unterguggenberger[1] [ID], and Stefan Mangard[1] [ID]

[1] Graz University of Technology, Graz, Austria
{moritz.waser,lukas.lamster,martin.unterguggenberger,
stefan.mangard}@tugraz.at
[2] Rivos Inc., Santa Clara, USA
davidschrammel@rivosinc.com

Abstract. The CHERI capability architecture is designed to implement the principle of least privilege at the hardware level, enabling fine-grain compartmentalization of resources in memory. Besides memory, capability-enhanced processors like the ARM Morello SoC rely on traditional ring-based isolation for instruction and register control. However, previous works have demonstrated that exploiting access to system registers or privileged instructions can allow attackers to break or bypass the memory isolation. Furthermore, ring-based isolation is too coarse-grain for software isolation that aims to enforce least privilege.

This paper presents CHERI UNCHAINED, a novel CHERI ISA extension that allows explicit management of (non-memory) hardware resources through software-controlled capabilities. Specifically, we introduce the new concept of *control capabilities*, which enforce the principle of least privilege by restricting access to instructions and registers while following CHERI's overarching design goals of provenance, integrity, and monotonicity. Our design enables fine-grain resource management for both, pure-capability and legacy software. Furthermore, CHERI UNCHAINED has the potential to replace traditional ring-based protection entirely, thus reducing complexity while providing a higher degree of privilege control flexibility. To demonstrate the feasibility of our design, we present a functional prototype based on the CHERI-QEMU simulator and evaluate the performance on the ARM Morello platform. Extending generic software running on Morello with fine-grain hardware resource management incurs a worst-case performance overhead of 2.76%. Additionally, we extensively analyze the security of all privilege-related mechanisms in our design, highlighting the flexibility of our generic approach.

Keywords: Memory Safety · Capability Architecture · Compartmentalization

---

D. Schrammel—The work was done while the author was at Graz University of Technology.

M. Dalla Preda et al. (Eds.): ARES 2025, LNCS 15993, pp. 149–170, 2025.
https://doi.org/10.1007/978-3-032-00627-1_8

1   Introduction

The principle of least privilege, a fundamental idea introduced in computer science several decades ago [31], guides the design of secure software systems. It ensures that each software component only receives the specific set of privileges required to fulfill its intended task. These privileges include access to dedicated memory locations, system resources such as system registers, and the ability to execute specific instructions. Consequently, an adversary exploiting software vulnerabilities cannot access resources beyond the defined set of privileges of the vulnerable software module, thereby effectively minimizing the overall attack surface of the system.

Traditionally, protection rings are used to establish distinct privilege levels for individual software components, controlling their access to dedicated instructions and hardware resources. The operating system runs at the highest privilege ring and has full access privileges, while applications operate at a lower-privileged ring with fewer privileges. However, today's monolithic kernels act as a single all-encompassing compartment with near full system access, which violates the principle of least privilege [48]. Considering operating systems run third-party kernel modules and browsers in user space run arbitrary code from potentially malicious websites, protection rings fail at restricting access at a suitable granularity. Attackers can abuse the insufficient access control granularity and mount powerful attacks by accessing system registers [9,28,45] or executing special instructions [7].

Capability systems [11,12] integrate the principle of least privilege into the system architecture. The seL4 microkernel [19], for instance, is designed for highly secure and reliable systems and implements capability-based access control. Capability architectures, such as CHERI [23] and the M-Machine [8], leverage capability-based addressing to enforce security in hardware.

The *Capability Hardware Enhanced RISC Instructions* (CHERI) capability system enables fine-grain privilege management for memory. CHERI achieves this by replacing traditional pointers with capabilities that enhance memory operations with range and privilege checks. A single-bit memory tag marks valid capabilities in memory and prevents forgery. Thereby, CHERI ensures memory safety [24] by restricting access to memory resources solely to the capabilities' specified address ranges. CHERIvoke [43] and Cornucopia (Reloaded) [14,15] implement capability revocation to achieve temporal memory safety. In addition, CHERI's capability sealing provides a mechanism for software compartmentalization.

CHERI's enforces the principle of least privilege for *memory access*, but for other hardware resources, it remains dependent on traditional protection rings. However, neglecting the isolation of (non-memory) hardware resources can lead to critical security problems [7,9,28,45]. For example, abusing access to RISC-V's `satp` register, which controls virtual memory, can compromise isolation. ISAs like x86 enable undervolting through access to system registers [25], and access to cache flushing instructions may allow adversaries to mount timing-based side-channel attacks [47]. As CHERI is incapable of enforcing least privilege within a protection ring, it must rely on inefficient countermeasures, such as binary scanning, before loading untrusted code [10, 16, 44].

Contributions. This paper presents CHERI UNCHAINED, a novel extension of the CHERI architecture that enables comprehensive privilege control specifically for non-memory system resources. We introduce dedicated *Control Capabilities* (CCaps), which enforce fine-grain policies for instruction execution and system register access. Our extension remains consistent with CHERI's design goals of provenance, integrity and monotonicity while enabling high flexibility with minimal system complexity. We achieve fine-grain compartmentalization within rings without the need of orthogonal techniques like binary scanning before loading untrusted code. Our design is able to establish software domains, e.g., sandboxes that can be efficiently combined and nested, and actually enforce the principle of least privilege for all system resources. Following CHERI's hybrid system approach, our CCaps can also be used to create sandboxes for legacy software, effectively isolating untrusted and potentially malicious code. Moreover, our design even facilitates ring-less compute systems with high access control flexibility in the future. We discuss how such an approach can reduce the overall complexity of hardware and privilege management, and elaborate on potential system design strategies that can leverage our ISA extension.

To prove the efficacy of our design, we implement a functional prototype based on the CHERI-QEMU simulator [1]. Furthermore, we showcase the efficiency of our design by evaluating the performance on the state of the art CHERI-based ARM Morello platform. Finally, our security analysis underlines the strong protection guarantees for different use cases (*i.e.*, safeguarding legacy systems and zero-ring computing).

In summary, our main contributions are as follows:

- We present CHERI UNCHAINED, a lightweight extension of the CHERI capability architecture that enforces the principle of least privilege for non-memory hardware resources through dedicated *control capabilities*.
- We detail how our extension enhances CHERI's compartmentalization for traditional, ring-based systems and efficiently sandboxes legacy code.
- We present different use-cases for our design, including its potential to eliminate the need of ring-based isolation.
- We implement a functional prototype based on CHERI-QEMU and evaluate the performance of our design with the ARM Morello platform. Adding support for CHERI UNCHAINED causes a negligible overhead of 0.15% while managing CCaps during function-granular compartmentalization in userspace increases runtime by 2.76%.
- We extensively analyze the security of our design, underlining the advantages of our approach.

Outline. The paper is structured as follows. Section 2 provides the background, and Sect. 3 the threat model of this paper. Section 4 presents the design of CHERI UNCHAINED and our compartmentalization approach. Section 5 elaborates on how our design can be used for different use-cases. Section 6 details the implementation and evaluation. Section 7 extensively analyzes the security of our design. Section 8 discusses related work, and Sect. 9 concludes this work.

2   Background

In this section, we detail the background on protection rings, software compartmentalization, and capability architectures.

2.1   Ring Model

Traditional ring-based isolation uses privilege levels, so-called *protection rings*, to manage access to system registers and critical instructions. Software components can operate on different privilege levels, *i.e.*, with full or reduced privileges. Typically, this is used to provide different levels of isolation for kernel and user applications. The privilege levels are enforced in hardware, and ring transitions are strictly controlled using call gates. During program execution, only instructions associated with the current privilege level can be executed.

2.2   Software Compartmentalization

To counteract the exploitation of memory errors [36], enforcing the principle of least privilege for software is crucial. The aim of compartmentalization is to effectively isolate different software modules from the rest of the system. This is achieved by exclusively limiting access to resources in memory needed by the respective module to fulfill its intended computational task. Many software isolation mechanisms have been proposed in the past [5, 10, 22, 27, 32, 33, 37–39, 41]. Isolating potentially malicious code that might be present in a software module, such as untrusted libraries, protects other modules, as an attacker cannot leak or corrupt data outside the vulnerable compartment. This reduces the attack surface in the scenario of software exploitation and prevents the attacker from compromising the entire target system.

2.3   CHERI Capability Architecture

Capability-based systems [5, 8, 11] integrate the principle of least privilege into the processor architecture, thereby enabling and enforcing fine-grain privilege management for system resources such as the access to code and data.

Capability Hardware Extended RISC Instructions (CHERI) [23] extends existing instruction set architectures (ISAs) with the integration of capability-based addressing. The current version of its specification focuses on RISC-V, however, the ARM Morello [21] project showcases that CHERI can also be adapted for ARM processors. CHERI integrates dedicated capability registers and capability instructions designed for performing access and permission checks in hardware. CHERI's *capabilities* use a fat pointer approach (*i.e.*, 128-bit capabilities on 64-bit architectures). In addition to the regular 64-bit address, these capabilities contain compressed bounds, permission bits, and an object type identifier. The bounds follow a custom format, called CHERI concentrate [42], which presents a trade-off between encodable range and alignment constraints.

The object type (otype) is an 18-bit identifier that can be used to group capabilities. A single-bit memory tag is used to identify CHERI capabilities in memory. This single-bit tag is associated with memory at a granularity of 128 bits and is stored and propagated through a tagged memory architecture [17].

In addition to the capability-based addressing, CHERI provides mechanisms for software isolation. First, capabilities can be sealed and unsealed by other capabilities (possessing respective permissions) with the CSeal and CUnseal instructions. Sealed capabilities are immutable and non-dereferenceable. Second, the CInvoke instruction, together with a sealed pair of code and data capabilities linked by otype, enables efficient software domain transition by unsealing both capabilities and loading the code capability into the *Program Counter Capability* (PCC) register.

CHERI's hardware checks restrict access to memory locations solely within the range defined by the capabilities' bounds, thereby enforcing spatial memory safety. In addition, CHERI enables the revocation of capabilities and, thus, access rights. Designs like CHERIvoke [43] and Cornucopia [14, 15] implement temporal memory safety for heap allocations through this revocation mechanism. Consequently, CHERI is able to address a variety of challenges of unsafe programming languages like C and C++, including memory safety [24] and fine-grain software compartmentalization [40]. However, since CHERI does not provide a sufficient mechanism to restrict access to instructions and control registers, it still relies on traditional protection rings. Within the active protection ring, the PERMIT_ACCESS_SYSTEM_REGISTERS permission controls access to all system registers at once. Besides protection rings, CHERI does not propose any mechanism to restrict access to specific instructions.

3   Threat Model

Our design supports complex software stacks running within different protection rings or compartments with varying privileges. These software modules may have different levels of trust. Software modules can range from individual functions to full libraries or entire binaries. Code running in a compartment can be categorized into three categories: legacy, CHERI-legacy, and CHERI UNCHAINED-aware. Legacy code refers to binaries that were compiled without the CHERI extension and, thus, uses regular pointers. CHERI-legacy code was built with CHERI capability support but without our CCaps. CHERI UNCHAINED-aware software makes full use of our CCap extension. We consider a sandbox scenario, in which an application intends to execute untrusted code modules without any security assumptions. An untrusted module can contain vulnerabilities that allow an adversary to arbitrarily run code, access memory and execute instructions, e.g., issue system calls. Note that this also includes all instructions introduced by the CHERI extension. In the sandbox scenario, both operating systems and user applications may intend to execute untrusted code. In the case of CHERI-legacy and CHERI UNCHAINED-aware code, the adversary is able to freely manipulate

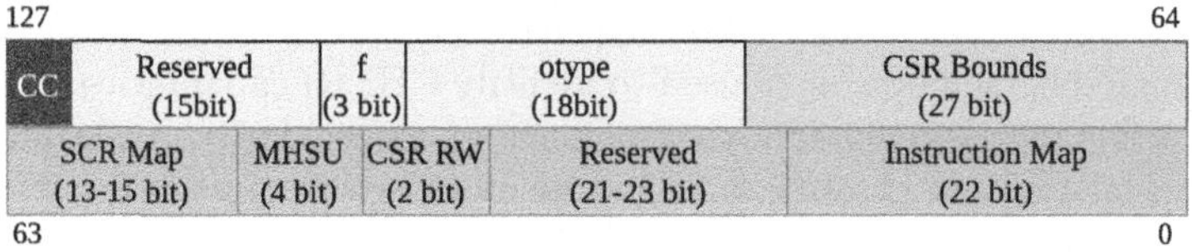

127   64

| CC | Reserved (15bit) | f (3 bit) | otype (18bit) | CSR Bounds (27 bit) |

| SCR Map (13-15 bit) | MHSU (4 bit) | CSR RW (2 bit) | Reserved (21-23 bit) | Instruction Map (22 bit) |

63   0

Fig. 1. Layout of our *Control Capabilities* (CCaps). The in-register and in-memory representations follow the CHERI concentrate 128 format [23,42]. All highlighted fields are modified compared to regular CHERI capabilities.

any capability that is available at the time of gaining arbitrary code execution. We assume that our proposed compartment model is used correctly. Malformed sandboxes that, e.g., feature exploitable compartment interfaces, are out of scope. Our design allows any piece of code, running with any degree of system privilege, to generate an arbitrary number of (nested) sandboxes without requiring support from an external, trusted code module, e.g., a compartment monitor. Moreover, we consider fault attacks [18,25] and side-channel attacks [29,47] out of scope, and orthogonal protection mechanisms must be used to address them.

4   CHERI UNCHAINED Design

In this section, we present CHERI UNCHAINED. We introduce flexible *Control Capabilities* (CCaps), which, in combination with regular CHERI capabilities, can enforce the principle of least privilege on all hardware resources by restricting access to memory, executable instructions, and control registers. We showcase the layout and general mechanism of CCaps, and list required extensions and modifications of the CHERI ISA. We introduce two mechanisms, *sandbox calls* and *controlled invocations*, that seamlessly blend existing CHERI compartmentalization with our CCaps.

4.1   Control Capabilities

CHERI neither provides a mechanism to restrict or filter the executable instructions within a domain, nor does it allow for fine-grain access rules to control registers. The ACCESS_SYSTEM_REGISTERS permission bit of the *Program Counter Capability* (PCC) only controls, whether the current context has access to all CSRs in its current privilege level, or none.

To address these shortcomings, we extend the CHERI architecture with CCaps. They improve on traditional CHERI compartments with fine-grain control over executable instructions and accessible control registers. Similar to regular CHERI capabilities, CCaps reside within general purpose registers. Software can load, modify, and store CCaps analogous to regular CHERI capabilities. They also follow the design principles of CHERI: provenance, integrity and monotonicity. Valid CCaps, which are marked by a tag bit both in memory and in the register file, may only be derived from other valid CCaps with equal or

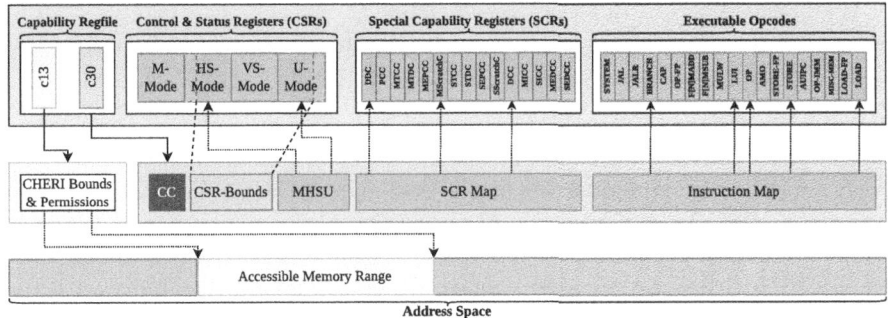

Fig. 2. High-level overview of CHERI UNCHAINED. Capabilities that reside within the general-purpose register file are distinguished between regular CHERI capabilities, and CCaps. Regular CHERI capabilities restrict access to memory regions, whereas our newly introduced CCaps implicitly enforce access permissions for CPU resources.

reduced permissions. Contrary to regular CHERI capabilities, CCaps are neither dereferenceable nor can they act as jump targets. When a valid CCap is loaded into register c30, it implicitly enforces access rules on the current execution context.

Layout. Figure 1 shows the layout of a CCap in the CHERI concentrate format. We reserve one of the four software-defined permission bits to mark a capability as a CCap, which we label CC bit. In terms of layout, the remaining 64 upper bits of the capability remain similar to normal CHERI capabilities. The bounds field is repurposed as bounds for CSR access. The address located in the lower 64 bits is split into several bitmaps that act as whitelists for instructions and CHERI's *Special Capability Registers* (SCRs). The MHSU and CSR RW further extend the CSR access rules with privilege levels and read/write permissions. Figure 2 presents an overview of the function of CCaps next to regular CHERI capabilities.

CSR Bounds. The accessible CSR range is encoded following a slightly modified version of the 128-bit CHERI concentrate format [23,42]. For normal capabilities, decompressing the encoded bounds requires the compressed bounds (consisting of a top and bottom field), an exponent and the address field. All CCaps use the fixed exponent 0, such that the bounds can be single-byte (*i.e.*, single-CSR) aligned. While the top and bottom fields can be up to 14 bits wide, we only use 12 bits for CCaps, as RISC-V defines a 12-bit address space for CSRs. When decompressing the bounds of CCaps, the actual data in the address field is ignored and assumed to be all zero. The bits [9:8] of RISC-V's CSR address encode the highest privilege level with permission to access the respective CSR. To sort the encoded CSR space in our CCaps based on privilege level, we interpret the bits [11:10] and [9:8] of the CSR address as flipped. Remapping these bits during a comparison with the CSR bounds in hardware is trivial.

While this design is tailored towards RISC-V, the exponent may be used to increase the addressable range of the CSR bounds for other ISAs like ARM. By limiting the CSR bound granularity, a wider CSR range can be achieved.

Permission Bitmaps. In addition to more fine-grain control over CSR access, the `Instruction Map` bitmap controls the types of instructions that are currently allowed. The individual bits of this field map directly to instruction classes defined by RISC-V opcodes, e.g., ALU operations. In addition to the regular read/write permissions of RISC-V CSRs, the `CSR RW` field enforces access rules for all CSRs within the encoded bounds. To enable greater flexibility with the allowed CSR range, the `MHSU` bits control access to CSRs associated with specific privilege levels. These permissions are enforced after the range specified in the bounds field. Since CHERI's *Special Capability Registers* (SCRs) reside in their own space, we require a separate `SCR Map` that control access to each SCR. We reserve 10 bits for CHERI's SCRs and add up to five additional SCRs in our map (see Sect. 4.2). The remaining bits of the capabilities' address field are reserved to extend the instruction or SCR maps with additional fields for future ISA extensions or the potentially higher number of required fields of other ISAs such as ARM platforms.

4.2 CHERI ISA Extension

In the following, we highlight all ISA changes that are required besides our newly introduced CCaps for CHERI UNCHAINED to function.

Control Capability Handling. Because the address field of the CHERI concentrate format is used as a bitmap in CCaps, we define several constraints that the hardware must enforce for CCaps. First, the only valid non-CHERI operation that may be performed on the address field (*i.e.*, lower 64 bits) is a logical AND. This constraint automatically enforces monotonicity on CCaps, as fields in the bitmap can only be cleared, but never set. Second, since regular arithmetic instructions may result in unrepresentable values for the CHERI concentrate format that would clear the tag, the AND operation must never clear the tag a CCap.

Special Capability Register (SCR) Extension. Depending on whether the system supports privilege levels or not, we add three to five additional SCRs. We add the *Default Control Capability* (DCC), *Machine Exception Default Control Capability* (MEDCC) and the *Machine Interrupt Control Capability* (MICC) SCRs for single privilege mode systems. Systems with privilege levels require the additional *Supervisor Exception Default Control Capability* (SEDCC) and *Supervisor Interrupt Control Capability* (SICC) SCRs.

The DCC holds a CCap that extends the permissions and bounds of the CCap in `c30`. Access is granted when at least one CCap provides the required permissions. DCC serves three purposes. First, CHERI UNCHAINED-aware code can use it to allow access to non-linear CSR ranges by defining non-overlapping bounds in both `c30` and DCC. When combined with the *MHSU* field, this may even be extended to multiple regions. Second, DCC receives and holds the CCap that is active during interrupt and exception handling. Finally, analogous to CHERI's *Default Data Capability* (DDC), our DCC is used to restrict the permissions of legacy code. When no valid CCap is present in either c30 or DCC, an exception is raised implicitly, as the running context lacks permissions to execute any instruction. MICC and SICC store CCaps that belong to a trap handling environment (see Sect. 4.2).

ABI Changes. The RISC-V calling convention lists the register c30 as a caller-saved, temporary register. We designate the register as the host for our CCap. Compilers must not use the register for normal operations, as this has direct implications for the access permissions of the running context. During normal, non-sandboxed function calls, the register is neither modified nor spilled onto the stack.

Interrupts. CHERI extends several RISC-V CSRs, which are related to interrupt handling, to full SCRs. For example, the xtvec CSR, which holds a pointer to the entry of the trap handler, is extended as *Trap Code Capability* (TCC). Analogous to the implicit SCR operations defined by CHERI, we add implicit CCap handling to trap entry and exit. Similar to new data and code capabilities, in a CHERI UNCHAINED system, the handler requires a new CCap with possibly elevated privileges. This capability is stored in the MICC or SICC for M- and S- mode respectively. When an exception or interrupt is raised, the CCap in DCC is copied to the MEDCC/SEDCC register. Simultaneously, the contents of MICC/SICC are moved to DCC, such that the trap handler has the necessary permissions to perform its task. As these operations are performed implicitly by the hardware, CHERI UNCHAINED does not add any additional overhead to trap handling. Like all other GPRs, the active CCap in c30 is spilled during trap handling and eventually restored when exiting the handler. DCC is restored from MEDCC/SEDCC when the handler returns.

System Startup. Systems must possess a valid CCap after a system reset. Software can then distribute derivates of this CCap to different compartments. Our design places the primordial, omnipotent CCap in the DCC SCR, when the system is reset. This ensures that, by default, the system does not trigger a CCap exception. Since CHERI requires the presence of another, primordial capability with access to system registers, the startup code always has access to the DCC SCR.

Multiple Control Capabilities and Non-contiguous Ranges. Our base design specifies a single capability register (c30) as the host for CCaps, to minimize the required hardware overhead of our design. However, in addition to DCC, several other general purpose registers may also be used to host CCaps. When all of them enforced, this allows for much greater flexibility in terms of permission management and non-linear CSR ranges. However, allowing more registers to host CCaps requires additional comparison logic per register. We leave this choice up to the specific hardware implementation.

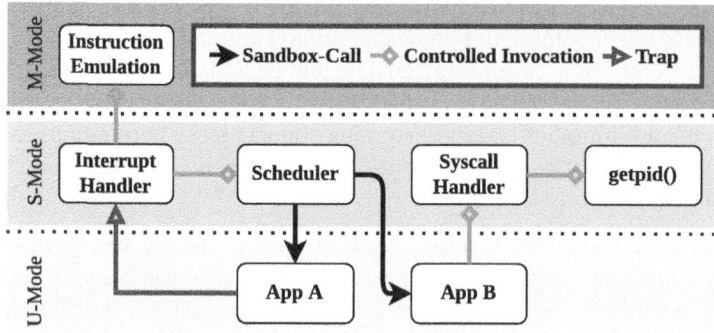

Fig. 3. Different types of compartment calls in our design. Sandbox calls keep or reduce the current privileges. Controlled invocation allows for intentional privilege escalation.

However, even with a single CCap host register (*i.e.*, c30), an application can use an arbitrary number of CCaps. The software can manage CCaps during runtime and ensure that the currently required CCap is loaded in the host register.

4.3   Compartment Management

CHERI's capability sealing mechanism combined with the CInvoke instruction provides a unified mechanism that enables efficient separation of software domains without additional intervention from the operating system or a trusted software component. Data and code capabilities are linked by their otype and present a clean entry point for a compartment. Any additional capability can be passed to a compartment as function argument. All other registers not involved in the compartment switch can be spilled onto the stack and should be cleared or invalidated afterwards. Since our CCap resides within a general purpose register, the caller can first spill its current CCap register alongside other registers and then optionally skip clearing it. This way, the enforced access permissions transition directly into the callee compartment. Hence, no changes to CInvoke are necessary to support CCaps. Note that a compartment requires a capability with the PERMIT_SEAL permission to create a sealed pair to be used with CInvoke. If a compartment should be able to constrain other functions in a sandbox, such a capability must be available within its scope.

Since the CInvoke instruction was designed to serve as a constrained form of non-monotonicity, we distinguish two cases. If it serves as a function call with monotonic permission changes, we call it *sandbox call*. Every call that elevates or changes privileges and, thus, behaves non-monotonic, is called *controlled invocation*. Figure 3 demonstrates this difference for an exemplary software stack. Apart from the additional management of CCaps, we treat both *sandbox calls* and *controlled invocations* as regular function calls. As specified by CHERI, a CInvoke call places the data capability into register c31, which we then use to

Listing 1.1. Setup and restore operations performed by the caller before and after a compartment switch. The otypes of both sealed pairs for call and return must match.

```
    s2 <- CSeal(sp) // otype A
    push cc
    sp <- CSetBounds(sp, ...)
    sp <- CSeal(sp) // otype B

    s3 <- AUIPCC(ret) // otype A
    s3 <- CSeal(s3)
    cc <- CSetBounds(cc, ...)
    ... // clear all caps except s2, s3, cc, and args
    CInvoke(sp, target)
ret:
    sp <- c31 // restore sp
    pop cc
```

Listing 1.2. Required steps for the callee upon entry and exit.

```
aware_target:
    ### only controlled invocation
    ... // load new cc with data capability
    ###

    push s2, s3
    ... // function
    pop s2, s3

    ### only controlled invocation
    cc <- CSetBounds(cc, ...) // reduce to minimum
    ###
    CInvoke(s3,s2) // return and unseal original sp
```

load a new CCap. Listing 1.1 highlights the callers steps for a generic compartment call. Listing 1.2 shows required steps by the callee upon compartment entry and exit.

Sandbox Calls. A sandbox call reduces the currently active permissions within the CCap. First, the caller creates a sealed capability from the current stack pointer, which can later be used to restore the state. Then, the currently active CCap is pushed to the stack. It then reduces the upper bound of the stack pointer capability such that it does not include the current call stack (including the previously spilled CCap) and seals the resulting capability. If the call requires more arguments than the amount that can be passed using registers, additional arguments are pushed onto the stack and the bounds of the stack pointer capability must be adapted accordingly. Next, it creates a return capability with the AUIPCC instruction and seals it as well. Together with a sealed version of the current stack pointer this return capability forms a sealed pair that provides the new compartment with a return path. Now the caller can reduce the permissions on the active CCap and clear all other registers besides the function arguments, the CCap, the target sealed pair and the return sealed pair. By using CInvoke with the sealed pair as arguments, control is transferred to the new compartment. After the callee eventually returns by using CInvoke with the return pair, the caller can simply restore its CCap from the stack again, alongside all other capabilities.

Controlled Invocation. *Controlled invocations* are similar to *sandbox calls* but they behave non-monotonic w.r.t. CCaps. The caller of such an invocation does not have access to the CCap of the callee, as it provides different privileges. In addition, especially for the case of different but not necessarily elevated privileges, the callee should also not get access to the CCap of the caller. For this reason, we require two additional steps to perform *controlled invocation*. First, after spilling its own CCap onto the stack, the caller must reduce the permissions of the currently active CCap to the minimum that is required to perform the CInvoke instruction and to load capabilities from memory. Second, the callee must have access to its own CCap directly after entry, through the unsealed data capability. When returning from a controlled invocation, the callee follows a similar approach of minimizing the privileges of the active CCap. The caller must restore its own CCap directly after the invocation returns.

Contrary to a *sandbox call*, the data capability used for *controlled invocation* is not a stack pointer. The callee must have access to its own stack through the invoked data capability. Restricting access to the caller's CCap is similar to *sandbox calls*. By pushing it to the stack, reducing the bounds of the stack pointer and using it as the sealed data capability for the return pair, the callee cannot access it.

5   CHERI UNCHAINED Use-Cases

Least Privilege in Traditional Systems. Traditional system designs filter instructions and restrict access to control registers through privilege levels. However, this does not enforce least privilege, as software, e.g., operating systems, often consists of a variety of modules with different purposes that all run with the same privileges. CHERI already improves this by enabling compartmentalization, which restricts access to memory regions. Access to all system registers of a privilege level, however, is either fully granted or fully revoked. If a software component requires access to a single control register, it receives access to all others. In addition, CHERI cannot limit executable instructions within a privilege level, again not providing least privilege. Hence, when loading untrusted code, e.g., third-party kernel modules, restricting access to privileged instructions would require expensive measures like binary scanning. Additionally, mechanisms like JIT or (e)BPF may generate code at runtime, which adds to this complexity.

With CHERI UNCHAINED, a ring-based software stack can be fully compartmentalized into modules that follow the principle of least privilege. By extending CHERI's compartmentalization for memory access, we sandbox modules within a protection ring to restrict access to security critical instructions or control registers. Every module is assigned a *Control Capability* (CCap), which may enforce

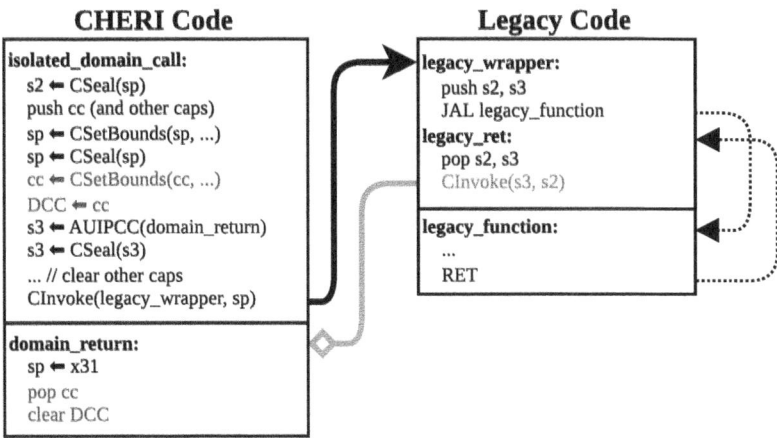

Fig. 4. Example of a legacy function call isolated within a sandbox. The legacy code is wrapped by a lightweight wrapper that manages the sealed capability pair used to return.

stronger restrictions than the privilege level of the running context. This also entails limiting access to memory and control registers of other, lower privilege levels. E.g., a kernel module can be stripped of all permissions regarding access to user mode resources. Similarly, compartments in user mode applications can be further sandboxed such that they only have access to instructions and resources that they actually require.

Sandboxing Legacy Code. While CHERI UNCHAINED requires recompilation of existing software to fully benefit from the added functionality, it is also capable of enforcing least privilege on legacy code in a hybrid setting. We define legacy code as any software that was compiled without notion of CHERI, e.g., an existing library. Legacy code may be executed in any privilege level. CHERI provides a *Default Data Capability* (DDC) SCR, which enforces capability permissions ranges on legacy memory accesses. Our DCC SCR allows us to extend this with fine-grain control over CSRs, SCRs, and executable instructions. We sandbox legacy code by executing function calls through a CHERI-based wrapper. This wrapper is responsible for controlled compartment entry and exit. Figure 4 visualizes this process. Before jumping into a legacy sandbox, the caller must set up the permissions within the DDC and DCC SCRs accordingly. To set up these wrappers correctly, we rely on either the linker or the loader for static or dynamic linking respectively. Specifically, the wrapper and the related legacy code must be placed such that the code capability used for the *sandbox call* covers both the wrapper and the related function. The (dynamic) linker can generate these for each shared (legacy) library in a program. In its simplest form, the wrapper pushes the capability required to return to the caller to the stack and calls the legacy function. After the legacy function returns, the wrapper restores the sealed capability pair to exit the sandbox and invokes it to return back to the caller's compartment.

5.1   Enabling Zero-Ring Computing

Combining CCaps with traditional protection rings is a compromise that tries to fix general design flaws of existing systems while maintaining compatibility. With a design primitive such as CHERI UNCHAINED, however, we can rethink established design choices and construct systems that do not require traditional privilege levels at all. Such systems, which replace the functionality of traditional, ring-based systems with capability-based hard- and software resource management, require less design complexity while providing a unified methodology to manage hardware privilege and software isolation. We call this *zero-ring computing*. While designing a new ISA without privilege rings is outside of the scope of this paper, this section discusses necessary changes to the CHERI-extended RISC-V ISA and elaborates on possible software design approaches.

Virtual Memory. In RISC-V, the `satp` CSR stores which page translation mode the CPU is currently running in (`MODE`), an address space identifier (`ASID`), and the physical page number (`PPN`) of the current root of translation. Following the RISC-V ISA, virtual memory translation is only active while the CPU is in U- or in S-mode.

In zero-ring systems we envision, this privilege mode-dependent behavior would be removed entirely. Changes made to `satp` are immediately active. Since toggling memory translation also affects instruction fetches, the software must ensure that any compartment that alters `satp.MODE` is mapped at the same location in both the physical and the current virtual address space. Capabilities retain their validity upon toggling memory translation, which may violate memory safety if access to `satp` is insufficiently constrained. To provide access to physical memory operations, similar to M-mode, we propose a special gate compartment. It is set up by boot code and kernel code must ensure that its virtual mapping mirrors the physical mapping. Upon entry, it deactivates virtual memory by setting `satp.MODE` to zero. Based on an argument, similar to a syscall number, it then calls a function/compartment that should be executed with physical memory access. Afterwards, the gate compartment activates virtual memory again, by setting `satp.MODE` to its previous value, and returns to the caller.

Control and Status Registers. In a zero-ring system, we can reduce the amount of required CSRs, as many of them are duplicated for every privilege level. First, we unify all CSRs related to interrupts and exceptions (`xstatus`, `xie`, `xip`, `xtval`, `xepc`, `xcause`, `xscratch`). We also do not need the `xideleg` and `xedeleg` CSRs anymore, as trap delegation can be replaced by a unified trap handler. Second, we can remove all CSRs related to RISC-V's physical memory protection (PMP), as traditional MPU-based memory isolation is obsolete in a CHERI system. Finally, we do not require a distinction between M-mode and U-mode performance counters anymore.

Without privilege levels, the two bits used to distinguish the privilege level in the CSR address space become part of the identifier. This removes the privilege split in the CSR address space and, thus, reduces hardware complexity while providing more design flexibility with space for custom CSRs.

Exceptions and Interrupts. In a traditional RISC-V system, the `xedeleg` and `xideleg` CSRs manage which exceptions or interrupts are directly delegated to a lower privilege level's trap handler. As we completely remove privilege levels, all interrupts and exceptions can share the same handler. This handler can be a small compartment that is only capable of invoking other compartments. Optionally, a scheduling compartment can either set individual handlers for each task or modify the capabilities of a universal handler to limit access to specific trap-related functionality.

System Calls. Without privilege levels syscalls (*i.e.*, the `ECALL` instruction) can be replaced by normal compartment invocations. With this, syscalls turn into regular function calls that invoke special compartments with elevated privileges. The specific access privileges of individual tasks regarding syscalls can be managed by limiting a task's access to capabilities for individual syscalls.

6   Implementation and Evaluation

In this section, we present our two CHERI UNCHAINED prototype implementations based on the CHERI-QEMU [1] simulator and the ARM Morello platform [21]. Furthermore, we evaluate the performance of our Morello prototype using the CheriBSD OS [2] and the SPEC-CPU 2017 benchmark suite [6].

6.1   Functional Prototype

As CHERI UNCHAINED cannot be implement purely in software, we present a functional prototype of our design based on the CHERI-QEMU system emulator. We extend the simulator with support for *Control Capabilities* (CCaps) and the required checks. Furthermore, we modify the CHERI LLVM compiler [3] to account for the usage of hardware capabilities.

CHERI-QEMU Extension. CHERI-QEMU [1] implements the CHERI specification and is, thus, a suitable starting point for our extension. We add support for CCaps to the emulator and implement multiple checks that enforce the limitations imposed by the CCaps, following Sect. 4.1. As we require new *Special Capability Registers* (SCRs), we extend the simulator with the registers described in Sect. 4.2, including the registers for S-mode. When executing an instruction, we ensure that every instruction that is disallowed by the currently active CCap causes an exception. We also trigger an exception when the running code attempts to dereference a CCap or use it as a jump target. Furthermore, every CSR and SCR access outside of the boundaries of the currently active CCap causes an exception as well. We extend capability-aware instructions to be aware of CCap restrictions. CHERI constitutes capability invalidation upon illegal modification, which we adhere to with our extension. Instructions that alter the address field (the lower 64 bits) of a capability (`CIncOffset`, `CIncOffsetImm`, `CSetAddr`, `CSetOffset`) automatically invalidate CCaps. Scaling down the bounds of a CCap, *i.e.*, reducing the accessible CSR range, with `CSetBounds`, `CSetBoundsExact`, or `CSetBoundsImm` will ignore the value of the address field and assume it to be all zero. All other capability-aware modifications of CCaps behave analogous to regular CHERI capabilities, *i.e.*, they are limited to operations that ensure the monotonicity of the target capability. Instructions like CAndPerm already enforce this by default. Similar to capability-aware instructions, regular integer instructions require additional care with regards to CCaps. Upon modification of the address field of regular capabilities, CHERI checks whether the bounds are still representable with the CHERI concentrate format. As CCaps hold bitmaps in the address field instead of addresses, we suppress this behavior to account for the altered semantics. Instead, we dictate that the only integer instruction that may modify CCaps is the AND instruction, which implicitly enforces monotonicity. All other non-CHERI instructions invalidate the CCap.

To enable interrupts and exceptions, following Sect. 4.2, we add the additional, implicit modifications of SCRs. At every trap, we implicitly exchange the *Default Control Capability* (DCC) with the *Exception Default Control Capability* (xEDCC). This mechanism saves the CCap of the interrupted context while simultaneously enabling the trap handlers' CCap.

CHERI Compiler Patches. To complement our QEMU prototype, we extend the CHERI-LLVM [3] to reserve the register c30 to host the currently active CCap. This prevents the compiler from placing regular capabilities or integer values into c30 during register allocation in the backend, which would remove all hardware permissions besides DCC. However, reserving one register increases the pressure on the remaining register file. Applications that already experience high register utilization will be more likely to require stack spills. Furthermore, we optionally instrument all function calls in the user-space, such that they enforce basic compartmentalization based on Sect. 4.3. We consider defining privileges for individual compartments orthogonal work and, thus, do not manage specific permissions for each compartment. However, we do insert the required instructions to facilitate correct compartment switches including management of CCaps. Concrete hardware access privileges for individual compartments may be defined through code annotations. Note that we chose functions as a boundary, since this is a sensible minimum granularity that recent works on sandboxing can support [26,33,46].

Software Modifications. Apart from compiling the CheriBSD kernel such that it does not use register c30, we compile all user-space binaries with full compartmentalization. To enable correct operation, we need to manually set up the correct CCap during boot time. After a reset, the primordial CCap is available from DCC. We modify the bootloader such that it copies this primordial CCap to the other SCRs related to interrupt handling (MICC, SICC, MEDCC, SEDCC). This way, as the exchange of CCaps during trap entry happens implicitly, we can never trigger an exception due to missing permissions while executing trap handling code.

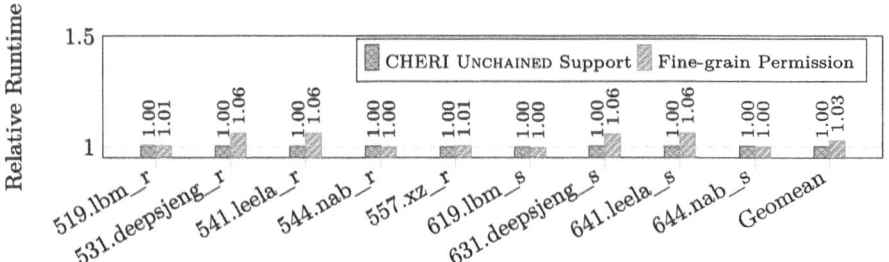

Fig. 5. Relative performance overhead of all functional SPEC CPU2017 benchmarks for different configurations.

6.2 Performance Evaluation

To evaluate the performance overhead of CHERI UNCHAINED, we build an evaluation prototype based on the ARM Morello platform and compare the performance of the SPEC CPU2017 benchmark suite [6] in different configurations.

Evaluation Prototype. We choose the ARM Morello platform [21] running CheriBSD [2] as a suitable target for our performance evaluation. This is the only taped-out processor with CHERI support, which allows us to achieve a reasonable estimation of real world performance implications of CHERI UNCHAINED. However, as we cannot modify the Morello ASIC, we evaluate the performance overhead of CCap management by defining an equivalent instruction sequence. To achieve this, we develop another CHERI-LLVM patch for the Morello SDK. We reserve the register C18, which the *ARMv8-A* ISA designates as platform register for platform-specific ABIs, to simulate the additional register pressure introduced by CCap management. CHERI's memory tagging does not cause additional overhead on the Morello platform, as the tag bits for capabilities are stored alongside ECC bits in memory.

For our evaluation, we use all benchmarks of the SPEC CPU2017 benchmark suite that can be successfully compiled using the Morello SDK and that terminate normally when run on CheriBSD. We compile all benchmarks with the SDK's *purespec-benchmark* ABI, which weakens the security guarantees related to program counter bounds to increase the amount of functional benchmarks. The baseline for our evaluation are all functional SPEC benchmarks running in an CheriBSD OS, both of which are compiled using the unmodified CHERI-LLVM compiler. We evaluate the performance overhead in two configurations. First, we evaluate the overhead of reserving the register C18 for CCaps, which leads to increased register pressure. Second, we measure the performance implications of managing CCaps at every function call. To achieve this, we spill the CCap before a function, modify it and restore it after returning. This serves as a worst-case overhead, as managing CCaps in practice does not require function-granular modifications.

6.3   Results

We distinguish between regular CHERI UNCHAINED support and *Fine-grain Permission*. Figure 5 visualizes the evaluated relative performance overhead of CHERI UNCHAINED compared to the baseline.

Full CHERI Unchained Support. To evaluate the performance overhead of reserving a register for a CCap, we compile all benchmarks with a patched LLVM compiler that reserves ARM's platform register C18. Apart from the smaller register file, this model is identical to the baseline and does not perform any CHERI-based compartmentalization. This emulates a system with full support for CHERI UNCHAINED but no utilization of its features. As ARMv8-A features 31 GPRs compared to other popular ISAs (x86_64 features 16), reserving one GPR causes a negligible geomean performance overhead of 0.15%. This demonstrates that CHERI UNCHAINED does not cause a significant amount of additional register spills due to the increased register pressure.

Fine-Grain Permission. This configuration highlights the overhead that stems from managing CCaps at function granularity. It represents the operating mode with the highest degree of security, as every function can enforce unique hardware resource access permissions, while causing the highest performance overhead due to frequent CCap modification. We aim to showcase the worst case overhead of our design by evaluating performance of CCap management without assuming any additional isolation. Since compartmentalization by itself introduces a significant performance overhead, the additional overhead of managing CCaps would be smaller relative to the baseline. Furthermore, CCaps can complement CHERI compartmentalization in different configurations and with diverse granularities. Enforcing the principle of least privilege, following our CHERI UNCHAINED design, would require a large-scale privilege analysis of a full system, which is infeasible for the scope of this work.

In this configuration, we observe a geomean overhead of 2.76% that can be considered as the upper-bound overhead, which, in practice, will never be reached. This overhead is comparable to other works related to software isolation [20,34]. However, we improve upon existing work and CHERI by including fine-grain hardware resource access permission management for individual domains and, thus, reducing the overall attack surface of a system.

7   Security Analysis

As with any isolation mechanism, it is imperative that it cannot be circumvented or otherwise exploited to gain more privileges than intended. Based on our threat model, we distinguish between legacy, CHERI-legacy, and CHERI UNCHAINED-aware software. We assume that any higher privileged software like interrupt handlers are correct and free of exploitable bugs. In the following, we discuss steps that a potentially malicious software compartment may attempt to gain more privileges and how our mechanism protects against them.

Capability Type Confusion. CCaps are different to regular CHERI capabilities as they do not represent a pointer with bounds and permissions. We distinguish normal CHERI capabilities and CCaps with the CC bit. The hardware enforces that CCaps can neither be dereferenced, nor can they be used as jump targets. When software attempts to use a CCap in an illegal manner, the hardware triggers an exception. Also, when attempting to modify a capability such that the CC-bit changes, the capability loses its tag and becomes invalid. Thus, CCaps can never be confused with regular capabilities.

Modifying Capabilities. Analogous to CHERI capabilities CCaps can also be modified when loaded in a register. Notably, CHERI capabilities have three key properties that are also upheld for our extension.

First, *Provenance*: Valid capabilities can only be derived from other valid capabilities. CCaps can only be copied from existing CCaps, but they cannot be generated without a pre-existing CCap.

Second, *Integrity*: Capabilities are clearly marked as such in the register file and also in memory using the 1-bit memory tag. Hence, regular memory or register content cannot be confused with (control) capabilities.

Third, *Monotonicity*: Capability derivation may only maintain or narrow permissions and bounds. For normal capabilities, this only concerns the upper 64 bits, which contain said permissions and bounds. As we also encode permissions in the lower 64 bits, our hardware extension ensures that CCaps can only be modified using capability instructions or arithmetic AND operations. For all other operations, the hardware strips the tag of the capability and thus invalidates it. Thereby it is ensured that whenever a capability is modified, it cannot increase the given permissions.

Sharing Capabilities. Analogous to the existing CHERI specification, capabilities may be freely shared with other software compartments either through shared memory or directly through registers. Notably, capabilities can only be shared to (shared) memory if the current software compartment holds a capability that covers the shared memory region and has the PERMIT_STORE and PERMIT_STORE_CAPABILITY permissions. It is the responsibility of a trusted monitor (or hypervisor/OS) to set up such shared memory only if needed. The compartments themselves need to ensure that they do not accidentally share or leak any capabilities through global variables, shared memory, or through registers (e.g., when calling an untrusted function via CInvoke).

Switching Permissions. As detailed in Sect. 4.3, changing permissions is possible through *sandbox calls*, where the caller merely restricts permissions, and *controlled invocations*, where permissions may be elevated. For both, we use the standard CInvoke CHERI instruction that takes a sealed pair (e.g., code and data) of capabilities, implicitly unseals them, and jumps to the code while also storing the data capability in c31. Assuming the caller has no unseal capability, they cannot use or dereference the capabilities in the sealed pair. Thus, they also cannot elevate their own permissions without also switching to the accompanied code location via CInvoke. The security for these switches, however, relies on the fact that these compartments are correctly defined (e.g., by the compiler).

Escalating Privileges. CCaps can be escalated in three possible ways. First, through `CInvoke` (see above). Second, through shared memory or through registers from other compartments (see above). And third, through interrupts and exceptions. In the latter case, the DCC register automatically gets replaced with a higher-privilege CCap such that the exception handler can perform its intended functionality. When returning (e.g., through `MRET`), the DCC register is again replaced with the original value from before. We assume that the exception handler works correctly and does not leave its own higher privileged capabilities in the register file or in memory that is available to the original compartment. Thus, the privilege escalation is strictly limited to the exception handler itself.

8   Related Work

In this section we discuss related work regarding CHERI-based software isolation and privilege control.

CHERI-Based Isolation. CompartOS [4] and CHERIoT [30] propose CHERI-based isolation methodologies for embedded platforms. CHERI-TrEE [35] introduces a CHERI extension to build software enclaves. Neither of them address the limited hardware access control. CompartOS' linkage-based approach should be easily extensible with our *Control Capabilities* (CCaps). Adapting CCaps for CHERIoT would require defining a new layout for its custom 64-bit CHERI concentrate encoding. CHERI-TrEE also enables nested compartments, but requires intrusive changes to the CHERI ISA.

Privilege Control for Instructions and Registers. ISA-Grid [13] analyzes the importance of fine-grain access control of system resources such as CSRs and instructions. It proposes a hardware architecture based on RISC-V and x86 that enforces access permissions on a single-bit granularity. Their design requires a control structure stored in memory and additional caches to avoid large memory overheads due to frequent accesses. In contrast, CHERI UNCHAINED requires only minimal hardware changes and is seamlessly integrated into the existing CHERI RISC-V ISA. Combined, it acts as a single unified isolation mechanism that does not only enhance existing ones but instead is able to replace them entirely.

9   Conclusion

In this paper, we presented CHERI UNCHAINED, a novel extension for the CHERI capability architecture that enables generic instruction and register control. We introduced dedicated *Control Capabilities* (CCaps) to constrain access to hardware resources in capability-enhanced processors. Thus, our design enforces the principle of least privilege for instruction execution and CSR access for individual software components. Our ISA extension allows the compartmentalization of both legacy computing systems and CHERI software, refining traditional ring-based isolation with fine-grain resource management. Additionally, we discussed the potential to implement privilege ring-free systems with our design.

Acknowledgements. We appreciate the feedback from our anonymous reviewers. This project has received funding from the Austrian Research Promotion Agency (FFG) via the SEIZE project (FFG grant number 888087) and the AWARE project (FFG grant number 891092). Additional funding was provided by generous gifts from Intel.

References

1. CHERI-QEMU (2024). https://github.com/CTSRD-CHERI/qemu. Accessed 05 Feb 2024
2. CheriBSD (2024). https://www.cheribsd.org/. Accessed 10 July 2024
3. The CHERI LLVM Compiler Infrastructure (2024). https://github.com/CTSRD-CHERI/llvm-project. Accessed 06 Feb 2024
4. Almatary, et al.: CompartOS: CHERI Compartmentalization for Embedded Systems. CoRR (2022)
5. Bittau, et al.: Wedge: splitting applications into reduced-privilege compartments. In: NSDI (2008)
6. Bucek, et al.: SPEC CPU2017: next-generation compute benchmark. In: ICPE (2018)
7. Bulck, et al.: Breaking virtual memory protection and the SGX ecosystem with foreshadow. IEEE Micro (2019)
8. Carter, et al.: Hardware support for fast capability-based addressing. In: ASPLOS (1994)
9. Chen, et al.: SgxPectre: stealing intel secrets from SGX enclaves via speculative execution. IEEE Secur. Priv. (2020)
10. Dautenhahn, et al.: Nested kernel: an operating system architecture for intra-kernel privilege separation. In: ASPLOS (2015)
11. Dennis, J.B., Horn, E.: Programming semantics for multiprogrammed computations. Commun. ACM (1966)
12. Fabry, R.S.: Capability-based addressing. Commun. ACM (1974)
13. Fan, et al.: ISA-grid: architecture of fine-grained privilege control for instructions and registers. In: ISCA (2023)
14. Filardo, et al.: Cornucopia: temporal safety for CHERI heaps. In: S&P (2020)
15. Filardo, et al.: Cornucopia reloaded: load barriers for CHERI heap temporal safety. In: ASPLOS (2024)
16. Hua, et al.: vTZ: virtualizing ARM TrustZone. In: USENIX Security (2017)
17. Joannou, et al.: Efficient tagged memory. In: ICCD (2017)
18. Kim, et al.: Flipping bits in memory without accessing them: an experimental study of DRAM disturbance errors. In: ISCA (2014)
19. Klein, et al.: seL4: formal verification of an OS kernel. In: SOSP (2009)
20. Koning, et al.: No need to hide: protecting safe regions on commodity hardware. In: EUROSYS (2017)
21. Limited, A.: Arm Architecture Reference Manual Supplement - Morello for A-Profile Architecture (2022)
22. Litton, et al.: Light-weight contexts: an OS abstraction for safety and performance. In: OSDI (2016)
23. Capability Hardware Enhanced RISC Instructions: CHERI Instruction-Set Architecture (Version 9). Technical report (2023)

24. MSRC Security Research: Security Analysis of CHERI ISA (2020). https://github.com/microsoft/MSRC-Security-Research/blob/master/papers/2020/Security%20analysis%20of%20CHERI%20ISA.pdf

25. Murdock, et al.: Plundervolt: software-based fault injection attacks against intel SGX. In: S&P (2020)

26. Narayan, et al.: Going beyond the limits of SFI: flexible and secure hardware-assisted in-process isolation with HFI. In: ASPLOS (2023)

27. Narayanan, et al.: LXDs: towards isolation of kernel subsystems. In: USENIX ATC (2019)

28. Ning, Z., Zhang, F.: Understanding the security of ARM debugging features. In: S&P (2019)

29. Osvik, et al.: Cache attacks and countermeasures: the case of AES. In: CT-RSA (2006)

30. Saar, et al.: CHERIoT: complete memory safety for embedded devices. In: Proceedings of the 56th Annual IEEE/ACM International Symposium on Microarchitecture (2023)

31. Saltzer, J.H., Schroeder, M.D.: The protection of information in computer systems. Proc. IEEE (1975)

32. Schrammel, et al.: Donky: domain keys - efficient in-process isolation for RISC-V and x86. In: USENIX Security (2020)

33. Schrammel, et al.: Jenny: securing syscalls for PKU-based memory isolation systems. In: USENIX Security (2022)

34. Sehr, et al.: Adapting software fault isolation to contemporary CPU architectures. In: USENIX Security (2010)

35. Strydonck, et al.: CHERI-TrEE: flexible enclaves on capability machines. In: EURO S&P (2023)

36. Szekeres, et al.: SoK: eternal war in memory. In: S&P (2013)

37. Vahldiek-Oberwagner, et al.: ERIM: secure, efficient in-process isolation with protection keys (MPK). In: USENIX Security (2019)

38. Vilanova, et al.: CODOMs: protecting software with code-centric memory domains. In: ISCA (2014)

39. Wang, et al.: Between mutual trust and mutual distrust: practical fine-grained privilege separation in multithreaded applications. In: USENIX ATC (2015)

40. Watson, et al.: CHERI: a hybrid capability-system architecture for scalable software compartmentalization. In: S&P (2015)

41. Witchel, et al.: Mondrix: memory isolation for linux using mondriaan memory protection. In: SOSP (2005)

42. Woodruff, et al.: CHERI concentrate: practical compressed capabilities. IEEE Trans. Comput. (2019)

43. Xia, et al.: CHERIvoke: characterising pointer revocation using CHERI capabilities for temporal memory safety. In: MICRO (2019)

44. Xia, et al.: Colony: a privileged trusted execution environment with extensibility. IEEE Trans. Comput. (2022)

45. Xu, et al.: Controlled-channel attacks: deterministic side channels for untrusted operating systems. In: S&P (2015)

46. Yang, et al.: Endoprocess: programmable and extensible subprocess isolation. In: NSPW (2023)

47. Yarom, Y., Falkner, K.: FLUSH+RELOAD: a high resolution, low noise, L3 cache side-channel attack. In: USENIX Security (2014)

48. Zonenberg, A.D., Yener, B.: Antikernel: a decentralized secure hardware-software operating system architecture. In: CHES (2016)

Exploring Speculation Barriers for RISC-V Selective Speculation

Herinomena Andrianatrehina$^{(\boxtimes)}$, Ronan Lashermes[ID], Joseph Paturel[ID], Simon Rokicki[ID], and Thomas Rubiano

Univ Rennes, Inria, CNRS, IRISA, Rennes, France
herinomena.andrianatrehina@inria.fr

Abstract. Speculative execution poses significant security risks to modern out-of-order cores, exemplified by attacks such as Spectre. Numerous countermeasures, including selective speculation in both software and hardware, have been proposed. This approach allows enabling or disabling speculative behavior based on circumstances. However, challenges such as evolving attack methods and the complexity of simulating out-of-order cores make these solutions difficult to reproduce and compare.

This paper investigates the use of RISC-V speculation fences to achieve selective speculation in a realistic scenario where the microarchitecture cannot distinguish between confidential and non-confidential data. We examine three aspects: the semantics of speculation fences (ranging from broad to selective constraints), the placement of fences in programs by compilers, and their hardware implementation in a modified NaxRiscv RISC-V out-of-order core. Using a new security metric, we compare configurations within a unified framework.

Our findings highlight that speculative execution of `load` instructions is critical for out-of-order core performance. Furthermore, we demonstrate that selective speculation without confidentiality-tagged data fails to achieve a meaningful security-performance trade-off.

1 Introduction

Modern microarchitectures employ speculative execution to boost performance by predicting and executing instructions before outcomes are confirmed. This allows continued execution along likely paths without delays. If a prediction is wrong, the processor rolls back, but residual changes in microarchitectural states, such as caches or branch predictors, can persist. This inability to clear all speculative traces can be exploited through vulnerabilities like Spectre [18], wherein an attacker influences speculative execution to leak sensitive information by leaving observable states within the microarchitecture.

Since the discovery of the Spectre vulnerability, numerous mitigation techniques have been proposed, as detailed in Sect. 3. However, these mitigations

The ARSENE project was funded by the "France 2030" government investment plan managed by the French National Research Agency, under the reference "ANR-22-PECY-0004".

often produce inconsistent results and are frequently difficult to reproduce, as noted in [24].

This inconsistency can be attributed to several factors. First, the significant impact of test environments on the results of certain mitigation measures, such as the benchmarks used. Second, the difficulty of openly experimenting on speculative microarchitectures, as researchers must choose between using simplified gem5 models of the most complex x86 cores or precise models of simpler RISC-V cores. Understandably, companies with access to RTL models of complex cores do not publish the security assessments of their products. Third, differing threat models and initial assumptions make it difficult to compare solutions designed to address different types of threats and varying levels of knowledge regarding which data requires protection.

Thus, although a variety of mitigation approaches have been proposed to address Spectre, the lack of reproducibility has made it challenging to accurately assess and compare the effectiveness of each solution.

A widely adopted approach is **selective speculation**. The goal is to delay the execution of instructions that potentially access or leak sensitive data, or contribute to leakage, until the processor is certain that it is not a misspeculation. This is achieved through various strategies such as inserting barrier instructions, also called fence instructions, or directly modifying the microarchitecture to handle this functionality in hardware.

In this article, we examine the potential of speculation barriers to achieve efficient selective speculation by providing a thorough and comprehensive analysis of their impact on both performance and security. We aim to address the critical question: **Is selective speculation with dedicated barrier instructions a viable solution to defend against Spectre attacks?**

To investigate this, we created a test environment for exploring and comparing different implementations of the selective speculation approach in a realistic testing environment. We varied the semantics of the barrier instructions, their placement policies, and the hardware implementations.

Our contributions include:

- The definition of different fence instructions for selective speculation, along with their hardware implementation in the open-source NaxRiscv [29] out-of-order processor.
- The modification of an LLVM-based compiler toolchain with several policies for inserting the aforementioned fences.
- The definition of a quantitative security metric used for fair comparison between different Spectre countermeasures, which relies on counting the number of vulnerable instruction sequences in execution traces.

A critical assumption in this work is that there is no way to differentiate a `load` instruction accessing a secret from a `load` instruction accessing innocuous data. As a consequence, our compiler passes cannot rely on security annotations and thus have to protect every `load` instruction, **as in realistic use cases**.

During our experimental study, we have evaluated the trade-offs between security and performance. **Our results indicate that—under our assumptions—there is no viable trade-off regardless of semantics, placement policy, or hardware implementation.** Fundamentally, the advantage of out-of-order cores over in-order cores appears to stem largely from load speculation, which should necessarily be delayed for security reasons.

These findings highlight the critical need for microarchitectures to distinguish between confidential data that must not be speculated on and other data, if we are to reconcile out-of-order execution with robust security.

As discussed, inconsistencies in existing results make a direct comparison between our proposed approach and prior work impossible. Therefore, the comparison cannot rely solely on results from the literature and must be conducted independently. To address this, we implemented the speculative load hardening (SLH) mitigation [8] due to its relatively straightforward integration, allowing us to assess it in our test environment and compare its effectiveness with our own results.

2   Security Issues with Speculative Execution

Speculative execution allows a processor to predictively execute instructions before it is fully certain of their necessity, established at the commit stage. All instructions are executed speculatively since execution is done prior to commit, but most are correctly speculated. Misspeculation means that some instructions have been executed when they should not have been, with the risk of leaving traces in the microarchitectural state that can be exploited. These traces can be observed and used in numerous ways to exfiltrate sensitive data out of its intended environment.

2.1   Covert and Side Channels

Covert channels and side channels are communication channels where information transfer should not be possible.

They correspond to two different threat models: a covert channel is a communication channel where the attacker controls both the emitter and receiver. In contrast, in a side channel, the attacker only controls the receiver, while the emitter is an innocent victim. Covert channels correspond to a stronger attacker model, capable of actively trying to emit information in the channel. As detailed in Subsect. 2.2, the Spectre attacker manipulates the microarchitecture to emit the target information, making the **covert channel** the primary threat model we aim to address in this paper.

In the context of microarchitecture security, most covert channels exploit timing differences to communicate information. The emitter tries to set up a component, e.g. a cache memory, in a state that can be observed by the receiver through timing variations, e.g. whether a cache line is present or not.

In the microarchitecture, any state can be exploited as a covert channel: cache memories [4,22], TLB [12], BTB [2], branch predictors [2], prefetchers [28], etc.

Countermeasures exist in the form of dedicated instructions to be applied during context switches that reset or partition the microarchitectural state [9,34]. Unfortunately, perfectly implementing these semantics implies applying formal methods during the hardware design to guarantee the absence of information leakage, a feat that is hardly feasible for the complex speculative cores.

2.2   Spectre

Spectre [18] attacks exploit speculative execution to bypass memory safety boundaries, reading and exfiltrating memory where it should not be possible. They work by tricking the processor into speculatively executing code paths that should not be executed, due to improper control flow or data flow predictions. Spectre attacks are generally categorized by the mechanism used to mislead speculative execution, such as branch prediction or return stack buffer misuse.

One of the most well-known forms of Spectre is Spectre-PHT [18], which involves manipulating the pattern history table (PHT) used for branch direction prediction. In Fig. 1, an attacker trains the branch predictor to assume a condition is true, causing speculative execution to proceed down a path where sensitive data is accessed.

```
if(x < array1_size){
    y = array2[array1[x] * 4096];
}
```

Fig. 1. Spectre-PHT attacks in C code

Spectre attacks proceed in two key phases:

Predictor Manipulation. The attacker manipulates the branch predictor to assume that the branch condition will likely be met (x < `array1_size`). This can be done by executing the branch in scenarios where the condition evaluates to true multiple times.

Data Exfiltration. The same code is executed again, but now with a condition that should evaluate to false (x ≥ `array1_size`), where x is controlled by the attacker. However, speculative execution still proceeds with executing the branch body due to a now incorrect branch direction prediction. During this phase, a `Spectre gadget` is executed; it built around three elements:

- **Speculation**: an instruction that triggers speculative behavior - the `if` condition.
- **Acquisition**: an instruction that can access a secret - a speculative `load` with the address `array1 + x` reads the secret value s.

- **Disclosure**: an instruction that translates the secret into a microarchitecture state - here, a second `load` exfiltrates the secret s into a tag field in cache memory.

Spectre attacks are especially challenging to mitigate because the mechanisms for speculative execution are integral to modern processor performance. Different variants of Spectre have emerged, each exploiting distinct speculative mechanisms:

- Spectre-PHT uses branch direction prediction via the PHT.
- Spectre-BTB leverages branch destination speculation via a branch target buffer (BTB).
- Spectre-RSB uses speculation from the return stack buffer (RSB).
- Spectre-STL exploits aliasing speculation in the Load Store Queue, known as store-to-load forwarding.

The adaptability of Spectre to exploit different speculative mechanisms makes comprehensive mitigation difficult without negatively impacting processor performance.

In our own nomenclature, the primary difference between microarchitectural data sampling (MDS) attacks [26] and Spectre attacks lies in the threat model. MDS attacks assume that the targeted application legitimately uses a secret value, whereas Spectre attacks assume only that a secret is accessible, even if not directly used by the application. Within this categorization, Meltdown [19] attacks are considered a subcategory of Spectre attacks, leveraging the speculation of non-occurrence of exceptions during execution. In these threat models, mitigating MDS attacks is essentially about mitigating covert channels, where Spectre attacks mitigation is more concerned with the speculation behavior. In this paper, we choose to focus on this latter issue.

3   Related Works Against Spectre Attacks

Spectre attacks that allow arbitrary memory reads are dangerous threats, and numerous countermeasures have been proposed to mitigate them. The existing solutions can be categorized into two broad categories: those that only use software structures and those that are based around the modification of the processor hardware.

3.1   Software Solutions

The `LFENCE` x86 instruction has seen its semantics changed after the publication of Spectre [18]. Previously a read ordering barrier, it is now effectively a speculation barrier, preventing all instructions following it from executing, even speculatively, until all earlier instructions have completed.

LLVM SESES (Speculative Execution Side Effect Suppression) [7] is a naive mitigation that prevents all possible Load Value Injection [31] attacks using misspeculated transient execution. This LLVM pass offers the option to add an `LFENCE` instruction before each memory read/write instruction and before the first branch instruction in a group of terminators at the end of a basic block. Benchmarks [23] show how drastically this mitigation affects performance but do not evaluate the actual security benefit it provides. We will discuss and compare these results in later sections.

Retpoline for "return trampoline" prevents Spectre attacks that exploit branch target injection. This variant leverages indirect branch predictions, such as function pointers or virtual function calls, to misdirect the CPU into executing unwanted instructions before the branch prediction is corrected. Retpoline disables speculation on indirect branches by trapping speculative execution in an infinite "safe loop" [1].

SLH is a software mitigation technique designed to protect against the Spectre-PHT variant. The main idea is to mask or "poison" either the pointer or the returned value of a speculated `load` to protect sensitive data. A predicate capturing the speculation status needs to be updated every time a conditional branch is taken. This predicate can also be transferred through function calls using some bits in the stack pointer. SLH is well-documented in LLVM and implemented for x86 [8].

Blade is a software mitigation technique that statically analyzes data flow from *potential sources* of secrets to *potential sinks* and "protects" them using different approaches. Various variants are proposed depending on the target architectures and available tools. Fence or SLH-like masks can be used. In [32], *potential sinks* are formally identified using a static type system that is "transient-aware".

3.2   Hardware Solutions

The hardware-based countermeasures can further be categorized into three groups: those that rely on cleanly reversing the changes that misspeculated instructions might have left in the microarchitecture, those that try to detect a Spectre-like leak, and those based on formal methods. It is worth noting that there is no open-source processor with a comparable complexity to Intel, AMD, or Arm cores. The results of the hardware-based solutions must then be extrapolated to these, without certainty about the relevance of this transposition. The literature is too extensive to be described in detail in this document, but pertinent state-of-the-art papers on the topic include [14] and [24].

Clean Reversal of Misspeculated Microarchitectural State. Spectre attacks are possible because transient instructions persistently modify the microarchitectural state, even when misspeculated. Therefore, a valid solution would be to revert the microarchitectural state exactly as it was before the misspeculated execution. While the concept is straightforward, implementing it is challenging, as all the possible states must be reverted. That includes caches, branch predictors, finie state machines, Load-Store Queues, etc.

Several works have explored this type of countermeasure, such as InvisiSpec [35], DAWG [17], and SafeSpec [16]. They all differ in their specific implementations, impacting both performance and security.

Delays Based on Speculative Secret Tracking. Another strategy is to identify the occurrence of a Spectre gadget in order to trigger the suspension of speculative behavior. The idea is to identify the risky behavior corresponding to the three elements of a Spectre gadget: speculation, acquisition, and disclosure: Taint tracking is necessary between acquisition and disclosure to detect if secret data is likely to leak. It is possible to follow these steps and act at each of them, either by preventing any speculation, forbidding speculative `load` instructions, or preventing the covert channel. The earlier the intervention, the safer but more costly the solution is in terms of performance.

Many proposals using this principle have been made, all differing in their implementations: NDA [33], STT [36], SpecShield [3], Efficient InvisiSpec [25], SpectreGuard [10], ConTExT [27], and DOLMA [20].

SpecTerminator [15] is the modern synthesis of this line of techniques that delay unsafe speculative execution with a hardware tainting mechanism and a way to delay some operations. Yet the reported performance penalty of +6% has not been reproduced, as reported in [24].

To enhance flexibility, software can be given greater control through dedicated speculation barriers. Our own implementations are described in this paper, but it was not the first speculation barrier implementation.

In Context-Sensitive Fencing [30], the authors propose automatically injecting speculation barriers in the micro-ops generated by the frontend, depending on pre-specified security policies. An example policy is to inject a barrier between control flow instructions and loads. Speculation barriers have also been proposed by established vendors: Intel's `LFENCE` or ARM's `SB`; ARM has patented this latter speculation barrier. Unfortunately, as far as we know, there is no proper public analysis on placement policies and associated trade-offs between performance and security.

While these solutions are interesting, they suffer from two major issues. The first one is that they are hard to reproduce and therefore to compare. For example, InvisiSpec [35] self-reports a performance penalty of +72%, Efficient InvisiSpec [25] tries to reproduce this first paper and measures a +50% performance penalty, NDA [33] does the same and reports +32%. The papers also differ on what they consider secure: some target specific variants, some all variants known at the time, etc. In practice, they cannot be compared with respect to security.

The second issue is that they are not all relying on realistic assumptions. For example, ConTExT [27] requires annotating secret data by marking with a dedicated bit in each page table entry. This is actually a strong assumption, since we do not have the infrastructure today to do that at scale.

Finally, most (but not all) of these previous works build demonstrators using the gem5 simulator with x86. This makes it actually hard to evaluate whether the corresponding implementations are realistic.

Use of Formal Methods. Given the complexity of modern microarchitectures, how can we ensure that secrets are never speculatively accessed or leaked to a covert channel?

Some approaches tackle this challenge by establishing hardware-software contracts for speculative behavior. The work of [13] formalizes the interaction between information leakage models and speculative behavior, demonstrating that simply delaying speculative `load` instructions is insufficient; other speculative behaviors must also be controlled. Speculative taint tracking is shown to be an effective method for ensuring security.

ProSpeCT [6] implements this speculative behavior contract in hardware. It ensures that secret values cannot be speculatively leaked by enforcing constant-time execution. This approach has been implemented on the out-of-order core Proteus, with performance overheads ranging from 0% to 45%, depending on the frequency of secret-related operations and the program's instruction-level parallelism (ILP).

4   Selective Speculation Semantics

In this work, we assume that the microarchitecture has no way to determine whether data in memory or in a register is secret or public. In Spectre attacks, the microarchitectural control flow is arbitrary since speculative, possibly influenced by the attacker. Therefore, all `load` instructions are at risk of loading secret data, even if the program normally forbids it. As a countermeasure, we propose inserting speculation barriers, also called speculation fences, which are specific instructions that act on the speculative behavior of the microarchitecture. If `load` instructions are not speculative, the invariants of the program remain enforced, and secrets are only handled when allowed by the application. Speculation is controlled through the insertion of these fences by the compiler.

4.1   Fences Instructions Semantics

In this paper, we distinguish between speculation fences, serialization fences, and conditional (speculation) fences.

Serialization fences: A register-based serialization fence `fence.ser rd, rs1` has the following semantics:

1. **Predecessor Dependencies**: this fence instruction depends on register `rs1` to be executed. It cannot be executed if `rs1` is not available. If `rs1 = x0`, then the instruction depends on all architectural registers (`x1`-`x31`).
2. **Successor Dependencies**: subsequent instructions that use `rd` depend on this fence instruction. If `rd = x0`, then the core should assume that the fence instruction touched all architectural registers (`x1`-`x31`), even if no values were modified.

There is no functionality associated with a serialization fence. Architecturally, it is a `nop` (no-operation). It limits the possibility to reorder instructions past the fence, hence its name.

Therefore, the serialization fence reduces the possible divergences between the architectural and the microarchitectural control flows. It reduces but does not eliminate all possible divergences:

- **Reordering with respect to source-only or destination-only instructions**: an instruction that has only sources or destinations (such as branches notably) can be reordered since there is no dependency relation. A `fence.ser` following a `branch` can be executed before it.
- **Delta between register availability and execution**: the fact that registers are available, necessary to resolve a dependency, does not imply that execution is not speculative. For example, a branch instruction can have both its registers available, but the condition is not yet computed. In this case, speculative execution based on this branch condition is possible, even for a limited speculation window.

In this paper, we only consider register-based serialization instructions. Another possibility is to have an instruction-based serialization fence, where dependencies are established purely from program order: the fence depends on all previous instructions, and all later instructions depend on the fence. It is worth noting that in modern x86 cores, the `LFENCE` instruction is an instruction-based serialization fence, in addition to being a speculation fence.

Register-based ordering gives more possibilities for the microarchitecture to reorder instructions, by giving finer-grained constraints on instruction dependencies, thus increasing the performances of the solution.

Speculation Fences: A speculation fence is a serialization fence that completes execution only in a non-speculative state, i.e. when the core is certain that it will commit.

We define it as the instruction `fence.spec rd, rs1` with the following semantics in addition to the rules given for serialization fences (**1** and **2** are the same as for `fence.ser`).

3. **Non-speculative Execution**: The execution of `fence.spec` can only terminate in a non-speculative state, meaning that the core is certain that the instruction will eventually commit (taking into account exceptions, interrupts, etc.).

Conditional Speculation Fences: A conditional speculation fence, defined as the instruction `fence.cond rs1`, is designed to prevent the Spectre-PHT attack, which exploits a conditional branch as the source of speculation. This version of the fence follows a conditional branch and uses a predicate stored in `rs1` to determine whether the branch results in misspeculation. Hence, additional computation is required to establish a correct predicate value based on the condition of the branch, which is inserted by the compiler. The conditional speculation fence must implement the following behaviors:

1. **Terminate Speculative Window**: If the predicate evaluates to a value other than 0, the instruction stalls its execution until a non-speculative state is achieved.
2. **Successor Dependencies**: All subsequent instructions with a source register depend on the conditional speculation fence instruction (equivalent to previous cases where `rd = x0`).

5   Hardware Implementation of Fences

This section details the modifications applied to a modern RISC-V core to implement the different behaviors of the fence instructions previously described.

The target of our work is the NaxRiscv core [29], an out-of-order, superscalar processor with branch predictors. Built with SpinalHDL, the NaxRiscv project has a decentralized hardware design that simplifies the integration of new features using a plugin system.

First, some background on how each relevant component of the NaxRiscv operates will be provided. Then, we will detail the modifications needed to implement the fence semantics described in Subsect. 4.1.

5.1   NaxRiscv Description

To manage instruction flow, the processor uses a reorder buffer (ROB) where each instruction is tracked by a unique RobId. Instructions are added in program order using a `push` pointer and committed using a `pop` pointer once execution completes. The ROB ensures in-order commitment, preserving architectural consistency despite out-of-order execution, and enabling correct handling of exceptions.

The processor needs to maintain a list of the dependencies between the instructions that are being processed to enable out-of-order execution. This is done using the Issue Queue and the Dispatch Unit. The Issue Queue stores the decoded instructions prior to their execution; it also keeps a representation of the dependencies between all the instructions it stores. The Dispatch Unit controls which instructions enter and leave the queue. When inserting new instructions, the Dispatch Unit retrieves the RobIds of all instructions that write to the source registers of the instructions being pushed and then computes the dependencies for the new instruction. When instructions are ready and the corresponding execution units are available, the Dispatch Unit pops these instructions from the Issue Queue and sends them to the adequate execution unit. The number of instructions that can be popped from the Issue Queue each cycle depends on the number of available execution units.

Note that in the ROB and Issue Queue, the registers are not the architectural registers (`x0`, ..., `x31`) - which correspond to the programmer-visible registers defined by the instruction-set architecture (ISA) - but physical registers. Physical registers are part of the microarchitecture and are mapped to architectural registers in the Rename stage. They are used to avoid data hazards during out-of-order execution.

5.2   Fences Implementations

The implementation of the proposed fences requires modifications to various elements of the microarchitecture. We will discuss these modifications for each fence type in the NaxRiscv core.

Serialization Fences: To satisfy the predecessor dependency semantic, the Dispatch Unit monitors whether `rs1 = x0` when inserting a `fence.ser` instruction. If this is the case, it reads all entries in the Issue Queue and creates a dependency with all valid instructions that have a destination register. Similarly, the Issue Queue manages the successor dependencies with respect to `rd`. If a newly pushed instruction is a fence and has `rd = x0`, this means that all architectural registers (`x1` - `x31`) depend on it. To represent this, we add a new flag called `isFullFence` to the associated instruction slots in the Issue Queue and set it to True. Any incoming instruction will automatically depend on any instruction in the Issue Queue that has the `isFullFence` flag set to True. Our `fence.ser` implementation uses the physical register of `rs2` to temporarily store the value of the *old physical register* of `rd`. During the execution stage, this value is written to the new physical register of `rd`. This ensures that the destination architectural register remains unchanged, even after the Rename stage, and the normal program behavior is not altered. The use of `rs2` is not visible at the architectural level.

Speculation Fences: Speculation fences operate in a similar fashion to the serialization fences. The key difference is that speculation fences cannot complete their execution while in a speculative state, causing them to stall at a specific stage in the pipeline. As the NaxRiscv CPU does not differentiate between speculative and non-speculative execution (i.e. all instructions are executed speculatively), a **speculation detector** module has been implemented to identify whether an instruction is considered speculative (when we cannot be sure that it will be committed or not). It uses the ROB to determine if an older instruction capable of triggering speculation has not yet been committed. The **speculation detector** takes the `RobId` of an instruction as an input and returns a boolean value indicating whether the instruction is speculative.

We have implemented three different approaches to implement speculation fences, depending on how they stall when considered speculative.

Execute-Stall Fence. Speculation fences cannot exit the execution stage of the pipeline while in speculative mode, thanks to the speculation detector. This approach minimizes performance loss by delaying the stall until the last possible stage before execution. However, this method has a significant drawback: it can deadlock the pipeline under certain conditions. If a speculation fence instruction B is speculatively executed before an older one A:

- Instruction B stalls on its execution unit until it is no longer in a speculative mode.

- Instruction A waits for the execution unit to become available as it is currently in use by the instruction B.
- Instruction A enforces the execution order, ensuring that the instruction triggering the speculation executes only after it completes.

To avoid this effect, the Dispatch Unit adds dependencies between each fence instruction to enforce in-order execution of fence instructions and avoid the deadlock.

Dispatch-Stall fence. The stall can be applied at the dispatch stage, before the fences enter the execution stage. This enforces in-order execution of the fence instructions. The Dispatch Unit holds the instruction until the speculation detector confirms a non-speculative state.

Operand-Stall Fence. Another implementation, called the Operand-Stall Fence, deviates from the original semantics of speculative fences described in Subsect. 4.1. Nevertheless, this mechanism may offer an alternative perspective on speculative fences. In this implementation, the fences can be dispatched to an execution unit as soon as the source register `rs1` is committed. Instead of confirming the execution states of the instructions, this implementation prioritizes the architectural correctness of source registers. In other words, it ensures the convergence state of the source register before allowing the execution of the instructions. Thus, this implementation allows the instructions to execute speculatively, which diverges from the original semantics.

Conditional Speculation Fences: Conditional Fences (`fence.cond`) are unique among the added fence instructions, as they use only a source register `rs1`. During the dependency computation in the Dispatch Unit, each subsequent register automatically depends on all conditional fences present in the Issue Queue (similar to the previous `rd = x0`). The execution units read the predicate from `rs1`, as the behaviour of a conditional fence depends on its value. If `rs1` $\neq 0$ (signaling a misspeculation), the execute unit stalls until the `pop` pointer of ROB reaches the conditional fence's `RobId`, forcing the previous conditional branch to commit and trigger a rescheduling first. Unlike SLH [8], this technique halts speculative execution entirely, ensuring no speculative traces are left on the microarchitecture.

6 Security Policies to Insert Fences

The proposed fence instructions enable the evaluation of various strategies at the compilation level. As noted in Sect. 3.1, prior work on compiler-based Spectre mitigations has focused mainly on x86 and ARM architectures [24]. Some mitigations are straightforward enough to adapt to RISC-V architectures and serve as our initial performance references.

Since memory instructions are the primary source of leakage in most Spectre attacks, we implemented an LLVM pass similar to SESES [7] that inserts `fence.spec` instructions near memory operations. However, we must ask ourselves: if only load instructions must be hardened, do stores also need to be protected? Furthermore, should fences be placed before or after the target instructions? Also, could fences be inserted around end-of-branch blocks, calls, or indirect jumps? Each stage of a Spectre gadget plays a crucial role in executing a Spectre attack. The speculation and disclosure stages can be carried out using various instructions and may vary significantly between different microarchitectures. However, the acquisition stage can only be performed using an instruction capable of loading the secret into a register - a `load` instruction.

These considerations result in numerous policies based on the combinations of options, including the various fence semantics introduced earlier. An exhaustive list of these policies can be found in Table 1.

To replicate SESES behavior in the LLVM `RISC-V` back-end, we replaced `LFENCE` with our new instructions, leveraging their similar semantics. For instance, `specall_before_load` uses `fence.spec.all` (`fence.spec x0`, `x0`), while policies prefixed with ser replace `fence.spec` with `fence.ser`. We then modified this pass to handle the cases where `rd` and `rs1` are not equal to `x0`.

To measure performance costs, we implemented a `nop` policy inserting `nop`s (a pseudo-instruction for `addi x0`, `x0`, `0`), which advances the program counter without architectural impact. Despite its simplicity, it affects both security and performance, serving as a baseline.

We implemented `spec_after_load` for comparing the placement of fences after memory instructions with respect to placing them before. Additionally, the `dependency` approach adds fences with operands based on branch conditions, such as `fence.spec rd`, `rs1` (`spec_dep_load`). Basic optimizations prevent redundant protection of non-redefined registers within the same basic block.

SLH, introduced in Sect. 3.1, can also be implemented on `RISC-V` architectures. On x86, "misspeculation predicates" are updated with `cmov` instructions, which are immune to prediction. Since `cmov` is absent in base `RISC-V`, it can be emulated using bitwise operations like `slt`, setting `rd` to 0 or 1 based on comparisons. Avoiding conditional branches prevents new speculation points, though this requires additional instructions compared to ^{cmov}.

SLH was previously translated for `RISC-V` by Moein Ghaniyoun [11] in the LLVM back-end. We modified their implementation to create `slh` and `slh-ip` policies, where the `-ip` suffix denotes *Inter-Procedural* predicate transfer via the stack pointer.

A conditional fence can be used to enhance this strategy: instead of poisoning the load's value or address, a$^{fence.cond}$ at the start of each block uses the SLH predicate (if a load exists) to prevent speculative execution of the entire block, ensuring no transient microarchitectural states. This can also be extended interprocedurally, forming the `spec_cond_ip` policy.

Gadget counts in Table 1 are the same ones as used to generate Fig. 3 but different than in Fig. 2. Indeed, in Fig. 2 two gadgets occurring at the same acquisition address are counted twice if they have different speculation sources, but are counted once in Table 1 and Fig. 3.

Performance is measured as the geometric mean of the number of hot cycles (after the warmup) for the benchmark suite.

7   Benchmark Results

To evaluate the effectiveness of the proposed fence semantics and insertion policies, we first need hardware that implements the former. The three different types of stalling mechanisms (execute-, dispatch- and operand-stall) were added in the Naxriscv core, making three different processors. We also need a set of benchmark programs to evaluate the potential security and performance implications of our methods. We have selected the Embench suite [5] for such purposes, as it is open-source and exercises a wide range of applications. Each program in the benchmark suite was evaluated using each processor and each fence insertion policy previously described. A "hardware-policy" configuration therefore corresponds to the specific benchmark binaries compiled with said policy and run on the simulator corresponding to said hardware. The simulations were carried out using the Verilator simulator, and execution traces were collected in a format closely resembling O3PipeView from Gem5. From these traces, different analysis passes were run to extract metrics: instruction mixes, performance, security, misspeculation windows, etc. These traces also enable the extraction of the microarchitectural state in case of any detected vulnerability.

Since execution traces only represent executed code, our results only apply to these executions. In particular, the absence of any Spectre gadget in the traces is no proof that no gadgets could appear, only that they have a low probability of doing so.

7.1   Security Metrics

Before analyzing the traces, we must define a security metric. Most of the previous work considers security as a binary value; the execution is either safe or unsafe with respect to a set of exploits (Spectre-PHT, Spectre-BTB, etc.). We propose a different strategy that is not tied to any exploit. We identify a Spectre gadget as the combination of 1) a misspeculation trigger, an instruction that initiates a misspeculation window, 2) a secret acquisition via a `load` instruction, and 3) the secret disclosure, where a value depending on the secret is leaked. In our case, a disclosed value is any value used as an issued `load` address, an issued `store` address or value, or an issued `branch` operand. During trace analysis, taint tracking is used for all potential secrets resulting from a `load` up to a disclosing instruction. To accurately assess policies that poison addresses (e.g. `slh`), we detect the cases where `load` instructions target the null address and rule out these gadget cases.

We consider that any such gadget *could* lead to an exploit and must be prevented.

It is possible to count the number of these Spectre gadgets in the execution traces for all benchmarks for each configuration. A gadget is identified by the address of the acquisition instruction, meaning that if two gadgets found in the execution trace share the same acquisition instruction, they are only counted once. This is required since all our benchmarks consist of a loop performing some operation: the same gadget may be found many times in the traces for each iteration of the loop. It would be a measure of the benchmark loop count, not a measure of security, if we counted repeating gadgets.

For any hardware-policy configuration, the security metric is the sum of Spectre gadgets detected across all benchmarks for this configuration.

Figure 2 depicts the proportions of speculation sources for the Spectre gadgets that were detected for several hardware-policy configurations.

We can observe in Fig. 2 that most of the gadgets found start from a misspeculated branch direction (*PHT*). It is also worth noting that some implementations are able to mitigate all the gadgets while others focus on disabling only some kinds of gadgets. For instance, `serall_*` policies will serialize store and load instructions, preventing any *STL* gadgets.

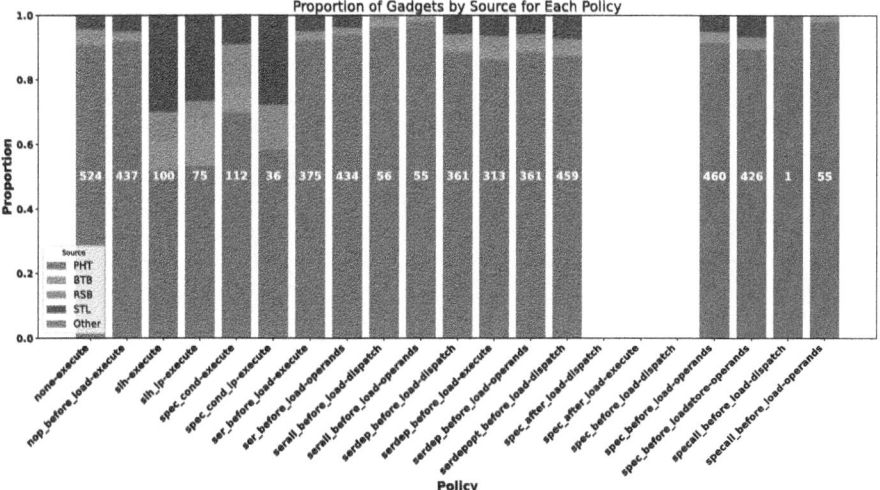

Fig. 2. Gadget speculation sources, the center number is the gadgets count

7.2 Security-Performance Trade-Off

Figure 3 represents where the different hardware-policy configurations stand in terms of gadget-count to performance loss ratio, compared to an unmodified processor. It is a graphical representation of the data contained in Table 1. We can observe a well-defined Pareto front that spans from the best-performing, unprotected configuration to the worst-performing, most-protected configuration. The latter is equivalent to in-order execution, according to McFarlin et al. [21].

Table 1. List of evaluated policies and results

Policy name	Description	Gadget counts			Benchmark duration geomean (hot cycles)		
		execute	dispatch	operands	execute	dispatch	operands
none	No policy applied (baseline).	514			3.6 M		
nop_before_load	Insert nop instruction before each load.	430			3.8 M		
ser_before_load	Insert fence.ser rA, rA instruction before each load rB, offset(rA).	369	428	428	3.9 M	3.8 M	3.8 M
serall_before_load	Insert fence.ser x0, x0 before each load.	16	55	55	7.0 M	5.8 M	5.8 M
serdep_before_load	Insert fence.ser rB, rA with rB used as address by the following load and rA register from the "most dominant branching instruction operands". It is a naive approach to add serialization between loads and most dominant branching instruction if there is one.	306	355	355	4.3 M	4.0 M	4.0 M
slh	SLH implementation for RISCV.	100			5.1 M		
slh_ip	SLH implementation with inter-procedural predicate transfer via a stack pointer.	75			5.3 M		
spec_after_load	Insert fence.spec rB, rB instruction after each load rB, offset(rA).	0	0	0	6.5 M	6.9 M	6.6 M
spec_before_load	Insert fence.spec rA, rA instruction before each load rB, offset(rA).	0	0	451	7.4 M	7.4 M	5.4 M
spec_before_loadstore	Insert fence.spec rA, rA instruction before each load rB, offset(rA) or store rB, offset(rA).	3	3	418	8.1 M	8.0 M	5.6 M
spec_cond	Insert $f^{fence.cond}$ rA at the beginning of each basic block that contains^{load}. It takes as operand rA, an always updated predicate computed as in slh policy.	108			5.2 M		
spec_cond_ip	As spec_cond with inter-procedural predicate transfer.	36			7.0 M		
specall_before_load	Insert $f^{fence.spec}$ x0, x0 before each^{load}.	0	1	55	8.4 M	8.2 M	5.8 M

Gadget counts in Table 1 are the same ones as used to generate Fig. 3 but different than in Fig. 2. Indeed, in Fig. 2 two gadgets occurring at the same acquisition address are counted twice if they have different speculation sources, but are counted once in Table 1 and Fig. 3. Performance is measured as the geometric mean of the number of hot cycles (after the warmup) for the benchmark suite.

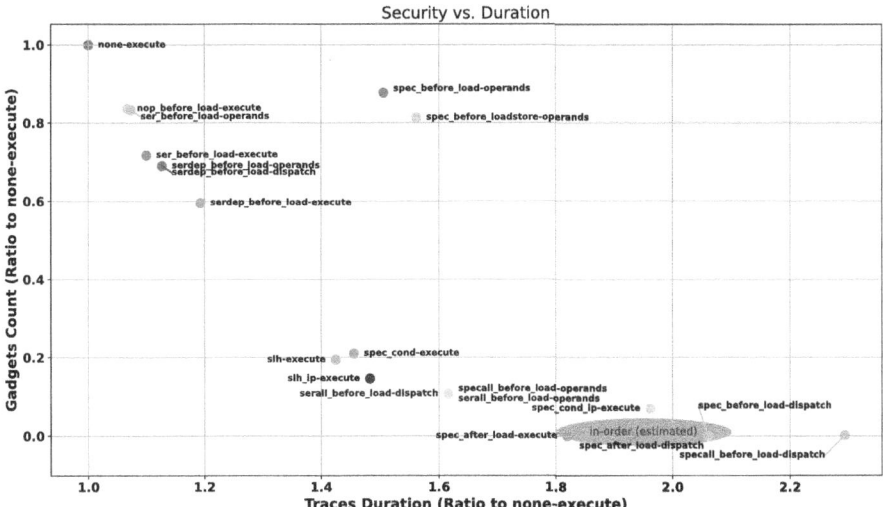

Fig. 3. The hardware-policy configurations according to both their security and performance metrics.

The `slh` policy, which does not use speculation barriers, is on the Pareto front. But this policy is not exempt from gadgets, an expected result since it targets the PHT variants only. Less expected, we can see in Fig. 2 that numerous PHT-variant gadgets are still present. Upon closer inspection, permitted by our tooling, it appears that most of these gadgets are due to the `slh` inter-procedural predicate being loaded from the stack. Furthermore, `slh` is done before register allocation with spilling that introduces new unmitigated `load`s. Our tests correctly determine that these `load`s could potentially be hijacked by an attacker, thus forming a Spectre gadget. More generally, proving a correct compiler mitigation pass can never be a perfect solution: the arbitrary control flow in the microarchitecture does not care about the proofs on the binary.

Our policy `spec_cond-execute` implements the same predicate technique but, using our new instruction `fence.cond`, has a security-performance trade-off close to `slh`. However, instead of poisoning load pointers, the `fence.cond` disables any speculative execution, incurring a slight overhead compared to `slh`.

Since widely different hardening techniques, compiler- or hardware-based, are aligned on Fig. 3, it is clear that the ability to execute memory requests speculatively is the main performance driver for the NaxRiscv core. In our case, configurations that achieve 0 gadgets have performance levels equivalent to those of an in-order core. **The indiscriminate use of speculation fences, which is the only viable strategy without microarchitectural knowledge of which data is confidential, does not allow for secure execution at out-of-order performance levels.**

Since microarchitectural control flow can be arbitrary, and thus any fence might be speculatively bypassed, one might expect that no policy could prevent all gadgets. Yet some policies, such as `spec_after_load-execute`, have successfully prevented all gadgets in our benchmarks. Therefore, even if no speculation barrier-based policy can guarantee the complete absence of gadgets, it may still offer strong security in practice.

7.3 Area Comparison

Since all the changes that were brought to the Naxriscv core are synthesizable, we can also measure the hardware costs of the proposed mechanisms. As a baseline, we considered the core configured as dual-issue with a 32-level deep Issue Queue, with support for single and double precision floating point operations, compressed instructions, and four execution units in total. A Xilinx XC7K325T was used as the target field-programmable gate array (FPGA), and synthesis was done using Xilinx Vivado 2023.1. In its base configuration, the NaxRiscv uses $\approx$ 26k look-up tables (LUTs) and $\approx$ 15k flip-flops (FFs), and the maximum operating frequency reported by Vivado is 51.6 MHz. As shown in Table 2, the overhead is relatively significant with +6.5k LUTs or +25% at best for the `execute-stall` hardware variant. The costs include the addition of an execution unit dedicated to our fences and the speculation detector ($\approx$ 0.9k LUTs).

When analysing the critical paths of our modified cores, we can observe that the modifications of the Dispatch Unit and the addition of a speculation detector play a major role in the operating frequency degradation. The speculation detector has to perform chained comparisons of all the possible `RobIds`, adding a significant amount of logic on the critical path.

Table 2. FPGA Resources Comparison for Fence Implementations

Fence Implementation	LUTs	FFs	FMAX
Baseline	25811	15105	51.6 MHz
`execute-stall`	32375 (+25%)	16241 (+8%)	38.1 MHz
`dispatch-stall`	29076 (+13%)	15437 (+2%)	50.0 MHz
`operand-stall`	31024 (+20%)	15318 (+1%)	32.9 MHz

7.4 Limitations

Given the significant effort required to experiment with both custom out-of-order cores and custom compilers, some of our choices have been dictated by technical feasibility and may limit the scope of our results.

First, we must note that, to achieve a secure implementation, the number of gadgets must be 0. Any other value implies that an attacker could potentially exploit the specific conditions that result in a gadget. Our security metric serves merely as an indication that the implementation is secure, not as a definitive proof.

Also, it is possible that a bigger Naxriscv configuration, with a wider issue width and a larger Issue Queue, could lead to better performance for the same level of security by enabling more reordering possibilities. However, in our hardware implementations that strictly adhere to the `fence.spec` semantics, fences cannot be reordered relative to one another, imposing a strict limit on reordering possibilities overall.

Finally, a known mitigation is `delay-on-miss`, where the core delays the execution of speculated^{load}s only if the target is not in cache memory. This countermeasure cannot be efficiently evaluated in our settings: the Embench benchmarks focus on hot execution paths, where instructions and data are already in cache if possible. But the `delay-on-miss` mitigation has a different threat model: that data in cache memories is public. In our own threat model where data in cache could be confidential, the `delay-on-miss` therefore appears as a new point that coincides with `none-execute`: fast and non-secure, which has been confirmed experimentally.

8 Conclusion

Despite the strong understanding of how Spectre leaks data, research into mitigation continues to face difficulties in providing complete protection against this vulnerability while maintaining a reasonable performance level. In this evaluation of selective speculation through speculation barriers, every `load` instruction is assumed to potentially access sensitive data and requires protection. However, results reveal that this approach is not efficient in such an attack model. By providing speculation barriers, the ISA shifts the responsibility for security to the developer and compiler, which are tasked with using them correctly. However, our results suggest that there is no way to use them correctly and efficiently, which significantly hinders their practical adoption. We recommend that any ISA specification for speculation barriers be accompanied by a thorough evaluation of their security and performance implications. Besides, the performance impact is so significant that adopting an in-order architecture may be a more viable solution for complete protection against Spectre. The main challenge of selective speculation is identifying which instruction or data must be restricted from speculative execution to avoid data leak.

Lack of insight into the program's secrets forces the hardware to overprotect itself, resulting in unnecessary performance losses. Yet, could this trade-off between performance and security be overcome if the architecture had precise knowledge of sensitive data?

References

1. Abdul Kadir, M.F., Wong, J.K., Ab Wahab, F., Abidin Bharun, A.F.A., Mohamed, M.A., Zakaria, A.H.: Retpoline technique for mitigating spectre attack. In: 2019 6th International Conference on Electrical and Electronics Engineering (ICEEE), pp. 96–101 (2019). https://doi.org/10.1109/ICEEE2019.2019.00026

2. Acıiçmez, O., Koç, Ç.K., Seifert, J.-P.: Predicting secret keys via branch prediction. In: Abe, M. (ed.) CT-RSA 2007. LNCS, vol. 4377, pp. 225–242. Springer, Heidelberg (2006). https://doi.org/10.1007/11967668_15

3. Barber, K., Bacha, A., Zhou, L., Zhang, Y., Teodorescu, R.: Specshield: shielding speculative data from microarchitectural covert channels. In: 28th International Conference on Parallel Architectures and Compilation Techniques, PACT 2019, Seattle, WA, USA, 23–26 September 2019, pp. 151–164. IEEE (2019). https://doi.org/10.1109/PACT.2019.00020

4. Bernstein, D.J.: Cache-timing attacks on AES (2005)

5. Burgess, A., et al.: Embench IoT: open benchmarks for embedded platforms (2020). https://github.com/embench/embench-iot. https://github.com/embench/embench-iot, gitHub repository

6. Daniel, L., Bognar, M., Noorman, J., Bardin, S., Rezk, T., Piessens, F.: Prospect: provably secure speculation for the constant-time policy. In: Calandrino, J.A., Troncoso, C. (eds.) 32nd USENIX Security Symposium, USENIX Security 2023, Anaheim, CA, USA, 9–11 August 2023, pp. 7161–7178. USENIX Association (2023). https://www.usenix.org/conference/usenixsecurity23/presentation/daniel

7. Developers, L.: LLVM SESES - speculative execution side effect suppression. https://groups.google.com/g/llvm-dev/c/EL8rUhvRCgo. Accessed 25 Oct 2024

8. Speculative load hardening. https://llvm.org/docs/SpeculativeLoadHardening.html. Accessed 25 Oct 2024

9. Escouteloup, M., Lashermes, R., Fournier, J., Lanet, J.: Under the dome: preventing hardware timing information leakage. In: Grosso, V., Pöppelmann, T. (eds.) Smart Card Research and Advanced Applications - 20th International Conference, CARDIS 2021, Lübeck, Germany, 11–12 November 2021, Revised Selected Papers. Lecture Notes in Computer Science, vol. 13173, pp. 233–253. Springer (2021). https://doi.org/10.1007/978-3-030-97348-3_13

10. Fustos, J., Farshchi, F., Yun, H.: Spectreguard: an efficient data-centric defense mechanism against spectre attacks. In: Proceedings of the 56th Annual Design Automation Conference 2019, DAC 2019, Las Vegas, NV, USA, 02–06 June 2019, p. 61. ACM (2019). https://doi.org/10.1145/3316781.3317914

11. Ghaniyoun, M.: Moein ghaniyoun's website. https://moeinghaniyoun.github.io/. Accessed 25 Oct 2024

12. Gras, B., Razavi, K., Bos, H., Giuffrida, C.: TLBleed: when protecting your CPU caches is not enough. In: Black Hat USA (2018). Slides=https://i.blackhat.com/us-18/Thu-August-9/us-18-Gras-TLBleed-When-Protecting-Your-CPU-Caches-is-Not-Enough.pdf Web=https://vusec.net/projects/tlbleed

13. Guarnieri, M., Köpf, B., Reineke, J., Vila, P.: Hardware-software contracts for secure speculation. In: 42nd IEEE Symposium on Security and Privacy, SP 2021, San Francisco, CA, USA, 24–27 May 2021, pp. 1868–1883. IEEE (2021). https://doi.org/10.1109/SP40001.2021.00036

14. Hu, G., He, Z., Lee, R.B.: SoK: hardware defenses against speculative execution attacks. In: 2021 International Symposium on Secure and Private Execution Environment Design (SEED), Washington, DC, USA, 20–21 September 2021, pp. 108–120. IEEE (2021). https://doi.org/10.1109/SEED51797.2021.00023

15. Jin, H., He, Z., Qiang, W.: Specterminator: blocking speculative side channels based on instruction classes on RISC-V. ACM Trans. Archit. Code Optim. 20(1), 15:1–15:26 (2023). https://doi.org/10.1145/3566053

16. Khasawneh, K.N., Koruyeh, E.M., Song, C., Evtyushkin, D., Ponomarev, D., Abu-Ghazaleh, N.B.: Safespec: banishing the spectre of a meltdown with leakage-free

speculation. In: Proceedings of the 56th Annual Design Automation Conference 2019, DAC 2019, Las Vegas, NV, USA, 02–06 June 2019, p. 60. ACM (2019). https://doi.org/10.1145/3316781.3317903

17. Kiriansky, V., Lebedev, I.A., Amarasinghe, S.P., Devadas, S., Emer, J.S.: DAWG: a defense against cache timing attacks in speculative execution processors. In: 51st Annual IEEE/ACM International Symposium on Microarchitecture, MICRO 2018, Fukuoka, Japan, 20–24 October 2018, pp. 974–987. IEEE Computer Society (2018). https://doi.org/10.1109/MICRO.2018.00083

18. Kocher, P., et al.: Spectre attacks: exploiting speculative execution. In: 2019 IEEE Symposium on Security and Privacy (SP), pp. 1–19 (2019). https://doi.org/10.1109/SP.2019.00002

19. Lipp, M., et al.: Meltdown: reading kernel memory from user space. In: 27th USENIX Security Symposium (USENIX Security 2018) (2018)

20. Loughlin, K., et al.: DOLMA: securing speculation with the principle of transient non-observability. In: Bailey, M.D., Greenstadt, R. (eds.) 30th USENIX Security Symposium, USENIX Security 2021, 11–13 August 2021, pp. 1397–1414. USENIX Association (2021). https://www.usenix.org/conference/usenixsecurity21/presentation/loughlin

21. McFarlin, D.S., Tucker, C., Zilles, C.B.: Discerning the dominant out-of-order performance advantage: is it speculation or dynamism? In: Sarkar, V., Bodík, R. (eds.) Architectural Support for Programming Languages and Operating Systems, ASPLOS 2013, Houston, TX, USA, 16–20 March 2013, pp. 241–252. ACM (2013). https://doi.org/10.1145/2451116.2451143

22. Percival, C.: Cache missing for fun and profit (2005)

23. Phoronix: Intel cxl r lvi benchmarking. https://www.phoronix.com/review/intel-cxlr-lvi. Accessed 25 Oct 2024

24. Randal, A.: This is how you lose the transient execution war. CoRR abs/2309.03376 (2023). https://doi.org/10.48550/arxiv.2309.03376

25. Sakalis, C., Kaxiras, S., Ros, A., Jimborean, A., Själander, M.: Efficient invisible speculative execution through selective delay and value prediction. In: Manne, S.B., Hunter, H.C., Altman, E.R. (eds.) Proceedings of the 46th International Symposium on Computer Architecture, ISCA 2019, Phoenix, AZ, USA, 22–26 June 2019, pp. 723–735. ACM (2019). https://doi.org/10.1145/3307650.3322216

26. van Schaik, S., et al.: RIDL: rogue in-flight data load. In: S&P (2019)

27. Schwarz, M., Lipp, M., Canella, C., Schilling, R., Kargl, F., Gruss, D.: Context: a generic approach for mitigating spectre. In: 27th Annual Network and Distributed System Security Symposium, NDSS 2020, San Diego, California, USA, 23–26 February 2020. The Internet Society (2020). https://www.ndss-symposium.org/ndss-paper/context-a-generic-approach-for-mitigating-spectre/

28. Shin, Y., Kim, H.C., Kwon, D., Jeong, J., Hur, J.: Unveiling hardware-based data prefetcher, a hidden source of information leakage. In: Lie, D., Mannan, M., Backes, M., Wang, X. (eds.) Proceedings of the 2018 ACM SIGSAC Conference on Computer and Communications Security, CCS 2018, Toronto, ON, Canada, 15–19 October 2018, pp. 131–145. ACM (2018). https://doi.org/10.1145/3243734.3243736

29. SpinalHDL: Naxriscv: an out-of-order RISC-V CPU core (2024). https://github.com/SpinalHDL/NaxRiscv. Accessed 11 July 2024

30. Taram, M., Venkat, A., Tullsen, D.M.: Mitigating speculative execution attacks via context-sensitive fencing. IEEE Des. Test 39(4), 49–57 (2022). https://doi.org/10.1109/MDAT.2022.3152633

31. Van Bulck, J., et al.: LVI: hijacking transient execution through microarchitectural load value injection. In: 2020 IEEE Symposium on Security and Privacy (SP), pp. 54–72 (2020). https://doi.org/10.1109/SP40000.2020.00089

32. Vassena, M., et al.: Automatically eliminating speculative leaks from cryptographic code with blade. Proc. ACM Program. Lang. **5**(POPL), 1–30 (2021). https://doi.org/10.1145/3434330

33. Weisse, O., Neal, I., Loughlin, K., Wenisch, T.F., Kasikci, B.: NDA: preventing speculative execution attacks at their source. In: Proceedings of the 52nd Annual IEEE/ACM International Symposium on Microarchitecture, MICRO 2019, Columbus, OH, USA, 12–16 October 2019, pp. 572–586. ACM (2019). https://doi.org/10.1145/3352460.3358306

34. Wistoff, N., Schneider, M., Gürkaynak, F.K., Benini, L., Heiser, G.: Microarchitectural timing channels and their prevention on an open-source 64-bit RISC-V core. In: Design, Automation & Test in Europe Conference & Exhibition, DATE 2021, Grenoble, France, 1–5 February 2021, pp. 627–632. IEEE (2021). https://doi.org/10.23919/DATE51398.2021.9474214

35. Yan, M., Choi, J., Skarlatos, D., Morrison, A., Fletcher, C.W., Torrellas, J.: Invisispec: making speculative execution invisible in the cache hierarchy. In: 51st Annual IEEE/ACM International Symposium on Microarchitecture, MICRO 2018, Fukuoka, Japan, 20–24 October 2018, pp. 428–441. IEEE Computer Society (2018). https://doi.org/10.1109/MICRO.2018.00042

36. Yu, J., Yan, M., Khyzha, A., Morrison, A., Torrellas, J., Fletcher, C.W.: Speculative taint tracking (STT): a comprehensive protection for speculatively accessed data. IEEE Micro **40**(3), 81–90 (2020). https://doi.org/10.1109/MM.2020.2985359

Do We Still Need Canaries in the Coal Mine? Measuring Shadow Stack Effectiveness in Countering Stack Smashing

Hugo Depuydt[1], Merve Gülmez[2], Thomas Nyman[3],
and Jan Tobias Mühlberg[4(✉)]

[1] ENS Rennes, Rennes, France
hugo.depuydt@ens-rennes.fr
[2] Ericsson Security Research, Stockholm, Sweden
merve.gulmez@ericsson.com
[3] Ericsson Product Security, Stockholm, Sweden
thomas.nyman@ericsson.com
[4] Université Libre de Bruxelles, Brussels, Belgium
jan.tobias.muehlberg@ulb.be

Abstract. Stack canaries and shadow stacks are widely deployed mitigations to memory-safety vulnerabilities. While stack canaries are introduced by the compiler and rely on sentinel values placed between variables and control data, shadow stack implementations protect return addresses explicitly and rely on hardware features available in modern processor designs for efficiency. In this paper we investigate whether stack canaries and shadow stacks provide similar levels of protections against sequential stack-based overflows. Based on the Juliet test suite, we evaluate whether 64-bit x86 (x86-64) systems benefit from enabling stack canaries in addition to the x86-64 shadow stack enforcement. We observe divergence in overflow detection rates between the GCC and Clang compilers and across optimization levels, which we attribute to differences in stack layouts generated by the compilers. We also find that x86-64 shadow stack implementations are more effective and outperform stack canaries when combined with a stack-protector-like stack layout. We implement and evaluate an enhancement to the Clang x86-64 shadow stack instrumentation that improves the shadow stack detection accuracy based on this observation.

1 Introduction

The urgency of mitigating memory-safety vulnerabilities in C and C++ software has grown under increasing regulatory scrutiny [25]. Memory-safety issues are one of the oldest problems in computer security and remain a persistent challenge despite decades of advances in both offensive and defensive techniques [29]. Stack canaries [12] stand out as one of the earliest systematic mitigations to achieve widespread adoption. In this paper, we reassess stack canaries in light of modern hardware-assisted mitigations, particularly shadow stacks [8], now operational in commodity x86-64 systems [21,22].

© The Author(s), under exclusive license to Springer Nature Switzerland AG 2025
M. Dalla Preda et al. (Eds.): ARES 2025, LNCS 15993, pp. 193–205, 2025.
https://doi.org/10.1007/978-3-032-00627-1_10

Stack canaries—a reference to the historic practice of bringing canary birds into coal mines to alert miners of toxic gases—are sentinel values placed between local variables and control data on the stack to detect buffer overflows. Shadow stacks, in contrast, specifically protect function return addresses, preventing exploits such as return-oriented programming (ROP) [27] that hijack a program's control flow. While shadow stacks target a different threat model, both techniques defend against sequential overflows that corrupt the stack canary or return address. We hypothesize that, with modern compiler optimizations omitting other control data from stack frames, stack canaries and shadow stacks offer comparable protection against sequential overflows.

This Paper and Contributions. This paper investigates whether conventional stack canaries are redundant in applications where hardware-assisted shadow stacks are enabled. We evaluate the effectiveness of both techniques on modern x86-64 systems using the NIST Juliet C/C++ Test Suite [7] which contains a wide range of C/C++ code examples with buffer-overflows among the 118 Common Weakness Enumeration (CWE) categories the suite covers. Our key contributions and findings include:

1. **Systematic evaluation between GCC and Clang.** We evaluate the effectiveness and performance of stack canaries and x86-64 shadow stack in GCC and Clang and show differences in the detection accuracy between the compilers. Across our sample set, Clang demonstrates a better detection rate with stack canaries than GCC, while shadow stacks alone detect significantly fewer buffer overflows compared to stack canaries. We further investigate the reasons for this difference.
2. **Impact of compiler stack layouts.** The stack layout generated by the compiler has a significant impact on detection accuracy for both stack canaries and shadow stack. The stack layout varies between the different compilers, the level of program optimizations used, and between different variants of the stack-canary instrumentation, i.e., the different option variants in the `-fstack-protector` family.
3. **Enhancements to Clang's shadow stack support.** To enhance the protection the x86-64 shadow stack offers against sequential buffer overflows, we propose new Clang compiler options that emulate stack-protector layouts while relying on shadow stack checks. Our evaluation shows these new options improve detection accuracy while allowing stack canary checks to be omitted and incur only a small performance degradation ($\approx 1.6\%$ and $\approx 0.4\%$ on the SPEC CPU 2017 intrate and intspeed test suites respectively) which is lower than that of the corresponding stack canaries ($\approx 3\%$ and $\approx 3.3\%$, when applied to all functions) and comparable to that of conventional x86-64 shadow stacks ($\approx 1.5\%$ and $\approx 0.6\%$).

Our observations have already been shared with security researchers in the GCC and Clang communities, with whom we confirmed that our findings can be disclosed and that the compiler features are working as intended. An extended version of this paper with additional technical details is available as [14].

2   Background

Over half a century since their discovery [2], memory-safety vulnerabilities have become the most prevalent class of software vulnerability [25]. Major software manufacturers, such as Microsoft and Google [16], attribute up to 70% of vulnerabilities discovered in their products to memory-safety issues [16, 24]. Examples of vulnerabilities, attacks, and outages attributed to memory-safety issues include the Heartbleed bug in OpenSSL [28], the BLASTPASS exploit chain used to deliver commercial spyware [9], and the CrowdStrike outage of 2024 [13].

2.1   Stack Canaries

As exploitation techniques for memory-safety vulnerabilities such as buffers overflows became prevalent, research into countermeasures resulted in several mitigation schemes of which *stack canaries* were eventually integrated into mainstream compilers [17, 31]. Stack canaries detect a stack buffer overflow before the execution of malicious code can occur: A function's stack layout is instrumented with canary values between local variables and the return address. A contiguous buffer overflow modifies the stack canary before corrupting the return address. A check inserted by the compiler before returning from a function detects if the canary has been modified and calls an error-handling routine, `__stack_chk_fail()`, that typically terminates the program, rather than returning with a corrupt return address. On x86-64 Linux with the GNU C library (glibc), the stack canary is a 64-bit random value with the final bytes zeroed to make it simultaneously act as a terminator canary. A survey of deployed compiler-based mitigations indicates that stack canaries are enabled in 85% of desktop binaries [32].

Allocation Placement. The placement of allocations in the stack frame relative to the stack canary and saved register values in the frame record is significant for the overflow detection efficacy of stack canaries. Both GCC and Clang use the following rules when deciding allocation placement for local variables with stack protector [23]:

- Large arrays and structures containing large arrays are nearest to the canary.
- Small arrays and structures containing small arrays are next nearest to the canary.
- Variables that have had their address taken are third nearest to the canary.
- Other variables whose sizes are known at compile time are further.
- Dynamically-sized variables, such as C99-style arrays, are the furthest.

Jiang et al. [20] observe that GCC and Clang can generate different layouts for allocation placement even when the stack protector feature is enabled and identify one instance in the RecIPE memory error defense benchmark where the differences in the relative placement of an allocations between GCC and Clang result in different outcomes in a benchmark test case.

2.2 Shadow Stacks

A shadow stack [8] is a mechanism to protect a function's stored return address while it resides on the call stack. To achieve this, a copy of the return address is stored in a separate, isolated region of memory area that is not accessible to the attacker. Before the function returns, its stored return address is compared against the protected copy on the shadow stack to ensure the original address has not been modified, for example as a result of a buffer overflow. If there is a mismatch between the return address on the call stack and its copy on the shadow stack, program execution is terminated.

By protecting the integrity of return addresses, shadow stacks ensure that returning from function calls leads back to the respective call site, a form of backward-edge Control-Flow Integrity (CFI) [1]. Attacks that violate CFI have been demonstrated at different levels of semantic granularity, across programming languages, and in the presence of defensive mechanisms [4–6,15,19,26]. The prevalence of ROP, in particular, have prompted processor manufacturers to incorporate hardware support for shadows stacks into all major processor architectures including x86-64 [10], AArch64 [11], and RISC-V [30]. On x86-64 hardware shadow-stack support is provided by Intel's Control-flow Enforcement Technology (CET) as well as AMD's Shadow Stack hardware features. At the time of writing, recent releases of commodity Linux distributions, such as Ubuntu 18.04 ship with the necessary software support for x86-64 shadow stacks, but software built with shadow stack support (`-fcf-protection=return` in GCC 8.0.1 and Clang 7.0.0 and later) must explicitly opt-in to shadow stack enforcement.

Comparison of Stack Canaries and x86-64 Shadow Stack. Table 1 shows a high-level comparison between stack canaries and the x86-64 shadow stack. The x86-64 shadow stack operates as a mechanism similar to stack canaries to protect the return address. However, due to its placement, the x86-64 shadow stack cannot protect the frame pointer, whereas stack canaries detect the corruption of the frame pointer and the return address. Stack canaries rely on heuristics to determine which functions receive the canary instrumentation based on the option shown in Table 1 (with the exception of `-fstack-protector-all` which applies to all functions). The x86-64 shadow stack applies implicitly to all functions. Stack canaries will detect any contiguous stack buffer overflows that overwrite the canary value. The canary check can be bypassed if the canary value becomes known to an adversary who can overflow the buffer and overwrite the canary with its original value, or if the buffer overflow is not contiguous the adversary can "skip" over the canary without overwriting it. The x86-64 shadow stack, in contrast, can prevent the replacement of the stored return address with arbitrary, or mismatched return addresses regardless of which kind of write primitive is used to manipulate the contents of the call stack.

Table 1. Comparison between stack canaries and the x86-64 shadow stack

Compiler option	Protection of frame record		Characteristics	
	Frame pointer	Return address	Protection coverage	Enforcement model
Stack Canaries				
`-fstack-protector`	✓	✓	Heuristic[1]	Probabilistic
`-fstack-protector-strong`	✓	✓	Heuristic[2]	Probabilistic
`-fstack-protector-all`	✓	✓	All functions	Probabilistic
Shadow stack				
`-fcf-protection=return`	✗	✓	All functions	Deterministic

[1]: `-fstack-protector` applies stack canaries to any function with character arrays that equal or exceed the `ssp-buffer-size` setting set via `-param=ssp-buffer-size` (8 by default).

[2]: `-fstack-protector-strong` applies stack canaries to any function that 1) takes the address of any of its local variables on the right-hand-side of an assignment or as part of a function argument, or 2) allocates a local array, or a struct or union which contains an array, regardless of the type of length of the array, or 3) has explicit local register variables.

3   Methodology

An often overlooked problem in validating compiler-based hardening features is test coverage and assurance of correctness. In normal application development, the codebase is finite and known; developers focus on ensuring that all code paths within their application are tested and function correctly. A compiler, in contrast, is used by countless developers to build a variety of applications. In reality, most security hardening features are tested by just a small number of regression or unit tests [3]. Even widely deployed features, such as stack canaries, can exhibit gaps that affect their effectiveness [18] as applying them to large amounts of code successfully does not necessarily establish their effectiveness; it just demonstrates the feature does not interfere with the normal operation of the code. To evaluate effectiveness, a common approach is to use vulnerable programs, i.e., known Common Vulnerability Enumerations (CVEs). However, CVE-based evaluation is limited both in scope, granularity, and scalability as proof-of-concept exploits are available for relatively few CVEs. A more systematic approach is to use a benchmark suite such as Juliet [7]. Previous work by Jiang et al. [20] focuses on evaluating different defenses across different types of memory locations, rather than over varying stack layouts and omit the x86-64 shadow stack from their evaluation. To the best of a knowledge, no prior work has attempted to perform a quantitative comparison of stack canaries and the x86-64 shadow stack.

3.1 Goal and Problem Statement

The goal of our evaluation is to answer the following research questions:

RQ1. Are the detection rates of stack canaries and the x86-64 shadow stack consistent across different compilers in large-scale tests.

RQ2. Is the detection rate of contiguous, stack-based buffer overflows comparable between the x86-64 shadow stack canaries.

RQ3. Is the impact on software performance in real-world use cases comparable between the x86-64 shadow stack and stack canaries.

Finally, since it is known that the efficacy of stack canaries is affected by the relative placement of a function's allocations on the call stack (see Sect. 2.1) we evaluate the impact of similar placement heuristics applied for stack canaries on the detection rate of the x86-64 shadow stack:

RQ4. Is the detection rate of the x86-64 shadow stack improved by a -fstack-protector-like stack frame layout?

Measuring Detection Rate. To evaluate RQ1 and RQ2, we use the Juliet test suite [7]. It is a collection of C/C++, C#, and Java programs with known defects organized by the corresponding CWE categories. The latest version released in 2017 covers 64099 C/C++ cases, 28942 C# cases, and 28,881 Java cases. Although the test cases in the Juliet suite are artificial, the defects in it are sourced from real-world applications, including known CVEs. That said, using Juliet for run-time evaluation, rather than the static analysis it was designed for, comes with a number of challenges. In this work, we focus on evaluating the *difference* of detection rate in RQ1 and RQ2. As such, the results in Sect. 4.1 should not be taken as indicative of the security of the schemes evaluated, merely as indications of their parity under conditions causing contiguous overflow.

Test Case Selection. Not all of the 118 CWE categories covered by the Juliet test suite exhibit buffer overflow defects. To keep the compilation and run-time of tests manageable, we had to narrow down the subset of test cases to evaluate those that exhibit contiguous buffer overflow behavior. Through empirical assessment, we narrow our evaluation to the five CWE categories in Table 2 which exhibit relevant defects.

Measuring Performance Impact. To evaluate RQ3, we use the SPEC CPU 2017 benchmark suite and report the results in Sect. 4.2, using -O2 -march=native for all cases, with 4 copies for rate tests, and 12 threads for speed tests, corresponding to the number of cores without simultaneous multi-threading (SMT). SMT and address space layout randomization (ASLR) were disabled for all tests.

Table 2. Relevant CWE categories in Juliet C/C++ version 1.3.

CWE Category		# Test Cases			
		Total	Excluded	Selected	Detectable
CWE121	Stack-Based Buffer Overflow	4944	96	4848	3562
CWE122	Heap-Based Buffer Overflow	5922	192	5730	1426
CWE124	Buffer Underwrite	2048	96	1952	604
CWE194	Unexpected Sign Extension	1152	384	768	192
CWE195	Signed-to-Unsigned Conversion Error	1152	384	768	288

Measuring Impact of Allocation Layout. To evaluate RQ4 we implemented a modification to the Clang compiler that applies the stack layout changes implied by the `-fstack-protector` family of options without enabling the stack canary instrumentation and checks. To achieve this, we reuse the analysis passes that the stack canary instrumentation uses, but remove the generation of the failure path, check, and stack canary allocation. These changes result in a `-fstack-layout` -family of options that make local allocations ordered by the rules described in Sect. 2.1, with large arrays and structures containing large arrays closer to the return address than small arrays and variables. We then evaluate x86-64 shadow stack detection accuracy when combined with the new `-fstack-layout` -family of options and report our results in Sect. 4.1.

3.2 Experimental Setup

We opted to use a source-based Linux distribution, Gentoo Linux, to ensure that the test cases and all dependencies were built with stack canary and x86-64 shadow stack options and the correct compiler. We used GCC 13.3.1_p20240614 p1 and Clang version 18.1.8 along with Gentoo's glibc 2.39-r6, on Gentoo's Linux Kernel version 6.6.51-gentoo-dist-hardened. Experiments executed on an Intel NUC 13 Pro Mini (NUC13ANK) with a Raptor Lake Intel Core[TM]i7-1360P and 14 GB random access memory (RAM).

4 Evaluation and Results

4.1 Results: Detection of Contiguous Overflows

Figure 1 illustrates the stack canary and shadow stack results for GCC and Clang under the optimization levels `-O2` and `-O0`. All test cases show better detection rates with `-O0` compared to `-O2`, as optimizations under `-O2` can exploit undefined behavior in test cases in ways which may suppress or contain the extent of buffer overflows. For example, in some CWE122 and CWE194 cases the offending buffers are not referenced by the test code after the initialization that overflows them, allowing the compiler to optimize away the entire array access as dead code. Overall, across all our tests, the combination of the x86-64 shadow stack and either `-fstack-protector-strong` or `-fstack-protector-all` using Clang at `-O0` has the highest detection rate, but only reaches $\approx 33\%$ detection of the selected cases in Table 2. Consequently, for comparison, it is more meaningful to compare the detection rates *within* a certain optimization level than the rates *across* optimization levels.

Stack Canary Detection Rates. An overall comparison of the plots in Fig. 1 reveals that Clang demonstrates better detection rate with stack canaries than GCC. The `-fstack-protector-all` and `-fstack-protector-strong` options consistently outperform the `-fstack-protector` option, which is expected. The `-fstack-protector-all` option does not perform significantly better than `-fstack-protector-strong`. We attribute the differences in detection results between GCC and Clang as follows:

Differences in Stack Layout Between Compilers: In GCC, an array may be placed before another array, while in Clang, the same array may be placed after. This difference in stack layout can result in arrays being positioned closer to the stack canary and return addresses, depending on the compiler. While [20] initially highlighted this variation between compiler stack-layout, our results offer a more quantitative analysis of its impact.

Differences in Handling of `alloca()` *Calls with Constant Values:* Clang treats `alloca` calls with constant values similarly to a local array declaration, optimizing the allocation accordingly. In contrast, GCC employs a dynamic implementation, which may allocate additional space, particularly at the `-O0` optimization level. This behavior can allow a buffer to overflow with a specific length without modifying the stack canary.

x86-64 Shadow Stack Detection Rates. When the x86-64 shadow stack is enabled without stack canaries present, its detection rates exceeds those of stack canaries in the `-O2` case for both GCC and Clang, but the `-O0` results are reversed with the best performing stack canary options (`-fstack-protector-all` and `-fstack-protector-strong`) detecting more overflows than the x86-64 shadow stack for both GCC and Clang. Considering all compilation options, there are 1217 tests that the x86-64 shadow stack detects successfully that stack canaries do not, and 163 tests that stack canaries detect that the x86-64 shadow stack does not.

x86-64 Shadow Stack with `-fstack-layout` Detection Rates. The results for Clang with `-O0` and `-O2` are shown in Fig. 1. They show a consistent improvement in x86-64 shadow stack detection accuracy when combined with the new options. We however, identified a specific limitation in our approach of reusing the existing `-fstack-protector` analysis passes: in some cases, such as when a function spills callee-saved registers the stack canary is not placed right next

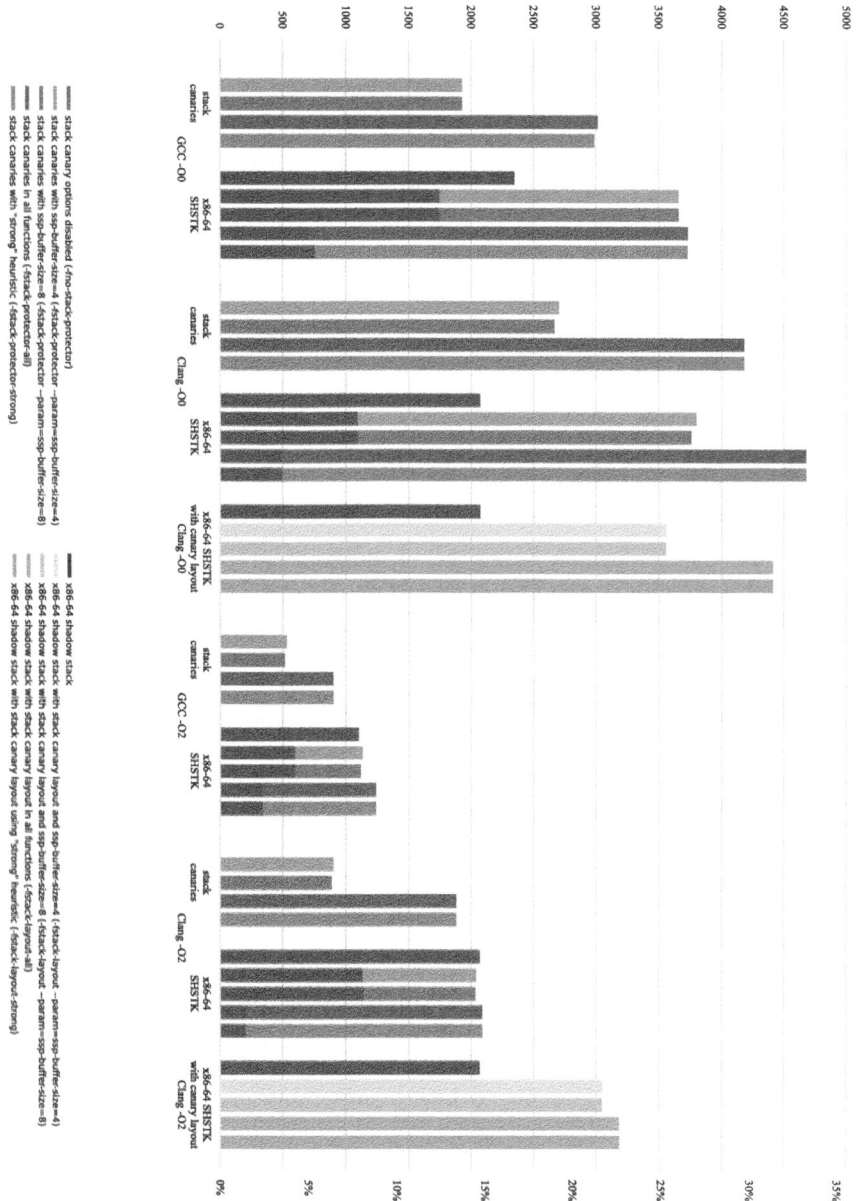

Fig. 1. Comparison of Juliet test results by compiler, optimization level, and options. The *stack canaries* bars show the detection rates for different stack canary options (indicated in the legend) with the x86-64 shadow stack disabled. The *x86-64 SHSTK* bars show the detection rate for the x86-64 shadow stack separately, and when combined with different stack canary options (indicated in the legend). The *x86-64 SHSTK with canary layout* bars show the detection rate for the x86-64 shadow stack when combined with the proof-of-concept -fstack-layout-family options for Clang -O0 and -O2 configurations. The left axis shows the number of test cases with detections, while the right axis shows the percentage of detected cases relative to the *Selected* test cases shown in Table 2.

to the return address, but also in such a way to protect any spilled register values. Our `-fstack-layout` options do not alter the placement of spilled registers leaving them unprotected by the x86-64 shadow stack.

Table 3. Geometric mean of performance degradation based on SPEC CPU 2017 results.

Protection variant	intrate	intspeed
stack canaries with "strong" heuristic (`-fstack-protector-strong`)	0.55%	0.27%
stack canaries in all functions (`-fstack-protector-all`)	3.05%	3.26%
x86-64 shadow stack	1.48%	0.57%
x86-64 shadow stack with stack canary layout using "strong" heuristic (`-fstack-layout-strong`)	1.55%	0.40%
x86-64 shadow stack with stack canary layout in all functions (`-fstack-layout-all`)	1.60%	0.41%

4.2   Results: Performance

We evaluate the performance impact of different stack canary implementations and the x86-64 shadow stack using the SPEC CPU 2017 intrate and intspeed benchmarks. For the performance evaluation we focus on the `-fstack-protector-strong` and `-fstack-protector-all` options as these outperformed the other `-fstack-protector` variants in the detection of contiguous overflows experiments (Sect. 4.1). To improve the consistency of results, we disabled ASLR and SMT. All benchmarks were compiled using Clang compiler with optimization level `-O2` and `-march=native`. We exclude the `548.exchange2_r` benchmark as it is written in Fortran and not supported by Clang.

Table 3 gives an overview of the performance results. Overall we found that the `-fstack-protector-strong` options degraded performance the least (on average $\approx$ 0.55% on intrate and $\approx$ 0.27% on intspeed) and `-fstack-protector-all` the most (on average $\approx$ 3.05% on rate and $\approx$ 3.26% on speed). The x86-64 shadow stack falls between these stack canary variants by degrading performance on average by $\approx$ 1.48% on intrate and $\approx$ 0.57% on intspeed. The x86-64 shadow stack with `-fstack-layout-strong` and `-fstack-layout-all` seems to have comparable performance to that of the conventional x86-64 shadow stack.

4.3   Conclusions from Evaluation

In Sect. 3 we set out to answer four research questions. Our conclusions regarding these questions and based on the above evaluation of detection and performance is:

RQ1. Are the detection rates of stack canaries and the x86-64 shadow stack consistent across different compilers in large-scale tests.
    No ✗: Our results show that different options exhibit different detection rates across compilers.

RQ2. Is the detection rate of contiguous, stack-based buffer overflows comparable between the x86-64 shadow stack canaries.
No ✗: The x86-64 shadow stack does not consistently outperform stack canaries in terms of detection rates.

RQ3. Is the impact on software performance in real-world use cases comparable between the x86-64 shadow stack and stack canaries.
No ✗: We measured consistently larger performance impacts for the x86-64 shadow stack compared to -fstack-protector-strong in our benchmarks.

RQ4. Is the detection rate of the x86-64 shadow stack improved by a -fstack-protector-like stack frame layout?
Yes ✓: We measured a consistent improvement in detection rate for the x86-64 shadow stack with our -fstack-layout-family of options.

5   Conclusion

We compared stack canaries and the x86-64 shadow stack for detecting contiguous overflows and return-address corruption across GCC and Clang at optimization levels -O0 and -O2, using the Juliet test suite and SPEC CPU 2017 benchmarks. Clang's stack canaries consistently outperformed GCC's, and both compilers detected more issues at -O0 than at -O2. At -O2, the shadow stack caught more overflows than canaries—with Clang again ahead of GCC—and by adopting Clang's canary-style stack layout (but without canary checks) we raised the shadow stack's detection rate well above standard canaries, at negligible runtime cost.

These findings suggest that, on supported hardware, a shadow-stack configuration could replace stack canaries, despite its return addresses being more predictable than random canary values. However, because the Juliet suite does not model real-world exploits—and GCC's lower detection may stem from either a more efficient stack layout or biases in the test suite—we acknowledge that our evaluation does not enable us to make strong claims regarding the security of the different configurations. We also show that stack-protector implementations influence code generation and stack ordering beyond inserting canaries, and recommend that similar layout effects be evaluated for other mechanisms, such as ARM Pointer Authentication.

Acknowledgements. We want to thank Kristof Beyls, William Huhn, Siddhesh Poyarekar and Niklas Lindskog for reviewing an earlier version of this paper. This research is partially funded by the CyberExcellence programme of the Walloon Region, Belgium (grant 2110186).

References

1. Abadi, M., et al.: Control-flow integrity. In: CCS 2005 (2005). https://doi.org/10. 1145/1102120.1102165
2. Anderson, J.P.: Computer Security Technology Planning Study Volume 1 - Executive Summary. Technical Report AD-758 206, James P. Anderson and Co. (1972). https://apps.dtic.mil/sti/citations/AD0758206
3. Beyls, K.: [RFC] BOLT-based binary analysis tool to verify correctness of security hardening. LLVM Discussion Forums (2024). https://discourse.llvm.org/t/78148
4. Bierbaumer, B., Kirsch, J., Kittel, T., Francillon, A., Zarras, A.: Smashing the stack protector for fun and profit. In: Janczewski, L.J., Kutyłowski, M. (eds.) SEC 2018. IAICT, vol. 529, pp. 293–306. Springer, Cham (2018). https://doi.org/10. 1007/978-3-319-99828-2_21
5. Bittau, A., et al.: Hacking blind. In: S&P 2014 (2014). https://doi.org/10.1109/ SP.2014.22
6. Bletsch, T., et al.: Jump-oriented programming: a new class of code-reuse attack. In: ASIACCS 2011 (2011). https://doi.org/10.1145/1966913.1966919
7. Boland, T., Black, P.E.: Juliet 1.1 C/C++ and Java test suite. Computer **45**(10), 88–90 (2012). https://doi.org/10.1109/MC.2012.345
8. Burow, N., Zhang, X., Payer, M.: SoK: shining light on shadow stacks. In: S&P 2019 (2019). https://doi.org/10.1109/SP.2019.00076
9. Citizen Lab: BLASTPASS: NSO Group iPhone Zero-Click, Zero-Day Exploit Captured in the Wild. Technical report, Citizen Lab, University of Toronto (2023). https://citizenlab.ca/2023/09/blastpass-nso-group-iphone-zero-click-zero-day-exploit-captured-in-the-wild/
10. Corbet, J.: Shadow stacks for user space. LWN.net (2022). https://lwn.net/ Articles/885220/
11. Corbet, J.: Shadow stacks for 64-bit Arm systems. LWN.net (2023). https://lwn. net/Articles/940403/
12. Cowan, C., et al.: StackGuard: automatic adaptive detection and prevention of buffer-overflow attacks. In: USENIX Security 1998 (1998). https://www.usenix. org/legacy/publications/library/proceedings/sec98/cowan.html
13. CrowdStrike: External Technical Root Cause Analysis—Channel File 291. Technical report (2024). https://www.crowdstrike.com/wp-content/uploads/2024/08/ Channel-File-291-Incident-Root-Cause-Analysis-08.06.2024.pdf
14. Depuydt, H., et al.: Do we still need canaries in the coal mine? Measuring shadow stack effectiveness in countering stack smashing (extended version) (2024). https:// doi.org/10.48550/arXiv.2412.16343
15. Evans, I., et al.: Control jujutsu: on the weaknesses of fine-grained control flow integrity. In: CCS 2015 (2015). https://doi.org/10.1145/2810103.2813646
16. Google: An update on Memory Safety in Chrome. Google Security Blog (2021). https://security.googleblog.com/2021/09/an-update-on-memory-safety-in-chrome.html
17. Guelton, S., Poyarekar, S.: Use compiler flags for stack protection in GCC and Clang. Red Hat Developer Blog (2022). https://developers.redhat.com/articles/ 2022/06/02/use-compiler-flags-stack-protection-gcc-and-clang#
18. Hebb, T.: CVE-2023-4039: GCC's-fstack-protector fails to guard dynamic stack allocations on ARM64. Meta Red Team X Blog (2023). https://rtx.meta.security/ mitigation/2023/09/12/CVE-2023-4039.html

19. Hu, H., et al.: Data-oriented programming: on the expressiveness of non-control data attacks. In: S&P 2016 (2016). https://doi.org/10.1109/SP.2016.62
20. Jiang, Y., et al.: RecIPE: revisiting the evaluation of memory error defenses. In: ASIACCS 2022 (2022). https://doi.org/10.1145/3488932.3524127
21. Larabel, M.: Intel Shadow Stack Finally Merged For Linux 6.6. Phoronix (2023). https://www.phoronix.com/news/Intel-Shadow-Stack-Linux-6.6
22. Larabel, M.: Glibc Updated For Recent Linux CET Shadow Stack Support. Phoronix (2024). https://www.phoronix.com/news/Glibc-Intel-CET-Shadow-Stack
23. Magee, J.: [cfe-dev] What do the different stack-protector levels protect in Clang? (2017). https://lists.llvm.org/pipermail/cfe-dev/2017-April/053662.html
24. MSRC: A proactive approach to more secure code. Microsoft Security Response Center Blog (2019). https://msrc.microsoft.com/blog/2019/07/a-proactive-approach-to-more-secure-code/
25. ONCD: Back to the Building Blocks: A Path Toward Secure and Measurable Software. Whitepaper, United States White House Office of the National Cyber Director (2024). https://bidenwhitehouse.archives.gov/wp-content/uploads/2024/02/Final-ONCD-Technical-Report.pdf
26. Roemer, R., et al.: Return-oriented programming: systems, languages, and applications. ACM Trans. Inf. Syst. Secur. **15**(1), 2:1–2:34 (2012). https://doi.org/10.1145/2133375.2133377
27. Shacham, H.: The geometry of innocent flesh on the bone: return-into-libc without function calls (on the x86). In: CCS 2007 (2007). https://doi.org/10.1145/1315245.1315313
28. Synopsys: Heartbleed Bug (2014). https://heartbleed.com/
29. Szekeres, L., et al.: SoK: eternal war in memory. In: S&P 2013 (2013). https://doi.org/10.1109/SP.2013.13
30. Traynor, B.: The RISC-V Instruction Set Manual Volume I: Unprivileged Architecture, Chapter 35. Control-flow Integrity (CFI) (2024). https://github.com/riscv/riscv-isa-manual/releases/tag/riscv-isa-release-ade2bfb-2024-11-28
31. Whitney, T.: /GS (Buffer Security Check). Microsoft Learn (2021). https://learn.microsoft.com/en-us/cpp/build/reference/gs-buffer-security-check?view=msvc-170
32. Yu, R., et al.: Building embedded systems like it's 1996. In: NDSS 2022 (2022). https://doi.org/10.14722/ndss.2022.24031

Supply Chain Security, Malware and Forensics

SoK: Towards Reproducibility for Software Packages in Scripting Language Ecosystems

Timo Pohl[1]([✉])[iD], Pavel Novák[2][iD], Marc Ohm[1,3][iD], and Michael Meier[1,3][iD]

[1] University of Bonn, Bonn, Germany
{pohl,ohm,mm}@cs.uni-bonn.de
[2] Masaryk University, Brno, Czech Republic
468940@muni.cz
[3] Fraunhofer FKIE, Bonn, Germany

Abstract. The disconnect between distributed software artifacts and their supposed source code enables attackers to leverage the build process for inserting malicious functionality. Past research in this field focuses on compiled language ecosystems, mostly analysing Linux distribution packages. However, the popular scripting language ecosystems potentially face unique issues given the systematic difference in distributed artifacts. This SoK provides an overview of existing research, aiming to highlight future directions, as well as chances to transfer existing knowledge from compiled language ecosystems. To that end, we work out key aspects in current research, systematize identified challenges for software reproducibility, and map them between the ecosystems. We find that the literature is sparse, focusing on few individual problems and ecosystems. This allows us to effectively identify next steps to improve reproducibility in this field.

Keywords: reproducible builds · software supply chain security · software packages · software security · library reproducibility

1 Introduction

Many programming ecosystems encourage the use of so-called *software packages* to improve development speed and reduce redundant work. These software packages, often libraries or frameworks, usually perform common tasks that can be generalized in a way that they can be used in a broad range of contexts, leading to some packages being part of hundreds of thousands of software projects. This of course makes them attractive for attackers, as infecting a single one of those packages could potentially infect all the machines running any of the dependent software. Such attacks are called software supply chain attacks, since they abuse the dependency relation between packages to indirectly infect a dependent package.

© The Author(s), under exclusive license to Springer Nature Switzerland AG 2025
M. Dalla Preda et al. (Eds.): ARES 2025, LNCS 15993, pp. 209–230, 2025.
https://doi.org/10.1007/978-3-032-00627-1_11

With ongoing research on detecting malicious snippets in source code [12, 25, 33], other attack vectors are explored to infect software packages. One of them is the infection of the build process. Software packages distribution usually happens via so-called *package registries*, where artifacts can be uploaded without any verifiable link to the source code they are supposedly built from. Therefore, even if the alleged source code of a package is carefully vetted, the distributed artifact could perform completely different tasks. There have been recent incidents exploiting exactly this circumstance, like the `ultralytics` Python package that was hit by a cache-poisoning attack on the GitHub Actions build process, leading to an artifact published on PyPI that contained functionality which was not present in the GitHub source code it was built from [13].

A strategy to combat this is to build the artifact at multiple independent builders and compare their artifacts. Ideally, all the artifacts would be the same when built from the published source code, suggesting that no builder has added any malicious changes. However, it has been shown that even if all parties are benign, differences occur across different builders [1, 2, 8]. This happens because the tools used for building the artifacts are not optimized for reproducibility, and often generate non-deterministic output, like a timestamp of the build time. Thus, to enable this strategy of combatting malicious or compromised build services, these build processes have to be made reproducible.

According to the StackOverflow Developer Survey 2024 [34], the most used programming languages are JavaScript (62.3 %), Python (51 %) and TypeScript (38.5 %), all of which are scripting languages. While compiled languages, especially in the context of Linux distribution packages for Debian and Arch Linux, have received a lot of attention regarding problems and solutions to achieve reproducibility [10], scripting language ecosystems for languages like JavaScript or Python, are not reproducible for the most part. This paper systematizes and collects the current research results regarding this topic, aiming to identify well researched areas, fields in which knowledge may be transferred from compiled language ecosystems, as well as future research directions. In particular, we will answer the following research questions:

RQ1 What are the key aspects of reproducibility research for software packages in scripting language ecosystems?

RQ2 What are common challenges for reproducibility in compiled and scripting language ecosystems?

RQ3 What are *additional* challenges for reproducibility in scripting language ecosystems?

The remainder of the paper is structured as follows: Sect. 2 provides background on reproducible builds, focusing on the definition, high-level approaches and the main differences concerning compiled and scripting language ecosystems. Section 3 then provides an overview of the current state of the art in reproducibility[1] research with respect to scripting language ecosystems, answering *RQ1*. Section 4 compiles and compares challenges regarding reproducibility in

---

[1] For brevity, we use the generic term "reproducibility" to mean "software reproducibility".

compiled and scripting language ecosystems, answering *RQ2* and *RQ3*. In Sect. 5 we discuss our findings, followed by an outlook on future research directions in Sect. 6. The paper is concluded in Sect. 7.

2   Background

In order to better understand our motivation and the contents of this paper, this section provides background on software reproducibility. We focus on its goals and their relation to different definitions found in the literature and the industry, as well as background on the differences between compiled and scripting language ecosystems in this context.

2.1   Software Reproducibility

The exact definition of software reproducibility varies across the literature and the industry. The main goals of software reproducibility, as stated by the Reproducible Builds project [32], are security and quality assurance. Regarding security, it aims to achieve resistance against attacks in the build process, which includes all the steps performed to create an artifact from given source code. In terms of quality assurance, it is supposed to guarantee that binaries behave the same, no matter on what system they were built.

The general idea behind reproducibility is always the same: Given the same input, the executable artifact resulting from the build process shall always behave the same. However, details in the definitions exhibit differences in the following three factors:

– How is behavioural equivalence tested or approximated?
– What exactly is part of the input?
– What is the build process?

Lakhotia et al. have shown that, in general, deciding whether two binaries behave equivalently is impossible [21]. For this reason, Dietrich et al. have formalized a set of criteria for equivalence relations between binaries, resulting in four assurance levels for behavioural equivalence [7].

Level 1 equivalence relations simply compare for bit-by-bit equivalence. *Level 2* equivalence relations perform bit-by-bit comparisons too but only in parts of the binary that are regarded as having a semantic effect on the binaries' behaviour. This excludes parts like embedded signatures, only used to check the authenticity of the binary by a third party. *Level 3* equivalence relations do not require any bit-by-bit comparisons. They regard semantically equivalent code sequences as equivalent. *Level 4* equivalence relations regard semantically *similar* code as equivalent [7].

Level 1 equivalence relations are easy to perform and check. However, it quickly happens that two binaries that behave the same are not regarded as equivalent by these relations. Level 2 and level 3 relations are less prone to falsely label equivalent behaviour as non-equivalent. Their drawback is that it is much harder to create relations that can reliably identify parts of artifacts with a semantic effect, or that are semantically equivalent than a simple bit-by-bit comparison, especially if these relations have to be generic over a heterogeneous set of artifacts. Level 4 equivalence relations do not actually test for behavioural equivalence but rather for behavioural similarity, thus being unable to achieve the goals stated above for reproducible software.

The most commonly used equivalence relation regarding reproducible builds is the level 1 bit-by-bit equivalence of the whole build artifact, used by almost all industry projects. Carnavalet et al. [4] introduce the notion of *verifiable builds* which allow omitting "unimportant details" from the comparison, corresponding to a level 2 equivalence relation. The Fedora Project [9] follow this notion, though still calling it reproducible builds, and ignore the embedded signatures of their software packages when comparing them. Pöll et al. also propose the notion of "accountable builds", ignoring all differences that are explainable and can be considered benign upon inspection [28], which would correspond to level 4 equivalence. We see no industry projects following this definition.

Regarding the definition of inputs, there are different granularities in how exact the input is defined. The Yocto Project [39] requires "build configurations" to be the same, while VMWare [19] says that "all states of the build" have to be controlled. The Reproducible Builds Project [32] defines the input as the "same source code, build environment and build instructions". The Fedora project also adds "metadata" to these required inputs.

Some projects also explicitly state what the reproducibility should *not* depend on. FOSSA Inc. [3] says that the build should not depend on the computer, the time or the available network services. The Yocto Project [39] states that builds should be reproducible regardless of the system they are run on.

Even though some of these definitions explicitly name inputs like "build configuration" or "build instructions", what exactly is part of them is not clearly defined. The Reproducible Builds project even explicitly states that maintainers have to choose the *relevant* parts of the build environment, and that these relevant parts should be as small as possible [32]. Thus, under all of these definitions it is still up to maintainers what exact parts of these inputs they provide.

At last, the definitions of what exactly is meant with the build process is mostly a concern of software packages in scripting languages. In compiled languages the build process consists of the compilation of the source code to an executable binary or bytecode, including all necessary pre- and post-processing. In scripting languages, some research considers the installation of a software package as part of a "reproducible build" [23], while other research considers the actual process of creating a package that can be distributed as an individual file to users of the software from the source code as the build process [2,14]. The relevant difference is that the latter only depends on *build dependencies*, while the former depends on *runtime dependencies*. In the context of scripting language ecosystems, the generic term *dependencies* usually refers to *runtime dependencies*, while in compiled language ecosystems, it often refers to *build dependencies*.

For this paper, we arrive at Definition 1 which is a more formal version of the definition given by the Reproducible Builds project. In particular, it explicitly states that reproducibility is a property of a tuple (source code, build instructions, build environment, artifacts). Throughout our paper, we consider tuples fulfilling this definition to have the *reproducible builds* property.

Definition 1. *A tuple (source code, build instructions, build environment, artifacts) is considered reproducible, if executing the build instructions on the source code within the build environment always produces the same artifacts when compared via bit-by-bit equality.*

However, proving reproducibility is difficult, as artifact equality would have to be proven under *all* circumstances. Therefore, the common practice to consider such a tuple as reproducible is what Lamb and Zacchiroli have coined "adversarial rebuilding" [22]—deliberately varying external factors, especially those known to cause irreproducibility, and checking whether the artifact stays the same. This can be achieved with tools like `reprotest`[2].

While the *reproducible builds* property is useful when trying to verify that a certain artifact was not illegitimately modified during the build process, it is neither strictly necessary nor sufficient, especially in ecosystems that do not (yet) aim to achieve build reproducibility. For this task, which we will call *artifact reproduction*, a software artifact is given as input and the goal is to reproduce this given artifact. This is commonly done for artifacts as they are distributed via registries. In ecosystems where it is not yet common to be concerned with build reproducibility, research in artifact reproduction may help to establish independent verifiers for distributed packages. This task can pose additional challenges, for example acquiring source code for an artifact, which reproducible builds assumes to be given.

2.2   Achieving Reproducibility

Lamb and Zacchiroli [22] split the reasons for irreproducibility in two broad categories: unstable inputs—for example build dependencies that are downloaded over the network during the build process, thus possibly returning different data in two distinct build runs—and non-determinism of the build tools, like compilers not always translating the same source code to the same machine code.

On a high level, the approaches to achieve build reproducibility can be split into proactive and reactive. The proactive approach involves controlling and stabilizing all inputs to the build process, as well as ensuring that all build tools are fully deterministic. While this approach should generically work for all build processes, guaranteeing access to all dependencies and the determinism of all involved build tools can be a demanding task. It typically involves containerization, dependency version pinning, and well-defined build scripts [24].

In the reactive approach, parts of the artifact known to be affected by nondeterminism are patched after the build to always contain the same content.

---

[2] https://salsa.debian.org/reproducible-builds/reprotest.

While this method does not require control over external factors, it needs a deep understanding of the concrete build process, to identify parts of the artifact affected by non-determinism and patch them without breaking the functionality of the program. Additionally, this method cannot resolve dependency-related issues [29,31]. Debian's `strip-nondeterminism`[3] is an example of a tool to perform such post-processing.

2.3 Artifacts in Compiled and Scripting Language Ecosystems

On a high level the build process in compiled and scripting language ecosystems is the same. A set of build instructions is executed on the source code, transforming it into one or few build artifacts. However, there are differences between artifacts in compiled and scripting language ecosystems that require dedicated research.

The main difference is that while build artifacts in compiled languages typically consist of machine or bytecode, artifacts for scripting languages are customarily some form of archive consisting of source code files. Additionally, ecosystems like NodeJS also commonly involve heavy preprocessing like transpilation, minification or bundling, posing unique challenges for reproducibility. Furthermore, archive formats often contain metadata both about themselves and the contained files.

Yet, many scripting language ecosystems also support so-called *native extensions*, meaning that some functionality is externalized into compiled binaries, often for performance reasons. Similarly, some ecosystems like Python also support pre-compiling parts of the source code into bytecode, which can be distributed in packages for performance benefits. As these binaries also have to be compiled from source code at some point, they may suffer from the same irreproducibility issues as software projects in compiled language ecosystems in general. We thus argue that the problems one may encounter in scripting language ecosystems is a superset of the problems encountered in compiled language ecosystems.

3   State of the Art in Reproducibility Research for Scripting Language Ecosystems

This section answers *RQ1* through a literature review of research investigating reproducibility in scripting language ecosystems. We start with reproducible builds, highlighting that discrepancies between artifacts exist, as well as categorizing these discrepancies. Afterwards research on artifact reproduction is investigated, mainly dealing with categorizing existing issues, as well as discovering the source code for a given artifact. At last, we show the development within popular scripting language ecosystems that assist build reproducibility.

Vu et al. [38] have investigated the differences between Python packages distributed on the PyPI registry and the corresponding source code. From the

---

[3] https://salsa.debian.org/reproducible-builds/strip-nondeterminism.

4000 most downloaded packages, they selected all packages with working, unique links to GitHub repositories, which contain a complete history of commits for the whole project lifetime. However, how exactly this commit completeness was evaluated is not clearly stated. This resulted in a sample of 2438 packages, and 93 252 artifacts considering all their versions.

They show that 65% of these artifacts exhibit differences compared to the linked source code repository. While this is not a direct violation of the reproducible builds property, it indicates that some preprocessing steps are performed before packaging the source code files. Regarding reproducibility verification, it also shows that reliably finding the source code that was used to create a package is not as easy as comparing the individual files of the software package to the files in the source code repository, and assuming that they should be equal.

Benedetti et al. [2] investigated reproducibility for software components across different ecosystems. The scripting language ecosystems they investigated are NodeJS, Python and Ruby. For these scripting languages, they investigated the number of reproducible packages, potential root causes and the influence of native extensions (c.f. Sect. 2).

They randomly sampled 4000 packages from the ecosyste.ms[4] project, for packages fulfilling the following criteria: Contains the respective ecosystem's metadata file like a `package.json` for NodeJS packages, has a working link to a source code repository, and a successfully terminating build process. Thus, general build failures would not count towards root causes for irreproducibility.

Using the tool `reprotest` to alter environmental conditions like the system time, build path and more, they built an artifact out of the most recent version of the repository code multiple times, and compared the results. They consider the immediate output artifacts of the native build commands as the artifact to compare, with no special post-processing like unpacking tarballs. A package is labelled reproducible, if all runs for all environmental variations with `reprotest` result in the same artifact [2].

They show that 100% of their tested NodeJS packages, 12.2% of Python and 0% of Ruby packages are reproducible without any modifications. Manually setting up the environment for reproducibility, for example by setting the SOURCE_DATE_EPOCH environment variable[5] increased reproducibility of Ruby packages to 97.1%, while not having an effect on Python package reproducibility. Additionally, patching the package manager `pip` to set predictable file permission bits increased reproducibility of PyPI packages to 98%. They also found that timestamps were responsible for 87.77% of Python, and 97.1% of unreproducible Ruby packages [2].

For the rest of unreproducible builds, they mainly blamed the ability to run arbitrary code during the packing process, expressing that fixing irreproducibility due to arbitrary code execution is hard to combat by nature [2]. While this is only explicitly mentioned for the Python and Ruby ecosystems, we note that npm has the same ability with their lifecycle scripts for the `pack` event, that would be

---

[4] https://ecosyste.ms.

[5] https://reproducible-builds.org/specs/source-date-epoch/.

automatically executed when calling `npm pack` [17]. However, as we will see later this section in the work of Goswami et al. [14], it has become common practice in the NodeJS ecosystem to use the `build` script instead of these lifecycle scripts. We assume that this is the reason why they do not affect the NodeJS ecosystem much in practice.

While this is valuable research, we argue that this tests the native build process of the ecosystem itself, rather than the reproducibility of individual packages. For example, the previously mentioned `build` scripts commonly employed in the NodeJS ecosystem are not automatically executed by the native build command `npm pack`. Since preprocessing with transpilers, bundlers, minifiers and other tools is common practice, an experiment testing the package managers' build commands in isolation does not give insight into the reproducibility of the whole process from published source code to distributed artifact. Still, testing the package managers in isolation is a valuable step in identifying parts of the process that lead to irreproducibility.

Regarding the influence of native extensions to reproducibility, Benedetti et al. find that native extensions do not change the distribution of irreproducible packages, even though the C and C++ compilation process has shown to have many issues regarding reproducibility, if not explicitly addressed [1,4,8,10,22, 28,30,35]. For NodeJS and Python this is attributed to their native extension toolchains, which are built with reproducibility in mind. However, Ruby does not have such a toolchain. They conjecture that native extensions are often a collection of small independent functions for very specific, computationally expensive workloads, and that this leads to little influence of typical irreproducibility causes [2].

In face of the little research regarding reproducible builds for interpreted language ecosystems, there is more work regarding artifact reproduction in this context. Goswami et al. [14] have investigated how many of the 1000 most depended upon packages in the npm registry they are able to reproduce, and established key challenges in doing so. To find the matching source code, they used the repository link given in the package metadata, if available. As all the available repositories pointed to GitHub, they used the GitHub releases to identify commits that presumably correspond to released artifacts on the npm registry. For all releases found on GitHub, they matched the release's name to a version released on npm. This way, they established a set of pairs of source code, and a corresponding distributed artifact. Afterwards, all packages that did not contain a `package.json` file, which is used to store package metadata, as well as all packages that do not contain a `build` script within the `package.json` were removed. Thus, the resulting dataset contained a total of 3390 versions for 226 packages.

To build the packages from the source code, they ran the commands `npm install` and `npm run build` [14]. The former command installs all the defined runtime dependencies, as well as development dependencies [16], while the latter runs an optional, user-defined script named `build`.

While the name might wrongfully suggest that this is a semantically meaningful script which is somehow standardized or encouraged to be used for the package build process, this is not the case [17]. This procedure also does not actually run the `npm pack` or `npm publish` commands, which are the commands to actually create the tarball artifact and publish it to the npm registry respectively [15]. Thus, they also skip all the lifecycle scripts a package maintainer might have defined for these operations. This also means that their resulting artifact used for later analysis is not the actual tarball that is distributed by the npm registry, but only its contents.

While it is not explicitly mentioned, we assume that they unpack the registry artifact for comparison, in order to at least have artifacts of the same form to compare. They use *diffoscope*[6] to examine the difference between their built artifact, and the corresponding registry artifact [14].

They find that almost 40% of package versions are not reproducible. For 492 packages (15%) the build process failed. For the remaining 2898 package versions, they investigated and categorized the differences in source code files, and analysed potential root causes, which are further discussed in Sect. 4 [14].

In 2021 Vu proposed *py2src* to investigate how to link Python packages to their corresponding source code [37]. This tool takes various information sources that may include a link to a source code repository into account, like information returned by the PyPI registry itself, or information from metadata files within the package, and rates them by how likely they are the correct link. They propose six heuristics to judge a single URLs reliability: Similarity of package and repository name, similarity of GitHub repository and PyPI package descriptions, "Python" being part of the GitHub repositories' reported languages, GitHub page containing badge that links to PyPI package, PyPI maintainer name being present in GitHub contributor list and GitHub repository tags matching versions released on PyPI.

These heuristic indicate that both, the GitHub repository and the Python package are actually maintained by the same author. However, they do not help to establish a trusted link between the artifact and the source code in case of a malicious author, nor do they contribute in finding the correct source code revision for a given version one may want to rebuild. Their reliance on package metadata also does not help to find source code for packages that do not link to a source code repository in their metadata.

Tsakpinis and Pretschner [36] picked up this last problem, and examined the availability of source code for the Python and NodeJS ecosystems. They collected all metadata for all packages in the PyPI and npm registries respectively, and analysed the values in the respective source URL metadata fields. If the given URL pointed to a repository on GitHub, they also analysed whether it was publicly available. They found that 42% of Python packages, and 54% of NodeJS packages have links that do not point to a valid GitHub repository, with 24% and 50% respectively having known invalid or missing links, further highlighting

---

[6] https://diffoscope.org.

the problem of relying on package metadata to find the corresponding source code.

Gao et al. [11] propose *PyRadar* aiming to find the corresponding source code repository to a Python package based on the code of the artifact, as well as validating a supposed link between a source code repository and a given artifact. Regarding the repository validation, they leverage so-called *phantom files*—files that appear in the registry artifact but not in the corresponding source code repository—as a metric. A file is considered a phantom file if the source code repository does not contain a file with the same SHA-256 hash [11].

To evaluate their approach, they take about 14 000 Python packages that are present on GitHub with at least 100 stars, for which they can find a corresponding package on PyPI, as the dataset with assumed correct links between the source code repository and registry artifact. To gather packages with incorrect links, they sample all Python packages that point to a repository already present in the presumed correct links dataset, but with a different listed maintainer. Furthermore, they add all Python packages that list the default `pypa/sampleproject` GitHub repository as their source code repository. This way, they end up with about 2000 packages in their presumed incorrect links dataset. These datasets are manually verified for a 95% confidence level and 5% confidence interval [11].

They show that there is a significant difference in occurrence of phantom files between artifacts and the source code from the correct source code repository compared to the source code from a different source code repository. They also show that certain files, like the Python package metadata files `setup.py` and `pyproject.toml` have a particularly high likelihood to be phantom files when comparing against incorrect source code repositories, while they are present within the correct source code repositories [11].

Including these findings, they come up with six features to train machine learning models on that can be used for classification whether a given link points to the correct source code repository or not. These are the number of phantom Python files, whether one of the Python package metadata files is a phantom file, whether the version of the package in question has a matching tag in the repository, the normalized Levenshtein similarity between the Python package name and the repository name, the number of maintainers of the package and the number of packages maintained by the package maintainers. Out of seven models they evaluated, a Random Forest model performs best with an *area under the ROC curve* of 0.995 [11].

While this is a promising approach to verify the correctness of the source code repository links, this is not a safe method to verify that a given registry artifact actually stems from the source code in the linked repository, but rather a plausibility check that the repository has not been accidentally mislinked.

Regarding source code retrieval for packages with no (correct) link to a source code repository, they leverage the *World of Code*[7] infrastructure to perform hash-based git repository queries. For a given Python artifact, they iterate over all Python files and calculate their SHA-256 hashes. They use these hash to look up

---

[7] https://worldofcode.org/.

all the commits the respective file is introduced in. Afterwards, these commits are mapped to unique repositories they appear in. If the file appears in less than a configurable amount of repositories, all those repositories are added to a set of candidate repositories for the artifact. Candidate repositories are then ranked by the amount of files from the artifact they contain. At last, the name similarity of the Python package and the top ranked source code repository name is calculated. If it is below a configurable threshold, no repository is returned. Otherwise, the top ranked source code repository is returned [11].

Using heuristically set values of 500 for the maximum amount of repositories a file may appear in, and 0.5 for the minimum name similarity between the package and the repository, 90.2% of repositories from their correct links dataset return a repository candidate, with an accuracy of 0.97 [11].

This is a promising approach to find source code repositories for python packages. It leverages the fact that in python the python ecosystem, individual files often appear unaltered in the resulting package. In other ecosystems like NodeJS, this is not necessarily the case, due to its common use of tools like minifiers or transpilers, transforming the source files before publishing them into registry packages. The transferability of this approach to other ecosystems is therefore to be evaluated.

Aside from these academic achievements, we have also observed efforts to work towards reproducible builds from within ecosystems. PEP 552 [26] was finalized in 2017, which outlines techniques to make compilation of python byte-code files more deterministic. Python core developers also created a tool called $Asaman$[8], aiming to produce reproducible wheels. However, according to its own documentation, this tool still has many limitations, and at the time of writing the latest commit was almost two years ago in April 2023, indicating that it may no longer be actively maintained.

Recently, two package registries also started to support *digital attestations of provenance information*. Namely, npm in early 2023 [6] and PyPI in late 2024 [18,27] introduced the ability to attach signed attestations to package releases, attesting that they were built from a certain source code revision with a specified build script. When these are signed by trusted entities, which could be for example the GitHub or GitLab organizations, they provide a trustworthy link between a package release and the corresponding source code, including the exact source code revision, build scripts and the build environment. If widely adopted, this could be very beneficial for artifact reproduction, as it eliminates the need to find the exact source code, build instructions and build environment a given artifact was built in.

In summary, we see that there is little research regarding reproducible builds in scripting language ecosystems, covering multiple ecosystems but investigating the isolated influence of package managers and their native build commands to reproducible builds. For artifact reproduction, there is a little more research, but individual topics often focus on a single ecosystem. Systematic analysis of challenges for artifact reproduction has only been done for the NodeJS ecosystem,

---

[8] https://github.com/kushaldas/asaman.

while research into discovering the source code for a given artifact is focused on the Python ecosystem. Overall, research in this context is very limited, and therefore hard to generalize over scripting language ecosystems as a whole.

> **Response to RQ1:** Research regarding reproducibility for software packages in scripting language ecosystems focuses on artifact reproduction. Two common subtopics are root cause analysis for irreproducibility, as well as identification of the source code for a given artifact. A single recent publication investigates the effect of package managers on reproducible builds.

4   Challenges for Reproducible Builds in Compiled and Scripting Language Ecosystems

After establishing the key aspects of reproducibility research in scripting language ecosystems, this section collects challenges for the more researched compiled language ecosystems, as well as for scripting language ecosystems. We aim to identify an overlap between the two, as well as additional challenges that scripting language ecosystems might be facing. To do so, we briefly summarize known challenges for reproducible builds, first in compiled and then in scripting language ecosystems. We then lay out which challenges they have in common, possibly with existing solutions, as well as challenges unique to scripting language ecosystems.

4.1   Reasons for Irreproducibility in Compiled Language Ecosystems

Regarding compiled language ecosystems, we first collect challenges identified for reproducible builds, following up with challenges for artifact reproduction.

Reproducible Builds. The reasons for build irreproducibility in compiled language ecosystems have been extensively researched. In 2019 Ren et al. [30] used system call tracing during the build process of 180 randomly chosen Debian packages, identifying five main categories causing irreproducibility: Timestamps, randomness, file ordering, locale and user- or hostnames in the artifact. A 2022 report by Lamb and Zacchiroli [22] also mentions build paths, archive metadata and uninitialized memory as main reasons for irreproducibility. In 2023, Bajaj et al. [1] created a comprehensive taxonomy of irreproducibility causes, as well as case studies on their frequency and impact on packages for the Linux distributions Arch Linux and Debian. Their taxonomy is displayed in Fig. 1. The Reproducible Builds project [32] and Debian [5] maintain continuously updated lists of causes for irreproducibility, matching this taxonomy.

An interview with participants of the Reproducible Builds project performed by Fourné et al. [10] has confirmed that the highest impact root causes of timestamps, build paths and general randomness are also perceived as the most pressing obstacles when trying to achieve reproducible builds. They additionally bring

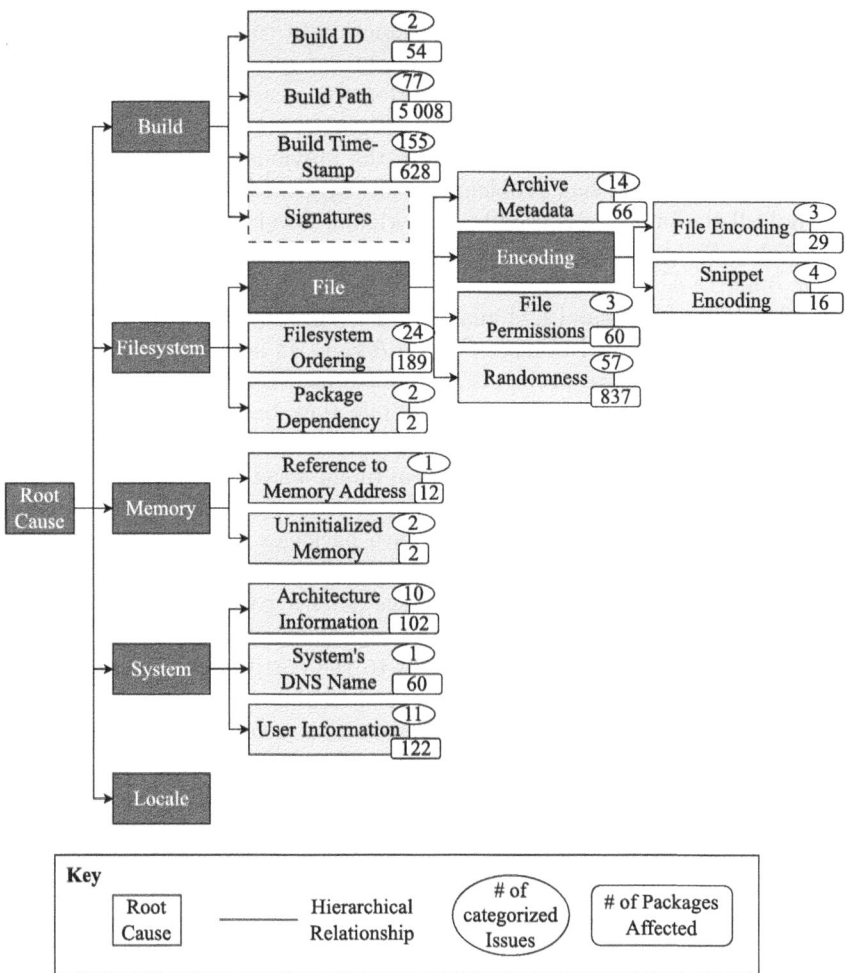

Fig. 1. Taxonomy of root causes for irreproducible builds in compiled language ecosystems by Bajaj et al. [1]. The number of issues belonging to a certain category is noted in the round box on the top right, with the number of affected packages noted in the rectangular box on the bottom right. The dashed box labelled "Signatures" has been amended by us as an additional root cause that has come up in other related work.

up signatures [10], which are sometimes part of the build artifacts. They do not appear in the previously mentioned taxonomy, because neither Arch Linux nor Debian include signatures as part of the package itself but rather as a separate detached artifact. However, other Linux distributions like Fedora do embed signatures into their packages [9]. We have therefore amended Fig. 1 to also include signatures as a root cause.

Artifact Reproduction. Artifact reproduction in compiled language ecosystems is not researched as well, with only three papers explicitly looking into the topic. In 2014 Carnavalet et al. [4] performed a case study, trying to reproduce the 16 most recent versions of the disk encryption software *TrueCrypt*[9]. Aside from reproducibility issues shown in the previously mentioned taxonomy displayed in Fig. 1, they had problems getting access to build tools. On the one hand, not all the build tools used by the original developers are free to use. On the other hand, older versions of the software required older, compatible versions of some build tools to build at all.

In 2024 Pöll and Roland [28] analysed the reproducibility of android builds at the example of so-called *Generic System Images*. In addition to the previously mentioned reproducibility problems, they also faced the challenge of matching the correct source code to the artifact. While they based their own builds on git tags matching the version of the image they want to rebuild, later analysis revealed that the respective Generic System Image was built from a later commit without a version tag.

Keshani et al. [20] tried reproducing Java packages from the Apache Maven registry. The main problems they experienced were missing links to source code repositories for given packages, missing tags denoting the exact revision of the source code that the package was built on, tags that by name match the version they try to rebuild but not actually point to the correct revision, and missing build environment definitions.

In summary, in addition to the challenges that general reproducible builds are facing, identified challenges unique to artifact reproduction are build tool availability and source code matching. While the low amount of studies combined the nature of these rather small case studies does not allow concluding that this is an exhaustive list of challenges regarding artifact reproduction in compiled language ecosystems, is serves our aim to map already identified challenges in this field to the field of scripting language ecosystems.

4.2   Reasons for Irreproducibility in Scripting Language Ecosystems

While fewer in number than for compiled language ecosystems, some studies also analysed reproducibility in scripting language ecosystems, for both reproducible builds and artifact reproduction. All the mentioned studies are described in detail in Sect. 3. This section highlights the mentioned reasons for irreproducibility.

Reproducible Builds. The only study to date that has performed an actual analysis of reproducible builds in scripting language ecosystems was performed by Benedetti et al. [2]. For the scripting language ecosystems surrounding Ruby, Python and NodeJS, they investigated how reproducible the native build pipeline of the ecosystem is, without external pre- or post-processing. They found that timestamps and file permissions were the largest contributors to irreproducibility.

---

[9] https://www.truecrypt.org/.

Some of these problems can be solved by configuration. For example, using the previously mentioned SOURCE_DATE_EPOCH environment variable is supported by pip. Likewise, pip can be configured to use different backends that actually perform the package builds, of which some deterministically fix the permissions for the packaged files, while others do not. However, none of the package managers under test have documentation indicating how to best configure them in order to achieve reproducible package builds [2].

As mentioned in Sect. 3 they also explicitly investigated how much native extensions—parts of the package written in a compiled language like C and called via foreign function interface—contribute to irreproducibility of these packages. While one might expect that these native extensions fall victim of the same reproducibility issues as the compiled language packages investigated in the beginning of this section, they actually found that native extensions do not affect the distribution of irreproducible packages, and furthermore, do not expose issues other than the timestamps and file permissions that packages without native extensions suffer from. They attribute this to the fact that for both, Python and NodeJS, the build systems building the native extensions have been optimized for reproducible builds already. For Ruby no such optimized build system is used, so they speculate that due to the nature of native extensions as dedicated functions usually performing a small isolated task, the root causes for irreproducibility identified for compiled language ecosystems, which were usually found in larger software packages, do not play a role [2].

Artifact Reproduction. A study of root causes for failing artifact reproduction has been performed by Goswami et al. [14]. As further described in Sect. 3, they tried reproducing all versions from the 1000 most depended upon packages. However, they excluded various packages from their analysis, due to no longer being publicly available in the npm registry, not exposing a link to the source code repository, or not explicitly defining a build script, resulting in a sample of 3390 versions for 229 distinct packages.

They find that almost 40% of package versions are not reproducible. This happened because the package was no longer publicly available in the npm registry, had no link to the source code For the remaining 2898 packages, they investigated the differences in source code files, resulting in the following categories:

- Different coding paradigms
- Different boolean expressions for the same logic
- Different number of statements or expressions
- Different variable names
- Different comments
- Different function or method order
- Different direct value assignments to variables

It is not further evaluated how much these differences in the code files cause differences in behaviour [14].

They derive three potential root causes: Version relaxation for build dependencies, unclear transpiler versions and unclear minifier versions, resulting in their own build process potentially using different build tool versions than the distributed artifact [14].

We argue that the latter two are just specializations of version relaxation, thus version relaxation of build tools being the overarching root cause of these observed diffs. Furthermore, we question the decision to exclude packages without a defined `build` script. As previously mentioned, the `build` script is an optional, user-defined script that is not required to successfully build a NodeJS package. At last, as noted in Sect. 3, the artifact they considered for their comparison is not the tarball that is actually distributed by the npm registry, but instead the individual files you get when unpacking this tarball, thus not taking any file metadata like timestamps or permission bits into account. However, as shown by Benedetti et al. [2], the `npm` package manager deterministically sets both of those, so it would likely not have come up as a problem anyway.

While not explicitly pursuing reproducible builds, the research by Vu et al. [37], Gao et al. [11] and Tsakpinis et al. [36] aiming to retrieve source code repositories for given packages, highlight that getting the source code at all, as well as getting the correct revision for a given version, is an unsolved problem. Even if registries were taking additional measures like enforcing links to source code or enforcing provenance information as specified by SLSA[10], giving strong guarantees for source code availability is hard. Not only does it depend on the willingness to publicly provide source code but also on external factors, like network availability to the source code hoster.

In summary, with regard to common problems for reproducible builds, we find that *build timestamps* and *file permissions* are identified as common causes for irreproducibility. As already mentioned by Benedetti et al. [2], an existing approach from the compiled language ecosystems, the `SOURCE_DATE_EPOCH` environment variable, is a viable solution to timestamp problems. Regarding artifact reproduction, acquiring source code, usually in the form of a git repository, as well as finding the correct revision corresponding to a given artifact within this repository are two identified problems. Additionally, unstable build dependencies resulting in other discrepancies are also found within both kinds of ecosystems.

In both cases, it has to be assumed that this is not a conclusive list. While reproducible builds have been analysed across multiple ecosystems, there was only a single study investigating the isolated effects of the native build command, disregarding potential pre- and post-processing steps. For example, any form of irreproducibility due to minification or transpilation, which is commonly used within NodeJS, is undetectable by the used methodology. Studies on artifact reproduction only investigate single ecosystems for their respective focus areas, making it hard to generalize their findings across other ecosystems even within scripting languages.

---

[10] https://slsa.dev/spec/v1.0/.

Response to RQ2: The common challenges regarding reproducible builds are build timestamps and file permissions. Common challenges regarding artifact reproduction are the acquisition of source code repositories, as well as the identification of matching repository revisions to a given artifact. Due to the low number of studies for scripting language ecosystems, as well as the nature of the existing research, this is not assumed to be a conclusive list.

Regarding challenges unique to scripting language ecosystems, none are identified for reproducible builds. For artifact reproduction, differences in source code files within artifacts are unique to scripting language ecosystems. However, as noted above, their suspected root cause, unstable versions of build dependencies, are a known problem in compiled language ecosystems too. Again, due to the small number of studies we assume this not to be a conclusive list, and that additional unique problems may be identified in the future, when a broader amount of ecosystems and build processes is analysed.

Response to RQ3: Regarding reproducible builds, no additional challenges are identified. Regarding artifact reproduction, additional challenges are various kinds of source code differences within released artifacts. Due to the low number of related studies within scripting language ecosystems, we cannot conclude that this is an exhaustive list.

5 Discussion

Reproducibility in compiled language ecosystems has been widely researched, and reproducibility in scripting language ecosystems is slowly catching up. However, ambiguities within the context of the reproducible builds ecosystem lead to ambiguous and inconsistent use of the same terms within the literature, making it hard to compare existing results.

It is not clear what exactly is meant with build reproducibility, and what it is applied to. The Reproducible Builds Project names it as a property of a *build*, without further specifying what exactly a build is [32], with other definitions not going into more detail either. We propose Definition 1 as a more precise definition, derived from the most common way we have seen the term used in practice, matching the broad definition of the Reproducible Builds Project. Additionally, current literature does not clearly differentiate between artifact reproduction and reproducible builds, as we have defined it. Common definitions of these terms help unifying what exactly is subject of reproducibility research, and what methodology is used to test it.

However, even this definition may be improved. It is undefined how exactly the build instructions are communicated to a building party. For example, in the NodeJS ecosystem, a build process would at least require running the commands `npm install` to install build dependencies, followed by `npm pack` to create the package from the source code. However, as noted before, there is a convention to also use the `npm build` command to execute build scripts, which is not explicitly endorsed by the ecosystem. If the entry point, the command the building party has to run in order to run the communicated build script, is unclear, different building parties may execute different commands, resulting in different conclusions about reproducibility. There appears to be the need for a universally agreed on entry point, at least within the scope of some context like an individual ecosystem, so that rebuilding parties know how to execute the build instructions.

Furthermore, we have also seen that the artifact to compare is not universally agreed on. While most research uses the artifact as it is distributed by the respective registry, some perform post-processing like unpacking the artifact archive and then comparing the contained files. An argument may be made that archive metadata is irrelevant to the behaviour of a certain artifact, since package managers often unpack them anyway. However, different file names or permissions might lead to different behaviour of the artifact during execution, but would not be caught by content only comparisons. Furthermore, especially when considering a malicious actor, the process of archive extraction may have unexpected side effects, which may not be noticed when comparing the apparent contents. For example, `tar` extraction may place files outside the current working directory without proper safeguards, possibly resultin in malicious files in places unnoticed by a user. We would therefore argue that the artifact to compare shall always be the artifact as it is distributed by the respective registry.

Doing such preprocessing of the distributed artifact may also be considered using a level 2 equivalence function instead of a level 1 equivalence function, leaving out the seemingly insignificant metadata. Inconsistent use of these comparison functions are also present across the industry, as for example the Fedora Project uses a level 2 equivalence function, disregarding embedded signatures [9], while the Reproducible Builds Project specifies the use of a level 1 equivalence function [32]. However, at least within the existing research, the term "reproducible builds" is always used in terms of level 1 equivalence, and any work deviating from this has coined their own term, like "verifiable builds" [4].

Furthermore, neither for reproducible builds, nor for artifact reproduction, there is a clear definition on when something counts as reproducible. Regarding reproducible builds, the most robust approach appears to be adversarial rebuilding (c.f. Sect. 2). However, there is no universal agreement on which external variables to change in what ways in order to label something as reproducible. Thus it could happen that builds are labelled as reproducible when they actually are not reproducible, if the irreproducibility causing external factors were not modified in the right way. For artifact reproduction, the case is less clear due to ambiguities like the aforementioned missing entry point. If building parties assume different entry points for the build script, they might come to different conclusions regarding the artifact's reproducibility.

This lack of standardization leads to difficulties when comparing research results, as they cause differences in methodologies in a way that results which appear to mean the same actually do not. Two studies claiming to analyse reproducibility of NodeJS packages, one concluding 100% reproducibility and the other claiming 10% reproducibility do not contradict each other, if one study performed registry artifact reproduction and the other compared adversarially rebuilt artifacts.

6   Future Research Directions

The provided review of literature allows us to identify multiple future research directions to advance the knowledge concerning reproducible builds in scripting language ecosystems.

With regard to the points of ambiguity mentioned in Sect. 5, procedures should be developed that allow for standardized research within and across ecosystems. While ambiguous naming is also a concern, research would mostly be required to create generic, standardized processes for both, registry artifact reproduction and adversarial rebuilding. A standardized format for communicating the build under test, as well as standard entry points for artifact reproduction have to be developed. Technologies that recently gained popularity, like provenance information with attestations or software bills of material might be promising candidates to contain parts of this information.

Regarding adversarial rebuilding, a set of environment variations shall be introduced which all builds under test should be subject to. If the artifacts stay the same under these variations, they can be labelled reproducible. This would help to standardize future reproducibility research, leading to more streamlined methodologies and more comparable results.

A taxonomy of root causes for irreproducibility regarding both artifact reproductions and reproducible builds, including a frequency and impact analysis similar to the work Bajaj et al. [1] have done for compiled language ecosystems, would be helpful to gain insights into categories of issues, and the ability to focus on high impact root causes. The work by Benedetti et al. [2] lays good groundwork regarding reproducible builds, and could be expanded to include more pre-processing steps, like executing the `build` script for NodeJS packages.

Finding root causes for discrepancies between artifact reproduction and reproducible builds results would also be helpful. Ideally, the registry artifact corresponding to any build that is regarded reproducible should also be able to be reproduced. However, we can see that this is not the case, for example comparing the results shown by Benedetti et al. [2] and Goswami et al. [14]. The reason for this probably lies in arbitrary pre- and post-processing steps executed by the project maintainer when creating the artifact that is distributed by the registry, but are not obvious to a rebuilding party. Finding out if there are typical steps in the respective ecosystems, like the aforementioned `build` script for NodeJS packages, could help to standardize build instructions rebuilding parties shall perform, and while this standardization process is ongoing, could also assist in closing the gap between artifact reproduction and reproducible builds research.

Once more reasons for irreproducibility in scripting language ecosystems have been established, more research into fixing these problems can be performed.

Again, the work by Benedetti et al. [2] shows a good example, transferring the use of the `SOURCE_DATE_EPOCH` environment variable from compiled language ecosystems to scripting language ecosystems, and proposing patches to package managers that fix non-deterministic file permission bits.

7   Conclusion

In this work we have analysed literature regarding reproducibility research, with a focus on scripting language ecosystems. We have shown that in general, research in this field is still sparse, but the concentration of publications in recent years indicates that it is gaining popularity. In contrast to compiled language ecosystems, the literature focuses more on reproducing distributed artifacts, than proving the reproducibility of the build process itself.

The identified reasons for irreproducibility so far only consist of a small subset of root causes identified for compiled language ecosystems, in addition to differences in source code files of the distributed artifact, which are unique to scripting language ecosystems by nature. However, due to the little research done so far and individual studies focusing on single ecosystems, we assume that more root causes may be discovered in the future.

Furthermore, we pointed out problems with comparability of research results, due to ambiguities in existing definitions of reproducibility, and resulting inconsistencies in their interpretation in the literature. We proposed more rigid notions of reproducible build and artifact reproduction, and advocate for more standardization in evaluation processes in the future.

References

1. Bajaj, R., Fernandes, E., Adams, B., Hassan, A.E.: Unreproducible builds: time to fix, causes, and correlation with external ecosystem factors. Empirical Softw. Engg. **29**(1) (2023)
2. Benedetti, G., et al.: An empirical study on reproducible packaging in open-source ecosystems (2025). https://www.cs.cmu.edu/~ckaestne/pdf/icse25_rb.pdf
3. Black, J.: The three pillars of reproducible builds. https://fossa.com/blog/three-pillars-reproducible-builds/. Accessed 05 Feb 2025
4. De Carné de Carnavalet, X., Mannan, M.: Challenges and implications of verifiable builds for security-critical open-source software. In: Proceedings of the 30th Annual Computer Security Applications Conference, ACSAC 2014, pp. 16–25. Association for Computing Machinery, New York (2014)
5. Debian: Notes on build reproducibility of debian packages. https://salsa.debian.org/reproducible-builds/reproducible-notes/-/tree/master. Accessed 21 Oct 2024
6. DeHamer, B., Harrison, P.: Introducing NPM package provenance (2023). https://github.blog/security/supply-chain-security/introducing-npm-package-provenance/. Accessed 29 Oct 2024
7. Dietrich, J., White, T., Hassanshahi, B., Krishnan, P.: Levels of binary equivalence for the comparison of binaries from alternative builds. arXiv preprint arXiv:2410.08427 (2024)

8. Drexel, J., Hänggi, E., Veiga, I.M.: Reproducible builds and insights from an independent verifier for arch linux. In: Sicherheit 2024, pp. 243–257. Gesellschaft für Informatik e.V., Bonn (2024)
9. Fedora Project: Fedora reproducible builds. https://docs.fedoraproject.org/en-US/reproducible-builds/. Accessed 05 Feb 2025
10. Fourné, M., Wermke, D., Enck, W., Fahl, S., Acar, Y.: It's like flossing your teeth: on the importance and challenges of reproducible builds for software supply chain security. In: 2023 IEEE Symposium on Security and Privacy (SP), pp. 1527–1544 (2023)
11. Gao, K., Xu, W., Yang, W., Zhou, M.: Pyradar: towards automatically retrieving and validating source code repository information for pypi packages. Proc. ACM Softw. Eng. 1(FSE) (2024)
12. Gonzalez, D., Zimmermann, T., Godefroid, P., Schäfer, M.: Anomalicious: automated detection of anomalousand potentially malicious commits on github (2021)
13. Gooding, S.: Ultralytics pypi package compromised through github actions (2024). https://socket.dev/blog/ultralytics-pypi-package-compromised-through-github-actions-cache-poisoning. Accessed 25 Feb 2025
14. Goswami, P., Gupta, S., Li, Z., Meng, N., Yao, D.: Investigating the reproducibility of NPM packages. In: 2020 IEEE International Conference on Software Maintenance and Evolution (ICSME), pp. 677–681 (2020)
15. NPM Inc.: CLI commands | NPM docs. https://docs.npmjs.com/cli/v11/commands. Accessed 27 Feb 2025
16. NPM Inc.: NPM-install | NPM docs. https://docs.npmjs.com/cli/v11/commands/npm-install. Accessed 27 Feb 2025
17. NPM Inc.: scripts | NPM docs. https://docs.npmjs.com/cli/v11/using-npm/scripts. Accessed 27 Feb 2025
18. Ingram, D.: Pypi now supports digital attestations (2024). https://blog.pypi.org/posts/2024-11-14-pypi-now-supports-digital-attestations/. Accessed 28 Feb 2025
19. Judge, R., Lock, J.: What makes a build reproducible, part 1 (2022). https://blogs.vmware.com/opensource/2022/07/12/what-makes-a-build-reproducible-part-1/. Accessed 05 Feb 2025
20. Keshani, M., Velican, T.G., Bot, G., Proksch, S.: Aroma: automatic reproduction of maven artifacts. Proc. ACM Softw. Eng. 1(FSE) (2024)
21. Lakhotia, A., Preda, M.D., Giacobazzi, R.: Fast location of similar code fragments using semantic 'juice'. In: McDonald, J.T., Preda, M.D. (eds.) Proceedings of the 2nd ACM SIGPLAN Program Protection and Reverse Engineering Workshop 2013, PPREW@POPL 2013, 26 January 2013, Rome, Italy, pp. 5:1–5:6. ACM (2013)
22. Lamb, C., Zacchiroli, S.: Reproducible builds: increasing the integrity of software supply chains. IEEE Softw. 39(2), 62–70 (2022)
23. Mukherjee, S., Almanza, A., Rubio-González, C.: Fixing dependency errors for python build reproducibility. In: Proceedings of the 30th ACM SIGSOFT International Symposium on Software Testing and Analysis, ISSTA 2021, pp. 439–451. Association for Computing Machinery, New York (2021)
24. Navarro Leija, O.S., et al.: Reproducible containers. In: Proceedings of the Twenty-Fifth International Conference on Architectural Support for Programming Languages and Operating Systems, ASPLOS 2020, pp. 167–182. Association for Computing Machinery, New York (2020)
25. Ohm, M., Boes, F., Bungartz, C., Meier, M.: On the feasibility of supervised machine learning for the detection of malicious software packages. In: Proceedings of the 17th International Conference on Availability, Reliability and Security. ARES 2022. ACM (2022)

26. Peterson, B.: Pep 552 - removing PGP from pypi. https://peps.python.org/pep-0552/. Accessed 28 Feb 2025
27. Pokorný, F.: Pep 710 – recording the provenance of installed packages (2023). https://peps.python.org/pep-0710/. Accessed 28 Feb 2025
28. Pöll, M., Roland, M.: Automating the quantitative analysis of reproducibility for build artifacts derived from the android open source project. In: Proceedings of the 15th ACM Conference on Security and Privacy in Wireless and Mobile Networks, WiSec 2022, pp. 6–19. Association for Computing Machinery (2022)
29. Randrianaina, G.A., Khelladi, D.E., Zendra, O., Acher, M.: Options matter: documenting and fixing non-reproducible builds in highly-configurable systems. In: Proceedings of the 21st International Conference on Mining Software Repositories, MSR 2024, pp. 654–664. Association for Computing Machinery (2024)
30. Ren, Z., Liu, C., Xiao, X., Jiang, H., Xie, T.: Root cause localization for unreproducible builds via causality analysis over system call tracing. In: 2019 34th IEEE/ACM International Conference on Automated Software Engineering (ASE), pp. 527–538 (2019)
31. Ren, Z., Sun, S., Xuan, J., Li, X., Zhou, Z., Jiang, H.: Automated patching for unreproducible builds. In: Proceedings of the 44th International Conference on Software Engineering, ICSE 2022, pp. 200–211. Association for Computing Machinery, New York (2022)
32. Reproducible Builds Project: Reproducible builds. https://reproducible-builds.org/. Accessed 21 Oct 2024
33. Sejfia, A., Schäfer, M.: Practical automated detection of malicious NPM packages (2022)
34. StackOverflow: Stackoverflow developer survey (2024). https://survey.stackoverflow.co/2024/technology/. Accessed 21 Feb 2025
35. Tomassi, D.A., et al.: Bugswarm: mining and continuously growing a dataset of reproducible failures and fixes. In: 2019 IEEE/ACM 41st International Conference on Software Engineering (ICSE). IEEE (2019)
36. Tsakpinis, A., Pretschner, A.: Analyzing the accessibility of github repositories for pypi and NPM libraries. In: Proceedings of the 28th International Conference on Evaluation and Assessment in Software Engineering, EASE 2024, pp. 345–350. Association for Computing Machinery, New York (2024)
37. Vu, D.L.: Py2src: towards the automatic (and reliable) identification of sources for pypi package. In: Proceedings of the 36th IEEE/ACM International Conference on Automated Software Engineering, ASE 2021, pp. 1394–1395. IEEE Press (2021)
38. Vu, D.L., Massacci, F., Pashchenko, I., Plate, H., Sabetta, A.: Lastpymile: identifying the discrepancy between sources and packages. In: Proceedings of the 29th ACM Joint Meeting on European Software Engineering Conference and Symposium on the Foundations of Software Engineering, ESEC/FSE 2021, pp. 780–792. Association for Computing Machinery, New York (2021)
39. Yocto Project: Reproducible builds. https://docs.yoctoproject.org/test-manual/reproducible-builds.html. Accessed 05 Feb 2025

Clustering Malware at Scale: A First Full-Benchmark Study

Martin Mocko[1,2]([✉]) [ID], Jakub Ševcech[4] [ID], and Daniela Chudá[2,3] [ID]

[1] Faculty of Information Technology, Brno University of Technology, Brno, Czechia
[2] Kempelen Institute of Intelligent Technologies, Bratislava, Slovakia
`martin.mocko@kinit.sk, daniela.chuda@stuba.sk`
[3] Faculty of Electrical Engineering and Information Technology, Slovak University of Technology, Bratislava, Slovakia
[4] Swiss Re, Bratislava, Slovakia
`jakub_sevcech@swissre.com`

Abstract. Recent years have shown that malware attacks still happen with high frequency. Malware experts seek to categorize and classify incoming samples to confirm their trustworthiness or prove their maliciousness. One of the ways in which groups of malware samples can be identified is through malware clustering. Despite the efforts of the community, malware clustering which incorporates benign samples has been under-explored. Moreover, despite the availability of larger public benchmark malware datasets, malware clustering studies have avoided fully utilizing these datasets in their experiments, often resorting to small datasets with only a few families. Additionally, the current state-of-the-art solutions for malware clustering remain unclear. Our study evaluates malware clustering quality and establishes the state-of-the-art on Bodmas and Ember - two large public benchmark malware datasets. Ours is the first study of malware clustering performed on whole malware benchmark datasets. Additionally, we extend the malware clustering task by incorporating benign samples. Our results indicate that incorporating benign samples does not significantly degrade clustering quality. We find significant differences in the quality of the created clusters between Ember and Bodmas, as well as a private industry dataset. Contrary to popular opinion, our top clustering performers are K-Means and BIRCH, with DBSCAN and HAC falling behind.

Keywords: Clustering · Malware · PE File · Public Malware Dataset · Ember · Bodmas

1 Introduction

Even in 2025, malware attacks and threats still represent a very relevant and pressing issue. Just recently, the security researchers from Human Security[1] have

---

[1] https://www.humansecurity.com/learn/blog/satori-threat-intelligence-disruption-badbox-2-0/.

M. Dalla Preda et al. (Eds.): ARES 2025, LNCS 15993, pp. 231–251, 2025.
https://doi.org/10.1007/978-3-032-00627-1_12

uncovered BADBOX 2.0 - the largest ever uncovered botnet of infected connected TV devices. This botnet contained over 1 million infected devices worldwide and was used for fraud schemes such as click fraud, ad fraud, and unauthorized proxy services. The amount of malware (but also of standard benign software) that is created daily makes it impossible to investigate all new incoming samples and assess their maliciousness *manually* by malware experts [1,18]. Therefore, there is a need to automate the analysis of incoming samples.

When looking at the malware domain from the machine learning perspective, two main ways of approaching the problem become apparent: either utilizing supervised models to classify data into (multiple) classes or utilizing unsupervised models to enable a different outlook on their data based on sample (cluster) similarity. The classification problems can be binary, such as malware detection, or into N classes, like malware family classification [1]. A similar distinction can be considered for the problems of clustering as well - however, most existing works that perform clustering of malware avoid considering benign samples in their experiments - the assumption is that benign samples have been previously filtered out by another mechanism (for example, a malware detection system).

Our work focuses on the under-researched area of *clustering incoming samples* - under no previous assumptions about their maliciousness. From our perspective, binary program clustering is the correct name for this task. However, given its close relation and conceptual overlap, we will primarily refer to the task as "malware clustering". Furthermore, some works have used the term malware clustering to mean binary program clustering before this work as well [2,21]. Utilizing such an approach makes the final solution more versatile - i.e., there is no assumption or reliance on any filtering approach used to filter out benign samples. This makes the entire solution more flexible, as it can, in theory, reveal interesting relationships between malware and clean software, as well as among malware families. The problem is also more complex to solve - the task is not just to differentiate different malware families from each other but also to distinguish these families from the relatively vast space of benign samples.

Utilizing malware clustering on the whole space of all samples (both benign and malicious) thus has the following benefits:

- can aid in analysis tasks done by malware experts[2];
- allows for generating signatures that cover the whole cluster or multiple clusters (See footnote 2);
- is unbiased by other systems (i.e., does not rely on the effectiveness of other systems for sample filtering);
- provides a different look at sample space via distance/similarity measures;
- and has the potential to create compressed datasets for further (ML or other) experimentation.

Furthermore, as will be shown in Sect. 2 and to the best of our knowledge, existing work lacks a comparison of malware clustering approaches on large public malware benchmark datasets. A few works exist which perform clustering on

---

[2] This also applies to regular malware clustering without benign samples.

public benchmark datasets. However, only a subset of the data is usually selected where the number of families is relatively low (i.e., less than 10) [12,13]. At the same time, the whole dataset contains at least two orders of magnitude more malware families. Such approaches do not provide the complete picture of the malware clustering quality in scenarios where the number of malware families is much greater. Therefore, a more thorough study on the *full* set of malware benchmark dataset samples is needed.

There are several more issues in the existing works that we, at least partially, try to address with our experiments. First, from the existing literature, it is not exactly clear what the state-of-the-art in malware clustering is (explained more in Sect. 2). Second, we identify Homogeneity as the primary metric for malware clustering evaluation because when clusters' label cohesion is high, the utility of such clustering is much greater for malware experts. Besides working with public benchmark malware datasets, we also employ a private industry real-world malware dataset. Therefore, our findings are also supported by experimental evidence on a real-world dataset.

The main contribution of this work is multi-fold and can be summarized as follows:

- To the best of our knowledge, our work is the first malware clustering study performed on *full* large public malware benchmark datasets (i.e., not on small subsets) - on Bodmas and Ember. Additionally, we also include a real-world private industry dataset in our experiments;
- We extend the usual malware clustering task by incorporating benign samples, extending the potential use cases of malware clustering. Our results suggest that the inclusion of benign samples does not have a significant negative effect on the clustering quality;
- Our experiments show that the malware clustering quality is highly dependent on the (sample) composition of the dataset - with the Ember dataset achieving sub-par results in Homogeneity compared to Bodmas. Our ablation study shows only a small Homogeneity increase when increasing the number of components, ruling out the number of clusters as a significant contributor to the low Ember cluster quality;
- Contrary to common assumptions, our experiments show that K-Means and BIRCH outperform other tested clustering approaches for malware clustering, while DBSCAN and Hierarchical Agglomerative Clustering exhibit lower Homogeneity.

This paper is organized as follows: Sect. 2 discusses the related work and provides the main ground on which the motivation for our experiments is based. Section 3 describes the methodology employed for our experiments. Experiments are conducted and results reported in Sect. 4. Discussion about the results can be found in Sect. 5. We conclude our work in Sect. 6.

2   Related Work

This section summarizes the existing research work relevant to our study. We examine related work in terms of the clustering task being solved, the datasets utilized in the study experiments, and from the perspective of clustering algorithms, achieved results and evaluation metrics. We identify gaps in existing research that motivate our work.

2.1   Clustering Task Perspective

In this subsection, we will look at existing research from the perspective of the clustering task that the research addresses. We will differentiate between malware clustering where no benign samples were used and refer to it as "malware clustering". When a research paper addresses the clustering of both malware and benign binary samples, we will refer to the task as "binary program clustering". If another task is being solved, it will be pointed out. Among existing studies on clustering, only one was identified that specifically addresses the task of binary program clustering [2]. On the other hand, there are a lot more works that focus on malware clustering [5,7,8,10,11,19]. Therefore, a thorough investigation of binary program clustering is warranted. Some works not only perform malware clustering but can also perform new malware family identification/discovery without the need to re-train the clustering approach [20,22]. However, they are also in a minority. The usual way new malware family identification is approached is that the solution combines a classification approach that filters out the known malware with a clustering approach that analyzes the rest of the samples. The latter approach performs the discovery process.

2.2   Dataset Perspective

To the best of our knowledge, no existing works perform binary program or malware clustering, *on the full benchmark datasets*. There are some works, however, that use some small subset of benchmark datasets. In the COUGAR paper by Wilkins et al. [23], experiments are performed on a subset of around 5,000 malware (only) samples from the Ember dataset. Their follow-up work extending COUGAR [14] utilizes 10,000 malware (only) samples from the Ember dataset. The most recent we found are two very similar works from 2024 by a very similar author collective [12,13]. In these works, the Ember dataset is utilized for experiments. However, it is only a subset that captures seven malware families out of more than 3,000 that can be found in Ember (although the number of malware samples is more decent).

Other identified works that do malware clustering usually utilize a small (i.e., thousands of samples) private industry dataset [8,10] or a dataset from a public malware source that usually is not very large either [19,22]. In most cases, this also means that the number of malware families in the dataset is relatively low (usually between 10 to 100). Only a few exceptions can be found. The work of Ali et al. [2] utilizes millions of samples - from 1 million up to 10 million.

We are not aware of a similar work. More importantly, the dataset used in the work is not publicly available, and information about the number of malware families is undisclosed. Hu et al. [11] utilize 132,234 malware samples from a public archive, and the two works by Jurečková et al. [12,13] utilize 7 Ember malware families totaling 112,651 malware samples in total. Conducting experiments under standardized benchmark conditions, particularly regarding data, helps the community compare proposed approaches and properly establish the state-of-the-art. Thus, the importance of conducting experiments on benchmark datasets cannot be overstated.

Looking at existing work, it is apparent that there is a wide range of used datasets - public and private, with static or dynamic features, smaller and larger. Most of the existing work utilized static malware datasets. Our work will primarily focus on two public malware benchmark datasets containing the same set of static features.

2.3 The Perspective of Clustering Algorithms, Results and Evaluation Metrics

From the perspective of clustering algorithms, many different clustering algorithms have been utilized. From K-Means [15], DBSCAN [6], Hierarchical Agglomerative Clustering (HAC) [16], OPTICS [4], BIRCH [25], clustering based on prototypes, and even LSH Bins. Even when using multiple clustering algorithms in a single research work, the winning algorithm is not always the same. Pitolli et al. [20] proposed using BIRCH to identify new malware families and achieved 81.9% Adjusted Rand Index. Faridi et al. performed a comparative study with HAC, K-Means++, DBSCAN, Spectral clustering, Affinity Propagation, and LSH Bins and achieved 92.1% V-Measure. Ali et al. [2] proposed a two-step approach of coarse clustering through K-Means combined with a fine-grained Threshold based Hierarchical Agglomerative Clustering (HAC-T) and achieved 98% Purity while clustering 66% of the dataset, therefore regarding the rest 34% as noise. A prototype-based approach was proposed by Hu et al. [11], and a Precision of 72% to 89% was achieved. An evolutionary approach was proposed by Wilkins et al. [23] and further extended in a follow-up work by MacAskill et al. [14] where Homogeneity of 73% and 79% was achieved on a very small Ember subset.

Another aspect of malware clustering is the number of clusters utilized. The default approach adopted in most works is to utilize the same number of clusters as the reported number of families. However, such an approach highly depends on the quality of the malware family labels. Moreover, multiple works have identified that clustering algorithms sometimes divide malware families into subfamilies [10,11].

Although many clustering approaches were tested, and even more evaluation metrics were used, it is still unclear what the state-of-the-art malware clustering approach is. One 2021 work [14] cited MutantX-S, a work from 2013 [11], as state-of-the-art. We have not found any more works mentioning state-of-the-art for malware clustering. Therefore, there is a clear need for a comparison performed on benchmark datasets to bring more clarity to the situation. The existing work makes it non-obvious to know whether the results achieved previously on other, primarily smaller, datasets translate to larger benchmark datasets.

3   Malware Clustering on Large Datasets

This section addresses the shortcomings introduced in Sects. 1 and 2 and describes the task and methodology employed to perform malware clustering experiments. Formally, we define the malware clustering task with the inclusion of benign samples as follows: let $D = \{(x_i, y_i)\}_{i=1}^{n}$ be a dataset of n samples, where $x_i \in \mathbb{R}^d$ represents the real-valued feature vector of the i-th sample with d dimensions and $y_i \in \mathcal{Y}$ is the ground truth label. The set of all possible labels is defined as $\mathcal{Y} = \{l_1, l_2, l_3, \ldots, l_m, b\}$, where $l_1, l_2, l_3, \ldots, l_m$ correspond to m malware families and b represents the benign class. The goal is to partition $\mathbb{R}^d$ into a set of clusters $\mathcal{C} = \{C_1, C_2, \ldots\}$, where each C_j is a subset of $\mathbb{R}^d$ and j corresponds to the j-th cluster.

3.1   Datasets

Based on the presented related work in Sect. 2, we defined criteria for a public malware benchmark dataset on which it makes sense to perform the experiments. The dataset's key criteria include:

- large(r) number of samples,
- large(r) number of malware families,
- availability of malware family labels,
- inclusion of both benign and malware samples,
- pre-extracted features (rather than the dataset containing only raw PE samples).

For the purpose of this study, a large number of samples is considered to be at least tens of thousands of samples. For the criteria defined above, we have found the following two public benchmark datasets that fit: Bodmas [24] and Ember [3]. Another large malware benchmark dataset, Sorel [9], does not fulfill one of the criteria - the availability of malware families. Therefore, we did not include it in this work. We also acquired a real-world industry malware dataset, further on referred to as Security, which the company used to train their actual AI models. It also fulfilled our dataset criteria (besides being publicly available). Therefore, we also used it in our experiments. Besides clustering the training sets of the respective datasets, we also predicted clusters for the respective test sets. Ember and Security come with pre-defined test sets, while for Bodmas, a train-test split with a ratio of 90:10 was created. Table 1 summarizes general information about the respective datasets used for our experiments.

Ember is the first real public malware benchmark dataset, published in 2018 [3]. More specifically, it is a collection of features extracted from various malware and benign samples - malware or benign samples were not made available. Together with the dataset, the authors also published a reusable codebase for extracting static features from PE files, making it a de facto feature standard for publishing malware datasets. Ember can be divided into two distinct datasets. One is an easier (for classification) dataset where the samples were collected up to 2017. The second, where samples were collected up to 2018, is a dataset where the samples were explicitly chosen in a way that the resultant training and test sets would be more challenging for machine learning algorithms to classify, according to the authors[3]. We are utilizing the more challenging 2018 version of the Ember dataset. Table 2 summarizes features that can be found in the Ember dataset.

Bodmas [24], a dataset published in 2021, tries to improve the public malware benchmark dataset situation in two ways. First, they include timestamps in their dataset. This enables researchers to study concept drift in the malware domain. It also enables researchers to perform their studies on a more fine-grained (i.e., multi-month or multi-year) basis. Second, they provide well-curated malware family information - their family labels were curated by their in-house scripts, and some were labeled manually by domain experts. Bodmas is published with Ember features. The last benefit of Bodmas is that the malware samples are made public - this increases the reusability of their dataset with other sets of features.

Security is a private malware dataset provided to us by a company from the software security industry. Therefore, we are not allowed to disclose very specific information. The oldest samples date back to 2001, and the latest to 2021. The features are based mostly on static analysis, but some may be based on emulation or dynamic analysis.

Table 1. Description of datasets that met the criteria for experiments conducted in this study. M/B ratio represents the ratio between malware and benign samples in the respective dataset.

Dataset	Year	# features	Dataset size	M/B ratio	# malware families
Bodmas	2021	2381[a]	134 435 total	43:57	581[b]
Ember v2	2018	2381[a]	600 000 train 200 000 test	50:50	~3000 AVclass
Security	2021	140	9.6 mil. train 100 000 test	37:63	~9800[c]

[a] Ember features
[b] determined by malware experts
[c] private labeling

---

[3] https://github.com/elastic/ember.

Table 2. Description of the 2381 Ember features that can be found both in the Ember and Bodmas dataset. Feature position numbers are also provided (with zero-based indexing).

Feature position	Feature category
0–255	Byte histogram
256–511	Byte entropy histogram
512–615	String extractor
616–625	General file info
626–687	Header file info
688–942	Section information
943–2222	Imports information
2223–2350	Exports information
2351–2380	Data directories information

3.2   Clustering Algorithms

Based on the presented related work in Sect. 2, we have decided to pick several representatives of different types of clustering used in malware clustering research: partitioning-based, density-based, and hierarchy-based. The most popular partitioning-based algorithm in the reviewed malware clustering literature was K-Means [2,8]. Among density-based clustering algorithms, the first place belongs to DBSCAN, which achieved top results in a few works [8,23]. Hierarchical Agglomerative Clustering (HAC), our choice for hierarchy-based clustering, also achieved top results [2,8]. Finally, we also chose a hybrid clustering algorithm - BIRCH. It is a hybrid combination of partitioning-based and hierarchy-based clustering. BIRCH was also the clustering algorithm of choice in multiple malware clustering works [5,19,20].

3.3   Representation Learning Techniques

The Ember feature set has a relatively high dimensionality of 2381. Therefore, a dimensionality reduction technique is appropriate. Existing research also does not specify which dimensionality reduction/representation learning technique is best for malware clustering. Therefore, we chose Principal Component Analysis (PCA), Autoencoder (AE), and UMAP [17] for our experiments. UMAP was also used for the COUGAR method [23] while PCA and Autoencoder are typical dimensionality reduction techniques used across many machine learning domains.

3.4   Experimental Setup

As mentioned earlier, we focus on the problem of clustering both malware and benign samples. Figure 1 shows a high-level description of our methodology. The

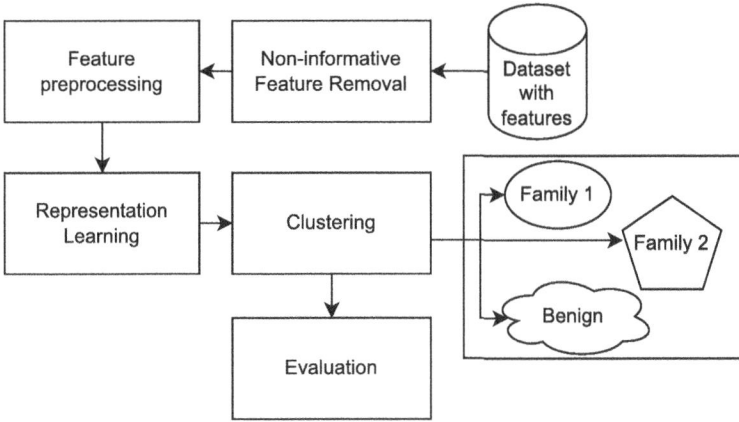

Fig. 1. Methodology for our malware clustering experiments. Our approach aims to form multiple clusters, separating diverse malware families from benign samples.

datasets identified in Sect. 3.1 were either already published with a train-test dataset split, or in the case of Bodmas, we created a train-test split with the ratio of 90:10. Our experiment pipeline takes all the samples from the train set of the respective datasets and first performs a feature elimination step. It removes all features that should not be used (i.e., label, family name, and so forth) or uninformative features and features that harm the representation learning process. During our preliminary phase of experiments, where we transformed features into a lower dimension, we discovered that some Ember features harmed the training process and decided to remove them. This resulted in utilizing 2235 features for Ember and Bodmas and 135 features in the case of Security.

The next step of our methodology is data preprocessing. For all three datasets, we perform the same preprocessing steps. We utilize a sequence of three preprocessors from the `sklearn`[4] library in the following order: RobustScaler (to first remove anomalies), StandardScaler (to standardize our features), and Min-MaxScaler (to lower the scale of features into a $[0; 1]$ range).

For representation learning, we used `sklearn` for PCA, `tensorflow`[5] for Autoencoder, and `umap-learn`[6] for training the UMAP representation. The embedding size was chosen to be 10, providing a great amount of compression as well as making it easier to compute distances compared to the original 2381 (2235) features.

DBSCAN, HAC, and BIRCH implementations were used from `sklearn`. For K-Means, we resorted to utilizing the RAPIDS cuML package to achieve a GPU speedup of the training process. In the end, for some DBSCAN computations,

---

[4] https://scikit-learn.org/.
[5] https://www.tensorflow.org/.
[6] https://umap-learn.readthedocs.io/.

we ended up utilizing the ELKI[7] implementation in Java. The implementation ran much faster and consumed less memory than the sklearn implementation, probably due to using the R-tree index structure.

We strived to achieve similar conditions for all the clustering algorithms, mainly regarding the number of clusters. Existing work in Sect. 2 shows that clustering algorithms often divide malware families into sub-families. Moreover, the extension of malware clustering by including benign samples poses a need to utilize more clusters than the reported number of malware families, thereby creating space for "benign" families. Therefore, we decided to include a broader range of the number of clusters to accommodate the potential need for a higher number of clusters. The number of clusters can be explicitly set for three out of the four algorithms chosen. In this case, we experimented with a wide range of clusters where $n\_clusters = [100, 500, 1000, 2000, 10\,000, 20\,000, 30\,000, 50\,000]$. These numbers of clusters were utilized for experiments with Ember and Security fully. However, for experiments with Bodmas, we resorted to utilizing only up to 2000 clusters. For Bodmas, going too far beyond these numbers is not desirable, as the theorized average number of samples per cluster would be relatively low.

For DBSCAN, the main two parameters affecting the number of created clusters (besides data itself) are the minimum number of points required to form a cluster (referred to as $MinPts$) and the maximum distance between two samples for them to be considered in the neighborhood of each other (referred to as $Epsilon$). It is hard to control DBSCAN's number of created clusters. Therefore, we defined various $Epsilon$ levels, which we trained on: $Epsilon = [3, 2, 1, 0.5, 0.3, 0.2, 0.1, 0.05, 0.02]$. $MinPts$ was set to 5. Combining three datasets, three representations, four clustering algorithms, and 8–9 cluster sizes resulted in around 300 clustering runs.

Furthermore, during the initial experimental phase, we discovered that HAC tends to use a lot of computer memory due to its large memory complexity. Usually, for a number of clusters greater than 2000, it demanded more than our server's available memory. Therefore, in the case of HAC, we resorted to training on a subset of the training dataset. Afterward, we trained a classification model on the cluster labels generated by HAC on the training data subset. This model was then used to assign clusters to the rest of the training data.

After training the clustering algorithms on the training set, we also perform a prediction for the test set. K-Means and BIRCH provide a prediction function in the implementation. For DBSCAN, we implemented the prediction function ourselves based on public consensus[8]. For HAC, we used the classifier that was used to classify the rest of its training data to predict the cluster assignment on new data. Our experiments were run on a CentOS 7 server with 64 CPU cores, 512 GB of RAM, and a 32GB VRAM graphics card. The source code for our experiments is also publicly available[9].

---

[7] https://elki-project.github.io/.

[8] https://stackoverflow.com/questions/27822752/scikit-learn-predicting-new-points-with-dbscan.

[9] https://github.com/kinit-sk/clustering-ares-2025.

3.5   Evaluation Metrics

The literature review in Sect. 2 showed that different works report different evaluation metrics for their malware clustering results. From our perspective, malware (and benign) clusters are useful when they are largely dominated by the same label (i.e., malware or benign). In the case of malware, they should be dominated by the same malware family. If one malware family was divided into several different sub-families using clustering, this does not constitute a huge problem. There is evidence from existing research that this division into sub-families happens in practice as well [10,11], thereby creating more clusters than the supposed number of malware families. Therefore, cluster "purity" is more important than cluster completeness for our experiments. Consequently, our *primary* metric for experiment evaluation is Homogeneity. It can be defined as:

$$h = \begin{cases} 1, & \text{if } H(C, K) = 0 \\ 1 - \frac{H(C|K)}{H(C)}, & \text{otherwise} \end{cases} \tag{1}$$

Similarly, Completeness can be defined as:

$$c = \begin{cases} 1, & \text{if } H(K, C) = 0 \\ 1 - \frac{H(K|C)}{H(K)}, & \text{otherwise} \end{cases} \tag{2}$$

In both equations H corresponds to entropy. The harmonic mean between Homogeneity and Completeness is V-Measure:

$$v = 2 \cdot \frac{h \cdot c}{h + c} \tag{3}$$

Completeness can inform us about how well the families are localized in one cluster – the more the families are spread into multiple clusters, the worse the score gets. Additionally, in the extreme case where every sample would become its cluster, we would get a perfect Homogeneity of 100% and a Completeness of 0%. However, such clustering is undesirable and would not be useful for any of the tasks presented in Sect. 1 where malware clustering is helpful. Therefore, besides reporting Homogeneity, we also report V-Measure, which we deem a balance between Homogeneity and cluster Completeness.

4   Experimental Evaluation

4.1   Quantitative Results

Running around 300 clustering runs yielded a large table of results. We summarize these results using multiple figures and tables. First, we share more general aggregated results about our experiment. Afterwards, results specific to each dataset are presented. If not further specified, we will generally refer to the evaluation metrics achieved on the *train* set of the datasets.

In the top-left graph of Fig. 2, we can see that, on average, the clustering algorithms achieved the highest Homogeneity on Bodmas - above 70%. Security, the private real-world industry dataset, achieved second place with Homogeneity being, on average, around 40%. Surprisingly, Ember was the worst of the three datasets to cluster, with mean Homogeneity only above 20%.

Looking at maximum Homogeneity (in the top-right graph of Fig. 2) achieved on the datasets, we can see that the difference between mean and maximum Homogeneity can often be quite large, above 20%. This is related to the relatively large spread of the number of clusters used in our experiments. Table 3 summarizes the best results achieved for the respective datasets. From it, we can see that K-Means consistently beat the other clustering algorithms in the race for best results. The best result overall, and the best result for Bodmas as well, was 92.5% Homogeneity achieved using UMAP representation. The best achieved Homogeneity on a real-world dataset, Security, was 77.64% - a relatively good result considering that this is the largest dataset in terms of samples and number of malware families. For Ember, all the clustering methods struggled to achieve a good clustering quality, with the best result being 42.66% Homogeneity. On all of the datasets, V-Measure stayed relatively low (8% to 16%) for the best results - a consequence of penalization through Completeness because of the utilization of more clusters than the reported number of malware families.

General aggregated results for the three utilized representations (lower-left graph of Fig. 2) show that PCA, on average, performed better than the other two representations. Interestingly, on average, UMAP and Autoencoder seem to have a very similar performance. A more telling story is when we look at results for the quality of representations grouped by datasets. Figure 3 shows mean and maximum Homogeneity for the three different representations grouped by datasets. The mean Homogeneity results suggest that UMAP could be considered the best representation for Ember and Bodmas. However, the most important information is which representation could achieve the best results. Indeed, for maximum Homogeneity, we see that PCA and Autoencoder achieved the best results on two out of three datasets. Bodmas shows a different story, with UMAP taking the first place. This could suggest that UMAP provides better representations when the dataset is not too large - as Bodmas is the smallest of the three datasets.

The lower-right graph in Fig. 2 shows the average performance of the four utilized clustering algorithms. We do not show maximum Homogeneity grouped by clustering algorithms because that would only show results achieved on Bodmas (as the results on the other two datasets were worse). The average performance graph shows that K-Means and BIRCH are the two best-performing clustering algorithms in our experiments. DBSCAN is a close third, and HAC was the worst-performing algorithm out of the four. Looking at Fig. 4, we can see that on Bodmas, all the algorithms had very similar high results. For Ember, there is a bigger gap between K-Means and BIRCH as the better performers and HAC and DBSCAN as the less performant algorithms. Clustering the Security dataset resulted in similar maximum performance for three clustering algorithms except for HAC, which performed significantly worse.

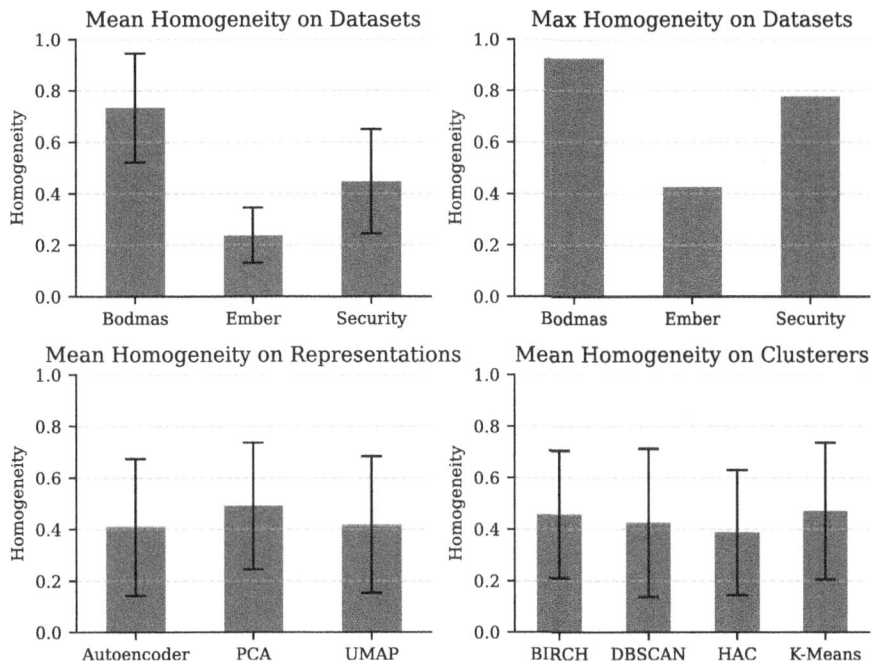

Fig. 2. Aggregated statistics of our experiments (using mean and maximum Homogeneity).

4.2   Ablation Experiment on the Number of Components

The wide range of results we observed on the datasets inspired us to perform an ablation study. We want to determine the influence of the number of components used in the representations on the clustering quality. Therefore, we performed an ablation experiment in limited conditions.

We picked K-Means as the clustering algorithm for this experiment - primarily because of its top performance in the main experiment. Regarding representations, UMAP took a long time to train, so we decided to restrict this ablation experiment to only PCA and Autoencoder representations. Besides 10 components that were utilized for the main experiments, we performed experiments with 30 and 50 components. We decided to utilize all three datasets for the experiment because of the large variance in Homogeneity observed between the datasets. Homogeneity was picked as the primary metric to show us the difference in quality (or lack thereof) in this experiment. Due to time constraints, we trained each representation only once. We also ran K-Means only once on the trained representations.

The results of the ablation experiment are reported in Table 4. For Bodmas, the Homogeneity seemed to increase with every increase in the number of components except for the case of Autoencoder and 30 components. For Ember, Homogeneity consistently increased with the increase in the number of com-

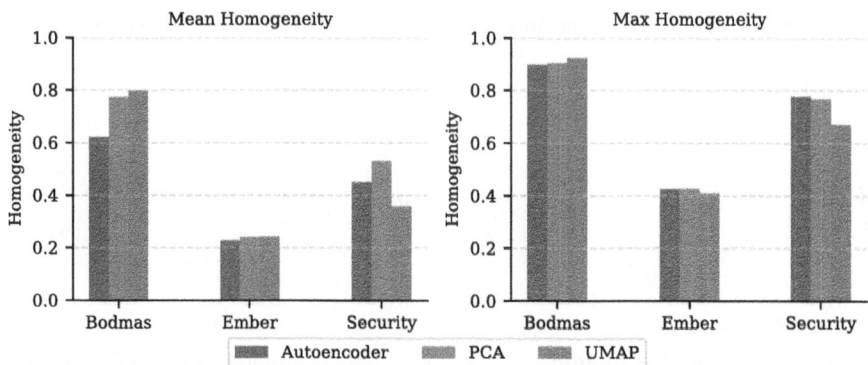

Fig. 3. Graphs representing mean and maximum Homogeneity on the three utilized representations.

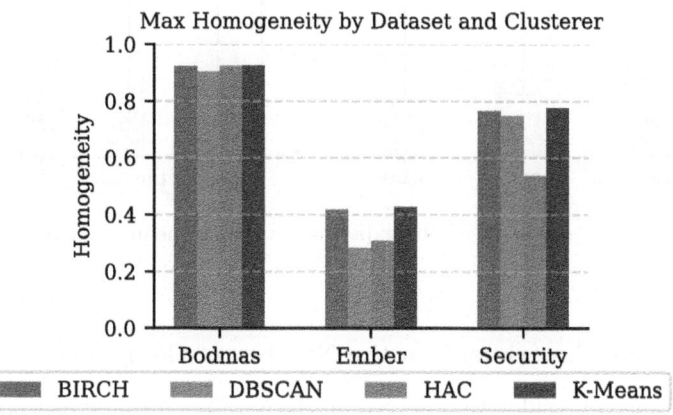

Fig. 4. The best results achieved for each dataset and each clustering algorithm.

ponents. The results for the Security dataset are the least consistent among the three datasets. In the case of PCA and 30 components, the Homogeneity decreased a little. On the other hand, for Autoencoder and 30 components, we saw an increase of more than 2% Homogeneity. For the case of 30 components, the Homogeneity increased in four out of six cases (of combinations of dataset and representation). The Homogeneity increased in all six cases for 50 components (compared to the 10-component baseline).

Table 3. The best results, based on the maximum Homogeneity (i.e. best "H-train") achieved, reported for each dataset

Dataset	Represent.	Clusterer	# clusters	H-train	H-test	VM-train	VM-test
Bodmas	UMAP	K-Means	2000	92.50%	92.80%	15.80%	16.01%
Ember	PCA	K-Means	50 000	42.66%	85.43%	8.89%	13.13%
Security	Autoencoder	K-Means	50 000	77.64%	86.61%	10.16%	12.02%

Table 4. Results achieved for an ablation experiment where the number of components was increased from 10 to 30 and 50. Homogeneity ("H-train-X") is reported for each dataset and two representations. X stands for the number of components.

Dataset	Representation	H-train-10	H-train-30	H-train-50
Bodmas	PCA	90.29%	90.52%	91.03%
	Autoencoder	89.74%	89.72%	92.02%
Ember	PCA	41.76%	43.73%	44.29%
	Autoencoder	42.56%	43.03%	43.77%
Security	PCA	76.69%	76.32%	78.64%
	Autoencoder	77.64%	79.91%	77.93%

5 Discussion

5.1 Interpretation of Results

The results presented in Sect. 4 provide multiple insights. The results clearly show that Bodmas was the easiest dataset to cluster, achieving above 90% Homogeneity for the top result. Contrastingly, Ember was the dataset where the worst results in terms of Homogeneity were achieved (i.e., only reaching 42% for the best result on Ember). This constitutes a considerable variance in results. Both of these datasets are public benchmark datasets and share the same set of 2381 Ember features. Moreover, they were gathered only roughly 2 years apart - from January 2017 to March 2018 for Ember and from August 2019 to September 2020 for Bodmas [24]. Furthermore, we determined that only 41 samples are shared between the Bodmas and Ember datasets. Therefore, the *main differentiating factor* are the samples inside the datasets. Thus, our key finding is that *malware clustering quality is highly dependent on the composition of the dataset.*

Our research modified the malware clustering scenario to include benign samples (drawing exclusively from those already supplied within the chosen datasets). We can make conclusions based on the results observed in our experiments and in the experiments found in the existing work presented in Sect. 2. Although often performed on much smaller datasets with much fewer malware families, the existing work showed 98% Purity, Precision between 72% to 89%, 92% V-Measure, and Homogeneity of 73% and 79%. Thus, our observed results for Bodmas and Security align with the existing literature's observations. We conclude that *the inclusion of benign samples did not have a dramatic effect on the clustering quality in terms of Homogeneity*. The result is different for Ember. As discussed earlier, the results on Ember are primarily affected by the composition of the dataset itself, and therefore, we see Ember as an exception to the conclusion.

Despite the existing work (Sect. 2) pointing to DBSCAN and HAC as the better clustering algorithms, we find that K-Means and BIRCH performed better on both the large public malware benchmark datasets and the private real-world industry dataset. In the case of HAC, this can be partially attributed to the necessity of utilizing workarounds to create HAC clustering assignments when using large amounts of clusters. This was needed due to the large memory requirements of the algorithm, which rapidly increase when the number of clusters increases. For DBSCAN, it is not an easy task to find an *Epsilon* value that will result in a reasonable number of clusters while keeping the level of noise small. Therefore, the search of hyperparameter space would have to be much more extensive in the case of DBSCAN.

In terms of representations, our results show that PCA tends to outperform the other representations on average. However, as was presented in Table 3, the best results were achieved each on a different representation. The lesson learned is that the utilization of UMAP could bring the best results for smaller malware datasets. In contrast, Autoencoder could help achieve the best results on very large datasets (e.g., Security).

The ablation experiment that studied how the increase in the number of components influences clustering quality led us to make multiple observations. First, our general observation is that increasing the number of components helps the clustering quality to some degree. The size of the effect on Homogeneity should be subject to further research. Our results suggest that the increase in Homogeneity could be anywhere between 0.2% to around 2.5%. Second, to decrease the uncertainty in the results, we would need to perform the training of the representations multiple times (ideally at least five times). For each trained representation, we would need to perform clustering multiple times. This could increase the time complexity of the experiment by 25 to 100 times.

Third, one of our primary motivations behind the experiment was also to see the impact of the increase in the number of components on the *Ember dataset*. Unfortunately, even for Ember, for which we have seen the worst results in terms of Homogeneity (in the main experiment), the increase in the number of components did not help much in increasing Homogeneity. Ideally, we would like to see that the number of components has a greater influence (i.e., at least 5%, ideally at least 10%) on the result Homogeneity, but this was not observed. This strengthens our previously stated argument that the influence of the samples (picked into the dataset) on the result Homogeneity cannot be overstated.

We have established the merit of the usage of a larger amount of clusters than the reported number of malware families in Sects. 2 and 3. The results presented in Sect. 4 point to a *potential positive effect of utilizing more clusters than the reported number of malware families.* This can be derived from the substantial increase in Homogeneity when the number of clusters increases.

However, we acknowledge that this result is nuanced. The Homogeneity metric is equal to 100% in the extreme case of every sample being in its own cluster. Such clustering would not be useful for any downstream task, but it illustrates that Homogeneity should increase with the number of clusters. Therefore, the best way to evaluate this result would be to have a Homogeneity metric adjusted for the *expected increase* when increasing the number of clusters. However, we are not aware of the existence of any such metric. Therefore, there is evidence that it *may* be beneficial to utilize a larger amount of clusters than the reported number of families (when cluster "purity" is the main objective).

5.2 Limitations

There are multiple limitations of our work. First, our work conducts experiments on datasets whose features are primarily based on static analysis. Static features can suffer when malware is obfuscated using packers and when malware variants are created that are syntactically very different but semantically very similar.

Both Bodmas and Ember are based solely on static analysis. For Security, a limited number of features are not based solely on static analysis, but most are. Therefore, the results presented and conclusions drawn primarily hold for datasets based on static features. We are not able to make conclusions about datasets that are based primarily on dynamic features.

Additionally, we experiment with two of the three most prominent public malware benchmark datasets. We did not include Sorel [9] primarily due to the unavailability of malware family labels. Moreover, it would be the largest of all datasets, around double the size of Security. In the interest of completeness of the results, performing malware clustering experiments on Sorel would also be beneficial.

Another issue that can be identified is that Ember and Bodmas were published a few years ago (2018 for Ember and 2021 for Bodmas). Even the Security dataset was created in 2021. Therefore, the clustering results presented here do not necessarily reflect the latest malware landscape, and we acknowledge this. However, we are not aware of any public benchmark up-to-date datasets. This is an ongoing problem in malware research.

A limitation of this research lies also in the selection of clustering algorithms. While K-Means, DBSCAN, BIRCH, and HAC were chosen due to their prevalence and suitability for malware clustering, other algorithms, such as Canopy clustering or OPTICS, could offer different perspectives on the data. Furthermore, the hyperparameter tuning (or, more specifically, the exploration of the number of clusters) for each algorithm was conducted within a specific range. A more comprehensive search of the numbers of clusters might reveal further improvements in clustering Homogeneity. Future research could address this limitation by evaluating a broader range of algorithms and employing more sophisticated optimization techniques, mainly in the case of DBSCAN and the search for the ideal *Epsilon* value.

5.3   Future Work

There are multiple possibilities for future extension of our work. Most of them are potential ways how to improve malware clustering quality. For example, our work could be extended by incorporating more clustering approaches. We have already mentioned OPTICS and Canopy clustering in the previous subsection. Approaches such as MutantX-S [11] and COUGAR [23] could also be explored.

Over the last few years, contrastive and self-supervised learning have become increasingly popular. Moreover, these solutions can often achieve near state-of-the-art performance in the computer vision domain. Therefore, adapting such techniques to help improve malware clustering quality is another possibility of extension.

Transfer learning is arguably even more popular these days than contrastive learning. Thanks to the shared feature set of the most prominent public malware benchmark datasets, transfer learning is also a viable avenue of exploration. For example, it would be interesting to see how well clustering algorithms trained on Bodmas can predict clusters for Ember or vice-versa.

A deeper investigation into the poor results on the Ember dataset is equally important. For instance, merging benign and malware samples from different datasets (e.g., Ember and Bodmas) and repeating the clustering experiments could offer better insights into malware clustering. This approach may help clarify the challenges associated with clustering different parts of these datasets.

Last, our experiments were conducted on features that come from static analysis for the most part. This was also the case in our analyzed existing work in Sect. 2. Therefore, we see great potential in employing dynamic features that can improve the observed results further.

6   Conclusion

Our full-benchmark study with large public (and one private) datasets is the first malware clustering study performed on the *whole* large public malware benchmark datasets, Bodmas and Ember. It does not rely on hand-picked subsets with a limited number of malware families and, therefore, is more realistic in the observed results. Furthermore, we extended the malware clustering task by incorporating benign samples. Our extension can be helpful for malware experts in their daily tasks of analyzing Portable Executables (PEs). It extends the use cases of malware clustering by introducing the ability to analyze new incoming unknown PE samples without a pre-filtering step. Additionally, it creates the potential to create compressed datasets for further (machine learning or other) experimentation. Moreover, we find that the inclusion of benign samples in the malware clustering task does not significantly affect the clustering quality of the solution.

We have established the state-of-the-art in malware clustering on large public malware benchmark datasets. The best results for Bodmas and Ember were achieved using K-Means and were 91% and 44% Homogeneity, respectively. Our results also indicate that K-Means and BIRCH achieve higher Homogeneity on these large datasets than DBSCAN and Hierarchical Agglomerative Clustering. Moreover, our findings show that the quality of malware clustering can vary considerably, even if they share the same set of features. This led us to conclude that malware clustering quality is highly dependent on the composition of the dataset. To examine the results more closely, we performed an ablation study, which increased the number of components of PCA and Autoencoder representations. The ablation results show that the increase in the number of components does not have a substantial effect on clustering Homogeneity, strengthening the result regarding dataset composition.

Moreover, we also utilized a higher number of clusters than the reported amount of malware families for the dataset. Our results indicate that utilizing a larger number of clusters than the number of families might improve clustering quality - as the results measured using Homogeneity show. However, this takeaway must be treated with caution since Homogeneity, as a metric, is not adjusted for the expected increase when increasing the number of clusters.

Last, we make recommendations regarding the utilized dataset representations - PCA, UMAP, and Autoencoder. Our experiments indicate that UMAP is best suited for smaller malware datasets to achieve the best clustering quality. We recommend utilizing PCA and Autoencoder when working with larger datasets.

The area of malware clustering still holds potential for future work, mainly in improving the clustering quality. This can be achieved in various ways. The most promising future direction is improving the underlying latent representation of the features. Therefore, our main suggestions for future work are utilizing contrastive learning, self-supervised learning, and transfer learning approaches.

Acknowledgements and Disclosure of Funding. Funded by the EU NextGenerationEU through the Recovery and Resilience Plan for Slovakia under the project No. 09I05-03-V02-00064.

References

1. Aboaoja, F.A., Zainal, A., Ghaleb, F.A., Al-Rimy, B., Eisa, T., Elnour, A.: Malware detection issues, challenges, and future directions: a survey. Appl. Sci. **12**(17), 8482 (2022). https://doi.org/10.3390/app12178482
2. Ali, M., Hagen, J., Oliver, J.: Scalable malware clustering using multi-stage tree parallelization. In: 2020 IEEE International Conference on Intelligence and Security Informatics (ISI), pp. 1–6. IEEE (2020). https://doi.org/10.1109/ISI49825.2020.9280546
3. Anderson, H.S., Roth, P.: Ember: an open dataset for training static PE malware machine learning models. arXiv preprint arXiv:1804.04637 (2018). https://doi.org/10.48550/arXiv.1804.04637
4. Ankerst, M., Breunig, M.M., Kriegel, H.P., Sander, J.: Optics: ordering points to identify the clustering structure. ACM SIGMOD Rec. **28**(2), 49–60 (1999). https://doi.org/10.1145/304181.304187

5. Aresu, M., Ariu, D., Ahmadi, M., Maiorca, D., Giacinto, G.: Clustering android malware families by http traffic. In: 2015 10th International Conference on Malicious and Unwanted Software (MALWARE), pp. 128–135. IEEE (2015). https://doi.org/10.1109/MALWARE.2015.7413693

6. Ester, M., Kriegel, H.P., Sander, J., Xu, X., et al.: A density-based algorithm for discovering clusters in large spatial databases with noise. In: KDD, vol. 96, pp. 226–231 (1996)

7. Fang, Y., Zhang, W., Li, B., Jing, F., Zhang, L.: Semi-supervised malware clustering based on the weight of bytecode and API. IEEE Access **8**, 2313–2326 (2019). https://doi.org/10.1109/ACCESS.2019.2962198

8. Faridi, H., Srinivasagopalan, S., Verma, R.: Performance evaluation of features and clustering algorithms for malware. In: 2018 IEEE International Conference on Data Mining Workshops (ICDMW), pp. 13–22. IEEE (2018). https://doi.org/10.1109/ICDMW.2018.00010

9. Harang, R., Rudd, E.M.: Sorel-20m: a large scale benchmark dataset for malicious PE detection. arXiv preprint arXiv:2012.07634 (2020). https://doi.org/10.48550/arXiv.2012.07634

10. Hu, X., Shin, K.G.: Duet: integration of dynamic and static analyses for malware clustering with cluster ensembles. In: Proceedings of the 29th Annual Computer Security Applications Conference, pp. 79–88 (2013). https://doi.org/10.1145/2523649.2523677

11. Hu, X., Shin, K.G., Bhatkar, S., Griffin, K.: {MutantX-S}: scalable malware clustering based on static features. In: 2013 USENIX Annual Technical Conference (USENIX ATC 2013), pp. 187–198 (2013)

12. Jurečková, O., Jureček, M., Stamp, M.: Online clustering of known and emerging malware families. arXiv preprint arXiv:2405.03298 (2024). https://doi.org/10.48550/arXiv.2405.03298

13. Jurečková, O., Jureček, M., Stamp, M., Di Troia, F., Lórencz, R.: Classification and online clustering of zero-day malware. J. Comput. Virol. Hacking Tech. **20**(4), 579–592 (2024). https://doi.org/10.1007/s11416-024-00513-5

14. MacAskill, N., Wilkins, Z., Zincir-Heywood, N.: Scaling multi-objective optimization for clustering malware. In: 2021 IEEE Symposium Series on Computational Intelligence (SSCI), pp. 1–8. IEEE (2021). https://doi.org/10.1109/SSCI50451.2021.9659925

15. MacQueen, J.: Some methods for classification and analysis of multivariate observations. In: Proceedings of the Fifth Berkeley Symposium on Mathematical Statistics and Probability, Volume 1: Statistics, vol. 5, pp. 281–298. University of California Press (1967)

16. Maimon, O., Rokach, L.: Data mining and knowledge discovery handbook, vol. 2. Springer (2005). https://doi.org/10.1007/b107408

17. McInnes, L., Healy, J., Melville, J.: Umap: uniform manifold approximation and projection for dimension reduction. arXiv preprint arXiv:1802.03426 (2018). https://doi.org/10.48550/arXiv.1802.03426

18. Or-Meir, O., Nissim, N., Elovici, Y., Rokach, L.: Dynamic malware analysis in the modern era–a state of the art survey. ACM Comput. Surv. (CSUR) **52**(5), 1–48 (2019). https://doi.org/10.1145/3329786

19. Perdisci, R., Ariu, D., Giacinto, G.: Scalable fine-grained behavioral clustering of HTTP-based malware. Comput. Netw. **57**(2), 487–500 (2013). https://doi.org/10.1016/j.comnet.2012.06.022

20. Pitolli, G., Laurenza, G., Aniello, L., Querzoni, L., Baldoni, R.: MalFamAware: automatic family identification and malware classification through online clustering. Int. J. Inf. Secur. **20**(3), 371–386 (2020). https://doi.org/10.1007/s10207-020-00509-4
21. Rezaei, T., Manavi, F., Hamzeh, A.: A PE header-based method for malware detection using clustering and deep embedding techniques. J. Inf. Secur. Appl. **60**, 102876 (2021). https://doi.org/10.1016/j.jisa.2021.102876
22. Rieck, K., Trinius, P., Willems, C., Holz, T.: Automatic analysis of malware behavior using machine learning. J. Comput. Secur. **19**(4), 639–668 (2011). https://doi.org/10.3233/JCS-2010-0410
23. Wilkins, Z., Zincir-Heywood, N.: Cougar: clustering of unknown malware using genetic algorithm routines. In: Proceedings of the 2020 Genetic and Evolutionary Computation Conference, pp. 1195–1203 (2020). https://doi.org/10.1145/3377930.3390151
24. Yang, L., Ciptadi, A., Laziuk, I., Ahmadzadeh, A., Wang, G.: Bodmas: an open dataset for learning based temporal analysis of PE malware. In: 2021 IEEE Security and Privacy Workshops (SPW), pp. 78–84. IEEE (2021). https://doi.org/10.1109/SPW53761.2021.00020
25. Zhang, T., Ramakrishnan, R., Livny, M.: Birch: an efficient data clustering method for very large databases. ACM SIGMOD Rec. **25**(2), 103–114 (1996). https://doi.org/10.1145/235968.233324

Advances in Automotive Digital Forensics: Recent Trends and Future Directions

Kim Strandberg[1,2](✉) and Mohamed Eldefrawy[2]

[1] Volvo Car Corp., Gothenburg, Sweden
[2] Halmstad University, Halmstad, Sweden
kim.strandberg@volvocars.com

Abstract. The automotive industry is increasingly facing growing cybersecurity challenges as vehicles become more connected and autonomous. Modern cars equipped with sophisticated electronic systems are becoming more susceptible to cyber threats. Enhancing detection and forensic capabilities within automotive systems is essential to mitigate these risks. This work builds on and extends a previous systematic literature review of automotive digital forensics, covering 2006 to early 2021. However, recent advances in the field have introduced new challenges and opportunities, particularly in light of an evolving, dynamic threat landscape and growing vehicle complexity. These developments have driven numerous advances, particularly in artificial intelligence, machine learning, and blockchain technologies. In response, we review the latest state-of-the-art developments from 2021 to 2025, addressing critical challenges and technical solutions to provide a comprehensive understanding of the evolving landscape and its implications for both researchers and practitioners. By categorizing and comparing these advancements with prior research, we highlight key trends and innovations, analyze security concerns, and ultimately offer valuable insights into future research directions and emerging trends.

Keywords: Automotive Digital Forensics · Cybersecurity · Systematic Literature Review

1 Introduction

1.1 Automotive Digital Forensics

Digital forensics, a subset of forensics, includes various domains, including automotive digital forensics (ADF), which focuses specifically on vehicles. Generally, digital forensics considers all devices that can store or process data and communication between such devices. Digital forensics investigations must follow a strict process, and the data used must meet cybersecurity requirements to ensure forensic soundness. The process can vary, but typically includes the following phases: *identification, preservation, acquisition, verification, analysis,* and *reporting* [34]. Cybersecurity requirements ensuring forensic soundness can include fulfilling

© The Author(s) 2025
M. Dalla Preda et al. (Eds.): ARES 2025, LNCS 15993, pp. 252–274, 2025.
https://doi.org/10.1007/978-3-032-00627-1_13

common security properties, such as Confidentiality (C), Integrity (I), and Availability (A), commonly known as the CIA triad. In addition, the CIA is typically extended with other properties, such as Non-Repudiation (N) and Privacy (P), where the former extends upon (I) to additionally ensure data origin, and fulfilling the latter infers that privacy-sensitive data is secured and all storage justified both considering the type of data and how long the data is kept [48]. A modern vehicle is a complex safety-critical system that can contain more than 150 computers, known as Electronic Control Modules (ECUs), and over 100 million lines of code. These ECUs, along with their code, control various functionalities, such as safety-critical steering, braking, and engine control, and more straightforward tasks, such as door nodes that check the status of open or closed doors. For instance, steering or braking typically involves a sensor that detects the position of the brake pedal or steering wheel and sends this data to an ECU. The data is processed and validated by the ECU, and a signal is sent from the ECU to an actuator that performs the actual response, such as aligning the wheel and brakes according to the signal. Infotainment systems tend to be more complex, with the potential to run various applications. ECUs are part of the vehicle's electrical/electronic (E/E) architecture, can run different operating systems, and use various communication buses. Vehicles are becoming more connected to the outside world via Vehicle-to-Everything (V2X) communication, including communication with other vehicles (V2V), infrastructure (V2I), the cloud (V2C), the grid (V2G), and pedestrians (V2P). Thus, forensically relevant data is not only found in the vehicle itself but also distributed across various locations. ADF is a distinct and rapidly evolving field, separate from similar fields such as the Internet of Things (IoT), i.e., devices with Internet connectivity, such as smartphones, sensors, and actuators. Although there are similarities, such as the use of IoT devices in vehicles, the main distinction is that vehicles are safety-critical cyber-physical systems (CPS) with real-time requirements. Therefore, failures can lead to serious and potentially fatal consequences for drivers, passengers, or people in the surroundings. As an example, a hypothetical scenario for forensic investigation follows:

The airbag system unexpectedly deploys, causing the driver to lose control and crash. The driver is seriously injured and placed in a medical coma. A forensic investigation reveals that the incident was caused by a cyberattack that targeted communication between airbag sensors and the control system, where signals were spoofed. Given the political importance of the driver and the complex routing of the attack through multiple servers, it is suspected that the attack originated from a foreign entity seeking to influence political outcomes.

For this hypothetical incident, it is imperative that the data is *Available (A)*, meaning sufficient data has been detected and logged. Furthermore, the data must be accessible only by authorized individuals, ensuring *Confidentiality (C)* and *Privacy (P)* considerations are maintained. Additionally, the data must be trustworthy, guaranteeing both *Integrity (I)* and *Non-repudiation (N)*. In summary, vehicle manufacturers are required to ensure the appropriate cybersecurity properties are in place, such as the aforementioned CIANP (Confidentiality,

Integrity, Availability, Non-repudiation, and Privacy) [47]. There are regulations and standards that include requirements affecting ADF, such as UN Regulation No. 155 [52] for cybersecurity and digital forensics, UN Regulation No. 156 [53] for vehicle software updates (which impact the ability to update and adapt mechanisms), UN Regulation No. 160 [54] for Event Data Recorders (EDRs), and the ISO 21434 [50] standard for vehicle cybersecurity. However, no standard specifically addresses ADF or defines key aspects such as data format, tools, and processes. While related standards and regulations exist, they offer limited detail, particularly with regard to ADF. As a result, vehicle manufacturers are responsible for demonstrating to authorities how regulations, such as UN Regulation No. 155, are being met.

1.2   Related Work

In [48], K. Strandberg et al. conducted a comprehensive systematic literature review (SLR) in the field of ADF, covering the most relevant related work from 2006 to 2021. A list of relevant data sources for ADF is identified and presented in Table 3 of the referenced SLR. Additionally, articles are organized into categories based on their purpose in Table 1 (technical solutions) and Table 2 (surveys), respectively. In addition, recommendations are provided for securing various data by maintaining security properties, and stakeholders are identified for the data. The SLR discusses that the automotive industry relies primarily on traditional methods for root cause analysis of incidents, such as examining component integrity, service history logs, and fault codes. Additionally, there are very few tools specifically adapted for vehicle data extraction. Examples include Berla iVE [12] for infotainment systems and the Bosch Crash Data Retrieval System for diagnostics and fault codes [6]. A few of the main challenges identified in the SLR include the lack of cybersecurity mechanisms to ensure trustworthy forensic data and considerations for privacy. There is a significant risk of data compromise and misuse, such as data tampering. Additionally, there is no standardization for ADF, for example, in terms of format, tools, or procedures. Currently, the ability to establish the chronological order of events across different communication buses and align with, for example, other vehicles potentially involved in an incident, is limited. The cost of securely detecting and storing forensic data is another significant challenge. Regarding the most relevant related work from the more recent period (2021-2025), this will fall within the scope of this work and will be addressed in the following sections.

2   Scope and Methodology

An extensive approach to an SLR was employed, using four databases along with backward and forward snowballing, covering the period from 2006 to early 2021 [48,56]. As shown in Fig. 1, this work adopts the same methodology, focusing on recent advances from 2021 to early 2025, and compares these developments with the findings of previous work included in the SLR. Papers were included based on relevance to the automotive domain, publications between 2021 and 2025, and being published in journals or conferences, and excluded based on being unrelated to automotive digital forensics, not written in English, or already included in the previous SLR [48].

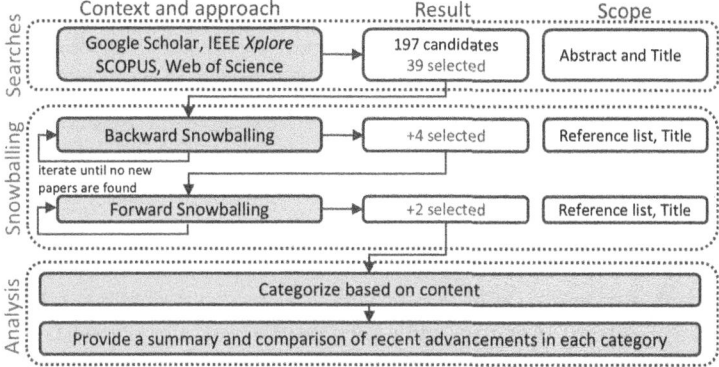

Fig. 1. Visualization of the methodology: Database searches, snowballing, and analysis.

We used the following search terms: *digital forensics* in conjunction with *vehicle*, *car*, or *automotive*. Google Scholar[1] returned 133 candidates, with 17 selected. IEEE Xplore[2] returned 41 candidates, with 16 selected. SCOPUS[3] returned 14 candidates, with 5 selected. Web of Science[4] returned nine candidates, with one selected. This resulted in 197 candidates, of which 39 were selected. We started with Google Scholar, which was less specific and returned most papers, but many were not relevant. The other three databases returned more specific and relevant articles, but due to duplicate removal, fewer articles were selected in each subsequent database search. Additionally, backward and forward snowballing [56] was performed, through which six additional papers were identified. With some adjustments to better reflect recent developments, the categories established in [48] are used to classify and analyze the publications, enabling comparison with the latest advances.

3   Contributions

Our main contributions are as follows:

- **Comprehensive Review of ADF:** We provide a detailed review of existing ADF research, focusing on critical challenges, technical solutions, and

---

[1] Google Scholar search performed on 2025-01-21.
[2] IEEE Xplore search performed on 2025-01-28.
[3] SCOPUS search performed on 2025-01-28.
[4] Web of Science search performed on 2025-01-28.

data collection methods, serving as a valuable resource for researchers and practitioners.

– **Categorization, Comparative Analysis, and Relevance Assessment:** We categorize and compare research from 2021–2025 with an SLR from 2006–2021 [48], highlighting trend shifts and innovations reshaping the field. We also assess the technical solutions in terms of security and practical relevance.
– **Recent Trends and Future Directions:** We provide a perspective on the future direction of ADF by analyzing recent developments, offering insights into emerging trends and key research areas, and providing practical guidance for researchers and engineers.

4 Categorization of Papers

We have divided the results into two main categories: technical solutions (Table 1) and surveys (Table 2). Articles proposing technical solutions are included in the former category, while all other articles are placed in the latter. Additionally, each paper is assigned to one or more identified focus categories. We also specify whether the papers were published in a conference or journal. Furthermore, we explicitly state whether the technical solution considers and emphasizes the CIANP properties and, if so, which ones. We begin with a summary of each category based on the period from 2006 to early 2021 [48], followed by the addition of the most recent advancements from 2021 to early 2025. We acknowledge that there is some overlap between categories, and we have chosen to summarize each paper under the category we believe is most applicable. Additionally, we use main categories when subcategories are more prone to overlap; for example, data collection and extraction are similar, with only a slight difference in emphasis.

1. Data: *different types of forensic data, data retrieval, and extraction techniques. 1a. Data Collection. 1b. Extraction Techniques*. This category discusses various aspects of data management and forensic techniques. Forensic data is considered from both the front- and back-end perspectives. The former focuses on data inside the vehicle, addressing challenges such as the lack of standardized interfaces for data extraction and formatting, as well as the absence of debug ports, which often require dismantling storage circuits. Additionally, it explores data extraction techniques, proposing methods using the JTAG (Joint Test Action Group) port, and mentions the issue that debug ports are commonly closed in production vehicles for security reasons. To some extent, tools related to data extraction, such as Alientech KTag [2], and PEmicro Cyclone [36], are discussed, with the compatibility issue highlighted. Blockchain for data management is explored, emphasizing both potential benefits and challenges, including security and privacy concerns.

Recent Trends. In [25], J. Lee et al. perform a study specifically on how data relevant to forensics are stored and transmitted in Tesla vehicles through the concept of software-defined vehicles (SDVs) and the centralized data storage provided by Tesla's SDV architecture. The study details the technical process of

Table 1. Selected papers concerning technical solutions

Ref.	Author	Publ. Year	Details	1a. Data: Data Collection	1b. Data: Extract. techniques	2a. Challenges: General	2b. Challenges: Req./Guidlines	3a. Com.: Cloud/Fog./Edge	3b. Com.: VANETs/V2X	4a. Software: App./SW	4b. Software: Tools	5a. Hardware: Architecture	5b. Hardware: Sensor	5c. Hardware: EDR/Blackbox	6a. Alg.: AI/ML	6b. Alg.: Other alg.	7a. Cryptography: Blockchain	7b. Cryptography: Other crypt.	8. Framework and Processes	9. Practical Experiments	10. Infrastruct./Smart Cities	11. TEE/Virtualization
[30]	Y.Li et al.	2025	Jo. C.I.P	•	•		•										•		•	•	•	
[41]	T.Reichel* et al.	2025	Co. I.	•								•	•	•	•				•			
[33]	T.Menard et al.	2024	Co. C.I.N.P.	•		•												•	•			
[25]	J.Lee et al.	2024	Jo. I.A.N.	•		•														•		
[57]	Y.Yoon et al.	2024	Co.	•					•											•		
[31]	J.Liang et al.	2024	Jo.	•													•		•	•		
[26]	J.Li et al.	2024	Jo. I.N.	•														•	•	•	•	
[49]	Q.Tao et al.	2024	Jo. I.N.P.					•									•		•			
[9]	Y.Chen et al.	2024	Jo.	•												•						
[40]	M.Rayno et al.	2024	Co. I.A.P	•		•	•						•						•			
[22]	J.Jung et al.	2024	Jo.	•					•	•									•			
[10]	Z.Chen et al.	2024	Jo.	•						•									•	•		
[1]	L.Ahmeti et al.	2024	Co. C.I.A.			•	•												•			
[14]	S.Ebbers* et al.	2024	Jo.	•															•			
[47]	K.Strandberg et al.	2023	Co. C.I.A.N.P.	•		•	•					•		•					•			
[39]	M.Rayno et al.	2023	Co. C.I.A.	•	•	•	•							•					•			
[13]	Y.A.Daraghmi et al.	2023	Jo. I.P.	•		•													•			
[4]	R.Amala et al.	2023	Jo.	•	•	•													•			
[5]	T.Bakhshi et al.	2023	Jo.	•		•	•												•			
[18]	J.Han et al.	2023	Jo.	•		•	•												•			
[17]	B.Gadekar et al.	2023	Co.	•		•	•	•		•										•	•	
[35]	M.Nicho et al.	2023	Jo.	•		•	•												•			
[20]	F.Iqbal et al.	2023	Co.											•					•			
[27]	M. Li et al.*	2023	Jo. C.I.A.N.P.	•		•											•	•	•			
[51]	R.Tyagi et al.	2022	Co. C.I.N.P.	•										•			•	•	•	•	•	
[3]	M.Y.AlKhanaf. et al.	2022	Co. C.I.P					•									•		•	•	•	
[55]	A.R.Vieira et al.	2022	Co. I.					•					•				•		•			
[7]	K.G.Buquerin et al.	2022	Co. I.	•	•					•									•			
[28]	M.Li et al.*	2022	Co. C.I.N.P			•	•										•	•	•	•	•	
[29]	X.Li et al.	2021	Co. I.	•		•	•										•		•	•		
[21]	S.Jabeen et al.	2021	Jo.	•	•	•	•							•						•		
[32]	T.Long et al.	2021	Co. I.	•									•						•	•		
[23]	C.Katsini et al.*	2021	Co. I.N.	•			•										•		•			

Table 2. Selected papers concerning surveys

Ref.	Author	Publ. Year		1a. Data: Data Collection	1b. Data: Extract. techniques	2a. Challenges: General	2b. Challenges: Req./Guidlines	3a. Com.: Cloud/Fog./Edge	3b. Com.: VANETs/V2X	4a. Software: App./SW	4b. Software: Tools	5a. Hardware: Architecture	5b. Hardware: Sensor	5c. Hardware: EDR/Blackbox	6a. Alg.: AI/ML	6b. Alg.: Other alg.	7a. Cryptography: Blockchain	7b. Cryptography: Other crypt.	8. Framework and Processes	9. Practical Experiments	10. Infrastruct./Smart Cities	11. TEE/Virtualization
[19]	S.Hussain et al.	2024	Co.			•			•								•					
[45]	M.A.Shayer et al.	2024	Co.	•						•	•		•									
[11]	N.I.Chowdhury et al.	2024	Co.	•					•				•									
[48]	K.Strandberg et al.	2023	Jo.	•	•	•	•	•	•	•	•	•	•	•	•	•	•	•	•	•	•	•
[24]	R.Kurachi et al.	2022	Co.	•	•	•	•						•							•		
[46]	C.Stathers et al.	2022	Co.	•	•	•	•		•	•	•								•			
[42]	J.Repas et al.	2022	Co.	•		•	•												•			
[43]	S.Rizvi et al.	2022	Jo.	•		•	•	•					•						•			
[44]	P.Sharma et al.	2022	Co.	•		•						•			•							
[38]	R.Rak et al.	2021	Jo.	•		•	•			•										•		
[15]	S.Ebbers et al.	2021	Co.	•	•	•			•	•										•		
[8]	K.G. Buquerin et al.*	2021	Co.	•	•	•				•			•						•			

Legend: *(C)Confidentiality (I)Integrity (A)Availability (N)NonRepudiation (P)Privacy*; *Retrieved from Snowballing*; *(Co)Conference (Jo)Journal* identifying, acquiring, analyzing, and verifying data from EDRs, multiple sensors, over-the-air (OTA) updates, and logs, with an emphasis on cross-referencing and integrating diverse data sets to strengthen the reliability of the forensic process. However, the legal and ethical concerns, particularly regarding privacy and the confidentiality of the data, require more attention. In [45], M.A. Shayer et al. conducts a comparative study of Generative Adversarial Networks (GANs), specifically DCGAN, VSGAN, and CGAN, for vehicle identification. The authors highlight VSGAN as an architecture specifically designed for vehicle image generation, emphasizing its superior performance in generating clearer and more accurate car images compared to DCGAN and CGAN. In [11], N.I. Chowdhury et al. analyze challenges, issues, and defenses for vehicles in three main areas: forensics, communication, and over-the-air updates. The Mitre ATTACK database is used to identify attack scenarios and mitigation. In [7] K.G. Buquerin et al. investigate the Tesla autopilot with an emphasis on its file system, addressing questions such as who, where, when, and how events occurred. They identify relevant timestamps, user accounts, media files, and system logs. The authors used Python and Magnet AXIOM [16] for their analysis, highlighting the integrity of the data while making assumptions, such as the accuracy of timestamps and the absence of tampering. In [46], C. Stathers et al. survey and perform practical experiments focusing on data extraction using mobile forensic techniques and On-Board Diagnostics (OBD) software on a 2008 Mitsubishi Colt. They examine data from sources such as the dashboard camera, the head unit, and other ECUs. The main conclusion is that even older cars contain a significant amount of data. In [38], R. Rak et al. focus on digital vehicle identifiers across various components in over 250 vehicle models and their applicability for forensic practices in identifying vehicles. The authors highlight the challenges and the need for standardization in the methods and devices used to collect such data. S. Ebbers et al. [14] propose a method for API-based forensic acquisition to extract vehicle data from manufacturer cloud systems. However, reliance on, for instance, insecure tokens raises concerns about data integrity and user privacy.

2. Challenges: *general challenges, requirements and guidelines*.

2a. General Challenges. 2b. Requirements, Guidelines. Automotive systems are becoming increasingly complex, with modern vehicles functioning as *computers on wheels*. However, many of these systems lack reliable security measures, making data extraction easier for forensic investigators. Still, these vulnerabilities present significant challenges, as the absence of security mechanisms in ADF reduces trust in the evidence and exposes data to cyberattacks. Major issues include the lack of authentication for in-vehicle communication, limited storage capacity, and difficulties in maintaining data integrity and authenticity during forensic investigations. The lack of standardization forces manufacturers to develop and implement their own strategies for data storage, interfaces, and forensic processes, further complicating forensic investigations. The vast amount of data and its distributed nature require extensive manual effort for collection and extraction. Adherence to laws for both privacy and data collection for digital forensics is a significant concern. The lack of forensic tools is also discussed.

Several suggestions have been made to improve the security of forensic data. For instance, the telematics unit is proposed to be used for storage with a circular buffer and additional memory. Requirements for event reconstruction and the need for detection and secure storage, such as using hashes to detect manipulation, are also highlighted. Machine learning (ML) is proposed to identify patterns, predict crimes, and link vehicles to individuals through data sources like cell phone logs and vehicle communication. A proposal for an organizational framework for traffic police is suggested to guide further research into accidents and crimes by integrating multiple data sources, such as vehicles, cell phones, and traffic data.

Recent Trends. In [19], S. Hussain et al. survey the potential integration of blockchain technology for vehicle communication, focusing on secure communication, forensic applications, secure data storage, trust and reputation management, and privacy. A comparison of Ethereum and Hyperledger consensus algorithms, along with challenges, is performed, with the author favoring Ethereum in terms of performance, efficiency, and scalability. In [42], J. Repas et al. conduct a study focusing on various challenges in ADF. The authors emphasize the increasing complexity in the evolution of vehicles and the need for new and better aligned methodologies to collect timely evidence in forensic investigations. In [44], P. Sharma et al. analyze the components of Connected Autonomous Vehicles (CAVs), including sensors, communication networks, and actuators, and discuss the current challenges. The paper reviews mitigation techniques, with a primary focus on security issues. It emphasizes the need for enhanced forensic solutions to detect, investigate, and understand security breaches, while also highlighting the critical role of strong cybersecurity measures in protecting forensic evidence and facilitating effective post-incident analysis.

3. Communication:*cloud, fog, edge node communication, Vehicular Ad hoc Networks, and Vehicle-2-Everything 3a. Cloud/Fog/Edge. 3b. VANETs/V2X.* The emphasis is on communication systems and cloud, fog, and edge computing, considering data transfer and storage, including VANETs for forensic data collection. For cloud computing, mechanisms for collecting and transferring data to the cloud using interfaces like Bluetooth or WiFi connected to the OBD-II port, are proposed, along with a discussion around the security risk introduced with such connections. The move toward fog/edge computing to reduce bandwidth by processing data closer to the source, such as utilizing RSUs (roadside units), is proposed to address issues with large data volumes. Still, issues remain in terms of security and data processing capacity. A solution for Multi-access Edge Computing (MEC) is proposed to improve accident handling by collecting driving data (position, speed, and acceleration) before and after an accident and analyzing data in an edge infrastructure to determine accident liability. An algorithm is introduced to embed location, timestamp, and other data, i.e., digital watermarking, into real-time accident photographs in VANETs, adding properties of authentication and integrity for digital evidence. However, privacy and trust issues due to the fact that potentially sensitive information, such as videos and photographs of individuals, may be present, remain significant challenges to making this feasible in a practical setting. A vehicle witness system is proposed to use moving vehicles and RSUs as witnesses for incidents, sending forensic data anonymously to the cloud to preserve privacy. However, videos and pictures can, as mentioned, contain sensitive information that must be taken into account. Thus, privacy concerns remain.

Recent Trends. In [30], Y. Lee et al. propose SA-Dedup, a Secure Approximate Deduplication scheme for forensic images in fog-assisted crowdsensing vehicular networks. The system divides the forensic region into geospatial grid cells based on vehicle positions, with the help of fog nodes. One key benefit is the reduction in storage requirements, as the system efficiently minimizes communication and storage overhead by detecting and eliminating near-duplicate images. The authors performed experimental validation to confirm the effectiveness and practicality of their approach. In [49], Q. Tao et al. propose a blockchain-based dynamic, extensible privacy protection and message authentication scheme for VANETs. The scheme uses elliptic curve-based point multiplication and batch message verification to reduce computational costs, while the Chinese Remainder Theorem (CRT) ensures secure message transfers and adaptive responses for RSUs. In [3], Alkhanafseh et al. propose a framework for securing VANETs using blockchain, intrusion detection systems (IDS), and forensic mechanisms. The framework is built upon four layers: blockchain for authentication, cluster formation to avoid data collisions, IDS enhanced with AI technology for attack detection, and forensics techniques to secure data collection and storage. Although solutions such as [3,30,49] seem promising, several challenges remain in making these approaches viable, such as infrastructural dependencies, high storage and bandwidth demands, and significant computational requirements, factors that come with high costs and may not be prioritized in practice.

4. Software: *applications, software, and tools. 4a. Applications and Software. 4b. Forensic Tools.* This category focuses on applications and software, specifically road safety systems and forensic tools. It covers systems monitoring vehicle data to detect road disturbances and accidents, highlighting security vulnerabilities, such as communication protocol issues. Forensic tools are essential for extracting forensically relevant data from sources like EDRs, OBD, USB, and JTAG ports. While several tools are available, many lack support for automotive-specific file systems like QNX. This highlights the need for more secure, automotive-compatible tools and solutions for ADF.

Recent Trends. In [22], J. Jung et al. propose a process for collecting automotive forensic data using an Android phone connected to a vehicle's OBD-II port. They utilize Android apps such as Infocar and Torque Pro, Bluetooth HCI snoop logs, and the Android system's main log buffer. The extracted data includes vehicle velocity, speed, braking events, refueling, and Bluetooth connection times. The authors claim that this data can be used to reconstruct driver behavior. Notably, the approach does not address security or privacy concerns. In [4], R. Amala et al. focus on Vehicle Tracking Systems (VTS) within the transportation domain, presenting methods for extracting and analyzing forensic data. They introduce the IoT Forensics Suite (IFS) and demonstrate its use for VTS. Data extraction was performed over the SPI interface, but whether these methods also apply to other interfaces remains uncertain. In [35], M. Nicho et al. simulate a use case involving a 2015 Toyota Land Cruiser SUV to demonstrate the application of established forensic tools for data extraction and analysis prior to a hypothetical incident. While the scenario effectively highlights the practical need for forensics in the automotive domain, it may not fully reflect real-world investigations due to its hypothetical nature. The authors emphasize the importance of ensuring security throughout the process, but the primary focus is on demonstrating the use of existing forensic tools and processes, rather than addressing broader security challenges. In [15], S. Ebbers et al. investigate vehicle assistant apps from various car manufacturers from a digital forensic perspective, such as reconstructing driver patterns, e.g., routes, parking, and unlock/lock. Their findings include that apps leave forensic traces, thereby demonstrating that data from vehicle assistant apps can be valuable for digital forensic investigations In [23], C. Katsini et al. introduce FoRePlan, a digital forensics tool designed to support security experts in preparing, selecting, and executing customized forensic readiness plans in real time. The tool aims to automate the collection and preservation of forensically sound evidence when cyberattacks are detected.

5. Hardware: *architectural digital forensic design. Solutions, and mechanisms for sensors such as GPS, LIDAR, and cameras. Requirements for Event Data Recorders (EDRs) and Blackboxes. 5a. Architecture. 5b. Sensor. 5c. EDR and Blackbox.* This category highlights different hardware solutions applicable to ADF. For instance, a blockchain architecture is proposed for use as a black box, utilizing a consensus algorithm to validate transactions. However, this approach is less practical due to the real-time requirements of vehicles and the cost of implementing a new architecture in which all ECUs would be able to sign and validate messages. In the context of forensic data sources, the CAN bus is emphasized, providing examples like error messages, and the infotainment system, which includes media content, internal logs, and GPS data. Dashboard cameras are also discussed in the context of ADF. For example, an algorithm is proposed to extract engine vibration patterns from video blur for vehicle identification, achieving around 90% accuracy. However, privacy concerns arise when the media content contains unrelated individuals or vehicles. Additionally, audio is proposed for vehicle identification, such as sound from the engine and air conditioner. However, challenges include sound disturbances and security and privacy concerns related to data collection and storage. Another important topic discussed is the use of data recorders, such as EDRs, and cryptographic methods, like encryption and hashing, to ensure data integrity for evidence.

Recent Trends. In [40] M. Rayno aims to improve the use of EDRs by identifying functional, privacy, and security requirements while also considering regulatory constraints. A model-based systems engineering (MBSE) approach is presented, using the MagicGrid V2 methodology. Challenges are highlighted, such as the issue of satisfying the availability of forensic data with privacy (e.g., GDPR [37]) and protecting the manufacturer's intellectual property. In

[39], M. Rayno et al. continue their work and present a system model detailing how to balance the need for forensic data, securing it, and protecting OEM's Intellectual Property (IP). They define specific EDR requirements and explain how these can address forensic investigation needs (e.g., data availability) and cybersecurity concerns (e.g., IP protection). In [10], Z. Chen et al. propose a model for digital forensic investigations of networked terminal devices to aid in determining liability in automobile accidents. The model is validated with three T-box devices, demonstrating its feasibility. However, the paper provides limited attention to security considerations regarding the model. In [47], K. Strandberg et al. propose the Automotive BlackBox architecture to support ADF, detailing data collection, storage, and analysis guidelines. The architecture introduces a specific data format and requirements within an automotive context, aligned with both current and envisioned future regulations and standards. The authors emphasize security while also recognizing several challenges, including balancing privacy with forensic capabilities and security.

In [17], B. Gadekar et al. investigate the challenges of event-based forensic analysis in automotive systems, driven by the growing number of vehicles, increasing data volumes, and real-time requirements, and propose a clustering-based architecture to improve data management efficiency in response to these challenges. T. Reichel et al. [41] highlight vulnerabilities in vehicle data storage systems for detecting GNSS spoofing and propose enhanced data collection and simulation approaches, although challenges remain with regard to data volume, privacy, detection accuracy, and integration with existing standards. In [32], T. Long et al. introduce a tampering detection framework that utilizes a dynamic watermarking technique. The framework was evaluated using real-world data, demonstrating its effectiveness in detecting tampered data. However, since static datasets were used, the framework's effectiveness in real-world driving scenarios remains unclear. Although the main goal is to ensure tampering detection, i.e., integrity, their solution could benefit from also addressing other security and privacy considerations. In [24], R. Kurachi et al. explore the potential of using EDRs for ADF, with an emphasis on detecting evidence tampering, such as hacking attempts. They also perform aligned experiments and propose security measures to counteract these threats, including message authentication and IDS. The authors conclude that while EDRs can be useful for forensic investigations, they need to be strengthened in terms of cybersecurity to ensure the trust in the data.

6. Algorithms: *Artificial Intelligence (AI), Machine Learning (ML), and other algorithms.* *6a. AI/ML. 6b. Other Algorithms.* This category emphasizes AI, ML, and other algorithms to improve forensic investigations and data analysis in contexts such as vehicle sensor data, driver behavior, and accident reconstruction. For instance, a protocol to detect sensor manipulation, such as spoofing and jamming, is proposed using deep neural networks. However, the analysis relies on simulated data rather than real-world sensor data, which raises questions about its practical value. ML is discussed for automating driver identification, but practical implementation remains challenging since a standardized forensic data format is not yet available. The CASE standard is proposed as a solution to address this challenge. Furthermore, the lack of a public specification for data communication in Vehicle Networks (IVN) is highlighted as a challenge. READ, an algorithm to reverse-engineer CAN messages to detect deviations, is proposed to help identify abnormal driving patterns before accidents. Additionally, a method is proposed to estimate the likelihood that a suspect was near a crime scene using data such as GPS, acceleration, and braking patterns. This approach aims to recalculate routes and determine suspects' locations in hit-and-run accidents, offering the main benefit of saving time compared to manual methods.

Recent Trends. In [9], Y. Chen et al. introduce the CPBW (Change-Point-Detection and Bag-of-Words-Based Mechanism) for driver identification, leveraging a smartphone's triaxial accelerometer. CPBW uses change point detection (CPD) and the Bag-of-Words (BoW) method to identify drivers based on driving behavior efficiently. The system was evaluated using real-world data from two vehicle models (Hyundai and Toyota) with around 400 km of driving. While the study focuses on efficiency and accuracy, the approach does not prioritize security, which may expose the system to potential cyberattacks and reduce trust in the data collected. Environmental factors, such as varying road and weather conditions, could also challenge the potential for driver identification. In [51], R. Tyagi et al. introduce a blockchain-based system to securely store forensic data while utilizing AI and ML techniques to process large volumes of data and ensure privacy by randomizing signatures to mask witnesses' true identities. Their approach is evaluated for feasibility through simulations on an Ethereum blockchain platform, which demonstrates that security and privacy concerns are addressed and that the AI/ML-based techniques improve data processing. The authors believe their approach is applicable to future 5G/V2X networks. However, although the evaluation shows improved processing, computational costs and communication overhead in a practical setting are likely to remain challenging.

In [43] S. Rizvi et al. explores the use of AI in the field of network forensics, focusing on the application of techniques such as ML, deep learning (DL), and hybrid approaches. While the primary focus is not specifically on automotive forensics, the authors highlight the relevance of AI in addressing challenges within the automotive domain. Specifically, AI is seen as a key solution for processing and analyzing the large amounts of data generated by modern vehicles, improving the accuracy of investigations, and ensuring the identification of authentic, relevant, and correct data. In [21], S. Jabeen et al. focus on the challenge of Vehicle Make and Model Recognition (VMMR) and use both structural and pattern-based feature descriptors. Four different descriptors are employed to capture both structural and textural features of vehicles, which are then processed using two classifiers: Support Vector Machine (SVM) and K-Nearest Neighbor (KNN). The evaluation demonstrates high accuracy in recognizing the vehicle make and model, with structural-based descriptors proving to be more effective than pattern-based. The paper also highlights various challenges, such as difficulties in obtaining high-quality frontal images and the required computational complexity. Additionally, security and privacy considerations need to be emphasized more for real-world applications. In [20], F. Iqbal et al. introduce a method for detecting and categorizing unusual events in audio recordings, including a dataset called the Unusual Occurrences in Audio Forensics Database (UOAFDB). The dataset consists of sounds from events such as car crashes, explosions, and gunshots, along with sounds from various background environments. Their method employs a deep-learning approach for sound event detection and classification, with the authors claiming to achieve a detection rate of over 80%. However, real-world conditions can present more complex and unpredictable noise scenarios, deep-learning models are also known to be resource-intensive, and security and privacy are not emphasized.

7. Cryptography: *blockchain technology or other cryptos*. *7a. Blockchain*. *7b. Other Cryptography*. The main content of this category focuses on various blockchain-based solutions to improve digital forensic investigations, including strengthening IVN security. A high-level traffic investigation framework is proposed using decentralized identity distribution on a blockchain with sensor data. However, its industrial use seems impractical due to its abstract nature. Another blockchain framework is proposed to secure IVN by tracking previous transactions in ECUs. While it offers historical traceability, its use is limited as it only covers actions from OEMs, service technicians, and communications with RSUs, and not events from other actors. A blockchain-based event recording system with Proof of Event mechanisms is proposed, where an election algorithm selects a verifier from a network of participants. The goal is to provide trust in event data related to accidents. However, considering the complexity of IVN data, it is likely only applicable to a small subset of forensic data. Another approach for collecting and storing forensic data, AVGuard, is proposed to secure integrity using hash chains and Bloom filters. However, the approach lacks further consideration of privacy and securing web communication and storage.

Recent Trends. In [33], T. Menard et al. highlight privacy challenges in ADF data collection, where previous approaches mainly prioritized user anonymity over data unlinkability, making them less efficient at preserving privacy. The authors' approach uses group signatures and secure communication to ensure both privacy and traceability to specific events. They claim their approach outperforms existing methods in terms of privacy and security and demonstrate its efficiency regarding computation and communication overhead. However, like other similar approaches, infrastructure dependencies and scalability issues exist, which may limit the practical applicability of their solution. J. Li et al. [26] propose a secure in-vehicle digital forensic scheme with public auditing to ensure data integrity and authenticity in cloud storage. Their approach utilizes verifiable delay functions (VDFs), which enable public verification of the data, allowing for the detection of tampering. The scheme aims to ensure that driving-related data uploaded to the cloud can be publicly audited and verified for authenticity. Future work should include incorporating trusted timestamps to ensure the correct time sequence of the data, as well as designing a more comprehensive vehicle forensics tool. While the scheme addresses data integrity and non-repudiation, it lacks emphasis on other security attributes such as confidentiality, availability, and privacy. Ming Li et al. introduce a systematic digital forensics framework that uses smart contracts on the Ethereum blockchain to model the process as a Finite State Machine (FSM), aiming to ensure traceability and tamper resistance [28]. A prototype deployed on the Rinkeby testnet demonstrates practical feasibility, though many real-world challenges remain.

In [55], A. R. Vieira et al. introduces BEDR, a blockchain-based distributed EDR solution for VANETs, designed as an alternative to traditional centralized EDRs. The paper presents a practical experiment using Hyperledger Iroha to simulate the BEDR solution and evaluate its feasibility, particularly in terms of performance. However, BEDR and similar solutions face several challenges for practical use in real-world scenarios, mainly related to scalability, bandwidth, computational demands, and the associated costs. In [29], X. Li et al. propose a blockchain-based cooperative transaction scheme designed to ensure data integrity, incorporating mechanisms to prevent malicious actors, enforced through blockchain and smart contracts. The authors highlight challenges such as intermittent internet connectivity, which prevents real-time updates and transaction validation, and the difficulties in ensuring security and scalability in dynamic environments. In [27], M. Li et al. propose Eunomia, the first blockchain-based scheme in this category to comprehensively address all CIANP properties, ensuring confidentiality through fine-grained access control, integrity via tamper-proof blockchain records, availability with distributed storage, non-repudiation through traceable identifiers, and privacy using anonymous credentials and zero-knowledge proofs.

8. Framework and Processes: *management of automotive digital evidence and simplification of automotive digital forensics processes.* This category focuses on incorporating ADF practices into systems to enhance accident prediction, traffic violation detection, and forensically sound data collection. Deep learning and blockchain are used in a proposal for a framework for road accidents, utilizing data from road conditions, climate, and driving patterns to predict incidents for specific road segments, accompanied by vehicle warnings from RSUs. Another framework uses a permission-based blockchain along with a public vehicle key infrastructure (VPKI) to securely collect various types of data, such as health data (e.g., from wearable devices) and automotive diagnostics. Yet another data collection system for distributed, decentralized, and mobile entities is proposed to ensure secure storage, including an algorithm for evidence integrity verification. A use case is outlined utilizing the OBD-II port and the tool WireShark, addressing forensic readiness, acquisition, analysis, and documentation. Another proposal applies a Desktop IT forensic process model to the automotive domain, including preparations, data gathering, investigation, and documentation, covering both live and static data from ECUs, sensors, and actuators. Lastly, a proposal for route reconstruction, considering data transmitted over the CAN bus, is suggested to either clear or link individuals to incidents.

Recent Trends. J. Liang et al. [31] proposes a block-chain based attribute-based access control model to ensure the integrity and authenticity of forensic data, along with an incentive mechanism based on reputational value creation to classify user behaviors and encourage participation. This aims to reduce insurance disputes and assist law enforcement investigations. A Raspberry Pi represents resource-constrained light nodes, and the framework is deployed via a Hyperledger Fabric blockchain platform. Experiments show that the proposed framework ensures data integrity and promotes user participation. However, challenges exist in terms of scalability, resource limitations, and ensuring fairness in the incentive-based mechanisms. In [13], Y. A. Daraghmi et al. propose a framework for the automatic analysis of dashcam videos, extracting data such as time, date, speed, and GPS coordinates. The framework enables mapping both temporal and spatial evidence to track vehicle routes. Still, as with all video data, privacy concerns arise, as unrelated information, such as individuals and license plates, may be captured.

In [5], T. Bakhshi et al. conducted a survey across law enforcement agencies and identified significant gaps in automotive forensics, such as a lack of standardized methods and reliance on invasive data extraction. In response, they introduced SAFE (Standardized Automotive Forensic Engine), an ML-based tool designed to guide forensic investigators through a step-by-step process. The authors aim to release SAFE as a public web-based application to improve forensic workflows. However, challenges remain, including differences in regulations and jurisdictions, as well as privacy concerns related to the data. Additionally, the framework does not emphasize security measures. In [18], J. Han et al. introduce a conceptual Vehicle Security Operations Center (VSOC) framework aimed at guiding future research and applications. The framework provides a structured approach for managing, detecting, orchestrating, and responding to cybersecurity threats. While the paper discusses various cybersecurity threats and existing countermeasures, the authors acknowledge the challenges of addressing security concerns due to the complex and evolving threat landscape. Additionally, they highlight practical challenges in integrating their solution, given the diversity of automotive technologies and regulatory environments.

In [1], L. Ahmeti et al. propose a forensic approach for handling incidents involving autonomous vehicles within the Gaia-X framework. They emphasize the importance of ensuring security and resilience. The authors present two key use cases: one involves manipulating the vehicle's control unit to enable unauthorized autonomous driving, and the other concerns a Distributed Denial-of-Service (DDoS) attack disrupting communication. The paper applies existing forensic guidelines, to these scenarios and suggests how the Gaia-X framework can assist in investigations. A key challenge discussed is the evolving nature of both autonomous vehicle technology (including V2X communication) and the Gaia-X infrastructure, which is decentralized and complex, making it difficult to establish standardized forensic approaches. In [8], K. G. Buquerin et al. propose a three-step methodology, comprising brainstorming, system archaeology, and expert interviews, to evaluate data completeness in automotive digital forensics. Additionally, survey results are presented to identify relevant data formats, highlighting the need for the development and improvement of forensic tools.

9. Practical Experiments: *practical cases for forensic investigation, or proposals for data management.* This category centers around practical experiments on ADF data and related components that can be used in digital investigations. One study explored vulnerabilities in a Skoda Octavia vRS and proposed that components and data, such as infotainment data, GPS, ECU memory, and diagnostics, could be useful for forensic investigations. Another study focused on forensic artifacts using the iVe tool from Berla Corporation [12] for two infotainment systems (Uconnect and Toyota Extension Box), revealing differences in the available data. The former provided only location data, while the latter contained additional information, such as contact and call logs, and GPS data. Additionally, crash data from the NHTSA database were analyzed in the proprietary EDRX format using a Bosch EDR tool [6]. The analysis revealed that post-2000, vehicle speed, airbag deployment, and engine throttle were recorded, and over time, more data, including diagnostic information, were added. Privacy and security issues were highlighted, raising concerns about the admissibility of such data in court. Other studies extracted data from infotainment systems and communication traffic from various networks (e.g., GSM/3G/4G) with the aim of identifying evidence, such as call records and packet captures (PCAP). Finally, a case study on a Volkswagen Golf highlighted issues, such as how to avoid data loss.

Recent Trends. In [57], Y. Yoon et al. conduct a forensic investigation of an Android Jellybean-based infotainment system installed in a Kia K5 2017. The focus is on collecting system logs and navigation logs to analyze their potential for reconstructing events and activities related to accidents or crimes. The system logs contain user data such as Bluetooth connections and navigation guidance, while the navigation logs provide detailed data from the navigation app, including user routes and search destinations. Notably, the approach lacks cybersecurity considerations, such as ensuring data integrity, and the general value is limited due to the study's focus on the specific Android Jellybean-based AVN system.

The categories 10–11 below, as derived from [48], have been outdated; for instance, infrastructure is included in other categories, while we did not find any recent research around ADF and smart cities. Neither TEE nor virtualization has been emphasized in recent research. Thus, we summarize previous research and refer to the discussion section.

10. Infrastructure/Smart Cities: *infrastructure communication and smart cities.* Issues are highlighted in handling forensic data from autonomous vehicles (AVs), such as the lack of integrity validation and unprofessional data extraction, compared to other forensic fields. It is argued that methods used both for analysis and for acquiring data for legal purposes are insufficient. A mechanism for securely acquiring AV sensor data and uploading it to the cloud is proposed as a response. Additionally, the integration of smart cars into smart city infrastructure is emphasized. As a case in point, a hypothetical use case is provided involving a reckless driver and its interaction with other smart entities, along with a forensic investigation process.

11. TEE/Virtualization: *securing digital evidence using Trusted Execution Environments (TEEs) and/or virtualization.* This category emphasizes isolated environments. One study proposes a data recording system for automotive applications, i.e., T-BOX, that operates inside a TEE with the purpose of detecting data manipulations, such as removal, replacement, replaying, and truncation of data. However, their approach remains platform-dependent and does not protect data against manipulation before storage. Additionally, confidentiality and privacy considerations are not addressed with regard to the stored data.

5   Discussion

Recent Trends. Recent trends emphasize the challenges of data collection and extraction [25,45]. Earlier studies used tools like Alientech KTag [2] and PEmicro Cyclone [36], while [7] demonstrates the successful use of Magnet AXIOM [16]. Current trends reflect a continued effort to adapt existing tools and methodologies to various vehicle systems, enhancing the accuracy and reliability of forensic data extraction. Recent challenges are linked to the increasingly dynamic threat landscape and the expanded vehicle ecosystem, where there is growing dependence on services and connections outside the vehicle (V2X), along with evolving complexities related to software and architectures [44]. There is an urgent need and a clear shift toward adopting newer technologies to address these challenges, with blockchain being notably emphasized [19]. We can also see a trend toward more advanced solutions, such as [30,49], and [3], which focus on reducing computational and storage demands, enhancing security utilizing blockchain technologies. However, challenges such as cost, infrastructure dependencies, and computational complexity remain.

The IoT Forensics Suite [4] is introduced, practical tool usage is demonstrated [15,35], and smartphones and apps, such as Android-based tools, are used for collecting vehicle data [22]. However, security remains a significant challenge. Various papers emphasize improving and extending EDRs while balancing privacy, security, and intellectual property protection, using models like MBSE and MagicGrid V2 [40]. Real-time analysis and scalability are highlighted through novel approaches like clustering [17] and tampering detection via watermarking [32]. Challenges remain, such as mitigating cyberattacks and detecting tampering to ensure trust in forensic evidence [24]. Recent trends highlight the need for more advanced approaches to address challenges such as managing large amounts of data. In response, advancements in AI/ML have emerged, along with solutions that integrate blockchain with AI/ML. For instance, the CPBW mechanism is introduced for driver identification using smartphones, and AI/ML integration with blockchain is explored for secure forensic data storage with real-world data [9]. Another blockchain-based solution also utilizes AI/ML techniques as a promising approach [51]. Other efforts focus on data integrity [31], dashcam video analysis for evidence mapping [13], and the SAFE tool for forensic investigations [5]. Additionally, responding to cybersecurity threats is emphasized in [18]. However, despite these advancements, challenges remain in making blockchain a practical solution. There is also a tendency to address challenges with privacy, traceability, and security for practical applications [26,29,33,55]. For instance, recent approaches focus on privacy through group signatures and secure communication [33], and enhanced integrity using verifiable delay functions [29].

Future Directions. The field of ADF is likely to move toward standardization, regulation, and more structured processes and frameworks for data handling (e.g., collection, extraction, and storage), ensuring that common tools and techniques can be applied universally across vehicle systems and manufacturers. As shown in Tables 1 and 2, there is a strong focus on these categories, along with practical experiments that demonstrate their value (categories 1, 2, 8, and 9). While blockchain continues to be explored as a potential solution for enhancing ADF and security, its cost, performance constraints, and infrastructure dependencies make it challenging for broad practical application. Despite its promise, blockchain suffers from various inherent limitations, such as scalability, and is unlikely to serve as a complete solution for ADF with the current limitations in mind. Nevertheless, it may serve as a supplementary technology when integrated with other approaches to enhance ADF. The integration of AI and ML is emerging as a critical response to address and extract value from the massive volume of data generated by modern vehicle systems due to increasing communication and the use of services (both in-vehicle and V2X data). These technologies will be invaluable in automating data analysis, identifying anomalies, and facilitating scalability for ADF.

However, as shown in Tables 1 and 2, there is an important gap in recent research regarding virtualization and TEE. These are cutting-edge technologies that could enhance ADF by securing sensitive data (such as cryptographic keys) through execution in isolation, thus enhancing tamper resistance and preventing data leakage. Additionally, the concept of smart cities has not been widely explored in the context of ADF. Future research is likely to consider how vehicles, through their V2X communication, interact with other smart systems, and the related forensic data that can be inferred from these interactions.

In summary, we forecast the field of ADF to evolve toward standardization and clearer regulations. The integration of AI/ML technologies will become imperative to address the increased volume of data, while blockchain will remain secondary but potentially useful for specific tasks. TEE and virtualization represent potential areas for further research to enhance ADF security. Lastly, as vehicles become more integrated into other smart systems, such as smart city ecosystems, future research will likely explore how this increasingly interconnected environment can benefit ADF with relevant data.

6   Conclusion

We have provided an updated and comprehensive SLR of the field of ADF, categorizing and comparing recent developments with prior research, while highlighting state-of-the-art trends, such as emerging solutions in artificial intelligence, machine learning, and blockchain. By analyzing these solutions from both a security and practical perspective, we offer valuable insights and implications for future research. This SLR not only emphasizes the latest advancements but also presents a forward-looking perspective on the future of ADF. As the automotive industry continues to evolve, we believe our work will be of value to both researchers and practitioners navigating this dynamic and critical field.

Acknowledgments. This research was partly supported by the MAGIC project (2024-03687) funded by VINNOVA, the Swedish Governmental Agency for Innovation Systems.

Disclosure of Interests. The authors have no competing interests to declare that are relevant to the content of this article.

References

1. Ahmeti, L., Dolos, K., Meyer, C., Attenberger, A., Hackenberg, R.: A forensic approach to handle autonomous transportation incidents within Gaia-X. Cloud Comput. **2024**, 51 (2024)
2. Alientech: K-tag ECU programming tool (2025). https://www.alientech-tools.com/k-tag/
3. AlKhanafseh, M.Y., Surakhi, O.M.: VANET intrusion investigation based forensics technology: a new framework. In: 2022 International Conference on Emerging Trends in Computing and Engineering Applications (ETCEA), pp. 1–7. IEEE, Karak, Jordan (2022)
4. Amala, R., Roy, K.R., Aravind, G.S., Dija, S., Manohar, K.: Digital forensics analysis of a vehicle tracking system. SN Comput. Sci. **4**(6), 835 (2023)
5. Bakhshi, T., Ghita, B., Kuzminykh, I.: SAFE: a standardized automotive forensic engine for law enforcement agencies. In: 2023 15th International Conference on Innovations in Information Technology (IIT), pp. 196–201. IEEE, Al Ain, United Arab Emirates (2023)
6. Bosch: Crash data retrieval (CDR) tool (2025). https://boschcdrtool.com/
7. Buquerin, K.G., Hof, H.J.: Digital forensics investigation of the Tesla autopilot file system. In: SECURWARE 2022: The Sixteenth International Conference on Emerging Security Information, Systems and Technologies (2022)
8. Buquerin, K.K.G., Corbett, C., Hof, H.J.: Structured methodology and survey to evaluate data completeness in automotive digital forensics. In: Proceedings of the 19th European Conference on Automotive Cyber Security (ESCAR Europe 2021), pp. 52–70 (2021)
9. Chen, Y.M., Lin, P., Yeh, E.H., Yang, S.R., Lu, R.: CPBW: a change-point-detection and bag-of-words-based mechanism utilizing smartphone triaxial accelerometer data for driver identification. IEEE Internet Things J. **11**(18), 29766–29780 (2024)
10. Chen, Z., et al.: Digital forensics for automotive intelligent networked terminal devices. IEEE Trans. Veh. Technol. **73**(4), 5128–5138 (2024)
11. Chowdhury, N.M.I., Hasan, R.: Security analysis of connected autonomous vehicles (CAVs): challenges, issues, defenses, and open problems. In: 2024 IEEE World Forum on Public Safety Technology (WFPST), pp. 81–86. IEEE, Herndon, VA, USA (2024)

12. Berla Corporation: iVe- vehicle system forensics (2025). https://berla.co/ecosystem/

13. Daraghmi, Y.A., Shawahna, I.: Digital forensic analysis of vehicular video sensors: dashcams as a case. Sensors **23**(17), 7548 (2023)

14. Ebbers, S., Gense, S., Bakkouch, M., Freiling, F., Schinzel, S.: Grand theft API: a forensic analysis of vehicle cloud data. Forensic Sci. Int. Digital Invest. **48**(Supplement S), 301691 (2024)

15. Ebbers, S., Ising, F., Saatjohann, C., Schinzel, S.: Grand theft app: digital forensics of vehicle assistant apps. In: Proceedings of the 16th International Conference on Availability, Reliability and Security, pp. 1–6. ACM, Vienna Austria (2021)

16. Forensics, M.: Magnet axiom, digital forensic software (2025). https://www.magnetforensics.com/products/magnet-axiom/

17. Gadekar, B., Dharaskar, R.V., Thakare, V.M.: An event based digital forensic scheme for vehicular networks. Int. J. Recent Innov. Trends Comput. Commun. **11**(5), 383–394 (2023)

18. Han, J., Ju, Z., Chen, X., Yang, M., Zhang, H., Huai, R.: Secure operations of connected and autonomous vehicles. IEEE Trans. Intell. Veh. **8**(11), 4484–4497 (2023)

19. Hussain, S., Tahir, S., Masood, A., Elahi, I.: Enhanced trust & risk based access control, in autonomous vehicles, by using ethereum vs hyperledger platforms consensus algorithms. In: 2024 IEEE 16th International Conference on Advanced Infocomm Technology (ICAIT), pp. 261–267. IEEE, Enshi, China (2024)

20. Iqbal, F., Abbasi, A., Javed, A.R., Srivastava, G., Jalil, Z., Gadekallu, T.R.: Identification and categorization of unusual internet of vehicles events in noisy audio. In: 2023 IEEE 97th Vehicular Technology Conference (VTC2023-Spring). IEEE, Florence, Italy (2023)

21. Jabeen, S., Jabeen, A., Adnan, S.M., Rao, W.A.: Vehicle make and model recognition using structural and pattern based feature descriptors. In: 2021 International Conference on Communication Technologies (ComTech), pp. 73–78. IEEE, Rawalpindi, Pakistan (2021)

22. Jung, J., Han, S., Park, M., Cho, S.J.: Automotive digital forensics through data and log analysis of vehicle diagnosis Android apps. Forensic Sci. Int. Digital Invest. **49**, 301752 (2024)

23. Katsini, C., Raptis, G.E., Alexakos, C., Serpanos, D.: Foreplan: supporting digital forensics readiness planning for internet of vehicles. In: Proceedings of the 25th Pan-Hellenic Conference on Informatics (PCI '21), p. 111. ACM (2021)

24. Kurachi, R., Katayama, T., Sasaki, T., Saito, M., Ajioka, Y.: Evaluation of automotive event data recorder towards digital forensics. In: 2022 IEEE 95th Vehicular Technology Conference: (VTC2022-Spring), pp. 1–7. IEEE, Helsinki, Finland (2022)

25. Lee, J.H., Lim, S.H., Hyeon, B., Jeon, O.Y., Park, J.J., Park, N.I.: Tesla log data analysis approach from a digital forensics perspective. World Electr. Veh. J. **15**(12), 590 (2024)

26. Li, J., Song, Z., Zhang, Z., Li, Y., Cao, C.: In-vehicle digital forensics for connected and automated vehicles with public auditing. IEEE Internet Things J. **11**(4), 6368–6383 (2024)

27. Li, M., Chen, Y., Lal, C., Conti, M., Alazab, M., Hu, D.: Eunomia: anonymous and secure vehicular digital forensics based on blockchain. IEEE Trans. Dependable Secur. Comput. **20**(1), 225–241 (2023)

28. Li, M., Weng, J., Liu, J.N., Lin, X., Obimbo, C.: Toward vehicular digital forensics from decentralized trust: an accountable, privacy-preserving, and secure realization. IEEE Internet Things J. **9**(9), 7009–7022 (2022)

29. Li, X., Tan, C., Liu, M., Luan, T.H., Gao, L., Qu, Y.: A Blockchain-based cooperative perception in internet of vehicles. In: 2021 IEEE 94th Vehicular Technology Conference (VTC2021-Fall), pp. 1–6. IEEE, Norman, OK, USA (2021)

30. Li, Y., Xue, L., Wang, L., Liu, J., Lin, X.: Secure approximate deduplication for forensic images in crowdsensing vehicular networks. IEEE Trans. Veh. Technol. **74**(4), 6624–6637 (2025)

31. Liang, J., Chen, J., Zhu, R., Miao, C., Lu, K., Jiao, L.: Reputation value-based converged dual-channel digital forensics for blockchain-enabled smart vehicles. IEEE Trans. Intell. Veh., 1–15 (2024)

32. Long, T., Xie, A., Ren, X., Wang, X.: Tampering detection of LiDAR data for autonomous vehicles. In: 2021 40th Chinese Control Conference (CCC), pp. 4732–4737. IEEE, Shanghai, China (2021)

33. Menard, T., Abouyoussef, M.: Towards privacy-preserving vehicle digital forensics: a Blockchain approach. In: 2024 12th International Symposium on Digital Forensics and Security (ISDFS), pp. 1–6. IEEE, San Antonio, TX, USA (2024)

34. Nelsons, B., Philips, A., Steuart, C.: Guide to computer forensics and investigations. Cengage (2018)

35. Nicho, M., Alblooki, M., AlMutiwei, S., McDermott, C.D., Ilesanmi, O.: A crime scene reconstruction for digital forensic analysis: an SUV case study. Int. J. Digital Crime Forensics **15**(1), 1–20 (2023)

36. PEmicro: Arm programming solutions (2025). https://www.pemicro.com/arm/arm_overview.cfm

37. Proton Technologies AG: Complete guide to GDPR compliance (2020). https://gdpr.eu/

38. Rak, R., Kopencova, D., Felcan, M.: Digital vehicle identity—-digital vin in forensic and technical practice. Forensic Sci. Int. Digital Invest. **39**, 301307 (2021)

39. Rayno, M., Daily, J.: Balancing digital forensic investigation with cybersecurity for heavy vehicle traffic crashes. INCOSE Int. Symp. **33**(1), 638–648 (2023)

40. Rayno, M., Daily, J.: Integrating model-based systems engineering for enhanced digital forensics in crash investigations. In: 2024 IEEE International Systems Conference (SysCon), pp. 1–8. IEEE, Montreal, QC, Canada (2024)

41. Reichel, T., Gerstner, M., Schiller, L., Attenberger, A., Hackenberg, R., Dološ, K.: A forensic analysis of GNSS spoofing attacks on autonomous vehicles. In: Proceedings of the Sixteenth International Conference on Cloud Computing, GRIDs, and Virtualization, pp. 1–6. IARIA, Valencia, Spain (2025)

42. Repas, J., Berek, L., Schmidt, M.: Autonomous vehicles forensics-the next step of the digital vehicles forensics. In: 2022 IEEE 1st International Conference on Cognitive Mobility (CogMob), pp. 67–72. IEEE, Budapest, Hungary (2022)

43. Rizvi, S., Scanlon, M., Mcgibney, J., Sheppard, J.: Application of artificial intelligence to network forensics: survey challenges and future directions. IEEE Access **10**, 110362–110384 (2022)

44. Sharma, P., Gillanders, J.: Cybersecurity and forensics in connected autonomous vehicles: a review of the state-of-the-art. IEEE Access **10**, 108979–108996 (2022)

45. Shayer, M.A., Mim, S.I., Anjum, N., Chowdhury, M.A.S., Preoshi, N.N.I., Mostakim, M.: The car image generation quality of DCGAN and VSGAN: a comparative study. In: 2024 7th International Conference on Informatics and Computational Sciences (ICICoS), pp. 143–148. IEEE, Semarang, Indonesia (2024)

46. Stathers, C., Muhammad, M., Fasanmade, A., Al-Bayatti, A., Morden, J., Sharif, M.S.: Digital data extraction for vehicles forensic investigation. In: 2022 International Conference on Innovation and Intelligence for Informatics, Computing, and Technologies (3ICT), pp. 553–558. IEEE, Sakheer, Bahrain (2022)

47. Strandberg, K., Arnljung, U., Olovsson, T.: The automotive BlackBox: towards a standardization of automotive digital forensics. In: 2023 IEEE International Workshop on Information Forensics and Security (WIFS), pp. 1–6. IEEE, Nürnberg, Germany (2023)

48. Strandberg, K., Nowdehi, N., Olovsson, T.: A systematic literature review on automotive digital forensics: challenges, technical solutions and data collection. IEEE Trans. Intell. Veh. **8**(2), 1350–1367 (2023)

49. Tao, Q., Ding, H., Jiang, T., Cui, X.: B-DSPA: a blockchain-based dynamically scalable privacy-preserving authentication scheme in vehicular AD HOC networks. IEEE Internet Things J. **11**(1), 1385–1397 (2024)

50. The International Organization for Standardization: Road vehicles – cybersecurity engineering (2022). https://www.iso.org/standard/70918.html

51. Tyagi, R., Sharma, S., Mohan, S.: Blockchain enabled intelligent digital forensics system for autonomous connected vehicles. In: 2022 International Conference on Communication. Computing and Internet of Things (IC3IoT), pp. 1–6. IEEE, Chennai, India (2022)

52. United Nations Economic Commission for Europe (UNECE: UN Regulation No. 155) (2022). https://unece.org/sites/default/files/2021-03/R155e.pdf

53. United Nations Economic Commission for Europe (UNECE: UN Regulation No. 156) (2022)

54. United Nations Economic Commission for Europe (UNECE: UN Regulation No. 160) (2023). https://unece.org/transport/documents/2023/01/standards/un-regulation-no160-revision-1-event-data-recorder-edr-01

55. Vieira, A.R., Farias, C.M., Melo, W.S., Madruga, E.L.: BEDR: blockchain event data recorder. In: 2022 IEEE 25th International Conference on Intelligent Transportation Systems (ITSC), pp. 2716–2721. IEEE, Macau, China (2022)

56. Wohlin, C.: Guidelines for snowballing in systematic literature studies and a replication in software engineering. In: Proceedings of the 18th International Conference on Evaluation and Assessment in Software Engineering. EASE '14, Association for Computing Machinery, New York, NY, USA (2014)

57. Yoon, Y., Jung, J., Cho, S.J., Choi, J., Park, M., Han, S.: Forensic investigation of an android jellybean-based car audio video navigation system. In: Proceedings of the 19th International Conference on Availability, Reliability and Security, pp. 1–8. ACM, Vienna, Austria (2024)

Exploring the Susceptibility to Fraud of Monetary Incentive Mechanisms for Strengthening FOSS Projects

Ben Swierzy[1,2]([✉]) [iD], Timo Pohl[1] [iD], Marc Ohm[1,2] [iD], and Michael Meier[1,2] [iD]

[1] University of Bonn, Bonn, Germany
{swierzy,pohl,ohm,mm}@cs.uni-bonn.de
[2] Fraunhofer FKIE, Bonn, Germany

Abstract. Free and open source software (FOSS) is ubiquitous on modern IT systems, accelerating the speed of software engineering over the past decades. With its increasing importance and historical reliance on uncompensated contributions, questions have been raised regarding the continuous maintenance of FOSS and its implications from a security perspective. In recent years, different funding programs have emerged to provide external incentives to reinforce community FOSS' sustainability. Past research primarily focused on analyses what type of projects have been funded and for what reasons. However, it has neither been considered whether there is a need for such external incentives, nor whether the incentive mechanisms, especially with the development of decentralized approaches, are susceptible to fraud. In this study, we explore the need for funding through a literature review and compare the susceptibility to fraud of centralized and decentralized incentive programs by performing case studies on the Sovereign Tech Fund (STF) and the tea project. We find non-commercial incentives to fill an important gap, ensuring longevity and sustainability of projects. Furthermore, we find the STF to be able to achieve a high resilience against fraud attempts, while tea is highly susceptible to fraud, as evidenced by revelation of an associated sybil attack on npm. Our results imply that special considerations must be taken into account when utilizing quantitative repository metrics regardless whether spoofing is expected.

Keywords: fraud · risk analysis · software metrics · software supply chain · open source · funding

1 Introduction

During the past decade, free and open source software (FOSS) has established itself as essential in modern digital systems. It is recognized as digital infrastructure, building the foundation for new developments. FOSS is viewed as a digital common good with society benefiting from it. While individuals are able to rapidly bootstrap new projects, developing products has become drastically cheaper for the industry as well. Overall, digital innovation is thriving. [14]

Compared to physical items, companies divest any liability claims for digital goods through mandatory legal agreements and users have no possibility to reliably judge security aspects [21]. In the past, commercial products have been criticized for this. With the majority of systems depending on FOSS, questions are raised on the maintenance and security of these projects. As a solution for the commercial case, areas of transparency are proposed [21] which already apply to FOSS: Openly available code facilitates independent audits, transparent development reveals best practices and open issue trackers disclose problems. While these incentives may work in a commercial context, free-time contributors have only limited capacity for the necessary maintenance. In this scenario, assistance or external incentives can improve the situation: Research has shown that several security practices in FOSS projects benefit from funding [4]. However, this topic is complex and multifaceted. For example, open source stewardship has a crux in finding the balance between private cost and public benefit [17] and fewer users are willing to support stable and established projects as they assume they are healthy and cared for [27].

External incentives can be established in many different ways. Central design questions are the eligibility criteria for funding and the method of allocating budget to eligible projects. As monetary support is the most common type of external incentive, fraud is inevitable if no preventative measures are deployed. The organizational structure (central or decentral) has important implications on possible fraud scenarios. In this work, we explore the susceptibility for fraud of external incentive mechanisms for FOSS projects. We focus on projects which fulfill the open source definition of the Open Source Initiative (OSI) [31] and restrict the scope to community FOSS projects. This confines to projects defined as commercial [6] or single-vendor OSS [39] which are fully backed by a commercial business model. We investigate the following research questions.

RQ1 Is there a need for external incentive mechanisms for strengthening maintenance of open source projects?

RQ2 How do processes and properties of centralized and decentralized incentive mechanisms compare?

RQ3 How susceptible are incentive mechanisms for FOSS projects to fraud?

Accordingly, our contributions are three-fold. We perform a meta study to show the need of FOSS funding without commercial interest, compile practical examples for automatic manipulation of impact metrics, and uncover a sybil attack on npm which could affect future research building on its registry data.

The remainder of the paper is structured as follows. Section 2 discusses whether there is a need for external incentive mechanisms. Section 3 compares centralized and decentralized mechanisms with the help of case studies. The susceptibility to fraud is examined in Sect. 4. Threats to validity and related work are discussed in Sects. 5 and 6. We conclude in Sect. 7.

2   Incentives for Open Source Contributors

There is a plethora of examples of successful and long-living FOSS projects backed by corporate support and even without any external incentives at all. With non-commercial funding gradually moving into the focus of software engineering research, there is little knowledge why such incentives are required. This motivates our first research question. To obtain an answer to this, we performed a keyword-based literature review on the research efforts of the past two decades into understanding the perspectives, motivations and development in FOSS projects. With an initial set of 12 papers obtained through the ACM digital library and DBLP using the keywords *open source maintenance*, we performed backwards snowball sampling to achieve a final collection of 21 papers. As a full systematic literature review is beyond the scope of this paper, we extract the key findings from each paper which contribute arguments to answer RQ1. Finally, all statements are grouped into a coherent order. This approach enables a longitudinal yet nuanced view, better suited to address the statements' diverse nature than quantitative characterizations.

Behind the success stories in FOSS, there is also a significant amount of failed projects. Through an interview study among impactful FOSS project maintainers from GitHub, Coelho *et al.* [11] compiled reasons why modern FOSS projects fail. Among the top 5 reasons—usurped by a competitor, obsolete, lack of time, lack of interest, and outdated technologies—external incentives can help in the majority of cases. Clearly, funding helps maintainers to invest more time on a project by not requiring them to work a full-time job in parallel. This also allows for necessary refactoring and for overcoming outdated technologies. Furthermore, it can be argued, that external incentives may help core maintainers see perspectives for a project in case commercial competition emerges. These results are in line with further interviews [22], identifying professional activities and financial aspects to be the major reasons why contributors switch from an active to a sleeping or even to a dead state. According to their own views, funding does not only compensate them for their time, but also helps them to dedicate more professional time towards their project [27]. Geer and Sieniawski find long-term commitment to open source stewardship to be essential for project success [17]. However, many projects have only few core developers, making them susceptible to dangers of a low bus factor [54], i.e., the minimum amount of contributors needing to stop working on a project until development halts. External incentives can be targeted towards community building, positively influencing the longevity and maintenance to sustain and grow the group of core developers. In this context, the subgroup within core developers which have administrative rights (called elite developers), show special correlations: While their investment into non-technical activities seems to negatively affect the productivity of a project [51], their time is invaluable for increasing the amount of (core) contributors [13]. Therefore, it is critical that elite developers have as few other professional obligations as possible with external incentives through funding a clear way of achieving this. However, it must be noted that lowering the barriers for participation may invite lots of low quality contributions [27] which would work against the intended target. Finally, several funding sources have been shown to improve the IT security, measured by increases in many categories on Open Secure Software Foundation (OpenSSF) scorecards [4]. The literature review results only in a single example of negative consequences of funding. Within an experimental initiative, parts of the Debian project tried to shorten release cycles through obtaining short-term sponsorships which created a complex conflict between contributors [18]. Overall, the reviewed research shows clear indications that funding increases quality, maintenance and, accordingly, the reliability and success chances for FOSS projects.

External incentives for FOSS projects, especially through funding, are prevalent for a long time. Already more than 10 years ago, half of the contributors of a project sample make at least 95% of their commits during regular working hours, suggesting they are paid for their contributions [40]. Most existing sponsorships may primarily be classified into individual and corporate sponsoring which exhibit different characteristics. For most projects, individual donors are shown to be more important than corporate donors in the long run [60]. At the same time, corporate donations are more significant than individual ones, which are considered to be a symbol of gratitude, and with neither being considered a sustainable source of income [27]. While these statements seem to partially contradict each other, GitHub's sponsor mechanism is shown to attract only individual donors, to scale with developer reputation and to only have a short-term effect on the project [56]. Therefore, individual donations seem to be an indicator for a strong project community with corporate sponsorship not achieving a comparable level of self-sustainability. This is backed by the observation that corporate domination shows a negative relationship with survival probability [59]. In addition, corporate involvement is always based on intrinsic motivation which can be subdivided into economic, technological and social dimensions [26]. This leads to prejudices from volunteers towards company-funded contributors which may cause frustration and conflicts [58]. Rust is an example where such an issue occurred, with several core developers leaving because of Amazon's participation [58]. To work against this, it is suggested that companies are highly transparent with their motivations and contributions [58]. Still, a FOSS project's sustainability is not in the focus of companies as seen on the example of OpenStack, where many companies withdrew as soon as their goals were achieved or have failed [57]. Further, Gonzalez-Barahona *et al.* suggest that conflicts may arise when multiple companies contribute to the same project which can lead to unfairness [20], although neither proven nor considered in depth. Tight corporate coupling can lead to highly restrictive contributor license agreements (CLAs), which may ask contributors to surrender rights to their contributions [2]. In addition, the copyleft license GPL sees less prevalence [3]. Overall, the literature review reveals numerous problematic aspects that corporate sponsorship may have on FOSS projects and their sustainability. In contrast, the arguments towards corporate funding are sparse. Capiluppi *et al.* find project management by a commercial entity to be a major success factor in FOSS [5]. Furthermore, company involvement positively influences project popularity [6]. Though, in the same work indicators for negative effects on software design quality and changes in governance are found [6].

> In conclusion, we can answer RQ1 positively. There are clear indicators that funding is important for the maintenance and longevity of FOSS projects. However, the common scenario of corporate sponsorship may have diverse negative effects on projects, especially, on their sustainability after the sponsorship ends. At the same time, it is rare that donations are able to provide an income above poverty thresholds and maintainers often save them instead of spending them [37]. Consequently, maintenance and sustainability funding driven without commercial motivations needs to be addressed to ensure optimal functioning of the FOSS ecosystem and its dependents.

3 Comparison of Incentive Mechanisms

There exists a variety of financial and organizational support opportunities for FOSS projects. The results of the previous section indicate the need for the special class of non-commercial and structured funding programs for community FOSS. In this section, we take a detailed look at two subclasses of such funding programs, namely, centralized and decentralized approaches. With respect to the risk of fraud, these face distinct challenges. We compare four essential components for these classes which each program requires: source of budget, eligibility to funding, the application and assessment process and the allocation of budget to applicants. Moreover, the Sovereign Tech Fund (STF) and the tea project are considered as case studies for the purpose of identifying exploitation possibilities by fraudulent actors.

3.1 Centralized Approaches

A funding program shows centralized characteristics if a single instance is in full control of at least one essential component. The component descriptions presented in this section are based on the STF [44], Open Technology Fund (OTF)'s FOSS sustainability fund [33], the Open Source Technology Improvement Fund (OSTIF) [32], and OpenSSF's Alpha-Omega's Alpha-Omega [49]. All of these are well-known representatives for centralized FOSS funding agencies and transparently document their economics and methods. In all cases, the centrality property exhibits by the programs' full control over the allocation of budget to interested projects.

Source of Budget. Centralized approaches have heterogeneous budget sources which can be split into governmental budget and sponsoring by companies or foundations. In most cases, the approaches are almost exclusively built on a single budget source, with OSTIF being the only exception where each category contributes a significant share. The financial resources of this approach are substantial, with a budget range of 1 to 100 million USD. Notably, this scope is beyond those of individual donors which are at most a negligible source of budget for these approaches.

Eligibility to Funding. Before FOSS projects may apply for funding, they must fulfill eligibility criteria. The exact requirements vary based on the political focus of the funding agency. In most cases, projects need to be established and impactful by some definition.

Application and Assessment. The eligibility needs to be self-assessed and part of an online application which is connected to a relevant amount of bureaucratic effort. Furthermore, the online application needs to propose activities to be funded. The degree of formality and the amount and design of application stages varies slightly. In special cases, the central party selects funded projects or a subset thereof directly and skips an open application process. Applications are reviewed in a single or multiple stages behind closed doors and their appropriateness is assessed with respect to predefined criteria.

Allocation of Budget. In central approaches, an application is either accepted or declined, i.e., either the cost estimate is fully allocated to the applicant or no funding is provided. Partial acceptance is not supported. While the decision is shared with the applicant, feedback is usually sparse [52]. Based on an internal ranking created during assessment, the program funds all projects in order until the budget is exhausted.

Case Study: Sovereign Tech Fund. The Sovereign Tech Agency (STA) was established in 2022 by the German government and offers the STF, in addition to other funding programs. Since its fund allocation and its impact are already outlined in prior work [36,41], this case study focuses on the process until funding is approved. If not clearly indicated as presumed, all information in this section is taken from the STA's website [44].

Source of Budget. The STF is completely publicly funded and has an annual budget of 17 million euros in 2024 at its disposal. Sponsorships by companies or foundations are not designed to be part of its budget.

Eligibility to Funding. The STF funds established FOSS digital base technologies, i.e., neither prototypes nor user-facing applications. According to own statements, development and maintenance work is primarily funded, but other activities such as security audits may also be encompassed. This aligns with an analysis of STF's funded projects [41].

Application and Assessment. The application itself is a questionnaire where the criticality, use cases, challenges, and planned activities including a cost estimate need to be comprehensively described. The 12 central questions are formulated rather openly which allows an applicant to choose how they want to prove impact, criticality and relevance themselves. After submission, the applications need to pass three official stages taking up to 6 months in total until a funding contract is finalized. Each of the stages is further subdivided into multiple internal steps with few details published. In the first step the eligibility is judged, while afterward the application is rated based on the internal criteria. This is handled by employed *technologists* with one of their tasks explicitly being technology assessment [45]. If this stage is passed, the STF team helps to refine the application and concretizing the planned activities. Then, external experts provide additional reviews which are taken into account for the final decision. Additionally, the STA actively scouts FOSS projects for funding.

Allocation of Budget. For budget to be allocated to an applicant, all application stages must be passed. While there is no explicit information, it can be inferred from other German funding programs, that STF applications are either completely accepted or declined.

3.2   Decentralized Approaches

A decentralized system is characterized by the absence of a central instance of power. In the context of incentive mechanisms, this manifests either as unstructured sponsorships or the transparent specification of a protocol. While the first lacks governance, the latter is able to provide decision-making capabilities by specifying a domain-specific algorithm or a employing consensus mechanism. Nonetheless, both are characterized by their low barriers for participation.

Source of Budget. Compared to central funding systems, the budget sources for decentral systems are more diffuse. In governance-less mechanisms, individuals or companies directly donate to a FOSS project. Therefore, this scenario does not have immediate budget at its disposal. If the construction relies on a protocol, the decentralized funding mechanism may be constructed similarly to cryptocurrencies. In detail, tokens managed on a distributed ledger are recognized by the community to have a value. As open-source maintainers should monetarily profit from the system, the monetary investments backing the token needs to be sponsored or crowdsourced. These investments can be incentivized with some sort of power obtainable within the system. While the perspective of profit could also be used to attract investments, this contradicts the concept of moving funds away from investors and towards open-source maintainers.

Eligibility to Funding. All packages within supported ecosystems or hosted on supported platforms are deemed eligible. Typically, there is no verification process in place to ascertain the existence of a FOSS license or the availability of the source code.

Application and Assessment. The low barriers for participation are particularly evident in the application process. Usually, a simple online registration is the only required step. In addition, decentralized approaches may require a proof of ownership. Although similar to before, this may be as easy as uploading an identifying file to your repository or connecting using an external identity provider such as GitHub.

Allocation of Budget. There are two primary ways of budget allocation in decentralized funding: impact metrics and reputation. The first are typically used to split a general budget among participants. Conversely, the latter builds the foundation and motivates funding in direct peer-to-peer scenarios.

Case Study: tea. tea is a novel project, aiming to provide incentive mechanisms for FOSS contributions. It builds upon a distributed ledger managing a custom-tailored cryptocurrency (TEA tokens). Its first implementation called *testnet* was launched in the beginning of 2024. tea consists of multiple processes such as staking tokens on a project, filing bug reports or participating in the decentral autonomous organization (DAO). In this case study, we focus on the subset of these processes which provides monetary incentives for FOSS maintainers. Other incentives share traits with gamification, which is not a type of incentive working towards the need identified in Sect. 2. If not stated otherwise, all information from this case study is extracted from the tea's documentation [47].

Source of Budget. While TEA token generation and deletion influences the budget within the ecosystem, only the exchange into widely accepted currencies will give the token its value. As tea is not yet in production mode, there is no value and therefore budget yet. For the future, it is planned that monetary value flows into the system through investors, public interest and parties interested in sponsorships [23].

Eligibility to Funding. All packages managed by "crates, npm, pkgx, hombrew (*sic*), pypi, apt-get, and rubygems" [48] are eligible to join. There are no requirements that a package must be FOSS or even source-available.

Application and Assessment. For registering a package, its metadata must refer to a GitHub repository URL which must contain a `tea.yaml` constitution file. It works as proof of ownership and connects the project to participants in tea. It must be noted that this repository does not need to contain the sources of the project.

Allocation of Budget. Besides providing the possibility for immediate donations of tokens, tea passively allocates budget to maintainers of impactful projects estimated through a metric called teaRank. It is based on the PageRank algorithm, but has been enhanced by additional parameters to combat some conceptual shortcomings. While there is a brief technical description available [48], the implementation is not openly available and details remain unclear. Therefore, we reverse engineer the teaRank calculation to be able to reliably assess the susceptibility to fraud. As the results are technical and do not contribute to answering the research questions, we refrain from presenting them here. Instead, they can be found in Appendix A to facilitate future work on this.

Answering RQ2, we find two major differences between the approaches. First, central programs require more bureaucracy than decentral programs with the latter benefiting from the absence of manual assessment. Second, the funding policies contrast each other. Decentral programs fund either impact or reputation, while central programs focus on funding maintenance work.

4   Incentive Mechanisms' Susceptibility to Fraud

In this section, we critically reflect on the presented incentive mechanisms and identify theoretical fraud scenarios. Afterward, the spoofability of the underlying metrics are considered before these results are being transferred back to the incentive mechanisms to assess the risk of the fraud scenarios.

4.1   Identification of Fraud Scenarios

The presented fraud scenarios are derived from three models for the fraudster:

F1 does not maintain a project.
F2 maintains a semi-impactful project.
F3 maintains an impactful project.

Centralized Approaches. To pass the eligibility stage, F1 is mandated to reference a FOSS project. For this, they can create a new project (C1.1), copy an existing project (C1.2) or impersonate a project by referencing a repository they do not have access to (C1.3). In comparison, F2 honestly passes the eligibility stage but would fall short during assessment. Therefore, they seek to deceive their reviewers (C2). F3 is able to honestly acquire funding but deliberately submits a cost estimate higher than the actual cost (C3). All fraudster models may try to place an insider in the central instance to manipulate internal processes (C-I).

Decentralized Approaches. Analog to the centralized approaches, F1 can pursue three scenarios: creating (D1.1), copying (D1.2) or impersonating (D1.3) a project. In contrast, there is no application to be assessed and, thus, F2 and F3 share a joint scenario, in which they try to illegitimately maximize the allocated budget (D2). A large advantage of decentralized approaches is the absence of a central party to be compromised. In practice, decentralized systems are often accessed through a uniform platform which could be susceptible to insider threats. However, as this scenario leans more towards technical IT security instead of fraudulent activities, we disregard it for the remainder of this work.

4.2   Reliability of Impact and Popularity Metrics for Software

Rating the criticality of a project and measuring its impact is an essential step for most centralized and decentralized approaches. It is important to consider the reliability of impact and popularity metrics for FOSS to be able to assess the likelihood of the presented fraud scenarios. In this section, we analyze 4 existing combined metrics, namely OpenSSF's criticality score [1], npm's quality/popularity/maintenance scores, teaRank, and CHAOSS's project popularity metric [8], by dissecting them into their components, referred to as *atomic metrics*. To cope with subtle differences between some atomic metrics, we categorize them by their underlying data source. All categories are visualized in Fig. 1. We discuss their reliability with respect to a project maintainer with write access to a project's repository contents and its presence on social coding platforms. This covers all fraud scenarios except impersonation (C1.3, D1.3) and insiders (C-I).

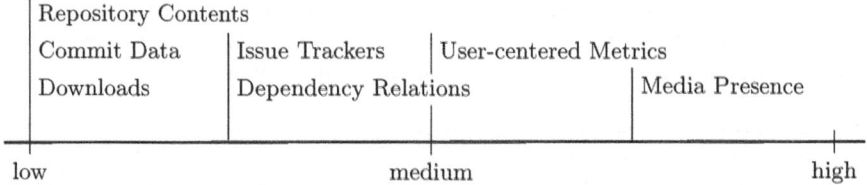

Fig. 1. Spoofing effort for categories of atomic metrics

Commit Data. A commit is the essential unit of a version control system (VCS). Active project maintenance implies regular commits. Therefore, atomic metrics derived from commit timestamps are commonly used. However, this type of data is highly unreliable and easily spoofed. Social coding platforms display commit data unaltered. This allows maintainers to create an arbitrary history and push that onto the platform to fulfill all desired metrics. While commits may be signed to verify the identity of the commit author, it does not help in the attacker model of a project maintainer. There are tools exploiting this behavior, for example, the `github-activity-generator` creating a commit history to obtain a custom activity graph in GitHub. It should be noted that the tool explicitly discourages its use to "misrepresent professional contributions or coding activity" [43].

Issue Trackers. Many FOSS projects facilitate the issue trackers provided on social coding platforms. While lots of open issues do not imply meaningful statements, an active usage of the issue tracker suggests interest and maintenance of a project. The lifetime of issues offers multiple atomic features to be extracted. Among the associated metrics, the ratio of open to closed issues and the average duration until an issue is closed are prime examples. All popular issue trackers offer APIs for automatic interactions and integration of external clients. A plethora of well-known large projects utilizes bots to assist with the issue management. Examples are TensorFlow[1] which automatically assigns

---
[1] https://github.com/tensorflow/tensorflow.

developers, and Go[2] which has an AI assistant automatically tagging the issue and searching links for related information. React[3] utilizes an officially provided GitHub Actions workflow to automatically close stale open issues. While we do not assume any malicious motives in this case, this directly boosts an atomic issue metric determining the maintenance score on npm. Other platform features such as publishing explicit releases offer comparable data for atomic metrics. For maintainers, these are as easily spoofable as issue-related data due to public APIs. Therefore, legitimate tools like `semantic-release`[4] increase the score in associated metrics.

User-Centered Metrics. Atomic metrics are considered to be user-centered if every user can increase this metric at most by one. They are platform-specific with examples being stars, forks, subscriptions or contributors. Of all categories with implemented measures, user-centered atomic metrics are the most difficult metric to spoof, requiring the attacker to automate account creation and violating the terms of service. Nonetheless, this can be outsourced to paid services. A report [15] describes stars to be successfully purchasable for 0.08 EUR each. However, the automatically created accounts for these are detected and removed along with the stars within a month. In contrast, "quality" stars cost 0.8 EUR each and are backed by accounts not as prone to bot detection. Services to buy forks and subscribers are found as easily. Therefore, given enough monetary or technical resources it seems to be possible to spoof user-centered metrics.

Downloads. Impactful projects are utilized by many users and, thus, deployed on many systems. Analyzing recent download counts is a proxy metric suggesting to approximate the deployment count. However, there is no clear connection and a widely deployed project does not need to have many recent downloads. More severely, the process of downloading is easy to automate. For npm, there even exist tools such as `npm-increaser-downloads`[5] offering an optimized implementation. Though it considerably wastes resources of the package registry, we did not find information on restricted counting, e.g., only once per IP address and day. While this does not defend against such an attack, it significantly increases the effort required by an attacker with only minor overhead for the registry.

Repository Contents. The quality metric of npm solely focuses on atomic metrics derived from the contents of a repository such as the existence of a license or the use of linters. The repository contents are trivial to adjust for a maintainer and, thus, it requires low effort to achieve a high score in this metric. Though in this case, we refrain from classifying such adjustments as spoofing, since no information is illegitimately represented.

---

[2] https://github.com/golang/go.
[3] https://github.com/facebook/react.
[4] https://github.com/semantic-release/semantic-release.
[5] https://github.com/MinhOmega/npm-increaser-downloads.

Media Presence. CHAOSS' project popularity metric [8] enhances its score by incorporating data from sources beyond social coding platforms and package registries. The atomic metrics range from social media mentions over job postings requesting project skills to event participation. Most are challenging to determine automatically and as such, their applicability is likely limited to the largest FOSS projects. Accordingly, these atomic metrics are difficult to spoof as their methods of measurement is not well specified.

Dependency Relations. Packages support an effective development process by providing functionality in a re-usable manner. Besides customer-facing end products, this also backs the development of new packages, resulting in a dependency network. This offers a unique view on the impact of projects and is integrated into all considered impact metrics. More specific, either the number of dependent projects or the more complicated and holistic view of teaRank [48] are employed. These metrics can be spoofed by creating bogus packages, referencing the maintainer's project either directly or transitively as dependency. For uncurated package repositories, we deem this attack to require low to medium effort, depending on the efficacy of its automatic spam detection mechanisms.

Sybil Attacks on npm. A passive rewarding system such as teaRank has the potential to incentivize maintainers to enhance their impact through dishonest methods. Its technical description [48] acknowledges two types of attacks. Width attacks introduce lots of dependents pointing to a single package. Tree attacks create long dependency chains. It is stated that both attacks are prevented by tracking the width and tree limit of a package and flagging it as potential spam if (secret) thresholds are surpassed. During our work, we manually inspected packages on the tea testnet and found the majority of the projects denoted as most impactful, i.e., having the highest teaRanks, to have either been unpublished or replaced with a security holding package on npm. When metadata was still available, the projects showed thousands of dependents with a record of less than 10 weekly downloads. This is a clear indicator for a sybil attack on teaRank.

To analyze this phenomenon, we examine package metadata from npm. As we try to approximate the order of magnitude for this attack, we employ the following heuristic-based methodology: Initially, all npm packages registered in the tea testnet are classified as sybil if they are published after 2024, have less than 10 published versions and fulfill one of the following three criteria:

- More than 95% of transitive dependencies must have been created within 4 weeks of the creation of the package under consideration.
- More than 80% of dependents must have more than 100 dependencies.
- The package was unpublished or marked as security holding.

In addition, we consider all transitive dependents of a sybil package to be sybil. This methodology is conservative and it can be assumed to be unlikely that a legitimate package is flagged as sybil. Overall, this results in the detection of 71,710 sybil packages on npm (2% of all listed). To confirm the reliability of the heuristic, we sample 100 potentially sybil packages uniformly at random and manually classify them. We do not find any erroneous classification. By calculating the one-tailed confidence interval for sample proportions, we can be 95% certain that the population contains at most 3% false positives. The sample reveals multiple classes of automatically generated packages (see Fig. 2). Partially, the generation scripts can still be found in the artifacts of the packages. Most commonly, boilerplate created by `create-next-app`, a bogus library detectable through `wallet.js` and `chains.js`, an artifact without JavaScript inside or a function returning a string are found. Comparing these with unpublished packages, we assume that these contents prevailed against npm's spam detection.

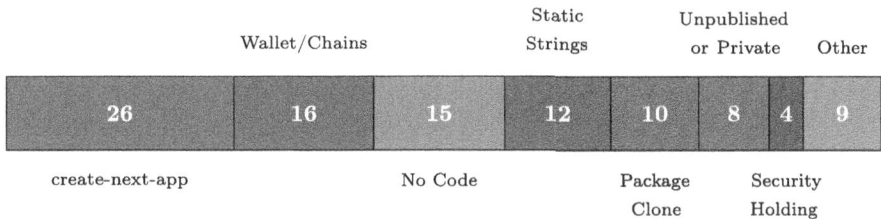

Fig. 2. Classes of sybil packages in a sample of 100 packages

These sybil attacks do not only increase the teaRank of projects but also affect other impact metrics. Past research has considered the top $N \leq 1000$ most depended upon packages as benign packages for evaluating malware protection [16,38], evaluating the adoption of security best practices [24] and others [7]. We find that, at the time of writing, 532 packages of the top 1000 most directly depended upon are in our sybil set. Though when taking transitive relationships into account, no package of the top 1000 most depended upon is marked as sybil by our approach. As a significant fraction of sybil packages was unpublished, the actual figures were likely to be higher in mid 2024. Since tea was introduced at the start of 2024, it is unlikely that the results of the referenced papers are affected by these sybil attacks. Still, this raises questions on the validity of using this or similar impact metrics for software package focused research.

4.3 Assessment of Fraud Scenarios

In this section, we assess the previously defined fraud scenarios by weighing the required effort and risks against the potential gains for the fraudster through a discussion. The assessment focuses on both case studies, since generalization abstracts essential details for an insightful fraud analysis. Nonetheless, we refrain from quantitative characterizations as risk is highly individual.

Sovereign Tech Fund. With respect to fraud, the most critical step within the application process of the STF is the assessment of applications. Although the details of this process are not disclosed, it can be expected that the technologist at least partially confirms the claims from the application while additionally confirming the criticality through a common methodology. Therefore, a successful case of fraud in C1.1 must spoof all considered impact metrics in a consistent way. In C1.2 and C2, this holds only for the subset of metrics which do not attest the necessary criticality. Slight inconsistencies may be fatal and cause a more detailed assessment. It is likely that technologists explicitly try to find dependents deemed to be trustworthy based on their prior experience. In the field of sybil detection, it is a standard assumption that links pointing from a benign to a sybil project are difficult to achieve [19]. Though most severely, the potential analysis of historic development of some quantitative metrics and qualitative metrics requires years of adversarial preparation. Consequently, we expect it to be unlikely that a fraudulent application withstands a thorough manual assessment of both, technologists and external experts.

An easier fraud attempt could be reached through impersonation (C1.3) of an existing impactful project. In this scenario, it is conceivable that all application stages may be passed. However, the funding is paid for achieving milestones which is unrealistic as an impersonator does not have the required access rights for this. While such long payment intervals have been criticized [34], they are an effective mechanism against fraud.

For the other potential weak points, the setup for successful fraud is much more complicated. In C3, the fraudulent applicant must already be responsible for an impactful core technology, overestimate the costs in bad faith and defend the argumentation in the later stages of application. In doing so, they risk being declined and act detrimental towards their own FOSS project. This does not fit the typical motivation and views of core maintainers [27]. In C-I, the fraudster places an insider threat in the STA. This provides a significant advantage to all other scenarios as an inconsistent presentation could be defalcated by the reviewer. However, we claim that the risks and efforts in this scenario clearly outweigh the potential gains, given that the allocation of budget is subject to the perspectives of several individuals.

tea. We start by assessing the susceptibility for impersonation (D1.3). Generally, proof of ownership is an effective concept for preventing impersonation. Still, it has two downsides. First, the project's artifact must be associated with an URL referencing a GitHub repository. Hosting sources on a different or custom platform as well as using a different VCS is not supported. Second, the first months after tea's testnet launch, hundreds of pull request in popular projects from unrelated users trying to push a `tea.yaml` containing themselves as maintainer have been created [50]. Since then, proof of ownership has been improved by requiring a direct commit of the file, reducing but not eliminating the chance of social engineering. Overall, we estimate this fraud scenario to have low chances of success, but it must be noted that effort and risk for trying are low as well.

The fraud scenarios D1.1, D1.2 and D2 share the same success condition, i.e., dishonestly increasing the teaRank as impact metric. While the teaRank can be increased by becoming a dependency of impactful packages, the fraudster controls none of them. Instead, it requires much less effort to create a lot of new dependent packages as it was done in the sybil attacks on the tea testnet. Most importantly, some persistence is required to keep a project's growth just below tea's spam detection thresholds and to deceive malware and spam detection mechanisms of the package registry. Both are achievable with low risk and medium effort through automation and generative AI. Essentially, this is a conceptual flaw of all quantitative impact metrics in this scenario as automatic abuse detection is weaker than automatic abuse, especially, if the detection algorithms are known. Here, Goodhart's law applies: When a measure becomes a target, it ceases to be a good measure [46]. Overall, the fraud scenarios D1.1, D1.2 and D2 have high chances of success with moderate effort and no risk for the fraudster.

Increasing Resilience Against Fraud. After identifying the largest risks for fraud in the STF and tea, we propose improvements to increase the resilience against fraud attempts. In the STF, the largest risk is the deception of the reviewing technologist leading to an incorrect assessment of the applicant's criticality. Therefore, we suggest 4 steps to minimize chances for successful fraud.

1. Target the focus towards the own impact assessment, not on the applicants' self-assessment.
2. Historic developments of impact metrics require the highest effort for spoofing and should be part of the analysis.
3. Maintain a high awareness for inconsistencies, e.g., many dependents but few downloads.
4. Acquire a set of trust anchors, i.e., confirmed benign projects, and try to obtain as many (transitive) references from the trust anchors to the applicant.

In tea, manipulation of the teaRank bears the largest risk for fraud. Unfortunately, we do not see a possibility to prevent fraud if any of the investigated impact metrics immediately decide the budget allocation. Nonetheless, there are several ideas how a similar incentive mechanism with increased fraud resilience could be designed. First, a distinct impact metric could be designed. All considered impact metrics are, at most, tied to digital identities which can be arbitrarily created. In contrast, binding an impact metric to physical identities does not fully fix the reliability but drastically increases the effort and cost required for spoofing. Second, an equivalent concept to trust-on-first-use can be employed to create a central invariant: At any point in time, benign projects have a voting power surpassing the power of sybil projects. If the growth of nodes is bounded in each time step, the benign projects can actively defend their majority by excluding sybil packages. Moreover, this concept allows a shift of the allocation policy from impact-based to work-based seen in centralized systems by facilitating votes on proposals. Although it must be noted, that such an approach places a burden of work on FOSS maintainers and, in this basic form, will likely fail to strengthen the maintenance level in FOSS.

Answering RQ3, the STF as a representative for central approaches has a low susceptibility to fraud if a thorough assessment of applications is performed. In contrast, our decentral case study tea appears to be susceptible to fraud since the underlying impact metrics are easily spoofable. All ideas to inherently improve its resilience of the approach require conceptual adjustments.

5   Threats to Validity

The highly empirical nature of research presented in this paper requires a discussion of its validity. RQ1 is answered based on a literature review. The results are one-sided and raise concerns on the internal validity. While the literature review does not follow all steps necessary for a systematic literature review, we argue that the most important methodological steps are employed and the methodology does not imply a bias. Instead, the results are explained by the absence of research on the benefits of commercial involvement for FOSS projects or, indeed, by the limited benefits that commercial involvement does offer. To a large extent, the analyses for RQ2 and RQ3 are based on case studies which is a potential threat to external validity. For the centralized approach, we argue that the STF is a good representative sharing traits with other instances. In the decentralized approach, tea is a unique concept and does not represent other decentral instances. However, to the best of our knowledge only reputation-based mechanisms do also qualify as decentral with their susceptibility to fraud being mainly prone to psychological attacks such as phishing. We minimize associated threats to validity by meticulously examining tea-specific statements before generalizing them. Still, it is imperative to carefully reflect case study related results when employing them in future work.

6   Related Work

Fraud facilitates similar techniques as attacks on IT systems. These techniques can be divided into social engineering, architectural and technical attacks. Zaoui et al. [55] compile a taxonomy for attacks and countermeasures of social engineering attacks. These are complementary to our fraud scenarios and proposed resilience strategies. More fundamentally, Longtchi et al. [28] analyze the underlying psychological factors of these attacks. We similarly include the motivations driving different groups in our argumentations.

For related architectural attacks, there is research on sybil attacks and sybil-resistant architectures. Similar to us, Müller et al. [30] propose binding digital to physical identities to reduce the susceptibility to sybil attacks. Friedman [10] proof that it is not possible to construct a symmetric sybilproofness reputation function for decentral networks, i.e., only considering the edges. This result is in line with our observations for sybil attacks on teaRank. Additionally, they show sybilproofness to be achievable for an asymmetric reputation function, e.g., with respect to a given node. In a related way, we suggest increasing the resilience in central approaches by following packages back to trust anchors through dependency relationships.

In this study, we have opted to exclude commercial open source products from our scope, given their distinct funding models and governance structures. Still, related work performs in-depth analysis of their motivations to explain their seemingly contradictory business model. West and Gallagher [53] reveal commercial FOSS to be driven strategically and provide possibilities to maximize the returns of internal innovation. For example, software components may be donated to provide an extensible platform for external contributors. Osborne [35] considers this strategy in detail for FOSS from the realm of artificial intelligence. They find the most important factor to be the governance democratization for technological and economic advantages. While outside our scope, such motivations are also responsible for companies and investors supporting FOSS maintenance initiatives beyond their sphere of authority.

Last, the design and analysis of impact and popularity metrics is related. Mujahid *et al.* [29] observe limitations of current popularity metrics such as stars and downloads and instead suggest employing package centrality. They successfully apply this approach to identify npm packages in decline which is a criterion to prefer alternative dependencies. Coelho *et al.* [12] present a machine learning model as a metric for measuring the maintenance status of GitHub software projects. As the input features are covered by the atomic metrics analyzed in this work, it is susceptible to the same degree of spoofing. In Sect. 4.2, the CHAOSS project popularity metric is considered. Besides that, CHAOSS [9] recently initiated a working group to develop methods for measuring funding impact. Similarly, Osborne [35] develops a toolkit for measuring the impact of public funding on FOSS. They argue that quantitative data has a "risk of creating perverse incentives through metric selection/optimisation" and suggests qualitative and mixed-methods to capture social, economic and technological impact. This is in line with our results that budget allocation based on quantitative impact metrics is highly susceptible to fraud.

7 Conclusion

In this study, we explored external incentive mechanisms for FOSS projects and their susceptibility to fraud. A comprehensive literature review reveals a clear necessity for incentive mechanisms to fund the maintenance of FOSS. Moreover, commercial funding can negatively affect the long-term self-sustainability FOSS projects, stressing the importance of alternative funds. We analyzed two structurally distinct approaches aiming to fill this gap. Central incentive mechanisms are backed by significant financial resources which are allocated on work packages proposed by applicants. On a case study of the STF, it is observed that applications are thoroughly reviewed and assessed before funding is approved.

Conversely, the sources of budget for decentral incentive mechanisms are more diverse and opaque, typically relying on individual or commercial investments. Though, the largest difference is observed for the funding policy with either impact or reputation being funded but not maintenance work. The case study on tea reveals a high risk of fraud due to the automatic allocation of budget through teaRank. Intuitively, it might be clear that all considered atomic metrics are theoretically spoofable. However, empirical evidence demonstrates the occurrence of spoofing also in practice. This renders it very complex if not impossible to create an impact metric suitable for this use case. Possible solutions require architectural changes such as impact metrics linked with physical identities or a voting-based system. Furthermore, there are also implications for academic research utilizing these metrics for dataset creation as shown on the example of a sybil attack on npm. We advocate to consider perils of mining software repositories [25] and discuss the implications of metrics [42] more thoroughly to increase the general significance of research results. In contrast, the STF shows more potential for resilience against fraud. If the impact assessment during the application process is thorough, there is a low risk of successful fraud.

We identify two major directions for future work based on our results. First, a compilation of quantitative data measured in regular intervals could be utilized to detect sybil attacks on package repositories. While, at first, this may sound contradictory to our result that all considered atomic metrics can be spoofed, we do not expect this to happen for no reason. Sybil attacks on repositories as observed in this work are usually targeted and only focus on the subset of relevant metrics. This enhances the probability of detection by an untargeted approach. Second, package repositories are popular data sources for academic research due to their size and (semi-)structured data. With the occurrence of sybil attacks on this dataset, the results' robustness in the presence of an attack is a novel and relevant research direction. For example, it is intuitively unclear how significant the performance of malware detection systems on npm degrades if they are partially trained on bogus packages.

A   teaRank

Inheriting the fundamental concept from PageRank, teaRank is built upon random walks in a Markov chain. The resulting scores represent the probability that a walk ends in a given state. For this, the dependency network is considered to be a graph $G = (V, E)$ with packages $V = \{p_1, p_2, \ldots, p_n\}$ as vertices and directed edges $E = \{(p_i, p_j), \ldots\}$ induced between packages if p_i depends on p_j. The translated adjacency matrix of this graph $A = (a_{ji})$ with $a_{ji} = \frac{1}{|E(i)|}$, $E(i) = \{e \in E | e = (p_i, *)\}$ if $(p_i, p_j) \in E$ is the central element of the calculation. Naturally speaking, all outgoing edges of a package have the same weight with each column summing to one if at least a single outgoing edge exists. teaRank utilizes a modified version of this matrix by introducing a parameter $0 \leq \kappa \leq 1$:

$$T = (1 - \kappa)A + \kappa \mathbf{1}_n$$

This adds κ-weighted self-edges to every vertex. Furthermore, PageRank has a decay factor $0 \leq d \leq 1$ which can be interpreted as a restart probability of the random walk. This factor is essential for the algorithm as G may be partitioned. In the algorithm, d represents a scaling factor for the uniform distribution $E = (\frac{1}{n}, \ldots, \frac{1}{n})^\top$.

Given a probability distribution vector v, the multiplication Tv denotes the transition in the Markov chain. A distribution vector v is considered stable if it is not altered by such a transition, i.e., $(1 - d)Tv + dE = v$. To find such an eigenvector, the power iteration method is often used: Starting with any vector v_0, the series $v_k = (1 - d)Tv_{k-1} + dE$ converges to a solution v. Despite a potentially large n, the algorithm is efficient since T is sparse and an iteration count in the order of 50 usually suffices to achieve a stable result. The resulting eigenvector v contains entries for all packages in the dependency graph. The web interface for the tea ecosystem does not display the raw teaRank, but applies the following function obtained through reverse engineering the frontend:

$$f(t) = 100 \cdot \left(\frac{\log_{10} t}{9} + 1 \right)$$

To check how well the described algorithm's output matches the real teaRank, we calculate the mean multiplicative error. As the concrete values for κ and d are not disclosed, we perform a grid search with a granularity of 0.05. We observe combinations that roughly fulfill the equation $d \approx 0.6 + \frac{\kappa}{3}$ to minimize the error with a value of 2.4. The minor deviation of our results to the project's scores are explainable by deviations in the underlying graph. tea's testnet supports multiple registries besides npm, although with 95% the clear majority of packages on tea is covered by our analysis.

References

1. Arya, A., Brown, C., Pike, R., The open source security foundation, open source project criticality score (2023). https://github.com/ossf/criticality_score
2. Birkinbine, B.J.: Incorporating the Digital Commons: Corporate Involvement in Free and Open Source Software. University of Westminster Press (2020)
3. Bonaccorsi, A., Lorenzi, D., Merito, M., Rossi, C.: Business firms' engagement in community projects. Empirical evidence and further developments of the research. In: First International Workshop on Emerging Trends in FLOSS Research and Development (FLOSS'07: ICSE Workshops 2007). IEEE (2007)
4. Brackett, S.A., Meyers, J.S., Scott, S.: O$$ security: does more money for open source software mean better security? A proof of concept. Technical report, Atlantic Council (2024)
5. Capiluppi, A., Stol, K.-J., Boldyreff, C.: Exploring the role of commercial stakeholders in open source software evolution. In: Hammouda, I., Lundell, B., Mikkonen, T., Scacchi, W. (eds.) OSS 2012. IAICT, vol. 378, pp. 178–200. Springer, Heidelberg (2012). https://doi.org/10.1007/978-3-642-33442-9_12
6. Capra, E., Francalanci, C., Merlo, F., Rossi-Lamastra, C.: Firms' involvement in open source projects: a trade-off between software structural quality and popularity. J. Syst. Softw. **84**(1), 144–161 (2011)
7. Chao, J., Tao, S., Ribbink, A.: Evaluating the evaluators: on package scores and their underlying metrics. Computing (EUC) (2019)

8. CHAOSS: Funding impact measurement working group (2025). https://github.com/chaoss/wg-funding-impact

9. CHAOSS: Project Popularity (2024). https://chaoss.community/kb/metricproject-popularity/

10. Cheng, A., Friedman, E.: Sybilproof reputation mechanisms. In: Proceeding of the 2005 ACM SIGCOMM workshop on Economics of peer-to-peer systems - P2PECON '05. P2PECON '05, p. 128. ACM Press (2005)

11. Coelho, J., Valente, M.T.: Why modern open source projects fail. In: Proceedings of the 2017 11th Joint Meeting on Foundations of Software Engineering. ESEC/FSE'17, pp. 186–196. ACM (2017)

12. Coelho, J., Valente, M.T., Silva, L.L., Hora, A.: Why we engage in FLOSS: answers from core developers. In: Proceedings of the 11th International Workshop on Cooperative and Human Aspects of Software Engineering. ICSE '18. ACM (2018)

13. Coelho, J., Valente, M.T., Milen, L., Silva, L.L.: Is this GitHub project maintained? Measuring the level of maintenance activity of open-source projects. Inf. Softw. Technol. **122**, 106274 (2020)

14. Eghbal, N.: Roads and bridges: the unseen labor behind our digital infrastructure, Technical report, Ford Foundation (2016). https://www.fordfoundation.org/work/learning/research-reports/roads-and-bridges-the-unseen-labor-behind-our-digitalinfrastructure/

15. Eldeeb, Y., Sikora, A.: How much are GitHub stars worth to you? (2023). https://the-guild.dev/blog/judging-open-source-by-github-stars

16. Ferreira, G., Jia, L., Sunshine, J., Kastner, C.: Containing malicious package updates in npm with a lightweight permission system. In: IEEE/ACM 43rd International Conference on Software Engineering, pp. 1334–1346. IEEE (2021)

17. Geer, D., Sieniawski, G.P.: Who will pay the piper for open source software maintenance? Can we increase reliability as we increase reliance? Login Usenix Mag. **45**(2) (2020). https://www.usenix.org/publications/login/summer2020/geer

18. Gerlach, J.H., Wu, C.-G., Cunningham, L.F., Young, C.E.: An exploratory study of conflict over paying Debian developers. Int. J. Open Sour. Softw. Process. **7**(3), 20–38 (2016)

19. Gong, N.Z., Frank, M., Mittal, P.: SybilBelief: a semi-supervised learning approach for structure-based Sybil detection. IEEE Trans. Inf. Forensics Secur. **9**(6), 976–987 (2014)

20. Gonzalez-Barahona, J.M., Izquierdo-Cortazar, D., Maffulli, S., Robles, G.: Understanding How companies interact with free software communities. IEEE Softw. **30**(5), 38–45 (2013)

21. Halderman, J.A.: To strengthen security, change developers' incentives. IEEE Secur. Priv. **8**(2), 79–82 (2010)

22. Iaffaldano, G., Steinmacher, I., Calefato, F., Gerosa, M., Lanubile, F.: Why do developers take breaks from contributing to OSS projects? A preliminary analysis. In: Proceedings of the 2nd International Workshop on Software Health. SoHeal '19, pp. 9–16. IEEE Press, Montreal, Quebec, Canada (2019)

23. Joslyn, H.: Is crypto the solution to paying open source developers? (2024). https://thenewstack.io/is-crypto-the-solution-to-paying-open-source-developers/

24. Kabir, M.M.A., Wang, Y., Yao, D., Meng, N.: How do developers follow security-relevant best practices when using NPM packages? In: 2022 IEEE Secure Development Conference (SecDev). IEEE (2022)

25. Kalliamvakou, E., Gousios, G., Blincoe, K., Singer, L., German, D.M., Damian, D.: An in-depth study of the promises and perils of mining GitHub. Empir. Softw. Eng. **21**(5), 2035–2071 (2015). https://doi.org/10.1007/s10664-015-9393-5

26. Li, X., Zhang, Y., Osborne, C., Zhou, M., Jin, Z., Liu, H.: Systematic literature review of commercial participation in open source software. ACM Trans. Softw. Eng. Methodol. **34**(2), 1–31 (2025)
27. Linåker, J., Link, G., Lumbard, K.: Sustaining maintenance labor for healthy open source software projects through human infrastructure: a maintainer perspective. In: Proceedings of the 18th ACM/IEEE International Symposium on Empirical Software Engineering and Measurement. ESEM '24, pp. 37–48. ACM (2024)
28. Longtchi, T.T., Rodriguez, R.M., Al-Shawaf, L., Atyabi, A., Xu, S.: Internet-based social engineering psychology, attacks, and defenses: a survey. Proc. IEEE **112**(3), 210–246 (2024)
29. Mujahid, S., Costa, D.E., Abdalkareem, R., Shihab, E., Saied, M.A., Adams, B.: Toward using package centrality trend to identify packages in decline. IEEE Trans. Eng. Manage. **69**(6), 3618–3632 (2022)
30. Müller, W., Plötz, H., Redlich, J.-P., Shiraki, T.: Sybil proof anonymous reputation management. In: Proceedings of the 4th International Conference on Security and Privacy in Communication Netowrks. Securecomm08, pp. 1–10. ACM (2008)
31. Open Source Initiative: The Open Source Definition (2024). https://opensource.org/osd
32. Open Source Technology Improvement Fund: Open Source Technology Improvement Fund (2025). https://ostif.org
33. Open Technology Fund: Localization LabFree and open source software sustainability fund (2025). https://www.opentech.fund/funds/free-and-open-sourcesoftware-sustainability-fund/
34. Osborne, C.: open source software developers' views on public and private funding: a case study on scikit-learn. In: 2024 Conference on Computer-Supported Cooperative Work and Social Computing. CSCW '24, pp. 154–161. ACM (2024)
35. Osborne, C.: Why companies democratise artificial intelligence: the case of open source software donations. arXiv preprint arXiv: 2409.17876 (2024)
36. Osborne, C., Sharratt, P., Foster, D., Boehm, M.: A toolkit for measuring the impacts of public funding on open source software development. arXiv preprint arXiv: 2411.06027 (2024)
37. Overney, C., Meinicke, J., Kästner, C., Vasilescu, B.: How to not get rich: an empirical study of donations in open source. In: Proceedings of the ACM/IEEE 42nd International Conference on Software Engineering. ICSE '20. ACM (2020)
38. Pohl, T., Ohm, M., Boes, F., Meier, M.: You can run but you can't hide: runtime protection against malicious package updates for Node.js. In: Sicherheit 2024, pp. 231–241. Gesellschaft für Informatik e.V., Bonn (2024)
39. Riehle, D.: The economic case for open source foundations. Computer **43**(1), 86–90 (2010)
40. Riehle, D., Riemer, P., Kolassa, C., Schmidt, M.: Paid vs. volunteer work in open source. In: 47th Hawaii International Conference on System Sciences. IEEE (2014)
41. Ruohonen, J., Choudhary, G., Alami, A.: An overview of cyber security funding for open source software. arXiv preprint arXiv: 2412.05887 (2024)
42. Sheoran, J., Blincoe, K., Kalliamvakou, E., Damian, D., Ell, J.: Understanding watchers on GitHub. In: Proceedings of the 11th Working Conference on Mining Software Repositories. ICSE '14, pp. 336–339. ACM (2014)
43. Shpota, S.: GitHub activity generator (2025). https://github.com/Shpota/githubactivity-generator
44. Sovereign Tech Agency: Sovereign Tech Fund (2025). https://www.sovereign.tech/programs/fund

45. Sovereign Tech Agency: Technologist (2025). https://www.sovereign.tech/jobs/
46. Strathern, M.: Improving ratings: audit in the British University system. Euro. Rev. **5**(3), 305–321 (1997)
47. TEA Association: TEA documentation (2025). https://docs.tea.xyz/tea
48. TEA Association: What is Proof of Contribution? (Technical) (2024). https://docs.tea.xyz/tea/i-want-to.../learn-about-proof-of-contribution/what-is-proof-ofcontribution-technical
49. The Linux Foundation: Alpha-Omega (2023). https://alpha-omega.dev
50. Tumbleson, C.: The disappointing tea.xyz (2024). https://connortumbleson.com/2024/02/26/the-disappointing-tea-xyz/
51. Wang, Z., Feng, Y., Wang, Y., Jones, J.A., Redmiles, D.: Unveiling elite developers' activities in open source projects. ACM Trans. Softw. Eng. Methodol. **29**(3), 1–35 (2020)
52. Warren, E.: FOSS Sustainability Fund 2024: the grant proposal is declined (2024). https://codeberg.org/forgejo/sustainability/pulls/48
53. West, J., Gallagher, S.: Challenges of open innovation: the paradox of firm investment in open-source software. R and D Management **36**(3), 319–331 (2006)
54. Yamashita, K., McIntosh, S., Kamei, Y., Hassan, A.E., Ubayashi, N.: Revisiting the applicability of the pareto principle to core development teams in open source software projects. In: Proceedings of the 14th International Workshop on Principles of Software Evolution. ESEC/FSE'15. ACM (2015)
55. Zaoui, M., Yousra, B., Yassine, S., Yassine, M., Karim, O.: A comprehensive taxonomy of social engineering attacks and defense mechanisms: toward effective mitigation strategies. IEEE Access **12**, 72224–72241 (2024)
56. Zhang, X., Wang, T., Yu, Y., Zeng, Q., Li, Z., Wang, H.: Who, what, why and how? Towards the monetary incentive in crowd collaboration: a case study of Github's sponsor mechanism. In: CHI Conference on Human Factors in Computing Systems. CHI '22, pp. 1–18. ACM (2022)
57. Zhang, Y., Liu, H., Tan, X., Zhou, M., Jin, Z., Zhu, J.: Turnover of companies in OpenStack: prevalence and rationale. ACM Trans. Softw. Eng. Methodol. **31**(4), 1–24 (2022)
58. Zhang, Y., Qin, M., Stol, K.-J., Zhou, M., Liu, H.: How are paid and volunteer open source developers different? A study of the rust project. In: Proceedings of the IEEE/ACM 46th International Conference on Software Engineering. ICSE '24, pp. 1–13. ACM (2024)
59. Zhang, Y., Stol, K.-J., Liu, H., Zhou, M.: Corporate dominance in open source ecosystems: a case study of OpenStack. In: Proceedings of the 30th ACM Joint European Software Engineering Conference and Symposium on the Foundations of Software Engineering. ESEC/FSE '22, pp. 1048–1060. ACM (2022)
60. Zhou, J., Wang, S., Kamei, Y., Hassan, A.E., Ubayashi, N.: Studying donations and their expenses in open source projects: a case study of GitHub projects collecting donations through open collectives. Empir. Softw. Eng. **27**(1), 1–38 (2021). https://doi.org/10.1007/s10664-021-10060-y

Machine Learning and Security

Multi-agent Simulation and Reinforcement Learning to Optimize Moving Target Defense

William Valentine$^{(\boxtimes)}$, Etienne Borde , and Mengmeng Ge

University of Canterbury, Christchurch, New Zealand
williamjohn.valentine@pg.canterbury.ac.nz

Abstract. As cyber threats continue to evolve, Moving Target Defense (MTD) strategies have emerged as a promising approach to enhancing network security by dynamically altering system configurations. However, optimizing MTD requires balancing security improvements with system availability. In this work, we propose a framework for optimizing MTD strategies, leveraging reinforcement learning (RL) and a cybersecurity simulation environment (named CybORG-MTD), to train defensive agents. Our approach introduces a reward function that explicitly models the trade-off between security and availability, enabling RL agents to learn effective defense policies. Through empirical evaluations, we demonstrate that our proposed methodology outperforms existing techniques in optimizing MTD strategies. While our results highlight the effectiveness of RL-based cyber defense, we also discuss key challenges, including scalability, and adaptive attacker behaviors.

1   Introduction

As cyber threats grow in complexity and persistence, defending networked systems has become increasingly challenging. *Moving Target Defense (MTD)* strategies offer a promising approach to counter these threats by continuously altering system configurations to increase uncertainty for adversaries. However, while MTD enhances security, it often introduces degradation in system performance and reduces services' availability. As such, optimizing MTD strategies requires careful balancing between improving defense effectiveness while maintaining availability.

MTD strategies optimization has been extensively studied, either using game theoretic approaches [2,5,7,8,12] and more recently using *Reinforcement Learning (RL)* approaches [3,4,14–18]. The former focuses on defining optimal policies to the price of complex computation and often statically defined policies. The latter requires less formalization and offers the potential to scale better, to the price of not guaranteeing optimality of the defense policy.

In this paper, we focus on RL as a powerful method for defensive agents to learn MTD strategies by dynamically adjusting their action probabilities based on the observed state and received reward. Training RL agents typically relies

© The Author(s), under exclusive license to Springer Nature Switzerland AG 2025
M. Dalla Preda et al. (Eds.): ARES 2025, LNCS 15993, pp. 299–320, 2025.
https://doi.org/10.1007/978-3-032-00627-1_15

on the use of a simulated environment, known as an **RL gym**, which provides state transitions, observations, and rewards in response to agent actions. The design of the reward function and the realism of the simulation are critical to producing effective defensive policies. Despite recent progress in applying RL to MTD optimization, existing approaches fall short in their effort to balance security with availability. Reward function definitions used in existing literature inadequately represent the trade-offs between security and availability, leading to poor MTD strategy optimization as we show in our evaluation results. In addition, there is currently no publicly available cyber defense RL gym designed to train agents on MTD techniques while accounting for their effects on both adversaries and legitimate users.

To address these gaps, we introduce a well-defined framework for MTD optimization and present **CybORG-MTD**, a cyber defense gym designed to support the evaluation and reinforcement learning of MTD strategies. The contributions of this work are as follows:

- **Formalization of Defender, Attacker, and User agent models for cyber defense simulations**: We introduce a formal definition of defender, attacker, and user agents within the RL framework. This formalization includes action spaces, observation models, and belief state representations tailored to cyber security applications. Building upon this formalization, we introduce an optimization objective function that accounts for the dual impact of MTD on both security and availability.
- **Development of CybORG-MTD, an RL gym with integrated MTD capabilities**: Built on the Cyber Operations Research Gym (CybORG) [6], CybORG-MTD provides a structured simulation environment where defensive agents operate in the presence of both attacker and user agents within an enterprise network. This enables the development and assessment of defensive policies that account for the dual impact of MTD on both security and availability.
- **Design of a reward function tailored to optimize the balance between security and availability in MTD strategies**: We use the activity of simulated user and attacker agents to learn an MTD policy that outperforms existing approaches in terms of its impact on the availability and security of the protected network.
- **Case study and benchmark results**: Building on the contributions presented here above, we propose a case study and an empirical evaluation of our solution, and compare it to the transposition of existing solutions to the specificity of our case study. Our results show that the approach we propose outperforms techniques presented in the literature.

The remainder of this paper is structured as follows: Sect. 2 presents the formalization of the problem, including agent models and network representations. Section 3 formalizes the optimization problem we target as a trade-off between security and availability. Section 4 describes the implementation of CybORG-MTD. Section 5 presents the case study we propose to evaluate our approach. Section 6 details our experimental setup and performance evaluation. Section 7

discusses the implications of our findings and the limitations of the current approach. Finally, Sect. 8 reviews related work, and Sect. 9 concludes the paper with
potential future directions.

2   Model Formulation

2.1   Network Model

We consider an enterprise **network** defined as a structured system of interconnected devices that communicate through a defined set of protocols. Formally,
such a network is represented as a graph $G = (H, V, E)$, where:

- H is the set of **hosts**, and each host $h \in H$ represents an end device such as
  a computer, server, or IoT device.
- V is the set of **nodes**, including hosts ($H \subseteq V$) as well as network devices
  such as routers and switches.
- E is the set of **edges**, representing communication links between nodes.

  Each node $v \in V$ has an associated network address, allowing it to be grouped
into **subnets**, defined as disjoint subsets $\mathcal{N} = \{N_1, N_2, \dots, N_k\}$ of V, where each
$N_i \subseteq V$ represents a group of nodes sharing a common routing prefix.

2.2   Agent Model

AG represents a set of agents where AG^D is the subset of defender agents,
AG^U is the subset of user agents, and AG^A is the subset of attacker agents.
Agent behavior is simulated inside a simulation **environment** that provides
observations to agents, and receives actions from agents, leading to an update of
the environment state which in turn leads to an update of agents' observations.
This observation/action/update is executed as one logical **timestep**, and the
environment executes this loop for a number of timesteps that defines the length
T of an **episode**. An agent $ag^\chi \in AG^\chi$ ($\chi \in \{D, U, A\}$) is therefore characterized
by an **action space** $\mathcal{A}^\chi$, an **observation space** $\mathcal{O}^\chi$, a **belief state space** $\mathcal{B}^\chi$,
and a **policy** π^χ that maps observations and beliefs into actions. We define these
concepts in the remainder of this section.

Action Space - $\mathcal{A}^\chi$. An agent's action space $\mathcal{A}^\chi$ represents the set of all possible
actions the agent is able to use. Once an action $a^\chi \in \mathcal{A}^\chi$ is chosen by an agent it
spends $a^\chi_{\text{prep}} \in \mathbb{Z}_{\geq 0}$ timesteps in an inconsequential **preparation** phase before
entering an **execution phase** for $a^\chi_{\text{exec}} \in \mathbb{Z}_+$ timesteps. If the final timestep of
the execution phase is successfully reached and the action still passes any validity
checks, the action is **completed** which results in the action terminating and the
final set of observations being returned to the agent, including an observation
that the action was successful.
   At timestep t

- $\mathcal{A}^\chi{}_{t,\text{select}}$ denotes the set of actions chosen by an agent at timestep t.

- $\mathcal{A}^{\chi}{}_{t,\text{prep}}$ denotes the set of an agent's actions in the preparation phase at timestep t.
- $\mathcal{A}^{\chi}{}_{t,\text{exec}}$ denotes the set of an agent's actions in the execution phase at timestep t, but not being completed.
- $\mathcal{A}^{\chi}{}_{t,\text{comp}}$ denotes the set of actions successfully completed by an agent at timestep t.
- $\mathcal{A}^{\chi}{}_{t,\text{fail}}$ denotes the set of actions failed by an agent at timestep t.

An action is defined as $action = (d_{prep}, d_{exec}, detectable, objective, remote)$ where $d_{prep} \in \mathbb{Z}_{\geq 0}$ is the number of timesteps the action spends in its preparation phase, $d_{exec} \in \mathbb{Z}_{+}$ is number of timesteps (at least 1) that the action spends in its execution phase, $detectable \in \mathbb{B}$ indicates whether the action can be flagged by an intrusion detection system, $objective \in \mathbb{B}$ indicates whether the action is an objective of the agent, and $remote \in \mathbb{B}$ indicates whether the action is remote (or otherwise local). Remote and local actions are defined in Sect. 2.3. Unless specified otherwise, by default, $detectable = False$, $objective = False$, and $remote = False$.

Observation Space - $\mathcal{O}^{\chi}$. An agent's observation space $\mathcal{O}$ represents the set of all possible observations the agent is able to receive from the environment.

Belief State Space - $\mathcal{B}^{\chi}$. A belief state is an agent's memorization, understanding and/or estimation of the state of the environment. This may be updated using a history of observations and/or previous actions. An agent's belief state space $\mathcal{B}^{\chi}$ represents the set of all possible belief states that the agent is able to internalize. We define transitions between belief states using a belief state.

Finite State Machine (FSM) $\mathcal{M}^{\chi}$. A belief state FSM $\mathcal{M}^{\chi}$ is typically too large to define explicitly, so we define it as the cartesian product of each FSM in a set of smaller FSMs M^{χ}, one per host $h \in H$.

$$\mathcal{M}^{\chi} = \prod_{h \in H} m_h^{\chi}$$

Where, $\forall h \in H$, we define $m_h^{\chi} \in M^{\chi}$ as follows:

$$m_h^{\chi} = (B_h^{\chi}, \Sigma_h^{\chi}, V_h^{\chi}, \delta_h^{\chi}, b_{h,0}^{\chi}, F_h^{\chi})$$

Where

- B_h^{χ} is the finite set of states. *e.g.* an attacker agent's attack stages with respect to an individual host, or possible intrusion detection alert states for an individual host in the case of a defender agent.
- $\Sigma_h^{\chi} \subset \mathcal{O}^{\chi}$ is the finite set of inputs.
- V_h^{χ} is the finite set of variables (used for guard conditions and update actions) of simple data type (boolean, integer).
- $\delta_h^{\chi} : B_h^{\chi} \times Guard_h^{\chi}(V_h^{\chi}) \times \Sigma_h^{\chi} \times Update_h^{\chi}(V_h^{\chi}) \rightarrow B_h^{\chi}$ is the state transition. $Guard_h^{\chi}(V_h^{\chi})$ represents the set of Boolean conditions over V_h^{χ}, expressed in propositional logic. $Update_h^{\chi}(V_h^{\chi})$ represents the set of updates of the value of variables in V_h^{χ} when the transition is taken.

- $b^\chi_{h,0} \in B^\chi_h$ is the initial state.
- $F^\chi_h \subseteq B^\chi_h$ is the set of terminal states.

The agent's belief state space can then be defined as the cartesian product of the set of states of each of these smaller FSMs:

$$\mathcal{B}^\chi = \prod_{h \in H} B^\chi_h$$

The belief state of an agent at time t is defined as $\mathcal{B}^\chi{}_t = \{b^\chi_{h,t} \in B^\chi_h \mid h \in H\}$, where $\forall h \in H, b^\chi_{h,t}$ is the current state of m^χ_h at time t.

Policy - π^χ. An agent's policy defines how an agent selects actions for each timestep of an episode. We define two types of agent policies.

1. **fixed stochastic policy** $\pi^\chi(a) = P(a)$ where each action a in the agent's action space $\mathcal{A}^\chi$ is selected at each timestep with probability $P(a)$. This type of policy does not depend on observations.
2. **belief-based policy** $\pi^\chi : \mathcal{B}^\chi \to \mathcal{A}^\chi$ where the agent's policy uses its current belief state to determine its next action to take. This type of policy does depend on observations since belief state FSM transitions are triggered by observations.

2.3   Sessions Model

Let AS be the set of **active sessions** running on hosts, and AS_t the current set of active sessions at timestep t.

A **remote session** $rs \in AS$ is defined as a temporal communication instance between two or more nodes, formally represented as: $rs = (ag, h, p, d)$ where: $ag \in AG$ is an agent owning the session, $h \in H$ is the host on which the session is operating. This is the target/remote host of the communication instance. $p \in AS$ is the parent session. This is the session that the agent ag used to create the communication instance. d is the session duration.

A **local session** $ls \in AS$ is defined as a temporal job instance on a node (*e.g.* a user logged in a local host), formally represented as: $ls = (ag, h, d)$ where $ag \in AG$ is an agent owning the session. $h \in H$ is the host on which the session is operating. d is the session duration.

Once an agent has a remote/local session on a host, they can execute actions from this host. **Remote actions** are actions that involve interacting with another host over the network. Note that some **remote actions** can create a **remote session** rs. **Local actions** are actions that take place on the session's host and do not involve using the network.

We distinguish between remote and local sessions as a way to implement persistent threat in our solution: local sessions cannot be removed by other agents than the one using the session, and therefore attacker agents always keep a foothold into the network once they establish a local session.

2.4   Intrusion Detection System (IDS) Model

We consider an IDS abstractly as an observer of network activity that probabilistically produces alerts where the alert probability depends on whether the activity comes from a malicious source or not. Observable network activity is the set of all actions in the attacker action space $\mathcal{A}^U$ and user action space $\mathcal{A}^A$ that are labeled as *"detectable"*. This will be illustrate in our case study in Sects. 5.4 and 5.5 respectively. In addition, the IDS is characterized with the following parameters: (i) *recall* - probability of flagging phenomena given it is malicious; (ii) *specificity* - probability of not flagging phenomena given it is not malicious.

3   Security vs. Availability Optimization

Our research aims to emphasize and capture the importance of balancing security with availability when optimizing MTD strategies. To facilitate the evaluation of a MTD defense strategy in terms of how it balances defense and availability, we propose the following objective function Obj.

$$Obj = \alpha \cdot (1 - Attack\_Efficiency) + (1 - \alpha) \cdot Availability$$

$\alpha \in [0, 1]$ specifies the degree of priority granted to defense relative to the priority of availability.

$$Attack\_Efficiency = \frac{\gamma \sum\limits_{0 \le t < T} |\mathcal{A}^A_{t,comp} \cap \mathcal{A}^A_{objective}|}{|H| \sum\limits_{0 \le t < T} |\mathcal{A}^A_{t,select}|} \quad \text{represents a normalized}$$

defense objective, where:

- $\mathcal{A}^A_{t,comp} \cap \mathcal{A}^A_{objective}$ is the set of all completed attacker agent objective actions at timestep t.
- $\mathcal{A}^A_{t,select}$ is the set of attacker agent actions selected at timestep t.
- γ is the average of the minimum number of actions required to complete an attack objective on each host. We believe this can be computed from an attack graph using an algorithm that finds the shortest path to attack objective completion from the initial state, as presented in [1].

$$Availability = \frac{\sum\limits_{0 \le t < T} |\mathcal{A}^U_{t,exec} \cap \mathcal{A}^U_{objective}|}{ag^U_\omega \cdot ag^U_\psi \cdot T \cdot |AG^U|} \quad \text{represents a normalized availability}$$

objective.

- $\mathcal{A}^U_{t,exec} \cap \mathcal{A}^U_{objective}$ is the set of user agent objective actions being executed at timestep t.
- $ag^U_\omega \cdot ag^U_\psi$ is the probability per timestep that a user agent executes an objective action.

The objective function Obj serves as a metric for the purpose of evaluating a defense policy.

4   Proposed Solution - CybORG-MTD

Cyber Operations Research Gym (CybORG) is a cybersecurity simulation environment designed to support the training and evaluation of autonomous cyber defense strategies. It provides a structured framework for simulating attack-defense interactions within enterprise networks. In order to design MTD policies using RL, we propose an extension of CybORG, CybORG-MTD. This extension integrates MTD into the action space of defender agents, define a RL method that relies on deep reinforcement learning, and provides a reward function that balances the defense and availability implications of MTD. In this work, we focus on IP address shuffling as the MTD technique available to the defender agent.

IP Shuffling Action - SwitchIP_Address$_h$ has the following effects on the environment state when completed by the defender agent:

1. Changes the IP address of host h to a random unallocated IP address within an IP address pool.
2. Disconnects any remote sessions running on host h at action completion.
3. Disconnects any remote sessions whose parent session was running on host h at action completion.
4. Disconnects any remote sessions whose parent session was disconnected.
5. Causes any remote actions to fail if their source session was disconnected.
6. Causes any remote actions to fail at action completion if the remote action's target host was host h.

Reward Function AO-UA - Attacker Objective and User Action. We propose this reward function as a way to incentivize the trained MTD strategy to balance defense and availability equally.

$$R_t^{\text{AO-UA}} = -1 \cdot \beta_{\text{AO-UA}} \cdot \frac{|\mathcal{A}_{t,\text{comp}}^A \cap \mathcal{A}_{\text{objective}}^A|}{|H|}$$
$$+ (1 - \beta_{\text{AO-UA}}) \cdot \frac{|\mathcal{A}_{t,\text{exec}}^U \cap \mathcal{A}_{\text{objective}}^U|}{ag_\omega^U \cdot ag_\psi^U \cdot T \cdot g|AG^U|}$$

Where $\beta_{\text{AO-UA}} \in [0,1]$ specifies the weight applied to the defense term, $\mathcal{A}_{t,\text{comp}}^A \cap \mathcal{A}_{\text{objective}}^A$ is the set of all completed attacker agent objective actions at timestep t, $\mathcal{A}_{t,\text{exec}}^U \cap \mathcal{A}_{\text{objective}}^U$ is the set of user agent objective actions being executed at timestep t, and $ag_\omega^U \cdot ag_\psi^U$ is the probability per timestep that a user agent should be executing an objective action.

Lastly, we propose a case study that illustrates the procedure to carry out the training of a MTD based defense policy for a specific network using the CybORG-MTD framework. Using our formal models, we implement defender, user, and attacker agents that interact in an enterprise network environment to train a defender agent policy to use MTD strategies that balance defense and availability. This and other information related to the case study are presented in the next section.

5   Case Study

In order to benchmark our solution against existing approaches, we propose a case study that elaborates on the model presented in Sect. 2.

5.1   Network

We consider two different networks in this case study: (i) a small network of 2 server hosts and 6 user hosts, and (ii) a large network of 5 server hosts and 60 user hosts. The first network was designed to be small to enable exploration of parameter values for parametric reward functions (e.g. $\beta_{\text{AO}-\text{UA}}$ in $R_t^{\text{AO}-\text{UA}}$) and select a good parameter value. The second network was designed to be representative of a realistic sub-network, in order to assess the usability of our approach where one defender agent would defend a sub-network.

With these networks, we aim at providing a meaningful benchmark of RL-derived policies based on multiple reward functions including ours and a significant subset of the related work. Extending this benchmark to even bigger networks is left as future work. This limitation on our results could however be mitigated by considering the deployment of multiple defending agents, each of them being responsible to independently defend a small subset of hosts in a larger network.

5.2   Agents

We consider a set of 8 (respectively 62) agents, *i.e.* $AG = \{ag^D, ag_1^U..ag_6^U, ag^A\}$ (resp. $AG = \{ag^D, ag_1^U .. ag_{60}^U, ag^A\}$). Each green agent is given a user session on its corresponding user host. We detail the action space, observation space, belief space, and policy of each agent in Sects. 5.3, 5.4, and 5.5.

5.3   Defender Agent Model

The defending agent is assigned a subset of hosts $H_{ag^D} \subseteq H$ which they are responsible for defending with the use of MTD.

Defender Agent Action Space - $\mathcal{A}^D$. The defender's action space is defined as the following set of actions:

$\mathcal{A}^D = \{\texttt{SwitchIP\_Address}_h \mid h \in H_{ag^D}\}$

The effect of $\texttt{SwitchIP\_Address}_h$ on the environment state is described in Sect. 4.

Further defender action details are described in Table 2.

We add the following constraint on action selection, which states that the defender agent cannot select an action at timestep t if this action is currently being prepared or executed: $\mathcal{A}_{t,\text{select}}^D \cap (\mathcal{A}_{t,\text{prep}}^D \cup \mathcal{A}_{t,\text{exec}}^D) = \emptyset$.

Defender Observation Space - $\mathcal{O}^D$. Defender observations are used to update the belief state of the defender agent. At each timestep t, any completed actions return a success flag letting the agent know whether the action was successful. The defender also receives the IDS alerts which specify for each host $h \in H_{ag^D}$ whether the IDS has identified h as having been the source of malicious activity, the target of malicious activity, or neither of these.

Defender Belief State Space - $\mathcal{B}^D$. The defender's belief state machine m_h^D is defined hereafter using notations introduced in Sect. 2 and is described in Fig. 1.

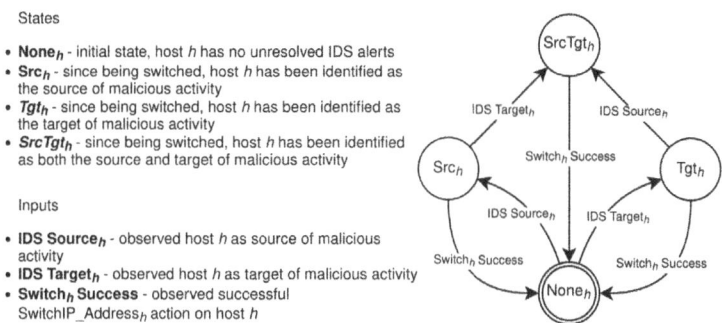

States

- **None$_h$** - initial state, host h has no unresolved IDS alerts
- **Src$_h$** - since being switched, host h has been identified as the source of malicious activity
- **Tgt$_h$** - since being switched, host h has been identified as the target of malicious activity
- **SrcTgt$_h$** - since being switched, host h has been identified as both the source and target of malicious activity

Inputs

- **IDS Source$_h$** - observed host h as source of malicious activity
- **IDS Target$_h$** - observed host h as target of malicious activity
- **Switch$_h$ Success** - observed successful SwitchIP_Address$_h$ action on host h

Fig. 1. Defender's belief FSM for a host's IDS alert status.

Defender Agent Policy $\pi^D : \mathcal{B}^D \to \mathcal{A}^D$. The defender agent's policy π^D is modelled as a fully-connected neural network defined with parameters θ^D. This policy maps from the defender agent's belief state space $\mathcal{B}^D$ to the defender agent's action space $\mathcal{A}^D$. Parameters θ^D control this mapping and are determined using deep reinforcement learning (DRL) techniques such that the defender's reward is maximized. The reward function to produce this environmental reward is discussed in detail in Sect. 4.

5.4   User Agent Model

User agents are tasked with acting as typical network users which in our simulation environment involves randomly performing local and remote actions.

User Agent Action Space - $\mathcal{A}^U$. The user action space is defined as follows:
$\mathcal{A}^U = \{\texttt{Sleep}\} \cup \{\texttt{LocalWork}\} \cup \{\texttt{AccessService}_h \mid h \in H_s\}$

$\texttt{AccessService}_h$ creates a remote session on a target host h in H_s for the duration of the action's execution.

$\texttt{LocalWork}$ represents work done using the green agent's local session's host.

$\texttt{Sleep}$ represents no activity.

Further user action details are described in Table 2.

We add the following constraints on action selection, which simply states that a user can select at most one action at any timestep t: $|\mathcal{A}_{t,\text{select}}^U| \leq 1$.

User Agent Policy - $\pi^U(a^U)$.

User agents are modeled using a fixed stochastic policy $\pi^U(a^U) = P(a^U)$ where each action in the user's action space $\mathcal{A}^U$ is selected with fixed probability such that $\sum_{a^U \in \mathcal{A}^U} P(a^U) = 1$.

$\texttt{AccessService}$ and $\texttt{LocalWork}$ actions are executed for a random (discrete) number of timesteps $d \in [d_{\min}, d_{\max}]$ where $d_{\min}, d_{\max} > 0$.

The average non-$\texttt{Sleep}$ action duration is denoted $\overline{d} = \frac{d_{\min} + d_{\max}}{2}$.

User agents each have an activity level $ag_\omega^U \in [0, 1]$ to control the probability that they are executing non-$\texttt{Sleep}$ actions at any given timestep.

User agents also each have a remote activity proportion $ag_\psi^U \in [0, 1]$ to control the probability that they are executing a $\texttt{AccessService}$ action given that they are executing a non-$\texttt{Sleep}$ action.

The probability of each action is calculated as follows:

$P(\texttt{AccessService}_h) = \frac{ag_\omega^U \cdot ag_\psi^U}{|H_s| \cdot \overline{d}} \quad \forall h \in H_s,$

$P(\texttt{LocalWork}) = \frac{ag_\omega^U \cdot (1 - ag_\psi^U)}{\overline{d}},$

$P(\texttt{Sleep}) = 1 - \frac{ag_\omega^U}{\overline{d}}$

5.5   Attacker Agent ag^A

Attacking agents aim to discover and exploit hosts on the network with the goal of achieving **data exfiltration** on hosts in the network.

Attacker Agent Action Space - $\mathcal{A}^A$. For a set of network hosts H, the attack action space $\mathcal{A}^A$ is based on the MITRE ATT&CK Framework[1] as follows:

$\mathcal{A}^A = \{\texttt{PingSweep}_N \mid N \in \mathcal{N}\} \cup \{\texttt{PortScan}_h \mid h \in H\}$
$\cup \{\texttt{RemoteProcessExploit}_h \mid h \in H\}$
$\cup \{\texttt{RemoteOperatingSystemExploit}_h \mid h \in H\}$
$\cup \{\texttt{OperatingSystemExploit}_h \mid h \in H\} \cup \{\texttt{DataExfiltration}_h \mid h \in H\}$

$\texttt{PingSweep}_N$ lists the names and current IP addresses of hosts in a target subnet $N \in \mathcal{N}$, (ATT&CK tactic TA0007 - *Discovery*).

$\texttt{PortScan}_h$ lists the vulnerable processes running on a target remote host $h \in H$, (ATT&CK tactic TA0007 - *Discovery*).

$\texttt{RemoteProcessExploit}_h$ creates a remote session with user privileges on a target remote host $h \in H$, (ATT&CK tactic TA0008 - *Lateral Movement*).

$\texttt{RemoteOperatingSystemExploit}_h$ creates a remote session with root privileges on a target remote host $h \in H$, (ATT&CK tactic TA0008 - *Lateral Movement*).

$\texttt{OperatingSystemExploit}_h$ elevates a session on host $h \in H$ with user privileges to root privileges, (ATT&CK tactic TA0004 - *Privilege Escalation*).

$\texttt{DataExfiltration}_h$ represents attack objective completion on a host $h \in H$, (ATT&CK tactic TA0010 - *Exfiltration*).

Further attacker action details are described in Table 2.

---

[1] https://attack.mitre.org/.

We add the following constraints on actions selection: an attacker agent can select at most one action at any timestep t, $i.e.$ $|\mathcal{A}^A_{t,\text{select}}| \leq 1$ and cannot select an action being prepared or executed, $i.e.$ $\mathcal{A}^A_{t,\text{select}} \cap (\mathcal{A}^A_{t,\text{prep}} \cup \mathcal{A}^A_{t,\text{exec}}) = \emptyset$.

Attacker Agent Observation Space - $\mathcal{O}^A$. Attacker observations are used to update the belief state of the attacking agent. Completion of actions results in a success flag letting the agent know whether the action was successful. Discovery actions ($\texttt{PingSweep}_N$ and $\texttt{PortScan}_h$) also provide observations of various details about each host. Controlling a session rs or ls on a host h will provide the attacking agent with session observations at each timestep which includes Operating System details of host h. If the attacker agent stops receiving observations of a particular session, this means the session has been disconnected.

Attacker Agent Belief State Space - $\mathcal{B}^A$. The attacker's belief state machine m^A_h is defined hereafter using notations introduced in Sect. 2 and is described in Fig. 2.

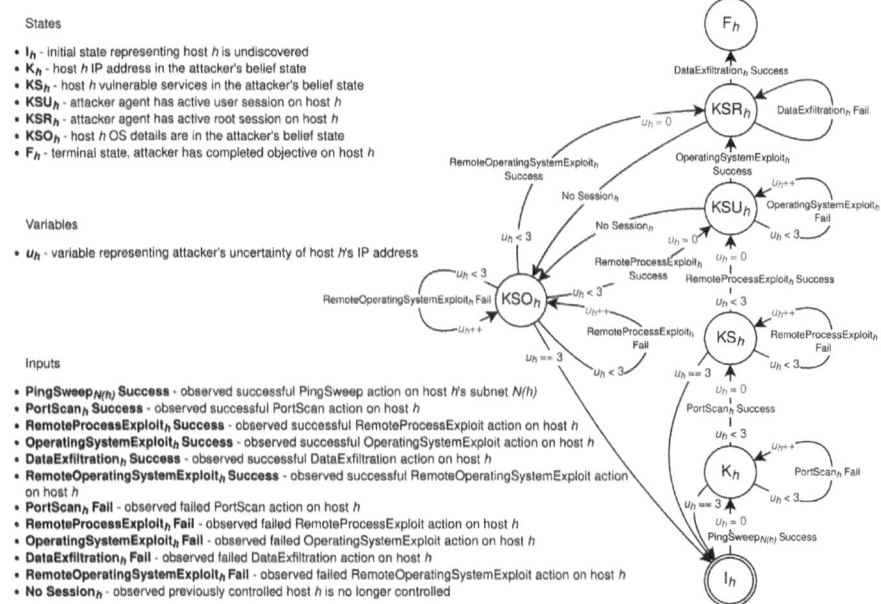

Fig. 2. Attacker's belief FSM on host h.

Attacker Agent Policy - $\pi^A : \mathcal{B}^A \to \mathcal{A}^A$. The attacking agent's policy produces an action at each timestep based on its current belief state. Attacker agent action probabilities are essentially determined randomly from the set of actions required for attack advancement for each host.

To determine action probabilities, we first define the following sets of hosts: $\forall \sigma \in \{\text{I}, \text{K}, \text{KS}, \text{KSU}, \text{KSR}, \text{KSO}, \text{F}\}$, $H^\sigma_t = \{h \in H \mid b^A_{h,t} = \sigma_h\}$. Then, action probabilities are as defined in Table 1. Note that if all hosts have their objectives completed, *i.e.* $H_t^F = H$, then the attacker selects no actions.

Table 1. Attacker Agent Action Probabilities

Action	Target	Probability
PingSweep$_N$	random subnet $N \in \mathcal{N}$	$\frac{|H_t^1|}{|H| - |H_t^F|}$
PortScan$_h$	random host $h \in H^K$	$\frac{|H_t^K|}{|H| - |H_t^F|}$
RemoteProcessExploit$_h$	random host $h \in H^{KS} \cup H^{KSO}$	$\frac{|H_t^{KS}|}{|H| - |H_t^F|} + \frac{|H_t^{KSO}|}{2(|H| - |H_t^F|)}$
OperatingSystemExploit$_h$	random host $h \in H^{KSU}$	$\frac{|H_t^{KSU}|}{|H| - |H_t^F|}$
RemoteOperatingSystemExploit$_h$	random host $h \in H^{KSO}$	$\frac{|H_{ht}^{KSO}|}{2(|H| - |H_t^F|)}$
DataExfiltration$_h$	random host $h \in H^{KSR}$	$\frac{|H_t^{KSR}|}{|H| - |H_t^F|}$

6   Performance Evaluation

6.1   Experimental Setup

To evaluate the effectiveness of different reward functions in optimizing policies for Moving Target Defense (MTD) strategies, we designed an experimental setup utilizing **Proximal Policy Optimization (PPO)** [10] as the RL algorithm, implemented using **RLlib** [13], a RL library for Python. RL parameters used for all experiments are shown in Table 3.

Table 2. CybORG-MTD Action Details

Action notation	Agent(s)	Target	Objective	Detectable	Remote	d_{prep}	d_{exec}
SwitchIP_Address$_h$	ag^D	$h \in H$			✓	0	2
AccessService$_h$	ag^U	$h \in H_s$	✓	✓	✓	0	[2..10]
LocalWork	$ag_{1..60}^U$	$h \in H_u$				0	[2..10]
Sleep	$ag_{1..60}^U$	none				0	1
PingSweep$_N$	ag^A	$N \in \mathcal{N}$			✓	0	1
PortScan$_h$	ag^A	$h \in H$		✓	✓	0	1
RemoteProcessExploit$_h$	ag^A	$h \in H$		✓	✓	2	2
RemoteOperatingSystemExploit$_h$	ag^A	$h \in H$		✓	✓	2	2
OperatingSystemExploit$_h$	ag^A	$h \in H$				2	1
DataExfiltration$_h$	ag^A	$h \in H$	✓			0	1

Simulation Environment. Our experiments are conducted using the CybORG-MTD gym. One environment configuration consists of a flat enterprise network with **8 hosts**, and another configuration is made up of **65 hosts**. In each configuration, a single defender agent is trained to protect the network using IP address shuffling as the MTD technique.

Table 3. RL Details

RL algorithm	PPO
Training batch size (episodes)	200
Evaluation batch size (episodes)	200
Episode length (timesteps)	500
Learning rate	5×10^{-5}
GAE parameter (λ)	1.0
Clipping parameter (ϵ)	0.2
Entropy coefficient	0.0
Value function loss coefficient	1.0
Gradient clipping	*none*
Hardware	NVIDIA RTX 4070 Ti 64 GB RAM Intel i5-14600KF
RLlib EnvRunner Actors (CPU threads used for parallel, independent simulation execution)	18

Defender Agent Model. The defender agent utilizes a fully connected neural network to map from the belief state space to the action space. The architecture of the policy network consists of input layer and output layer the size of the defender's belief state space $\mathcal{B}^D$ and the defender's action state space $\mathcal{A}^D$ respectively, as well as two hidden layers, each of size 256.

Intrusion Detection System (IDS) Configuration. The environment includes an IDS with a recall of 0.9 and specificity of 0.99.

User Agent Behavior. User agent behavior is parameterized with an activity level of 0.5 indicating users engage in work 50% of the time, and remote work proportion of 0.5 representing 50% of total time spent on working is spent on remote work.

Objective Function Weighting. To balance the trade-off between security and availability, we set the **defense-availability trade-off parameter** to $\alpha = 0.5$, indicating that defense and availability are considered equally important in the evaluation process.

6.2 Benchmarked Reward Functions

This section defines the reward functions to be compared. The selection criteria for these reward functions is that they are used in previous works for reinforcement learning of MTD and are able to be defined for a MTD policy space that includes both proactivity and reactivity.

$\forall \omega \in \{AO - UA, I - DA, DA - UA\}$, reward function R^ω uses hyperparameter β_ω to specify how the defense and availability terms of the reward are weighted. In order to optimize each reward function such that performance (as measured by the objective function) is maximized, we conduct a search for $\beta_\omega^* \in [0,1]$ where $R_\omega(\beta_\omega^*)$ produces a policy that achieves a better evaluation score than $R_\omega(\beta_\omega)$ for any other $\beta_\omega \in [0,1]$.

Reward Function AO-UA - Attacker Objective and User Action. This reward function is the one we propose, as described in Sect. 4. Training trajectories of policies trained using reward function AO-UA for different values of $\beta_{\mathrm{AO-UA}}$ are shown in Fig. 3a.

Reward Function I-DA - Intrusion Alert and Defense Action. This reward function is based on the reward functions used by Yunglaicela-Naula et al. [16] and Cao et al. [3] where IDS flags are used to calculate the defense component of the reward, while the cost of using MTD is simply a constant value subtracted when MTD is used. We have produced the following reward function using these principles.

$$R_t^{\mathrm{I-DA}} = -1 \cdot \beta_{\mathrm{I-DA}} \cdot |\{c_{h,t} \in \mathcal{C}_t \mid c_{h,t} \neq \mathrm{None}_h\}| - 1 \cdot (1 - \beta_{\mathrm{I-DA}}) \cdot |\mathcal{A}_{t,\mathrm{comp}}^D|$$

Where $\{c_{h,t} \in \mathcal{C}_t \mid c_{h,t} \neq \mathrm{None}_h\}$ is the set of host IDS alerts at timestep t and $\mathcal{A}_{t,\mathrm{comp}}^D$ is the set of defender actions completed at timestep t.

Training trajectories of policies trained using reward function $\mathrm{I-DA}$ for different values of $\beta_{\mathrm{I-DA}}$ are shown in Fig. 3b.

Reward Function AA - Attacker Action. This reward function is based on the reward function used by Zhang et al. [17] where the defender is incentivized to use host address mutation to prevent attackers from successfully scanning hosts. This is done by providing a constant positive reward if hosts avoid being scanned by attackers, and if any hosts are successfully scanned the reward is a negative value, linearly proportional to the number of successful scans.

We represent this approach using the following reward function.

$$R_t^{\mathrm{AA}} = -1 \cdot |\{a \in \mathcal{A}_{t,\mathrm{comp}}^A \mid a \in \{\mathrm{PortScan}_h \mid h \in H\}|$$

Where $\{a \in \mathcal{A}_{t,\mathrm{comp}}^A \mid a \in \{\mathrm{PortScan}_h \mid h \in H\}$ is the set of successfully completed PortScan actions at time t. A training trajectory obtained with reward function AA is shown in Fig. 4b.

Reward Function AS - Attacker Session. This reward function is based on the reward functions used by Zhang et al. [18] and Xu et al. [14] where the reward is determined based on the number of nodes compromised by an attacker.

In [18], the defender uses service function chain migration to mitigate attacks. The reward function provides a positive reward when no service function chains are compromised, while a negative reward linearly proportional to the number of compromised nodes is returned if any service function chains are compromised.

In [14], the defender uses route mutation to mitigate attacks. The reward function provides a positive reward when no routes are being attacked and otherwise returns a negative reward proportional to the number of nodes compromised by the attacker.

We use the following reward function to represent this approach.

$$R_t^{\text{AS}} = -1 \cdot |\{rs \in AS_t \mid rs(ag) = ag^A\}|$$

Where $\{rs \in AS_t \mid rs(ag) = ag^A\}$ is the set of remote sessions belonging to the attacker agent active at timestep t. A training trajectory obtained with reward function AS is shown in Fig. 4.

Reward Function DA-UA - Defense Action and User Action. This reward function is designed to most closely represent the reward function used by Xu *et al.* [15] who use routing randomization as the MTD technique. Here, the reward function is constructed such that if a routing scheme mutation introduces enough uncertainty, the reward is proportional to traffic volume minus delay. If

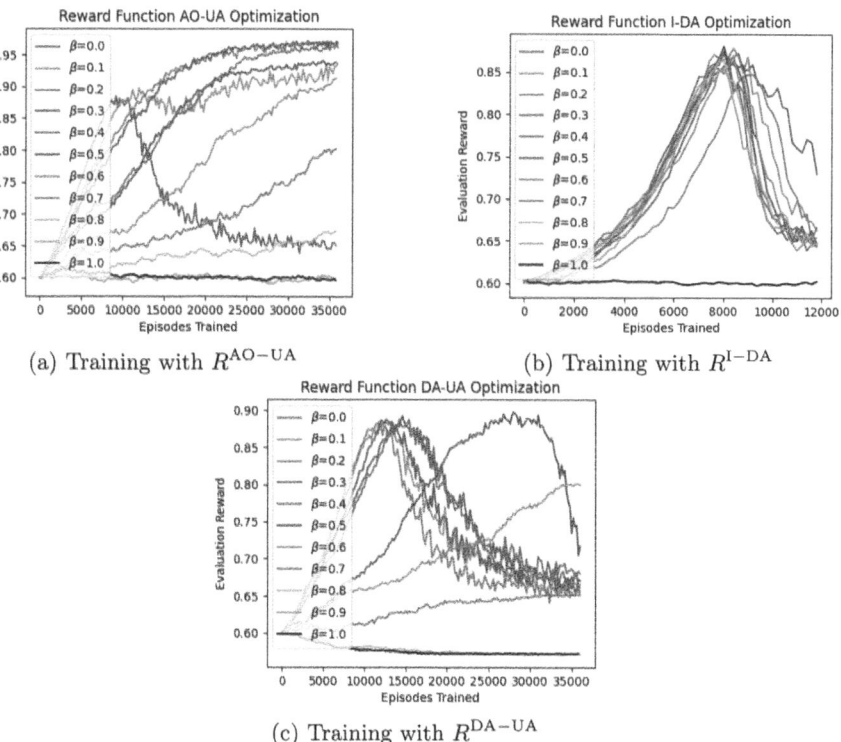

(a) Training with $R^{\text{AO-UA}}$

(b) Training with $R^{\text{I-DA}}$

(c) Training with $R^{\text{DA-UA}}$

Fig. 3. Reward functions optimization.

the routing scheme switch does not meet the mutation threshold, the reward is a large negative constant. To approximate this approach in the context of IP shuffling, we use the following reward function.

$$R_t^{\text{DA}-\text{UA}} = -1 \cdot \beta_{\text{DA}-\text{UA}} \cdot \frac{|\mathcal{A}_{t,\text{comp}}^D|}{T} + (1 - \beta_{\text{DA}-\text{UA}}) \cdot \frac{|\mathcal{A}_{t,\text{exec}}^U \cap \mathcal{A}_{\text{objective}}^U|}{ag_\omega^U \cdot ag_\psi^U \cdot T \cdot |AG^U|}$$

Where $\mathcal{A}_{t,\text{comp}}^D$ is the set of defender actions completed at timestep t, $\mathcal{A}_{t,\text{exec}}^U \cap \mathcal{A}_{\text{objective}}^U$ is the set of user agent objective actions being executed at timestep t, $ag_\omega^U \cdot ag_\psi^U$ is the probability per timestep that a user agent should be executing an objective action, T is the episode length in timesteps, and AG^U is the set of all user agents being simulated.

Training trajectories of policies trained using reward function DA − UA for different values of $\beta_{\text{DA}-\text{UA}}$ are shown in Fig. 3c.

6.3   Comparison Results

Figure 4a shows a comparison between reward functions $R^{\text{AO}-\text{UA}}$, $R^{\text{I}-\text{DA}}$ and $R^{\text{DA}-\text{UA}}$ regarding how their respective β hyperparameter affects the maximum evaluation score achieved during training. Reward Functions $R^{\text{I}-\text{DA}}$ and $R^{\text{DA}-\text{UA}}$ achieve best performance with $\beta_{\text{I}-\text{DA}} = \beta_{\text{DA}-\text{UA}} = 0.5$ while reward function $R^{\text{AO}-\text{UA}}$ achieves best performance with $\beta_{\text{AO}-\text{UA}} = 0.3$

A comparison of the best training trajectories of each reward function are shown in Fig. 4b. These results show that the reward function we propose, *i.e.* AO − UA, outperforms reward functions transposed from the literature, in terms of maximization of the objective function. However, we can also note that training with reward function AO − UA takes longer than with reward function I − DA.

Although reward functions I-DA and DA-UA achieve similar maximum evaluation scores during training, reward function I-DA achieves peak performance of 0.881 after roughly 8,000 episodes trained, while reward function DA-UA achieves peak performance of 0.898 after roughly 27,000 episodes trained. The greatest evaluation score of 0.972 is achieved by reward function AO-UA after 35,000 episodes trained and appears to be still increasing. Reward functions AA and AS saw no improvement in evaluation score during training.

Table 4 shows the performances of important policies in the small (8 host) and large (65 host) networks with respect to evaluation functions using $\alpha = 0.5$, $\alpha = 1.0$, and $\alpha = 0.0$. The policies considered include those trained using each reward function that achieved the highest evaluation score, the latest subsequent policy resulting from further training, an untrained policy, and a policy that uses no defending actions.

7   Discussion and Limitations

Our approach to objective-based reward function definition demonstrates significant advantages over existing methods.

Table 4. Policy Evaluation

	Policy	Balanced Evaluation ($\alpha = 0.5$)	Defense Evaluation ($\alpha = 1.0$)	Availability Evaluation ($\alpha = 0.0$)
small network (8 hosts)	AO-UA *best*	0.972	0.980	0.964
	I-DA *best*	0.881	0.839	0.924
	I-DA *last*	0.647	0.303	0.992
	DA-UA *best*	0.898	0.925	0.871
	DA-UA *last*	0.718	0.452	0.983
	AA *best*	0.605	0.991	0.218
	AA *last*	0.600	0.991	0.209
	AS *best*	0.602	0.992	0.213
	AS *last*	0.576	0.991	0.160
	Untrained (random)	0.601	0.991	0.210
	No Defense	0.500	0.000	1.000
large network (65 hosts)	AO-UA *best*	0.853	0.879	0.827
	I-DA *best*	0.860	0.893	0.827
	I-DA *last*	0.694	0.395	0.992
	DA-UA *best*	0.716	0.742	0.689
	Untrained (random)	0.609	0.993	0.224
	No Defense	0.500	0.000	1.000

7.1 Discussion of Key Findings

Previous works tend to approach the optimization of the attack success mini-mization and availability maximization trade-off either by using reward terms that approximate attack success and/or availability, or they define defense or performance thresholds that limit MTD actions outside of the defense policy being learned. Our proposed AO − UA reward function definition closely aligns with the desired security-availability trade-off as it specifically involves the same phenomena that are measured in the evaluation function. Our results clearly demonstrate the potential to improve policy learning, as evidenced by the trend in evaluation function values in our benchmark comparisons.

Small Network (8 Hosts). As shown on Fig. 4b, reward function I-DA achieved the highest rate of performance increase during training of any reward function we tested, with a relatively early peak performance of 0.881 achieved after roughly 8,000 episodes trained. Reward function I-DA also exhibited the lowest sensitivity with respect to the balancing parameter β. Reward function DA-UA required over 3 times as many episodes (roughly 27,000) to achieve a maximum score of 0.898, however lower values of β_{DA-UA} allowed performance to peak in roughly half this time with little loss to the maximum score. The highest evaluation score of 0.972 is achieved by reward function AO-UA after $35,000$ episodes trained and appears to be still increasing.

Large Network (65 Hosts). As shown on Fig. 4c reward function I-DA again achieved the highest rate of performance increase during training with a peak score of 0.860 after roughly 70,000 episodes trained. Reward function AO-UA

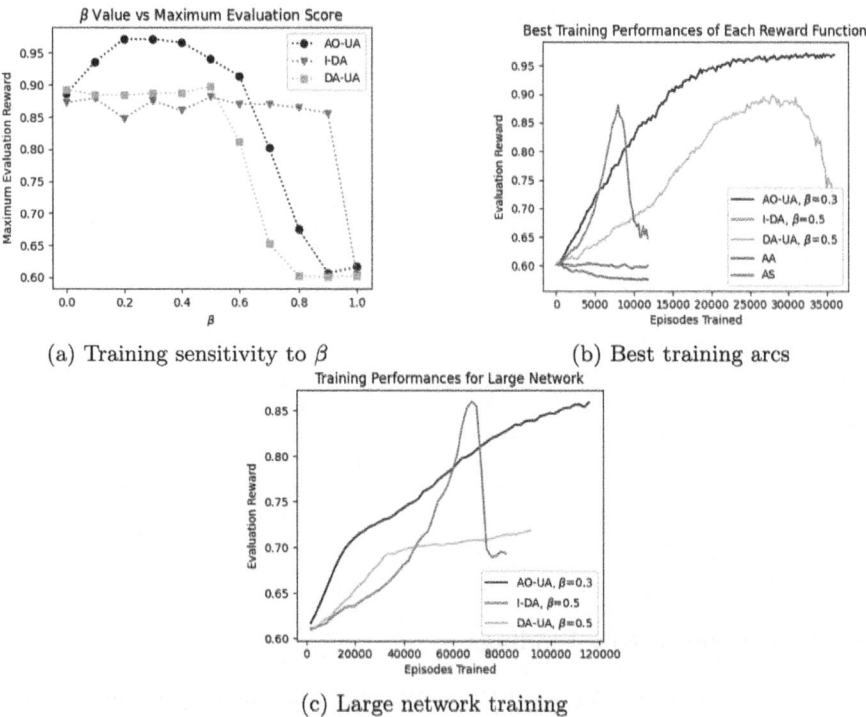

(a) Training sensitivity to β

(b) Best training arcs

(c) Large network training

Fig. 4. Reward functions comparison.

achieved a maximum score of 0.853 after over 100,000 episodes trained, however it appears that with more training a higher evaluation score might be achieved. In addition, it appears that I-DA achieved similar best scores on the small network and on the large network. This tends to show that the best reward obtained with I-DA is unlikely to change with different training hyper-parameters. In addition, and as opposed to I-DA, the difference between the best scores obtained with AO-UA on the small and large networks as well as the apparent gradient of the evaluation of AO-UA over time suggests that an improvement margin still exists to improve the results obtained on the large network.

Summary. A breakdown of performances of policies in Table 4 shows how moving from their best policies to their last policies, reward functions I-DA and DA-UA both experience the same problem where the defense score drops and the availability score increases. This suggests that MTD is being overly discouraged by the reward functions in the later stages of training. The policies of reward functions AA and AS produce policies very similar to the untrained policy. As expected, moving from their best policies to their last policies shows a slight decrease in availability with negligible change to defense. While the defense score of AO-UA is lower than the defense score of a random, untrained policy, we have shown with the results obtained with the small network that through RL and the AO-UA reward we are able to sacrifice just 0.011 from a policy's defense score to improve the availability score by 0.754. On the large network, the AO-UA reward sacrifices 0.114 from a policies defense to improve the availability score by 0.603.

7.2 Limitations

Despite these positive outcomes, our work has several limitations that should be acknowledged and addressed in future research.

- **Scalability**: Our evaluation uses a small network as well as a larger, more realistic one. Training using the realistic network takes longer due to both the increased computational load to simulate the larger network, as well as more training episodes needed to achieve a given evaluation score as seen by comparing Figs. 4b and 4c. There exist lots of opportunities to improve our current results such as hyper-parameter tuning, and using computation clusters for training.
- **Fixed Attacker Behavior**: The attacker agents in our experiments operate under predefined behavioral models that remain consistent between training and evaluation. In practice, attackers can adapt their strategies dynamically in response to defensive measures. Incorporating adaptive adversarial learning into our framework would provide a more robust assessment of RL-based MTD strategies against sophisticated attackers.
- **Generalization With Different MTDs**: Our experiments focus on a specific MTD technique (IP address shuffling). While our methodology is generalizable, additional work is needed to validate its effectiveness across several MTD techniques, such as web-services technological stack reconfigurations or mutation of operating systems.

To overcome these limitations, future research should focus on scaling up our approach for larger networks, integrating adaptive attacker models, and refining our defense strategies to work with real-time network data. Overall, our work presents a significant step forward in the application of RL to MTD optimization. By addressing the above limitations, we can further enhance the robustness, efficiency, and practical applicability of RL-based cyber defense strategies.

8   Related Work

When deploying an MTD strategy, it is important to minimize attack success while maximizing availability (alternatively minimizing defense cost). Therefore, RL reward function definition for training an MTD policy should consider both attack success and availability.

The reward function definitions in [3,16], and [4] approximate attack success using IDS alerts and their resolution. False positives and false negatives of IDS alerts mean that the defense component of the reward definitions does not exactly align with the ground truth when it comes to attack success. In [3,16], the negative effects of MTD are approximated using a constant value reduction when MTD is used. A constant penalty for MTD use is limited in its ability to represent how availability is impacted in complex scenarios.

Maintaining availability in [17,18], and [14] is handled by limiting the action space to actions that do not violate network constraints. Here, the RL process simply learns to maximize defense within the network operation constraints. This approach does not recognize network availability as something to maximize in balance with defense. The limitation with this approach to reward function definition is highlighted with the example that a MTD policy is not seen as better if it improves availability without affecting defense.

The approach to reward function definition used by Xu *et al.* [15] is the only one that uses network user activity to represent the availability component of the reward. The defense component of the reward is dependent on the degree to which the routing scheme is randomized. To extend this approach to other MTD techniques, we see that essentially the defending agent is being explicitly rewarded for its use of MTD. Instead of basing the reward off an action's outcomes, this approach rewards the use of actions directly. This approach discards the ability of RL to optimize action selection for specific scenarios with respect to their outcomes.

No approaches explicitly include both main phenomena we aim to prevent and preserve when deploying MTD. Our goal is to prevent attack objective success, however this is not explicitly included in any reward functions. Typically, the negative impact of MTD is reduced availability which is only explicitly included by Xu *et al.* [15]. Our approach to reward function definition includes both of these phenomena.

Reti *et al.* [9] implemented host address mutation into the NASim framework [11] in order to evaluate the effectiveness of MTD. Addresses of hosts in a subnet are simultaneously mutated in a time-based fashion by the defender. The authors claim that the effect of these address switches is that the attacker does not know which hosts they have exploited. It is unclear whether the implementation of host address mutation disrupts the reconnaissance phase of attacks. The evaluation of the defense is based on the success of the attackers and does not include the impact of MTD on QoS. The defense policy space is limited to the selection of switch periodicity. The defending agent is not able to apply address mutation to a proper subset of hosts on a subnet. This is an important limitation if IDS alerts or vulnerability information of specific hosts is available to the defender and the impact of address mutation on QoS is considered in the evaluation of the MTD policy.

Our work addresses these limitations by allowing the defender agent to select any subset of hosts to undergo an IP switch, and the reward and evaluation use the simulated user agent activity to determine an availability metric.

9   Conclusion

In this work, we have introduced a cyber defense simulation framework for optimizing MTD strategies that balance defense and availability. By developing the CybORG-MTD gym and designing a uniquely objective-based reward function, we have demonstrated the feasibility of training RL agents to generate adaptive and effective defense policies. The approach to MTD reward function definition outperforms existing methods in terms of optimizing the trade-off between defense and availability. Despite the promising results, challenges such as scalability, and adaptive attacker behaviors remain limitations of our results. Future research should explore ways to address these limitations and extend our approach to more complex and realistic environments. By refining RL-based MTD strategies, we aim to contribute to the advancement of automated and intelligent cyber defense mechanisms.

References

1. Ammann, P., Wijesekera, D., Kaushik, S.: Scalable, graph-based network vulnerability analysis. In: Proceedings of the 9th ACM Conference on Computer and Communications Security, pp. 217–224. CCS '02, Association for Computing Machinery, New York, NY, USA (2002). https://doi.org/10.1145/586110.586140
2. Ayrault, M., Borde, É., Kühne, U., Leneutre, J.: Moving target defense strategy in critical embedded systems: a game-theoretic approach. In: 2021 IEEE 26th Pacific Rim International Symposium on Dependable Computing (PRDC), pp. 27–36 (2021). https://doi.org/10.1109/PRDC53464.2021.00014
3. Cao, Y., Liu, K., Lin, Y., Wang, L., Xia, Y.: Deep reinforcement learning based self-evolving moving target defense approach against unknown attacks. IEEE Internet Things J. (2024)
4. Celdrán, A.H., et al.: RL and fingerprinting to select moving target defense mechanisms for zero-day attacks in IoT. IEEE Trans. Inf. Forensics Secur. (2024)
5. Feng, X., Zheng, Z., Mohapatra, P., Cansever, D.: A StackelBerg game and Markov modeling of moving target defense. In: Rass, S., An, B., Kiekintveld, C., Fang, F., Schauer, S. (eds.) Decision and Game Theory for Security, pp. 315–335. Springer, Cham (2017)
6. Kiely, M., et al.: Exploring the efficacy of multi-agent reinforcement learning for autonomous cyber defence: a cage challenge 4 perspective. In: Thirty-Nineth AAAI Conference on Artificial Intelligence, AAAI 2025, Thirty-Seventh Conference on Innovative Applications of Artificial Intelligence, IAAI 2025, Fifteenth Symposium on Educational Advances in Artificial Intelligence, EAAI 2015, February 25-March 04, Philadelphia, Pennsylvania, USA. AAAI Press (2025)
7. Lei, C., Ma, D.H., Zhang, H.Q.: Optimal strategy selection for moving target defense based on Markov game. IEEE Access 5, 156–169 (2017). https://doi.org/10.1109/ACCESS.2016.2633983
8. Li, H., Zheng, Z.: Optimal timing of moving target defense: a StackelBerg game model. In: MILCOM 2019 - 2019 IEEE Military Communications Conference (MILCOM), pp. 1–6. IEEE Press (2019). https://doi.org/10.1109/MILCOM47813.2019.9020963

9. Reti, D., Fraunholz, D., Elzer, K., Schneider, D., Schotten, H.D.: Evaluating deception and moving target defense with network attack simulation. In: Proceedings of the 9th ACM Workshop on Moving Target Defense, pp. 45–53 (2022)
10. Schulman, J., Wolski, F., Dhariwal, P., Radford, A., Klimov, O.: Proximal policy optimization algorithms. arXiv preprint arXiv:1707.06347 (2017)
11. Schwartz, J., Kurniawatti, H.: NASim (2019). https://github.com/Jjschwartz/NetworkAttackSimulator
12. Sengupta, S., et al.: A game theoretic approach to strategy generation for moving target defense in web applications. In: Proceedings of the 16th Conference on Autonomous Agents and MultiAgent Systems, pp. 178–186. AAMAS '17, International Foundation for Autonomous Agents and Multiagent Systems, Richland, SC (2017)
13. Wu, Z., Liang, E., Luo, M., Mika, S., Gonzalez, J.E., Stoica, I.: RLlib flow: distributed reinforcement learning is a dataflow problem. In: Conference on Neural Information Processing Systems (NeurIPS) (2021). https://proceedings.neurips.cc/paper/2021/file/2bce32ed409f5ebcee2a7b417ad9beed-Paper.pdf
14. Xu, C., Zhang, T., Kuang, X., Zhou, Z., Yu, S.: Context-aware adaptive route mutation scheme: a reinforcement learning approach. IEEE Internet Things J. **8**(17), 13528–13541 (2021)
15. Xu, X., Hu, H., Liu, Y., Tan, J., Zhang, H., Song, H.: Moving target defense of routing randomization with deep reinforcement learning against eavesdropping attack. Digital Commun. Netw. **8**(3), 373–387 (2022)
16. Yungaicela-Naula, N.M., Vargas-Rosales, C., Pérez-Díaz, J.A.: SDN/NFV-based framework for autonomous defense against slow-rate DDoS attacks by using reinforcement learning. Futur. Gener. Comput. Syst. **149**, 637–649 (2023)
17. Zhang, T., Xu, C., Shen, J., Kuang, X., Grieco, L.A.: How to disturb network reconnaissance: a moving target defense approach based on deep reinforcement learning. IEEE Trans. Inf. Forensics Secur. (2023)
18. Zhang, T., Xu, C., Zhang, B., Li, X., Kuang, X., Grieco, L.A.: Towards attack-resistant service function chain migration: a model-based adaptive proximal policy optimization approach. IEEE Trans. Dependable Secure Comput. **20**(6), 4913–4927 (2023)

LeaX: Class-Focused Explanations for Locating Leakage in Learning-Based Profiling Attacks

Qi Lei[iD] and Christian Wressnegger[(✉)][iD]

KASTEL Security Research Labs, Karlsruhe Institute of Technology (KIT),
Karlsruhe, Germany
c.wressnegger@kit.edu

Abstract. Machine learning can significantly improve power side-channel attacks that derive cryptographic keys from hardware devices. The attacker learns a model that maps side-channel information (e.g., a device's power consumption) to the computation's intermediate states/values, which in turn serve as evidence for the actual key. The model implicitly learns which portions of the power traces leak information and which are mere noise. This knowledge is of great interest to the designer of the cryptographic hardware. Knowing the "leakage points" allows them to tweak the implementation to prevent the leakage. The community has thus investigated the use of "Explainable AI" (XAI) to derive the machine-learning model's knowledge about existing leakage. Unfortunately, with limited success for protected (masked) implementations as used in practice so far. In this paper, we show that very much like for a side-channel attack itself, model analysis using XAI must focus on intermediate values rather than keys, accumulate evidence for all intermediates, and make an informed choice at the end. Doing so successfully, however, requires class-discriminative explanations—a fact overlooked up to now. We present a novel analysis method, LeaX, that uses this observation to precisely pinpoint leakage, especially for masked cryptographic implementations, which prior work has failed to do.

1 Introduction

Machine learning has emerged as a powerful tool in power side-channel analysis (SCA) to retrieve secret keys from cryptographic hardware [3,6,7,18,19,39, 40]. Side-channel attacks correlate side-channel information, such as the power consumption [e.g., 16,35] or electromagnetic emissions [e.g., 3,4,25], with intermediate values of the cryptographic computation, which are used as evidence to derive secret keys. While traditional methods, such as differential power analysis (DPA) [15] and correlation power analysis (CPA) [5], perform statistical analysis to uncover this correlation, learning-based attacks train a machine-learning model to do so [26]. Proficiency in identifying these correlations is critical to reduce the number of traces required for a successful attack. For defense, in

© The Author(s), under exclusive license to Springer Nature Switzerland AG 2025
M. Dalla Preda et al. (Eds.): ARES 2025, LNCS 15993, pp. 321–342, 2025.
https://doi.org/10.1007/978-3-032-00627-1_16

turn, we strive to additionally identify the source of the leakage and fix it (e.g., avoid moving the mask and the masked value to the same register [3]).

Side-channel traces represent the executed instructions over time. Thus, it is possible to precisely link leakage occurrence in time to the executed instruction in the implementations [28,30]. However, doing so is particularly difficult for learning-based attacks. While the used machine-learning models hold unique knowledge about leakage that the hardware designer requires to protect against (or at least increase the difficulty of) learning-based attacks, they are mostly operated as black-box oracle and do not expose their internal "reasoning" easily.

"Explainable AI" (XAI) holds great promise in this setting as it allows to reveal what the machine-learning model "looks at" during a successful attack, and thus, can point out where information leaks. Prior work [7,12,22,24,38,40] has explored transferring XAI techniques from the image domain to side-channel analysis, such as "Simple Gradients" [31], "Layer-wise Relevance Propagation" [2], or "Weight Visualization" [36,40]. We find that these methods fall short of accurately locating leakage points in protected (masked) implementations. The reason is two-fold: First, unlike in the image domain, neither instance-based explanations [2,31], that explain a single input trace, nor model-based explanations [36,40], that explain the underlying model using its parameters and/or activations, are directly applicable in side-channel analysis because the machine-learning models used here operate on comparably low confidence [25]. SCA-based attacks, hence, accumulate evidence gathered from intermediate values across multiple power traces. Second, applying this logic of accumulating results to explanations must not solely focus on the correct key [12] but all classes. As it is well known in the SCA community, all classes of all traces contribute to the ranking of each key candidate. Similarly, all classes of all traces contribute to the final explanation, and thus, all classes need to be considered for model analysis (without pre-filtering by key). We find that the success of such *class-focused aggregation of explanations* is, however, dependent on using class-discriminative explanations—a type of explanation method that can attribute feature-relevance specific to a single class and suppress the influence from other classes [11,17]. Most explanation methods [2,31,41] used in SCA so far [7,12,24,40] are specific to the predicted class but are *not* class-discriminative.

Contribution. In this paper, we revisit the use of XAI techniques in the field of side-channel analysis and provide new insights in how to use them for learning-based profiling attacks. We point out the limits of key-focused explanations (that filter explanations based on the correct key) for locating leakage points in protected/masked hardware implementations. Additionally, we propose a novel approach for locating leakage, LeaX, that uses class-focused explanations and is suitable for the particularities of side-channel analysis. We extensively evaluate our explanation strategy on the community benchmarks ASCAD [3], AES_HD [25], and DPA_v4 [4], showing that LeaX significantly outperforms instance-based and key-focused explanations across different learning-based SCA attacks.

2   Side-Channel Analysis

In this paper, *we focus on the classical setting where side-channel analysis is used to derive encryption keys from cryptographic hardware* [5,8,15]. Although the encryption scheme is provably secure, it is possible to derive the used key via information leaked during the hardware's computations. In this setting, the side-channel commonly is the hardware's power consumption, referred to as power traces. We specifically consider learning-based profiling attacks [3,6,7,19,40], meaning, attacks that learn a machine learning model on power traces observed during profiling a cloned device [26].

We elaborate on the considered attacker model and provide more details on learning-based attacks in Sects. 2.1 and 2.2, respectively. Moreover, side-channel attacks can also serve to locate leakage points, that is, the specific time samples that allow to derive the secret key. This information is of paramount importance for hardening the implementation, as we explain in Sects. 2.3.

2.1   Attacker Model

Side-channel attacks operate on cryptographic hardware, implementing a specific, known cryptographic function for which side-channel information can be gathered. We consider power consumption as the side-channel measured over time, yielding power traces. Moreover, the encryption key is not hardcoded in the device but is configurable, and the attacker cannot read the key from the device's memory.

In addition to the *"target device,"* the adversary is assumed to have an identical cryptographic device, the *"clone device,"* that can be reconfigured at will and unlimitedly queried. It hence is possible to gather side-channel information, such as power traces, for different configurations and keys as a preparatory step for the attack, giving rise to so-called profiling attacks. In contrast to non-profiling attacks [e.g., 5,15], profiling attacks better cope with defense strategies such as "masking." We refer the reader to related survey [26,27] for more details.

For the actual attack against the target device *for which the key is not known*, the adversary collects side-channel information to derive a ranking of possible key candidates. The more evidence the adversary collects (number of power traces), the higher the correct (actually used) key rises in the derived ranking and thus, can be identified. The likelihood of success can be estimated using the "guessing entropy," which in turn is estimated through the mentioned key rank. Below, we sketch the principle and again refer the reader to related work [21,33] for details.

2.2   Learning-Based Attacks

In recent years, learning-based attacks have yielded promising results in SCA [18, 39,40]. Thereby, a machine learning model represented as its parameters θ and a decision function $f_\theta : \mathbb{R}^d \to [0,1]^{256}$, takes a single power trace $\mathbf{x}$ consisting out of d time samples as its input and predicts the probabilities scores for abstract representations of a cryptographic intermediate value used as label $y = \varphi(z)$.

An *intermediate value* z can result from any intermediate computational step, for instance, $z = S(p_i \oplus k_i)$, where S refers to an S-box. Its representation, in turn, can be thought as a map φ, implemented as either the hamming weight [24], least significant bit (LSB) [34], or simply the identity function [3,25,40]. In the remainder of the paper, we consider the latter as it is the most effective among the three with the least loss of information [3].

Note that a thoroughly trained model can still *not* predict the intermediate value perfectly but provides imprecise clues only. Hence, a successful learning-based profiling attack accumulates prediction results across multiple inputs. *In this setting, the above observation on the indirection from intermediate value z to key byte k_i is crucial.*

Depending on the plaintext byte p_i, a different intermediate value z represents the correct key byte k_i^* in the model's output. Hence, when cumulating results over a set of inputs $X = \{x_1, \ldots, x_n\}$ it is imperative to resolve this indirection per input trace $\mathbf{x}$ individually.

For the remainder of the paper, we abstract away details of the encryption scheme (e.g., the use of S-Boxes) and introduce a plaintext-dependent map ϕ, using a message $m_{\mathbf{x}}$ that represents the used plaintext of a specific input trace $\mathbf{x}$, so that $z = \phi(k_i ; m_{\mathbf{x}})$. Next, we sum up the yield log-probabilities over all traces in X to measure the attack performance, forming a single experiment's "distinguishing vector":

$$\mathbf{v}_X = \sum_{\mathbf{x} \in X} \left(\log f_\theta(\mathbf{x})_{\phi(k_i ; m_{\mathbf{x}})} \right)_{k_i \in \{0, \ldots, 255\}} , \tag{1}$$

where each element of the vector refers to the likelihood of a specific key byte k_i to be correct. The map ϕ links keys (associated with the vector's dimensions) with the classifier's predictions of intermediate values.

Finally, we approximate the guessing entropy and thus the success of a learning-based SCA attack after processing n traces in X (the attack budget) across N experiments as: $Rank(k_i^*, \mathbf{v}_X) = \frac{1}{N} \sum_{l=1}^{N} rank(k_i^*, \mathbf{v}_X{}^{(l)})$. For evaluation, one commonly shows the average rank on the y-axis over the number of traces in X used on the x-axis. Hence, the "faster" an attack approaches $Rank = 0$ (meaning the fewer input traces are needed to reach an approximated guessing entropy of 0), the better the attack.

2.3   Locating Leakage

Side-channel traces represent the executed instructions over time, and thus, it is possible to pinpoint the instruction responsible for the observed effect in the trace. Consequently, knowing the precise time samples where leakage occurs allows for identifying problematic instructions or constructs in the implementation [28,30]. These indicative time samples of a power trace that correspond to information leakage are commonly referred to as "leakage points" or "points of interest" [26].

Locating leakage thus is of particular interest to the analyst, striving to improve the concealment of information in hardware. A large strain of research on side-channel analysis hence attempts to precisely locate leakage points [12, 22, 28, 30]. Our paper also falls in this category, presenting methods to locate leakage based on learning-based profiling attacks.

Most straightforwardly, the analyst can use the signal-to-noise ratio (SNR) to point out leakage locations [20]. *However, such an analysis requires knowledge about the used encryption key and the masking scheme (including the involved random values) that is deployed as a defense.* In learning-based profiling attacks, the attacker has access to a clone device and thus, controls the key during profiling. The masking scheme, however, is obstructed in the implementation and initialized through randomness so that an attacker or external analyst *cannot* compute the SNR directly [1, 37].

3   XAI for Side-Channel Analysis

Explainable AI (XAI) can show what a machine learning model "looks at" when deriving the correct key. An explanation method $h_\theta(\mathbf{x}, c)$ provides a *prediction-specific* relevance vector $\mathbf{R} \in \mathbb{R}^d$ of the same dimensionality as the input trace $\mathbf{x}$ based on the model θ. This means that each input feature x_i receives a relevance value R_i, showing how important that feature is to class c. Consequently, these methods can indicate leakage points, and thus, the problematic instructions to be adjust in the implementation to prevent the leak [28, 30]. *However, prior work on using XAI methods for leakage localization [7, 12, 22, 24, 38, 40] had limited success in correctly pointing out points-of-interest in protected (masked) implementations as we show in our evaluation (cf. Fig. 2).*

Informative time samples including leakage are sparsely distributed. Hence, an explanation method needs to highlight specific time samples accurately rather than rough regions. Figure 1 provides an example of an ideal attribution $\mathbf{e}$ using XAI (orange) with the SNR-over-time as ground truth showing the masking's random value r and the masked S-box output depicted in red and gray color.

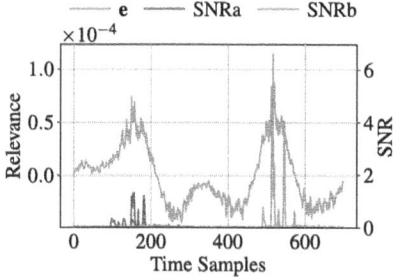

Fig. 1. Locating leakage points using XAI (orange) for a recent learning-based attack [12] on the ASCAD dataset [3]. Ground truth is provided in red and gray color based on the signal-to-noise ratio (SNR). *Note that information about the SNR is not available in practice but is provided by the benchmark.* (Color figure online)

In further follow, we describe common strategies found in literature and highlight shortcomings of existing attempts to use XAI in side-channel analysis.

Explanation Strategies. In the past, various explanation methods and strategies have been used for locating leakage points [7,12,22,24,38,40], split into two rough categories: intrinsically explainable machine-learning models and "post-hoc explanations" of ML models.

While the former promises a tight coupling of explanations to the reasoning of the learning-based attack, these approaches are currently limited in handling low-dimensional inputs with as little as twelve time samples only [38]. The large majority [7,12,24,40], however, uses post-hoc explanations for locating leakage, which is also in line with the XAI community where most approaches fall into this category [2,29,31,41]. We distinguish three explanation strategies for SCA:

A. **Instance-based explanations.** Most straight-forwardly one takes a single input (a power trace) and uses XAI to highlight what the machine-learning model considers to be important for deriving the encryption key [22]. In the image domain, instance-based explanations are used with great success [2,29,41]. For side-channel analysis, however, a single input carries too little information to derive the correct key with certainty [25], and thus, the explanation based on one individual power trace cannot locate the true leakage as we demonstrate. As an example, Fig. 2a shows three traces explained using Gradient Visualization [22], exhibiting drastic variance from one to another.

B. **Model-based explanations.** In SCA, we strive to know what the model in its entirety has learned about all the individual power traces that contain little clues about the occurring leakage. Model-based explanations [7,40] promise to provide this insight so that their application in SCA feels somewhat natural. Unfortunately, the models in learning-based attacks provide predictions with comparably low confidence [25], and hence, model-based explanations replicate this low confidence, failing to satisfactorily locate leakage. For instance, Fig. 2b shows the "Layer-wise Correlation" method [7] indicating areas where no sensitive information/leakage exists.

C. **Aggregation-based explanations.** In line with the learning-based attack's common practice of cumulating predictions to derive the correct encryption key, another strain of research proposes to cumulate explanations to locate leakage [12,24]. This middle way uses instance-based explanations to extract model knowledge as striven for in model-based explanations. Such an explanation strategy is unique to the field of side-channel analysis and is not employed in the image domain. Figure 2c and 2d provide two examples: First, attribution-based explanations [12] fail to indicate clear positive or negative regions of relevance in the trace, and also the "Layer-wise Activation" method [24] equally struggles to highlight "points of interests."

Unfortunately, none of those directions has yielded satisfactory results for masked implementations so far, leaving the community with effective key extraction but without the means to use these tools to locate leakage.

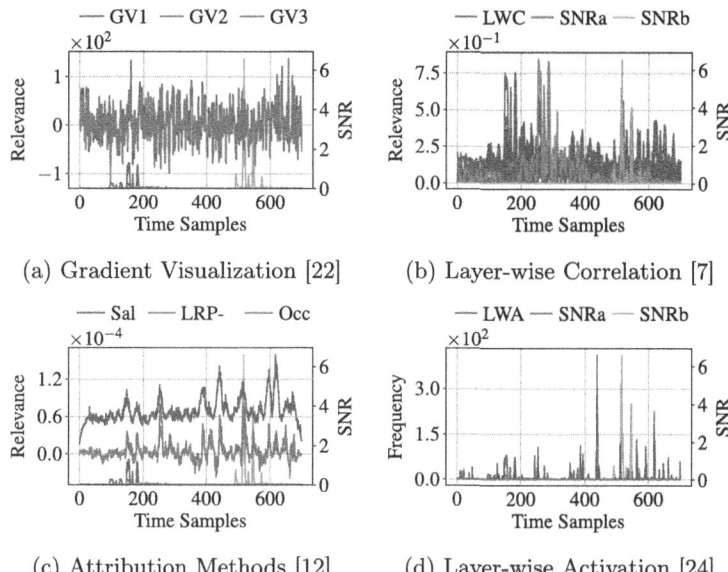

(a) Gradient Visualization [22]

(b) Layer-wise Correlation [7]

(c) Attribution Methods [12]

(d) Layer-wise Activation [24]

Fig. 2. Explanations of pior work: (a) Instance-based "Gradient Visualization" [22], (b) model-based "Layer-wise Correlation" [7], and two aggregation-based techniques using (c) different attribution methods [12] including salicency maps ("Sal"), LRP-ϵ, and Occlusion ("Occ"), and (d) Layer-wise Activation [24].

4   Revisiting Aggregation-Based Explanations

In this section, we specifically look at aggregation-based explanations that cumulate relevance values across multiple input traces similar to how attacks in SCA are typically conducted [3]. We detail key-focused explanations as presented in related work [12] and derive our proposal of *class-focused explanations* that better resembles the community's knowledge of SCA-based attacks.

Key-Focused Explanations. Hettwer et al. [12] propose to average explanations across all inputs $\mathbf{x} \in X$ whilst considering the mapping from the correct key byte k_i^* to the respective intermediate value $z = \varphi(\phi(k_i^* ; m_\mathbf{x}))$. However, we assume $\varphi(.)$ to be the identity map in further follow, so that $z = \phi(k_i^* ; m_\mathbf{x})$. An instance-based, prediction-specific explanation method $h_\theta(\mathbf{x}, z)$ then derives the time samples' contribution to the decision for value z:

$$\mathbf{e}_{k_i^*} = \frac{1}{|X|} \sum_{\mathbf{x} \in X} h_\theta(\mathbf{x}, \phi(k_i^*; m_\mathbf{x})). \tag{2}$$

This derivation, unfortunately, does not allow us to conclusively determine the correct leakage points in masked implementations, as we show in our evaluation. However, it gives rise to connecting explanation strategies with the common attack strategy in SCA. In line with the computation of the key ranking to approximate the guessing entropy, this approach can be extended to finding the correct averaged explanation based on label-to-key mapping ϕ among all key candidates $k_i \in K = \{0, \ldots, 255\}$:

$$E_K = \left\{ \frac{1}{|X|} \sum_{\mathbf{x} \in X} h_\theta(\mathbf{x}, \phi(k_i; m_\mathbf{x})) \mid k_i \in K \right\}. \tag{3}$$

Note that $\mathbf{e}_{k_i^*} \in E_K$ because k_i^* is one (of multiple) key hypothesis.

Class-Focused Explanations. We propose an alternative explanation strategy for side-channel analysis: Rather than focusing too rigidly on the label-to-key mapping, ϕ, it instead is better to explain the neural network's prediction, $f_\theta(\mathbf{x})_c$ for the specific classes $c \in C$, irrespective of the assigned key byte $k_i = \phi^{-1}(c; m_\mathbf{x})$. This rationale follows the intuition that all predicted classes (intermediate values) of all traces contribute to the ranking of the individual key candidates [26]. However, as we are not interested in the final key but in the model's insights/explanation, we consider all predicted classes of all traces *without* pre-filtering by keys. There are two crucial observations to make:

1. *While the classifier might be wrong overall, the individual locations it "looks at" (i.e., the corresponding features) can still be correct.*
2. *Predictions are influenced by features from the correct class and any other (wrong) class. Hence, indicative features can be obstructed by wrong features.*

A class-discriminative explanation method $h'_\theta(\mathbf{x}, c)$ that subtracts the influence of classes not matching the actual prediction [11] can highlight these indicative features. Cumulating over multiple inputs $\mathbf{x} \in X$ then gathers all the class-discriminative clues/features that the model is aware of, no matter how small:

$$E_C = \left\{ \frac{1}{|X|} \sum_{\mathbf{x} \in X} h'_\theta(\mathbf{x}, c) \mid c \in C \right\}. \tag{4}$$

Moreover, without relying on the correct key byte k_i^* each class $c \in C$ seems equally likely, so that we require a method for finding the most indicative explanation $\mathbf{e} \in E_C$. Formally, we denote this method as $H_\theta(X)$ and describe a novel approach in Sect. 5.

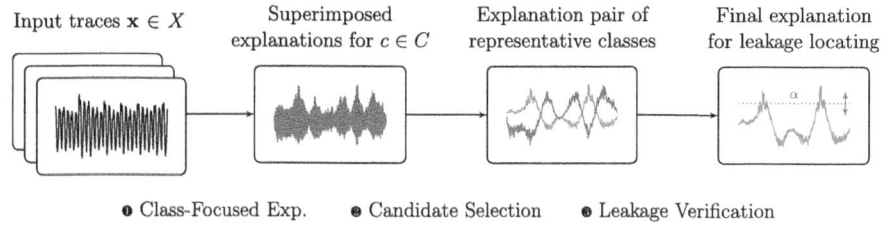

Input traces $\mathbf{x} \in X$ Superimposed   Explanation pair of   Final explanation
                       explanations for $c \in C$ representative classes   for leakage locating

❶ Class-Focused Exp.   ❷ Candidate Selection   ❸ Leakage Verification

Fig. 3. Schematic depiction of LeaX: We ❶ employ our class-focused explanation strategy, ❷ select two maximally contradicting groups of candidates, and ❸ verify which of those describe leakage by analyzing different cut-off thresholds α.

5   LeaX: Locating Leakage Using XAI

Our method LeaX determines the most indicative explanation $\mathbf{e} = H_\theta(X)$ that shows leakage points ("points of interest"), thus implementing the function H_θ on an attack dataset X. Often, there is not a single explanation, though, but a group of similar explanations that stand out so that we average across the most indicative candidates from E_C in practice.

Locating leakage with out method, LeaX, involves three steps as depicted in Fig. 3:

❶ We determine the class-focused explanations for all possible classes $c \in C$ as described in Sect. 4. We do so by averaging across an attack dataset of power traces X gathered from the clone device (Sect. 5.1).

❷ Interestingly, these (aggregated) class-focused explanations occur in two opposing groups with varying intensity. We choose the explanations that differ the most, yielding the most promising "explanation candidates" (Sect. 5.2).

❸ These candidates have low/high relevance values for the correct leakage points already. However, we cannot tell which one of the two is correct, so that we verify leakage by incrementally removing least to most relevant time samples (according to the explanations) and inspect the progression of attack success. Only the candidate yielding more effective attacks across increasing α indicates the correct leakage points (Sect. 5.3).

5.1   Class-Focused Explanations

While the reasoning for class-focused explanations is based on difficile details of side-channel analysis (cf. Sect. 4), the computation itself is rather straightforward. However, the specific choice of the used explanation method h_θ is crucial, though: We require so-called class-discriminative explanation methods as we strive to focus on the involved classes (and their individual prediction scores). Interestingly, most explanation methods are *not* class-discriminative.

Methods such as Simple Gradients [31], SmoothGrad [32], or "Layer-wise Relevance Propagation" (LRP) [2,23] indicate features relevant to the decision *but* do not focus on features distinguishing it from other classes [11]. Consequently, these are unsuitable for our use case. There exist class-discriminative extensions to some of the mentioned methods, though, e.g., "Softmax Gradient LRP" (SGLRP) [14] or "Contrastive Layer-wise Relevance Propagation" (CLRP) [11]. For LEAX, we use the latter and provide further details below.

In our evaluation (cf. Sect. 6.3), however, we show results for both variants (LEAX with CLRP and SGLRP) to shed light on the differences in practice.

Contrastive Layer-Wise Relevance Propagation (CLRP). As the name suggests, CLRP [11] builds upon LRP [2,23], which is founded on the so-called conservation property, stating that the relevance of all the units of a neural network's layer l need to sum up to the relevance values of all the units in the next layer $l + 1$ for all L layers of the network:

$$\sum_i R_i^{(1)} = \sum_i R_i^{(2)} = \ldots = \sum_i R_i^{(L)}.$$

Here, $R_i^{(l)}$ denotes the relevance of unit i in layer l. LRP determines relevance for all classes, which unfortunately results in low sensitivity to the predicted class [11]. To highlight features for the target class, CLRP introduces negative values to non-target classes and conducts multiple runs of the above calculation. CLRP initialize the relevance values of the last layer as follows:

$$R_i^{(L)} := \begin{cases} g_\theta(\mathbf{x})_c & i = c \\ -\frac{g_\theta(\mathbf{x})_c}{|C|-1} & \text{otherwise,} \end{cases}$$

where $g_\theta(.)$ represents the logits of the neural network before any softmax operation. The currently investigated class is denoted as c, and $|C|$ refers to the total number of classes. Note that only the relevance for the particular class c is set to the model's output, and all remaining values of classes $c' \neq c$ are set so that the overall sum of relevance values is zero:

$$R_c^{(L)} + \sum_{c' \neq c} R_{c'}^{(L)} = 0.$$

This construction guarantees that features indicative for class c' are highlighted rather than other classes' features. Moreover, similarly to LRP, positive values mean that the features speak in favor of the classification of class c, while negative values (from the wrong classes' "penalty values") speak against it. Eventually, we will use positively valued input features for determining leakage points with LEAX as these speak in favor of the classification.

5.2   Candidate Selection

Due to the use of class-discriminative explanations and the aggregation of input traces, class-focused explanations $e \in E_C$ exhibit some interesting properties:

(1) Positive values that speak in favor of the classification and negative values that speak against the classification cancel each other out when averaged across classes $c \in C$. (2) Positive and negative values are spread out over the entire input range due to the noise involved in learning-based SCA attacks. Considering positive values only and averaging these, hence, is not helpful. Consequently, we have to indeed select one/some of the classes rather than average across E_C. (3) Class-focused explanations form opposing clusters with varying intensity, that is, we have multiple pairs of c_1 and c_2, so that $\mathbf{e}_{c_1} \approx -\mathbf{e}_{c_2}$. In other words, some explanations show very high while other explanations show very low relevance values for the same time samples.

The third and last property is crucial for identifying the most indicative class (representative) and its class-focused explanation, respectively. We calculate the pair-wise Euclidean distance for all explanations $\mathbf{e}_1, \mathbf{e}_2 \in E_C$ to find the opposing (groups of) explanations. We then choose the pair, P_{max}, with the largest distance. However, it may happen that doing so captures stark outliers that are not good candidates. We hence determine the l-nearest neighbors[1] [9] to form two groups/neighborhoods of explanations, E_{C1} and E_{C2}, that show similar explanation patterns. Finally, we use the center class of E_{C1} and E_{C2} as our explanation candidates $\mathbf{e}_a$ and $\mathbf{e}_b$, respectively, for the final step.

5.3   Leakage Verification

At this stage, the candidates $\mathbf{e}_a$ and $\mathbf{e}_b$ are equally likely, and we cannot decide based on the mere explanation output which one shows true leakage points. We, thus, take recourse to established techniques for evaluating XAI methods [13] and adapt them to class-focused explanations.

We follow the intuition that a learning-based attack will not succeed if we remove time samples that leak information from the considered input traces. Put differently, if we remove time samples that do *not* leak information, the attack still works. However, in learning-based SCA attacks, we may have multiple leakage points (e.g., repetitive leakage [4] or combined leakage [3]) that may serve as an indicator for the used key. Even worse, the machine-learning model may or may not consider this redundancy. Hence, the mere removal of certain time samples is insufficient.

We propose to take/keep presumably indicative (regions of) time samples according to a "take ratio" α while rejecting the rest and retrain an attack model on this data. We refer to this process as "Take and Retrain" (TART) that we describe below in more detail. Based on this, we then demonstrate how to identify the correct explanation candidate by observing attack performance over increasing values of α.

Take and Retrain (TART). We construct two datasets $X_{\mathbf{e}_a}$ and $X_{\mathbf{e}_b}$ based on the explanation candidates $\mathbf{e}_a$ and $\mathbf{e}_b$, and train separated models θ_a and θ_b on

---

[1] Note that we use the well-known k-nearest neighbors algorithm [9] but avoid using k to prevent confusion with the encryption key as used before.

these datasets. More specifically, we filter out time samples with low relevance according to a "take ratio" α yielding $T_{\mathbf{e}} = \{i \mid e_i > \alpha \cdot \max(\mathbf{e})\}$ for an explanation $\mathbf{e}$. This set of highly relevant time samples serves as a reference to judge which time samples (i.e., input features) to take/keep in the new datasets:

$$X_{\mathbf{e}} = \left\{ (x_i)_{i \in T_{\mathbf{e}}} \mid \mathbf{x} \in X \right\}.$$

For each candidate $\mathbf{e}_a$ and $\mathbf{e}_b$, we construct individual training datasets, $X_{\mathbf{e}_a}^{(train)}$ and $X_{\mathbf{e}_b}^{(train)}$, and attack datasets $X_{\mathbf{e}_a}$ and $X_{\mathbf{e}_b}$, respectively. While the former is used for training, the latter we use to measure the attack performance of the new models θ_a and θ_b. The model architecture remains identical except for the input size. Comparing the performances of these models then allows us to pick the candidate that shows the leakage points used by the original model.

Note that retraining on these datasets is crucial for the success of TART, and the original model must not be used to classify the modified data. Without retraining, it is impossible to tell whether the dataset modification itself causes a change in performance or it stems from the removed input features [13]. In other words, retraining allows the model to adapt to the changed dataset distribution.

Assuming $\mathbf{e}_a$ as the more suitable explanation, we have three possible outcomes of the final comparison of models:

1. One model performs a successful attack while the other does not:

$$Rank(k_i^*, \mathbf{v}_{X_{\mathbf{e}_a}}) = 0 \;\wedge\; Rank(k_i^*, \mathbf{v}_{X_{\mathbf{e}_b}}) \neq 0,$$

   where $\mathbf{v}_{X_{\mathbf{e}_a}}$ and $\mathbf{v}_{X_{\mathbf{e}_b}}$ are the "distinguishing vectors" of the respective models, and $Rank$ determines the averaged rank of the correct key byte k_i^* as discussed in cf. 2. A successful attack is indicated by a rank of 0, meaning that the model has learned the leakage correctly as revealed by the explanation candidate.
2. Machine-learning models do not necessarily capture redundancy if a subset suffices for successful prediction. In our scenario, a model may derive the correct key using one of multiple leakage points. This circumstance may lead to the situation where both models are successful:

$$Rank(k_i^*, \mathbf{v}_{X_{\mathbf{e}_a}}) = 0 \;\wedge\; Rank(k_i^*, \mathbf{v}_{X_{\mathbf{e}_b}}) = 0,$$

   which means that both explanations capture leakage points. Here, we are in favor of the explanation enabling faster rank convergences to 0.
3. Finally, it may happen that both models fail to derive the correct key:

$$Rank(k_i^*, \mathbf{v}_{X_{\mathbf{e}_a}}) \neq 0 \;\wedge\; Rank(k_i^*, \mathbf{v}_{X_{\mathbf{e}_b}}) \neq 0.$$

In this case, either the underlying explanation method cannot show the real leakage or the take ratio α is too restrictive/high.

Verification. For verifying explanation candidates, we repeat TART for different take ratios $\alpha \in [0, 1]$ applied to $\mathbf{e}_a$ and $\mathbf{e}_b$. We measure the average number of traces required for a successful attack (normalized to the attack budget n) indicated on the y-axis per take ratio on the x-axis and determine the area under this curve denoted as TART-AUCe$_a$ and TART-AUCe$_b$, respectively. The lower the ..., the preciser the explanation—thus, the explanation candidate yielding the lower value indicates the correct leakage points.

Obviously, the ...can only be approximated in discrete steps for increasing the α in practice. In the remainder of the paper, we thus use steps of 0.1. Examples are provided in Figs. 4, 5 and 6. *Note that the figures in the remainder of the paper show the absolute number of traces used on the y-axis rather than the normalized value to better compare the attack success to related work.*

6   Evaluation

In this section, we evaluate LeaX across different model structures and leakage scenarios. We begin by introducing the used datasets in Sect. 6.1, before presenting our main results of LeaX under different leakage scenarios in Sect. 6.2. Finally, the ablation study in Sect. 6.3 investigates the choices of LeaX's major components and elaborates on the insufficiency of key-focused explanations.

6.1   Experimental Setup

Benchmarks used in the SCA community typically consider implementations of the "Advanced Encryption Standard" (AES) [10] to compare side-channel attack methods. In our experiments, we apply our method to attack models from related work that use (a) convolutional neural networks (CNNs) [12,40][2] and (b) simple multi-layer perceptrons (MLPs) [36]. We evaluate LeaX on three datasets covering different types of leakage. Note that each dataset has a specific MLP and a CNN model, and that all models applied to demonstrate the general applicability of LeaX have been proposed in related work.

Datasets. In our evaluation, we cover three leakage types from varying software and hardware implementations described below:

1. *Combined Leakage* means that information from multiple, disjunct time frames must be combined to infer sensitive data. The hardware implementation from the ASCAD dataset [3] uses first-order masking so that the adversary requires both the mask r and the masked S-box output, $S(m_\mathbf{x} \oplus k^*) \oplus r$, to obtain the correct key.

---

[2] The model architecture for AES_HD is inspired by Zaid et al. [40]. It has one convolutional layer with kernel size 1 and a pooling size of 25. The model is trained *without* (0,1)-scaling [36].

2. *Single Leakage* refers to a situation where one specific time frame reveals sensitive information. The AES_HD dataset [25] shows power traces of an FPGA-based, unprotected (i.e., no masking) implementation, where leakage occurs through writing a register in the last round of the AES decryption.

3. *Repetitive Leakage* occurs if multiple time frames leak identical sensitive information. The DPA Contest v4.2 (DPA_v4) dataset [4] has been recorded based on a masked software implementation of AES for a smart card. Here, the masking values are know, so that the community [e.g., 25, 40] often treats it as unprotected implementation and reduces it to a subset of 4000 time samples per trace. Each input trace contains three groups of time samples that leak the S-box output in the first round of AES.

Among the public benchmark datasets, ASCAD dataset [3] is most commonly used for demonstrating machine learning-based side-channel attacks [3, 7, 18, 25, 39, 40] and explanation techniques in this domain [12, 22, 24, 38].

Learning Setup. We follow the common setup in deep-learning based SCA, where attack models are customized to each dataset. 90% of a training set (the "profiling dataset") is used for actual training and 10% for validation. Each benchmark dataset mentioned above additionally provides a test dataset to measure attack performance. The input traces are preprocessed to have zero mean and unit variance before training. For all datasets, we average the guessing entropy across 100 repetitions of the attack and shuffle the attack traces randomly for each experiment.

6.2   Explanation Performance

We apply LEAX to different MLP-based and CNN-based attack models [12, 36, 40] and use the same explanation parameterization/configuration across different datasets. More specifically, we use CLRP for ❶ class-focused explanation, set the number of nearest neighbors to 5 for ❷ candidate selection, and present explanation results indicated by ❸ leakage verification. The choice of these parameters is further explained in the ablation study in Sect. 6.3.

Combined Leakage. We show LEAX on the most commonly investigated dataset ASCAD [3] that records combined leakage where the mask and the masked output are required to infer sensitive data. We present results of LEAX on an MLP model [36] and CNN model [12] in Fig. 4 and discuss the details in the subsequent paragraphs.

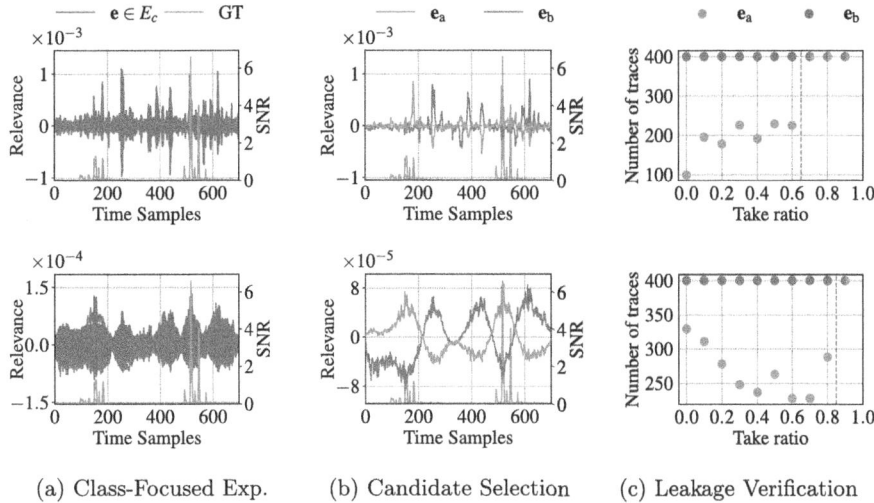

(a) Class-Focused Exp.   (b) Candidate Selection   (c) Leakage Verification

Fig. 4. Our method using CLRP for ASCAD on the MLP model [36] (top row), and CNN model [12] (bottom row).

MLP. Figure 4a (top row) shows class-focused explanations using CLRP for each class, that is, for each of the 256 possible key bytes. Based on these, LeaX's candidate selection obtains the representative explanation pair $(\mathbf{e}_a, \mathbf{e}_b)$ as presented in Fig. 4b (top row), that show opposing relevance scores across the x-axis. Consequently, only one of them can be correct.

We apply leakage verification with different take ratios $\alpha \in [0, 1]$ and present the attack performances in Fig. 4c (top row). Orange and blue dots represent models trained on time samples positively indicated by $\mathbf{e}_a$ and $\mathbf{e}_b$, respectively. When the take ratio α increases to 0.7 to construct $X_{\mathbf{e}_a}$, the attack fails as we start to exclude time samples corresponding to the masking at time sample 180. Therefore, there is not sufficient information to learn the real leakage based on $\mathbf{e}_a$ anymore. In contrast, when taking time samples based on $\mathbf{e}_b$, the trained models fail consistently across take ratios (blue dots in Fig. 4c top row). We use the attack budget of 400 traces to indicate failure.

In summary, leakage verification yields a ...for $\mathbf{e}_a$ and $\mathbf{e}_b$ of 0.64 and 1.0, respectively, indicating that $\mathbf{e}_a$ is the correct explanation. The presence of two peaks (close to time samples 180 and 514) in $\mathbf{e}_a$ suggests that we are dealing with a combined leakage scenario, where two distinct sets of leakage information are required for a successful attack.

CNN. Again, we show all class-focused explanations and the distilled representative explanations $(\mathbf{e}_a, \mathbf{e}_b)$ in Figs. 4a and 4b (bottom row), respectively. We then apply leakage verification to reveal which explanation matches the leakage. The attack performance in Fig. 4c (bottom row) shows that taking time samples based on $\mathbf{e}_a$ allows us to reliably identify the correct key, whereas $\mathbf{e}_b$ does not lead to a successful attack. We yield a ...for $\mathbf{e}_a$ and $\mathbf{e}_b$ of 0.70 and 1.0, respectively, indicating that $\mathbf{e}_a$ is the correct explanation. Also, $\mathbf{e}_a$ nicely overlaps with the ground truth visually. Only when the take ratio α equals 0.9, the critical leak close to time sample 149 (i.e., the mask) is omitted. Therefore, the model is unable to learn the correlation between traces and target classes.

Single Leakage. Next, we present how LEAX locates a single leakage on the AES_HD dataset [25] in Fig. 5. We show results on a MLP-based [36] and a CNN-based attack model [40] in three steps as before.

MLP. We retrained attack models based on $\mathbf{e}_a$ and $\mathbf{e}_b$, as extracted from the 256 class-focused explanations shown Fig. 5a (top row), using different take ratios $\alpha \in [0, 1]$. In Fig. 5c (top row), we present the number of traces on the y-axis needed to perform a successful attack for different values of α on the x-axis. Here, TART-AUC($\mathbf{e}_a$) = 0.55 and TART-AUC($\mathbf{e}_b$) = 0.96, meaning that selecting time samples based $\mathbf{e}_a$ highlights the leaking samples best. Visually, there also is a high peak in $\mathbf{e}_a$ close to time sample 960 in accordance to the ground truth.

CNN. Fig. 5 (bottom row) shows the three steps of LEAX. During leakage verification, we obtain TART-AUC($\mathbf{e}_a$) = 0.52 and TART-AUC($\mathbf{e}_b$) = 1.0, and thus, $\mathbf{e}_a$ as the correct explanation. This is a similar difference in attack performance between $\mathbf{e}_a$ and $\mathbf{e}_b$ as in the MLP model (cf. Fig. 5 top row). The results on MLP and CNN models demonstrate LEAX can address a single leakage scenario.

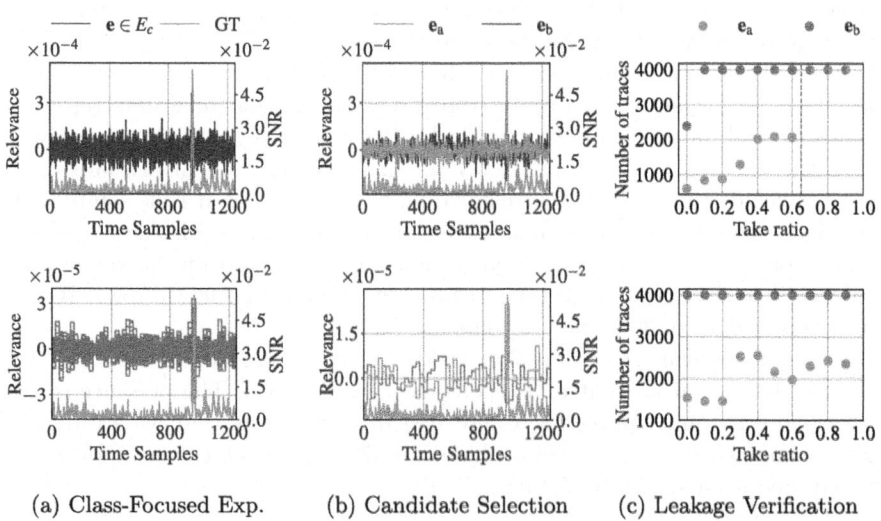

(a) Class-Focused Exp.   (b) Candidate Selection   (c) Leakage Verification

Fig. 5. LEAX using CLRP for AES_HD on the MLP model [36] (top row), and CNN model [40] (bottom row).

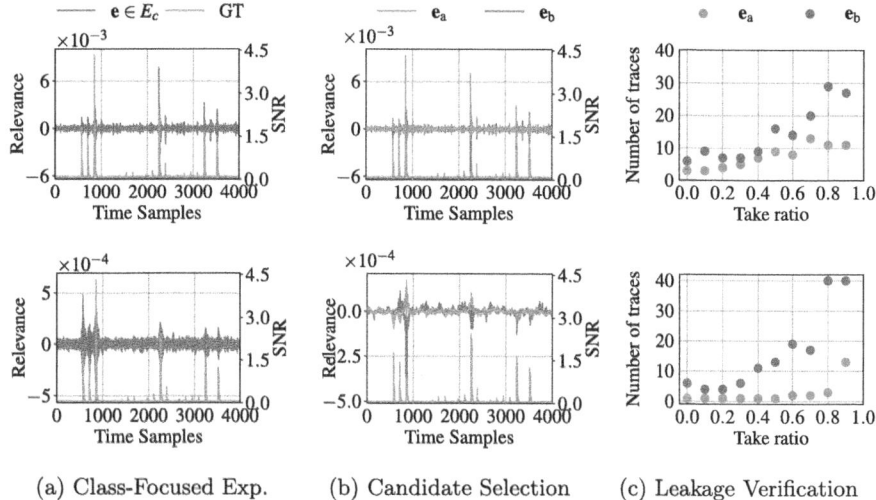

(a) Class-Focused Exp.   (b) Candidate Selection   (c) Leakage Verification

Fig. 6. LeaX using CLRP for DPA_v4 on the MLP model [36] (top row), and CNN model [12] (bottom row).

Repetitive Leakage. DPA_v4 dataset [4] has three groups of leakage representing the same information leak. We present the results of LeaX on an MLP model [36] and a CNN model [12] in Fig. 6.

MLP. After applying CLRP to all classes, we obtain a representative explanation pair $(\mathbf{e}_a, \mathbf{e}_b)$ as shown in Fig. 6b (top row). Leakage verification identifies $\mathbf{e}_a$ as the correct explanation, with a ...of 0.18. The explanation candidate $\mathbf{e}_b$, in turn, yields a ...of 0.36. As can be seen in Fig. 6c (top row), trimming time samples according to both explanations does not make the attack fail, indicating the presence of multiple leakages within the dataset.

CNN. Leakage verification for the selected candidates $\mathbf{e}_a$ and $\mathbf{e}_b$ (cf. Fig. 6b bottom row) yields TART-AUC$(\mathbf{e}_a) = 0.07$ and TART-AUC$(\mathbf{e}_b) = 0.40$, and thus, identifies $\mathbf{e}_a$ as the final explanation result. In Fig. 6c (bottom row), the model retrained on $X_{\mathbf{e}_a}$ always performs better than $X_{\mathbf{e}_b}$, meaning the model learns the leakage mainly from time samples close to 850.

6.3 Ablation Study

We proceed to analyze each component of LeaX, focusing on the influence of class-discriminative explanation methods and the cluster size used for candidate selection. Finally, we also discuss the insufficiency of key-focused explanations.

Class-Discriminative Explanations. To clarify why class-discriminative methods are crucial to class-focused explanations, we apply class-discriminative methods and not class-discriminative methods to explain all classes on the benchmark dataset ASCAD. Additionally, we investigate LEAX when using a method that is not class-discriminative, Grad × Input, and another class-discriminative method, SGLRP, and present the results in Fig. 7.

When using Grad × Input, LEAX yields a ...of 0.80 and 0.95 for e_a and e_b, respectively. The former thus is selected as the correct explanation. However, both ...values are relatively high, implying that both explanations are subpar. As shown in Fig. 7c (top row), the attack based on e_a fails with a take ratio of 0.4 already. Also visually comparing with the ground truth (cf. Fig. 7b top row) reveals that neither explanation candidate highlights the masked output at time sample 514.

For SGLRP, in contrast, leakage verification results in ...values of 0.62 and 0.99 for e_a and e_b, respectively, indicating e_a as the correct explanation. Explanations based on SGLRP are clearly more indicative: The TART-AUC(e_a) is significantly lower when using SGLRP than it was with Grad × Input. In Fig. 7b (bottom row), e_a again highly overlaps with the ground truth.

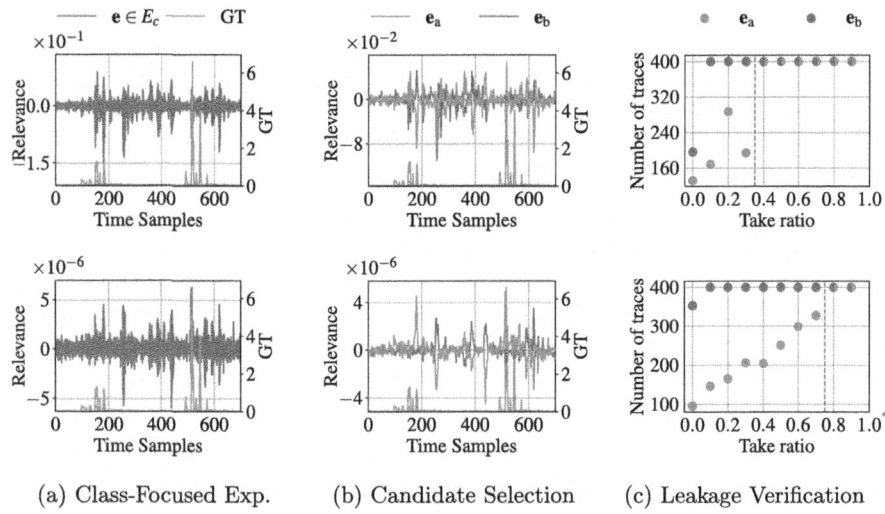

(a) Class-Focused Exp.   (b) Candidate Selection   (c) Leakage Verification

Fig. 7. LEAX using Grad × Input (top row) and SGLRP (bottom row) on the MLP model [36] for ASCAD dataset.

Size of Candidate Clusters. Assuming that high positive values in the explanation indicate high classification confidence, we select explanations of high relevance to indicate leakage time samples. Given the limited size of only 256 classes, exhaustively searching for suitable candidates emerged as a suitable options. Our candidate selection seeks to identify class pairs with the highest Euclidean distance P_{max} as potential representatives. Since explanations across different classes are similar, we use simple nearest neighbors clustering to find similar explanation groups based on P_{max}.

While the number of clusters is fixed to two (to find two opposing groups of explanations), we perform a grid search for the best neighborhood size in $[5, 10, 20, 40, 60, 80, 100, 120, 140]$. Interestingly, all these values perform reasonably well for locating leakage when selecting the center explanation. Averaging across classes, however, is not. The reason is that the larger the neighborhood gets, the more low-relevance explanations are included, flattening any explanation peaks present. In our experiments, we thus fix the neighborhood size to 5.

Insufficiency of Key-Focused Explanations. With the successful use of class-discriminative explanations, a natural thought is, if we can improve key-focused explanations using class-discriminative explanation also. We present two case studies: (1) using CLRP in key-focused explanations and (2) using LeaX's candidate selection based on key-focused explanations.

Case Study 1. We incorporate CLRP into the key-focused explanation strategy. Specifically, we choose the class corresponding to the correct key for each trace and aggregate the relevance scores to obtain $\mathbf{e}_{k_i^*}$ as described in Eq. (2). Figure 8 shows the key-focused explanations on MLP and CNN models retrieved this way. Both fail to indicate the correct leakage as compared to the ground truth. The explanation of the MLP points to non-leakage time samples $[200, 300]$ and $[600, 700]$, the one for the CNN highlights time samples $[200, 300]$ and $[400, 500]$.

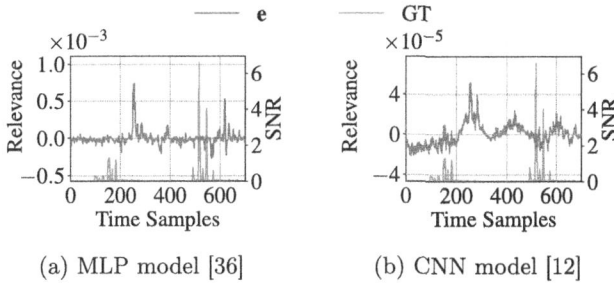

(a) MLP model [36]   (b) CNN model [12]

Fig. 8. Key explanations using CLRP on ASCAD with the correct key.

Case Study 2. Finally, we generate key-focused explanations for all 256 key hypotheses (i.e., $\mathbf{e}_{k_i} \in E_K$) and apply candidate selection to observe how well the explanation candidates align with the ground truth. Again, the key-focused explanation strategy fails to highlight leakaging time samples on MLP and CNN models. Compared to class-focused explanations, they simply are not as indicative. Key-focused explanations cannot help locate leakage even when equipped with class-discriminative explanations or LeaX's candidate selection.

7 Conclusion

Existing approaches for locating leakage points using learning-based attacks fall short in precision. We analyze the reasons and revisit the use of XAI techniques for this task. Two aspects are crucial: First, naively applying instance-based or model-based explanations is prone to fail as the accuracy of the SCA attack models is low in comparison to other classification tasks where XAI is applied. Second, accumulating explanations just like we do for attacks to compensate for low classification accuracy, in turn, must focus on the model's classes (the intermediate values) rather than the key, giving rise to *class-focused explanations*. The feasibility of class-focused explanations, however, is fundamentally dependent on class-discriminative explanations (e.g., CLRP). We have developed a thorough understanding of the relations of SCA attacks and traditional XAI techniques, effectively bridging disciplines. The resulting technique, LEAX, allows to precisely locate leakage, improving the state of the art decisively.

Acknowledgments. We gratefully acknowledge funding by the Helmholtz Association (HGF) within topic "46.23 Engineering Secure Systems."

Data Availability Statement. For the sake of reproducibility, we make the implementations of our method, LEAX, publicly available at:https://intellisec.de/research/leax.

References

1. Azouaoui, M., et al.: A systematic appraisal of side channel evaluation strategies. In: Proceedings of the International Conference on Security Standardisation Research (SSR) (2020)
2. Bach, S., Binder, A., Montavon, G., Klauschen, F., Müller, K.R., Samek, W.: On pixel-wise explanations for non-linear classifier decisions by layer-wise relevance propagation. PLoS ONE **10**(7), 1–46 (2015)
3. Benadjila, R., Prouff, E., Strullu, R., Cagli, E., Dumas, C.: Deep learning for side-channel analysis and introduction to ASCAD database. JCEN **10**(2), 163–188 (2020)
4. Bhasin, S., Bruneau, N., Danger, J., Guilley, S., Najm, Z.: Analysis and improvements of the DPA contest v4 implementation. In: Proceedings of the International Conference on Security, Privacy, and Applied Cryptography Engineering (SPACE) (2014)
5. Brier, E., Clavier, C., Olivier, F.: Correlation power analysis with a leakage model. In: Proceedings of the International Workshop on Cryptographic Hardware and Embedded Systems (CHES) (2004)
6. Cagli, E., Dumas, C., Prouff, E.: Convolutional neural networks with data augmentation against jitter-based countermeasures - profiling attacks without preprocessing. In: Proceedings of the International Workshop on Cryptographic Hardware and Embedded Systems (CHES) (2017)
7. Cao, P., Zhang, C., Lu, X., Gu, D., Xu, S.: Improving deep learning based second-order side-channel analysis with bilinear CNN. IEEE Trans. Inf. Forensics Secur. **17**, 3863–3876 (2022)

8. Chari, S., Rao, J.R., Rohatgi, P.: Template attacks. In: Proceedings of the International Workshop on Cryptographic Hardware and Embedded Systems (CHES) (2002)

9. Cove, T., Hart, P.: Nearest neighbor pattern classification. IEEE Trans. Inf. Theory **13**(1), 21–27 (1967)

10. Daemen, J., Rijmen, V.: The Design of Rijndael: AES - The Advanced Encryption Standard. Information Security and Cryptography, Springer, Berlin, Heidelberg (2002). https://doi.org/10.1007/978-3-662-60769-5

11. Gu, J., Yang, Y., Tresp, V.: Understanding individual decisions of CNNs via contrastive backpropagation. In: Proceedings of the IEEE/CVF Asian Conference on Computer Vision (ACCV) (2018)

12. Hettwer, B., Gehrer, S., Güneysu, T.: Deep neural network attribution methods for leakage analysis and symmetric key recovery. In: Proceedings of the International Conference on Selected Areas in Cryptography (SAC) (2019)

13. Hooker, S., Erhan, D., Kindermans, P., Kim, B.: A benchmark for interpretability methods in deep neural networks. In: Proceedings of the Annual Conference on Neural Information Processing Systems (NeurIPS) (2019)

14. Iwana, B.K., Kuroki, R., Uchida, S.: Explaining convolutional neural networks using softmax gradient layer-wise relevance propagation. In: Proceedings of the IEEE/CVF International Conference on Computer Vision (ICCV) Workshops (2019)

15. Kocher, P.C., Jaffe, J., Jun, B.: Differential power analysis. In: Proceedings of the Annual International Cryptology Conference (CRYPTO) (1999)

16. Kwon, D., Hong, S., Kim, H.: Optimizing implementations of non-profiled deep learning-based side-channel attacks. IEEE Access **10**, 5957–5967 (2022)

17. Lee, J.R., Kim, S., Park, I., Eo, T., Hwang, D.: Relevance-CAM: your model already knows where to look. In: Proceedings of the IEEE Conference on Computer Vision and Pattern Recognition (CVPR) (2021)

18. Lu, X., Zhang, C., Cao, P., Gu, D., Lu, H.: Pay attention to raw traces: a deep learning architecture for end-to-end profiling attacks. IACR TCHES **3**, 235–274 (2021)

19. Maghrebi, H., Portigliatti, T., Prouff, E.: Breaking cryptographic implementations using deep learning techniques. In: Proceedings of the International Conference on Security, Privacy, and Applied Cryptography Engineering (SPACE) (2016)

20. Mangard, S.: Hardware countermeasures against DPA – a statistical analysis of their effectiveness. In: Proceedings of the Cryptographers Track at RSA Conference (CT-RSA) (2004)

21. Massey, J.L.: Guessing and entropy. In: IEEE International Symposium on Information Theory (ISIT) (1994)

22. Masure, L., Dumas, C., Prouff, E.: Gradient visualization for general characterization in profiling attacks. In: Proceedings of the International Workshop on Constructive Side-Channel Analysis and Secure Design (COSADE) (2019)

23. Montavon, G., Lapuschkin, S., Binder, A., Samek, W., Müller, K.: Explaining nonlinear classification decisions with deep Taylor decomposition. Pattern Recogn. **65**, 211–222 (2017)

24. Perin, G., Ege, B., Chmielewski, L.: Neural network model assessment for side-channel analysis. IACR Cryptology ePrint Archive, p. 722 (2019)

25. Picek, S., Heuser, A., Jovic, A., Bhasin, S., Regazzoni, F.: The curse of class imbalance and conflicting metrics with machine learning for side-channel evaluations. IACR TCHES **2019**(1), 209–237 (2019)

26. Picek, S., Perin, G., Mariot, L., Wu, L., Batina, L.: SoK: deep learning-based physical side-channel analysis. ACM CSUR **55**, 1–35 (2023)
27. Prouff, E., Rivain, M.: Masking against side-channel attacks: a formal security proof. In: Proceedings of the Annual International Conference on the Theory and Applications of Cryptographic Techniques (EUROCRYPT) (2013)
28. Pundir, N., Park, J., Farahmandi, F., Tehranipoor, M.M.: Power side-channel leakage assessment framework at register-transfer level. IEEE Trans. VLSI **30**(9), 1207–1218 (2022)
29. Selvaraju, R.R., Cogswell, M., Das, A., Vedantam, R., Parikh, D., Batra, D.: Grad-CAM: visual explanations from deep networks via gradient-based localization. In: Proceedings of the IEEE/CVF International Conference on Computer Vision (ICCV) (2017)
30. Shelton, M.A., Samwel, N., Batina, L., Regazzoni, F., Wagner, M., Yarom, Y.: Rosita: towards automatic elimination of power-analysis leakage in ciphers. In: Proceedings of the Network and Distributed System Security Symposium (NDSS) (2021)
31. Simonyan, K., Vedaldi, A., Zisserman, A.: Deep inside convolutional networks: visualising image classification models and saliency maps. In: Proceedings of the International Conference on Learning Representations (ICLR) Workshop Track Proceedings (2014)
32. Smilkov, D., Thorat, N., Kim, B., Viégas, F.B., Wattenberg, M.: SmoothGrad: removing noise by adding noise. arXiv preprint arXiv:1706.03825 (2017)
33. Standaert, F., Malkin, T., Yung, M.: A unified framework for the analysis of side-channel key recovery attacks. In: Proceedings of the Annual International Conference on the Theory and Applications of Cryptographic Techniques (EUROCRYPT) (2009)
34. Timon, B.: Non-profiled deep learning-based side-channel attacks with sensitivity analysis. IACR TCHES **2019**(2), 107–131 (2019)
35. Wei, L., Luo, B., Li, Y., Liu, Y., Xu, Q.: I know what you see: power side-channel attack on convolutional neural network accelerators. In: Proceedings of the Annual Computer Security Applications Conference (ACSAC) (2018)
36. Wouters, L., Arribas, V., Gierlichs, B., Preneel, B.: Revisiting a methodology for efficient CNN architectures in profiling attacks. IACR TCHES **2020**(3), 147–168 (2020)
37. Wu, L., Perin, G., Picek, S.: Not so difficult in the end: breaking the lookup table-based affine masking scheme. In: Proceedings of the ACM Symposium on Applied Computing (SAC), vol. 14201 (2023)
38. Yap, T., Benamira, A., Bhasin, S., Peyrin, T.: Peek into the black-box: interpretable neural network using SAT equations in side-channel analysis. IACR TCHES **2023**(2), 24–53 (2023)
39. Zaid, G., Bossuet, L., Carbone, M., Habrard, A., Venelli, A.: Conditional variational autoencoder based on stochastic attacks. IACR TCHES **2023**(2), 310–357 (2023)
40. Zaid, G., Bossuet, L., Habrard, A., Venelli, A.: Methodology for efficient CNN architectures in profiling attacks. IACR TCHES **2020**(1), 1–36 (2020)
41. Zeiler, M.D., Fergus, R.: Visualizing and understanding convolutional networks. In: Proceedings of the European Conference on Computer Vision (ECCV) (2014)

Large Language Models Are Unreliable for Cyber Threat Intelligence

Emanuele Mezzi[1]([⊠])(iD), Fabio Massacci[1,2](iD), and Katja Tuma[3](iD)

[1] Vrije Universiteit Amsterdam, Amsterdam, The Netherlands
{e.mezzi,f.massacci}@vu.nl
[2] University of Trento, Trento, Italy
fabio.massacci@ieee.org
[3] Eindhoven University of Technology, Eindhoven, The Netherlands
k.tuma@tue.nl

Abstract. Several recent works have argued that Large Language Models (LLMs) can be used to tame the data deluge in the cybersecurity field, by improving the automation of Cyber Threat Intelligence (CTI) tasks. This work presents an evaluation methodology that other than allowing to test LLMs on CTI tasks when using zero-shot learning, few-shot learning, and fine-tuning, also allows to quantify their consistency and their confidence level. We run experiments with three state-of-the-art LLMs and a dataset of 350 threat intelligence reports and present new evidence of potential security risks in relying on LLMs for CTI. We show how LLMs cannot guarantee sufficient performance on real-size reports while also being inconsistent and overconfident. Few-shot learning and fine-tuning only partially improve the results, thus posing doubts about the possibility of using LLMs for CTI scenarios, where labelled datasets are lacking and where confidence is a fundamental factor.

1 Introduction

The number of vulnerabilities is becoming overwhelming: de Smale et al. [61] report that companies have reduced the raw intake of vulnerability information by 95%. In the quest to only do the work that really matters [17], Cyber threat intelligence (CTI) seems to be the new coping strategy. Unfortunately, despite standardization efforts such as STIX [5], TAXII [15], and MISP [65], CTI still requires humans to manage the massive amount of natural language information [49].

Large Language Models (LLMs) seem to be the solution to tame the CTI data deluge [57,58] compared to pre-trained language models (PLM) such as BERT, used to automate the identification of Advanced Persistent Threat (APT) attack events [10,71] and the extraction of knowledge graph (KG) [66]. Recent papers report high accuracy levels of LLMs processing CTI. Patsakis et al. [52] report 89% accuracy for extracting indicators of attack compromise and Hu et al. [27] used few-shot learning and fine-tuning in both named entity recognition and MITRE's Tactics, Techniques and Procedures classification, with precision

M. Dalla Preda et al. (Eds.): ARES 2025, LNCS 15993, pp. 343–364, 2025.
https://doi.org/10.1007/978-3-032-00627-1_17

Table 1. LLMs extracting CTI info: papers vs reality. LLM performance is strong when evaluated on inputs shorter than the abstract of this manuscript. However, in realistic scenarios involving full-length cybersecurity reports such as CISA's Emergency Directive 21-01 (SolarWinds) [14] or the 350 MITRE's APT reports analyzed in [17], averaging 3,009 words LLM performance degrades significantly due to the increased input length and complexity.

Dataset	Input type	Words	Precision
Wang et al. [68]	Sentence	20	0.89
Wang et al. [67]	Sentence	18	0.83
Fieblinger et al. [22]	Sentence	54	miss.
Hu et al. [27]	Paragraph	106	0.88
The abstract of this paper	Paragraph	174	-
Emergency Directive 21-01 (SolarWinds) [14]	Report	1764	-
Our evaluation	Report	**3009**	**0.76**

of 88% and 97%, respectively. Prompt engineering [9] and model benchmarking for CTI tasks [30] also produced promising results. CTI extraction is being augmented to use the LLM as a chatbot and requests to furnish information regarding a specific subject [21]. LLMs are known to hallucinate [28] but their CTI applications seem immune.

Unfortunately, *such promises are not based on real CTI reports*. Table 1 shows the lengths of inputs employed to perform CTI extraction, and compares them to the CISA's emergency directive on SolarWinds. Previous claims analyzed sentences instead of reports or at best small paragraphs, shorter than the abstract of this paper. Hence our first question:

RQ1: How do LLMs perform extraction on real CTI reports?

We use the open access datasets of reports by Di Tizio et al. [17] which includes 350 reports on all Advanced Persistent Threats (APT)s reported by MITRE up to 2020 (and therefore should be known to the LLMs). Real, raw reports are two orders of magnitude larger than what is tested on the considered papers. The last column of Table 1 leaks the answer to our evaluation: LLMs are not great. Few-shot learning, prompt engineering, and fine-tuning do not significantly improve the results.

A different dimension of analysis is the consistency in the presence of repeated questions which is critical if the LLM is to be used as a chatbot. LLMs' output generation is potentially not deterministic [40,62] and the possibility of receiving different results when extracting information from the same CTI report, poses severe risks in CTI such as for patch management.

RQ2: How to evaluate the CTI consistency of LLMs?

Finally, even if the LLM may hallucinate overconfidently [73] we would like to have an estimate of its uncertainty which is normally required when reporting risks [24]. This analysis is also not reported in related work [22,27,36,62].

RQ3: Are LLMs over(under)confident when making predictions in CTI?

To address these challenges we: 1) design and deploy a novel evaluation pipeline to test the effectiveness, consistency and confidence calibration of LLMs for pre-attack CTI practices by extracting information from CTI reports and generating information regarding APTs, 2) run a validation experiment leveraging an existing open-source dataset consisting of 350 threat intelligence reports structured in STIX standard [17] as ground truth where we evaluate OpenAI, Google, and Mistral LLMs, 3) presents the result of the analysis on (i) the ineffectiveness of few-shot learning and fine-tuning for CTI, (ii) the inconsistency of LLMs, when used for information generation, and (iii) the low LLM confidence calibration in the extraction and generation of CTI information.

1.1   Threat Model and Non-Goals

A current focus of LLMs security research [60] is to implement adversarial attacks on LLMs such as prompt injection [23] and data poisoning [11] whose goal is to alter LLMs' behaviour by deceiving them into making incorrect predictions. The corresponding mitigation measures to prevent adversarial attacks [13], include adding guardrails that can control LLMs output avoiding harmful outputs [56].

While interesting, we consider it a *non-goal* of our study, because there are already big security problems without calling attackers into play. We show that (uncompromised) LLMs may jeopardize the security of organizations using them to summarize CTI due to lack of consistency [73] and calibration [62]. The intuitive cause is that real reports contain additional information besides the entities which the LLM must retrieve. While a report concerns a particular attack scenario which involved a specific APT, the vulnerabilities they exploited, and the attack vectors they used in that particular scenario, it often contains information about other APTs that might have used the same vectors in other occasions or other attack vectors used by the same APT in other scenarios. The irrelevant information in the report is easily confused as relevant and thus raises the number of False Positives (FPs) and False Negatives (FN).

2   Examples of Unreliable LLMs in CTI

Longer Reports, Worse Output. The analyst prompts the LLM with the following instructions: *Given the following CTI report, extract the name of the APT, the starting date of the campaign, the CVE of the vulnerabilities exploited and the attack vector employed.* However, the final result can be compromised by the ambiguity of natural language CTI reports, shown in Figure 1, that makes automated extraction of CTI challenging. The correct (human) interpretation of this information is that spear-phishing links are the attack vector (as shown in

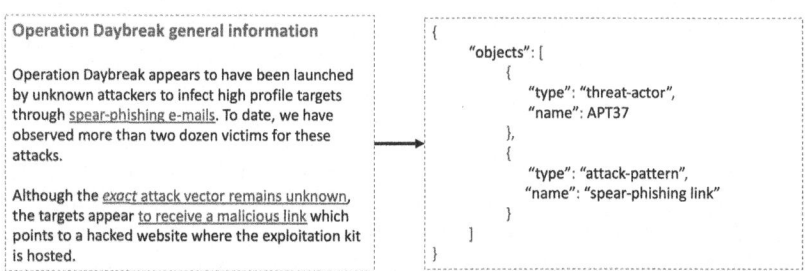

Fig. 1. Excerpt of a CTI report (top) and STIX format (bottom). CTI reports can deceive tools by conveying contradictory information: **spear-phishing link** or **unknown attack vector**? The text fragment shown in the picture is extracted from a report about a campaign by APT37.

the STIX format), but if taken out of context, the CTI report can be contradictory. This ambiguity, which can be reduced on small-size reports, forces to evaluate LLMs on real-size threat reports, to avoid the capacity of the models being overestimated due to the evaluation on small reports that do not represent the complexity of real CTI documents. Figure 2 shows the effects of report length on the LLM performance. The user prompts the LLM first by giving in input a paragraph of a threat report. The result reported by the LLM is perfect, as all the requested entities are extracted. The user then asks to repeat the same task with a complete report, and the result is disappointing, as the APT and starting date of the attack campaign should be one, thus raising the FP.

Ask Twice and Patch Two Different CVEs. It is possible that when the user prompts the LLM twice with the same instructions the information extracted differs between the two iterations [62,72], creating uncertainty in the patching steps. If we focus on the information regarding the vulnerabilities, this lack of determinism brings uncertainty concerning the CVE that is necessary to patch, thus delaying the fixing process. However, the delay in patching the right vulnerabilities will result in a higher chance of being attacked [18]. A key information is assessing the type of threat actor (e.g. nation-state actor or criminal organization), as that implies different attacker resources, and requires proportional defences [46]. Lack of consistency in this type of information can have ominous consequences.

(Un)sure about the (Right)Wrong CTI. When an LLM is employed it associates a number corresponding to the confidence about the predicted token(s). For example, the LLM may associate confidence of 0.90 for the *APT* K3chang and 0.20 to the *CVE* CVE-2014-6321. Model confidence is the parameter used to decide whether to accept or not the prediction when no dataset is available. Model confidence can only be trusted if the model is calibrated: the estimated probabilities are then representative of the true correctness likelihood [25]. When automated CTI pipelines blindly rely on the model confidence level, we do not know whether a high/low confidence value is justified or the model is over or

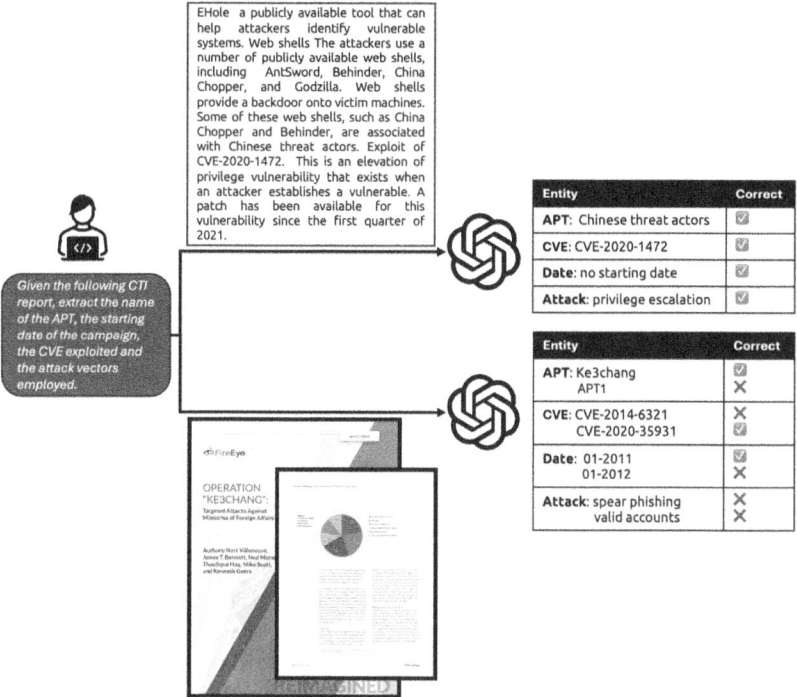

First, the analyst inputs the LLM with a paragraph of a threat report and the LLM extracts all the information contained in it. Then, the input consists of the entire report. Even though the input is better in terms of completeness, the result is worse as the number of FP and FN rises. The LLM is thus unable to distinguish the important information from the irrelevant ones.

Fig. 2. More Information, worse output.

underconfident. The model could return medium to high confidence levels about a specific APT extracted from a CTI report. An automated CTI pipeline does not know if the model is overconfident, and thus if the high confidence expressed reflects the true correctness likelihood. The model might be attributing an attack campaign from a report to a threat actor that probably did not implement it, *introducing false positives*. The opposite case is also possible. If the model returns low confidence regarding an extracted vulnerability, an automated CTI pipeline will likely discard the prediction. If the model is underconfident, the confidence level does not reflect the true correctness likelihood. Thus, an automated pipeline may discard the prediction regarding a vulnerability that could be correct with a higher chance, *raising the number of false negatives* and thus leading to failing to repair a vulnerability that can be attacked in the future [3].

3   Related Work

We searched on Scopus for all papers with CTI keywords and either NLP or LLM over the last five years.

NLP and LLMs in CTI. The increasing scale and complexity of cyber attacks lead to the necessity to automate CTI practices and sharing [4,7,38]. Thus, researchers invented formats to structure datasets containing CTI, which can be used to test new emerging methodologies for the automation of CTI analysis. Some datasets can be employed for specific tasks such as named-entity recognition (NER) in CTI, such as [42,67]. Other general-purpose datasets can be employed for KG extraction [2,68]. Husari et al. [29], propose an NLP-based analysis to reconstruct the chains of the attacks composed by the actions performed by the APT. In contrast, Zhang et al. [75] propose EX-Action a framework to extract threat actions from cyber threat reports. Abdi et al. [1] propose an NLP-based system to automatically highlight a CTI report with the responsible actor. Important tools offered by the world of NLP to researchers consist of PLMs and LLMs. One of the first activities to which PLMs were applied was called entity recognition in cyber threat reports. Quiao et al. [55] employs BERT-based models to annotate nine different categories of entities. Researchers also employed LLMs to help analysts respond to incoming attacks or threat campaigns, for instance automating the labelling of network intrusion detection systems rules, and the consultation of frameworks such as ATT&CK and D3FEND [16]. Researchers also tested the capacity of LLMs to automate the generation of threat reports [53] or to retrieve recovery steps from threat reports [36]. Finally, researchers employ PLMs [32,45,59] and LLMs [41] to extract entities and connections from threat reports, thus automating the operation of KG extraction. Fieblinger et al. [22], Hu et al. [27], and [41] tests LLMs on the task of KGs from cyber threat reports reporting promising performances. LLMs are also starting to be employed as CTI assistants to assign the correct CWE to a specific CVE [21,44]. Current approaches that employ LLMs for CTI extraction from threat reports show promising performance. However, they test LLMs on single sentences and report paragraphs that are less complex than real-size reports. Moreover, even though LLMs are starting to be used as CTI assistants, there is still the necessity to perform proper evaluation. In this work, we address this gap by evaluating LLMs in the task of information extraction on real-size reports and in the task of CTI assistants that will build the APT profile given the given APTs' names.

Consistency Quantification in LLMs. Considering the lack of determinism of LLMs [28,62], a complete branch of research is dedicated to quantifying the consistency characterising their outputs [20,72,74]. It is possible to highlight two categories of consistency quantification in the realm of LLMs, where the first concerns the general characteristics of LLMs as free-form generation, while the second looks a the capacities of the LLMs regarding more limited and close-ended applications such as classification and information extraction. Examples of the first case are the scientific research published by Kuhn et al. [37] who introduce the concept of semantic entropy, helping to measure the uncertainty

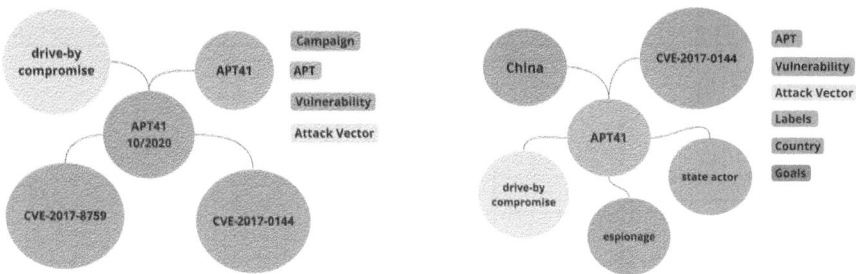

(a) KG extracted from CTI reports.   (b) KG from information generation.

Figure 3a and Figure 3b picture the graphs created when extracting information from cyber threat reports and generation information from the names of APTs. The graph resulting from information extraction is characterized by the entity *Campaign* that is composed by the name of the APT and by the starting date of the campaign, while the graph resulting from information generation is characterized by the *country* of origin of the APT, by its *goals* and by its *labels* which correspond to the type of APT.

Fig. 3. KG extracted (a) and generated (b) when performing CTI tasks.

regarding sentences and outputs which have the same meaning, and Lin et al. [40] who propose different metrics to evaluate the uncertainty in black-box LLMs. Examples of the second path of research can be seen in the scientific articles written by Wang et al. [69], concerned with uncertainty quantification in the realm of text-regression, and in the research carried on by Jiang et al. [31] and Kamath et al. [33], concerning uncertainty quantification in the case of PLMs employed for question answering. Current approaches in CTI measure performance with point value metrics and do not consider issues due to a lack of determinism. We address this gap and present an evaluation step that quantifies LLM consistency.

Calibration in LLMs. Lack of calibration is a characteristic of contemporary Deep Learning (DL) models [25]. However, even though new methods to improve calibration for LLMs have been suggested [73], in security this is still an unexplored problem. To the best of our knowledge, only one article explored LLMs' calibration and how to improve it for code generation [63]. Lack of calibration can have consequences in case LLMs are deployed in the absence of a labelled dataset, where the prediction confidence is used to choose whether to consider or discard their predictions. No previous work analysed calibration when LLMs are involved in CTI tasks. We address this gap by performing a calibration analysis to determine whether LLMs are (under)overconfident.

4   Overview of the Approach

We design our five-step evaluation pipeline for two critical tasks.

Information Extraction. When the LLM is given a *single* unstructured CTI report it is asked to extract entities from this report such as the APT the report is about or the attack vector it has exploited according to the report. This task

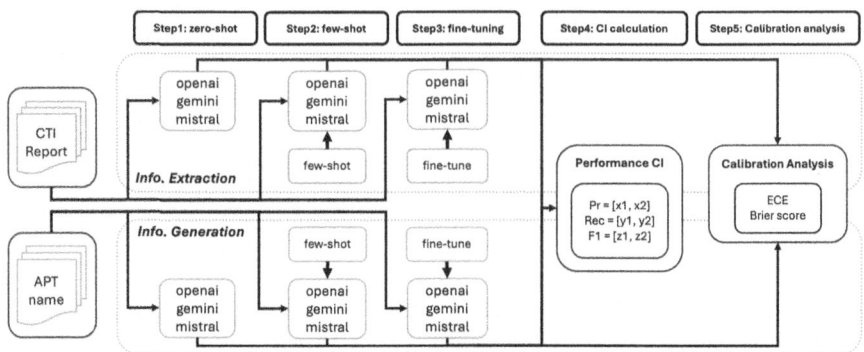

Each evaluation step involves two selected CTI tasks: information extraction from threat reports and information generation from APT names, respectively represented by the orange and the green frame. The 1st step evaluates LLMs with zero-shot learning, the 2nd with few-shot learning, and the 3rd after fine-tuning the model. Performance is registered as point values. In the 4th step, we quantify LLM performance consistency by calculating performance confidence intervals (CI). During the 5th step, we compute the expected calibration error (ECE) and Brier Score (BS).

Fig. 4. Illustration of the LLMs evaluation.

is essential to transform natural language text into a structured format such as STIX. Figure 3a, shows an example of the expected outcome.

Information Generation. When the LLM is asked to provide information related to an APT (e.g., the used attack vectors, the country of origin etc.) based on the knowledge embedded in its weights. Figure 3b shows an example output.

Figure 4 shows the evaluation steps. The first step consists of evaluating each LLM with zero-shot learning. The second step uses few-shot learning. To control for *prompt overfitting*[1], we evaluate the LLMs on the part of the dataset from which we do not gather any few-shot examples, mimicking the division between train and test datasets, and checking whether the model can generalize from given examples. The same approach is performed for fine-tuning: we fine-tune the LLM on the dedicated dataset section and then test it on the remaining part of the dataset. The fourth step calculates the confidence intervals (CIs) regarding the performance, and quantifies the oscillation in model performance, an aspect overlooked in previous work evaluating LLMs on CTI tasks [22,27].

Precision and recall are sufficient only when models can be evaluated with a labelled dataset. When models must be used in real-world scenarios, knowledge regarding calibration is needed to know whether the predictions can be trusted [63]. The fifth step consists of deriving model confidence by analyzing the log

---

[1] With prompt overfitting, we refer to the case in which an LLM can perform well on the data from which the few-shot examples that enrich the prompt are gathered, but it is not able to use those few-shot examples to generalize its performance to data samples that do not contain those same few-shot examples [12].

probabilities generated by the LLMs. We can thus check whether the models are calibrated and whether few-shot learning and fine-tuning improve the calibration level, an aspect overlooked in previous work on LLMs for CTI [22,27,36,64].

5   Evaluation Metrics

Traditional Metrics of Performance. For evaluating the impact of the size of the report we use the traditional metrics used in the literature (See Sect. 3 and Table 1): *Precision* $P = \frac{TP}{TP+FP}$ is the portion of extracted elements of a specific class which were correctly extracted; *Recall* $R = \frac{TP}{TP+FN}$ is the portion of elements of a specific class which have been extracted by the model; *F1* is the harmonic mean of precision and recall.

Confidence Intervals. We measure the consistency of LLM output when prompted several times with identical inputs. To obtain measures beyond point estimates, we build confidence intervals from our observations by relying on a multi-sample method [37]. We draw sample values from the population with bootstrapping [19] with replacement, and calculate the sample mean. We repeat this process where n is the population size and k is the size of the sample drawn. Then, we create a list with the sample means, the 5th and 95th percentile (lower and upper bound of the interval).

Calibration Metrics. We evaluate the LLMs calibration with expected calibration error (ECE) and Brier score (BS). The ECE [48] and BS [6], are two measures of calibration that quantify the deviation from perfect calibration. From Jiang et al. [31], given an input X and true output Y, a model output $\hat{Y}$, and a probability $PN(\hat{Y}|X)$ calculated over this output, a perfectly calibrated model satisfies the condition:

$$P(\hat{Y} = Y | PN(\hat{Y}|X) = p) = p, \forall p \in [0,1] \tag{1}$$

which is that the confidence p of the model, corresponding to the calculated probability of its prediction that the output is $\hat{Y}$, equals the empirical fraction p of the cases where the actual output Y correctly matches the prediction $\hat{Y}$ [63]. The best obtainable value for ECE and BS is zero, indicating perfect calibration. The higher the value is, the lower the calibration.

6   Experimental Pipeline

Prompt Preparation. To ensure the quality of the prompts we rely on the practices from prompt engineering (Table 2). The techniques used are role specification, which instructs the LLM to embody the role of CTI analyst, input subdivision and step specification, which allows to specify a different task for each section of the prompt. We apply world closing by reducing, based on the dataset in [17], the possible values that entities can be assigned to by the LLM during information extraction and generation.

Table 2. Prompt engineering techniques employed taken from [9,50].

Technique	Description	Example
Role specification	Instructing the LLM on the role.	`You are a Cyber Threat Intelligence (CTI) analyst.`
Step specification	Specify the steps required to accomplish a task.	`Step 1 - Extract the starting date of the campaign, the Advanced Persistent Threat (APT), the CVE codes of the vulnerabilities exploited by the APT ...`

Input subdivision	Split the steps into different and separated sections.	`Step 2 - Return the information filling in this JSON format:`
		`"nodes": {`
		`    "APT": [{"name": ""}],`
		`    "attack_vector": [{"name": ""}], ...`

World closing	Reducing the values an LLM can assign to an entity, indicating the possible alternatives.	`The name of the attack vector can only be one of the following: drive-by compromise, supply chain compromise, spear-phishing via service, spear-phishing attachment ...}`

Few-shot learning	Providing a small number of labelled examples to the LLM from which it can generalize.	`Examples to understand which attack vector the APT used.`
		`- ... employed legitimate user credentials`
		`    to access its targets: valid accounts.`
		`- ... has been linked to a watering hole`
		`    attack: drive-by compromise. ...`

Zero-Shot Learning. We evaluate the capacity of the LLMs to perform the selected tasks without providing any examples through the prompt to help the LLM to extract and classify the information contained in the threat reports or the description of the APTs [35]. To perform information extraction, the LLM receives in input the prompt which instructs it regarding the entities to extract, and the cyber threat report from which they are to be extracted. For information generation, the LLM receives in input the name of the APT, the description of the APT, and the instructions indicating the information to recover.

Few-Shot Learning and Fine-Tuning. In the second and third steps, we repeat the tasks, by applying few-shot learning [8] and fine-tuning [47], measuring to what extent these techniques affect the performance of the LLMs for information extraction and generation. To implement few-shot learning for information extraction and generation, we respectively extract few-shot examples from threat reports and APTs' descriptions. We evaluate the LLMs on the dataset section from which few-shot examples were not extracted, to ensure that prompt over-fitting is avoided. To fine-tune LLMs we randomly select a portion of the threat reports and APTs' descriptions and create the training dataset composed of the prompts and the correct answers to be generated. At the end of the fine-tuning, we evaluate the models on the test dataset, consisting of the dataset section not

Table 3. Dataset [17] key Indicators.

Entities	Num	Report Size	
		Mean	Max
# of reports	350		
# Campaign	350	# words 3 009	21 569
# APT	86	# tokens 4 002	27 794
# Vulnerability	123		
# Attack Vector	170		
# Country	17		
Max vulns/campaign	6		
Max attack vectors/campaign	4		

used for the training. We rely on supervised fine-tuning (SFT) [51] instead of more recent techniques based on reinforcement learning, such as Reasoning with REinforced Fine-Tuning (REFT) [43] as they suffer from reward hacking.

Generation of Confidence Intervals (CI). Since LLMs suffer from a lack of determinism [62], our evaluation measures their capacity to generate consistent results over multiple iterations. To this aim, we rely on a multi-sample approach [37,72], by repeating the process of information extraction and information generation multiple times on the same input, registering the performance and then generating CIs. For each task, we re-prompt each LLM ten times on the same input, with *temperature=0* and the same seed to guarantee maximum determinism, derive precision, recall, and f1-score, and then employ the bootstrapping method [19] to empirically build CIs. The bootstrapping method avoids assumptions over the distribution of data samples represented by metrics values gathered during the iterations. We re-prompt the LLM ten times to balance the necessity of checking for lack of consistency in model output with expense limits that would allow researchers to reproduce experiments.

LLM Calibration Analysis. In the last step, we analyse whether LLMs are calibrated regarding the selected CTI tasks. We perform this analysis for zero-shot learning, few-shot learning and the fine-tuned model, to check whether few-shot learning and fine-tuning help in improving model calibration in CTI tasks [34,63]. We implement calibration analysis by extracting the log probabilities that the LLM assigns to the tokens composing the generated response. Considering that the response is in the JSON format, and each field of the JSON file corresponds to a different entity, we isolate the tokens and the probabilities of each section of the JSON file corresponding to a specific entity, multiply the token probabilities of that JSON file section, and derive the overall confidence for each entity. Finally, we calculate the ECE [48] and BS [6], to measure the deviation from the ideal confidence level.

7   Dataset and Models

Dataset Selection. For our evaluation, we use the APT dataset from Di Tizio et al. [17]. We report in Table 3 the characteristics of interest for our study.

We have selected the dataset as it is open source, it has been manually curated for correctness and presents characteristics in terms of length of reports and heterogeneity that allow us to test the LLMs on real-size CTI reports. The dataset guarantees heterogeneity by selecting 86 of the 163 APT groups on the MITRE ATT&CK. The selected APTs are the ones that launched at least one campaign during 2008 and 2020. The amount of attack campaigns and thus of CTI reports is 350. Each CTI report is associated with the following entities that can be extracted: *APT, Campaign, Vulnerability,* and *Attack vector.* The *APT* is the actor responsible for the attacks, the *Campaign* is composed of the name of the APT responsible for the attacks and its starting date, the *Vulnerability* corresponds to the *CVE* codes of the vulnerabilities exploited by the APT, and the *Attack Vectors* are the techniques employed by the threat actor.

The origin and structure of the textual sources widely vary: from cyber threat reports written by cybersecurity providers to blog posts shared by cybersecurity enthusiasts. Other than the threat reports, the dataset is equipped with information regarding the 86 APTs. Each APT is associated with the *country* of origin of the APT, the *label* of the APT which refers to whether the APT is a criminal, a nation-state actor or a spy, its *goals* such as espionage, the *vulnerabilities* they exploited over their campaigns, and the *attack vectors* employed.

Dataset Division. We randomly select 70% of the dataset, thus mimicking the splitting which is typical of ML and DL model validations. In ML and DL, the splitting would have been in training, validation, and testing respectively in portions of 70%, 20%, and 10%. Since we do not train from scratch our model we assign 70% to the few-shot examples section and fine-tuning and 30% for the testing. We employ this division to avoid overfitting both for fine-tuning and for few-shot learning, if the few-shot examples are gathered directly from the dataset on which testing is conducted [12].

Models. We implement all the experiments by employing LLMs which are state-of-the-art at the time of writing, that can be fine-tuned, and for which it is available the JSON modality: *gpt4o* from OpenAI, *gemini-1.5-pro-latest* from Google, and *mistral-large-2* from Mistral, that can digest even the longest threat report given their large context windows (128k, 2M, and 128k tokens).

8   RQ1. Performance of LLMs in CTI

Tables 4 and 7 (in the Appendix) show the results related to the first research question for entity extraction and entity generation respectively. We test LLMs with zero-shot learning, few-shot learning, and after fine-tuning.

Information Extraction. Focusing on information extraction, Table 4 shows that zero-shot learning does not bring positive performance. Focusing on the

Table 4. Results for information extraction.

	Model	Zero-shot			Few-shot			Fine-tuning		
		P	R	F1	P	R	F1	P	R	F1
campaign	gpt4o	0.72	0.72	0.72	0.72	0.72	0.72	0.58	0.58	0.58
	gemini	0.77	0.77	0.77	0.73	0.73	0.73	0.61	0.61	0.61
	mistral	0.74	0.74	0.74	0.69	0.69	0.69	0.58	0.58	0.58
APT	gpt4o	0.87	0.87	0.87	0.84	0.84	0.84	0.68	0.68	0.68
	gemini	0.89	0.89	0.89	0.82	0.82	0.82	0.80	0.80	0.80
	mistral	0.89	0.89	0.89	0.82	0.82	0.82	0.68	0.68	0.68
CVE	gpt4o	0.67	0.87	0.76	0.74	0.92	0.82	0.71	0.69	0.70
	gemini	0.69	0.90	0.78	0.75	0.89	0.81	0.81	0.63	0.71
	mistral	0.72	0.90	0.80	0.79	0.91	0.85	0.71	0.69	0.70
attack vector	gpt4o	0.53	0.75	0.62	0.44	0.77	0.56	0.69	0.65	0.67
	gemini	0.68	0.74	0.71	0.71	0.78	0.74	0.89	0.84	0.87
	mistral	0.67	0.83	0.74	0.67	0.85	0.75	0.69	0.65	0.67

recall in the best case is equal to 0.90, when *gemini* and *mistral* retrieve CVEs, meaning that 10% of the vulnerabilities will be overlooked. Recall can be as low as 0.72 when *gpt4o* is employed to retrieve *campaigns* entities, thus overlooking 28% of the campaigns. Even more worrying is the lack of benefits of few-shot learning and fine-tuning. When applying few-shot learning the performance can decrease below the performance obtained with zero-shot learning. The maximum decrease is obtained when considering the *APT* specifically for the models *gemini* and *mistral* for which the performance decreases by 7.87% from 0.89 to 0.82. The decrease in performance means that employing LLMs for CTI tasks will cause overlooking *APT* names, *CVEs*, and *campaign* and thus to an error in comprehension of the scenario and in the attack attribution. The same and even worsened negative trend is evident when analyzing the performance model after fine-tuning. The table shows that the recall decreases as low as 0.58 from 0.72 when *gpt4o* is applied to retrieve *campaign*, leading to overlooking the 42% of the *campaign* entities. However, the worst decrease is obtained when *gpt4o* and *mistral* are used to extract *APT* names with precision and recall decreasing from 0.87 to 0.68, with a decrease of 21.84%.

Information Generation. Table 7 (in the Appendix) shows the results for information generation. Generally, the recall is considerably low, with the lowest level registered when the LLM is used to generate the type of *APT*, with 0.02 reached by *gemini* and *mistral*. The effect of few-shot learning and fine-tuning is limited and can also be detrimental, with the only exception represented by the *goals* entity. For few-shot learning, the maximum decrease in performance is obtained when *mistral* is used to generate the country of the threat actor, starting with precision and recall of 0.78 and ending with precision and recall of 0.64, and thus 36% of APTs' countries are wrongly predicted. Low performance is obtained when the LLM is fine-tuned. The worst case is represented by the application of *gpt4o* and *mistral* to generate *CVEs*, when the registered recall is 0.00, meaning that after fine-tuning the LLM is completely unable to generate and highlight the CVEs exploited by threat actors.

Table 5. Performance CI calculated with the bootstrapping techniques, for information extraction. LLMs lack complete determinism.

	Model	Few-shot			Fine-tuning		
		P	**R**	**F1**	**P**	**R**	**F1**
campaign	gpt4o	[0.69, 0.70]	[0.69, 0.70]	[0.69, 0.70]	[0.55, 0.56]	[0.55, 0.56]	[0.55, 0.56]
	gemini	[0.73, 0.74]	[0.73, 0.74]	[0.73, 0.74]	[0.58, 0.60]	[0.58, 0.60]	[0.58, 0.60]
	mistral	[0.67, 0.68]	[0.67, 0.68]	[0.67, 0.68]	[0.55, 0.56]	[0.55, 0.56]	[0.55, 0.56]
APT	gpt4o	[0.84, 0.84]	[0.84, 0.84]	[0.84, 0.84]	[0.66, 0.68]	[0.66, 0.68]	[0.66, 0.68]
	gemini	[0.84, 0.84]	[0.84, 0.84]	[0.84, 0.84]	[0.78, 0.79]	[0.78, 0.79]	[0.78, 0.79]
	mistral	[0.82, 0.82]	[0.82, 0.82]	[0.82, 0.82]	[0.66, 0.68]	[0.66, 0.68]	[0.66, 0.68]
CVE	gpt4o	[0.74, 0.74]	[0.89, 0.90]	[0.81, 0.82]	[0.72, 0.74]	[0.71, 0.74]	[0.72, 0.74]
	gemini	[0.74, 0.75]	[0.89, 0.89]	[0.80, 0.81]	[0.80, 0.81]	[0.62, 0.63]	[0.70, 0.71]
	mistral	[0.80, 0.81]	[0.91, 0.91]	[0.85, 0.85]	[0.72, 0.74]	[0.72, 0.74]	[0.72, 0.74]
attack vector	gpt4o	[0.42, 0.43]	[0.77, 0.77]	[0.54, 0.55]	[0.71, 0.73]	[0.67, 0.69]	[0.69, 0.71]
	gemini	[0.72, 0.73]	[0.77, 0.78]	[0.74, 0.75]	[0.90, 0.91]	[0.85, 0.86]	[0.87, 0.88]
	mistral	[0.66, 0.66]	[0.83, 0.84]	[0.73, 0.74]	[0.71, 0.73]	[0.71, 0.73]	[0.71, 0.73]

9   RQ2. Consistency of LLMs Output

Here we analyze the results concerning the consistency quantification for LLMs generated output. The larger the CI computed the lower the consistency. Thus, we attribute an LLM perfect determinism or perfect consistency when the width of the CI is zero, indicating that the LLM returns the same output given the same input over multiple iterations.

Tables 5 and 8 (in the Appendix) show the performance CI for the two tasks. For both tasks and most entities the LLMs are not consistent. Between the two tasks, information generation shows a greater lack of consistency. For information extraction in the worst case, the difference between the lower and upper bound of the CI is 0.02. The highest width can only be found between fine-tuned models, for instance when *gemini* is used to retrieve *campaign* with a precision and recall CI of [0.58, 0.60] with a difference between the lower and upper bound of 3.39% or when *mistral* is used to retrieve *CVE* codes, with precision and recall of [0.72, 0.74] and thus a difference between lower and upper bound of 2.74%.

For the task of information generation, the maximum difference between the lower and upper bound is 0.06, when few-shot learning is applied to *gemini* to generate *CVE* codes with a recall CI of [0.19, 0.25] and thus a 27.27% percentage difference between the lower and upper bound.

10   RQ3. Analysis of LLMs Calibration Level

The calibration analysis is performed by reporting the values of ECE and BS, which indicate the deviation of the model from perfect calibration. The best possible value for ECE and BS is zero, thus the higher their value the lower the calibration. Table 6 shows the results related to the calibration analysis.

Information Extraction. Few-shot learning is detrimental to the model calibration, as seen by the variations in the ECE and BS. An increase in ECE and BS is seen when considering *campaign* entity in which the ECE and BS increase from 0.25 and 0.26 to 0.26 and 0.28 respectively. The same can be seen for the *attack vector* where ECE and BS increase from 0.13 and 0.46 to 0.19 and 0.49. The *CVE* entity presents the worst increase for ECE and BS, as they increase from 0.28 and 0.32 when zero-shot learning is used to 0.35 and 0.37 when employing few-shot learning.

Also fine-tuning worsens the LLM calibration. The only exception that shows improvement is the *CVE* entity, which diminishes both the ECE and BS when evaluating the fine-tuned LLM. All the other entities worsen their performance, with the maximum increase reached by the *campaign* entity, which registers an ECE and BS of 0.48 when calculated on the fine-tuned model performance. An increase of 92% in ECE and 84.62% for BS, compared to the ECE and BS registered when zero-shot learning is applied.

Information Generation. The LLM employed for information generation offers a similar scenario. The only exception is the *goals* entity, in which few-shot learning and fine-tuning improve the ECE and BS. All other entities worsen their performance. An example of this pattern is the *labels* entity, which registers an ECE and BS of 0.45 and 0.44 when zero-shot learning is used, which rises to 0.57 and 0.53 when few-shot learning is used. This pattern is evident also for *attack vector* where the ECE raises from 0.47 to 0.48.

More concerning are the effects of fine-tuning on model calibration. The worst case is highlighted by the *CVE* and *attack vector* entity. For CVE the fine-tuned LLM registers an ECE and BS of 0.91 and 0.98 signalling a complete misalignment between performance and confidence level. For generation *attack vector*, the ECE and BS are 0.87 and 1.00 respectively rising from 0.47 and 0.43.

Table 6. ECE and BS with *gpt4o* for information generation and extraction.

	Information extraction						Information generation					
	Zero-shot		Few-shot		Fine-tuning			Zero-shot		Few-shot		Fine-tuning	
	ECE	BS	ECE	BS	ECE	BS		ECE	BS	ECE	BS	ECE	BS
campaign	0.25	0.26	0.26	0.28	0.48	0.48	goals	0.13	0.14	0.04	0.03	0.08	0.05
APT	0.16	0.15	0.17	0.15	0.25	0.23	labels	0.45	0.44	0.57	0.53	0.48	0.49
CVE	0.28	0.32	0.35	0.37	0.18	0.21	country	0.19	0.22	0.38	0.27	0.35	0.29
attack vector	0.13	0.46	0.19	0.49	0.27	0.58	CVE	0.15	0.29	0.13	0.22	0.91	0.98
							attack vector	0.47	0.43	0.48	0.42	0.87	1.00

11   Discussion

Regarding information extraction, we could see how for *campaign* entity the recall of each model is below 80%, meaning that the *campaign* entity is in more than 20% of the cases overlooked. Regarding the *CVE* codes we could see how the maximum recall is 0.90 (*gemini* and *mistral*) and the minimum is 0.87 (*gpt4o*), meaning that LLMs overlook at least the 10% of the vulnerabilities contained in the threat report and exploited during threat campaigns. The same phenomena concern *attack vector*, in which the maximum recall is 0.83 and the minimum is 0.74, meaning that 26% of the techniques used to exploit CVEs are overlooked. Few-shot learning and fine-tuning do not improve LLM performance and present detrimental effects after their use, as can be seen in Table 4 focusing on the maximum decrease brought by few-shot learning and fine-tuning of respectively 0.07 and 0.19 related to the *APT*.

The same pattern can be seen in information generation, when the LLM is used to recover the APT profile starting from its name and description, allowing to gather strategic and tactical information. The lowest recall and precision registered are 0.02 when the LLM is used to generate the label of the APT, meaning that the lack of knowledge regarding the type of APT (e.g., nation-state actor, criminal organization, etc.) is almost complete. Low and precision are also present when dealing with *CVE* entity as the minimum precision and recall are 0.10 and 0.06 (*gpt4o*) and the maximum precision and recall are 0.21 and 0.17 (*mistral*). With *country* entity the recall oscillates between 0.70 (*gpt4o*) and 0.78 (*mistral*), meaning that the best LLM in the 20% of the cases wrongly derives the country of an APT, leading to errors in the attribution of the cyber attacks. As for information extraction, the performance is rarely improved by the application of few-shot learning and fine-tuning, and their use can also be detrimental as shown by Table 7 (in the Appendix), where in the worst case few-shot learning decreases precision and recall of 0.14 (*labels* entity) and fine-tuning of 0.21 for precision and 0.17 for recall (*CVE* entity) leading to recall and precision of 0.00 when *mistral* generates CVEs exploited by APTs.

Our analysis highlights the (in)consistency of LLMs outputs. The repeated iteration and bootstrapping techniques are effective in building performance CIs that quantify LLM consistency. The computed CI show that in the task of information extraction from unstructured threat reports, LLMs lack complete determinism, with a maximum CI width of 0.02 (Table 5), posing an additional burden to their use in real-world environments, where repeated analysis could generate contradictory answers regarding the same threat report. Even larger lack of consistency, involves information generation, with a maximum CI width of 0.06, posing limitations to the use of LLMs as CTI chatbots and assistants.

Finally, our work shows that LLMs are not calibrated for CTI as shown by ECE and BSs. Few-shot learning and fine-tuning do not improve model calibration and can also be detrimental. The lack of calibration poses a third burden to using LLMs in real-world scenarios, where a labelled dataset is not available and thus the parameter used to accept or reject the model prediction consists of the confidence assigned to the information extracted or generated.

12 Limitations

Regarding the performance evaluation, a limitation is posed by evaluating LLMs on only one dataset, as evaluating LLMs on more intelligence reports would allow us to gain a deeper comprehension of the limitations posed by different types of CTI reports. We tried to handle this limitation by selecting a dataset characterized by great heterogeneity in terms of length and report source to reproduce a real-world scenario on which to test LLMs. Another limitation is posed by the limited number of LLMs, which we mitigated by choosing three state-of-the-art LLMs characterized by different architecture and from different providers.

Second, we consider limitations of the consistency quantification, where we highlight the cost-precision trade-off, as the higher the number of re-prompting the higher the precision and the higher the computational and economical costs. As we quantify the LLM consistency by re-prompting them ten times there is a risk of obtaining unreliable confidence intervals due to bootstrapping with a relatively small sample size. Raising the number of re-prompting would cause higher costs which would lead to the impossibility of reproducing the experiments. However, since the distribution of the samples is unknown, this is, to the best of our knowledge, the most appropriate method. We perform the calibration analysis only with *gpt4o* as it is the only closed-source model between the ones used that allows extracting log probabilities and thus calculating the confidence level assigned by the LLM to tokens. This characteristic of closed-source models also limits the application of post-processing calibration methods such as Platt Scaling which requires access to logits [25,54]. We chose closed-source models as they can be run directly on the cloud of proprietary companies, simplifying experiment reproducibility and reducing computational time and economic cost as open-source models need powerful and expensive hardware to be run [22].

13   Conclusion and Future Work

We show that LLMs are not ready for real-world CTI tasks. Regarding information extraction, performed on a dataset of real-size reports, given the low precision and recall, the performance cannot guarantee a faithful reconstruction of an attack scenario. Few-shot learning and fine-tuning does not seem to help. We observe the same pattern for information generation, used to build the profile of an APT, indicating that it would be risky to use LLMs as CTI assistants. A further worrying aspect consists in the performance oscillations measured and in the lack of calibration which further limits the trustworthiness posed in LLM predictions in a context where few evaluation datasets are available thus model confidence is a fundamental factor in choosing whether to rely on or not on model predictions.

In future work we plan to extend our experiments to other datasets, such as vulnerability databases, and to more LLMs, to generalize our results regarding the performance limitations that characterize them. Moreover, we plan to experiment with other prompting techniques such as Chain-of-Thought (CoT) [70], with other AI frameworks such as Retrieval Augmented Generation (RAG) [39] to improve information generation, and with approaches involving more than one LLM contemporarily, such as LLMs-based multi-agent systems [26]. Regarding measuring the consistency of LLMs, we plan to improve the empirical analysis by relying on the combination of different consistency quantification methods

[72] gaining more insights regarding the model's consistency. At the same time, we also plan to integrate the empirical work with a formal analysis, thus complementing the empirical investigation.

Acknowledgements. This work was partially supported by the *Nederlandse Organisatie voor Wetenschappelijk Onderzoek (NWO)* under the KIC HEWSTI Project under grant no. KIC1.VE01.20.004, and the Horizon Europe Sec4AI4Sec Project under grant no. 101120393.

Disclosure of Interests. The authors have no competing interests to declare that are relevant to the content of this article.

CRediT Author Statement. Conceptualization: EM, FM, KT; Methodology: EM; Software: EM; Validation: EM; Formal analysis: na; Investigation: EM; Resources: KT, FM; Data Curation: FM; Writing - Original Draft: EM, FM, KT; Writing - Review & Editing: FM, KT; Visualization: EM; Supervision: KT, FM; Project administration: FM, KT; Funding acquisition: KT, FM.

A   Additional Tables

Table 7. Results for information generation. Few-shot learning and fine-tuning have limited performance improvement and their effect can be detrimental, as we can see for the entities *country* and *labels*. When a fine-tuned model the performance considerably decreases, even under the performance obtained with zero-shot learning, as it happens with *CVE*, and *labels*.

	Model	Zero-shot			Few-shot			Fine-tuning		
		P	R	F1	P	R	F1	P	R	F1
goals	gpt4o	0.85	0.85	0.85	0.96	0.96	0.96	0.96	0.96	0.96
	gemini	0.72	0.72	0.72	0.83	0.83	0.83	0.84	0.84	0.84
	mistral	0.77	0.77	0.77	0.92	0.92	0.92	0.96	0.96	0.96
labels	gpt4o	0.50	0.50	0.50	0.44	0.44	0.44	0.44	0.44	0.44
	gemini	0.02	0.02	0.02	0.54	0.54	0.54	0.40	0.40	0.40
	mistral	0.02	0.02	0.02	0.36	0.36	0.36	0.44	0.44	0.44
country	gpt4o	0.70	0.70	0.70	0.56	0.56	0.56	0.60	0.60	0.60
	gemini	0.73	0.73	0.73	0.81	0.71	0.76	0.68	0.68	0.68
	mistral	0.78	0.78	0.78	0.64	0.64	0.64	0.60	0.60	0.60
CVE	gpt4o	0.10	0.06	0.08	0.08	0.07	0.07	0.00	0.00	0.00
	gemini	0.13	0.13	0.13	0.23	0.19	0.21	0.17	0.36	0.23
	mistral	0.21	0.17	0.19	0.24	0.24	0.24	0.00	0.00	0.00
attack vector	gpt4o	0.37	0.52	0.43	0.37	0.51	0.43	1.00	0.09	0.16
	gemini	0.24	0.54	0.33	0.27	0.56	0.36	0.52	0.84	0.64
	mistral	0.22	0.58	0.32	0.20	0.75	0.32	1.00	0.09	0.16

Table 8. Performance CI for the task of information generation.

	Model	Few-shot			Fine-tuning		
		P	**R**	**F1**	**P**	**R**	**F1**
goals	gpt4o	[0.96, 0.96]	[0.96, 0.96]	[0.96, 0.96]	[0.96, 0.96]	[0.96, 0.96]	[0.96, 0.96]
	gemini	[0.87, 0.90]	[0.87, 0.90]	[0.87, 0.90]	[0.84, 0.84]	[0.84, 0.84]	[0.84, 0.84]
	mistral	[0.92, 0.92]	[0.92, 0.92]	[0.92, 0.92]	[0.96, 0.96]	[0.96, 0.96]	[0.96, 0.96]
labels	gpt4o	[0.44, 0.44]	[0.44, 0.44]	[0.44, 0.44]	[0.44, 0.44]	[0.44, 0.44]	[0.44, 0.44]
	gemini	[0.54, 0.56]	[0.54, 0.56]	[0.54, 0.56]	[0.39, 0.40]	[0.39, 0.40]	[0.39, 0.40]
	mistral	[0.36, 0.36]	[0.36, 0.36]	[0.36, 0.36]	[0.44, 0.44]	[0.44, 0.44]	[0.44, 0.44]
country	gpt4o	[0.57, 0.59]	[0.57, 0.59]	[0.57, 0.59]	[0.60, 0.61]	[0.60, 0.61]	[0.60, 0.61]
	gemini	[0.82, 0.86]	[0.71, 0.74]	[0.76, 0.79]	[0.68, 0.68]	[0.68, 0.68]	[0.68, 0.68]
	mistral	[0.64, 0.64]	[0.64, 0.64]	[0.64, 0.64]	[0.60, 0.61]	[0.60, 0.61]	[0.60, 0.61]
CVE	gpt4o	[0.08, 0.09]	[0.07, 0.08]	[0.07, 0.08]	[0.00, 0.00]	[0.00, 0.00]	[0.00, 0.00]
	gemini	[0.21, 0.26]	[0.19, 0.25]	[0.20, 0.25]	[0.16, 0.19]	[0.32, 0.37]	[0.21, 0.24]
	mistral	[0.23, 0.24]	[0.24, 0.24]	[0.23, 0.24]	[0.00, 0.00]	[0.00, 0.00]	[0.00, 0.00]
attack vector	gpt4o	[0.37, 0.37]	[0.51, 0.52]	[0.43, 0.44]	[1.00, 1.00]	[0.09, 0.10]	[0.16, 0.18]
	gemini	[0.24, 0.27]	[0.55, 0.58]	[0.34, 0.36]	[0.49, 0.50]	[0.82, 0.84]	[0.61, 0.63]
	mistral	[0.20, 0.20]	[0.74, 0.75]	[0.31, 0.31]	[1.00, 1.00]	[0.00, 0.00]	[0.00, 0.00]

References

1. Abdi, H., et al.: Automatically labeling cyber threat intelligence reports using natural language processing. In: Proceedings of ACM DocEng-2023, pp. 1–4 (2023)
2. Alam, M.T., et al.: Looking beyond IoCs: automatically extracting attack patterns from external CTI. In: Proceedings of RAID-2023, pp. 92–108 (2023)
3. Ami, A.S., et al.: False negative - that one is going to kill you: understanding industry perspectives of static analysis based security testing. In: Proceedings of IEEE SS&P-2024, pp. 3979–3997. IEEE (2024)
4. Bairwa, A.K., et al.: Enhancing cyber threat intelligence and security automation: a comprehensive approach for effective protection. In: Proceedings of ISBM-2023, pp. 297–306. Springer (2023)
5. Barnum, S.: Standardizing cyber threat intelligence information with the structured threat information expression (stix). Mitre Corp. **11**, 1–22 (2012)
6. Brier, G.W.: Verification of forecasts expressed in terms of probability. Mon. Weather Rev. **78**(1), 1–3 (1950)
7. Bromander, S., et al.: Investigating sharing of cyber threat intelligence and proposing a new data model for enabling automation in knowledge representation and exchange. ACM DTRAP **3**(1), 1–22 (2021)
8. Brown, T., et al.: Language models are few-shot learners. Adv. Neural. Inf. Process. Syst. **33**, 1877–1901 (2020)
9. Chen, B., et al.: Unleashing the potential of prompt engineering in large language models: a comprehensive review. arXiv preprint arXiv:2310.14735 (2023)
10. Chen, J., et al.: Automatically identifying sentences with attack behavior from cyber threat intelligence reports. In: Proceedings of DSC-2023, pp. 491–498. IEEE (2023)

11. Chen, X., et al.: The Janus interface: how fine-tuning in large language models amplifies the privacy risks. arXiv preprint arXiv:2310.15469 (2023)
12. Cho, Y., et al.: Make prompts adaptable: Bayesian modeling for vision-language prompt learning with data-dependent prior. arXiv preprint arXiv:2401.06799 (2024)
13. Chowdhury, A.G., et al.: Breaking down the defenses: a comparative survey of attacks on large language models. arXiv preprint arXiv:2403.04786 (2024)
14. CISA: Emergecy directive 21-01: mitigate solarwinds Orion code compromise, Technical report, Cybersecurity and Infrastructure Security Agency (CISA) (2020)
15. Connolly, J., et al.: The trusted automated exchange of indicator information (taxii). The MITRE Corporation, pp. 1–20 (2014)
16. Daniel, N., et al.: Labeling NIDS rules with MITRE ATT&CK techniques using ChatGPT, pp. 76–91 (2024)
17. Di Tizio, G., et al.: Software updates strategies: a quantitative evaluation against advanced persistent threats. IEEE TSE **49**(3), 1359–1373 (2022)
18. Dissanayake, N., et al.: Why, how and where of delays in software security patch management: an empirical investigation in the healthcare sector. In: Proceedings of ACM CSCW2-2022, pp. 1–29 (2022)
19. Efron, B.: Bootstrap methods: another look at the jackknife. In: Breakthroughs in Statistics: Methodology and Distribution, pp. 569–593. Springer (1992)
20. Fadeeva, E., et al.: LM-Polygraph: uncertainty estimation for language models. arXiv preprint arXiv:2311.07383 (2023)
21. Ferrag, M.A., et al.: Generative ai and large language models for cyber security: all insights you need. arXiv preprint arXiv:2405.12750 (2024)
22. Fieblinger, R., et al.: Actionable cyber threat intelligence using knowledge graphs and large language models. In: Proceedings of IEEE EuroS&PW-2024, pp. 100–111. IEEE (2024)
23. Greshake, K., et al.: Not what you've signed up for: compromising real-world LLM-integrated applications with indirect prompt injection. In: Proceedings of ACM AISec-2023, pp. 79–90 (2023)
24. Guikema, S.: Artificial intelligence for natural hazards risk analysis: potential, challenges, and research needs. Risk Anal. **40**(6), 1117–1123 (2020)
25. Guo, C., et al.: On calibration of modern neural networks. In: International Conference on Machine Learning, pp. 1321–1330. PMLR (2017)
26. Guo, T., et al.: Large language model based multi-agents: a survey of progress and challenges. arXiv preprint arXiv:2402.01680 (2024)
27. Hu, Y., et al.: LLM-TIKG: threat intelligence knowledge graph construction utilizing large language model. Comput. Secur. **145**, 103999 (2024)
28. Huang, L., et al.: A survey on hallucination in large language models: principles, taxonomy, challenges, and open questions. arXiv preprint arXiv:2311.05232 (2023)
29. Husari, G., et al.: Learning APT chains from cyber threat intelligence. In: Proceedings of HotSoS-2019, pp. 1–2 (2019)
30. Ji, H., et al.: SevenLLM: benchmarking, eliciting, and enhancing abilities of large language models in cyber threat intelligence. arXiv preprint arXiv:2405.03446 (2024)
31. Jiang, Z., et al.: How can we know when language models know? On the calibration of language models for question answering. TACL **9**, 962–977 (2021)
32. Jo, H., et al.: Vulcan: automatic extraction and analysis of cyber threat intelligence from unstructured text. Comput. Secur. **120**, 102763 (2022)
33. Kamath, A., et al.: Selective question answering under domain shift. arXiv preprint arXiv:2006.09462 (2020)

34. Kapoor, S., et al.: Calibration-tuning: teaching large language models to know what they don't know. In: Proceedings of UncertaiNLP-2024, pp. 1–14 (2024)
35. Kojima, T., et al.: Large language models are zero-shot reasoners. Adv. Neural. Inf. Process. Syst. **35**, 22199–22213 (2022)
36. Kucsván, Z.L., et al.: Inferring recovery steps from cyber threat intelligence reports. LNCS, vol. 14828, pp. 330 – 349. Springer (2024)
37. Kuhn, L., et al.: Semantic uncertainty: linguistic invariances for uncertainty estimation in natural language generation. arXiv preprint arXiv:2302.09664 (2023)
38. Leite, C., et al.: Automated cyber threat intelligence generation on multi-host network incidents. In: Proceedings of IEEE BigData-2023, pp. 2999–3008. IEEE (2023)
39. Lewis, P., et al.: Retrieval-augmented generation for knowledge-intensive NLP tasks. In: Proceedings of NeurIPS-2020, vol. 33, pp. 9459–9474 (2020)
40. Lin, Z., et al.: Generating with confidence: uncertainty quantification for black-box large language models. arXiv preprint arXiv:2305.19187 (2023)
41. Liu, J., et al.: Constructing knowledge graph from cyber threat intelligence using large language model. In: Proceedings of 2023 IEEE BigData-2023, pp. 516–521. IEEE (2023)
42. Liu, Y., et al.: APTTOOLNER: a Chinese dataset of cyber security tool for NER task. In: Proceedings of ACCTCS-2023, pp. 368–373. IEEE (2023)
43. Luong, T.Q., et al.: REFT: reasoning with reinforced fine-tuning. arXiv preprint arXiv:2401.08967 (2024)
44. Madden, C.: Using GENAI for efficient CVE mitigation. In: Presentation at EPSS Sig (2024)
45. Marchiori, F., et al.: STIXnet: a novel and modular solution for extracting all STIX objects in CTI reports. In: Proceedings of ARES-2023, pp. 1–11 (2023)
46. Mavroeidis, V., et al.: Threat actor type inference and characterization within cyber threat intelligence. In: Proceedings of CyCon-2021, pp. 327–352. IEEE (2021)
47. Mosbach, M., et al.: Few-shot fine-tuning vs. in-context learning: a fair comparison and evaluation. arXiv preprint arXiv:2305.16938 (2023)
48. Naeini, M.P., et al.: Obtaining well calibrated probabilities using Bayesian binning. In: Proceedings of AAAI-2015, vol. 29 (2015)
49. Nainna, M.A., et al.: Factors amplifying or inhibiting cyber threat intelligence sharing. In: Proceedings of EMCIS-2023, pp. 204–214. Springer (2023)
50. OpenAI: Prompt engineering (2024). https://platform.openai.com/docs/guides/prompt-engineering/strategy-write-clear-instructions
51. Pareja, A., et al.: Unveiling the secret recipe: a guide for supervised fine-tuning small LLMs. arXiv preprint arXiv:2412.13337 (2024)
52. Patsakis, C., et al.: Assessing LLMs in malicious code deobfuscation of real-world malware campaigns. Expert Syst. Appl. **256** (2024)
53. Perrina, F., et al.: AGIR: automating cyber threat intelligence reporting with natural language generation. In: Proceedings of IEEE Big Data-2023, pp. 3053–3062. IEEE (2023)
54. Platt, J., et al.: Probabilistic outputs for support vector machines and comparisons to regularized likelihood methods. Adv. Large Margin Classif. **10**(3), 61–74 (1999)
55. Qiao, Z., et al.: Improving cybersecurity named entity recognition with large language models. In: Proceedings CSECS-2023, pp. 01–06. IEEE (2023)
56. Rebedea, T., et al.: Nemo guardrails: a toolkit for controllable and safe LLM applications with programmable rails. arXiv preprint arXiv:2310.10501 (2023)

57. Saddi, V.R., et al.: Examine the role of generative AI in enhancing threat intelligence and cyber security measures. In: Proceedings of ICDT-2024, pp. 537–542. IEEE (2024)

58. Sai, S., et al.: Generative ai for cyber security: analyzing the potential of ChatGPT, dall-e and other models for enhancing the security space. IEEE Access (2024)

59. Sewak, M., et al.: CRUSH: cybersecurity research using universal LLMs and semantic hypernetworks (2023)

60. Shayegani, E., et al.: Survey of vulnerabilities in large language models revealed by adversarial attacks. arXiv preprint arXiv:2310.10844 (2023)

61. de Smale, S., et al.: No one drinks from the firehose: how organizations filter and prioritize vulnerability information. In: Proceedings of IEEE SS&P-2023, pp. 1980–1996. IEEE (2023)

62. Song, Y., et al.: The good, the bad, and the greedy: evaluation of LLMs should not ignore non-determinism. arXiv preprint arXiv:2407.10457 (2024)

63. Spiess, C., et al.: Calibration and correctness of language models for code. arXiv preprint arXiv:2402.02047 (2024)

64. Tihanyi, N., et al.: CyberMetric: a benchmark dataset based on retrieval-augmented generation for evaluating LLMs in cybersecurity knowledge. In: Proceedings of CSR-2024, pp. 296–302 (2024)

65. Wagner, C., et al.: MISP: the design and implementation of a collaborative threat intelligence sharing platform. In: Proceedings of ACM WISCS-2016, pp. 49–56 (2016)

66. Wang, G., et al.: KnowCTI: knowledge-based cyber threat intelligence entity and relation extraction. Comput. Secur. **141**, 103824 (2024)

67. Wang, X., et al.: APTNER: a specific dataset for ner missions in cyber threat intelligence field. In: Proceedings of IEEE CSCWD-2022, pp. 1233–1238. IEEE (2022)

68. Wang, X., et al.: DNRTI: a large-scale dataset for named entity recognition in threat intelligence. In: Proceedings of IEEE TrustCom-2020, pp. 1842–1848. IEEE (2020)

69. Wang, Y., et al.: Uncertainty estimation and reduction of pre-trained models for text regression. TACL **10**, 680–696 (2022)

70. Wei, J., et al.: Chain-of-thought prompting elicits reasoning in large language models. In: Proceedings of NeurIPS-2022, pp. 24824–24837 (2022)

71. Xiang, G., et al.: An APT event extraction method based on BERT-BiGRU-CRF for APT attack detection. Electronics **12**(15), 3349 (2023)

72. Xiong, M., et al.: Efficient and effective uncertainty quantification for LLMs. In: Proceedings of Safe Generative AI Workshop NeurIPS-2024 (2024)

73. Yang, H., et al.: Can we trust LLMs? Mitigate overconfidence bias in LLMs through knowledge transfer. arXiv preprint arXiv:2405.16856 (2024)

74. Ye, F., et al.: Benchmarking LLMs via uncertainty quantification. arXiv preprint arXiv:2401.12794 (2024)

75. Zhang, H., et al.: EX-action: automatically extracting threat actions from cyber threat intelligence report based on multimodal learning. Secur. Commun. Netw. **2021**, 1–12 (2021)

Augmented Tabular Adversarial Evasion Attacks with Constraint Satisfaction Guarantees

Nour Alhussien[1]([✉]) [ID], Gagan Agrawal[2][ID], and Ahmed Aleroud[3][ID]

[1] University at Albany, Albany, NY 12222, USA
nalhussien@albany.edu
[2] University of Georgia, Athens, GA 30602, USA
gagrawal@uga.edu
[3] Augusta University, Augusta, GA 30904, USA
aaleroud@augusta.edu

Abstract. Evasion attacks are among the most widely studied attacks within the general domain of Adversarial Machine Learning (AML). While there is a very active line of research on generating new more efficient attacks on unconstrained domains, where attributes of a record can be modified arbitrarily, work on tabular constrained domains is significantly more limited. Specifically, to date, there is no general technique for adapting a given attack generation method to any new tabular constrained domain, while ensuring the validity and evasiveness of the generated adversarial examples. Addressing this issue, this paper introduces the Tabular Constraint Guaranteed Evasion (TCGE) algorithm. Our algorithm harnesses the full evasive power of unconstrained attacks by ensuring that the maximum possible perturbation is applied without violating domain constraints, leading to attacks that are both evasive and valid. TCGE accommodates linear, nonlinear, correlated dependencies, and relational constraints. We incorporate TCGE into white-box and black-box threat models in four constrained domains. TCGE shows its plug-and-play compatibility within various existing unconstrained attacks and guarantees the generation of valid evasive adversarial examples without introducing significant time overheads, making TCGE adaptable also for real-time attack generation methods. Despite its generality, TCGE is demonstrated to be more effective and efficient over a specialized attack method for constrained tabular domains.

Keywords: Adversarial Machine Learning · Constrained Domain · Evasion Attacks · Tabular Attacks

1 Introduction

Machine learning (ML) and deep learning (DL) models are increasingly applied to tabular data across various domains, including fraud detection [10], risk scoring systems [14], network intrusion detection [4], phishing detection [1], healthcare diagnostics [5], and credit scoring [15]. However, adversarial attacks threaten

© The Author(s), under exclusive license to Springer Nature Switzerland AG 2025
M. Dalla Preda et al. (Eds.): ARES 2025, LNCS 15993, pp. 365–386, 2025.
https://doi.org/10.1007/978-3-032-00627-1_18

the integrity of these models by exploiting vulnerabilities in their training or inference processes. Evasion attacks are a category of adversarial attacks that operate by introducing perturbations in input samples with the goal of producing misclassifications, allowing malicious activities to evade a victim classifier. While research into adversarial attacks is extensive, it has predominantly focused on unconstrained data domains such as images, audio, and text [2,8,17,24,33,38]. In contrast, studies on adversarial attacks in tabular constrained data domains remain limited [7,21,37].

Tabular data, also referred to as structured data, has unique characteristics that distinguish it from unstructured domains, including:

Heterogeneous Data Types. Tabular datasets typically include a mix of numerical (with varying ranges and scales), categorical, binary, and textual features. Crafting adversarial attacks requires careful handling of these diverse feature types.

Imperceptibility. Defining imperceptibility in tabular data is complex. Unlike in images, where slight perturbations may go unnoticed by humans, even small changes in tabular data (e.g., numerical or categorical values) are often easily spotted by domain experts.

Domain Constraints. Tabular data is subject to domain-specific constraints, such as value ranges, relational dependencies, and immutability rules. Unlike unstructured adversarial attacks, which often perturb input data freely, adversarial attacks on tabular data must ensure that generated examples adhere to constraints. For example, a network traffic record with an invalid port number will not even be carried by a network protocol, making it irrelevant whether it can evade the classifier.

Given these characteristics, effective tabular adversarial attacks must account for these properties, particularly domain constraints. However, existing research has yet to fully address this challenge. Kireev et al. [21] propose cost-and-utility-aware tabular attacks, defining attack utility and the associated cost rather than focusing on imperceptibility. While significant, their framework does not enforce domain constraints, a critical property for tabular data. Moreover, their approach heavily relies on domain expertise, limiting its adaptability to broader use cases. Ballet et al. [7] introduce imperceptible tabular attacks guided by feature importance, perturbing less-critical features to create adversarial examples. However, their method similarly neglects the enforcement of domain constraints, undermining its practical applicability.

The enforcement of domain constraints is a crucial and often-overlooked aspect of developing tabular adversarial attacks. Research on adversarial attacks in constrained domains does exist [16,34], but it tends to focus on specific datasets or domains, limiting generalizability. Although Simonetto et al. [35] proposed a generalizable framework for constrained attacks, it requires modifying the objective function for each specific attack and does not guarantee the generation of valid and evasive adversarial examples.

To address these limitations, a generalized algorithm is essential to adapt existing unconstrained attacks for constrained tabular domains. Such an algorithm first, leverages advancements in state-of-the-art adversarial attack techniques without requiring custom solutions for each new domain. Second, guarantees that generated adversarial examples satisfy domain constraints, ensuring they are both deceptive (fooling the victim model) and structurally valid. Third, operates with minimal performance overhead while efficiently producing evasive adversarial examples.

In this paper, we propose a novel tabular adversarial attack framework, **TCGE** : **T**abular **C**onstrained **G**uaranteed **E**vasion, designed to achieve both evasiveness and validity. Evasiveness ensures that inputs are misclassified to evade the victim model, validity enforces adherence to domain-specific constraints, generating adversarial examples that are valid and evasive.

A key innovation of TCGE is the introduction of a Graph-Based Constraint Encoding. TCGE defines a dependency map to encode domain constraints in a graph-based representation. This dependency map plays a crucial role in enforcing constraints efficiently while generating adversarial examples. By modeling constraints as a graph where nodes represent feature indices and edges capture constraint relationships, the algorithm partitions features into disjoint groups, each connected by one or more constraints. During attack generation, TCGE verifies the validity of adversarial perturbations within each group: if the adversarial value satisfies all constraints, it is retained; otherwise, the original value is restored, ensuring only the affected group undergoes modification. This structured approach enables precise control over constraint enforcement while maintaining attack effectiveness. Our contributions are summarized as follows:

- We define representations for encoding diverse features with respect to tabular domain constraints, including immutability, linear and non-linear relationships, correlated dependencies, relational constraints, and for capturing constraint dependencies.
- We define a dependency map to capture relationships between mutable constraints, enabling efficient constraint verification and enforcement. TCGE employs a graph-based modeling approach to partition features into disjoint groups, allowing localized constraint verification and retaining valid perturbations.
- We introduce the TCGE algorithm, which extends existing adversarial attack techniques to constrained tabular domains. The algorithm is agnostic to target classifiers, data domains, and threat models, leading to broad applicability.
- We show that TCGE achieves superior performance compared to existing methods [35], generating valid adversarial examples with minimal latency overhead.

2   Background and Solution Overview

2.1   Key Definitions

Data Format and Domain. We require an input dataset $\mathcal{D}$ of pre-labeled records. Each record in the dataset contains a set of ordered features, with values in $\mathbb{R}$, and an associated class label. Although we focus on binary classification, multi-class scenarios are in scope. Feature values can be normalized or unnormalized, but we assume them to be unnormalized for this study. Various data formats may be considered, e.g., tabular, image, or temporal. Categorical data must be preprocessed to numeric format through binarization.

Constraints. A set of satisfiable constraints, denoted as $\mathcal{C}$, applies to the dataset. A constraint specifies an invariant on a subset of features. For example, a constraint may state "the age of a loan applicant must be 18 years or over". We require records in $\mathcal{D}$ satisfy constraints in $\mathcal{C}$.

Victim Classifier. The classifier is an existing pre-trained supervised learner. The classifier performs inference by mapping inputs to a discrete set of labels occurring in $\mathcal{D}$.

Adversarial Attack. We consider evasion attacks, a category of attacks that involve modifying records of $\mathcal{D}$ with carefully crafted perturbations, to obtain $\mathcal{D}'$, intended to cause misclassification during inference. Misclassification implies that the classifier assigns a different label to a record compared to its original unperturbed counterpart.

Although we do not explicitly restrict the attack threat model, it must be compatible with a selected victim classifier – a white-box attack requires information about classifier internals, a black box attack requires information about input/output into/from classifier, tree-based attack requires a tree classifier, etc. The minimum requirement for our problem is the ability to access the perturbed adversarial examples, $\mathcal{D}'$.

2.2 Solution Overview

This paper creates tabular constrained attacks from existing unconstrained evasion attacks as depicted in Fig. 1. The pseudo-code here is a generic depiction of a typical evasion sample generation algorithm for an unconstrained domain. As shown here, by simply inserting a function call to `enforce` (whose implementation is unrelated to the logic of attack generation method itself), the method become now capable to handle domain constraints. This guarantees that generated adversarial examples also satisfy constraints.

3 Constraints and Their Dependencies

Domain constraints define restrictions that data records must always satisfy. For example, when a categorical feature is replaced by several binary features (i.e. 5 choices of color replaced by 5 binary features), only one of these features can be true. Constraints can also capture enforceable properties of data, such as a limit of 65,535 bytes size for a IPv4 network packet; a higher value is not permissible and such packet would be dropped by a network.

3.1 Representing Constraints

We distinguish three categories of constraints. An *immutability* constraint is satisfied if and only if a feature's value matches the corresponding value of an original

```
def tabular_attack(records, labels, constraints):
    # initialize a return value from inputs
    best_batch = records.copy()
    best_score = calculate(records, labels)
    while condition:
        # generate adversarial examples
        adv_records = generate(records)
        # new: enforce constraints
        enforce(records, adv_records, constraints)
        # score adversarial examples
        batch_score = calculate(adv_records, labels)
        # keep batch with the highest score
        if batch_score > best_score
            best_batch = adv_records
            best_score = batch_score
    return best_batch
```

Fig. 1. Integrating TCGE into adversarial attack frameworks. TCGE can be introduced to existing unconstrained evasion attacks, following adversarial example generation, to ensure the generated examples satisfy domain constraints.

unperturbed record. In the context of adversarial manipulation, this implies that perturbations must be applied to features not restricted by an immutability constraint. Conversely, a *mutable* constraint permits features to be perturbed under certain conditions - this can include restrictions on a single feature or multiple features. Mutable constraints must be evaluated after adversarial perturbation to determine if the constraint is satisfied. The third implicit category is *permissive*; it allows unrestricted perturbations. We formalize the notions of constraint categories with their logical equivalents in Definition 1.

Definition 1 (Constraint). *Let n be cardinality of features in a domain, and $\mathcal{I} = \{1, \ldots, n\}$ the set of feature indices, and $\mathcal{V} = \{\mathcal{V}_i, i \in \mathcal{I} \mid \mathcal{V}_i \in \mathbb{R}\}$ the feature values. A k-tuple of feature indices is $\mathcal{I}^k = \{(i_1, \ldots, i_k) \mid i_j \in \mathcal{I} \text{ for } 1 \leq j \leq k\}$. A predicate P is a Boolean constant $(\top, \bot)$; or a function type, evaluated at a k-tuple of feature values $\mathcal{V}^k = (\mathcal{V}_i)_{i \in \mathcal{I}^k}$, that maps to a Boolean, $P : \mathcal{V}^k \to \mathbb{B}$. A constraint C over k-features is an ordered pair, $C : \mathcal{I}^k \times P$.*

Expressiveness. In Sect. 5 we discuss how we encoded constraints in four practical domains, including all constraints from two previous studies [31,35] using this representation. These experiments demonstrate that a substantial set of constraints can be expressed in a straightforward fashion.

In Fig. 2, we show our constraints representation in natural language form and a corresponding encoding form (predicate), derived from a real-world network connections dataset, UNSW-NB15 dataset. The figure illustrates two network traffic constraints, C1 and C2. C1 ensures that there is an internal consistency between protocol type and associated TCP-specific features. If the protocol is

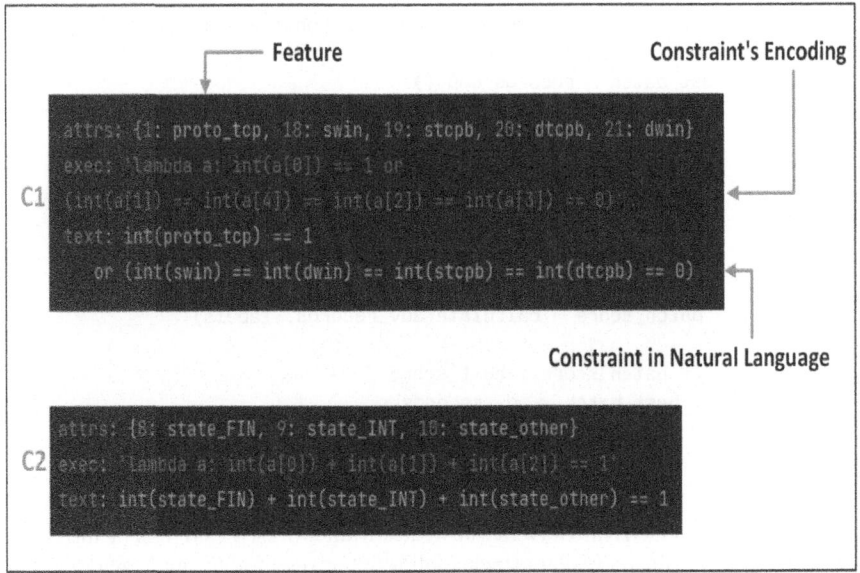

Fig. 2. Constraint representations.

TCP, the constraint is satisfied. Otherwise, it requires that the related TCP-specific features (swin, dwin, stcpb, dtcpb) be 0. C2 enforces mutual exclusivity among connection states: a packet should only be in one state at a time. Exactly one of the state indicators (FIN, INT, or other) should be set to 1 (active), and the others should be 0. Using our constraint representation, it is possible to construct arbitrarily complex in-lined expressions, perform function calls, and apply multiple predicates on any subset of features. However, a limitation is that constraints must be specified on individual records, e.g., aggregation and multi-record constraints are out of scope.

3.2 Dependency Maps

We define a dependency map for capturing relationships between mutable constraints. A dependency map allows detecting precisely the impact of a constraint when it is not satisfied. A dependency map consists of feature groups, each of which a disjoint subset of features connected by at least one constraint. If features are vertices and constraints are edges, then feature groups are the connected components of a graph, cf. Fig. 3. The dependency map corresponding to it is $C_1 \mapsto \{1, 2\}$; $C_2 \mapsto \{3, 4, 5\}$; $C_4 \mapsto \{3, 4, 5\}$.

The construction procedure, Algorithm 1 begins by representing the features and their corresponding constraints as a graph, where nodes represent feature indices, and edges represent the fact that the two features are involved in a constraint. We used a depth-first search to identify disjoint sets of connected

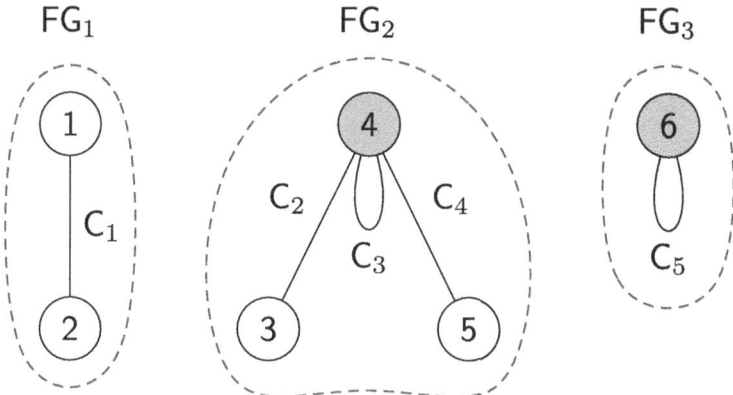

Fig. 3. Constraint dependencies. The nodes are features (1–6) and edges are constraints (C_1–C_5). Feature groups (FG_1 – FG_3) identify disjoint groups of features connected with at least one constraint. Features 3 and 5 do not occur in a shared constraint, but are connected through feature 4. Constraint satisfaction is evaluated individually for each feature group. A permissible perturbation of FG_2 requires both C_2 and C_4 are satisfied. An immutability constraint applies to features 4 and 6.

feature indices, forming groups of features such that there are no constraints across the groups.

Algorithm 1. Build a constraint dependency map

Input: associative array of mutable constraints $\mathcal{C} : k \mapsto v$
Output: associative array of constraint dependencies

1: **function** DEPENDENCY MAP($\mathcal{C}$)
2:    $D \leftarrow \text{Array}\{\}$ ▷ Stores dependencies
3:    $G \leftarrow \text{Graph}(\mathcal{C})$ ▷ Construct graph
4:    $S \leftarrow \text{DEPTH-FIRST SEARCH}(G)$ ▷ Return disjoint indices
5:    **while** $S \neq \text{NULL}$ **do**
6:        $I \leftarrow S.\text{POP}()$ ▷ Disjoint indices
7:        **for all** $k \in C$ **do**
8:            **if** $I \cup \{C_k.i\} \neq \varnothing$ **then**
9:                $D_k \leftarrow I$ ▷ Associate I with the constraint at k
10:    **return** D

---

4 Tabular Constraint Guaranteed Evasion Algorithm

Tabular Constraint Guaranteed Evasion, TCGE, transforms existing uncon-strained evasion attacks into constrained tabular ones.

4.1   Constraints Enforcement

The detailed steps of constraint enforcement are outlined in Algorithm 2. We will explain the steps of this algorithm through an example in Fig. 4. Constraint enforcement requires two inputs: a reset array, M^R, of initial valid records, and their adversarially generated perturbed variants, M^A, produced by the original evasion attack generation algorithm. The top row in Fig. 4 displays M^R and M^A, with perturbed values highlighted (8, 5, -4, 2, 3).

The challenge lies in determining the best choice between two extremes: at one end, the reset array examples that satisfy constraints but are not evasive, and on the other, adversarial examples are mostly evasive but may not satisfy constraints. The goal of TCGE is to produce adversarial examples that maintain constraint satisfaction and allow the maximal degree of perturbation.

$$
\text{Reset } M^R \quad
\begin{bmatrix} 4 & 2 & 5 & 0 \\ 6 & -7 & 1 & 8 \\ -1 & 3 & 0 & 2 \end{bmatrix}
\quad
\text{Adversarial } M^A \quad
\begin{bmatrix} 4 & 2 & 8 & 5 \\ 6 & -4 & 1 & 8 \\ 2 & 3 & 3 & 2 \end{bmatrix}
\quad
\text{Validation map } M^V \quad
\begin{bmatrix} 1 & 1 & 1 & 0 \\ 1 & 0 & 1 & 1 \\ 1 & 1 & 1 & 1 \end{bmatrix}
\quad
\text{Valid adversarial } M^{A'} \quad
\begin{bmatrix} 4 & 2 & 8 & 0 \\ 6 & -7 & 1 & 8 \\ 2 & 3 & 3 & 2 \end{bmatrix}
$$

Fig. 4. Constraint Enforcement Example

To achieve the goal, the key idea is to construct a validation map, M^V, to trace the decision boundary between reset and adversarial inputs. The algorithm accepts adversarial values, unless a predicate evaluates to false, then it reverts to values of the reset array. In M^V, value 1 means that the corresponding value in M^A is acceptable, whereas the value 0 denotes inadmissible perturbed values - these will be substituted with values from M^R.

A critical consideration is handling unsatisfied constraints when predicate evaluation returns false, cf. line 9. Since constraints can have dependencies, unsatisfiability of one constraint has potential ripple effects on others. The algorithm addresses the insatisfiability by employing a reset strategy, line 12, to choose values from the reset array to rectify the validation state. Here we deploy the dependency map to determine the right features to reset. Reset is applied to all features of an affected feature group. This action is justified since feature groups are disjoint; false evaluation impacts only features of its associated feature group.

The output is represented in the adversarial array $M^{A'}$. Returning to the example in Fig. 4, inadmissible values have been reset (0, -7; boxed), whereas acceptable perturbations are preserved (8, 2, 3; underlined). It is possible that certain features of the same record are reset and others are preserved (0 and 8), since the dependency map identifies feature dependencies and allows fine-grained corrective reset.

Algorithm 2. Enforce constraints

Input: reset array M^R, adversarial array M^A
Parameters: constraints $\mathcal{C} : k \mapsto v$, feature value ranges $\mathcal{F}$
Output: valid adversarial array M^A

Require: Immutable, Mutable $\leftarrow$ CATEGORIZE $(\mathcal{C})$
Require: $D \leftarrow$ DEPENDENCY MAP (Mutable)
Require: $\forall r \in M^R, C \in$ Mutable, $C(r) = \top$
Require: $\#M^R = \#M^A = \#M^V$
1: **function** ENFORCE(M^R, M^A)
2:    $M^V \leftarrow 1$ ▷ Initialize validation map
3:    **for all** $i \in$ Immutable **do**
4:        $M_{*i}^V \leftarrow 0$ ▷ Mark immutable
5:    $M^A \leftarrow M^A \otimes M^V + M^R \otimes (1 - M^V)$ ▷ Apply validation map
6:    $M^V \leftarrow 1$ ▷ Re-initialize
7:    **for all** $k, i \times P \in$ Mutable **do**
8:        $v \leftarrow M_{*i}^A \otimes \mathcal{F}_i$ ▷ Scale values
9:        $b \leftarrow P(v)$ ▷ Evaluate constraint
10:       **for all** $j \in 1 \dots len(b)$ **do**   ▷ Propagate
11:           **if** $b_j = 0$ **then**
12:               $M_{jD_k}^V \leftarrow 0$ ▷ Reset invalid values
13:    $M^A \leftarrow M^A \otimes M^V + M^R \otimes (1 - M^V)$ ▷ Apply final validation
14:    **return** M^A

4.2 Correctness

The primary property of TCGE is that it guarantees adversarially generated examples are correct, the specified constraints are satisfied in the Algorithm 2's output, as formalized below.

Theorem 1. *Given constraints $\mathcal{C}$, reset array M^R, adversarial array M^A, and $M^{A'} = $ ENFORCE(M^R, M^A), then $\forall C \in \mathcal{C}, C = i \times P \implies M_i^{A'} = M_i^R \lor P(M_i^{A'}) = \top.$*

Proof ((sketch)). Recall a constraint C is a pair of feature indices and predicate P; the proof is by cases of constructing C. Case 1: C is *permissible*. Right condition holds immediately. Case 2: C is *immutable*. Line 4 handles immutable features and line 5 resets them to values of M^R. The left condition holds. Case 3: C is *mutable*. Evaluating P has two return values. On $\top$, the right condition holds immediately. On $\bot$, correction is required: every dependent feature is reset to value from M^R. Reset is irreversible by execution line order. As feature dependencies are defined by disjoint subsets, the reset does not impact the correctness of features outside the subset. Simultaneously, it ensures the correctness of features within the subset. Given that mutable constraints are known to hold in M^R, they also hold for $M^{A'}$ after correction. Both left and right conditions hold.

5   Experimental Evaluation

We evaluated TCGE by integrating it into three unconstrained evasion attacks—Projected Gradient Descent (PGD) [25], Zeroth Order Optimization (ZOO) [12], and HopSkipJump Attacks (HSJ) [11]—against two victim classifiers across four data domains. Additionally, we evaluated projected gradient descent modified with TCGE against an alternative state-of-the-art attack, constrained projected gradient descent (C-PGD) in [35].

Moreover, we updated exiting tabular attack, lowprofool (LPF) [7], to include domain constraints using our algorithm and compare it with the unconstrained lowprofool attack. To ensure reproducibility, we have made our implementation of the TCGE algorithm, along with all experimental data, configurations, comparison studies, and evaluation results publicly available.[1]

5.1   Tested Evasion Attacks

Although any evasion attack within the problem specification could be considered, we focus on the following three attacks because they represent different threat models and attack strategies. We obtained initial implementations from Adversarial Robustness Toolbox [30], modifying them to use TCGE. In all other aspects the modified attacks match their initial versions. We prepend to the attack's name the term *Valid* (abbreviated as "V") to identify the TCGE-enhanced variants.

Projected Gradient Descent. A white-box attack, PGD [25] iteratively seeks a perturbation that maximizes the model's loss for a given input, while ensuring the magnitude of the perturbation remains within a specified limit. Furthermore, the perturbed samples are constrained to be within the permissible data ranges [25]. For VPGD, we modified the attack's compute method that runs on each iteration.

Zeroth Order Optimization. A black-box attack which assumes that class label probabilities are accessible [12]. The attack queries a victim classifier to obtain class label confidence scores, then it uses the scores to estimate gradients of the victim classifier and generate adversarial examples. For VZOO, we introduced constraint enforcement during the attack's binary search step, immediately before scoring adversarial examples.

HopSkipJump. A black-box attack, with emphasis on query efficiency [11]. Its threat model is more restrictive than ZOO, only requiring predicted class labels. The attack employs a binary search to identify a decision boundary, then estimates a gradient at that boundary, and uses geometric progression to generate adversarial examples. For VHSJ, we introduced a call to enforce constraints as the final operation of an internal attack method.

LowProFool. A white-box attack, it was developed to generate adversarial examples for tabular data by iteratively applying perturbations to an original

---

[1] https://github.com/aucad/cge.

sample until the perturbed sample is misclassified by the classifier [7]. The algorithm also incorporates feature importance to guide the perturbation process, prioritizing features based on their significance to the classifier.

Feature importance is calculated using Pearson correlation, where greater perturbations are applied to less important features and smaller perturbations to more important ones. LPF enforces only feature range constraints on the generated adversarial examples, ignoring relational and dependency constraints. For VLPF, we enforce domain constraints within the generation of the best perturbed sample using a call for our algorithm.

5.2   Other Evaluation Details

Datasets. We selected four pre-labelled tabular datasets for binary classification. These datasets were selected because they represent different domains and various kinds of constraints. Futhermore, they have been used in previous studies focusing on adversarial evasion attacks in constrained domains [31,35], thus allowing us to reuse of the same constraints as the previous works.

1. IoT-23 is a modern realistic capture of benign and malicious network traffic flows of Internet of Things Devices [16]. 2. UNSW-NB15 is a network intrusion dataset, comprising traditional network traffic with normal activities and synthetic attack behaviors [26–29,32]. 3. URL contains properties of website addresses for website phishing detection [18]. 4. LCLD includes submitted loan applications with financial and personal information; the class label determines if the application was approved or declined [20].

Table 1. Experiment constraint configurations. Feature density is the average number of features involved in mutable constraints; it is more revealing than number of constraints alone.

Datasets	IoT-23	LCLD	UNSW	URL		
Constraints count	18	29	6	14		
Feature density, μ	3.9	3.2	4.2	3.3		
Performance tests	Single-feature		Multi-feature			
Constraints count	3	6	12	3	6	12
Feature density, μ	1.0	1.0	1.0	2.0	2.3	2.5

We preprocessed all datasets, applying feature selection and binarization to categorical attributes, to obtain numeric and unnormalized data. We took the entire URL dataset because its class distribution is balanced by default. For the rest, we applied random sampling without replacement to obtain an equal class distribution. The data sizes were 10K–20K records.

Constraints. For each dataset, we identified constraints of types including linear, non-linear, relational, and feature value constraints. Multiple sets of constraints could be defined for one dataset. We defined two sets of experimental constraints, details in Table 1. 1. *Realistic constraints*, respective of the four datasets, based on domain knowledge. We obtained these constraints from two previous related studies. The constraints for URL and LCLD were defined in [35] and IoT-23 and UNSW-NB15 in [31]. The only required adjustment was encoding the constraints in our representation, but otherwise the constraints are the same. 2. *Synthetic constraints*, on UNSW-NB15, to stress-test TCGE under different conditions for performance evaluation.

Here, we systematically increased the number of mutable constraints to measure constraint impact on adversarial success and attack latency. We defined two scenarios, one employing *single-feature constraints* and the other using *multi-feature constraints*. In the single-feature scenario, each constraint involves only one feature, while in the multi-feature scenario, a constraint involves multiple features simultaneously. In addition, we introduce the concept of *feature density* (denoted by μ), defined as the average number of features involved in each mutable constraint. This metric is more revealing than the total number of constraints alone, as it provides insight into the complexity of the constraint set.

Victim Classifiers. We evaluated two classifiers, a tree-based ensemble-learner XGBoost and Keras Deep Neural Network (DNN). They are widely used in practice, sufficiently different to be experimentally interesting, and compatible with the selected attacks (except PGD and XGBoost). We trained XGBoost models with soft probability objective for 20 boost rounds. We trained DNN models using Adam optimizer, varying the construction slightly based on dataset dimensionality—1 to 3 hidden layers and 32 to 64 neurons each—using ReLU activation and lastly softmax activation at the output layer. The precise configurations are detailed in our GitHub repository.

Comparison Attack. Although existing research on constrained attacks largely focuses on specific attacks and particular domains, our approach is different. TCGE is designed to adapt any unconstrained attack into a constrained tabular one. Therefore, we chose to benchmark it against general attacks and without restrictions on specific domains [35]. We focused on white-box C-PGD attacks as they offer a sufficient variety for a fair comparison.[2]

Constrained Projected Gradient Descent (C-PGD) attack is a variant of PGD. It enhances the attack's loss function by incorporating a penalty based on differentiable constraints, enabling it to maximize generated examples to account for non-differentiable constraints.

Although constraint-aware, C-PGD does not make assertions regarding constraint satisfiability. C-PGD is a suitable comparison target because it permits meaningful comparison with PGD and VPGD. Attacks based on PGD are generally of high interest, since past research [22] shows multistep gradient attacks are one of the most powerful categories of adversarial attacks. Using the original implementation of C-PGD [36], we applied only minor modifications to internal

---

[2] We specifically omit comparison to Simonetto et al. MOEVA attack, since it uses a grey-box threat model; it does not permit meaningful comparison with the other evaluated attacks operating under different threat models.

parameters of C-PGD, to account for dependency upgrades in the Adversarial Robustness Toolbox.

VLowProFool is our enhanced version of the LowProFool attack [7], incorporating constraint satisfaction into the adversarial example generation process.

Metrics. We used 5-fold cross validation, reserving 80% of input data for classifier training and 20% holdout for classifier testing and for applying an attack. For each fold, we measured 1) *classifier accuracy*, the fraction of correctly classified unperturbed records. 2) *Evasive rate*, the fraction of perturbed records that are misclassified by the classifier and do not adhere to domain constraints. 3) *Valid-Evasive rate*, the fraction of evasive records that are also valid and satisfy the constraints.

We report all measurements as averages of the 5 experiment folds. We ran all experiments on a virtual instance of Linux Ubuntu v20.04 Focal, with x86-64 architecture, 8 CPU cores and 32 GB RAM, in a cloud environment.

5.3   Evaluation Results

Using the defined experimental setup, we evaluated TCGE in four research questions.

1. What is the impact of TCGE on the attack evasion success?
2. How does TCGE affect attack execution time?
3. How does VPGD compare to C-PGD?
4. How does increasing the number of constraints impact VPGD and C-PGD performance?
5. How does VLPF compare to LPF?

RQ1: TCGE Impact on Evasion Success. We measured evasion rates for all considered compatible attacks, classifiers, and datasets, in 20 experiment combinations. We considered two cases: (a) without constraint enforcement, where the generated examples were scored afterward to determine constraint satisfiability; and (b) with constraint enforcement, attacks enhanced with TCGE, where we enforce domain constraints during adversarial example generation. We reported the *Valid-Evasive* and *Evasive* rates for 2 classifiers, 4 datasets, and three attacks.

Figure 5 (a) shows the unconstrained attacks had only a moderate success – large fractions of examples, although evasive, did not satisfy the constraints. The overall *Evasive* rate, which shows the average success across the classifiers, attacks, and datasets, is 31%. In this case, the default attack can produce valid examples by chance. Conversely, Fig. 5 (b) shows that the adversarial examples discovered by TCGE-variants always satisfy the constraints. The overall *Valid-Evasive* rate is 49%, the attacks show improved success at discovering valid adversarial examples in 14 out of 20 experiments. The overall *Valid-Evasive* rate improved by 1.6x, rising from 31% to 49%, for the TCGE-enhanced attack variants. This improvement shows the benefits of our approach.

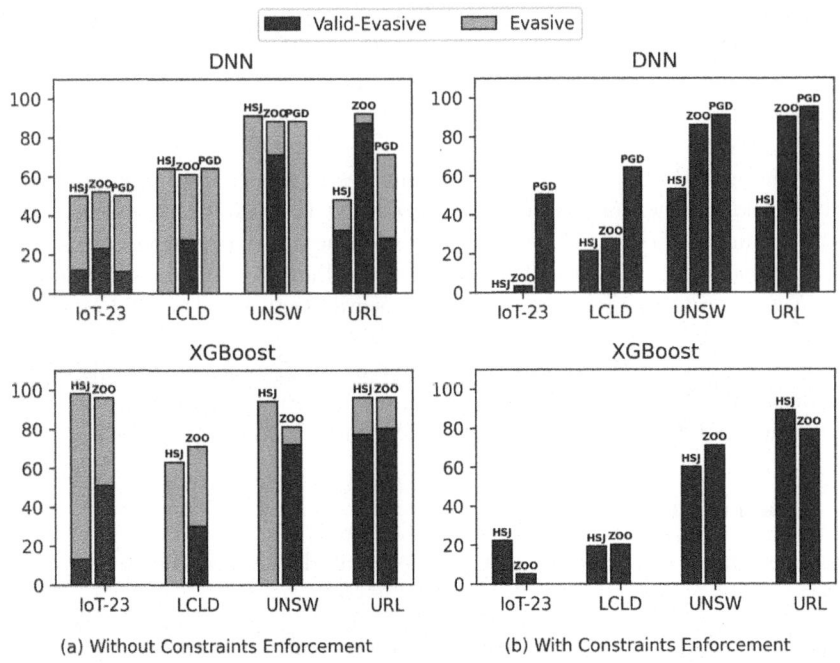

Fig. 5. Attack evasion success. (a) No awareness of constraints during attacks, and adversarial examples are scored for constraint satisfiability after the attack. (b) Enforcement of constraints during example generation.

RQ1 Summary. TCGE-enhanced attacks improved discovery of *Valid-Evasive* adversarial examples 1.6x.

RQ2: TCGE Impact on Attack Performance. We inspected again the 20 experiment combinations introduced in RQ1 to evaluate execution time overhead introduced by TCGE. We measured the wall time for the enhanced attacks, E, and compared it against the baseline unconstrained attacks, B. The results for both the enhanced and baseline versions of each attack across the four datasets are presented in Table 2.

The black-box attacks, VZOO and VHSJ, demonstrated negligible overhead in execution time for ZOO and HSJ. The white-box attack VPGD added 2.8–5x overhead compared to PGD. However, considering the trade-off between the improved *Valid-Evasive* success of the enhanced attacks and the accompanying computational overhead, the fraction of the generated *Valid-Evasive* adversarial examples outweigh the cost.

RQ2 Summary. The overhead introduced by TCGE is comparable to state-of-the-art for white-box attacks and has no significant impact on black-box attacks.

Table 2. Attack Execution Wall Times.

Model	Attack	IoT-23		LCLD		UNSW		URL	
		B	E	B	E	B	E	B	E
XGB	VHSJ	78	78	184	187	91	90	112	110
	VZOO	151	163	305	334	163	175	209	226
DNN	VHSJ	507	483	1008	1000	850	771	477	441
	VZOO	2875	2916	4236	4080	3560	3430	2479	2351
	VPGD	41	144	34	165	21	57	31	107
	CPGD	45	105	78	451	52	97	47	256

RQ3: VPGD and C-PGD Comparison.

We compared VPGD and C-PGD,[3] with the results presented in Fig. 6, highlighting their *Valid-Evasive* and *Evasive* rates. While VPGD successfully generates *Valid-Evasive* adversarial examples, C-PGD lacks this guarantee.

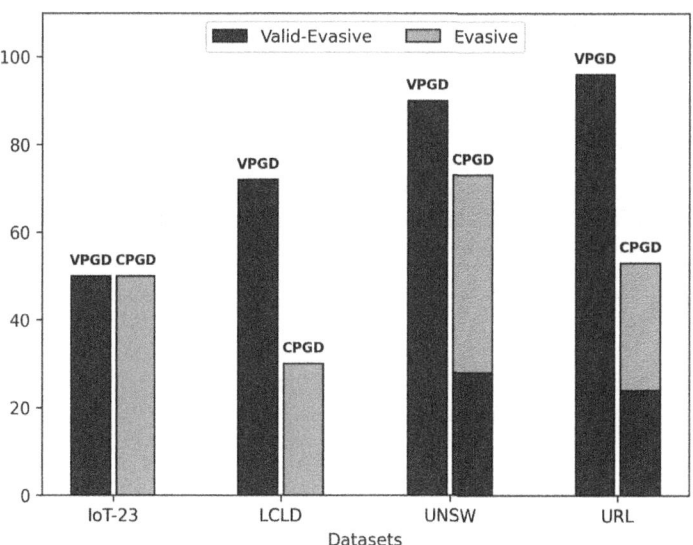

Fig. 6. Attack evasion success for VPGD and C-PGD. The victim classifier is a Deep Neural Network.

Across the four datasets, the overall *Valid-Evasive* rate for VPGD was 75%, and consistently succeeded in generating *Valid-Evasive* examples for each

---

[3] Differences in experimental setup with C-PGD: 1) we used balanced and sampled data of 20K records vs. unbalanced 915K testing and 305K training in previous study, and 2) the victim models are slightly differently configured in terms of layers and optimizer.

dataset. In contrast, C-PGD demonstrated an overall *Evasive* rate of 53%, but only 15% of the generated adversarial examples were *Valid-Evasive*. On IoT-23 and LCLD datasets, C-PGD failed to generate any *Valid-Evasive* adversarial examples.'

RQ3 Summary. The TCGE-enhanced attack variant, VPGD, guaranteed domain constraint satisfaction and C-PGD did not.

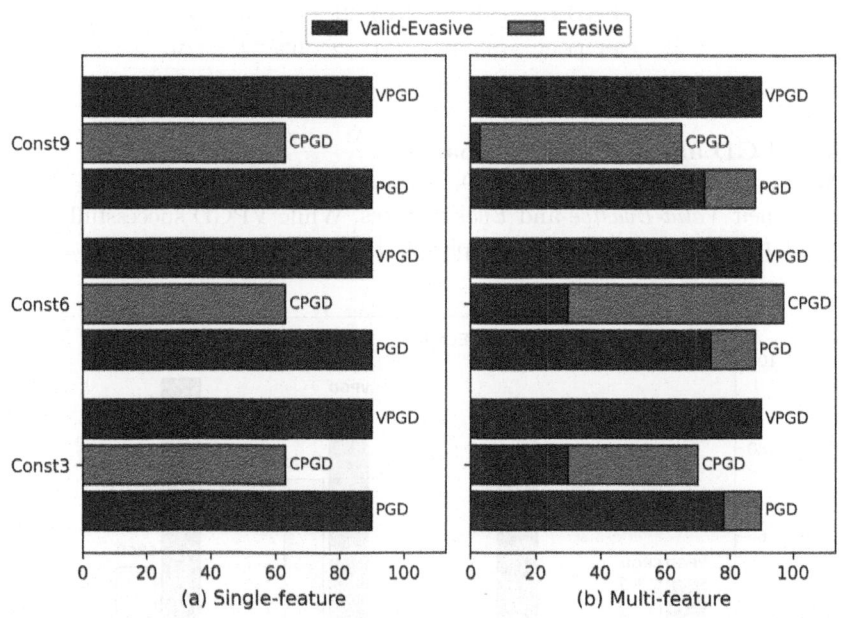

Fig. 7. Evasion success rates for varying constraints. Comparison of evasive success rates, for PGD-variant attacks, against a DNN trained on UNSW-NB15 data, with increasing number of constraints.

RQ4: Increasing Number of Constraints. Using a fixed dataset and a neural network classifier trained on UNSW-NB15, we gradually increased the constraint count to measure the impact on attack performance. This comparison used VPGD, since it could be compared with the baselines PGD and C-PGD. We configured two scenarios; single-feature and multi-feature mutable constraints, resulting in a total of 6 experiment cases.

In single-feature constraint scenario, as illustrated in Fig. 7 (a), both VPGD and PGD exhibit similar behavior, surpassing the performance of C-PGD, which failed to generate any *Valid-Evasive* adversarial examples when the number of constraints varied. In multi-feature constraint scenario, as illustrated in Fig. 7 (b), 11–22% of *Evasive* examples generated by PGD failed to satisfy constraints. For C-PGD, 70% of *Evasive* examples failed to satisfy constraint with counts of 3 and

6, while all evasive examples failed in 12 constraint counts. VPGD demonstrated constraint satisfaction across all 6 experiments, consistently outperforming PGD and C-PGD in generating *Valid-Evasive* examples. In particular, VPGD did not impose a limit on the number of constraints it could handle, reliably producing valid examples regardless of the number of constraints.

The comparison of attack execution wall times between C-PGD and VPGD while varying constraint counts is illustrated in Table 3. The results showed that the C-PGD attack introduces significantly more overhead compared to VPGD across various constraint counts. Specifically, C-PGD incurs an average time increment of approximately 70 s, while VPGD's average increment is substantially lower at about 31 s. This indicates that C-PGD is more computationally intensive, particularly as the number of constraints increases, with overhead growing by up to 103 s when 12 constraints enforced. Conversely, VPGD showed a moderate overhead, demonstrating a more efficient trade-off between generating *Valid-Evasive* adversarial examples and ensuring feasible execution time.

Table 3. Execution times for varying constraints. The "+" indicates the additional time taken by the enhanced attacks compared to the baseline.

Attack	Single-feature			Multi-feature		
Constraints	*3*	*6*	*12*	*3*	*6*	*12*
C-PGD	+36	+57	+98	+45	+74	+103
VPGD	+13	+24	+50	+18	+28	+56

RQ4 Summary. As the number of constraints increased, VPGD consistently demonstrated greater efficiency compared to C-PGD, with significantly lower execution times in both single-feature and multi-feature scenarios.

RQ5: VLPF and LPF Comparison. We evaluated the *Valid-Evasive* and *Evasive* rates for VLPF and LPF across four datasets. Since LPF is a tabular attack that enforces only one type of constraint (feature range constraints), we conducted a separate comparison to ensure a meaningful analysis against unconstrained attacks. Specifically, we compare the existing LPF with our enhanced version, VLPF, which incorporates our proposed algorithm.

The results in Fig. 8 demonstrate the superior performance of VLPF, particularly in the UNSW dataset where LPF failed to generate any *Valid-Evasive* adversarial examples. Despite achieving an 89% evasion rate, the adversarial examples generated by LPF were impractical, as they did not satisfy the network domain constraints. In the IoT-23 dataset, VLPF outperformed LPF by generating 26% more *Valid-Evasive* adversarial examples. However, in the and LCLD datasets both VLPF & LPF exhibited similar *Valid-Evasive* rate.

The relatively high *Valid-Evasive* rates of LPF in these cases can be attributed to its design as a tabular adversarial attack and its use of a clipping

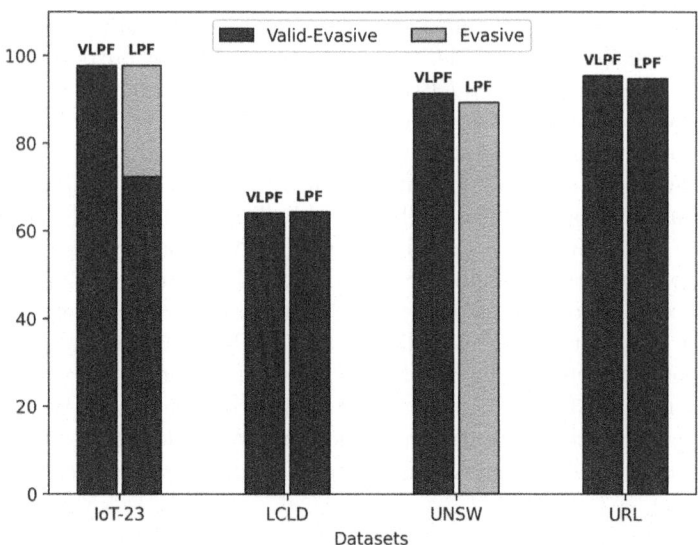

Fig. 8. Attack evasion success for VLPF and LPF. The victim classifier is a Deep Neural Network.

function, which ensures adversarial examples remain within feature range limits. However, LPF does not explicitly enforce domain-specific constraints, limiting its applicability in scenarios requiring strict adherence to domain rules.

RQ5 Summary. VLPF outperformed LPF, matching its performance in two domains, while significantly surpassing it in UNSW (VLPF: 92% vs. LPF: 0%) by successfully generating *Valid-Evasive* examples, and showing better results in a IoT domain (VLPF: 98% vs. LPF: 72%).

6   Related Work

As stated previously, the current work in evasion attacks for constrained domains can be categorized into two broad categories – we summarize the existing work in each below.

Adapting Unconstrained Attacks for Domain Constraints. In [34], the authors modified two adversarial algorithms—the adaptive Jacobian-based saliency map and Histogram sketch generation—to incorporate network domain constraints. However, the presented algorithm has limitations in addressing binary features, value bounds, and nonlinear feature dependencies. In [19], the authors developed an algorithm to create constrained adversarial examples for anomaly-based network intrusion detection systems. Three manipulation techniques were used: splitting payloads, delaying packets, and injecting decoy packets. The approach is applicable to a specific constrained domain with no efforts towards generalization.

Teuffenbach *et al.* [39] extended the work by [19]. However, besides not being adaptable, it is specifically designed for the C&W attack, unlike our attack-independent approach. In [16], the authors proposed a Restricted Traffic Distribution Attack method, to protect network data from traffic analysis attacks. Their perturbation techniques are more limited than what can be handled through our approach.

The study in [3] conducted a detailed analysis of constrained adversarial examples within network domains. Introducing network constraints and evaluating their effectiveness in different attack settings, including success rates, transferability, targetability, and defense analysis. While the study was comprehensive, the valid rate for the generated adversarial examples was 100% only for zoo attacks, whereas white-box attacks achieved valid adversarial rates of 81% and 76%. In contrast, our algorithm consistently guarantees a 100% valid adversarial rate.

Developing New Constrained-Domain Adversarial Attacks. CaFA [9] presents a cost-aware framework for generating feasible adversarial attacks specifically designed for tabular data. It achieves cost efficiency by perturbing fewer features with lower magnitudes and ensures feasibility by adhering to domain constraints. However, the framework is limited to a single attack method, TabPGD, which restricts its generalizability across diverse attack scenarios.

In [13], the authors introduced FENCE framework, which involves an iterative gradient-based adversarial attack to generate adversarial examples complying with network domain constraints. To maintain feature dependencies, the approach includes feature-update algorithms for each dependency type. FENCE requires extensive modifications for different classifiers, involving defining optimization objectives, feature families, constraints, update functions, and projection functions.

Within cyber-physical systems domain, Li *et al.* [23] introduced the ConAML threat model, generating adversarial examples that comply with physical constraints in water treatment and power grid systems. For phishing website detection, [6] employed evasion attacks adhering to constraints based on website semantics, ensuring perturbations do not violate inter-feature dependencies. However, again, these strategies are domain-specific.

7   Conclusions

This paper introduces a novel general algorithm for adapting unconstrained evasion attack generation methods to new constrained tabular domains, working independently of threat models and victim classifiers. The efficacy of the approach is demonstrated by capturing constraints from four different tabular domains, and their associated datasets; and by adapting four known evasion attacks to operate within these domains against two victim classifiers.

The TCGE-algorithm achieves 1.6x increase in the generation of valid evasive adversarial examples, without introducing significant computational latency for black-box attacks, and with modest increase for white-box attacks. A key advantage of TCGE is its ability to create a dependency map, enabling precise constraint assessment. Instead of solving the complex satisfiability hard problem, TCGE efficiently verifies adversarial examples for constraint compliance and resets unsatisfiable ones to a known valid state.

Potential future directions include exploring the advantages constraint-awareness could offer in adversarial example generation. In particular, using constraints to directly guide the adversarial example generation offers a plausible avenue for improved evasion success rates in constrained tabular domains.

References

1. Abu-Nimeh, S., Nappa, D., Wang, X., Nair, S.: A comparison of machine learning techniques for phishing detection. In: Proceedings of the Anti-Phishing Working Groups 2nd Annual eCrime Researchers Summit, pp. 60–69 (2007)
2. Akhtar, N., Mian, A.: Threat of adversarial attacks on deep learning in computer vision: a survey. IEEE Access **6**, 14410–14430 (2018)
3. Alhussien, N., Aleroud, A., Melhem, A., Khamaiseh, S.Y.: Constraining adversarial attacks on network intrusion detection systems: transferability and defense analysis. IEEE Trans. Netw. Serv. Manag. (2024)
4. Almseidin, M., Alzubi, M., Kovacs, S., Alkasassbeh, M.: Evaluation of machine learning algorithms for intrusion detection system. In: 2017 IEEE 15th International Symposium on Intelligent Systems and Informatics (SISY), pp. 000277–000282. IEEE (2017)
5. Alvi, R.H., Rahman, M.H., Khan, A., Rahman, R.M.: Deep learning approach on tabular data to predict early-onset neonatal sepsis. J. Inf. Telecommun. **5**(2), 226–246 (2021)
6. Apruzzese, G., Conti, M., Yuan, Y.: Spacephish: the evasion-space of adversarial attacks against phishing website detectors using machine learning. In: Proceedings of the 38th Annual Computer Security Applications Conference, pp. 171–185. ACM (2022). https://doi.org/10.1145/3564625.3567980
7. Ballet, V., Renard, X., Aigrain, J., Laugel, T., Frossard, P., Detyniecki, M.: Imperceptible adversarial attacks on tabular data. arXiv preprint arXiv:1911.03274 (2019)
8. Behjati, M., Moosavi-Dezfooli, S.M., Baghshah, M.S., Frossard, P.: Universal adversarial attacks on text classifiers. In: ICASSP 2019-2019 IEEE International Conference on Acoustics, Speech and Signal Processing (ICASSP), pp. 7345–7349. IEEE (2019)
9. Ben-Tov, M., Deutch, D., Frost, N., Sharif, M.: CaFa: cost-aware, feasible attacks with database constraints against neural tabular classifiers. In: 2024 IEEE Symposium on Security and Privacy (SP), pp. 227–227. IEEE Computer Society (2024)
10. Cartella, F., Anunciacao, O., Funabiki, Y., Yamaguchi, D., Akishita, T., Elshocht, O.: Adversarial attacks for tabular data: application to fraud detection and imbalanced data. arXiv preprint arXiv:2101.08030 (2021)
11. Chen, J., Jordan, M.I., Wainwright, M.J.: HopSkipJumpAttack: a query-efficient decision-based adversarial attack. In: 2020 IEEE Symposium on Security and Privacy, pp. 1277–1294. IEEE (2020). https://doi.org/10.1109/SP40000.2020.00045
12. Chen, P.Y., Zhang, H., Sharma, Y., Yi, J., Hsieh, C.J.: ZOO: zeroth order optimization based black-box attacks to deep neural networks without training substitute models. In: Proceedings of the 10th ACM Workshop on Artificial Intelligence and Security, pp. 15–26. ACM (2017). https://doi.org/10.1145/3128572.3140448

13. Chernikova, A., Oprea, A.: FENCE: feasible evasion attacks on neural networks in constrained environments. ACM Trans. Priv. Secur. **25**(4), 1–34 (2022). https://doi.org/10.1145/3544746
14. Clements, J.M., Xu, D., Yousefi, N., Efimov, D.: Sequential deep learning for credit risk monitoring with tabular financial data. arXiv preprint arXiv:2012.15330 (2020)
15. Dastile, X., Celik, T.: Making deep learning-based predictions for credit scoring explainable. IEEE Access **9**, 50426–50440 (2021)
16. Granados, A., Miah, M.S., Ortiz, A., Kiekintveld, C.: A realistic approach for network traffic obfuscation using adversarial machine learning. In: Decision and Game Theory for Security, pp. 45–57. Springer (2020). https://doi.org/10.1007/978-3-030-64793-3_3
17. Guo, C., Sablayrolles, A., Jégou, H., Kiela, D.: Gradient-based adversarial attacks against text transformers. arXiv preprint arXiv:2104.13733 (2021)
18. Hannousse, A., Yahiouche, S.: Towards benchmark datasets for machine learning based website phishing detection: an experimental study. Eng. Appl. Artif. Intell. **104**, 104347 (2021). https://doi.org/10.1016/j.engappai.2021.104347
19. Hashemi, M.J., Cusack, G., Keller, E.: Towards evaluation of NIDSs in adversarial setting. In: Proceedings of the 3rd ACM CoNEXT Workshop on Big DAta, Machine Learning and Artificial Intelligence for Data Communication Networks, pp. 14–21. ACM (2019). https://doi.org/10.1145/3359992.3366642
20. Kaggle: All lending club loan data (2019). https://www.kaggle.com/datasets/wordsforthewise/lending-club
21. Kireev, K., Kulynych, B., Troncoso, C.: Adversarial robustness for tabular data through cost and utility awareness. arXiv preprint arXiv:2208.13058 (2022)
22. Kurakin, A., Goodfellow, I., Bengio, S.: Adversarial Machine Learning at Scale. arXiv preprint arXiv:1611.01236 (2016)
23. Li, J., Yang, Y., Sun, J.S., Tomsovic, K., Qi, H.: ConAML: constrained adversarial machine learning for cyber-physical systems. In: Proceedings of the 2021 ACM Asia Conference on Computer and Communications Security, pp. 52–66. ACM (2021). https://doi.org/10.1145/3433210.3437513 pp. 52–66. ACM (2021). https://doi.org/10.1145/3433210.3437513
24. Ma, X., et al.: Understanding adversarial attacks on deep learning based medical image analysis systems. Pattern Recogn. **110**, 107332 (2021). https://doi.org/10.1016/j.patcog.2020.107332
25. Madry, A., Makelov, A., Schmidt, L., Tsipras, D., Vladu, A.: Towards deep learning models resistant to adversarial attacks. In: International Conference on Learning Representations, pp. 1–23. OpenReview (2018). https://openreview.net/forum?id=rJzIBfZAb
26. Moustafa, N., Creech, G., Slay, J.: Big data analytics for intrusion detection system: statistical decision-making using finite dirichlet mixture models. In: Data Analytics and Decision Support for Cybersecurity, pp. 127–156. Springer (2017). https://doi.org/10.1007/978-3-319-59439-2_5
27. Moustafa, N., Slay, J.: UNSW-NB15: a comprehensive data set for network intrusion detection systems (UNSW-NB15 network data set). In: 2015 Military Communications and Information Systems Conference (MilCIS), pp. 1–6. IEEE (2015). https://doi.org/10.1109/MilCIS.2015.7348942
28. Moustafa, N., Slay, J.: The evaluation of network anomaly detection systems: statistical analysis of the UNSW-NB15 data set and the comparison with the KDD99 data set. Inf. Secur. J. A Glob. Perspect. **25**(1–3), 18–31 (2016). https://doi.org/10.1080/19393555.2015.1125974

29. Moustafa, N., Slay, J., Creech, G.: Novel geometric area analysis technique for anomaly detection using trapezoidal area estimation on large-scale networks. IEEE Trans. Big Data **5**(4), 481–494 (2017). https://doi.org/10.1109/TBDATA.2017. 2715166

30. Nicolae, M.-I., et al.: Adversarial robustness toolbox v1.15.0 (2023). https://github. com/Trusted-AI/adversarial-robustness-toolbox

31. Rusch, N., Jodeiri Akbarfam, A., Maleki, H., Agrawal, G., Dorai, G.: Classify me correctly if you can: evaluating adversarial machine learning threats in NIDS. In: Security and Privacy in Communication Networks. Springer (2023)

32. Sarhan, M., Layeghy, S., Moustafa, N., Portmann, M.: NetFlow datasets for machine learning-based network intrusion detection systems. In: Big Data Technologies and Applications, pp. 117–135. Springer (2020). https://doi.org/10.1007/ 978-3-030-72802-1_9

33. Schönherr, L., Kohls, K., Zeiler, S., Holz, T., Kolossa, D.: Adversarial attacks against automatic speech recognition systems via psychoacoustic hiding. arXiv preprint arXiv:1808.05665 (2018)

34. Sheatsley, R., Papernot, N., Weisman, M., Verma, G., McDaniel, P.: Adversarial examples in constrained domains. arXiv preprint arXiv:2011.01183 (2020)

35. Simonetto, T., Dyrmishi, S., Ghamizi, S., Cordy, M., Le Traon, Y.: A unified framework for adversarial attack and defense in constrained feature space. In: Proceedings of the Thirty-First International Joint Conference on Artificial Intelligence, IJCAI-22, pp. 1313–1319. International Joint Conferences on Artificial Intelligence Organization (2022). https://doi.org/10.24963/ijcai.2022/183

36. Simonetto, T., Dyrmishi, S., Ghamizi, S., Cordy, M., Le Traon, Y.: Constrained attacks (C-PGD) source code, v0.1.2 (2023). https://github.com/serval-uni-lu/ constrained-attacks

37. Simonetto, T., Ghamizi, S., Cordy, M.: Constrained adaptive attack: effective adversarial attack against deep neural networks for tabular data. arXiv preprint arXiv:2406.00775 (2024)

38. Taori, R., Kamsetty, A., Chu, B., Vemuri, N.: Targeted adversarial examples for black box audio systems. In: 2019 IEEE Security and Privacy Workshops (SPW), pp. 15–20. IEEE (2019). https://doi.org/10.1109/SPW.2019.00012

39. Teuffenbach, M., Piatkowska, E., Smith, P.: Subverting network intrusion detection: crafting adversarial examples accounting for domain-specific constraints. In: Machine Learning and Knowledge Extraction, pp. 301–320. Springer (2020). https://doi.org/10.1007/978-3-030-57321-8_17

TTP Classification with Minimal Labeled Data: A Retrieval-Based Few-Shot Learning Approach

Dzenan Hamzic[1]([✉]) [ID], Florian Skopik[1] [ID], Max Landauer[1] [ID],
Markus Wurzenberger[1] [ID], and Andreas Rauber[2] [ID]

[1] AIT Austrian Institute of Technology, Vienna, Austria
{dzenan.hamzic,florian.skopik,max.landauer,
markus.wurzenberger}@ait.ac.at
[2] Vienna University of Technology, Vienna, Austria
rauber@ifs.tuwien.ac.at

Abstract. Cyber threat intelligence (CTI) reports are critical for understanding adversarial behaviors but are often unstructured and lack sufficient labeled data, which makes automated extraction of Tactics, Techniques, and Procedures (TTPs) challenging. This paper addresses these issues by introducing TTPFShot, a novel retrieval-based few-shot learning framework that classifies TTPs from CTI texts with minimal labeled data. TTPFShot leverages a vector database to retrieve semantically similar examples from a sentence-based dataset derived from the MITRE ATT&CK framework. These examples are used to construct few-shot prompts that guide large language models to accurately map CTI sentences to the appropriate TTP categories. Comprehensive evaluations on both sentence-based and document-based datasets demonstrate that TTPFShot outperforms existing approaches, such as TTPXHunter, by achieving higher precision, recall, and F1 scores. These results underscore the framework's ability to mitigate data scarcity issues and improve TTP classification accuracy in real-world settings.

Keywords: cyber threat intelligence · ttp classification · large language models · few-shot learning

1 Introduction

Cyber Threat Intelligence (CTI) reports provide critical information about how attackers perform cyberattacks, often including details like indicators of compromise (IoCs) such as domain names, IP addresses, and Tactics, Techniques, and Procedures (TTPs) used by attackers. These reports help organizations better understand the methods and goals of cybercriminals [20,24]. Since they are primarily meant for human consumption, they are usually unstructured, written in everyday language, and put little effort in providing machine readable information.

An example of such a report is Trend Micro's "Pawn Storm's Lack of Sophistication as a Strategy" [15]. This report covers the tactics of the advanced persis-

© The Author(s) 2025
M. Dalla Preda et al. (Eds.): ARES 2025, LNCS 15993, pp. 387–408, 2025.
https://doi.org/10.1007/978-3-032-00627-1_19

tent threat (APT) group Pawn Storm, also known as APT28[1]. It describes how the group uses brute force techniques (T1110)[2] to break into accounts, either by guessing passwords or using password hashes they have obtained [3]. The report includes a detailed technical breakdown with code examples, IoCs, and related files, making it a valuable resource for spotting attack patterns. Many CTI reports from security companies, blogs, and forums use informal language, which can make it difficult to pull out useful information for automated security tools [18,25].

Organizations rely on these CTI reports to prepare for possible attacks. However, analyzing these reports to find useful information is a complex and time-consuming task for security analysts [25]. To understand attacks better and build stronger defenses, analysts often map the information from CTI reports to frameworks like MITRE ATT&CK. This framework organizes TTPs at different stages of an attack, such as initial access, execution, and persistence, and categorizes the goals of attackers, like stealing data or spying [19]. By using MITRE ATT&CK as a standard reference, organizations can understand the steps in an attack and evaluate their security measures [7,9].

Recognizing TTPs from CTI reports is challenging due to rapidly evolving attacker techniques, limited structured data, and language differences that complicate context and mapping to the MITRE ATT&CK framework [2,23]. Moreover, one-to-one mapping often misses relevant TTPs.

In this paper, we introduce **TTPFShot**[3], a framework designed to automatically extract TTPs from CTI texts. CTI reports are usually designed for human readers, thus they mostly lack structured data, making it hard to accurately classify the TTPs they describe in an automated manner at scale. TTPFShot tackles this issue by using Few-Shot Learning (FSL) [4], a method that requires only a small number of labeled examples, which is essential when labeled data is limited. This technique is efficient and enables our model to classify TTPs even with minimal labeled data by finding similar sentences that were extracted from labeled data and stored in a vector database.

The TTPFShot framework (Fig. 1) works in several steps:

1. **COLLECT**: Extract sentences and corresponding labels from the MITRE ATT&CK framework.
2. **EMBED**: Embed the sentence and store the embeddings, along with their labels as metadata, in a vector database.
3. **QUERY**: Search the database for the N sentences that are most similar to the input sentence from a CTI report, and return their similarity scores.
4. **CLASSIFY**: Use the most similar sentences and their labels to create a few-shot prompt for the Large Language Model (LLM) to classify the new sentence according to the MITRE ATT&CK Technique or subtechnique.

---

[1] https://attack.mitre.org/groups/G0007/.

[2] https://attack.mitre.org/techniques/T1110/.

[3] https://github.com/ait-cti/TTPFShot.

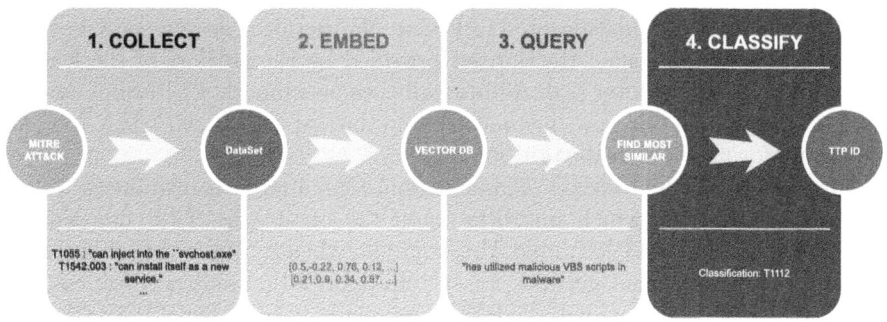

Fig. 1. TTPFShot Concept.

This approach is especially innovative in TTP classification. Traditional models, like BERT (Bidirectional Encoder Representations from Transformers) [8], need a large number of labeled examples to perform well; for instance, TTPHunter notes that at least 50 sentences per TTP are required for fine-tuning a BERT model [22]. However, some TTPs in the MITRE ATT&CK framework have very few available examples. For example, the technique T1093 has only two sentences describing it, which would typically be insufficient for traditional models. TTPFShot, on the other hand, overcomes this limitation by relying on the vector database to supply additional context through similar examples, which the LLM can then use for FSL.

By making use of FSL in this way, TTPFShot significantly reduces the dependency on large datasets and offers a more flexible solution for classifying TTPs with minimal data. This framework has the potential to accelerate the process of analyzing CTI reports, making it easier for organizations to identify and respond to threats quickly and efficiently.

Our contributions collectively advance the state-of-the-art in TTP classification, addressing limitations in current approaches and offering resources and methods applicable to both research and practical cybersecurity applications. In detail, the main contributions of this paper are as follows:

1. A Novel Retrieval-Based FSL Approach for TTP Classification: We introduce an innovative approach that leverages retrieval-based FSL to classify TTPs, even when only a few labeled samples are available.
2. Extended Classification to MITRE ATT&CK Subtechniques: Unlike previous research, which primarily focuses on high-level TTPs, our approach extends to the classification of MITRE ATT&CK subtechniques.
3. Contribution of Two New Datasets: To facilitate TTP classification and further research, we publish two newly developed datasets: a sentence-based dataset (DSA)[4] and a document-based dataset (DSC)[5] from CTI reports.

---

[4] https://zenodo.org/records/14907305.
[5] https://zenodo.org/records/14659512.

4. Comprehensive Evaluation of TTPFShot: We perform an extensive evaluation of TTPFShot using the dataset provided by the authors of the leading approach, TTPXHunter [23]. Additionally, we benchmark TTPFShot against TTPXHunter on our new document-based dataset DSC from CISA to compare performance in real-world settings.

5. Adaptation to One-to-Many Classification: Our approach introduces a one-to-many classifier, which improves upon the one-to-one TTP mapping in TTPHunter and TTPXHunter. For example, when a sentence such as "Payload scans system and network for system information and network connection discovery" is provided, TTPXHunter maps it to either T1082 (System Information Discovery) or T1049 (System Network Connection Discovery). However, TTPXHunter's one-to-one TTP mapping limits its capacity, as it only links each sentence to a single TTP, potentially missing other relevant TTPs in a document [22]. Our one-to-many classification approach overcomes this limitation by enabling the classification of multiple relevant TTPs from a single sentence, capturing a more comprehensive view of the ground truth TTPs within CTI reports.

The remainder of the paper is organized as follows. Section 2 provides background and related work on CTI and the challenges of TTP classification. It discusses existing tools such as TTPHunter, TTPXHunter, and TRAM, as well as the relevance of FSL and Retrieval-Augmented Generation (RAG) [13] in enhancing TTP classification. Section 3 outlines the datasets used in this study, including the DSC dataset from CISA, as well as the methodology of our TTPFShot approach, which combines vector databases, FSL, and LLMs for TTP classification. Section 4 describes the evaluation results of TTPFShot compared to other models, such as TTPXHunter, using both DSB and DSC datasets. Finally, Sect. 6 discusses the conclusions and future work.

2 Background and Related Work

In CTI reports[6, 7] analysts find important information about new and ongoing cyber threats, including details on specific attacks and the TTPs attackers use. These reports often explain how attackers break into systems, stay hidden, steal data, and cover their tracks. They may also include Indicators of Compromise (IoCs), such as IP addresses or domain names, which signal possible threats [16].

For security analysts, CTI reports are essential tools for planning defense strategies. Analysts review TTPs in each report to see how these methods might affect their organization's setup and IT systems. For example, if a CTI report describes how attackers use techniques like credential dumping (e.g. T1003) or phishing (e.g. T1566) to gain access, analysts can check if their own detection systems are prepared to spot these threats [6].

---

[6] https://github.com/blackorbird/APT_REPORT/blob/master/BlindEagle/
APT_Blind_Eagles_Malware_Arsenal_Technical_Analysis_of_the_New.pdf.

[7] https://github.com/blackorbird/APT_REPORT/blob/master/lazarus/
CryptoCore-Lazarus-Clearsky.pdf.

By matching TTPs from CTI reports to their organization's systems, analysts can take measures to close security gaps and improve defenses. This may involve updating detection rules, refining security policies, or training response teams on these attack methods. However, because CTI reports are often written in everyday language, it can be hard to quickly extract TTPs for automated tools. Tools that can automatically read and pull out TTPs from CTI reports are capable of reducing the workload for analysts and help organizations respond faster to new threats, but often fail to provide accurate results due to the following challenges [23]:

- Unstructured Language: CTI reports often use varied, everyday language, making it hard for automated tools to extract TTPs consistently [10].
- Rapidly Evolving Techniques: Attackers frequently modify or create new techniques, requiring models to stay up-to-date to recognize the latest TTPs [5].
- Limited Labeled Data: Many TTPs lack sufficient labeled examples, especially less common ones, making training difficult [22].
- Context-Dependent Classification: TTPs can mean different things based on context, requiring models to understand context to avoid misclassification [14,22].
- Multilabel Complexity: Actions often map to multiple TTPs, needing models that can handle multiple labels per instance [22].

These challenges underline the need for flexible approaches that can interpret unstructured text, adapt to new techniques, and classify TTPs with minimal data.

FSL is a machine learning approach designed for scenarios where only a small amount of labeled data is available. Unlike traditional models that require large datasets for effective training, FSL can classify new examples by learning from just a few instances per category. This makes it especially relevant for TTP classification, where labeled examples for each technique are often limited or sparse. In the context of CTI, some TTPs may only have a handful of examples, making traditional, data-hungry models like BERT less effective. However, a key limitation of retrieval-augmented FSL is that queries need to be sufficiently similar to the stored vectors in order to retrieve relevant examples. If the query differs too much from the existing data, the model might fail to recognize its similarity, leading to misclassifications. This can be problematic in other domains where the diversity of input data is large and unpredictable. In the case of CTI reports, however, this issue is somewhat mitigated. CTI texts often contain structured descriptions of common attack techniques, and the semantic similarity between sentences in these reports tends to be more predictable compared to other domains. As a result, FSL can still perform well in CTI applications despite this limitation, as the range of variations in the language used to describe TTPs is relatively narrow, and many of the techniques are described using similar phrasing or terminology across different reports.

TTPHunter [22], TTPXHunter [23], and TRAM [17] are tools developed to enhance the classification of TTPs in CTI domain. TTPHunter, for example, leverages BERT-based contextual feature extraction combined with a linear classifier to map CTI sentences to specific TTP categories. While this method has proven effective in processing unstructured CTI reports, it faces limitations, such as its reliance on a substantial amount of labeled data and its inability to handle multi-label classification effectively. TTPXHunter builds on this by incorporating SecureBERT, which improves dataset augmentation through masked word prediction, helping to address the scarcity of labeled data and enhance the representation of underrepresented TTPs. However, its single-label classification approach still poses challenges when multiple TTPs are relevant in a single sentence. TRAM uses FastText embeddings and BERT-based models. It initially applies FastText with logistic regression for single-label classification of unstructured text, while multi-label classification is handled with multi-output logistic regression. For more complex tasks, TRAM uses BERT-based feature extraction, improving classification accuracy by capturing contextual nuances in sentences. However, BERT requires more labeled data and computational resources, limiting scalability. Despite these challenges, TRAM offers a flexible solution for TTP classification, dependent on data quality and feature extraction.

Our approach combines techniques from RAG and FSL to improve TTP classification in CTI. RAG operates in two parts: a retrieval step that searches a database to find relevant examples (sentences and corresponding TTP labels) and a generative model that uses these examples to make more accurate label predictions. In our method, the retrieval step is used to create or enhance the Few-Shot template. A Few-Shot template is a set of examples (sentences and their corresponding TTPs) that the model uses to understand the task with minimal labeled data. It retrieves sentences from the database that are similar to the input text and their associated TTPs, which serve as context for the classification task. These examples are then fed into a LLM, allowing it to classify the TTPs more accurately by leveraging the context provided in the Few-Shot template.

3   Methodology

In this section, we explain the methodology used to develop the design of our TTPFShot approach.

3.1   Retrieval Augmented Few Shot Template

In this study, we apply retrieval-augmented few-shot learning, a technique that combines retrieval-based methods with a prompting technique to classify CTI sentences into corresponding TTP ID labels. Figure 2 depicts the four steps of our approach and provides samples. In Step 1, the input sentence, such as "Payload scans system and network for system information and network connection discovery" is provided for classification. This sentence[8] describes an action that needs to be classified according to the MITRE ATT&CK framework. Step 2

---

[8] https://attack.mitre.org/techniques/T1049/.

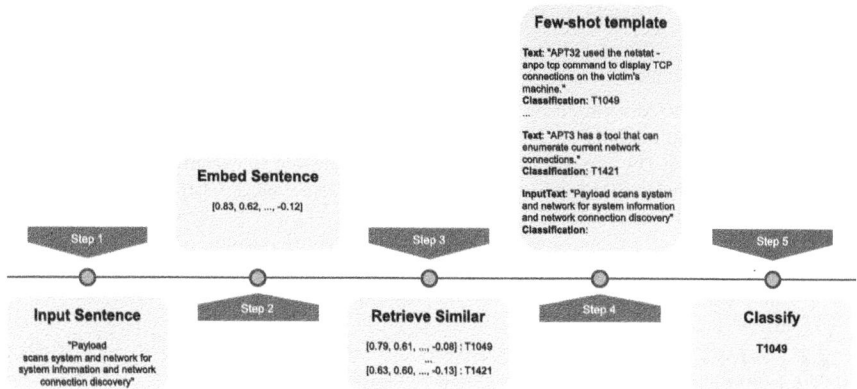

Fig. 2. Retrieval-based Few-Shot Templating.

involves converting this sentence into an embedding vector, which is a numerical representation that captures the semantic meaning of the sentence in a high-dimensional space. This transformation allows for better comparison between sentences. Step 3 follows, where a search is performed to retrieve similar sentence embeddings from a pre-existing dataset. Along with these similar vectors, their corresponding TTP IDs are returned. For example, similar sentences may be linked to TTP IDs such as T1049 and T1421, representing actions like "Network service scanning" and "Network connection enumeration" In Step 4, a few-shot template is constructed using the examples retrieved in Step 3, as well as the input sentence. These retrieved examples (such as "APT32 used the netstat -anpo tcp command to display TCP connections on the victim's machine" with classification T1049) are used to build a template that helps in classifying the input sentence. Finally, in step 5, the input sentence is classified based on the patterns learned from these few examples. The generative model uses these examples to make better predictions for the input sentence.

3.2 Data Sets

Sentence-based datasets, such as DSA and DSB, differ from document-based dataset DSC primarily in their granularity and structure. While document-based datasets contain full reports or articles with TTP references scattered throughout the text, sentence-based datasets break these reports down into individual sentences, each labeled with a specific TTP ID. This granular approach enables more precise classification, as each sentence is treated as a standalone instance for retrieval and prediction. In contrast, document-based datasets require models to understand broader context across the entire document, making them more complex and challenging to process due to the varying levels of relevance and context in different parts of the text. Sentence-based datasets, therefore, simplify the task by focusing on smaller, more manageable chunks of information, which is especially beneficial for techniques like retrieval-augmented few-shot learning.

Table 1. Example TTP with description

TTP ID	Sentence
T1574.012	[Blue Mockingbird] has used textttwmic.exe and Windows Registry modifications to set the COR_PROFILER environment variable to execute a malicious DLL whenever a process loads the .NET CLR. (Citation: RedCanary Mockingbird May 2020)

Table 2. Rules, Examples, and Replacements

Rule	Example	Replacement
re.sub(r'\[.*?\]\(https://attack.mitre.org/software/.*?\)', 'Software', text)	[Some Software](https://attack.mitre.org/software/S1234)	Software
re.sub(r'\[.*?\]\(https://attack.mitre.org/groups/.*?\)', 'Attacker', text)	[Some Group](https://attack.mitre.org/groups/G1234)	Attacker
df['Value'].str.replace(r'\((?)]*\)', '', regex=True)	This is a test (with some extra information)	This is a test
df['Value'].str.replace(r'\[.*?\]', '', regex=True)	This is a test [extra information]	This is a test
df['Value'].str.strip()	Extra spaces at start and end	Extra spaces at start and end

To build the DSA retrieval dataset, we utilized the MITRE ATT&CK framework, specifically version 15.1 of the enterprise data set[9]. From this framework, we extracted descriptions of techniques and examples of textual procedures associated with each technique. To improve the dataset's granularity, the textual descriptions were split into individual sentences, creating a sentence-based dataset. Each sentence was then automatically assigned to a specific technique or sub-technique ID, allowing for precise alignment and easier retrieval when querying the vector database (see example in Table 1).

Since most procedure description sentences contain group names (replaced with Rule 2), software names (replaced with Rule 1), corresponding URLs (replaced with Rules 1 and 2), and brackets (replaced with Rules 3 and 4), the preprocessing rules in Table 2 were applied to clean and standardize the data. Rule 5 removes the extra spaces at start and end. The DSA dataset includes a total of *780 unique techniques and sub-techniques*, significantly expanding the number of labels compared to the 193 technique labels in TTPXHunter and the 50 techniques in TRAM. Overall, the dataset contains 19,747 rows. As can be seen from the Fig. 3, the highest number of sentences are associated with the following TTPs: T1105, T1082, T1071.001, T1059.003, and T1083, with sentence counts of 468, 387, 349, 345, and 324, respectively. On the other hand, the TTPs with the fewest sentences are T1093, T1079, T1028, T1182, and T1195.003, each with only 2 or 3 sentences.

---

[9] https://raw.githubusercontent.com/mitre-attack/attack-stix-data/refs/heads/master/enterprise-attack/enterprise-attack-15.1.json.

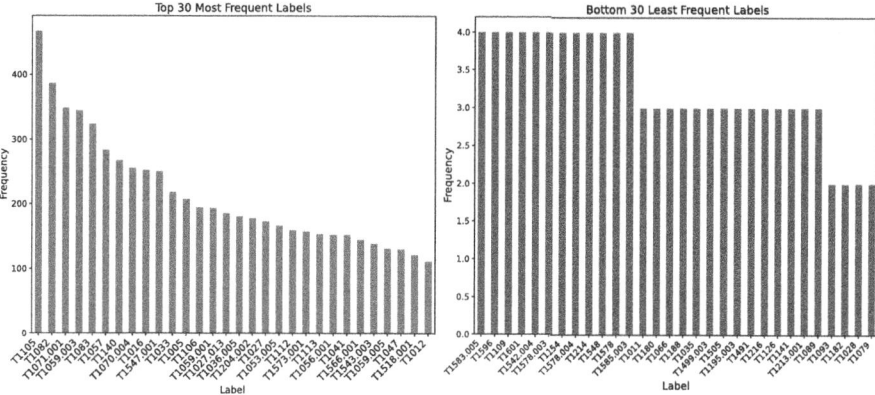

Fig. 3. Label Distribution.

We used the sentence-based TTPHunter dataset[10] (DSB) to determine the optimal number of examples (shots) needed for FSL and to perform an initial comparison with the current leading text-to-TTP classification framework, TTPXHunter. The dataset uses the standard MITRE ATT&CK knowledge base as a data source to collect text data and their corresponding TTPs. The Indicators of Compromise (IOC) are replaced with their base names, e.g., the email adress xyz@pqr.com is replaced with the word "Email". This dataset consists of 8,387 rows, with two main columns: TTP ID and Sentence. It includes only 50 unique TTP IDs, selected by the TTPHunter authors based on the availability of at least 50 sentences for each TTP, covering 177 unique MITRE ATT&CK techniques [22]. The dataset preparation methodology differs from ours (DSA dataset), since we did not remove the IOCs, and we included TTP labels having less then 50 sentences, i.e., we included all TTP labels.

The DSC dataset comprises 77 cybersecurity articles sourced from the public CISA website, published between July 2020 and February 2024. Each article explicitly mentions MITRE ATT&CK Tactics, Techniques, and Procedures (TTPs), providing valuable insights into adversary behaviors. The dataset includes the following columns:

- RawText: The unfiltered text extracted from the main content of each article.
- TTP: A set of MITRE ATT&CK TTP IDs found within the article's RawText. This column serves as a ground truth for multilabel classification.
- CleanText: A cleaned version of the RawText, with tables and TTP IDs removed for clarity. Sentences from this column serve as input to be classified.
- URL: The URL to the original article.

---

[10] https://github.com/nanda-rani/TTPHunter-Automated-Extraction-of-Actionable-Intelligence-as-TTPs-from-Narrative-Threat-Reports/blob/main/Dataset/TTPHunter_dataset.csv.

To standardize the text and facilitate analysis, TTP mentions were extracted and replaced with empty spaces using the regex pattern:

```
(?:TA\d{4}|T\d{4,5}(?:\.\d{3})?)
```

The extracted TTP IDs serve as labels or ground-truth of the corresponding document. This step is crucial as it removes the ground truth labels from the text, effectively preventing the model from directly relying on these labels during classification. By doing so, we ensure that the classification algorithms are evaluated purely on their ability to infer TTPs from the context of the report, rather than using predefined labels that may influence the outcome. This approach helps in assessing the model's actual performance in detecting and classifying TTPs without bias from the known ground truth labels. The sentences which contain no TTP labels are left intact.

3.3   Classification Approach Design

The workflow for our TTP classification system (Fig. 4) starts with preparing a dataset of sentences from a DSA, each labeled with its corresponding TTP ID (TTP Sentences). These sentences, which describe specific TTPs used in cyber-attacks, are then processed into embeddings using SecureBERT [1]. SecureBERT generates vector embeddings with a dimension of 1x768 for each sentence, capturing its semantic meaning. These embeddings are stored in a vector database (or "vector DB").

When a user or system sends a new sentence (e.g., from a CTI report that needs TTP labeling) for classification, the sentence is first embedded using the same SecureBERT model to ensure consistency with the stored embeddings. This new sentence embedding is then used to query the vector store, retrieving the N most similar sentences based on semantic similarity. These retrieved sentences provide relevant context and examples. The FSL template is created by organizing these examples in a structured format that helps the model make accurate predictions. This template plays a crucial role in guiding the model by providing relevant context to classify the new sentence effectively.

The Few-Shot Template, now containing the N similar sentences as examples, is sent as a prompt to a LLM. The LLM processes this prompt and classifies the input sentence by predicting the appropriate TTP ID. The output returned by the LLM is solely the TTP ID label (or multiple TTP IDs, depending on the prompt setting), which represents the best match for the queried sentence based on the examples provided in the Few-Shot template.

Querying on a sentence level is more effective relative to whole document querying because it allows for precise and granular classification, focusing on specific TTP descriptions that are clearly defined within individual sentences. This approach reduces ambiguity and makes it easier to match the sentence to the correct TTP ID, as each sentence is a self-contained unit with a clear context. Since the dataset for retrieval is sentence-based, the model is optimized for this level of granularity, whereas whole document querying could introduce noise and require more complex context handling.

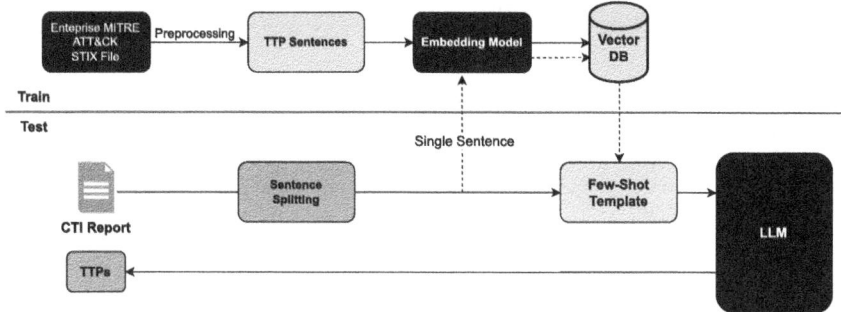

Fig. 4. TTPFShot Concept Overview.

3.4   Configuration of TTPFShot's Few Shot Template

In our experiment, we simulated varying numbers of Few-Shot samples (FS number) to evaluate their impact on the model's performance metrics: F1 Score, Precision (Micro), and Recall (Micro). Few-Shot samples refer to a small number of labeled examples used by the model to learn and make predictions. Figure 5 illustrates these metrics across different Few-Shot numbers, showing how the model's performance stabilizes as we increase the number of Few-Shot samples. For this evaluation, we used a dataset split with 80% for training and 20% for testing. The 80/20 dataset split is a commonly used approach in machine learning, as it provides a good balance between training the model on a sufficient amount of data (80%) while retaining enough data (20%) for testing, ensuring effective evaluation of the model's generalization capability [22].

We chose the number 65 as the parameter setting for the number of shots in Few-Shot algorithm because it provides a balance between performance and computational efficiency. At 65 (Fig. 5), the micro F1 score, precision, and recall show optimal or near-optimal values, indicating a high level of accuracy and consistency. This ensures that the model performs well without excessive computational costs or diminishing returns at higher few-shot numbers.

3.5   Few-Shot Template

The Few-Shot template (Fig. 6) is designed to help the LLM classify CTI sentences into specific MITRE ATT&CK TTP categories. This template includes 65 examples of TTP-labeled sentences, retrieved using a vector retriever, providing context to guide the model's classification decision. These 65 examples are the most similar to the input text that is to be classified. The similarity of each example to the input text (query) is given by the retriever, measured by the L2 distance in float, with a lower score representing higher similarity. Each example consists of a sentence, a similarity score, and its corresponding TTP classification label. The template begins by instructing the LLM that it is acting

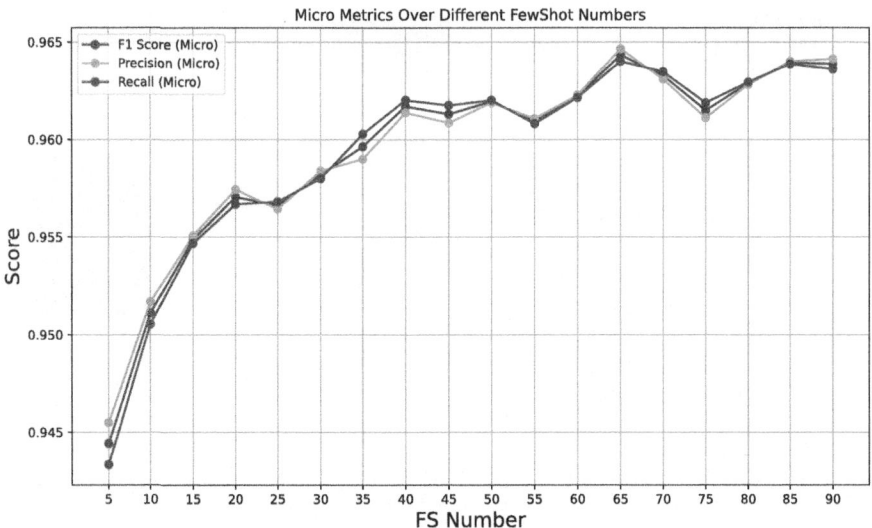

Fig. 5. Evaluation of Varying Few-Shot numbers on Prediction Performance.

as a "MITRE ATT&CK TTP classification expert." Its task is to classify an input text based on examples provided in the template. Each example follows a structured format:

- **Text**: The sentence itself, which describes a specific tactic, technique, or procedure observed in a cyberattack.
- **Similarity**: The similarity score between the example sentence("Text") and the input sentence ("InputText"). This score indicates how closely the example matches the input, with lower values representing higher similarity.
- **Classification**: The TTP label that corresponds to the example sentence. This label starts with "T" and is followed by a unique identifier number from the MITRE ATT&CK framework (e.g., T1082).

If the LLM finds that the "InputText" is not related to any of the examples provided, it is instructed to return the label "T0000". The similarity score acts as a threshold, guiding the model to avoid assigning a TTP label if the input text does not sufficiently match any example.

Below is the properly formatted template (Fig. 6), showing a sample of the structure. Note that in the actual implementation, 65 examples would be included, providing a robust reference set for the LLM to classify the input sentence accurately.

```
You are a MITRE ATT&CK TTP classification expert. Your task is to classify the
'InputText' based on the provided examples below. Each example shows:
- a sentence (InputText),
- inverse similarity to InputText (the lower the better) (Similarity),
- and its corresponding classification label starting with 'T'.
Use these examples to determine the correct classification for the given text
(InputText). If 'InputText' is completely not related to any of the provided examples,
return class 'T0000'. To determine if the 'InputText' is not related to the given
examples, you can use the 'Similarity' property of the examples. Low 'Similarity'
values indicate high similarity between strings.Return only the classification label
starting with 'T' or 'T0000' if you found no appropriate class for 'InputText'.

Text: tajmahal has the ability to identify hardware information, the computer name,
and OS information on an infected host.[1]
Similarity: 0.09965219
Classification: T1082

Text: runningrat gathers the OS version, logical drives information, processor
information, and volume information.[1]
Similarity: 0.11707238
Classification: T1082
...
InputText: reaver collects the victim's IP address.[1]
Classification:
```

Fig. 6. TTPFShot Prompt Template.

4 Evaluation

This section presents a comprehensive evaluation of TTPFShot and competing methods across both sentence-based (DSB) and document-based (DSC)
datasets, utilizing a diverse set of metrics—including accuracy, precision, recall,
F1-score, Hamming accuracy, as well as novel measures such as coverage and
bad coverage—to capture the nuances of multilabel classification in cybersecurity threat intelligence.

4.1 Evaluation Metrics

As previously mentioned, TTPFShot is evaluated on two distinct datasets: a
sentence-based dataset (DSB) and a document-based dataset (DSC). For the
DSB, we consider the test set as the ground truth for comparison. The DSC
dataset, however, consists of a comprehensive crawl from the CISA website, fea-
turing Cybersecurity Alerts & Advisories articles that have been manually annotated with TTP IDs. This dataset serves as a rigorous benchmark to evaluate
the performance of our approach alongside TTPXHunter.

To assess the models' performance comprehensively, we employ several evaluation metrics: Accuracy [26], Precision [11], Recall [21], F1-score [27], as well as
Hamming Accuracy [12]. The latter is particularly useful for evaluating multilabel classification in the DSC dataset. These metrics help us gauge the effectiveness of TTPFShot in correctly identifying relevant TTPs within each document.
To provide additional insights into the model's ability to perform multilabel

classification tasks, we propose two novel metrics called Coverage and Bad Coverage, which we define and explain in the following.

Coverage. measures how much of the ground truth is correctly captured by the predicted labels (see Eq. 1). It calculates the proportion of elements in the ground truth that are also present in the predicted set. In other words, it tells us how well the model covers the correct answers.

$$\text{Coverage Ratio} = \frac{|y_{\text{true}} \cap y_{\text{pred}}|}{|y_{\text{true}}|} \tag{1}$$

Bad Coverage. measures how much of the prediction is incorrect or missing when compared to the ground truth (see Eq. 2). It calculates the proportion of elements in the predicted set that do not match or are missing from the ground truth. Essentially, this metric highlights the errors or omissions in the model's predictions.

$$\text{Bad Coverage Ratio} = \frac{|y_{\text{pred}} \setminus y_{\text{true}}|}{|y_{\text{pred}}|} \tag{2}$$

4.2   TTPFShot Evaluation

In this section, we present an evaluation of TTPFShot's performance on both the sentence-based DSB (single-label) dataset and the DSC (multilabel) dataset.

4.3   Evaluation on DSB Dataset (Sentence-Based)

Fig. 7 illustrates the evaluation results of TTPFShot, TTPHunter, and TTPX-Hunter on DSB across three metrics: Precision, Recall, and F1-Score. The scores demonstrate that TTPFShot consistently outperforms the other two methods, achieving the highest values (0.96 for all three metrics) compared to TTPHunter (Precision: 0.89, Recall: 0.88, F1-Score: 0.88) and TTPXHunter (Precision: 0.94, Recall: 0.92, F1-Score: 0.92). This highlights the effectiveness of default setting (SL - Single Label) TTPFShot, which uses the GPT-4o model, in accurately extracting and classifying TTPs from CTI sentences on the DSB dataset.

4.4   Evaluation on DSC Dataset (Document-Based)

Evaluation on DSC (Table 3) is more challenging and reflects real-world CTI reports. The abbreviations next to TTPFShot represent different configurations: "Multi-Label" (ML), "Zero-Shot" (ZS), "Single Label LLaMA 3 70B-Instruct" (SL L), and "Single Label Mixtral 7x8B-Instruct v0.1" (SL M).

The following configurations of TTPFShot were evaluated, each with different settings for handling the classification task:

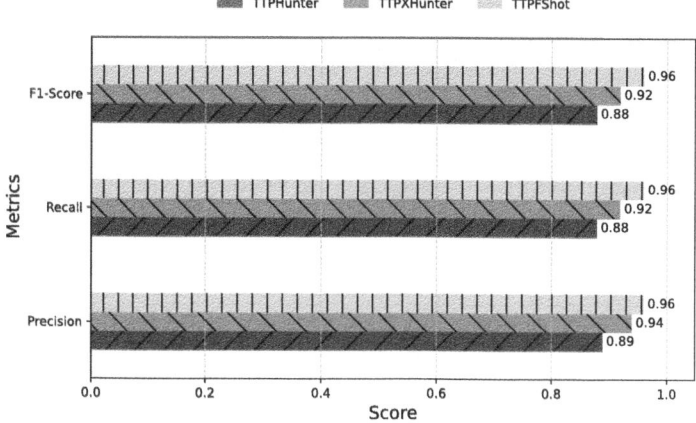

Fig. 7. Performance Comparison on DSB Dataset.

Table 3. Evaluation Metrics for Models on DSC Dataset

Model	Hamming Acc.	F1	Precision	Recall	Jaccard	Coverage	B. Coverage
TTPXHunter	0.91	0.09	0.13	0.10	0.06	0.11	0.85
TTPFShot SL	0.92	0.28	0.19	0.35	0.14	0.38	0.78
TTPFShot ML	0.93	0.26	0.16	0.35	0.12	0.37	0.81
TTPFShot ZS	0.91	0.17	0.16	0.21	0.10	0.24	0.80
TTPFShot SL L	0.82	0.08	0.09	0.25	0.07	0.26	0.87
TTPFShot SL M	0.92	0.24	0.15	0.30	0.11	0.33	0.82

- **Multi-Label (ML):** In this setting, TTPFShot's prompt was modified to include a sentence instructing the model to output multiple labels starting with "T" if applicable. This setting uses OpenAI's GPT-4o model.
- **Zero-Shot (ZS):** In this configuration, TTPFShot's prompt was adjusted to exclude any Few-Shot examples. This setting uses GPT-4o model as well.
- **Single Label LLaMA 3 70B-Instruct (SL L):** TTPFShot was executed using the LLaMA 3 70B-Instruct model instead of the ChatGPT 4o model.
- **Single Label Mixtral 7x8B-Instruct v0.1 (SL M):** TTPFShot was executed using the Mixtral 7x8B-Instruct v0.1 model instead of the ChatGPT 4o model.

Table 3 shows that while TTPXHunter achieves a high Hamming Accuracy (0.91), its F1 (0.09), Precision (0.13), Recall (0.10), and Jaccard (0.06) scores are very low, with a Coverage of only 0.11 and a high Bad Coverage of 0.85—indicating many missed or misclassified TTPs. In contrast, TTPFShot SL improves recall (0.35) and F1 (0.28), with better Coverage (0.38) and lower Bad Coverage (0.78), suggesting it more effectively captures true positives while reducing errors. Similarly, TTPFShot ML achieves the highest Hamming Accuracy (0.93) with comparable recall (0.35) and balanced Coverage (0.37) and Bad Coverage (0.81). The Zero-Shot variant (TTPFShot ZS) and the single-

Table 4. Evaluation Metrics for Models using Subset of Data

Model	Hamming Acc.	F1	Precision	Recall	Jaccard	Coverage	B. Coverage
TTPXHunter	0.78	0.36	0.36	0.32	0.20	0.29	0.58
TTPFShot SL	0.75	0.50	0.38	0.62	0.31	0.65	0.56
TTPFShot ML	0.74	0.48	0.36	0.62	0.30	0.65	0.57
TTPFShot ZS	0.76	0.46	0.38	0.55	0.29	0.58	0.55
TTPFShot SL L	0.60	0.24	0.22	0.50	0.18	0.49	0.70
TTPFShot SL M	0.72	0.45	0.33	0.58	0.27	0.58	0.61

label models based on LLaMA 3 (SL L) and Mixtral (SL M) show lower overall performance—especially SL L with an F1 of 0.08, Coverage of 0.26, and the worst Bad Coverage (0.87). Overall, TTPFShot SL and ML offer the best trade-offs, delivering higher recall and coverage with fewer incorrect predictions compared to the alternatives. The F1 scores across all models are relatively low (Table 3), reflecting the inherent challenges in achieving a balance between precision and recall in this complex task. While F1 provides a valuable summary of the trade-off between these two metrics, it alone does not fully capture the nuances of model performance, particularly in real-world CTI scenarios (DSC dataset). Similar to TTPHunter, where document-based evaluation (F1-score: 0.75) performed worse than sentence-based evaluation (F1-score: 0.88), we observe a performance drop when evaluating on DSC compared to DSB. This may be due to the polymorphic nature of words—whose meanings vary with context in CTI reports often marked by broad, vague descriptions—and language differences that further complicate TTP identification [2, 22, 23].

Refining the Evaluation to only Important Techniques Without Subtechniques. We refined the scope of the evaluation to focus exclusively on techniques, excluding subtechniques, to streamline the task and improve consistency. Furthermore, we prioritized important or more frequently referenced techniques by limiting the evaluation to those with over 50 sentences in their MITRE ATT&CK descriptions. This ensures that the analysis concentrates on widely recognized techniques with sufficient descriptive context, enhancing the relevance and robustness of the evaluation.

Table 4 shows that although TTPXHunter achieves the highest Hamming Accuracy (0.78), its overall performance is weaker—particularly in the Coverage metric (0.29), which indicates that it captures only a small portion of the ground truth labels in the documents. In contrast, TTPFShot SL stands out with the highest F1 score (0.50) and recall (0.62), paired with the best coverage (0.65) and low bad coverage (0.56)—indicating it not only captures more of the relevant TTPs but also minimizes incorrect predictions. TTPFShot ML performs similarly, effectively handling multi-label cases, whereas the zero-shot version and alternative single-label variants (SL L and SL M) lag behind, particularly in coverage quality and error rates.

Overall, the results indicate that TTPFShot SL and TTPFShot ML offer the best trade-offs between various metrics. Their performance makes them particularly well-suited for real-world CTI applications that require an efficient balance between precision, recall, and multi-label classification.

To gain a more nuanced understanding of the model's performance, additional metrics such as coverage and bad coverage were introduced, providing valuable insights into how well the models capture relevant TTPs and avoid incorrect predictions in multilabel classification tasks. This approach ensures a balanced evaluation that goes beyond traditional metrics.

Figure 8a shows how coverage varies across models as the threshold for matching ground truth increases (from 0.5 to 1.0). As the threshold increases, fewer labels are assigned because the retrieved examples are not similar enough to the input sentence. TTPFShot SL consistently achieves the highest coverage, maintaining strong performance even at stricter thresholds. TTPFShot ML and TTPFShot ZS perform competitively but fall short of TTPFShot SL, especially at higher thresholds. TTPXHunter starts strong at lower thresholds but declines significantly as the threshold tightens. Single-label variants, TTPFShot SL L and SL M, exhibit the lowest coverage, struggling to match the performance of other models. Overall, TTPFShot SL proves to be the most robust and reliable model across varying threshold levels. Figure 8b highlights the proportion of incorrect or irrelevant predictions across models as the threshold for matching ground truth increases (above 0.5 to 1.0). TTPFShot SL exhibits the lowest bad coverage across all thresholds, indicating minimal errors in its predictions even under stricter conditions. TTPXHunter and TTPFShot ZS have higher bad coverage, particularly at lower thresholds, but improve slightly as thresholds tighten. In contrast, TTPFShot SL L and SL M show the highest bad coverage, reflecting significant prediction errors compared to other models.

Unlike traditional metrics like F1-score, Accuracy, Precision, and Recall, which assess classification correctness at the sample level, Coverage and Bad Coverage offer a broader view of how well a model retrieves relevant TTPs while minimizing incorrect predictions. The coverage and bad coverage plots (see Fig. 8a and Fig. 8b) highlight these aspects, capturing the percentage of ground truth retrieved and the proportion of incorrect classifications—insights not provided by Recall, which ignores false positives, or F1-score, which balances Precision and Recall but does not distinguish between missing relevant TTPs (low Coverage) and assigning incorrect labels (high Bad Coverage). TTPFShot SL emerges as the most reliable model, achieving high coverage with minimal bad coverage across all thresholds.

5   Discussion

Our experiments with TTPFShot highlight both the strengths and limitations of using a retrieval-augmented few-shot learning approach for TTP classification. In early implementations, TTPFShot employed standard BERT embeddings; however, evaluations on the DSB dataset revealed that SecureBERT embeddings significantly enhance precision, recall, and F1 scores by better capturing

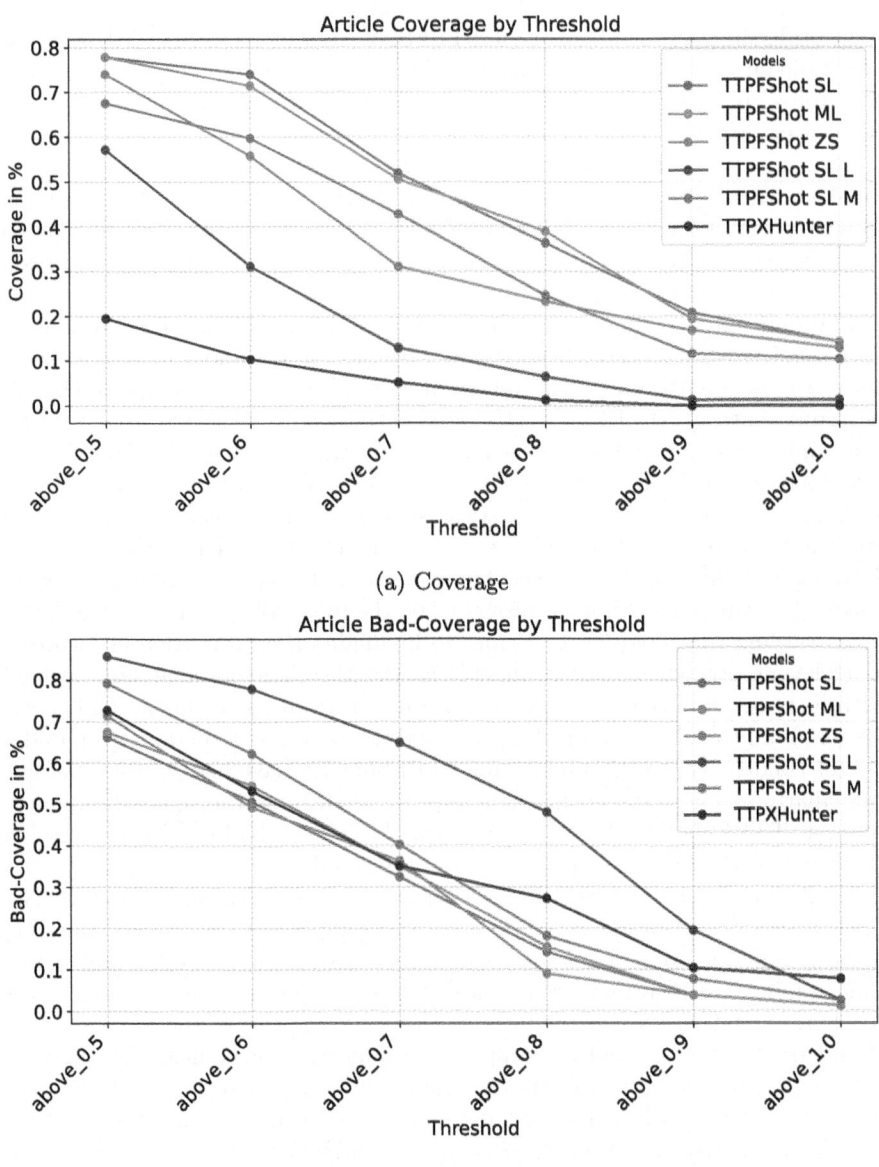

(a) Coverage

(b) Bad Coverage

Fig. 8. Comparison of Coverage and Bad Coverage.

cybersecurity-specific language. Efforts to improve retrieval via vector database partitioning did not yield further benefits (see Sect. 3.1). We are aware that LLMs struggle with floats, but we found out that including L2 distance in few-shot template as "Similarity" improves classification in our case. For the few-shot

Table 5. Mean and Standard Deviation of document processing times (in minutes) for each tool

Model	Mean	Std
TTPFShot SL	3.2	1.5
TTPFShot ML	2.9	1.3
TTPFShot ZS	1.8	0.8
TTPXHunter	0.7	0.4

Table 6. Comparison of Pros and Cons: TTPFShot vs. TTPXHunter

Aspect	TTPFShot	TTPXHunter
Pros	Minimal labeled data requirement; supports one-to-many (multi-label) classification; no fine-tuning needed; easily updatable retrieval dataset.	Fast execution speed.
Cons	Slower processing time; higher computational cost; dependent on internet latency and shared LLM resources.	Requires time-intensive fine-tuning upon framework updates; requires time-intensive dataset construction;.

classification stage, we evaluated several OpenAI models. Notably, models such as `gpt-4o-mini` and `o1-preview` underperformed relative to `gpt-4o`, which demonstrated superior generalization from few-shot examples. Consequently, `gpt-4o` was adopted as the default model in TTPFShot.

Execution performance is a key consideration for real-world CTI applications. We measured the average sentence classification times on the DSC dataset for different TTPFShot configurations, as compared to TTPXHunter. Table 5 summarizes these results. The results indicate that TTPFShot in both single-label and multi-label modes is notably slower than TTPXHunter. Although the zero-shot variant improves speed, it does so at the expense of classification performance (see Table 3 and Table 4). The slower processing time of TTPFShot is largely due to reliance on online LLM APIs and internet latency; with dedicated LLM instances, we expect execution times to improve.

A side-by-side comparison of TTPFShot and TTPXHunter is provided in Table 6. TTPFShot's main advantages include its minimal need for labeled data, support for one-to-many (multi-label) classification, elimination of fine-tuning, and ease of updating the retrieval dataset when the MITRE ATT&CK framework is revised. In contrast, TTPFShot's drawbacks are its slower processing speed and higher computational cost. TTPXHunter benefits from fast execution and simplicity but requires time-intensive fine-tuning to adapt to framework updates.

In summary, TTPFShot is well-suited for scenarios with scarce labeled data and where multi-label classification is essential, offering flexibility and ease of updates. However, its slower processing speed and higher operational costs may limit its applicability in real-time settings, where TTPXHunter's rapid execution can be advantageous despite its fine-tuning and dataset construction overhead. As for the practical dimension, TTPFShot will be integrated into Taranis AI[11], where it will operate as an asynchronous bot that periodically processes newly collected CTI data, showcasing its potential for real-world deployment.

6   Conclusion

In this paper, we introduced TTPFShot, a novel retrieval-based few-shot learning framework for classifying TTPs in CTI reports. TTPFShot leverages a vector database to retrieve semantically similar examples from a labeled sentence-based dataset (DSA), which are then used to construct a Few-Shot template for an LLM-based classification model. This approach allows TTP classification with minimal labeled data, making it highly effective for cybersecurity applications where annotated datasets are scarce.

To validate its real-world applicability, we evaluated TTPFShot using DSC, a real-life CTI dataset containing cybersecurity reports from CISA. The framework demonstrated its capability to classify 780 MITRE ATT&CK techniques and subtechniques, significantly expanding the scope of previous approaches. We conducted a comparative evaluation against existing models like TTPHunter and TTPXHunter, using multiple datasets (DSB and DSC) and standard classification metrics such as F1-score, Precision, Recall, and Hamming Accuracy. In addition, we evaluated the approaches with two novel metrics proposed in this paper, namely Coverage and Bad Coverage, which measure the proportions of correct answers and errors respectively.

The evaluation showed that TTPFShot outperforms TTPXHunter and other baselines, particularly in multi-label classification and recall, indicating higher effectiveness in capturing relevant TTPs from unstructured CTI texts. Our results highlight the advantages of retrieval-augmented few-shot learning over traditional supervised approaches, reducing dependence on large labeled datasets while improving classification accuracy.

Future work will explore enhancing retrieval mechanisms, optimizing classification prompts, and integrating more cybersecurity-specific embeddings to further improve performance and adaptability.

Acknowledgments. Funded by the European Union under the European Defence Fund (GA no. 101121403 - NEWSROOM and GA no. 101121418 - EUCINF). Views and opinions expressed are however those of the author(s) only and do not necessarily reflect those of the European Union or the European Commission. Neither the European Union nor the granting authority can be held responsible for them. This work is co-funded by the Austrian FFG Kiras project ASOC (GA no. FO999905301).

---

[11] https://taranis.ai/.

References

1. Aghaei, E., Niu, X., Shadid, W., Al-Shaer, E.: Securebert: a domain-specific language model for cybersecurity. In: Security and Privacy in Communication Networks: 18th EAI International Conference, SecureComm 2022, pp. 39–56 (2023)
2. Alam, M.T., Bhusal, D., Park, Y., Rastogi, N.: Looking beyond IoCs: automatically extracting attack patterns from external CTI. arXiv preprint arXiv:2211.01753 (2022)
3. ATT&CK Mitre: Brute force, technique t1110 - enterprise. https://attack.mitre.org/techniques/T1110/
4. Brown, T., et al.: Language models are few-shot learners. Adv. Neural. Inf. Process. Syst. **33**, 1877–1901 (2020)
5. Chen, F., et al.: Adapting to cyber threats: a phishing evolution network (pen) framework for phishing generation and analyzing evolution patterns using large language models. arXiv preprint arXiv:2411.11389 (2024)
6. CISA: Best practices for Mitre att&ck mapping (2023). https://www.cisa.gov/sites/default/files/2023-01/Best%20Practices%20for%20MITRE%20ATTCK%20Mapping.pdf
7. Picus Security: Noise to knowledge tackling challenges in cyber threat intelligence (2023). https://www.picussecurity.com/resource/blog/from-noise-to-knowledge-tackling-challenges-in-cyber-threat-intelligence
8. Devlin, J., Chang, M.W., Lee, K., Toutanova, K.: BERT: pre-training of deep bidirectional transformers for language understanding. In: Proceedings of the 2019 Conference of the North American Chapter of the Association for Computational Linguistics: Human Language Technologies, vol. 1, 4171–4186 (2019). https://doi.org/10.18653/v1/N19-1423
9. DISA: The Mitre Att&ck framework: using TTPS to understand cyber threats (2023). https://www.disa.mil/mitre-attack
10. Fieblinger, R., Alam, M.T., Rastogi, N.: Actionable cyber threat intelligence using knowledge graphs and large language models. arXiv preprint arXiv:2407.02528 (2024)
11. Flach, P.A.: Precision-recall and ROC curves. Mach. Learn. **68**(2), 227–243 (2006). https://doi.org/10.1007/s10994-006-6676-4
12. Hamza, W., Zhang, Y.: Hamming accuracy for classification models in multi-class problems. J. Comput. Res. **4**(3), 24–32 (2013). https://doi.org/10.1016/j.jcr.2013.04.002
13. Lewis, P., et al.: Retrieval-augmented generation for knowledge-intensive NLP tasks. Adv. Neural. Inf. Process. Syst. **33**, 9459–9474 (2020)
14. Mavroeidis, V., Hohimer, R., Casey, T., Jøsang, A.: Threat actor type inference and characterization within cyber threat intelligence. In: 13th International Conference on Cyber Conflict (CyCon) (2021). https://doi.org/10.48550/arXiv.2103.02301
15. Micro, T.: Pawn storm uses brute force and stealth against high-value targets (2024)
16. Microsoft: What is cyber threat intelligence? https://www.microsoft.com/en-us/security/business/security-101/what-is-cyber-threat-intelligence
17. MITRE: Att&ck threat report annotation model (tram): automatically annotating cyber threat intelligence reports (2020). https://github.com/mitre-attack/tram
18. AGIR: Automating Cyber Threat Intelligence Reporting with Natural Language Generation. arXiv preprint arXiv:2310.02655 (2023)

19. Palo Alto Networks: Cyber threat intelligence and Mitre Att&ck framework (2024). https://www.paloaltonetworks.com/resources/cyber-threat-intelligence-mitre-attack

20. Orbinato, V., Barbaraci, M., Natella, R., Cotroneo, D.: Automatic mapping of unstructured cyber threat intelligence: an experimental study (2022)

21. Powers, D.M.W.: Evaluation: from precision, recall and f-score to roc, informedness, markedness and correlation. J. Mach. Learn. Technol. **2**(1), 37–63 (2007). https://doi.org/10.1016/j.jmlr.2007.10.003

22. Rani, N., Saha, B., Maurya, V., Shukla, S.K.: Ttphunter: automated extraction of actionable intelligence as TTPS from narrative threat reports. In: ACSW '23: Proceedings of the 2023 Australasian Computer Science Week, pp. 126–134 (2023). https://doi.org/10.1145/3579375.3579391

23. Rani, N., Saha, B., Maurya, V., Shukla, S.K.: Ttpxhunter: actionable threat intelligence extraction as TTPS from finished cyber threat reports. arXiv preprint arXiv:2403.03267 (2024)

24. Rastogi, N., et al.: Inferring cyber threat intelligence – a knowledge graph-based approach (2023)

25. Siracusano, G., et al.: Time for action: automated analysis of cyber threat intelligence in the wild. arXiv preprint arXiv:2307.10214 (2023)

26. Sokolova, M., Lapalme, G.: A systematic analysis of performance measures for classification tasks. Inf. Process. Manag. **42**(5), 1316–1342 (2006). https://doi.org/10.1016/j.ipm.2005.08.001

27. Sokolova, M., Lapalme, G.: A systematic analysis of performance measures for classification tasks. Inf. Process. Manag. **42**(5), 1316–1342 (2016). https://doi.org/10.1016/j.ipm.2016.04.002

C2 Beaconing Detection via AI-Based Time-Series Analysis

Jeetesh Gupta[✉], Jan Pfeifer, Anum Talpur, and Mathias Fischer

University of Hamburg, Hamburg, Germany
{jeetesh.gupta,jan.pfeifer,anum.talpur,mathias.fischer}@uni-hamburg.de

Abstract. Command and Control (C2) beaconing, which provides early warning of potential cyber threats, plays a significant role in cybersecurity. However, detecting these hidden communications remains a major challenge for traditional security solutions. To address this issue, we conduct a comprehensive study of C2 beaconing detection using artificial intelligence (AI)-based solutions. We experiment with an existing traditional time series-based approach, propose a long short-term memory (LSTM) model to effectively identify periodic and anomalous communication patterns, and also experiment with transformer-based GPT models to effectively capture temporal dependencies and improve the detection accuracy. We utilize multiple publicly available intrusion detection datasets, and also tested these approaches using real-world anonymized customer data from the cybersecurity services company, achieving higher accuracy in detecting malicious beaconing devices in real-world traffic.

Keywords: Command and Control (C2) · Intrusion Detection Systems (IDS) · Time Series Analysis · Cyber Threat Detection

1 Introduction

Detecting Command and Control (C2) [6] beaconing in real-world scenarios is a crucial task with far-reaching implications for various domains, including wireless networks, cybersecurity, and Internet of Things (IoT) systems. The variety of devices, their behaviors, and the ever-present threat of interference and noise make it challenging. The importance of C2 beaconing detection lies in its ability to reveal the presence and behavior of rogue devices, which can compromise network security, disrupt communication protocols, or even facilitate malicious activities such as data theft or denial-of-service attacks. In real-world contexts, the detection of C2 beaconing is complicated by various environmental [18] factors. These include dynamic channel allocations, fluctuating signal intensities, and the coexistence of multiple devices exhibiting overlapping transmission patterns. Despite the significance of detecting C2 beacons in different areas, controlled experiments with simulated data are often not realistic. They cannot accurately represent the complex, ever-changing environments that exist in the real world. Traditional intrusion detection systems (IDS) mainly use signature-based methods to recognize [11] attacks. These methods frequently prove ineffective when challenged by advanced C2 techniques or novel zero-day attacks that lack established signatures. Machine learning further enhances this process by analyzing traffic patterns and identifying beaconing activity. Another widely used detection method is time series analysis [20] [2], which is a powerful approach for detecting C2 beaconing activities within network traffic. This method utilizes the periodic nature of beaconing, whereby malware on a compromised host regularly communicates with a C2 server, thereby enabling the identification of patterns and anomalies in sequential data. However, when applied to real-world data, time series analysis for C2 beaconing detection faces several limitations due to its complex and dynamic environments [18], with diverse device types, varying signal strengths, and multiple interference sources. These factors have the potential to considerably influence the effectiveness of time series analysis, resulting in reduced accuracy, an increase in false positives, or missed detections. With this, the main contributions of our C2 beaconing detection framework are as follows:

– We address the challenge of detecting C2 beaconing in noisy real-world network traffic, overcoming limitations of traditional methods such as BAY-WATCH [9] and Global Analysis [21].
– We propose a time series analysis approach utilizing advanced deep learning models—LSTM, a multivariate time series (MVTS) transformer classifier, and time generative pre-trained transformer (TimeGPT)-1 [7].
– We evaluate the proposed models alongside conventional techniques on diverse datasets, including CSE-CIC-IDS2018 [17], CTU-13 [4], and IoT-23 [5].
– We also evaluate it on anonymized real-world network traffic data from our project partner company to demonstrate the impacts of time-series analysis.

The rest of the paper is organized as follows. Section 2 provides an overview of the related work in the literature. Section 3 describes the system design overview, feature extraction, data pre-processing, and proposed neural network models. Section 4 details the evaluation, and Sect. 5 makes concluding remarks.

2   Related Work

To address the problem of detecting beaconing behavior, researchers widely use time series analysis. Fine-grained detection [2] involves examining individual source-destination pairs, while global analysis [21] aggregates network data from multiple organizations. However, these methods may struggle with noise and data volume in real-world networks. Traditional statistical analysis and spectral analysis, including UPNSCA [10], BAYWATCH [9], and RobustPeriod [20], have been used to identify periodic patterns, but require careful noise management and may encounter limitations in high-noise settings.

Time series and periodicity analysis are used to detect malicious domains by identifying consistent temporal signatures in beaconing traffic. A probabilistic method [19] is used to identify domain names generated by Domain Generation Algorithm (DGA) families, which display high entropy and randomness.

Entropy-based detection [16] assists in identifying botnet C&C activities, but is limited in detecting advanced [3] C2 beaconing communications.

Clustering and capturing group activities (CCGA) [14] is designed to detect DGA-based botnets, but has limitations, including difficulty differentiating between botnets from the same DGA family and limited visibility into network topology. Real Intelligence Threat Analytics (RITA) [1] excels in detecting C2 beaconing activities through machine learning-driven analysis, but is limited by proprietary feeds and human analysis biases. A robust random forest classifier [12] achieves high precision and recall, but is ineffective for identifying new unknown attacks.

Unlike existing literature, our study introduces and evaluates deep learning models—LSTM, MVTSTransformerClassifier, and TimeGPT-1. By leveraging advanced neural architectures with pre-training and attention mechanisms, our approach achieves significantly higher accuracy, efficiency, scalability, and robustness, setting it apart from prior efforts that often overlook the complexities. Our work also performs a wide set of experiments to demonstrate the efficacy of detection systems using publicly available datasets along with real-world network traffic.

3   System Design

In this section, we explain the system model, pre-processing steps and feature extraction, and the experimented AI models.

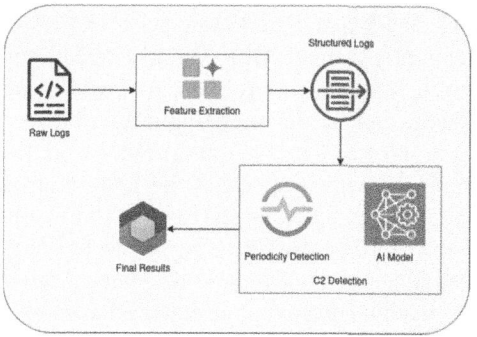

Fig. 1. System Design Overview

3.1   Basic Overview

The basic overview of our proposed system model is shown in Fig. 1. At first, the idea is to transform the overwhelming volume of raw network data into a structured, analyzable form, alleviating the burden on analysts tasked with identifying threats in real-time. At its core, the model design comprises three integrated components. First, a time-based feature extraction module distills log data into meaningful attributes, such as temporal patterns, port details, and packet metrics. Second, a periodicity detection module uncovers rhythmic signatures in C2 beaconing, separating them from routine traffic using techniques like Median Absolute Deviation and Bowley Skewness Measure. Finally, a detection component uses AL-based methods, including RNN and transformer-based models, to identify deviations that signal potential threats and highlight malicious communication. This system demonstrates the capability of detecting C2 beacons by leveraging temporal patterns, ensuring high accuracy in identifying malicious activity.

3.2   Feature Extraction/Data Pre-processing

We used labeled network flows from multiple real-world network traffic collections, each containing a mix of benign and malicious activities. These datasets provide a diverse foundation for analyzing network behavior under realistic conditions, allowing us to evaluate the effectiveness of our security-oriented model in different network scenarios.

Features were extracted using a CICFlowMeter [13] tool designed to process raw packet captures (PCAPs) into a comprehensive set of over 80 behavioral metrics. These metrics capture nuanced patterns, enabling the differentiation of normal network activity from suspicious anomalies. In another collection, binary network flow files were aggregated into a unified CSV format, preserving critical labels and features for analysis. Similarly, labeled log files were consolidated into a single CSV, ensuring consistency and facilitating streamlined processing across all data sources.

To optimize model performance and align with the research objectives, the feature set was subsequently refined. Our system extracts four key types of features from network traffic data: Temporal Features, which include granular time components such as year, month, day, hour, minute, and second; Port Features, which provide directional flow insights through source and destination port numbers; Protocol Information, which specifies the communication protocol type; and Packet Information, which includes metrics such as average forwarded packets and average packet size to characterize packet-level behavior.

To ensure compatibility across diverse data sources, we converted hexadecimal port numbers to decimal format and enforced consistent column naming. The preprocessing pipeline utilized a ColumnTransformer to standardize numerical features and encode categorical variables, such as protocol types, using StandardScaler and OneHotEncoder. This harmonized approach established a robust foundation for training the model, enhancing its ability to accurately classify network traffic across real-world scenarios.

3.3   AI Models

This research evaluates the performance of two deep learning model architectures, Recurrent Neural Networks (RNNs) and Transformers, to detect C2 beaconing through time series analysis. RNNs capture dependencies in time series data, while Transformers leverage attention mechanisms to uncover long-range dependencies and parallelize computations, offering a complementary approach to identifying temporal patterns and anomalies in network traffic.

Long Short-Term Memory Model. LSTM [8] networks are a specialized type of Recurrent Neural Network (RNN) designed to capture long-term dependencies in sequential data through the use of gated mechanisms. The gates in a Long Short-Term Memory (LSTM) network include the Forget Gate, which determines which information to discard from the cell state, the Input Gate, which decides which new information to store in the cell state, and the Output Gate, which controls the information output from the cell state to the hidden state. Our LSTM model consists of two Bidirectional LSTM layers with 64 units each, which capture context from both past and future sequences. We also include Batch Normalization layers to stabilize and accelerate the training process, Dropout layers with a rate of 0.5 to mitigate overfitting, and a final Dense layer with a softmax activation function for classification. Our model is trained using the Adam optimizer and sparse categorical crossentropy loss function, with early stopping to enhance generalization.

MVTSTransformerClassifier. MVTSTrans, implemented within the sktime Python library [15], represents an advanced deep-learning approach tailored for multivariate time series classification. This model adapts the Transformer architecture originally developed for natural language processing—to handle the complexities of time series data, making it a promising candidate for detecting C2 beaconing patterns in network traffic.

Unlike traditional models that rely solely on sequential processing, the MVTSTransformerClassifier leverages the Transformer's attention mechanism to capture both short and long range dependencies across multivariate time series. This capability is particularly suited for identifying periodic and anomalous behaviors in C2 communication, where temporal relationships span varying timescales.

Our model operates through three key steps. First, it processes multivariate time series data, preserving inter-dependencies among dimensions. Next, it uses attention-based feature extraction to weigh the importance of different temporal points, extracting contextual features that highlight periodicity and trends. This involves computing attention weights, incorporating positional encoding, and using multi-head attention to capture diverse temporal relationships. Finally, the extracted features are fed into a fully connected layer with a softmax activation to classify the time series as benign or indicative of C2 activity.

TimeGPT-1. TimeGPT, a foundation model, has been designed specifically for time series forecasting and anomaly detection. Leveraging the Transformer architecture, originally developed for natural language processing, TimeGPT-1 [7] utilizes a sophisticated framework that enables it to evaluate the importance of different parts of the input sequence when making predictions.

The model's architecture is based on an encoder-decoder structure, where the encoder processes the input time series to identify key features and temporal relationships. The decoder then uses this processed information to generate forecasted values. Both the encoder and decoder consist of multiple layers, enhanced with residual connections and layer normalization to address vanishing gradient issues and stabilize the training process. TimeGPT-1 also incorporates local positional encoding to convey the relative positions of time steps in the input sequence, which is essential for capturing temporal patterns. A final linear layer maps the decoder's output to the forecasting horizon, producing the model's predictions.

To train TimeGPT-1, a massive dataset of over 100 billion data points was collected from various domains. The model was trained on a high-performance computing environment using a cluster of NVIDIA A10G GPUs, requiring several days to complete. Extensive hyperparameter tuning was conducted to optimize performance, with larger batch sizes and smaller learning rates proving effective in improving training stability and accuracy. The Adam optimizer was used with a learning rate decay strategy to ensure stable convergence.

4 Evaluation

This section evaluates LSTM, TimeGPT-1, and MVTSTransformerClassifier along with baseline methods like Global Analysis [21] and BAYWATCH [9]. The evaluation employs standard classification metrics—accuracy, precision, recall, and F1-score—to measure each model's performance. The following subsections outline the datasets used and results, providing a comprehensive analysis of the system's capability to meet its design requirements and objectives.

4.1 Datasets

In this paper, we assess four different datasets, including three widely utilized publicly accessible datasets and one real-world dataset obtained from a partner company.

The public datasets used are- CSE-CIC-IDS2018 [17], CTU-13 [4], and IoT-23 [5]. These datasets serve as essential benchmarks for evaluating intrusion detection systems, offering a foundation to assess our model's effectiveness in detecting C2 beaconing activities. As shown in the Table 1, we extracted specific scenarios that represent C2 beaconing behavior in these datasets,. In the

Table 1. Characteristics of Datasets used for C2 Beaconing Detection

Dataset	Source	Data Type	Volume	Relevance
CSE-CIC-IDS2018	CIC and CSE	Packet Captures	16M+ records	Labeled botnet C2 traffic
CTU-13	Czech Technical University	NetFlow	2.8M+ flows	Real botnet C2 scenarios
Aposemat IoT-23	Stratosphere Lab	Packet Logs	325M+ packets	IoT-specific C2 activity
Real-World Data	Company's SOC Team	Anonymized Logs	90M+ flows	Multi-variate C2 activity

CSE-CIC-IDS2018 [17] dataset, we focused on the botnet attack scenario, where compromised devices establish covert communication channels with a command-and-control (C2) server. Similarly, in the CTU-13 [4] dataset, we analyzed various botnet scenarios that involve periodic beaconing traffic. Additionally, in the IoT-23 [5] dataset, we extracted C2 malware communication scenarios, where infected IoT devices maintained persistent contact with remote C2 servers. To further validate the robustness of our model, we leveraged anonymized customer data from a cybersecurity services company. This dataset included nine injected malicious beaconing devices (using Sliver C2) within anonymized real-world network traffic, providing a highly realistic testing environment. By evaluating our model in this real-world setting, we ensured its capability to detect C2 beaconing across various network infrastructures and malware types.

4.2   Results

This section presents the performance metrics of three time series analysis approaches—LSTM, TimeGPT-1, and MVTSTransformerClassifier—for detecting C2 beaconing in network traffic data. Table 2 summarizes the results on different datasets. For a fair comparison, we also evaluate the existing solutions of Global analysis [21] and BAYWATCH [9] on all datasets.

Performance on Different Datasets. We assess model performance on various datasets using accuracy, precision, recall, and F1-score to evaluate their robustness in detecting malicious patterns in diverse network flows. In Table 2, we compare model performance on the CSE-CIC-IDS2018 dataset for C2 beaconing detection. TimeGPT-1 excels with 99.7% accuracy, 99.8% precision, 99.4% recall, and 99.3% F1-score, outperforming LSTM (97.3% accuracy, >97% F1-score) and MVTSTrans (97.5% accuracy, >97% F1-score). Traditional methods like Global Analysis (42.6% accuracy) and BAYWATCH (35.9% accuracy) show significantly weaker performance in complex network traffic.

In Table 2, we compare model performance on the CTU-13 dataset for C2 beaconing detection. TimeGPT-1 leads with 99.6% accuracy, 99.3% precision, 99.1% recall, and 99.4% F1-score, showing robust detection. LSTM follows with 96.9% accuracy and 96.6% F1-score, while MVTSTrans achieves 92.7% accuracy and 92.0% F1-score, both outperforming traditional methods. Global Analysis [21] and BAYWATCH [9] struggle, with accuracies of 42.8% and 35.7%, respectively, highlighting their limitations in handling diverse botnet-driven C2 communications.

In Table 2, we compare model performance on the IoT-23 dataset for C2 beaconing detection in IoT environments. TimeGPT-1 leads with 95.6% accuracy and 95.4% F1-score, followed by MVTSTrans with 93.6% accuracy and 93.5% F1-score, both excelling in IoT contexts. LSTM shows a decline, with 79.4% accuracy and 78.1% F1-score, struggling with IoT traffic diversity. Traditional methods, Global Analysis [21] and BAYWATCH [9], perform poorly, with accuracies of 31.4% and 25.7%, respectively, underscoring their limitations in complex IoT C2 detection.

Table 2. Performance Comparison of Models Across Different Datasets

Model	CSE-CIC-IDS2018 Dataset			
	Accuracy	Precision	Recall	F1-Score
Global Analysis [21]	42.6%	39.8%	37.7%	39.8%
BAYWATCH [9]	35.9%	33.8%	33.5%	34.6%
LSTM	97.3%	96.6%	96.4%	97.1%
TimeGPT-1	99.7%	99.8%	99.4%	99.3%
MVTSTrans	97.5%	96.1%	96.1%	97.2%
Model	CTU-13 Dataset			
	Accuracy	Precision	Recall	F1-Score
Global Analysis [21]	42.8%	39.6%	37.9%	40.1%
BAYWATCH [9]	35.7%	33.6%	33.8%	34.9%
LSTM	96.9%	95.3%	96.0%	96.6%
TimeGPT-1	99.6%	99.3%	99.1%	99.4%
MVTSTrans	92.7%	91.4%	90.7%	92.0%
Model	IoT-23 Dataset			
	Accuracy	Precision	Recall	F1-Score
Global Analysis [21]	31.4%	30.9%	29.2%	30.5%
BAYWATCH [9]	25.7%	24.2%	24.9%	24.0%
LSTM	79.4%	81.0%	79.6%	78.1%
TimeGPT-1	95.6%	95.3%	95.2%	95.4%
MVTSTrans	93.6%	92.8%	92.3%	93.5%

Performance of the Pre-trained Models on the Real-World Data. In Table 3, we evaluate pre-trained models (trained on CSE-CIC-IDS2018) on real-world partner company data for C2 beaconing detection. The LSTM model, using its recurrent architecture, achieves 78.9% accuracy, 78.2% precision, 77.4% recall, and 78.3% F1-score on real-world data, effectively detecting short-term C2 beaconing patterns but with increased false negatives for longer sequences due to a trade-off in detection capability. The MVTSTransformerClassifier, utilizing transformer architecture with multi-head attention, achieved 91.7% accuracy, 90.1% precision, 90.0% recall, and 91.1% F1-score, effectively capturing short- and long-range C2 patterns. TimeGPT-1, adapted from time series forecasting, recorded 95.6% accuracy, 94.8% precision, 94.3% recall, and 94.9% F1-score, excelling in anomaly detection over extended periods but with slightly lower precision due to a higher false positive rate from its forecasting bias, demonstrating robustness in C2 detection.

MVTSTransformerClassifier, leveraging attention mechanisms for multivariate dependencies, closely followed TimeGPT-1 with strong performance but was limited by training constraints. TimeGPT-1 and MVTSTransformerClassifier's high recall ensures reliable C2 detection, minimizing missed threats, while their precision reduces false positives. LSTM showed moderate proficiency in sequential data modeling but lacked the precision of Transformer-based models, partic-

Table 3. Comparison of Pre-trained models on the Real-World Dataset

Model	Accuracy	Precision	Recall	F1-Score
Global Analysis [21]	20.8%	19.3%	18.7%	18.9%
BAYWATCH [9]	13.9%	13.4%	12.7%	13.2%
LSTM	78.9%	78.2%	77.4%	78.3%
TimeGPT-1	95.6%	94.8%	94.3%	94.9%
MVTSTrans	91.7%	90.1%	90.0%	91.1%

ularly for long-term dependencies. Global Analysis (20.8% accuracy, 18.9% F1-score) and BAYWATCH (13.9% accuracy, 13.2% F1-score) performed poorly, overwhelmed by real-world dataset noise, rendering them impractical for C2 detection without significant improvements.

Performance of Different Set of Features on the Real-World Data
Figure 2 and Fig. 3 illustrate the performance of a C2 beaconing detection model across different feature sets, evaluating precision and recall metrics to assess its effectiveness in identifying malicious activity. In the Model Precision chart (Fig. 2), the C2 beaconing detection model achieves a peak precision of 0.96 with "All features", effectively minimizing false positives. Precision drops to 0.92 without IP features ("No IP"), 0.98 with only time series and protocol features ("Only TS and Proto"), and 0.94 with only time series ("Only TS"). In the Model Recall chart (Fig. 3), the model reaches perfect recall of 1.00 with "All features", detecting all C2 beacons. Recall falls to 0.85 with "No IP", 0.62 with "Only TS and Proto", and 0.64 with "Only TS". Using all features, particularly time series, protocol, and IP data, optimizes precision and recall for robust C2 detection.

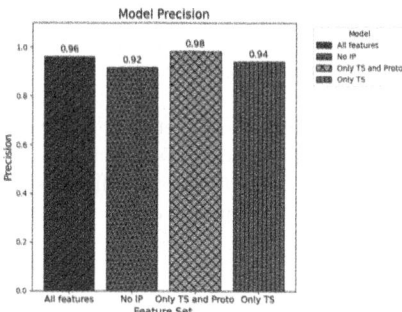

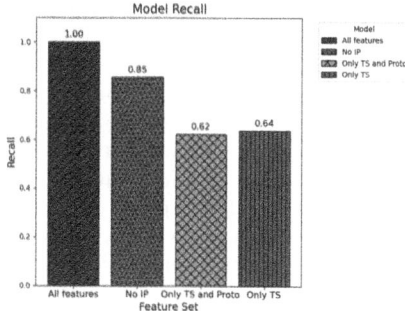

Fig. 2. Model Comparison - Precision   **Fig. 3.** Model Comparison - Recall

5   Conclusion

In this paper, we conducted a study that performs time series analysis to detect stealthy C2 beaconing, while addressing the challenge of effectively reducing noise in network traffic data to improve analysis accuracy. We applied deep learning models- LSTM, TimeGPT-1, and MVTSTransformerClassifier-along with a baseline technique of time analysis method. We conclude that TimeGPT-1 achieved exceptional performance with 95.6% accuracy, followed by MVTSTransformerClassifier's 91.7% accuracy, while LSTM delivered moderate results with 78.9% accuracy. In contrast, Global Analysis struggled, achieving 20.8% accuracy, particularly in the presence of uncontrolled noise. The success of TimeGPT-1 and MVTSTransformerClassifier suggests that advanced architectures using pre-training and attention mechanisms can effectively mitigate noise in real-world data and isolate C2 patterns from benign traffic.

Acknowledgement. This work was partially funded by the German Federal Ministry of Research, Technology and Space under Grant No. 16KISA068K and partially by the Agentur für Innovation in der Cybersicherheit GmbH (Cyberagentur) as part of the SOVEREIGN (https://sovereign-project.de) project. The Agentur für Innovation in der Cybersicherheit GmbH did not interfere in the research process and its results. We also gratefully acknowledge the DCSO GmbH for providing anonymized real-world data and supporting our research with real-world insights.

References

1. Active Countermeasures: RITA: real intelligence threat analytics (2025). https://www.activecountermeasures.com/free-tools/rita/
2. Apruzzese, G., Marchetti, M., Colajanni, M., Zoccoli, G.G., Guido, A.: Identifying malicious hosts involved in periodic communications. In: 2017 IEEE 16th International Symposium on Network Computing and Applications (NCA) (2017)
3. Eisenberg, D.A., Alderson, D.L., Kitsak, M., Ganin, A., Linkov, I.: Network foundation for command and control (c2) systems: literature review. IEEE Access (2018)
4. Garcia, S., Grill, M., Stiborek, J., Zunino, A.: An empirical comparison of botnet detection methods. Comput. Secur. **45** (2014)
5. Garcia, S., Parmisano, A., Erquiaga, M.J.: Iot-23: a labeled dataset with malicious and benign IoT network traffic. http://doi.org/10.5281/zenodo.4743746
6. Gardiner, J., Cova, M., Nagaraja, S.: Command and control: understanding, denying and detecting-a review of malware c2 techniques, detection and defences (2014). arXiv preprint arXiv:1408.1136
7. Garza, A., Mergenthaler-Canseco, M.: TimeGPT-1 (2023). arXiv preprint arXiv:2310.03589
8. Hochreiter, S.: Long short-term memory. Neural Comput. (1997)
9. Hu, X., et al.: Baywatch: robust beaconing detection to identify infected hosts in large-scale enterprise networks. In: 2016 46th Annual IEEE/IFIP International Conference on Dependable Systems and Networks (DSN) (2016)
10. Huynh, N.A., Ng, W.K., Ulmer, A., Kohlhammer, J.: Uncovering periodic network signals of cyber attacks. In: 2016 IEEE Symposium on Visualization for Cyber Security (VizSec) (2016)

11. Ioulianou, P., Vasilakis, V., Moscholios, I., Logothetis, M.: A signature-based intrusion detection system for the internet of things. Inf. Commun. Technol. Form (2018)
12. Känzig, N., Meier, R., Gambazzi, L., Lenders, V., Vanbever, L.: Machine learning-based detection of C and C channels with a focus on the locked shields cyber defense exercise. In: 2019 11th International Conference on Cyber Conflict (CyCon). IEEE
13. Lashkari, A.H., Draper-Gil, G., Mamun, M.S.I., Ghorbani, A.A.: Characterization of TOR traffic using time based features. In: Proceedings of the 3rd International Conference on Information System Security and Privacy (ICISSP) (2017)
14. Liu, Z., Yun, X., Zhang, Y., Wang, Y.: CCGA: clustering and capturing group activities for DGA-based botnets detection. In: 2019 18th IEEE International Conference On Trust, Security and Privacy in Computing and Communications/13th IEEE International Conference on Big Data Science and Engineering (TrustCom/BigDataSE)
15. Löning, M., Bagnall, A., Ganesh, S., Kazakov, V., Lines, J., Király, F.J.: sktime: a unified interface for machine learning with time series (2019). arXiv preprint arXiv:1909.07872
16. Richer, T.J.: Entropy-based detection of botnet command and control. In: Proceedings of the Australasian Computer Science Week Multiconference (2017)
17. Sharafaldin, I., Lashkari, A.H., Ghorbani, A.A.: Toward generating a new intrusion detection dataset and intrusion traffic characterization. In: International Conference on Information Systems Security and Privacy (2018)
18. Talib, M.A., Nasir, Q., Nassif, A.B., Mokhamed, T., Ahmed, N., Mahfood, B.: APT beaconing detection: a systematic review. Comput. Secur. **122** (2022)
19. Vishvakarma, D.K., Bhatia, A., Riha, Z.: Detection of algorithmically generated domain names in botnets. In: Advanced Information Networking and Applications: Proceedings of the 33rd International Conference on Advanced Information Networking and Applications (AINA-2019), vol. 33. Springer
20. Wen, Q., He, K., Sun, L., Zhang, Y., Ke, M., Xu, H.: Robustperiod: Robust time-frequency mining for multiple periodicity detection. In: Proceedings of the 2021 International Conference on Management of Data (2021)
21. Zhang, Y., Dong, H., Nottingham, A., Buchanan, M., Brown, D.E., Sun, Y.: Global analysis with aggregation-based beaconing detection across large campus networks. In: Proceedings of the 39th Annual Computer Security Applications Conference (2023)

Fooling Rate and Perceptual Similarity: A Study on the Effectiveness and Quality of DCGAN-based Adversarial Attacks

José Areia⬡, Leonel Santos⬡, and Rogério Luís de C. Costa⁽⊠⁾⬡

CIIC, ESTG, Polytechnic of Leiria, Leiria, Portugal
{jose.a.areia,leonel.santos,rogerio.l.costa}@ipleiria.pt

Abstract. Deep neural networks (DNNs), while widely used for classification and recognition tasks in computer vision, are vulnerable to adversarial attacks. These attacks craft imperceptible perturbations that can easily mislead DNN models across various real-world scenarios, potentially leading to severe consequences. This paper explores the use of deep convolutional generative adversarial networks (DCGANs) with an additional encoder to generate adversarial images that can deceive DNN models. We trained the DCGAN using images from three different adversarial attacks with varying perturbation levels and tested them on four DNN models. Our experiments demonstrate that the generated adversarial images achieved a high fooling rate (FR) of up to 91%. However, we also assessed image quality using the Fréchet Inception Distance (FID) and Learned Perceptual Image Patch Similarity (LPIPS) metrics. Our results indicate that while achieving a high FR is feasible, maintaining image quality is equally important—*yet more challenging*—for generating effective adversarial examples.

Keywords: Adversarial Attacks · Deep Neural Networks · Generative Adversarial Networks · Perturbation-based Attacks

1 Introduction

Deep neural networks (DNNs) have achieved remarkable success in computer vision [1]; however, they are widely recognised for their vulnerability to adversarial examples [2,3]. These adversarial examples, often imperceptible perturbations, can severely disrupt DNN predictions [4], particularly in image recognition tasks [5], causing the target model to misclassify a given image. This vulnerability threatens the reliability and robustness of DNN models [1]. Researchers have developed methods to design adversarial perturbations that are transferred across different DNN models [6,7]. However, these perturbations are often image-specific, limiting their effectiveness against unseen samples [8,9]. To overcome this, universal adversarial perturbations (UAPs) were introduced [10]. UAPs create perturbations that can deceive several DNN models across different images, enhancing their real-world applicability and usefulness in evaluating model robustness [11,12]. Although adversarial perturbations have become a prominent topic in the context of machine learning security and privacy [4], generative artificial intelligence also holds significant relevance in this area [13]. Generative models, such as adversarial generative networks (GANs) [14] and deep convolutional GANs (DCGANs) [15], are capable of rapidly producing high-quality images [16]. Moreover, they can replicate human-imperceptible image features similar to those introduced by adversarial attacks [17].

This study introduces a generative model, specifically DCGAN, to learn the characteristics of various adversarial attacks and generate images that can deceive different DNN models. The model's effectiveness is validated against four well-known DNN architectures and evaluated under three perturbation magnitudes. The primary contributions of this study are: *i*) a generative model that extracts adversarial characteristics to create new adversarial examples on demand; *ii*) an evaluation of how different perturbation magnitudes affect fooling rate and visual quality; and *iii*) an assessment of three attack types in four established DNN models.

The rest of the paper is organised as follows. Section 2 reviews related work. Section 3 details our methodology. Section 4 describes the experimental setup, results, and discussion. Finally, Sect. 5 summarises the study and suggests future research directions.

2   Related Work

Adversarial Approaches with DCGAN. Xiao *et al.* [18] introduced Adv-GAN, aiming to generate adversarial examples using a GAN. Instead of traditional attacks, they hypothesised that a GAN trained to exploit the discriminator's misclassifications could produce adversarial samples. By training the generator with adversarial loss to mislead the classifier, their network achieved on what they call "impressive results," by fooling the public MNIST black-box attack challenge with 92.76% accuracy. Deng *et al.* [19] proposed using DCGAN to extract and learn features from FGSM-based adversarial images to generate adversarial examples for attacking deep learning models. Their study showed that DCGAN-generated adversarial examples could bypass conventional defences, highlighting the potential of generative models in adversarial learning research. Their experiments achieved an 89.10% success rate, indicating that the generated adversarial samples were both more effective and aggressive. Nevertheless, to the best of our knowledge, no prior work has systematically evaluated generative models with an auxiliary encoder using a diverse set of attacks as inputs to assess their effectiveness across different target models.

Black-Box Attacks with DCGAN. Liu *et al.* [13] presented a novel method for black-box data poisoning attacks using an Enhanced Conditional DCGAN (EC-DCGAN). Their research involves poisoning the training dataset with mislabelled data to degrade model performance without accessing its internal structure. The proposed approach enhances the Conditional DCGAN by adding more conditioning information, enabling the creation of more realistic and targeted adversarial examples. This work addresses the challenge of generating effective poisoned data in black-box scenarios, where the attacker can only access the model's predictions.

Defensive Strategies with DCGAN. Yan *et al.* [17] proposed a defence mechanism against adversarial attacks by utilising a DCGAN. Their approach employs a generator to reconstruct clean signals from adversarial inputs, thereby mitigating the impact of adversarial perturbations. Experimental results demonstrate that this method effectively neutralises adversarial interference while maintaining high localisation accuracy, enhancing the robustness of indoor localisation systems against adversarial threats. However, these studies did not evaluate the quality of the generated images using proper metrics, focusing primarily on misclassification accuracy.

3   Methodology

This section introduces key concepts for designing universal perturbations to generate adversarial images, followed by a description of the proposed adversarial generative architecture.

3.1   Preliminary

As stated in Sect. 2, to deceive a given CNN model f, UAP-based attacks [1,9,10] seek to identify a universal perturbation δ derived from a perturbation vector v within a data distribution $\mathbb{R}^d$. This perturbation δ is designed to maximise the classification loss $\mathcal{L}$ (*e.g.*, cross-entropy) and mislead the classifier f on nearly *all data points* sampled from μ, where μ represents the distribution of images in $\mathbb{R}^d$. That is, these attacks seek to:

$$f(x + v) \neq f(x) \text{ for "most" } x \sim \mu, \tag{1}$$

where $f(x)$ represents the output of the model f, *i.e.*, the predicted label for each image $x \in \mathbb{R}^d$. Moreover, it is important to recall that these attacks seek to find v that satisfies a main constraint, as defined in Eq. 2.

$$\|v\|_p \leq \xi \ , \ \underset{x \sim \mu}{\mathbb{P}} \left(f(x + v) \neq f(x) \right) \geq 1 - \delta \tag{2}$$

The hyperparameter ξ controls the magnitude of the perturbation vector v, while δ, representing the universal perturbation, also specifies the desired fooling rate across all images sampled from the distribution.

However, this approach requires computing δ beforehand and applying it manually to each image. At scale, this is computationally intensive, as it involves both generating δ for each $x \in \mathbb{R}^d$ and ensuring proper scaling by ξ. Furthermore, the resulting perturbation may not generalise well across models; a perturbation optimised for model f may perform poorly on a different model g.

3.2   DCGAN to Generate Adversarial Images

As conventional DCGANs generate images based on features learned from a discriminator, while traditional adversarial attacks apply perturbations directly to an image, we hypothesise that a trained DCGAN can generate adversarial images capable of misleading a given CNN model. Unlike UAP-based methods, our approach does not solely focus on generating a perturbation δ. Instead, we aim to train an entire model capable of generating adversarial images on demand, with the potential for transferability to deceive multiple models. We validate our approach with a five-stage methodology: i) data gathering and preparation, ii) attack generation, iii) generative model training, iv) encoder training, and iv) testing and evaluation of the generated images.

For the first two stages, we utilise a pre-existing dataset and apply various adversarial attacks. To evaluate the impact of each perturbation factor ϵ on the models, we generate separate adversarial datasets for each attack, with each dataset corresponding to a different perturbation magnitude. The resulting adversarial images are then organised based on the attack type, forming a diverse n-set of perturbed images, categorised accordingly.

In the third stage, we develop a DCGAN comprising a discriminator (D), and a generator (G), designed to produce adversarial images. The D network adopts a deep convolutional neural network (CNN) architecture, structured as a sequence of five convolutional layers with progressively increasing depth. Each convolutional layer is followed by a non-linear activation function—LeakyReLU in all layers except the final one, which employs a Sigmoid activation. Additionally, batch normalisation is applied to stabilise training, except in the first and last layers. Similarly, the G network follows an inverse architecture to D, consisting of five convolutional layers with progressively decreasing depth. Each convolutional layer is followed by batch normalisation, except for the last layer, and a non-linear activation function—ReLU in all layers except the last one, where Tanh is used.

Since G produces images from a latent space vector as input, and our objective is not to generate random images—which could introduce errors during the evaluation phase due to the high likelihood of generating similar images, leading to identical outcomes—but rather to mimic real images, an encoder, denoted as E, is necessary. By design, an encoder learns structured latent representations of real data, which helps the generator produce more realistic and diverse outputs. Therefore, instead of relying on $y = G(z)$ to generate an adversarial image, we use $y = G(E(x))$, where $E(x)$ is the encoder's output using the real image x as input. In the fourth stage, we proceed with training the encoder. For this training, we utilise both the real images from the dataset and G for each test iteration.

3.3   Evaluation Metrics

To assess if the generated images can mislead a given CNN model, we first verify the correct classification of original images x and then test their adversarial counterparts x'. This approach identifies potential false positives, ensuring reliable evaluation and yielding a variation of the FR [11,20]. Since generative models create visually distinct images inspired by the reference set, their quality can not be accurately judged by direct pixel-by-pixel comparison with training images. To address this, we employ two metrics: the Fréchet Inception Distance (FID) [21] and the Learned Perceptual Image Patch Similarity (LPIPS) [22].

The FID metric compares the means and covariances of features from the deepest layer of the Inception v3 network [2], capturing high-level semantic information. It compares two image sets via the Fréchet distance between their Gaussian-modelled feature distributions [21]:

$$\text{FID} = \|\mu_r - \mu_g\| + \text{T}_r(\Sigma_r + \Sigma_g - 2(\Sigma_r \Sigma_g)^{1/2}), \tag{3}$$

where μ_r, μ_g are the means of real and generated image distributions, and Σ_r, Σ_g are their covariance matrices. A lower FID score indicates greater similarity between generated and real images in terms of feature distributions.

The LPIPS metric measures perceptual similarity between two images using features from a pre-trained deep neural network, unlike FID which compares image sets [22]. It calculates a weighted distance between the deep features of the images. Feature maps F_i and F_j from layer l for images I_i and I_j are normalised as $\hat{F}_{ij} = F_{ij} / \|F_{ij}\|_2$. After normalisation, the image distance is calculated as:

$$d^l = \frac{1}{H_l W_l} \sum_{h,w} \left\| \hat{F}^l_{i,hw} - \hat{F}^l_{j,hw} \right\|_2^2, \tag{4}$$

where H_l and W_l represent the spatial dimensions of the feature maps at layer l. The final LPIPS score is a weighted sum of distances across all layers:

$$\text{LPIPS}(I_i, J_i) = \sum_l w_l \cdot d^l \tag{5}$$

Weights w_l are learned from human perceptual judgments, aligning LPIPS more closely with human visual perception than traditional metrics.

4   Experiments

This section presents the experimental aspects of our study. It begins with the experimental setup, followed by a description of the conducted experiments. It concludes with the results and a discussion of the findings.

4.1   Experimental Setup

Dataset. We used the publicly available Imagewoof dataset [23], a subset of the well-known ImageNet dataset [24], containing images of 10 dog breeds. Approximately 10 000 images were used for training and 5 000 for validation. Pre-processing techniques were applied to improve data quality.

Attacks. The generative model is trained on perturbed images instead of original ones, enabling it to learn adversarial characteristics from the modified data. The perturbations δ were generated using three attacks: UAP [10], and two UAP-based variants—TRM-UAP [9] and SGA [1]. These were produced with three perturbation magnitudes, $\epsilon \in [0.01, 0.10, 0.20]$. TRM-UAP boosts CNN activations TRM-UAP enhances CNN activations via truncated ratio maximisation without requiring data, while SGA stabilises gradients through multi-step noisy forward gradient aggregation and single-step quantised updates per iteration.

Hyperparameters. Several hyperparameters were carefully selected to optimise performance and stability. The batch size was set to 128, and the image dimensions were reduced to 64×64. The number of channels was fixed at 3, the latent space vector nz was set to 100, and the size of the feature maps in both D, G and E was set to 64. The Adam [25] optimiser was utilised with a learning rate lr and two momentum parameters: β_1 and β_2. The lr was initialised at 2×10^{-4}, while β_1 was set to 0.5, and β_2 was set to 0.999. Separate Adam optimisers were employed for both D and G, but each used the same values for lr, β_1 and β_2. The parameters were fine-tuned using Optuna, which was also leveraged to determine the optimal patience parameter p for the *ReduceLROn-Plateau* function. The minimum learning rate for this function was set to $lr/10$. Finally, the training process was carried out for a total of 60 epochs. Further insights into the model parameters and training methodology can be found in our publicly available repository[1].

Evaluation Models and Metrics. We employed the FR method proposed by data-free universal methods [11,20], along with a modified variation (see Sect. 3.2), to assess false positives in our results. Additionally, the FID [21] and LPIPS [22] metrics were used to evaluate the similarity between the generated images and the original ones. Moreover, we evaluate four widely used models, namely VGG-16 and VGG-19 [26], ResNet18 and ResNet152 [27].

Setup. All experiments were conducted using Python 3.12 with PyTorch 2.6. Additionally, manual verification was employed to monitor the training process and analyse loss behaviour. The study was carried out on a workstation equipped with a single NVIDIA GeForce GTX 1650 GPU, utilising CUDA 12.4.

4.2   Adversarial DCGAN Performance

This section details DCGAN's performance across various tests conducted under the experimental setup described in the previous section. Figure 1 shows the FR results from different test iterations, comparing attack effectiveness.

All three UAP-based attacks yielded consistent results. ResNet152 proved the most resistant, with FR between 87.23% and 89.03%, while ResNet18 was the most susceptible, consistently exceeding 90% FR across all perturbation magnitudes. The VGG-16 and VGG-19 models showed minimal variation, with FR ranging from 88.17% to 89.41% across all attacks and perturbation levels.

---

[1] The corresponding repository: https://github.com/ipleiria-ciic/adversarial-dcgan

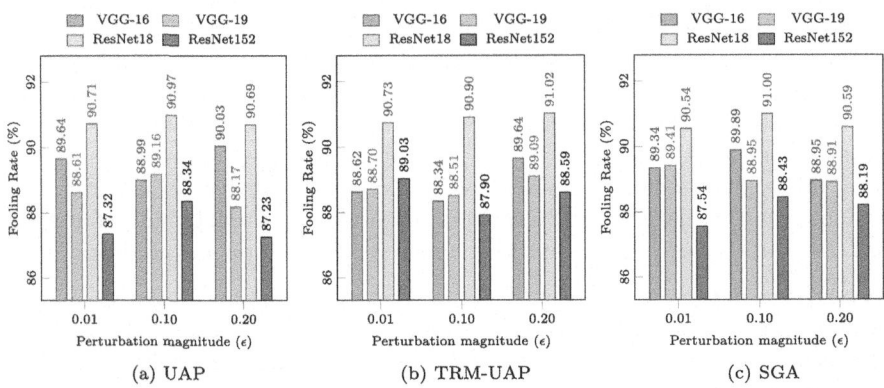

Fig. 1. Performance results for the FR across VGG-16, VGG-19, ResNet18, and ResNet152 models under different perturbation magnitudes (ϵ) for UAP, TRM-UAP, and SGA attacks. Higher FR (%) means better attack effectiveness.

Regarding the LPIPS metric, Fig. 2 presents the results obtained under the same experimental setup. These results provide insights into the perceptual similarity between the generated adversarial images and their original counterparts, further assessing the quality of the perturbations beyond fooling rates.

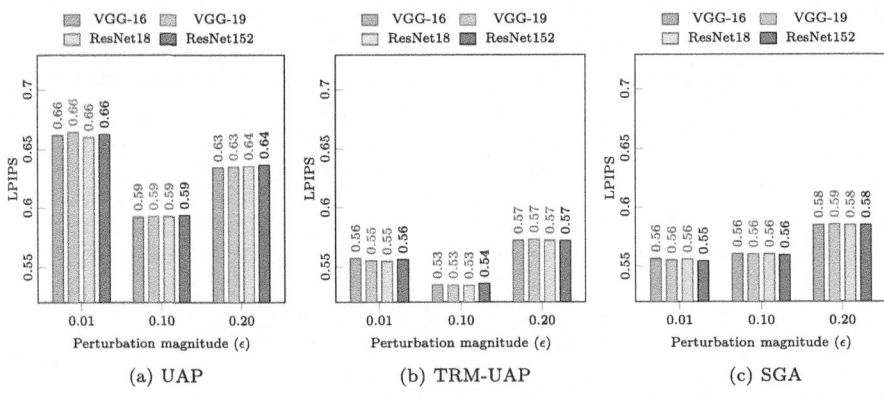

Fig. 2. Performance results for the LPIPS across VGG-16, VGG-19, ResNet18, and ResNet152 models under different perturbation magnitudes (ϵ) for UAP, TRM-UAP, and SGA attacks. Lower LPIPS means better image quality.

For all models, the LPIPS results were relatively similar. However, different perturbation magnitudes led to varying outcomes in this metric, as did the different attack types. TRM-UAP and SGA achieved the best results, with an interesting slight decrease in LPIPS at magnitude $\epsilon = 0.10$. Conversely, the UAP attack yielded the worst results, with an average LPIPS of 0.63. Interestingly, the lowest LPIPS score within all the attacks occurred at a perturbation magnitude of $\epsilon = 0.10$, which contradicts theoretical expectations, suggesting potential inconsistencies in how perturbations impact perceptual similarity in this specific attack.

Lastly, Fig. 3 presents the results obtained regarding the FID metric across the different attacks and perturbation magnitudes.

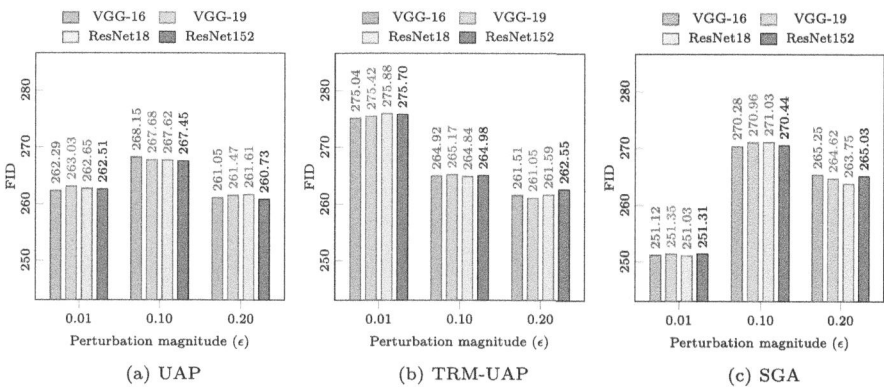

Fig. 3. Performance results for the FID across VGG-16, VGG-19, ResNet18, and ResNet152 models under different perturbation magnitudes (ϵ) for UAP, TRM-UAP, and SGA attacks. Lower FID means better image quality.

Similar to LPIPS, the scores did not differ much from model to model. However, from perturbation magnitude to another, the results changed. Within both UAP and TRM-UAP attacks, inconsistent results were acquired, with special attention to the 0.20 magnitude, which scored the lowest, contrary to the theoretical reason behind it. Similar to SGA, an increase in the FID metric across the first two magnitudes can be seen, but a decrease in the last magnitude was observed, presenting an average difference of 8 points.

4.3 Evaluating Adversarial Image Quality

Upon analysing the extracted results and computing all evaluation metrics, real-world image inference was necessary. The previous section introduced two metrics relevant to this evaluation: LPIPS and FID. By examining these metric results, it is evident that the scores were quite poor despite the FR achieving high values. Figure 4 presents a comparison between real images from the dataset and those generated by the model, specifically under the TRM-UAP attack with a perturbation magnitude of $\epsilon = 0.10$ applied to the ResNet18 model, alongside their predicted labels. Notably, the labels for real images correspond to their correct classifications, achieving 100% accuracy.

Fig. 4. Comparison of images generated by the DCGAN using the TRM-UAP attack with a magnitude of 0.10, targeting the ResNet18 model, alongside real images. The top row displays the original samples with their correct labels. The bottom row shows images generated by the DCGAN, with the classification labels attributed by the model.

Despite achieving an average FR of 90.87% under the specific test conditions, the generated images exhibit a significant amount of noise, making it challenging to discern the forms they represent. Although colour and silhouette can occasionally be identified, the discrepancy from real images remains substantial. This underscores a clear gap in the hypothesis of generating perturbations "imperceptible to the human eye." When crafting such images, the goal should not solely be to achieve a high FR, as observed in this case, but also to minimise LPIPS and FID scores, which would indicate more realistic image generation.

5   Conclusion

In this paper, we tested using a DCGAN with an encoder to generate adversarial samples to deceive four different CNN models. The DCGAN was trained using three established adversarial attacks. We generated perturbations with varying magnitudes, crafted the training data, and used the DCGAN and encoder to produce adversarial images. Experimental results showed a high FR across all attacks and perturbation magnitudes, with the best performance reaching 91% for the SGA attack on the ResNet18 model, and a variation of 4.19% from the lowest, corresponding to the UAP attack on the ResNet152 model. However, image quality metrics such as FID and LPIPS were poor. This highlights the need to balance a high FR with good image quality, as fooling models with poor-quality images can inflate FR scores and neglect the goal of creating imperceptible perturbations. Additionally, contrary to theoretical expectations, varying perturbation magnitudes did not significantly impact any of the metrics tested. Future research should focus on optimising both objectives: achieving a high FR while maintaining high image fidelity. This can be done through multi-objective training strategies that balance adversarial effectiveness with perceptual quality.

Acknowledgments. This work is partially funded by FCT - Fundação para a Ciência e a Tecnologia, I.P. through project UIDB/04524/2020 and under the Scientific

Employment Stimulus - Institutional Call - CEECINS/00051/2018, and by the European Union/Next GenerationEU through the project Sustainable Stone by Portugal - 02/C05-i01.02/2022.PC644943391-00000051.

References

1. Liu, X., Zhong, Y., Zhang, Y., Qin, L., Deng, W.: Enhancing generalization of universal adversarial perturbation through gradient aggregation. arXiv preprint arXiv:2308.06015 (2023)
2. Szegedy, C., Vanhoucke, V., Ioffe, S., Shlens, J., Wojna, Z.: Rethinking the inception architecture for computer vision. arXiv preprint arXiv:5120.0567 (2015)
3. Goodfellow, I.J., Shlens, J., Szegedy, C.: Explaining and harnessing adversarial examples. arXiv preprint arXiv:1412.6572 (2015)
4. Al-Rubaie, M., Chang, J.M.: Privacy-preserving machine learning: threats and solutions. IEEE Secur. Priv. **17**(2), 49–58 (2019). https://doi.org/10.1109/MSEC.2018.2888775
5. Moosavi-Dezfooli, S.M., Fawzi, A., Frossard, P.: DeepFool: a simple and accurate method to fool deep neural networks. arXiv preprint arXiv:1511.04599 (2016)
6. Madry, A., Makelov, A., Schmidt, L., Tsipras, D.: Towards deep learning models resistant to adversarial attacks. arXiv preprint arXiv:1706.06083 (2019)
7. Chakraborty, A., Alam, M., Dey, V., Chattopadhyay, A., Mukhopadhyay, D.: A survey on adversarial attacks and defences. CAAI Trans. Intell. Technol. **6**(1), 25–45 (2021). https://doi.org/10.1049/cit2.12028
8. Carlini, N., Wagner, D.: Towards evaluating the robustness of neural networks. arXiv preprint arXiv:1608.04644 (2017)
9. Liu, Y., Feng, X., Wang, Y., Yang, W., Ming, D.: TRM-UAP: enhancing the transferability of data-free universal adversarial perturbation via truncated ratio maximization. In: 2023 International Conference on Computer Vision (ICCV), pp. 4739–4748 (2023). https://doi.org/10.1109/ICCV51070.2023.00439
10. Moosavi-Dezfooli, S.M., Fawzi, A., Fawzi, O., Frossard, P.: Universal adversarial perturbations. arXiv preprint arXiv:arXiv1610.08401 (2017)
11. Mopuri, K.R., Garg, U., Babu, R.V.: Fast feature fool: a data independent approach to universal adversarial perturbations. arXiv preprint arXiv:1707.05572 (2017)
12. Creswell, A., White, T., Dumoulin, V., Arulkumaran, K., Sengupta, B., Bharath, A.A.: Generative adversarial networks: an overview. IEEE Sig. Process. Mag. **35**(1), 53–65 (2018). https://doi.org/10.1109/MSP.2017.2765202
13. Liu, H., Li, D., Li, Y.: Poisonous label attack: black-box data poisoning attack with enhanced conditional DCGAN. Neural Process. Lett. **53**(6), 4117–4142 (2021). https://doi.org/10.1007/s11063-021-10584-w
14. Goodfellow, I., et al.: Generative adversarial nets. In: Advances in Neural Information Processing Systems, vol. 27, Curran Associates, Inc. (2014)
15. Radford, A., Metz, L., Chintala, S.: Unsupervised representation learning with deep convolutional generative adversarial networks. arXiv preprint arXiv:1511.06434 (2016)
16. Liu, B., Lv, J., Fan, X., Luo, J., Zou, T.: Application of an improved DCGAN for image generation. Mobile Inf. Syst. **2022**(1) (2022). https://doi.org/10.1155/2022/9005552

17. Yan, Q., Xiong, W., Wang, H.M.: Secure indoor localization against adversarial attacks using DCGAN. IEEE Commun. Lett. **29**(1), 130–134 (2025). https://doi.org/10.1109/LCOMM.2024.3503721

18. Xiao, C., Li, B., Zhu, J.Y., He, W., Liu, M., Song, D.: Generating adversarial examples with adversarial networks. arXiv preprint arXiv:1801.02610 (2019)

19. Deng, B., Ran, Z., Chen, J., Zheng, D., Yang, Q., Tian, L.: Adversarial examples generation algorithm through DCGAN. Intell. Autom. Soft Comput. **30**(3) (2021)

20. Mopuri, K.R., Ganeshan, A., Babu, R.V.: Generalizable data-free objective for crafting universal adversarial perturbations. arXiv preprint arXiv:arXiv1801.08092 (2018)

21. Heusel, M., Ramsauer, H., Unterthiner, T., Nessler, B., Hochreiter, S.: GANs trained by a two time-scale update rule converge to a local Nash equilibrium. In: Advances in Neural Information Processing Systems, vol. 30, Curran Associates, Inc. (2017)

22. Zhang, R., Isola, P., Efros, A.A., Shechtman, E., Wang, O.: The unreasonable effectiveness of deep features as a perceptual metric. arXiv preprint arXiv:1801.03924 (2018)

23. Howard, J., Husain, H.: Imagewoof (2020). https://github.com/fastai/imagenette

24. Russakovsky, O., et al.: ImageNet large scale visual recognition challenge. arXiv preprint arXiv:1409.0575 (2015)

25. Kingma, D.P., Ba, J.: Adam: a method for stochastic optimization. arXiv preprint arXiv:1412.6980 (2017)

26. Simonyan, K., Zisserman, A.: Very deep convolutional networks for large-scale image recognition. In: International Conference on Learning Representations (2015)

27. He, K., Zhang, X., Ren, S., Sun, J.: Deep residual learning for image recognition. In: IEEE Conference on Computer Vision and Pattern Recognition (CVPR), pp. 770–778 (2016). https://doi.org/10.1109/CVPR.2016.90

Author Index

The manufacturer's authorised representative in the EU is Springer
Nature Customer Service Centre GmbH, Europaplatz 3, 69115 Heidelberg,
Germany. If you have any concerns regarding our products, please
contact ProductSafety@springernature.com

Printed and bound by CPI Group (UK) Ltd, Croydon, CR0 4YY
24/04/2026
02096367-0016